PENGUIN BOOKS

Chromorama

Riccardo Falcinelli is an award-winning graphic designer and best-selling author whose work has been highly acclaimed in Italy and around the world. He teaches at the ISIA Faculty of Design in Rome.

PENGUIN BOOKS

UK | USA | Canada | Ireland | Australia
India | New Zealand | South Africa

Penguin Books is part of the Penguin Random House group of companies whose addresses can be found at global.penguinrandomhouse.com.

penguin.co.uk

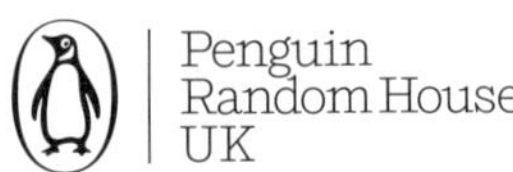

First published in Italy as *Cromorama* by Giulio Einaudi s.p.a., Torino 2017
This translation first published in Great Britain by Particular Books 2022
Published in Penguin Books 2025
002

Design by Riccardo Falcinelli

Typeset by Jouve (UK), Milton Keynes

Printed in Latvia by Livonia Print SIA

A CIP catalogue record for this book is available from the British Library

Penguin Random House UK, One Embassy Gardens,
8 Viaduct Gardens, London SW11 7BW

The authorized representative in the EEA is Penguin Random House Ireland,
Morrison Chambers, 32 Nassau Street, Dublin D02 YH68

978-1-802-06030-0

Penguin Random House is committed to a sustainable future for our business, our readers and our planet. This book is made from Forest Stewardship Council® certified paper.

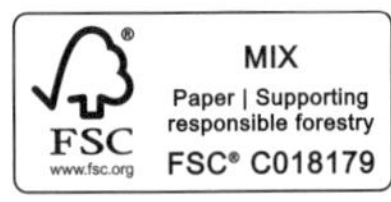

Riccardo Falcinelli

Chromorama

How Colour Changed Our Way of Seeing

Translated by Simon Carnell and Erica Segre

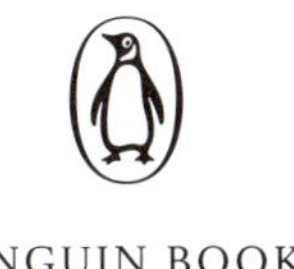

PENGUIN BOOKS

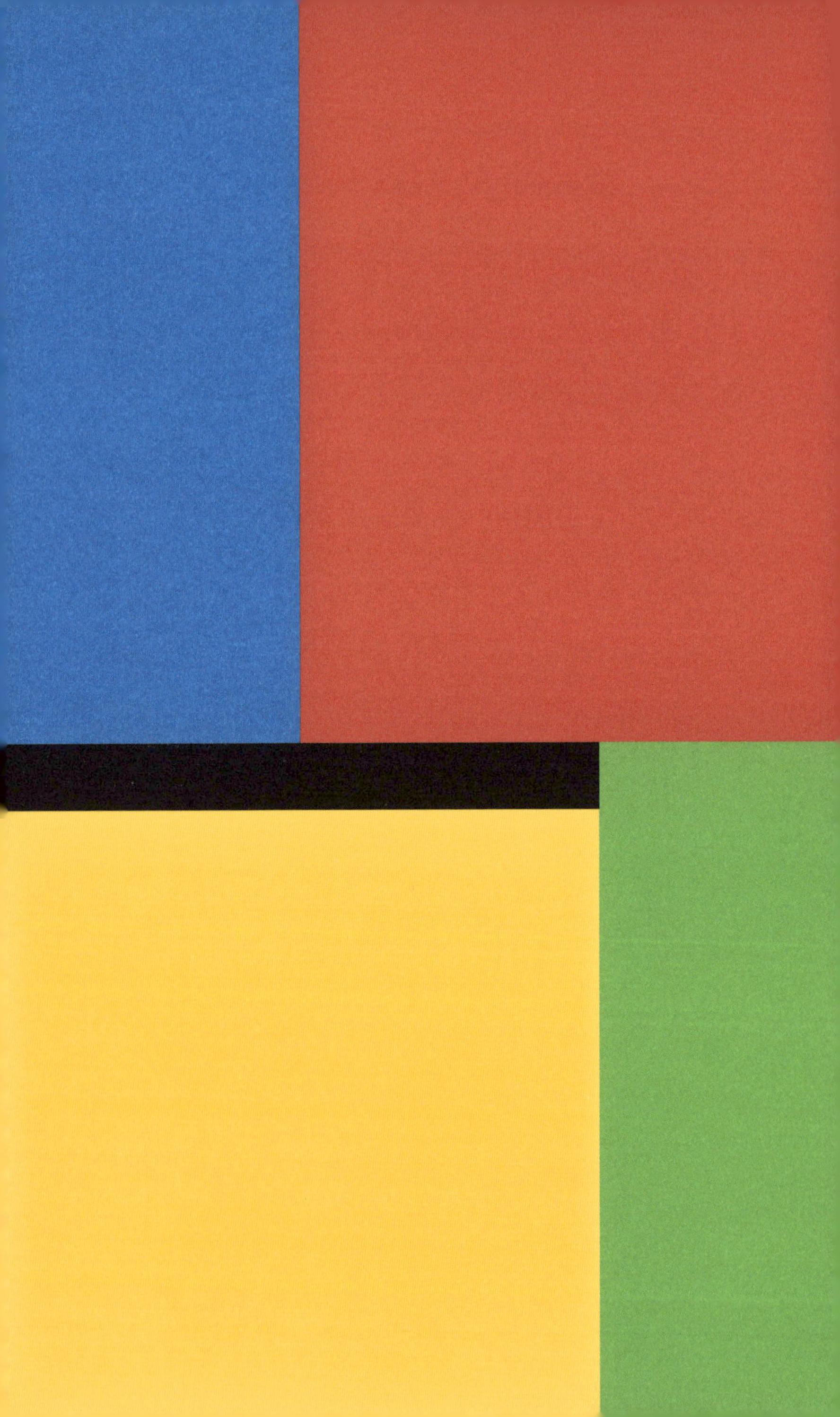

Contents

1

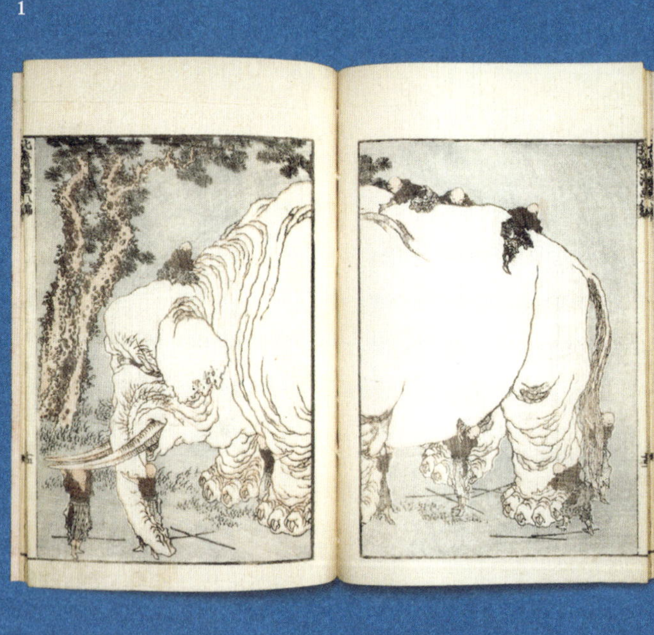

Chromorama

PART ONE

Looks

2

L&C. Hardtmuth's
"Koh-i-Noor"
Pencils.
Perfection in Pencils.

3

Facebook
Twitter
Apple
Lg
Messenger

4

Google
pencil

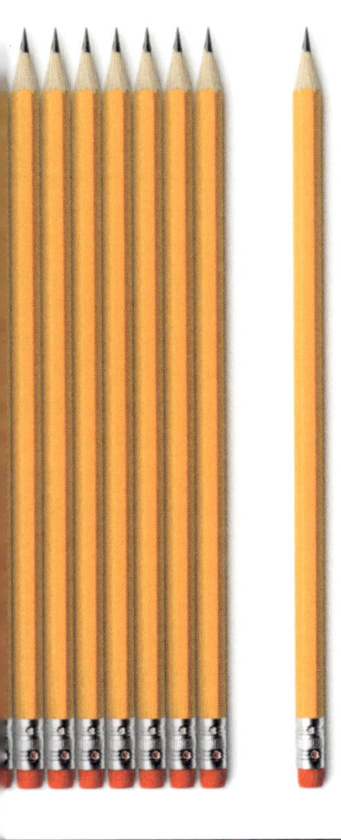

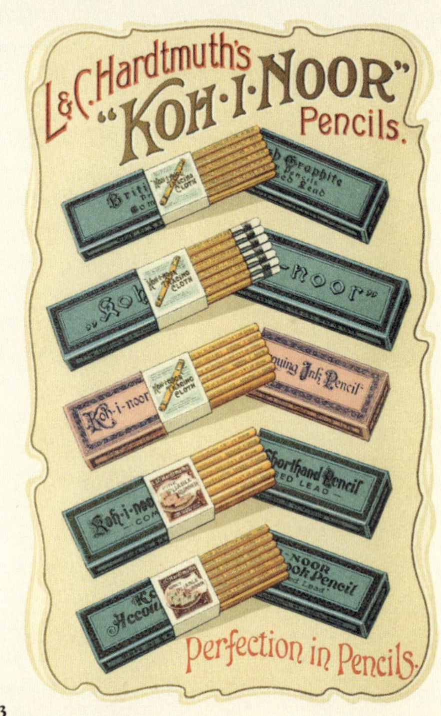

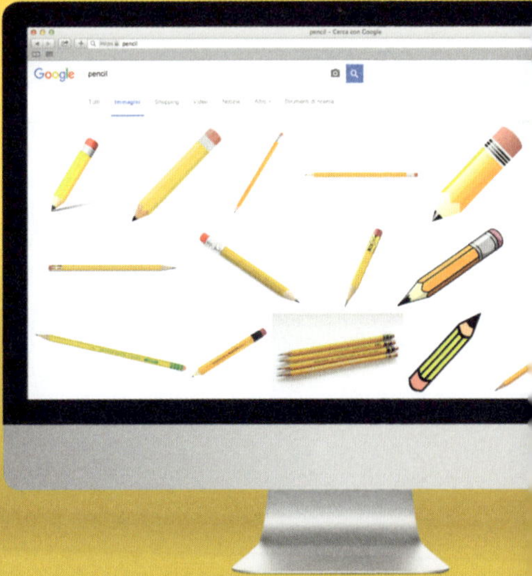

5

Industrial Yellow

Society's Design

Lying on a table in front of me there is a yellow pencil. 2
Actually, it would be more accurate to say that it is a wooden lead pencil painted yellow. On one of its ends its grade or hardness is marked. That end is a little chewed – a sure sign that, where objects are concerned, we often have relationships with them that are more emotional and neurotic than we might allow ourselves to admit. Seeing it lying there, we are liable to think of it as a 'classic' pencil. But what is it, exactly, that inclines us to such a conclusion? Its *yellowness* is surely significant – a sign that we should definitely not overlook. In fact, if this were a crime scene, any detective worth their salt would start from here, with this colour.

PETROSKI, 2002

The pencils we currently have – with their graphite encased in a wooden sheath – were first introduced in 1790. Before that, we had carbon brushes, pastels or sticks of graphite without any kind of casing. It was Nicolas-Jacques Conté who first had the idea of using graphite *dust* – mixing it with clay and sheathing it in wood – rather than purchasing from England significantly more costly blocks of pure graphite.

The design of such an object, in a century in which drawing explodes as a recreational activity, responds to the demand for implements that do not dirty the hands and clothes of non-professionals, above all the hands and clothes of women. The wood encasing the lead is ultimately a practical choice made in response not so much to the needs of artists as to those of a huge constituency of amateurs. And it is this thinking about potential buyers that turns Conté into a designer.

The first pencil sold with its wooden casing painted would
not appear until a century later, launched at the Chicago
3 Columbian Exposition in 1893 by Koh-I-Noor, the firm
that is still today one of the world's most prestigious makers of writing implements. This use of colour probably had something to do with hiding material imperfections, given how unlikely it was that the finest wood would be used to make such an inexpensive object. And what was the colour of this first painted pencil? Yellow, of course.

According to some design historians, the choice of this particular colour was a nationalistic one: echoing, that is, the emblematic yellow of the Austro-Hungarian Empire, where Kohl-I-Noor was based, first in Vienna and then in Bohemia. According to others, it is something of an oblique, metaphorical choice referring to China – since graphite traditionally came from China and yellow was the colour of its imperial family. Whatever the actual reason for its selection, the colour proved to be immensely successful. Millions of yellow pencils have been sold all over the world.

Today, more than a century later, wooden pencils continue to enjoy almost universal popularity – even in an era in which many other highly sophisticated writing instruments are produced. The pencil's main drawback, the inconvenience of having to sharpen it, is in itself a ritual not without its charm. The lightness of the wood remains very efficient for both writing and drawing. Not to mention the fact that, unlike a mechanical pencil, the classic pencil loses its sharpness as we use it, resulting in ever thicker lines and in the process affording unexpected expressiveness. Perhaps surprisingly, to this day two thirds of the pencils produced on the planet happen to be yellow.

PETROSKI, 2002

There is an anecdote that may help us to understand why this is the case. A few years ago, as part of market research in American offices, new pencils were handed out – some yellow, some green. After a week of using them, people were asked which of the two they preferred. The vast majority complained about the green ones: because the lead continuously split; because they were more difficult to sharpen; because the wood was harder and would more readily break. And yet, perhaps needless to say, the green and yellow pencils were actually the same. It was only their external finish – their colour – that was different.

In contemporary society, colour is not just a perception or a mere physical attribute of things. Colour is frequently also an idea or an expectation. Which is to say that certain colours become so fused with the objects that bear them that it is difficult to think of them otherwise. It is no accident that
if we Google an image of a pencil, the first one we get is 5
yellow. Or that the pencils used for the most popular emojis 4
are pure yellow. A yellow pencil is in fact simply more *pencil-like* than any other. It is an archetype, a mental model to which all others must be compared. Like some Platonic archetype, we could say that the yellow pencil is the very Idea of a pencil – and that the green, red or blue ones are merely pale copies or imitations. And it is this that makes it a classic.

Today, the majority of things that we come into contact with have been mass-produced. Whether it is shoes, mobile phones, T-shirts, frozen food or indeed pencils, they have all been manufactured and marketed in substantial numbers of units.

This is not just the case with objects. Television broadcasts, films and video games are designed to be viewed on many different screens, and our words, when they circulate on social networks, come to be read on hundreds of contemporary devices. Not to mention the events and famous people who live thanks to the millions of reproductions – photos, gadgets, videos – disseminated by the mass media. Our modern society is characterized by the multiplication of discourse via means of mass production and reproduction.

This does not mean that there are no longer any unique works or singular experiences – simply that they are no longer the norm, or are relatively rare in people's lives. What is new about our world, however, is not just the prevalence of this *copying* and the existence of copies. It is the type of mentality that it produces and shapes.

Industry is mainly characterized by the regulation of pro- DORFLES, 2001
duction for economic reasons above all else. Contrary to
what we might assume, this does not apply only to human
artefacts; even supposedly 'natural' products are involved
in a similar process. Many fruits, for example, such as apples or oranges, are passed through a ring determining an
average size before being sent to the supermarket: if the
fruit does not pass through and conform – because it is too
large or eccentrically shaped – it is immediately rejected
and used for making juice or in the manufacture of other
beverages. This is why the oranges displayed on our shelves
6 always end up being perfectly round, as well as the same
size and shade of colour.

The fact that we have oranges with a regular and regulated appearance means that they are not so different
from objects that have issued machine-made from a mould,
7 like tennis balls. Standardization is not actually just one FALCINELLI, 2014
of the necessary phases of production: the market itself
finds it easier to sell things that are the same, because
commerce has a need precisely for both 'things' (products)
and their coherent representation. The selection made by

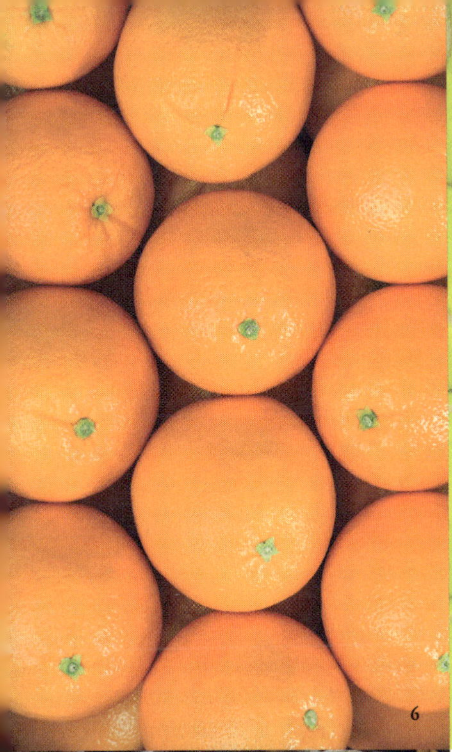

6

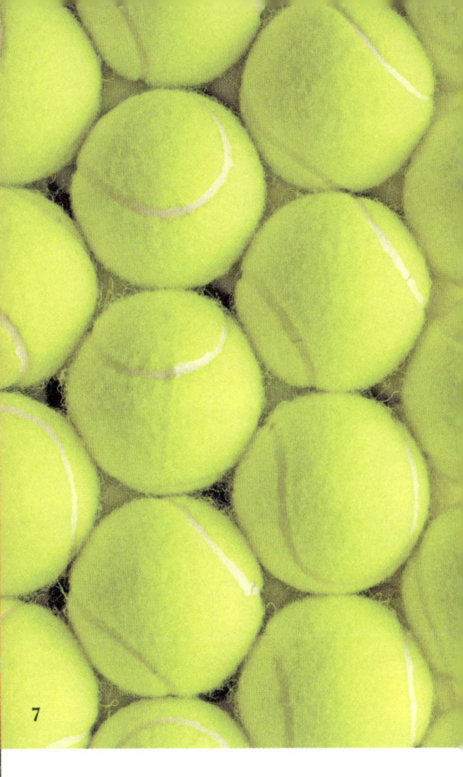

7

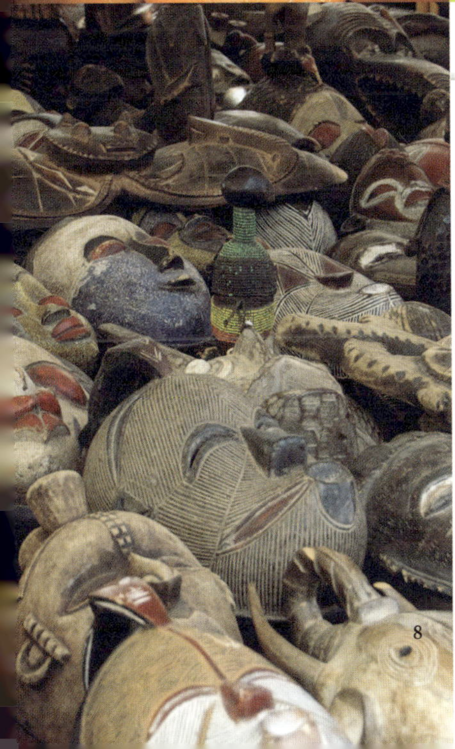

8

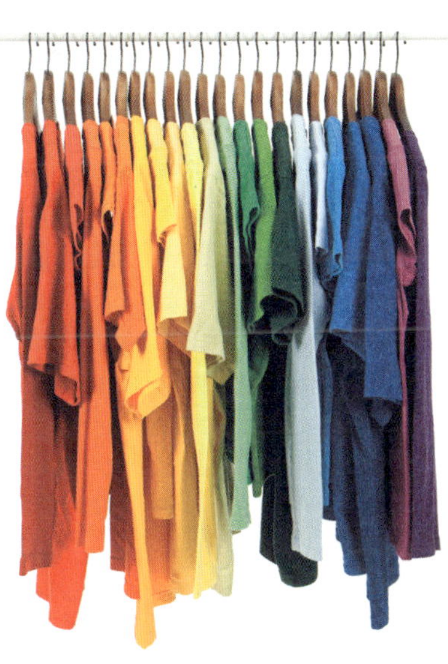

9

the distribution chain is effectively an act of design, since it projects and determines the way in which those fruits will be seen.

In this way, industry standardizes our perception of things, so that without realizing it we end up treating an orange as if it were an artefact. The mass-produced series effectively provides us with mental templates with which we think about the world.

If, for example, we were to pick up in a shop a disposable biro such as a Bic, and notice an error in the moulding at the top, we would almost certainly choose another one instead. We have learned that a visible flaw indicates that something is not quite right. Yet this does not altogether explain our choice. The small defect in the plastic does not mean that the pen will write less well. In reality, we have internalized the idea that such objects must be identical, and we are inclined and conditioned to always prefer an individual item that is exactly like all the others. Demanding series without exceptions, we want not the single object but its very idea. We seek the prototype of which that individual pen is a manifestation or example. This, at any rate, is how most consumers behave, so that objects with the slightest flaw are effectively unsaleable and immediately withdrawn.

We are not talking here about a form of neurosis but about a historical condition. And it is easy enough to see how deviations from the norm have a way of confirming it: how the exception proves the rule. In recent years, for example, in order to escape the monopoly of the gigantic production lines, there have been groups of 'zero miles' suppliers, offering only produce sourced locally. The fruit and vegetables that they offer are often inconsistent, irregular, perhaps even slightly gnawed by the odd snail or insect. These imperfections, which are unacceptable to the large distributors, are greeted by consumers as a sign of authenticity, to the extent that generic regularity in a box would actually cause suspicion. But this is because regularity has become in our minds an essential quality of the modern world and of advanced capitalism. The zero-miles approach is in the end only thinkable in relation to the supermarket, because we can no longer separate our view of things from the idea that we have of the 'standard'.

Wandering in big European cities we frequently come across vendors of carved wooden figures and masks made by African artisans. Even though we are dealing here with 8
genuinely hand-made, individually carved artefacts, they are nonetheless virtually identical. And this is because they have been designed for our market: on the one hand, to cater for European expectations and even prejudices with regard to Africa; on the other, to take account of our way of buying things. African artisans have in effect embraced the notion of serial production, and however much the sale of their work proposes itself as an alternative to standardization, that work must nevertheless take account of it and reflect it.

This shows how the essence of design lies not in the fact that work is done by machinery but in the serialization of production processes. Many objects that appear to be highly industrial, such as mobile phones, are actually hand-assembled by underpaid workers in the factories of the Third World.

An orange, an African statue, a mobile phone. They seem to be very different objects. As commodities, we consider the first to be a fruit of nature, the second a piece of craftwork and the third an industrial product. Yet today all three share a similar condition and have come to be *consumed* in almost the same way. Design, through the iteration of ideas and models, projects above all 'representations', which is to say things that present themselves to our actual gaze but that end up lodged or dwelling in our minds. That is why design, even before producing objects, produces *discourses*:

a set of knowledge, convictions, myths, behaviours and social practices shared on a mass scale. And our means of communication have played a fundamental role in this, in the first place through the invention of graphics, cinema and advertising that for at least a century have been a constitutive part of our experience of reality. It is certainly not without significance that in 1912 Picasso and Braque inaugurate the Cubist revolution by inserting remnants of fabric and wallpaper, train tickets and newspaper cuttings into their paintings – not as generic components of a collage but as pieces of the world. The piece of newspaper is there, glued to the canvas, to signify an actual newspaper placed on a table. These are scraps of reality ushered directly into a still life that takes for granted the fact that in modern society there are tables, bowls, fruit – and the mass media.

From these observations we can begin to see how the chromatic imagination is constructed: to make an object in a certain colour – one choice among many possibilities – may or may not meet the approval of the public. But if it does, it begins to dwell in our imagination, and over a few decades that colour becomes a category by which we judge everything else. As in the case of the yellow pencil. That particular colour turns into an archetype, making us think that it is the pencil par excellence, even if we never actually use yellow pencils.[1]

The crucial aspect of this rapport between colours and things lies precisely in this depositing of the colour in our

[1] The role of colour in objects is not just one-dimensional or just symbolic. For example, the bi-coloured, red and blue pencil on the one hand helps us to understand which way to hold it without looking at the point, and on the other has become a cultural icon with multiple associations: homework, grammar, more or less grave mistakes. The coupling of colours plays various roles: informative, seductive, iconic and rhetorical, as the red and blue, which evoke the school environment, function like a synecdoche – that rhetorical figure in which a part (in this case the combination of colours) stands for and recalls the whole.

collective memory – it continues to reside and signify there even when its original meaning has been lost in the folds of history. To verify this, we could try making a list of all the now famous yellow things that are typical of our cultural world, yet whose origins we either ignore or do not need to know. The *Yellow Pages*, for instance, which was published thus more by chance than choice – because their first editor, in Wyoming, only had paper of this colour at his disposal. Or we could think of such disparate things as Van Gogh's *Sunflowers*, a packet of banana-flavoured Nesquik, or New York taxis. The list of iconic yellow things is endless.

Many common habits – such as thinking in solid colours, or considering blue to be a 'cold' colour – are actually very recent inventions, frequently determined by technical necessity. And yet they seem like obvious facts to us, like givens, as if there were no other way of conceiving colour. In order to understand how we got here we need to leap back into the past, to take account of what colour was and how it functioned for those living before the advent of mass society.

For the past 3,000 years, the most diverse men and women have taken an interest in colour, and built upon it nothing less than complete visions of the world. The chromatic dilemmas and concerns of a dyer living in the second century BC are clearly quite remote from those of a seventeenth-century painter or a contemporary biologist. Every area or discipline has posed its own problems and constructed an appropriate lexicon. This means that today we often find ourselves with contradictory knowledge about colour, and with a terminology that is multivalent and frequently imprecise.

If we find ourselves talking to an artist, for instance, we might hear them define as 'saturated' a colour which in common parlance is called 'bright'. Or we might find

that a designer will refer admiringly to the 'luminosity' of FROVA, 2000
a colour, whereas a physicist would explain that this is an approximate term, and that it would be better and more precise to speak of its 'brilliance'.[2] To say nothing of the common opinion, taken for granted since Newton, that a
rainbow contains all colours. Recent science, as we shall OLEARI, 2008
soon see, has demonstrated in fact that very intense red – that of poppies, say, and of Coca-Cola – does not actually exist on the chromatic spectrum.

These contradistinctions – at once both terminological and conceptual – are an important aspect of the history of colour. The multitude of approaches, of studies and of expertise accumulated over the centuries have in fact constructed a great fortress of meanings yet also produced a good deal of debris and detritus. But these are themselves extremely valuable cultural incrustations: a mixture of illuminations and of commonplaces, of innovation and of preconceptions – all living material in our perception and experience of colour. And how could we even communicate if there was not the kind of consensus – perhaps scientifically unfounded, perhaps even a little foolish – telling us that red is linked to love and to passion? Anyone observing our society will know well enough that a stereotype is in fact more packed with meaning, and conveys more to us, than an exact idea.

The world of colour reminds us of that marvellous print
1 by Hokusai in which a huge, old, decrepit elephant is
being felt by the hands of eleven blind men. One touches him, one brushes against him, another embraces him; all are intent on gleaning an idea of what they are dealing

[2] I will use the term 'brightness' rather than the more precise 'clarity' to refer to the appearance of hues within a context (see Appendix A 7.3.2). It is a deliberate choice, given that 'brightness' is the most used in common parlance, and therefore the most appropriate to the themes of this book, namely the ideas and discourses that formed the chromatic imagination of contemporary society.

with. Yet none of them is able to 'see' the elephant whole, because the experience of the senses only furnishes fragments rather than the thing in its entirety. This elephant of Hokusai's is a witty metaphor of the impossibility of ever knowing the thing in itself.

Similarly, in order to understand colour we must abandon all pretence of seeing the whole story, or of arriving at a single truth, and think instead of these blind men – because everyone will have something different to say, some part of the picture to reveal. If we want to understand how colour is coded today, we must ask ourselves not only how it functions, but what kind of ideas humanity has had about it both now and in the past. And it goes without saying that the convictions of specialists and those of laypeople will need to be considered in parallel to each other, given that for our purposes science and myth are simply two ways of looking at reality. We will have to listen to philosophers and dyers, biologists and artists, writers and entrepreneurs, physicists and astrologists, as well as to shop assistants, pastry chefs and our relatives.

PASTOUREAU, 2011

Let me be clear about what follows. This is not a historical essay but a story in which some specific historical facts are used to highlight certain characteristics of our contemporary world. Even though history is made up of successive continuities and breaks, I will focus on those rupturing, revolutionary phenomena that have determined society as we know it. This book is intended to be a kind of history of the modern gaze, of modern looking, and of how it has been shaped.

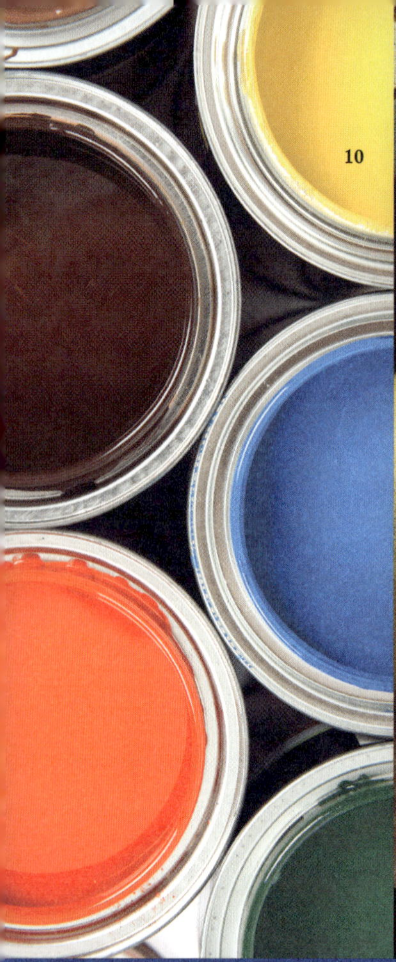

10

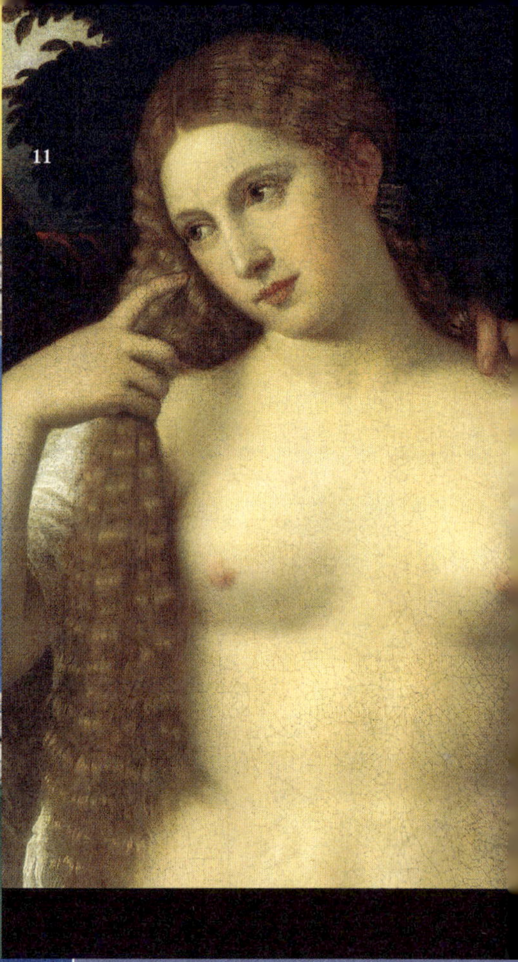

11

12 Oil on canvas

13 Offset print

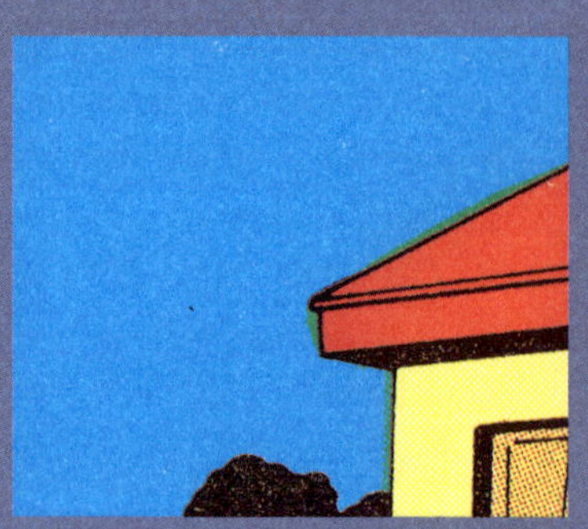

Solid Red

The 21st-Century Eye

Recently I was in a pastry shop and, partly in order to make conversation, partly out of curiosity, I asked the owner if there was one single cake that she tends to sell more of than any other. This was how she came to tell me that, in Italy, people no longer buy a tray of twelve pastries but a tray of six, and that this reduction is proportionate to the number of those attending mass on a Sunday; that the rum in the typical Neapolitan sponge cake has a festive significance now lost on the young; and that the 'queen' of pastries continues to be the 'diplomat cake',[1] a slice of liqueur sponge cake with puff pastry and custard – an epic dessert, with a complicated structure seen as a symbol of a bygone age. Which is to say that the diplomat, even for our grandmothers, is the pastry par excellence.

If we think about it for a moment, we can see that this complexity has to do not so much with the pastry in itself, with its recipe and constituent parts, as with the way in which it is tasted. When we bite into the diplomat cake the icing sugar immediately hits our palate. Then we feel with our teeth the crunchiness of the puff pastry. Once broken, it reveals the moistness of a filling that when

[1] Depending on where you are in Italy, it is called a *diplomatico* ('diplomatic'), a *veneziana* ('Venetian'), or a *zuppetta* ('little soup').

chewed releases in turn a liqueur that oozes onto the tongue. This is a pastry which requires of us a certain amount of time. From when we bite into it to when it is swallowed, it produces multiple effects and sensations: dryness and moistness, sweetness and an ooze of liqueur. It has no single taste but several articulated tastes that persist and change, even after we have swallowed it.

The fact that it is an old-fashioned pastry is down, perhaps, precisely to this slowness, to the duration required to experience it. If we compare it with something like Nutella, the latter 'lasts', like almost every industrial sweet, for the duration of the time that we hold it in our mouths. The contrast between the two is that between an exquisite luxury product and a mass-produced inexpensive one, between artisanal tradition and contemporary mass production. Above all, though, they embody the contrast between two rhythmically dissimilar mentalities: the slow, leisurely unfolding of the one versus the immediacy of the other.

The point here, however, is not to establish hierarchical degrees of value. Homogeneous or multiform, rapid or extended: these are simply different ways of thinking about matter, each pleasurable in its particular way. It is rather that, in many areas of invention, speed is the sign of our times. In art and design, the languages that achieve most success are those that can be grasped at once – 'at a glance', as we say. We might conclude that if the diplomat cake is a symphony, Nutella is a jingle. And we can translate the metaphor into chromatic terms: if the diplomat is an articulated and shimmering colour, then Nutella is a solid one.

From a technical point of view, a solid colour is the uniform look of a surface upon which we recognize the same colour at every one of its points. But for all its use in common parlance, it is difficult to say where the concept of solid colour begins: a pair of opaque woollen stockings almost certainly possesses it, whereas one of more or less sheer tights backed by the changeability of skin colour does not. In everyday terms, we tend to use it of something, such as a sweater, that lacks something else, implicitly contrasting it with a pattern, a design or a mixture.

A solid colour makes itself instantly understood. To
prove this we need only compare the colour of a sky painted by Fragonard in the seventeenth century with the sky 12
in a comic book: the first is worked, insistent, full of 13
miniscule tonal variations, and to appreciate it (as with our diplomat cake) requires *time* spent carefully looking, whereas the second is homogeneous and immediate, like Nutella. This is not just a perceptual characteristic, however, but a category with which we think more generally about colour. A revolution, above all, of the gaze, of how we look at things.

Familiarity with industrial languages has brought about,
without our realizing it, the fact that we refer predomin-
antly to single colours: their red, yellow or blue appearance.
When we refer to 'colour', we almost take for granted that 10
it is solid. Together with synthetic pigments, this idea of consistency is perhaps the true and most important novelty of the modern world. Something so obviously part of our world that we struggle with the idea that it has not always existed.

The creation of unique pieces – and before industrialization almost everything was a unique piece – was characterized by the use of *non*-solid and -consistent colours. The taste for non-homogeneous colour is a constant quality in the artefacts of the past. Think of the golden backgrounds in Byzantine painting, so rich and so changeable as to elude summary in a single word. Or think of

medieval jewellery, in which colour speaks with layered
and simultaneous voices. In the case of gemstones, the invention of various techniques of cutting serves to multiply
the tonal possibilities of the material: just as the faceting
of diamonds creates distinct chromatic moments within
the interior of a single substance. With so-called 'cabo- GRAMACCINI, 2003
16 chon' mounting, for instance, an oval stone is cut in two
and hollowed out, so that the light entering from beneath
reverberates throughout the whole volume of the gem, revealing an evanescent iridescence. It makes little sense in
the end to wonder if a cabochon-mounted garnet is ver- CASTELNUOVO, 1994
milion or burgundy, because it is both things at once.
Similarly, in Gothic cathedrals we experience dynamic
light and colour effects that are quite remote from modern uniformity – such as so-called *doublé*, in which two
layers of glass, one white, one red, are used one on top of
the other, producing variable effects depending on their
thickness and the angle of incidence of the light passing
through them.

Reflecting on artisanal inventions such as these that escape chromatic homogenization allows us to understand
key characteristics of our modernity. It is clear that such
doubling, with all its irregularities, was intended to pro-
18 duce effects a world away from the lustre of Plexiglas. If
we look at the transparent plastic used by Philippe Starck
for his chairs, we can appreciate its crystalline coherence,
but we hardly find this in the throbbing elusiveness of a
17 stained-glass window in Chartres. These are languages
and choices that are very remote from each other, issuing
from completely different existential conditions. On the
one hand, we have a smooth glass impossible to produce
in the thirteenth century, on the other, Gothic colour
participating metaphorically in a system in which divin-
ity speaks intermittently and desires to escape definition.

Japan, nineteenth century

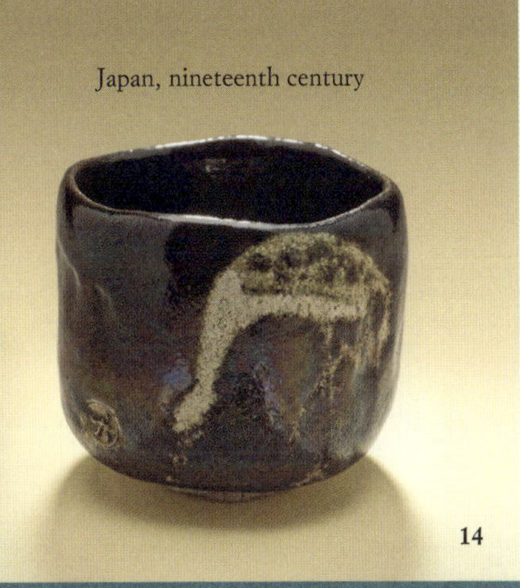

14

15

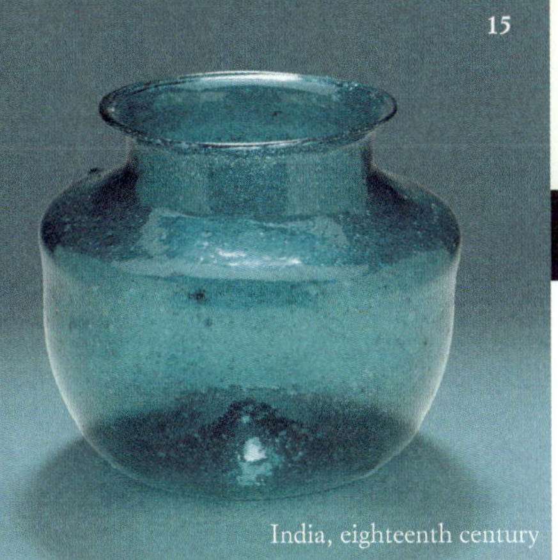

India, eighteenth century

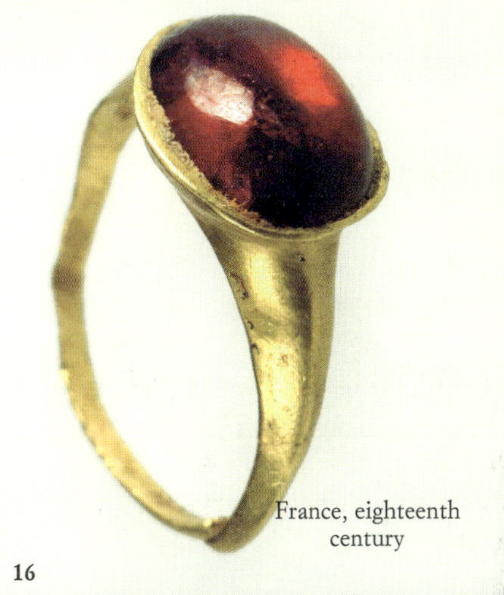

France, eighteenth century

16

17

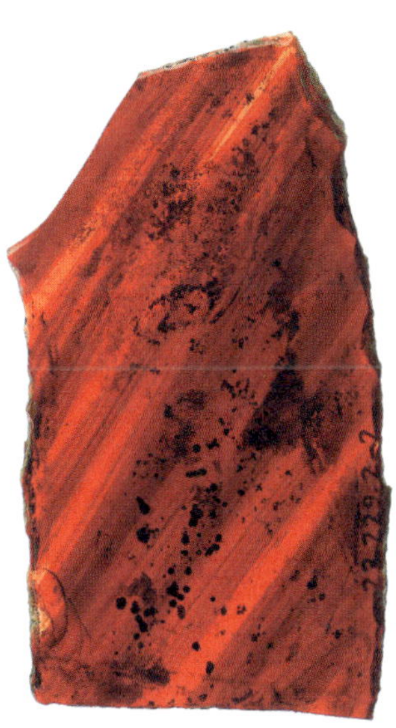

Chartres, France, eighth century

18

Twenty-first century

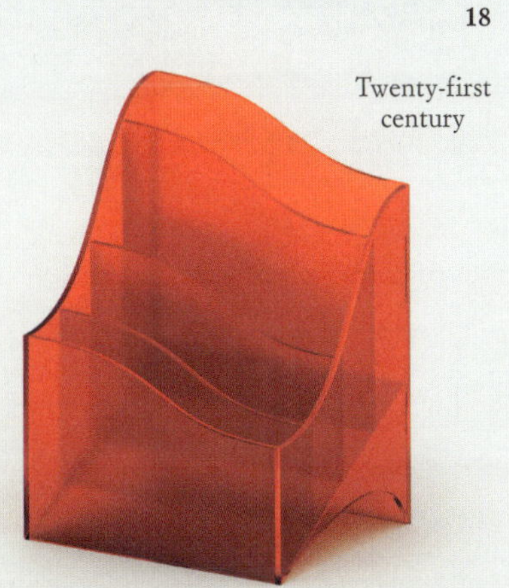

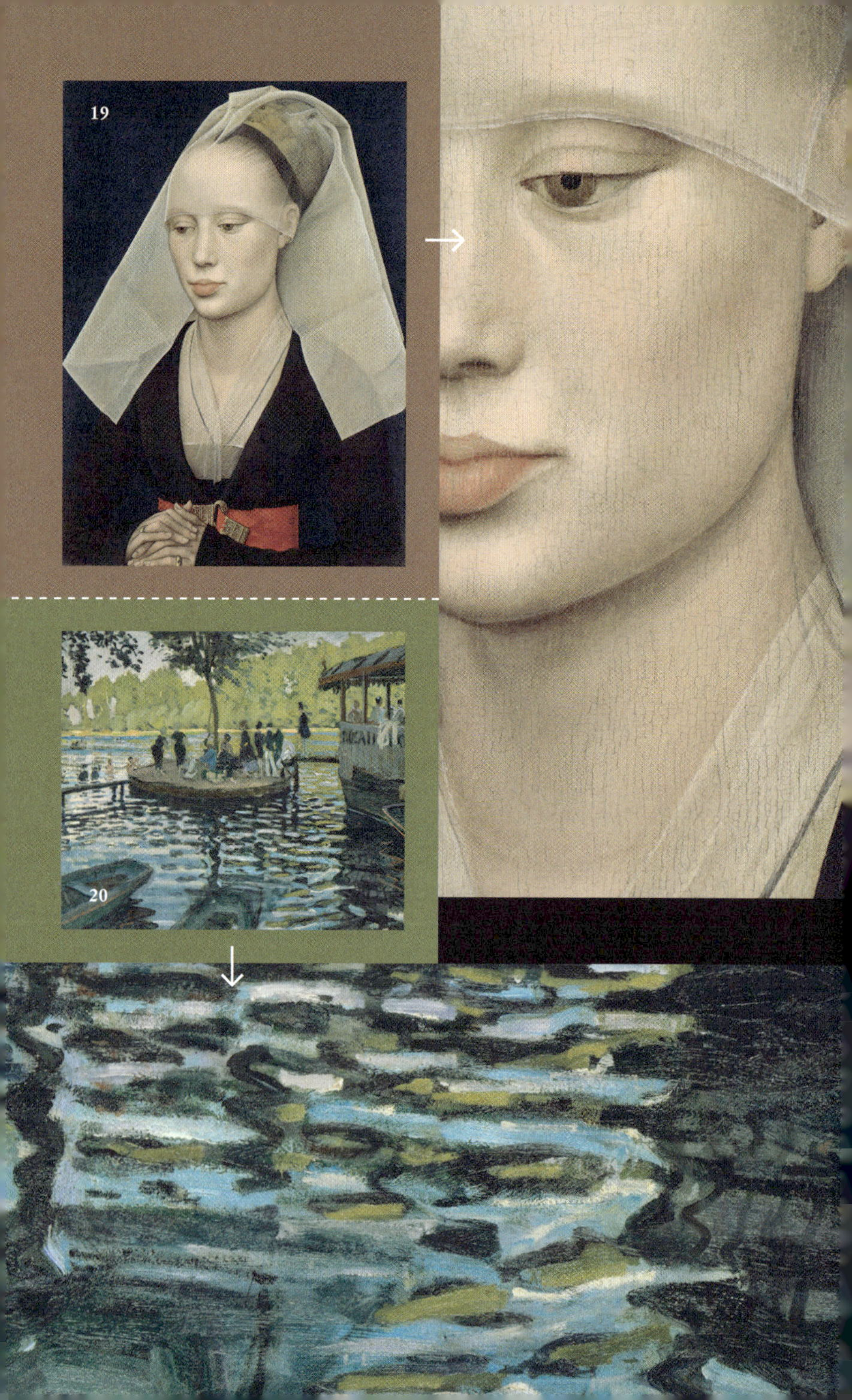
19
20

Starck's chair, in complete contrast, is a finished and de-
finable thing because it inserts itself as a technological
and partly ironic moment in a society that has no doubts
about the concreteness of the world.

For similar reasons, the glaze of a traditional Japanese
Raku ceramic has a chromatic interiority that situates it 14
within the magmatic flow of life, whereas a plate from Ikea
exudes a compact and immobile defiance of time (and of
the dishwasher) with its impeccable, standardized, endlessly reproducible smoothness.

It is in painting, however, that the most significant dif- 11
ACTON, 2009
ferences with modernity reveal themselves. If we examine
up close (if possible with the actual canvas before us) the
finish of an Old Master painting, we soon notice that the 19
colour has a materiality that does not end with the paint
but seems to penetrate into the very canvas instead, in a
manner consistent with an organic surface. In Renaissance
paintings there is a mellow and articulated unfolding that
ELKINS, 2000
provides a rich and vibrant texture. This is due, in a way
that's peculiar to oil painting, to the so-called 'glazing technique' – the way in which colour is applied in successive
transparent layers, with fresh and perhaps diluted coats
overlaid upon others that have dried, so that the underlying
colour more or less shines through. It is as if the pictorial surface were varnished and we were looking through
PINOTTI, 2007
that glaze. If we compare such an effect with the work of
a twentieth-century artist, the difference is striking. We
need only to think of Jackson Pollock applying paint to
the canvas directly from the tube or tin. Historically, however, the real change begins with Impressionism, when for 20
the first time colour is used like a dense body, with precise tints that have no depth but only relief: applied in
flecks, in touches, or in relatively broad strokes. It is not

by chance that the era of the Impressionists is also that of new forms of pigments sold ready to use. Leonardo had to grind his own colours; Monet no longer needed to – and this is why the paint can be spread just as it comes out of the tube, breaking with tradition and allowing the paintings to speak the accelerated language of nascent mass society.

REWALD, 1991

In the ancient world, solid colours were impossible or extremely difficult to produce. Success in doing so is more of an exception than the norm. Solid colour is more of an imagined, theoretical horizon than an everyday reality. With the development of serial or mass production the situation is reversed: producing uniform colour is often easier than avoiding it. The reason for this, both technical and historical, is not far to seek: having to reduce everything to repeatable procedures, industry has an intrinsic tendency to simplify forms and finishes. In the case of colour, the process is also facilitated by the development of modern pigments created in laboratories and devoid of impurities. In many ways, solid or uniform colour is not (or not only) a choice, a taste or a fashion, but one of the inevitable consequences of mass production. This does not mean that industry cannot do otherwise, only that it is simply its default position.

If we take a random object from among the many we deal with every day, we will notice that more often than not it will have solid colours, and that even the presence of a printed motif or pattern will follow a rule of regular and orderly repetition. This is why, from a historical point of view, we can say that solid colour is the principal charac-
21 teristic of modern objects – from Lego bricks and plastic bowls to the bodywork of cars. Turning to contemporary writing implements provides further confirmation of this:
25 felt-tip markers, for instance, produce marks that are solid

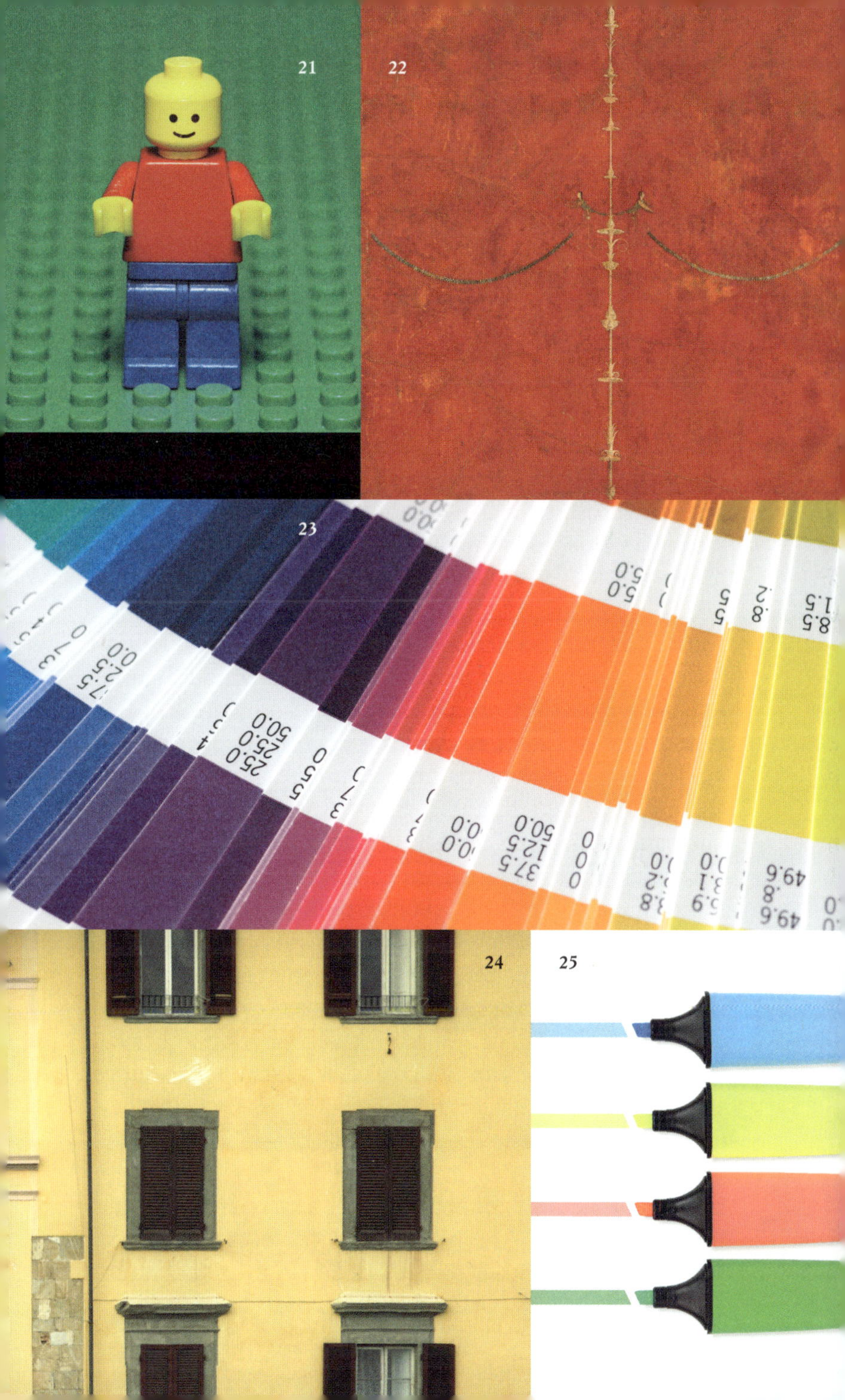
21
22
23
24
25

compared to the colours produced in the past by pencils, chalks or pastels, and even though the latter continue to be used, homogeneity now reigns supreme in our lives.

This is scarcely an inevitable or 'natural' outcome. Apart from the sky and the petals of some flowers, we have evolved in a world in which chromatic solidity and uniformity are actually very rare. Stones and soil, trunks and vegetation, are always variegated in colour. It is industrialization that has effectively transformed solid colour from an exception into an everyday fact, to the extent that it has now become the norm against which everything else is defined. The very idea of a shade, for instance, is only conceivable in relation to the possibility of a solid background.

Standardization has caused something else besides. As a consequence of becoming accustomed to solid colours, we have come to use colour itself like an abstraction. In order to confirm how obvious this is, we need only think of Pantone's sample books or guides, part of the most popular and famous colour-matching system in which all possible shades are included, and it is taken for granted that colour can be assessed using solid swatches. EISEMAN, 2011 If this works for the many objects we are surrounded by, it is of distinctly limited use for artefacts from the past. To say that
22, 23 the frescoes in a Pompeian villa are number-1805 red is an approximation that we can immediately see is quite inadequate, since it fails to recover the reality of our experience of the colour. To label a Lego brick number-032 red, on the other hand, more or less sums up its essence, and conveys in a few letters and characters everything we need to say about it.

Beyond the needs of production, there is a further question as to why it is that modernity has such a liking for solid colours. In order to provide an answer, let's try to reverse the problem and imagine what our world would be like if they did not exist.

Thinking of our houses, of our walls, of our textiles, the first thing that comes mind is that without uniform surfaces everything would seem a little on the old side, worn out or dirty. I am not talking about the chaotic variegation of a multicoloured textile, or of an artfully painted wall; I am thinking more of the faded aura that adheres to a fabric after prolonged use, or of the dark stripes that radiators leave on walls where they have heated the dust. Dirtiness is obviously relative: every culture establishes its own regulations as to cleanliness, in relation to norms. It is obvious that someone living in the third century would have a very different idea about hygiene in domestic spaces than someone living in the twenty-first. And for similar reasons, in a residence in the city we are less tolerant of dirt and dust on the floor compared to our attitude to a holiday let, where the sand on the floor is acceptable. And, when in a rural dwelling we appreciate its fired-brick flooring, we are naturally applying an idea of cleanliness very different from that with which we instinctively evaluate the marble beneath our feet in an outpatients department.

Hygiene, regularity, expected standards are some of the pillars on which modern society is based; they are forms of control as powerful as they are invisible, because they are often crudely equated with the virtues of progress. It is a story initiated 150 years ago. Against the worn and faded clothes of the peasant world, against the lime-washed walls of the poorer neighbourhoods, nineteenth-century culture proposes to the emergent petit-bourgeois and middle classes an alternative model in which order is central. In this universe – presented as progressive and aesthetically unprecedented – the logic of the market invites us to throw away what is old and to replace it with something new. This kind of renewal is an unprecedented model, and anyone who opposes it is soon branded as reactionary. This is reinforced by advances in medical knowledge, causing dirt to be looked at with thoroughgoing suspicion. In the end, the dirty, the old and the worn-out – three different concepts – end up becoming equivalent and sharing the same moral condemnation. If you want to be modern, you must aspire to the new and the clean.

And yet, if we stop to think about it, this is based partly on a deception. It is of course inevitable that everything gets worn out and dirty, but before the nineteenth century we did not make a drama out of the fact. It was industrialization that emphasized the transience of all inanimate objects, causing that subtle and widespread neurosis provoked by a chipped plate or scratched bodywork, reminding us of the transience and mortality of everything. And among the many weapons honed by advertising, this anxiety is one of the most powerful.

TANIZAKI, 2000

So we can say that solid colour embodies qualities that are not just chromatic. It is also an aspect of our idea of the 'new' on a perceptual level. The relationship between them is not deterministic: the mania for the new did not call forth solid colour but has contributed rather to its ubiquity – including through plastics, acrylic resins and paints. Familiarity with domestically consumed mass-produced objects has fostered the development of new categories with which to think about the world. And in accordance with our expectation that things should be new, modern finishes and materials actually seem to suffer the passage of time more than ancient ones, and plastic seems to age less well than glass or wood.

If we look at contemporary suburban buildings painted with synthetically bound emulsions, for instance, we notice that with time they become stained and cracked, but that

BISSON, 2005

the colour remains solid and plasticky. By contrast, the walls of buildings in historic centres are directly impacted 24
by weather conditions, and even shortly after restoration begin to stain in fascinating ways, revealing a dynamic interplay between tempera and environment. The difference between (attractive) inhomogeneity in the historic centre and 'dirtiness' in the suburbs goes with the difference between our concepts of the 'antique' and the 'old'. The old presupposes and is eclipsed by the new, whereas the antique faces off only with the eternal.

Reflections such as this are possible both because every technology produces its own specific outcome, and because our way of conceiving, feeling and judging things is no longer independent of the mark that industrialization has made on history. If we see a Renaissance painting we do not tend to think of it as dirty (even though it might be), whereas in front of many works of art of the 1950s and 1960s, such as those of Pop Art, we are keenly aware of their dustiness or shabbiness, and that it is not restoration they are in need of so much as a good cleaning. We are able to think this precisely because they are made with the materials of industrialization, and inhabit, much like we do, the same mental spaces.

26

24 GIANT SIZE PKGS.
New!
Brillo®
soap pads
WITH RUST RESISTER
SHINES ALUMINUM FAST
24 GIANT SIZE PKGS.
New!
Brillo®
soap pads
WITH RUST RESISTER

27

Nuovo Politecnico 66 Einaudi 1975
ROLAND BARTHES
IL PIACERE
DEL TESTO
Contro le indifferenze della scienza e il puritanesimo
dell'analisi ideologica

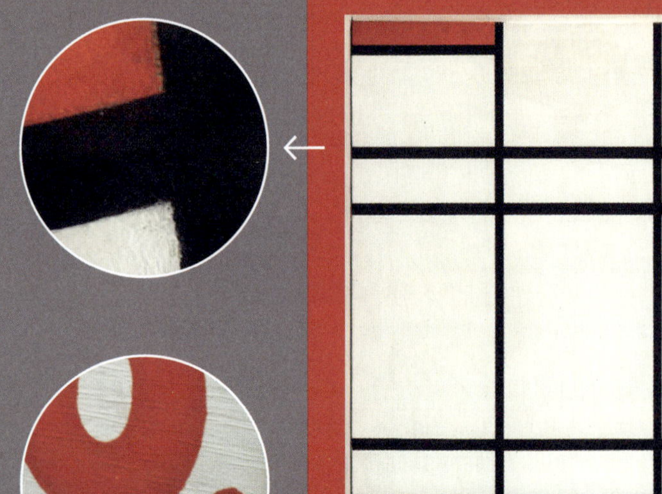

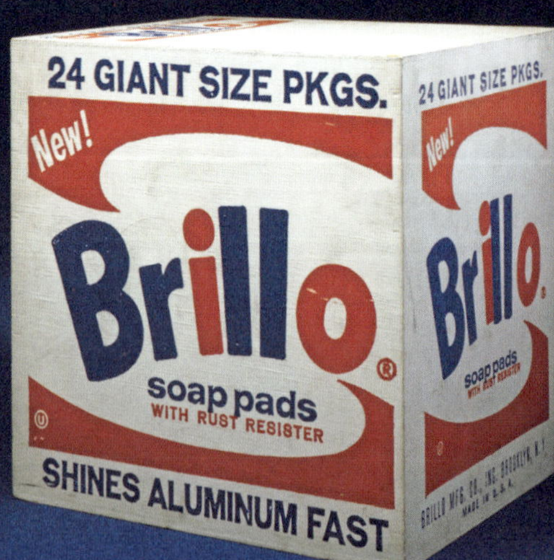

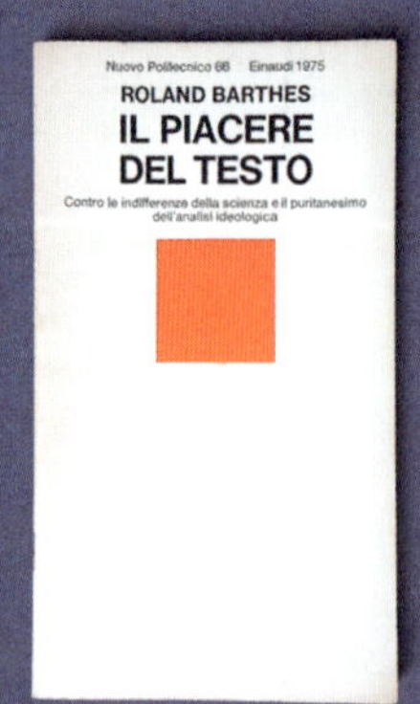

28

Complex Black

The Possibility of Industrial Colour

From what we have said so far, it would seem that our status as industrialized beings might restrict our taste to artefacts of relatively simple design: if the complex glazes of Old Master paintings speak to connoisseurs of the most refined kind, solid colour addresses everyone, without distinction, levelling us all down to the role of instant consumers.

Still, however much we might regret lost complexity, and believe that standardization has ultimately impoverished our aesthetic sense, that is not quite right. Our contemporary world possesses other kinds of richness. To understand this, it is worth looking at a handful of works encapsulating some of the qualities of the languages of mass culture.

A work that vividly illustrates the conflict between chromatic complexity and the logic of serial or mass production
is Andy Warhol's *Brillo Box* (1964), one of the best-known 27
examples of Pop Art. It is a replica, the same only in appearance, of the cardboard boxes used to distribute Brillo pads to shops and supermarkets. Warhol studies and reproduces them in an almost identical fashion. But it is precisely this 'almost' that is crucial.

BOATTO, 2008

The real Brillo boxes are made of white cardboard on which the brand logo is screen-printed in two colours. Warhol's boxes are made from plywood, are slightly larger, and have also been screen-printed – but individually and by hand, so that here and there they exhibit slight imperfections and differences. And it is this that makes us think. DANTO, 2010

Industrial printing, especially of large numbers of units, almost always produces irregularities; but no one notices them, because they are considered to be intrinsic to the technique with which they are realized. They are not defects, but merely a reality of this particular language.

Warhol's inaccuracies appear instead to be intentional and poetic. In other words the printing imprecision which in the real Brillo boxes is part and parcel of the technology that produced them, in Warhol becomes painting, becomes a human gesture, revealing the trembling border of the solid colours in our contemporary collective imagination. 'Look at how gorgeous all this printed colour is with a little blurring' – Warhol seems to be saying – 'look at how much expressivity there is even in a supermarket, if only we had eyes to see.' Ultimately, Warhol is a romantic of sorts: he loves these mass-produced objects so much as to want to restore them to us as unique pieces, to have us recognize their unexpected allure, and their status as perhaps the real art of our times.

This aspect of contemporary colour can also be approached from a completely different angle. There is
26 another artist, Piet Mondrian, whose popularity has been equal to that of Warhol's, and whose paintings – through constant and ubiquitous reproduction – have become representative of artistic modernity itself. In the 1980s, even L'Oréal launched a line of hair products blatantly inspired by the Dutch master.[1]

One of the reasons for Mondrian's success is the fact that his pictorial style has an affinity with modern graphic

[1] The Studio Line, which is still in production.

design, with what has historically been the language of industry. His pictures, when reproduced, are bi-dimensional, compact, solid, just like factory-made objects. The constant presence of his paintings in manuals, books and magazines has created, however, an enormous misunderstanding. A Mondrian-style red rectangle might resemble, in aesthetic presence, a square of printed red – like one on a Bruno 28
Munari cover, for instance. But Mondrian's is a *painted* red, and this should not be forgotten. If we look closely at the actual painting itself, we become aware – not accidentally – of many intentional and decidedly pictorial discontinuities in the apparent solidity of the colour.

If Mondrian had wished to devise merely graphic grids, he would have made his work using screen-printing or stencils. He could even have become a graphic designer. Instead, after starting out as a figurative artist, he arrived at abstraction through a series of successive simplifications, deciding to stop just before the painterly crosses the border into industrial colour. His sense of his works resides precisely in this vital contradiction: he makes images for mass society that resemble its quotidian lexicon and mimic its layout and lineaments, that *almost* resemble design, but which, when looked at close up, reveal a pulsating nature. The same matter engaged with by the Renaissance Masters.

Flat colours are effectively taken in and appreciated at a glance, whereas worked and painterly colour requires a kind of slow and patient looking. Making worked colour and the glance coincide, Mondrian and Warhol engage in their different ways with the problem of an increasingly decentralized contemporary public and propose their own personal aesthetic solution. Paradoxically we could say that they both make graphic, design-led use of the material of painting.

Precisely because of its natural predisposition towards
solid colours, graphic art has sought various ways of establishing a new kind of chromatic richness that could
be properly and uniquely its own. One such method of
achieving this was the use of overprinting: after one ink
has been used, another is immediately laid over it, with-
32 out cancelling it completely. This is a common enough
procedure that nevertheless may be transformed into an
expressive element. It means that there are two colours,
both 'solid', producing a vibrant new colour that displays AMBROSE, 2009
a variegated surface, especially when contrasted with its
two constituents. The result of this overprinting is not
just a third colour, a pure mixture, but one which reveals,
sometimes to a surprising degree, the manner in which it
has been produced.

There is an outstanding example of this in a 1922 litho-
29 graph by Wassily Kandinsky, from his *Kleine Welten* (Small
Worlds) series: the green emerges from a superimposition
of yellow upon blue, becoming in the process something
fluid, dynamic, even pulsating. There is another such example, in a more refined and painterly mode, in a portrait
30 of a woman made by Egon Schiele in 1910, in which the
redness of her hair is achieved by laying down a deep,
grainy and irregular pink upon a yellow ground, captur-
ing in the process its smoky lustre through the imperfect
coincidence of the two impressions.

If we look at graphic art designed for a wide circulation we can find significant examples of this technique in HOLLIS, 2002
33 the work of Albe Steiner (1913–74) – in the formidable
first page of *Il Contemporaneo*, for instance, in which the
enlarged date 1917 is overprinted on the text and photographs, amplifying the significance and the impact of the
entire layout. And it is worth looking too at the famous
31 Monza racing poster by Max Huber (1919–92), in which

29

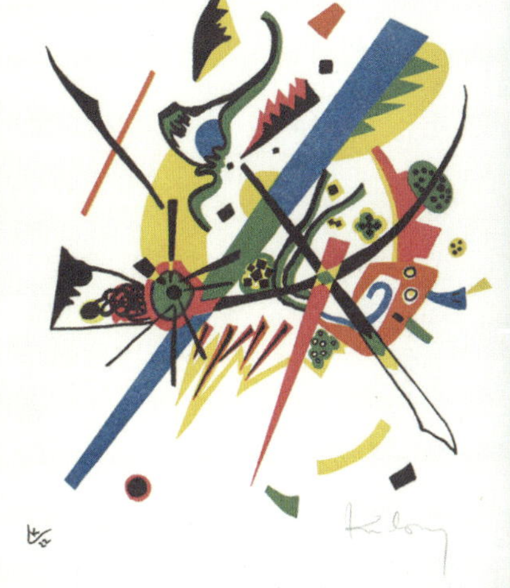

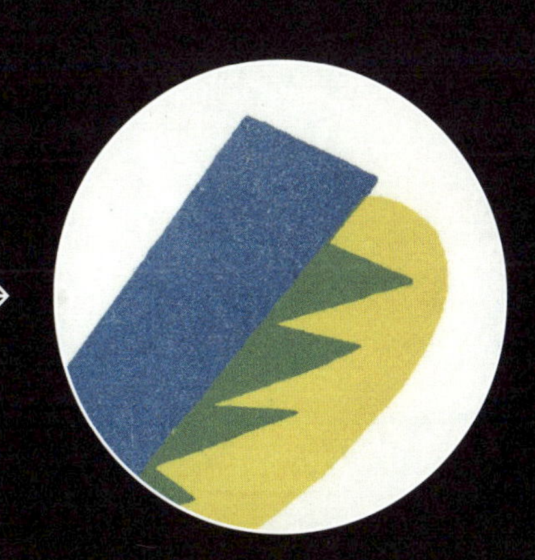

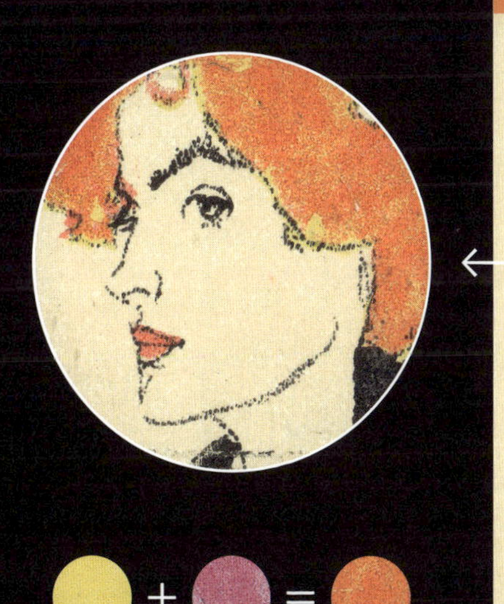

30

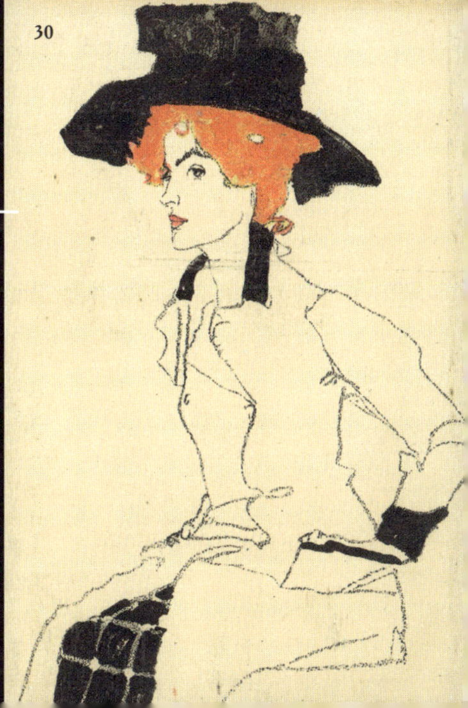

31

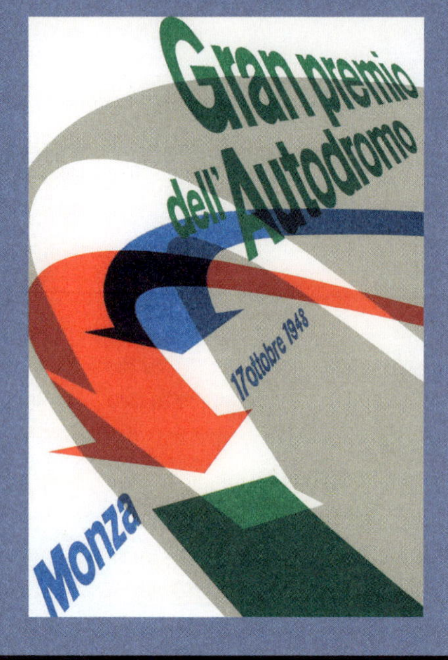

32

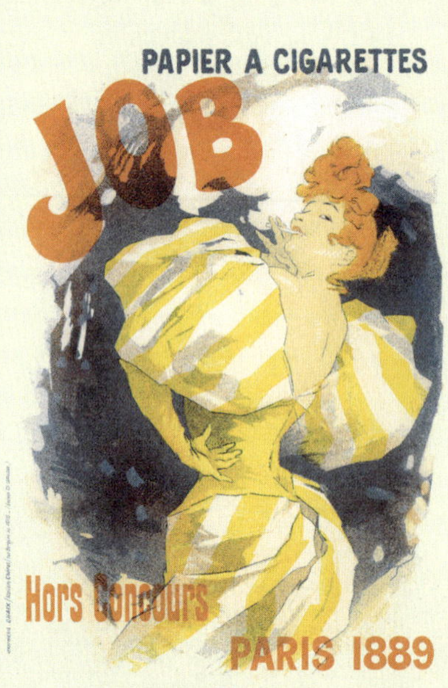

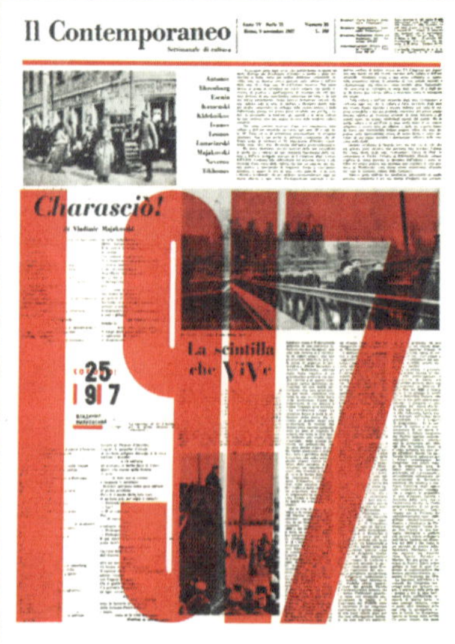

Il Contemporaneo

Charasciò!

di Vladimir Majakovski

1917

La scintilla che ViVe

25
1917

33

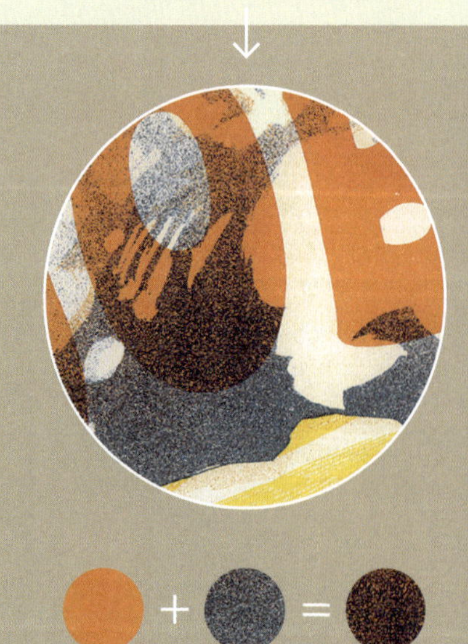

the overprinting intensifies the temporal dynamics of the arrows, as if we really had before us the trails left behind by racing cars.

A more recent example can be found in the work of Blex-bolex (b. 1966), a sophisticated French illustrator whose 34
books, including the magnificent *L'imagier des gens*, turn the superimposition of differently coloured inks into the syntax with which the story is told, transforming a technical given into a narrative element. In all these cases, the overprinting has the charm of a mechanism that we seem to get pleasure from by seeing its workings, in a way that is typically modern.

Illustration – which by definition is painting conceived with reproducibility in mind – has in turn found original ways to give life to rich and articulated colour within the limitations of industrial design, especially when in the hands of real artists.

Simone Rea (b. 1975), one of the most gifted of con- 35
temporary illustrators, has developed a highly individual technique in which he superimposes multiple layers of acrylic – now thickly, now subtly – which are sanded several times and coated with oil varnishes in a way that allows the underlying colours to show through. The result is a design orchestrated by defined backgrounds similar to flat colours, but within which there is a febrile and undulating dust stirring – reintroducing something of the play of glazes, rethought with the logic of printing.

On a completely different front there is the work of
Shout (b. 1977): made on a computer, it reintroduces com- 36
plexity by superimposing granularity and dirt upon digital surfaces that are by their very nature flat and without texture. On the one hand, this confers a vintage patina to the design, like that of a sheet of old paper found in a drawer;

on the other hand, it creates a virtuoso short circuit between the constancy of colour and those unexpected events that occur in the making of art, emphasizing errors in printing as an essential requisite for contemporary figuration.

If we find the works of such artists suggestive, it is perhaps because our minds have always been torn between a need for order and the need to break it, between the desire for a smooth background and for unpredictable variation. On the one hand, the success of modern colours is due precisely to the beauty of uniformity, which gives us an ideal and almost mathematical dimension, reinforcing our tendency towards abstraction. But on the other, we look for this to be roughened and dirtied – for the imperfection that makes colour alive and human.

Returning to the words of the pastry chef with which we began the last chapter, we should not forget an important detail in her account: her 'diplomat cake' is so popular because each generation feels it to be the pastry of a bygone era, and its apparently outmoded status is not so much an actual fact as a psychological one. Its presumed old-worldliness is one of the seductions that help to sell it to us. Memory is just a point of view, another way of dealing with contemporaneity. It's a way of saying that, since the past is always something of an invention, nostalgia is not by definition to be condemned. In the end, only those familiar with industrial colours are able to appreciate the imperfections and noise to which there was perhaps no alternative in the Renaissance. The point is not to prefer the 'diplomat cake' over Nutella but to recognize the aesthetic specificity of each while remaining men and women of our own time.

When I first attended art school, I had a teacher of graphic design who asked me to paint square after square using blacks of various kinds: tempera, charcoal, oils,

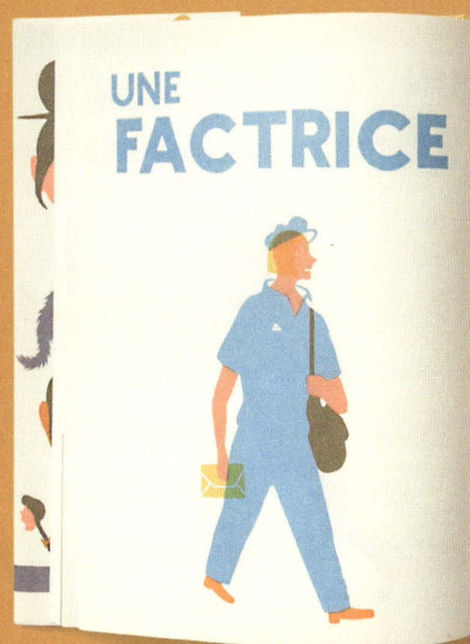
UNE
FACTRICE

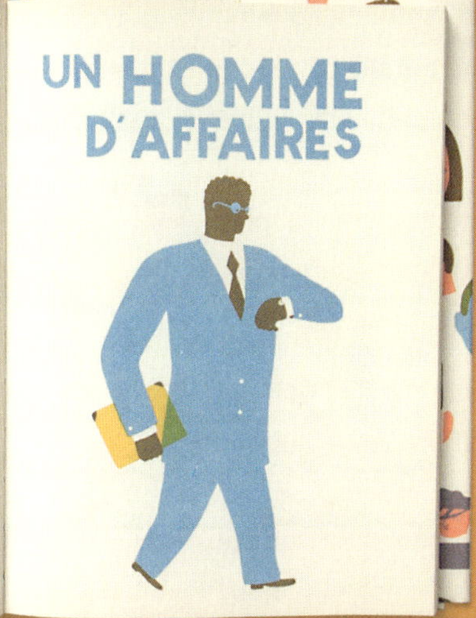
UN HOMME
D'AFFAIRES

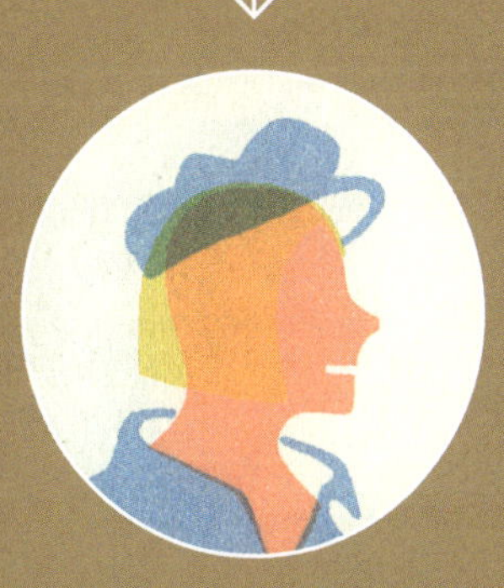

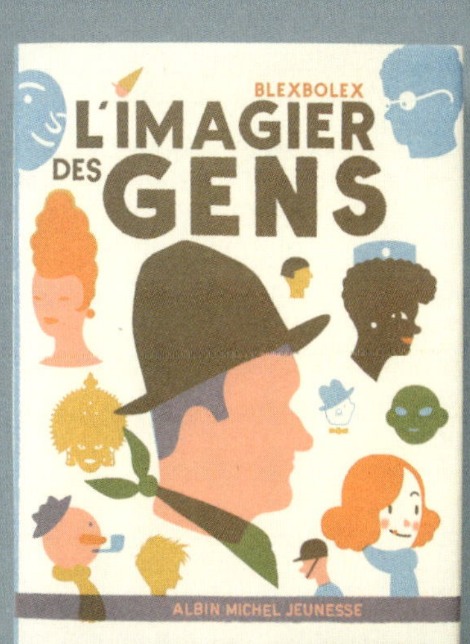
BLEXBOLEX
L'IMAGIER
DES GENS
ALBIN MICHEL JEUNESSE

35

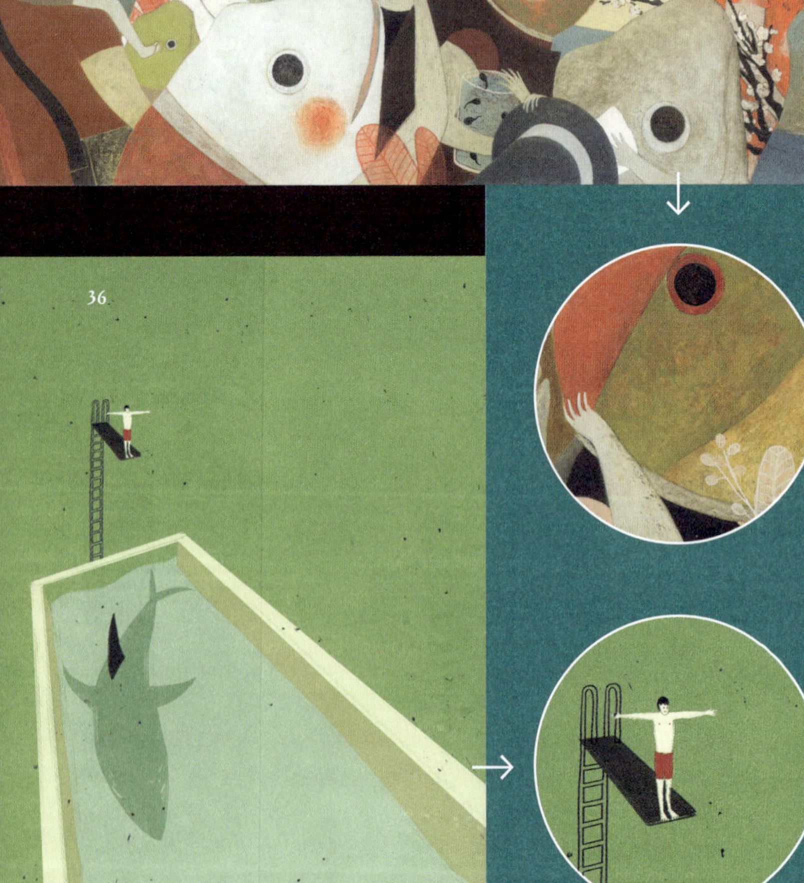

watercolour, soft and hard graphite. And in doing so he cited Hokusai's manual of painting, written in 1895, according to which there was old black and shiny black, a black illuminated by the sun and one as dark as a shadow. We wanted to get onto our computers, but he insisted that in order to become good graphic artists we must first colour in these squares with the greatest possible number of blacks: shiny and matte, silkily smooth and grainily textured, brilliant and opaque. We spent an entire week on producing those squares in an infinite variety of blacks, and commenting upon their effects. This professor was teaching an industrial- and digitally minded generation that black is not something given once and for all, and that there are infinite ways, now inert and now pulsating, in which colour can reveal itself. Even in design.

Understanding the inventive logic of the past can teach us, by way of contrast, about new uses of colour in mass-produced artefacts. To understand, however, it is not enough just to look. It is essential to relate the colour to its context, and to ask questions about the world and the ways of thinking that produced it. And this is what we will be doing in the following chapters.

PART TWO

Histories

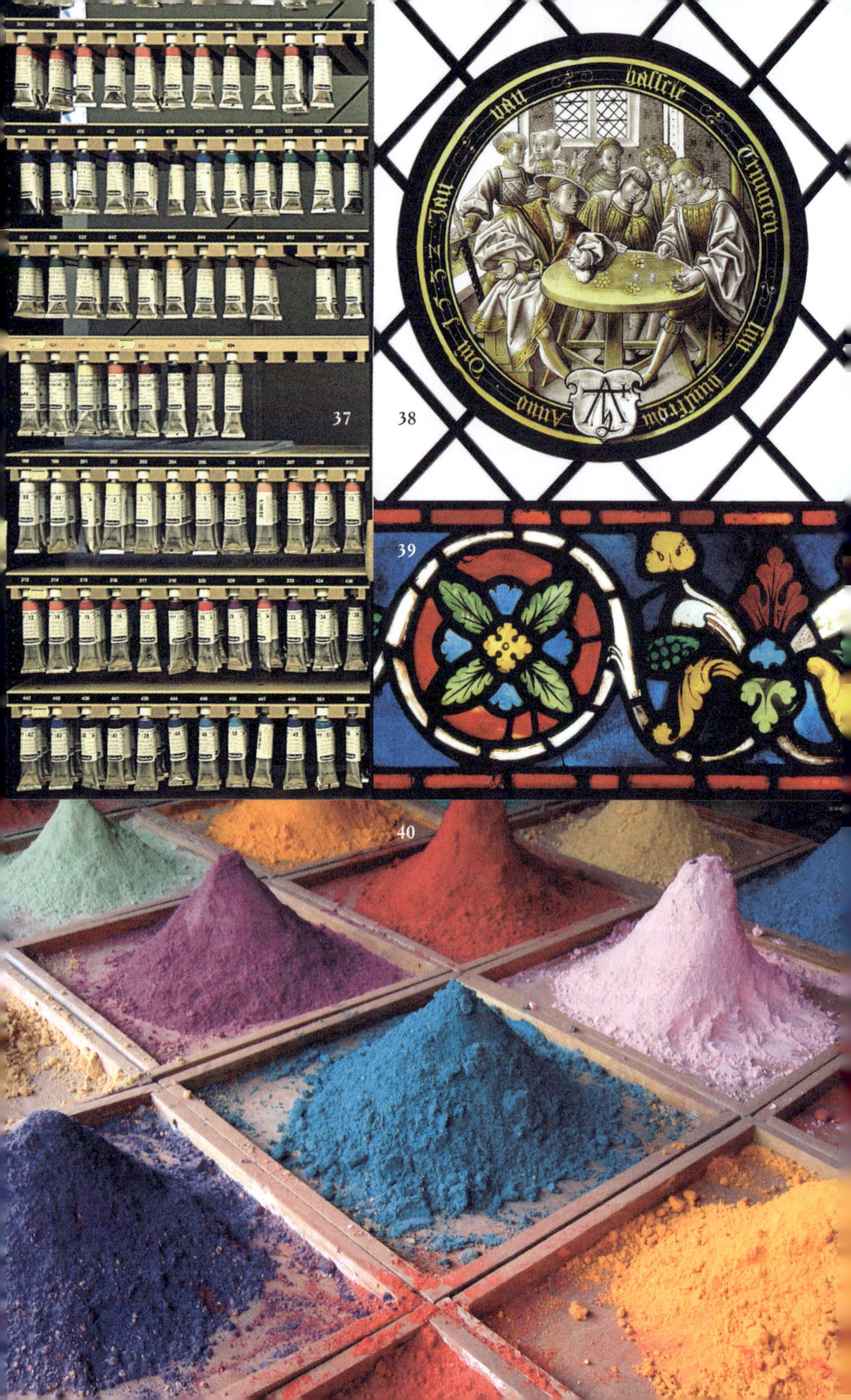
37
38
39
40

Luxury Blue

Dyes and Pigments before Modernity

By one of those coincidences that as children we like to attribute to fate, I was born above a shop selling artists' materials that I could pop down to every time I needed paper or a coloured pencil. When I reached the age to graduate from felt-tips to grown-up colours, I was struck and somewhat disoriented at first by their peculiar names: burnt Sienna, Van Dyke brown, cadmium yellow, ultramarine blue. Compared to the lexicon to which I was accustomed, these were difficult words, hinting at an esoteric world that was both seductive and awe-inspiring.

The names were not only extravagant; they were too numerous. There were at least three kinds of white, for instance – zinc, titanium and lead – which all seemed to be the same, so it was unclear which one I should go for and why.

As I was accustomed to sets of crayons in which colours had generic rather than particular names, for me colour up to this point was a mere question of perception, of 'how it looked'. Red, yellow and blue were sensations. They were not concrete things.

Fine art names evoked instead not so much the appearance of colours as their origin. Burnt Sienna was named after the place where, at the time, this ferrous soil abounded; Van Dyke brown got its name in homage to the painter who used that dark tone best; cadmium yellow was so called because it was made using cadmium sulphide. These were not simply names for colours, they were certificates of provenance – and for a child growing up in an industrialized world, provenance was part of a logic that was difficult to understand. The first and foremost difference about these colours of the past, often encoded in their names, was this: that before chemistry colour was above all a precious material substance.

For more than thirty-five millennia, colours were sourced from the three realms of nature. From mineral deposits extracted from the earth, carbon and stones were obtained for grinding. From the animal kingdom, molluscs and insects were sought to be squeezed and crushed. And from the vegetable world came all those plants whose juices revealed their power to stain and dye.

The fact that certain colours could be found only in
particular places and not in others is something that has
frequently left its mark on human artefacts, in a way that
always needs to be taken into account. In the Romanesque
windows of Germanic areas, for instance, we find many
38 greens and yellows, whereas in similar French ones it is
39 blue and red that predominate. This is not a question of
taste or of style – it is a reflection instead of the actual
availability of certain substances in certain geographical
areas.

CASTELNUOVO, 1994

Today, whether for artistic or industrial use, colours are synthetic products: molecules created in a laboratory through chemical reactions. For the first time in human history, it is possible to access all colours without scouring the world for them. All we need now is access to the internet and a credit card.

LUZZATTO, 2001

But this is not all: in the past, objects could only be certain colours, meaning that the colour was seen as consubstantial with their being, and not an adjective or a sensation added to

their concreteness or contingency. When we speak of colour today, on the other hand, we are referring to a concept that is partially abstract. We use yellow, red and blue as adjectives that can be applied to anything: a yellow skirt, a red table, a book with a blue cover. We have a general sense of colours unfettered from precise objects, and we can conceptualize and name the yellow that comes before all yellow *things*. But this is not just about the capacity of our minds for abstraction, it also relates to a historical condition – because it is
industry that allows us to see that a skirt, a table and a book 9
can potentially come in any colour.

This may seem like an obvious fact, and yet it is a recent achievement. As recently as the 1930s, nylon stockings had to wait to enter the marketplace, as it wasn't at all clear how to colour the synthetic fibre from which they were made – unlike those made of silk, a fabric that had been successfully dyed since the Middle Ages.

To get an idea of the nature of these mythic and heterogeneous origins, it is worth considering the biographies of some of the most eminent colours.

BRUNELLO, 1968

The first pigments[1] used by humankind were derived 40
from the earth. Procuring them was relatively easy: we only needed to dig. They have been used since prehistoric times to paint or to change the appearance of artefacts. It is these earthy colours that give life to such prehistoric paintings as the magnificent Lascaux bison, and that are found in some of the oldest burials. The so-called Red Lady of Paviland,

[1] Colours are divided into two groups: 'dyes' and 'pigments'. The first are substances that dissolve in liquids (such as water) and are used to colour textiles, for drawing on paper and to colour food. The second, since they have particles that are larger than those of dyes, do not dissolve but spread out in liquid, and are used for painting or as the basis for cosmetics. In other words: the sap extracted from plants is a dye and is used to colour textiles that are then fixed so as not to fade with washing; earth and powdered stone are pigments that are mixed with other substances such as gesso, egg and oil to make a paste that can be applied with brushes.

a skeleton dating to 33,000 BC, is covered across its entire surface with a layer of red ochre, chosen in all probability in connection with the belief that this oxide, like blood, was vitally connected to life.[2]

41 From plants we extract substances that are adapted to colouring paper, foodstuffs and textiles. From madder, for instance, comes a vibrant red perfect for dyeing fabrics; from saffron we obtain a variety of tones from yellow to orange; while from woad, a plant found mostly in northern Europe, we extract a blue dye. The latter was a colour little loved in classical times, probably because it was difficult to obtain and to fix – but also because of its association with those barbarians who coloured their faces blue before going into battle, as Julius Caesar records in his *Gallic Wars*. The word 'Britons' itself, in fact, can be derived from 'brythen' meaning 'painted men', a detail lodged in the popular imagination and cited by Mel Gibson in *Braveheart* (1995). (No matter that the blue-painted face of the film's Scottish national hero is completely anachronistic for its thirteenth-century setting.) NORDENFALK, 2012

Other colours come to us from the animal kingdom, such as the red derived from cochineal beetles, not only the most-used dye for centuries but even now one of the most widespread food colourings, commercialized today with the name E120. It is to this that we owe, among many others things, the splendour of Campari red, as well as of gummy bears and many fruit juices. Even the colour of the strawberry Frappuccino sold by Starbucks was for a long time vividly enhanced by cochineal – before protesting vegans in the United States successfully persuaded the coffee giant to replace it with a synthetic additive. ECKSTUT, 2013

[2] The use of red ochre to colour the bones of the dead has also been discovered in prehistoric North America and in Japan.

41

PIGMENTS

DYES

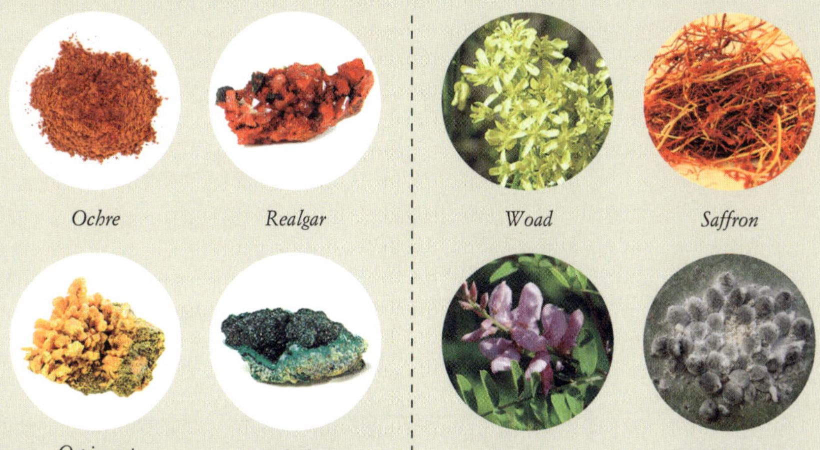

Ochre · *Realgar* · *Woad* · *Saffron*

Orpiment · *Malachite* · *Indigo* · *Cochineal*

42 NATURAL DEPOSITS

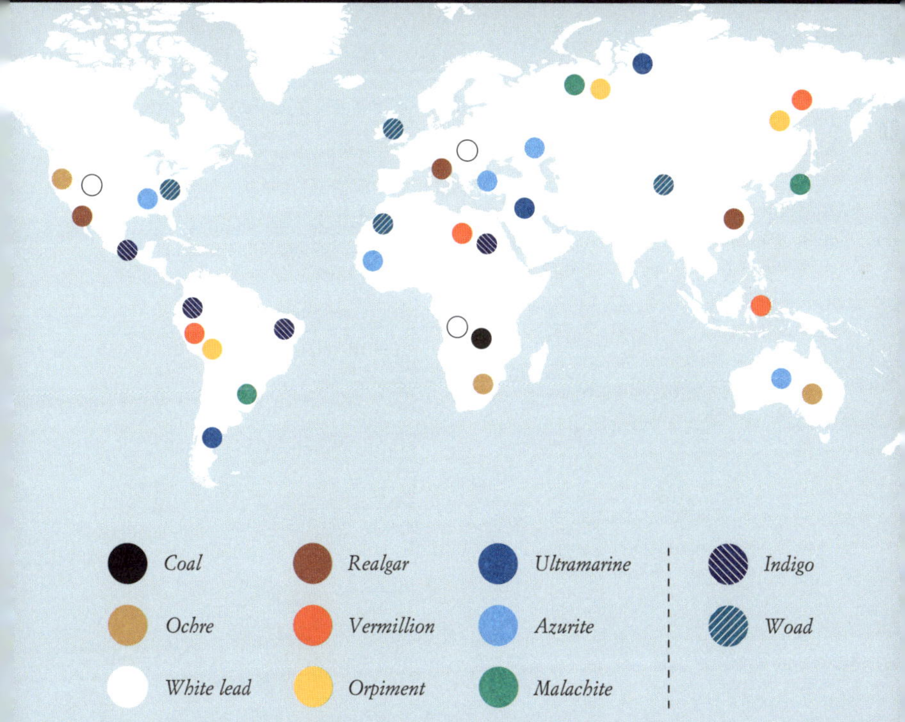

Coal

Ochre

White lead

Realgar

Vermillion

Orpiment

Ultramarine

Azurite

Malachite

Indigo

Woad

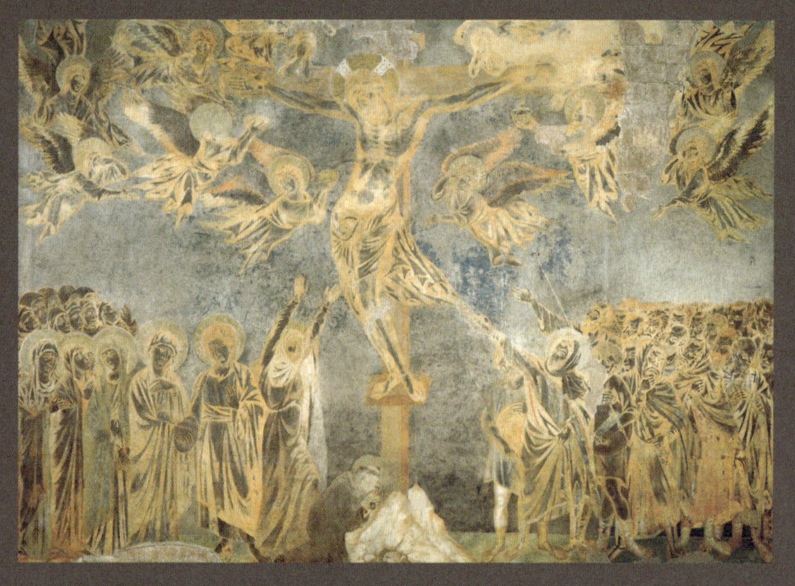

43

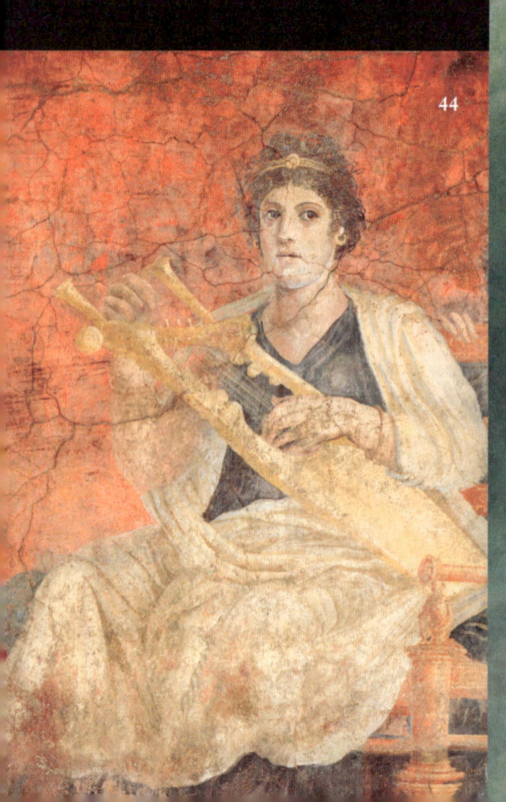

44

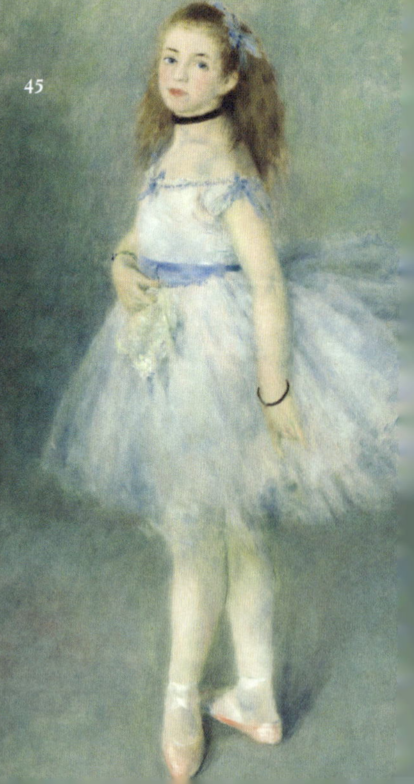

45

There are colours that are created by combining the animal and vegetable kingdoms, such as the exquisite Indian yellow that is produced by feeding cows exclusively on mango leaves and preventing them from drinking water, in order to extract from their dried urine a yellow powder with intense strength as a colourant. Or at any rate that is how it was done in India in the fifth century: now Indian yellow is manufactured using a chemical formula.

Still, even in the ancient world, colours were not just 42
sourced from our environment: at some point we also began to fabricate them.

The oldest artificial pigment, 'Egyptian blue', dates from 3,000 BC and was the most commonly used blue for
MALTESE, 1991
centuries.[3] Even more successful was white lead, the most important paint from the classical age all the way down to the nineteenth century, when it was discovered to be toxic and removed from sale.[4] It is the white that we find in the
frescoes of Imperial Rome, as well as in the palette of Renoir 44
where it softens and clarifies the blues and pinks. Apart 45
from its toxicity, it has another serious defect: when used in frescoes it is prone to turn dark. We can see an example of
this catastrophic effect in Cimabue's *Crucifixion* (1277– 43
ZECCHINA, 2012
83) in Assisi, where the plaster has absorbed the damp and turned the carbon into black lead sulphide. In the process, the image has become inverted like a photographic negative.

[3] We are talking about a mixture of calcium carbonate, copper and silica heated to 900 degrees, from which one obtains a glassy paste that, once cooled, is made into a powder and used like any other pigment.

[4] White lead is a basic lead carbonate, a soft paste giving good coverage, easy to lay down and very quick to dry, hence ideal for painting and as a base for canvases. To make white lead, the process used until the nineteenth century consisted of putting vinegar and thin strips of lead into holes filled with fresh manure, where the vapours from the manure, reacting with the ascetic acid, produced a white powder from the lead. Today the sale of white lead powder is illegal in almost all countries because of its toxicity. The whites that have become most common since lead fell out of use are those made from zinc and from titanium.

Toxicity and instability account for many of the problems encountered by those working with colours in the premodern world. Theirs is a history fraught with danger and pitfalls, a path strewn with poisonings, arduous effort and stench. On the one hand, the harmful properties of some chemical combinations are completely ignored – white lead is even used in Rome as face make-up or foundation, causing serious skin reactions – on the other, in order to fix colours, recourse is made to acidic substances such as urine, hence making the process extremely unpleasant. The famous expression *pecunia non olet* (money has no smell) refers precisely to Vespasian's reply when his son complained about the urine tax he had imposed for tanning and painting, revealing how large the turnover in such bodily fluid must have been.

RINALDI, 1986

LUZZATTO, 2001

Whoever worked with colours effectively belonged to a low and foul-smelling class, and the more that varicoloured fabrics were appreciated, the more those responsible for their colours were stigmatized – as happens in many societies where those working manually must get their hands filthy. These were workers at the bottom of the social ladder, beneath artisans and artists and categorized as mere 'mechanicals'. In Sparta, wool was left white and undyed, partly in order not to succumb to the frivolity of colour – but also to avoid having to admit dyers into Spartan society.

BRUNELLO, 1968

From this handful of stories we can see how in the past colour was thought of in a profoundly different way than it is now. Above all because, as with anything that does not come readily to hand, the more difficult colours were to obtain, the more expensive they were.

In the ancient world, every colour had a specific cost which came to define it. Lampblack, obtained from carbon, is very easy to procure and was therefore available at an affordable price; the red of porpora (derived from a certain kind of mollusc) and the blue of lapis lazuli – both imported substances of an exotic and precious kind – had prohibitive prices that placed them at the other end of the economic scale.

The palette did not consist of colours that were equal with each other – it was distinctly hierarchical instead, with the differences in their cost and value continuing to count in finished artefacts such as paintings, clothes and tableware. Cost and provenance effectively defined colours, as they do today with foodstuffs: the radish that comes from Treviso; the hazelnuts from Piedmont; the mango from India. The availability of synthetic colours has effectively annulled the kind of economic education that we still have today with foodstuffs (at least in Europe) and that teaches even children, long before it is a question of taste, that wine sold in cartons is not champagne.

Today a tube of lampblack and one of ultramarine will cost more or less the same; in the Renaissance the difference between them was like the difference between a potato and a white truffle. Which is to say that, in the past, blue was not only worth more than black, but the difference was immediate and obvious – registered at a glance, without even thinking about it.

PASTOUREAU, 2002

Ultramarine blue is not only more expensive; it is first and foremost a mythic substance. So much so, in fact, that Marco Polo included it among the marvels discovered on his voyages. It is after all the reduction to powder of a semiprecious stone, lapis lazuli and it arrives in Europe fetched 51
from distant countries 'beyond' the Mediterranean. 'Ultramarine', as it is dubbed in the Renaissance, refers in a vague way to how it gets to the market from an imprecise 'overseas' place. Today we know that in the ancient world the only source of this mineral was actually in what is now Afghanistan, and that it reached Italy via the silk route, arriving

like all kinds of exotic goods in Venice, the most important trading hub in Europe.[5]

Although it was known since antiquity, in the Europ- HALL, 1994
ean imagination ultramarine is the blue of the Renaissance:
that intense azure that we find in Giotto's paintings in
the Scrovegni Chapel, in Leonardo's *Last Supper*, on Michelangelo's Sistine ceiling and in the skies of so many
46 paintings by Bellini and Titian, to mention only the most
celebrated examples.

To make this colour all the more precious, it did not
come readymade but required a long and laborious prep-
aration. In its natural state, lapis lazuli is found mixed
51 with other minerals, and before use it is essential to sep- BRUNELLO, 1968
arate out the pigment from all impurities. So it must first
be ground before oil, wax and resin are added and the resulting paste is kneaded several times before undergoing
multiple rinses from which, after drying, a very fine powder
of a brilliant azure is obtained. This process is described
by Cennino Cennini (1370–1427), a Giotto-esque painter
and author of *The Book of Art*. Cennini's book is an extraordinary account of workshop practices in which he gives
detailed technical advice, revealing the difficulties faced
by those working with colour at the time, and allowing us
47 to reconstruct the prestigious palette that characterized
and defined Italian painting from the fourteenth to the
sixteenth centuries.

Reading Cennini is like going behind the scenes in a great Renaissance studio. Here even the names of colours are fascinating: orpiment, minium, dragon's blood. These

[5] According to Pliny the Elder, lapis lazuli came from Persia, but this was probably just the centre of its distribution. The etymology of the word, however, is indeed Persian, from *lajward*, which is to say 'blue'. That it passed through Samarkand en route is witnessed to by the fact that it is sometimes referred to as Samarkand. In the nineteenth century, new sources of lapis lazuli were found in Siberia and in Chile, but by this time it was already possible to produce it artificially.

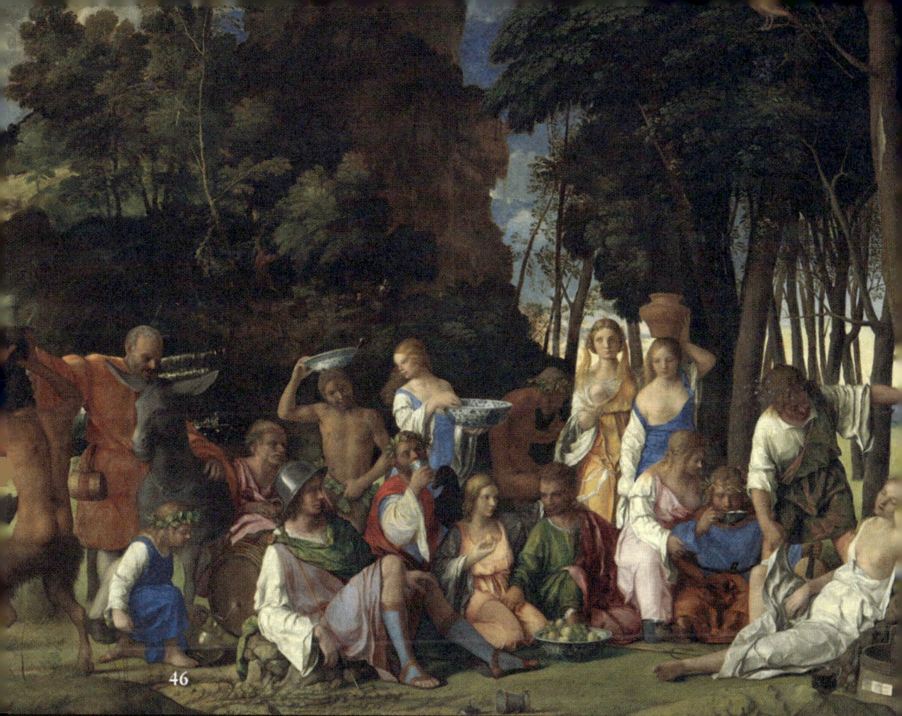

46

47 THE RENAISSANCE PALETTE AFTER CENNINO CENNINI

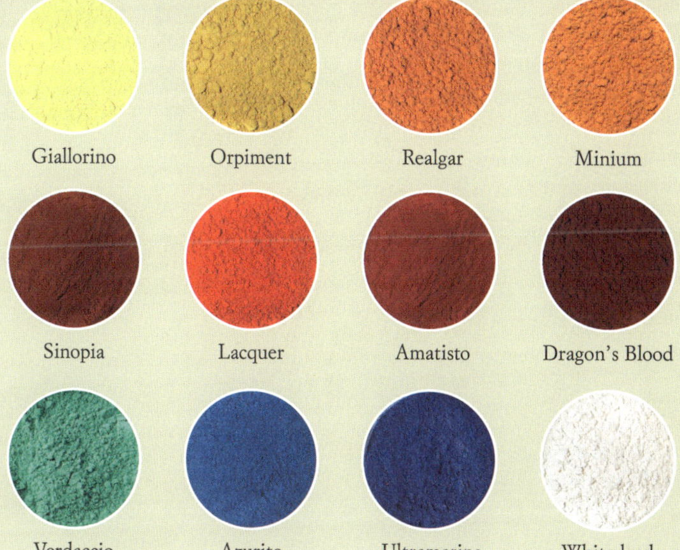

48

49

50

WINSOR
&
NEWTON
Artists'
OIL COLOUR™
FRENCH ULTRAMARINE
OUTREMER FRANÇAIS
ULTRAMAR FRANCÉS
Permanence A
Series/Série 2
37 ml ℮ 1.25 US fl oz

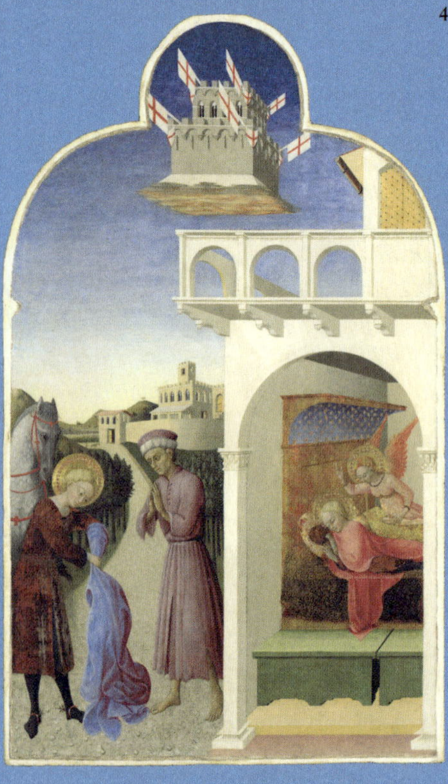

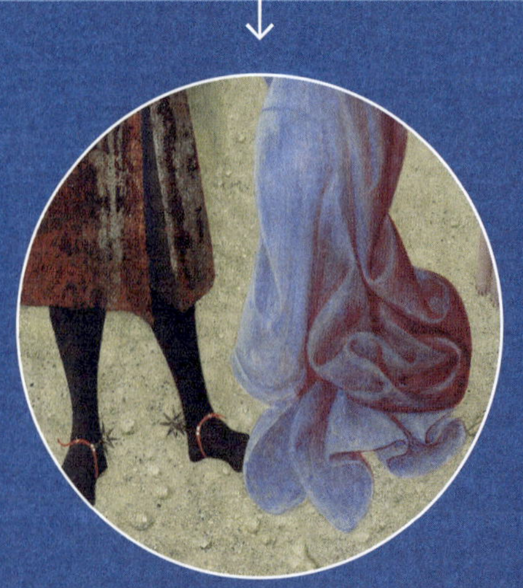

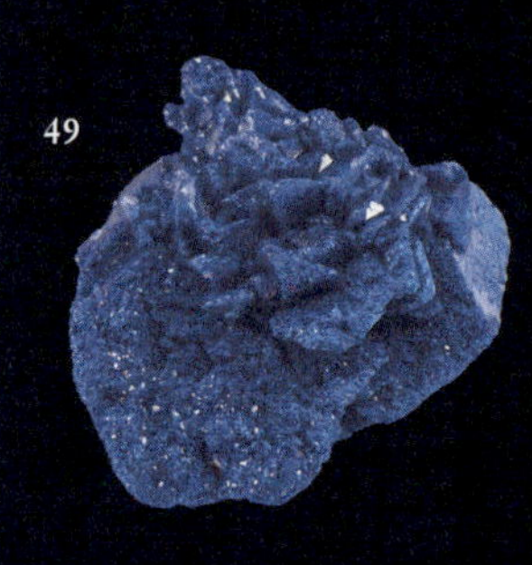

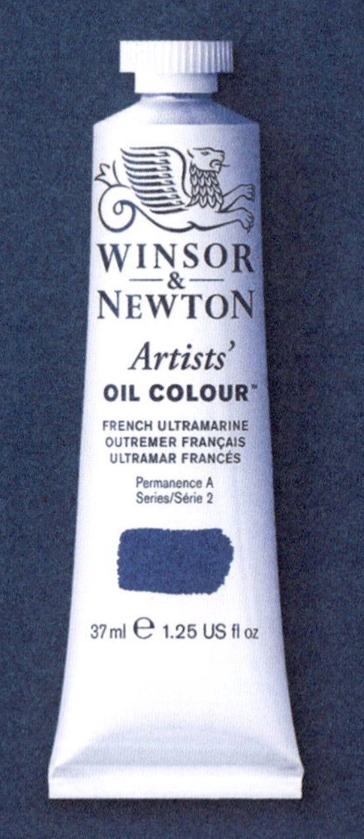

51

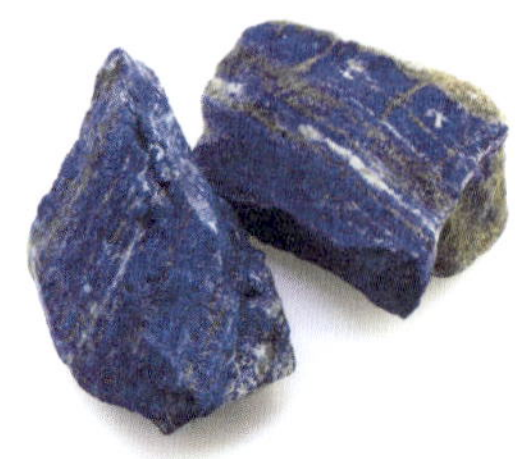

CENNINI, 1982

were elements of an order – practical and then conceptual – that established many of the chromatic conventions of Western art to which our imagination is still indebted. That this culture remains the basis of our modern visual society is remarkable, but to understand the extent of the deeper traces that it has left, we have to take into account complex social dynamics. Dynamics in which lapis lazuli had a major role to play.

ANTAL, 1960

The majority of customers for paintings in the fifteenth century are merchants and bankers whose fortunes come from borrowing and lending at interest. For the Catholic Church, such 'usury' is a grave sin, above all for a theological reason: it consists of charging interest that grows with time, but since time is an attribute of God, it cannot be bought and sold. To save themselves from damnation, these highly refined loan sharks (who answer to such distinguished names as Medici and Rucellai) dispose of some of their wealth in benevolence or charity, and some of it in patronage of the arts – by commissioning paintings and works of architecture, or by supporting humanistic publications and research. The aim was to exhibit their munificence and demonstrate their power, and in the process give back to society some of what they had taken from it. It was a way of securing their place in paradise, or at any rate among the great and the good.

These were not mere financiers but collectors of a particularly interested kind, mindful not only of the aesthetic value of artefacts but of the ways in which artists work. The choice of prestigious materials was vital: art must show talent, and at the same time it must conspicuously show how costly it is. And the final say is had by whoever actually puts up the money.

We almost always tend to see the Renaissance from the artists' point of view, but if we try to think of ourselves as clients for paintings at the time we soon realize that the relationship between the Medici and Botticelli is not so different to the one we currently have with a builder tasked with altering our apartment. BAXANDALL, 2001 We put our faith in the builder and leave the work up to them – but we choose the floor tiles and the design ourselves. Botticelli has achieved renown as a great artist, but in the fifteenth century an artist is socially closer to a builder than to an intellectual, and art is so politically important that it cannot be left entirely in the hands of a mere painter.

51 It is here that our lapis lazuli enters the picture, at the
intersection between financial concerns and symbolic sig-
48 nificance. In Sassetta's *Saint Francis Giving a Cloak to a
Poor Soldier (1437–44), for instance, we see the saint re-
linquishing an azure cloth, handing it over to the other
figure in the painting with a pious gesture. But what for
us is simply a colour like any other was for the fifteenth-
century viewer emphatically 'ultramarine'. The gift being BAXANDALL, 2001
made by Saint Francis is metaphorically reinforced and
elevated by the use of this expensive pigment. This is
how the superior value of blue to that of black would be
immediately communicated, understood at a glance. Lapis lazuli carries over its marketplace value *into* works of
art, allowing colour to assume meanings that are not just
symbolic but more widely cultural.

But there is more to it than this. The particular type of colour used may also establish significant gradations within a single painting. Contracts from the period reveal how lapis lazuli had different grades of purity and correspondingly different prices – from one to four florins an ounce. The most expensive would be recommended for the mantle of the Madonna, while the less costly would serve for things of lesser importance.[6] Colours that to our eye appear to be identical can establish through their differing costs distinctions of a theological kind. This is why ultramarine soon becomes not only a mythical colour but an obsession.

To understand how much lapis lazuli can be worth, we need
only think of how Winsor & Newton, still today one of the
most important manufacturers of fine art materials, marketed and sold 'real' ultramarine as well as its synthetic version 50
throughout the whole of the nineteenth century. But whereas an ounce of the latter cost a pound sterling, the real thing
would set you back 120 pounds per ounce.

That artists of the Renaissance worked with such precious materials, perhaps needless to say, meant that they
found themselves encountering problems of logistics and
'setting' similar to those faced by jewellers. The cost of materials is on the one hand the responsibility of the artist,
and on the other borne directly by the client, who must
specify the exact quantity of every substance that will be
used. A bit of gold dust or lapis lazuli fraudulently stint-
ed in its making can detract significantly from a work's
ultimate value. Economic considerations are a key ingre-
dient for all parties involved, and Cennini never fails to
warn artists against potential fraud. Speaking of blue, for
instance, he says that we must be wary of azurite, a less 49
costly and less stable mineral that may easily be substituted for ultramarine, and one that is less durable when used
in frescoes because humidity will cause it to crumble or

[6] The commission given to Ghirlandaio to depict *The Adoration of the Magi* stipulated the exclusive use of ultramarine costing four florins. An even more revealing contract is the one that Botticelli signed in 1485, specifying that he will be paid two florins for blue, thirty-eight for gold and thirty-five 'for his brushwork', or rather for his artistry. From which it can be gathered that Botticelli's talent, which for us is inestimable, was at the time worth thirty-three florins more than the blue he was to use, but three less than the gold.

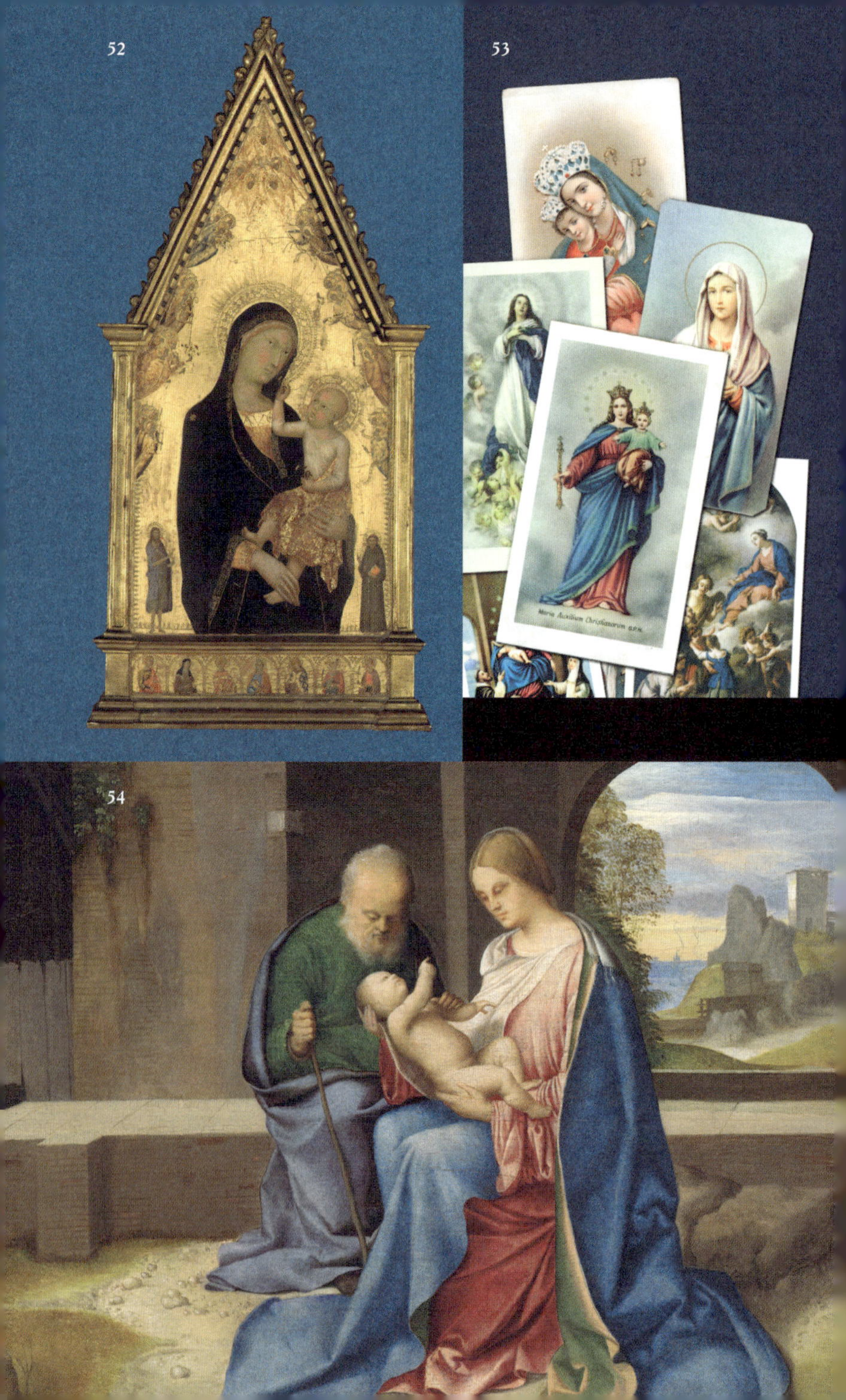
52
53
Maria Auxilium Christianorum o.p.n.
54

CENNINI, 1982

become greenish.[7] The only way to live peacefully and remain on good terms with one's fellow men, according to Cennini, is to know which places are best equipped for and most knowledgeable about the production of colour. An artist had to be exceptionally talented, but also good at shopping for materials.

The prestige of ultramarine changes the fate of blue, which goes from being seldom used in antiquity to becoming in the Renaissance the most noble and appreciated of colours – to the extent that it is chosen to become a signature aspect of the mantle of the Madonna herself. And 54
this is a complete novelty.

Until the fifteenth century the official habit of the Virgin was dark, symbolizing mourning for her son. We need 52
only glance at paintings and icons prior to this century for proof of this. And it is the case even in paintings in which she is holding the infant Jesus – as if she already knew what was in store for him. Then, in the 1400s, there is a complete change of direction, when the lavish generosity of patrons determines that Mary should now invariably appear draped in blue, which is to say adorned with lapis lazuli.

PASTOUREAU, 2002

The Museum of Liege hosts a Madonna sculpted in lime wood that clearly shows this oscillation in chromatic taste. The sculpture has been repainted many times, in keeping with changes in iconographic fashion. The deepest, oldest layer is black, because it belongs to a time when the Virgin was depicted as a mother in mourning. On top of that there is a layer of Renaissance blue, signifying that she is no longer simply a mother but above all the Queen of Heaven. Then comes a layer of Baroque gold from the period when Mary

[7] In the Renaissance, in order to distinguish between ultramarine and azurite it was necessary to heat the stones until they were incandescent before grinding them; azurite on cooling turns black, lapis lazuli remains blue. It was common practice, however, to use a base of azurite with a thin layer of lapis lazuli. This is what Bellini does, for instance, in his *Madonna del prato* (1505).

becomes identified with the Church itself and is enveloped in an ostentatiously imposing mantle in emphatic contrast with Protestant visual plainness and impoverishment. And finally, there is a layer of white, probably overpainted after the proclamation of the Immaculate Conception in 1854, reinventing the Virgin as a symbol of purity. The statue beneath has remained the same for almost five centuries. It is the colours that have made it speak in such different ways.

Conventions change to reflect wider changes in the culture, but what is worth underlining here is how the ideas that we have about things have always been constructed starting from the concrete uses of the things themselves. The Madonna continues to wear a blue mantle in all her recent
53 representations: in the figures distributed in parish churches or spread throughout the world by missionaries; in the little framed pictures in the corridors of hospitals in Italy, or in the infinite number of statues mass-produced for nativity scenes, whether in precious ceramic or on sale at the supermarket in moulded plastic. But the Virgin is blue because a concrete condition of the marketplace has been sublimated by art into a theological question.[8]

Even making the sky blue is an option that becomes BARASCH, 1992
normative when it begins to be painted with lapis lazuli, rendering it darker and more intense than it actually is. This is a stylistic choice initiated by Bellini and used to
46 perfection by Titian.

And yet the sky has no precise colour, and it is hardly ever this blue: it is white at dawn, red with the setting sun, grey in the winter months and light blue on a beautifully

[8] The relation between appearance and economic value has a complex history: gold, with its brilliance and lustre, has been synonymous with luxury and riches since ancient times. This is in large part due to its visual characteristics. Gold is effectively the only metal that does not darken on contact with the air, constantly maintaining its colour and shine. It is therefore a perceptual characteristic that has caused it to be the most noble and costly metal.

sunny day. The sky by its very nature changes constantly, and in painting it has been depicted in many different ways: in Byzantine icons it is red, sometimes black, and more frequently gold in order to signify with a scintillating material the luminous grandeur of the universe, and to express clearly the equivalence between God and light.

The desire that signs should have something to do with reality is strong, and it is always easy to convince ourselves that a convention is a natural phenomenon. When we suggest to children that they should colour the sky blue with their felt-tip pens, we believe that this will evoke a physical fact, without recognizing that we are applying a particular fashion, undoubtedly of a poetic kind, but one that was first codified by the elegant moneylenders of the Renaissance.

The collective imagination of industrialized society is criss-crossed with the traces of 500 years of material history. The chromatic past continues to speak in modern usages and conventions. But in order to understand just how much has changed we need to investigate those ideas and theories of colour that pre-date the scientific revolution.

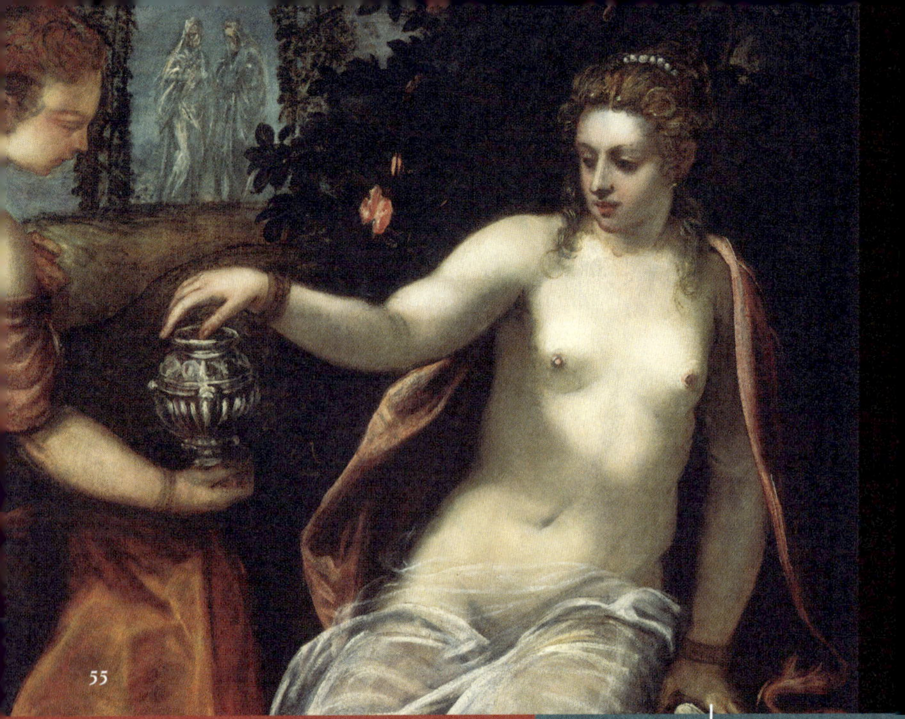

55

56

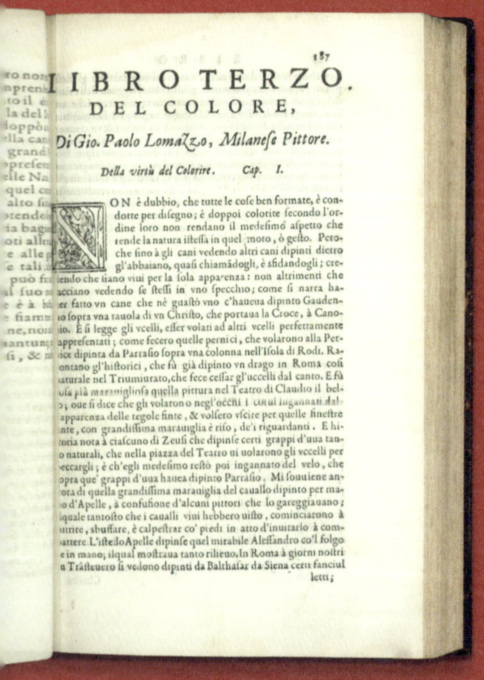

187

IIBRO TERZO.

DEL COLORE,

Di Gio. Paolo Lomazzo, Milanese Pittore.

Della virtù del Colorire. *Cap. I.*

NON è dubbio, che tutte le cose ben formate, è condotte per disegno; è doppoi colorite secondo l'ordine loro non rendano il medesimo aspetto che rende la natura istessa in quel moto, ò gesto. Peroche fino à gli cani vedendo altri cani dipinti dietro gl'abbaiano, quasi chiamãdogli, è sfidandogli; credendo che siano viui per la sola apparenza: non altrimenti che acciano vedendo se stessi in vno specchio; come si narra haer fatto vn cane che nè guastò vno c'haueua dipinto Gaudenio sopra vna tauola di vn Christo, che portaua la Croce, à Canoio. È si legge gli vcelli, esser volati ad altri vcelli perfettamente appresentati; come fecero quelle pernici, che volarono alla Perice dipinta da Parrasio sopra vna colonna nell'Isola di Rodi. Raontano gl'historici, che fù già dipinto vn drago in Roma cosi aturale nel Triumiurato, che fece cessar gl'uccelli dal canto. E fù osa più marauigliosa quella pittura nel Teatro di Claudio il belo; oue si dice che gli volarono negl'occhi i corui ingannati dal apparenza delle tegole finte, & volsero vscire per quelle finestre nte, con grandissima marauiglia è riso, de'i riguardanti. E historia nota à ciascuno di Zeusi che dipinse certi grappi d'uua tanto naturali, che nella piazza del Teatro ui uolarono gli vcelli per eccargli; è ch'egli medesimo restò poi ingannato del velo, che opra que' grappi d'uua hauea dipinto Parrasio. Mi souuiene ancora di quella grandissima marauiglia del cauallo dipinto per mano d'Apelle, à confusione d'alcuni pittori che lo gareggiauano; iquale tantosto che i caualli viui hebbero uisto, cominciarono à nitrire, sbuffare, è calpestrar co' piedi in atto d'inuitarlo à combattere. L'istesso Apelle dipinse quel mirabile Alessandro co'l folgo e in mano; ilqual mostraua tanto rilieuo. In Roma à giorni nostri n Trãsteuero si vedono dipinti da Balthasar da Siena certi fanciul letti;

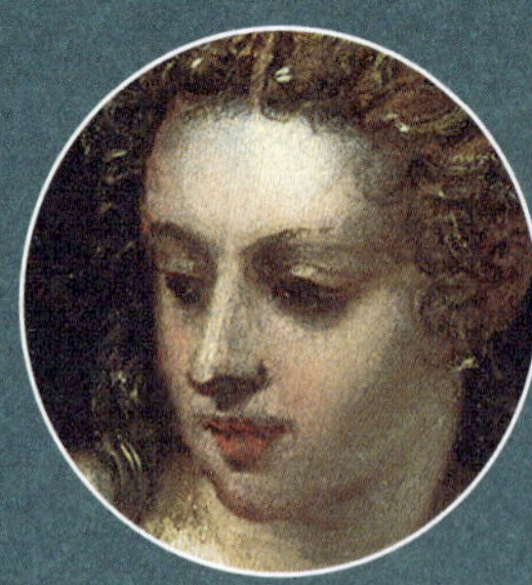

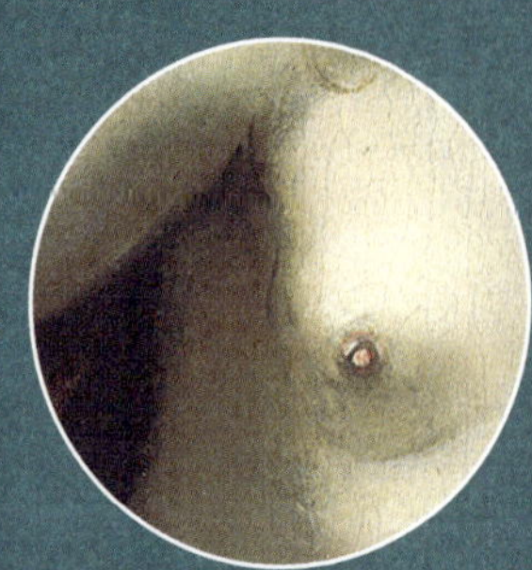

Symbolic Purple

Ideas and Myths of the Ancient World

BARASCH, 1992

To those familiar with the secrets of art, the colour market in the sixteenth century offered goods with extraordinary powers, closed to the uninitiated. Alongside the most well-known pigments, next to those derived from the earth and from powdered stones, some artists are accustomed to buying a dark substance, as expensive as it is macabre: a powder made from mummified human remains, smuggled to Europe out of Egypt at the time of the crusades. It is called 'mummy brown', a term that reveals its human, mortuary origin, and it has been so successful that it became commercialized as a pharmaceutical to be ingested or inhaled, like tobacco.

BRUSATIN, 2005

Legend would have us believe that Tintoretto (1519–94) 55
was disposed to pay more than lapis lazuli for a bit of this 'mummy brown' that he mixes with other pigments, convinced that it has an occult power capable of penetrating into the material and essence of paintings, and of rendering his name immortal and his fame undying. And he is not alone in believing that painting requires a little magic as well as talent: Giovanni Paolo Lomazzo (1538–92), for example, 56
one of the most important theorists of the sixteenth century, maintained that very finely ground mummy powder was ideal for painting shadows. And this is a point worth dwelling on.

When depicting a human figure, in order to draw a credible shadow what matters is the tonal relationships between
the light areas and the dark: the darker tones must appear to
55 recede and the lighter ones to come towards us. Shadows are
substantially an optical phenomenon that we can achieve with
any pigment that is brown or earthy. Tintoretto and Lomazzo, although reasoning correctly and almost photographically
about shadows, are persuaded that the Egyptian mixture
confers upon painting an additional merit that is invisible
in the picture itself and yet prodigious in its effect. To their
way of thinking, these coloured mixtures are not just practical but also ritual substances, and the boundaries of what
is deemed to be a colour are decidedly blurred compared to
how we think of them today. In our world, it is inconceivable
that in order to cure a fever we might choose to go either to
a pharmacy or to a shop selling artists' materials: paint and
aspirin belong in completely distinct categories, because the
system of production has separated them into sectors, standardizing and rationalizing them in the process.[1]

BAXANDALL, 2003 GOMBRICH, 1996 CALABRESE, 1984

In antiquity, the majority of people were familiar in everyday life with colours that were natural or faded: ecru, beige, the browns and the many dirty whites that today seem chic but that for many centuries were simply the norm for common clothes. Hence anything coloured was exceptional and miraculous, and not just in a metaphorical sense.

ANDREUCCETTI, 1996

Many of the ideas developed about colours in the past are fascinating precisely because of the magical properties that were ascribed to them. The power of magnets is only the most obvious manifestation of the capacity that was

[1] Even though, to tell the truth, both colours and drugs are produced in similar laboratories, through chemical synthesis.

felt to be operating in all substances. For this reason the power of colour is deemed to be just one of the attributes that things possess, together with other attributes that have important agency but are not visible.[2] According to this way of thinking, colour is something that is bound up with the things that possess it, and concerns the ontology of matter, which is to say its essence.

GRAMACCINI, 2003

To say 'purple', for instance, is always to indicate a concrete thing together with a perception, and when we read that a robe is of this colour we are being referred not so much to a wavelength as to information on how that fabric has been made. According to how it has been treated, the pigment – extracted from a mollusc – can actually dye a fabric red, orange, brown or violet. Purple is therefore a 'colour', but one which corresponds to *many hues* and brings with it above all its economic and spiritual characteristics. In order to dye a single robe, many thousands of mollusc shells are needed, a process so extravagant that strict sumptuary laws determine which classes may wear the colour and which may not, as tends to happen with luxury goods.[3]

LUZZATTO, 1997

This privileged status gives rise to myths and legends passed down through the centuries. Isidore of Seville (560–636) – the author of a vast encyclopaedia[4] in which concepts are ordered according to the etymology of words – maintains that the term 'purple' comes from *puritate luci* (purity of light), signifying

[2] Lapis lazuli was also ingested, for remedial purposes, to the extent that pieces of it have been found in various pharmacies, such as Santa Fina in San Gimignano.

[3] The first to have commercialized this seem to have been the Phoenicians, and it made the fortune of the cities of Tyre and Sidon as well as that of others cities in the Mediterranean. In Rome it was used to embellish the clothes of aristocrats, and as the hallmark of the senatorial toga: which was white with a purple border. Almost 12,000 shells are needed to make a couple of grams of purple. In the third century a pound of purple-dyed wool cost the annual salary of a baker.

[4] It is entitled *Etymologiae* and for centuries was one of the key reference texts of encyclopaedic medieval culture.

that behind this sensation there is a prerogative that is not given to anyone. This exquisitely medieval logic clarifies how the origins of colours, whether geographic or mythic, were so important at the time: how going back to first principles reveals the deeper significance of things.

Bestiaries, lapidaries, herbariums: medieval people compiled endless collections in which the knowledge displayed did not reside in verifiable data but in allegorical resonance. What seems unthinkable for the premodern mind is arbitrary signification: while for us moderns a red traffic light means 'stop' according to a chosen convention, for the medieval mind red, like everything else, belongs to an established order that precedes agreements between men. One does not choose a colour because it goes with another one; each pigment has ulterior properties that must justify its use. And for this reason there is always a hierarchy among materials, whether mystical, moral or purely economic.

CALVESI, 1986

In pre-industrial society the heterogeneous origins of pigments and dyes preclude the mixing together of colours: combining the red of purple with the blue of lapis lazuli would not produce the violet that we get today but a mere mishmash of animal (shellfish) paste and powdered stone, with the two remaining separate or resulting in an unstable concoction. It is above all this irreducibility of one colour to another that gives precedence to their peculiarity as substances, with the concept of tinting and their optical aspects remaining distinctly secondary. A universal theory of colour that could contain them all in an orderly way, as in a colour wheel or Pantone's samples, in which individual colours are entities freed from objects and can be spoken about in an abstract way, is simply unthinkable.

Today, if we ask in a shop for 'purple', we are only referring to a tonality of red. We can acquire it as a tube of oil paint, as a felt-tip pen, as a ball of wool, as a food colouring for desserts – without needing to be informed of its origin, as we would be in the ancient world.[5] We are not buying a material but a sensation. When we meet our neighbour in a purple sweater, we assume that it has been chosen on the basis of factors that have to do with taste, sensibility and even psychology. But beyond such deductions we do not have colours that signify so much more than their retinal effect, as used to be the case from the first century onwards with the purple that was immediately synonymous with prestige and majesty.[6]

In the ancient world, the symbolic reading of the universe was not confined to an erudite elite but was part of a fund of knowledge on which the whole of society drew. It is how both artists and the general public thought, the highly cultivated and the uneducated, when they looked at artefacts. We are dealing with a world that, from the perspective of our more precise universe, may appear incoherent or vague but becomes fascinating if we attend to it carefully. In medieval recipes, for instance, we read that after it has been prepared a colour must be left to rest for three days or for nine months. This is purely symbolic reasoning: three days as in the Resurrection of Christ, or the nine months because that is the duration of a human pregnancy. In essence, the recipe tells us that the mixture must have time to mature and transform, and that this is something that cannot be measured: everyone should follow their own intuition and

BRUNELLO, 1968

FANTETTI, 2001

[5] The commercialization of colour according to an agreed list of names and numbers was unthinkable in the past. Today the process is such that in dictionaries we are often given the primary colours that when mixed together make another colour. Purple, for Wikipedia, is: RGB 178, 27, 28.

[6] The only area in which this idea has been preserved is gastronomy, which may help us to enter into this premodern mentality. When we see the words 'Happy Birthday' piped in chocolate fondant on a cake covered in icing, we do not limit ourselves to recognizing the tonal contrast between white and brown, but immediately recognize that the brown is a precise substance with a value, a taste, a cost, with characteristics that are not confined to visual effect. It is brown in colour, but it is above all chocolate.

judgement. Such generic vagueness is not so different from 'season to taste' in our own culinary recipes.

The highest positions in the hierarchy of prestigious coloured substances were occupied by those deriving from hard stones, and each one has its particular powers: chalcedony BIANCO, 1992 keeps away melancholy; in the hands of the uncultivated, opal can release uncontrollable energies; jasper provides protection from epilepsy. From the Hellenistic to the medieval world, gemstones are considered to be living creatures – masculine or feminine, domesticated or wild. It is no accident that coral – which really is 'animal' – enters into this system, where its red variety becomes associated with Christ's blood and is therefore frequently used in the manufacture of amulets.

Stones refer to virtues, because when they are illuminated
they display an unexpected chromatic quality of an almost
divine kind. Colour in medieval aesthetics is a manifestation ECO, 1987
of theological mysteries, and light is always a metaphor for
God: one adage asserts that just as sunlight passes through
glass and makes it shine without damaging it, so the Holy FUMAGALLI BEONIO BROCCHIERI, 2002
Spirit entered into Mary without compromising her vir-
ginity. According to the Book of Revelations, the walls
of the Heavenly Jerusalem are constructed with precious
stones of many different colours; hence it is appropriate
57 that the covers of liturgies and illuminated bibles should
be studded with them. And it is above all for its luminos-
59 ity that gold is held in such high regard: in Byzantine and
medieval paintings it acts like a mirror, seeming to be on
a different level to the pictorial surface. The shimmer of a
gold background breaks the illusionism of representation,
signifying the presence of the divine in the concreteness of
a world of two-dimensional colours. And in fact it is precisely when they are combined with homogeneous colours
that the virtues of metals are frequently seen in their best

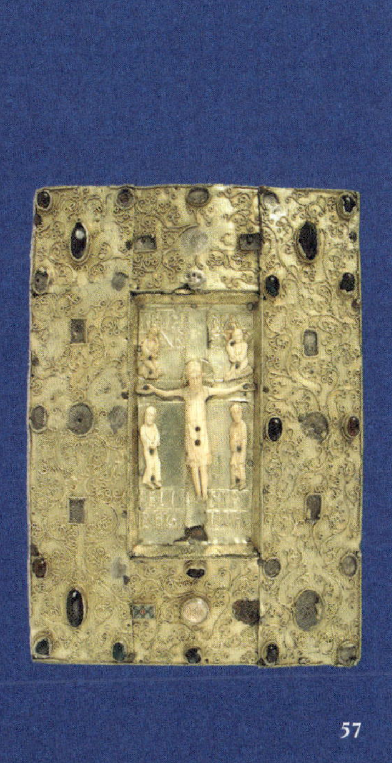

57

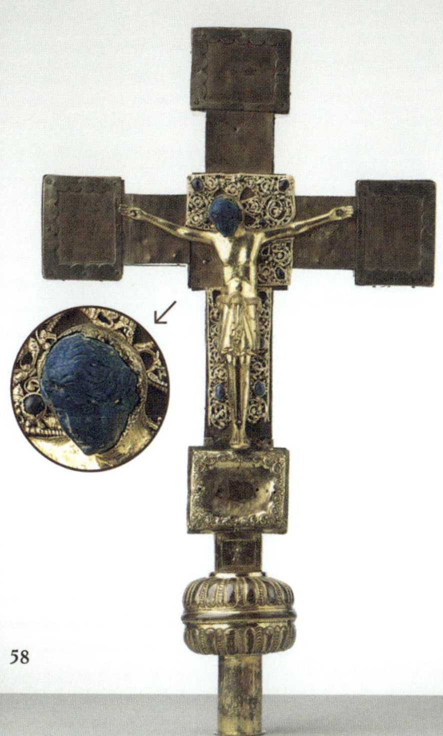

58

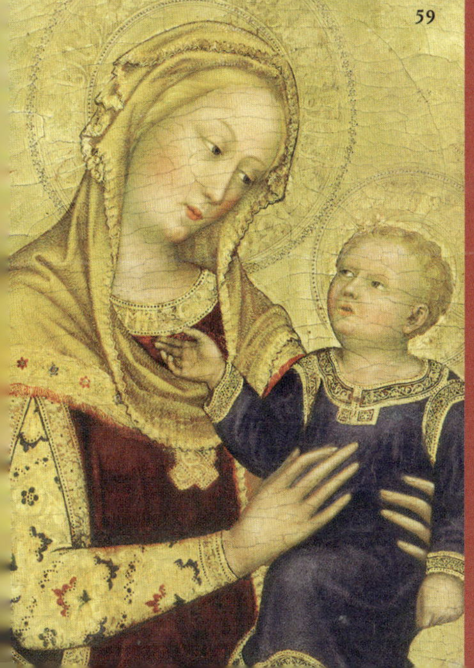

59

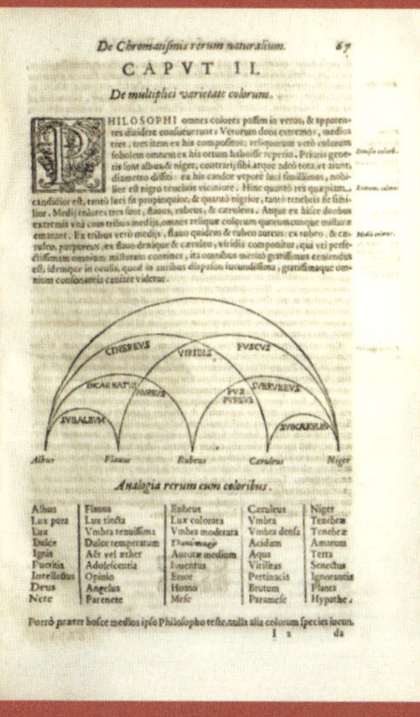

60

De Chromatismis rerum naturalium. 67

CAPVT II.

De multiplici varietate colorum.

PHILOSOPHI omnes colores passim in veros, & apparentes diuidere consueuerunt: Verorum duos extremos, medios tres, tres item ex his compositos; reliquorum verò colorum sobolem omnem ex his ortum habuisse reperio. Prioris generis sunt albus & niger, contrarij sibi atque adeò tota, vt aiunt, diametro dissiti: ex his candor vtpote luci simillimus, nobilior est nigro tenebris viciniore. Hinc quantò res quæpiam candidior est, tantò luci fit propinquior, & quantò nigrior, tantò tenebris fit similior. Medij colores tres sunt, flauus, rubeus, & cæruleus. Atque ex hisce duobus extremis vnà cum tribus medijs, omnes reliquæ colorum quorumcunque mixturæ emanant. Ex tribus verò medijs, flauo quidem & rubeo aureus: ex rubeo, & cæruleo, purpureus, ex flauo denique & cæruleo, viridis componitur, qui vel perfectissimam omnium mixturam continet, ita omnibus meritò gratissimus censendus est, idemque in oculis, quod in auribus diapason iucundissima, gratissimaque omnium consonantia censere videtur.

Analogia rerum cum coloribus.

Albus	Flauus	Rubeus	Cæruleus	Niger
Lux pura	Lux tincta	Lux colorata	Vmbra	Tenebræ
Lux	Vmbra tenuissima	Vmbra moderata	Vmbra densa	Tenebræ
Dulce	Dulce temperatum	[illegible]	Acidum	Amarum
Ignis	Aër vel æther	Auroræ medium	Aqua	Terra
Pueritia	Adolescentia	Iuuentus	Virilitas	Senectus
Intellectus	Opinio	Error	Pertinacia	Ignorantia
Deus	Angelus	Homo	Brutum	Planta
Nete	Parenete	Mese	Paramese	Hypathe.

Porrò præter hosce medios ipso Philosopho teste, nulla alia colorum species iucun-

I 2 da

light, breaking the plane of the composition and suggesting sudden gaps and unexpected depths.

Suger (1082–1151), Abbot of Saint-Denis, openly celebrates the sensual pleasure inspired by such splendid objects, not as a luxury for its own sake but as a means of attaining higher truths. On the bronze door of his cathedral were inscribed the words: *Mens hebes ad verum per materialia surgit*: 'the dull mind rises to the truth through material things'. Matter, in the end, is never just about itself, and the aesthetic experience is always a channel to an ecstatic one.

There is an object that perfectly exemplifies the pre-modern fascination with precious things. It is a small
58 eleventh-century crucifix preserved in the Kolumba Museum of Art in Cologne, a unique piece of its kind. The body of Christ is moulded in metal, and the head – 1,000 years older than the rest – is a piece of lapis lazuli carved in the first century. It is hardly atypical of the jeweller's art to mount such a hard stone in a metal setting. But there is rather more going on here: it is the Hellenistic head of a woman that has been mounted on this masculine body – and not just any body, but that of Christ himself. For the anonymous medieval sculptor, the conflict of gender and sexuality, the contrast of materials and of colours (body of gold, blue face), are not alienating, jarringly incompatible or kitsch: what matters is how the bringing of an ancient and precious colour to a modern setting makes it spiritually eloquent. The face of Christ exercises in the end a spell that is bound up with its material status as something costly, prestigious and remote.

From as early as the fifth century, theories investigating the physical nature of colour begin to appear in which we can recognize aspects that will become typical of modern thought. These are ideas that are now cosmological, now naturalistic, that reveal intentions of a decidedly scientific kind. What is radically new about them is their handling of colour in the abstract – not regarding it, as theologians, merchants and dyers had done, as a *thing* – but as a characteristic of the visible world.[7]

ARISTOTELE, 2002

Aristotle tells us that colours are the fruit of a dynamic relationship between light and dark: to such an extent that they are not even visible if there is too much light or not enough. It is the mixture of light and darkness that generates them and gives them consistency. Violet is much closer to darkness, yellow to light – while red is found somewhere in the middle.

GAGE, 2001

BRUSATIN, 1983

Associating colours with the quantity of light they reflect is an essential move in uncoupling them from concrete things, in order to arrive at a description of them via general attributes, as we do today by specifying brightness, hue and saturation. But Aristotle does not stop there: he maintains that between the poles of darkness and of light there are seven fundamental colours. This is a crucial step. For a merchant there are as many reds as there are things that produce red (purple, kermes, madder), whereas for Aristotle there are seven colours regardless of specific things that might exhibit them: seven phenomenal qualities, one of which is the category of *redness*. This is one of the first attestations that colours exist in a limited and defined number, thus anticipating the idea that they may also follow some kind of order.[8]

[7] The two principal, opposed currents of thought belong to those who maintain that colour is a property of things, and those who, in contrast to this, believe that colour does not in fact exist outside of the heads of those looking at it. This dualism, which opposes a physical reading of reality to a psychological one, has been reprised many times throughout history, and is currently manifested in modern neuroscience.

[8] If we remember that the discovery of a progression in the spectrum of colour

Hence Aristotle concludes that colour is an *accident*, that is to say something 'added' to things that belongs to an object in a casual and contingent way without being part of its essence. This is not yet colour as we know it today: the 'accident' of which Aristotle speaks is effectively a given of matter, whereas the great revolution of the twentieth century, as we shall soon see, is to understand that colour is an accident of our psyche, or something that becomes constructed within our brain from the data furnished by reality.

CARDANO, 1562

These intuitions of Aristotle's will be elaborated twenty centuries later by the mathematician Girolamo Cardano (1501–76), who indicates with numbers the relative luminosity of colours,[9] maintaining that white contains 100 parts of light, scarlet fifty and black none, and so on for every colour.[10]

This is a remarkably modern idea. As recent neuroscience has in fact demonstrated, the capacity to split luminous characteristics from chromatic ones is a central aspect of the way in which our brain thinks about colour.

Perhaps it is no accident that Cardano's ideas developed during a century that saw a growing interest in tonalism in painting – that attention to the relationships between light and dark from which the heavy contrasts of first Caravaggio and then the Baroque will emerge.

will have to wait for Newton, some 2,000 years later, we cannot help but admire Aristotle's prescience.

[9] Cardano writes of this in his *De gemmis et coloribus* (1562).

[10] A century later, in 1645, Athanasius Kircher proposes the first diagram in which the relations between colours are ordered on the basis of luminosity and along the lines of musical intervals.

The transition of colour from magical cosmos to abstract
system was also facilitated by medical knowledge, which in
the ancient and medieval worlds is based upon the theory
of the four humours: blood, phlegm, and yellow and black 61
bile. It is analogous to the four fundamental elements of air,
water, earth and fire, transposed to the physiological realm.
The free combination of these elements, of which every individual is composed, determines our personality. To the
melancholic type, who has an excess of black bile, certain
associated zodiacal signs, favourite stones and a predestined
colour are also attributed.

KLEIN, 1975 KLIBANSKY, 2002

This is a body of knowledge and a discourse that has left deep traces in European languages: we can still say that someone bad-tempered is 'choleric' (or in Italian, 'gnaws his liver') or that someone is 'incandescent with rage'. Not to mention the fact that we still point to the heart as the location of our affections, despite knowing full well that our sentiments occur in our brain rather than being distributed among the various organs of the body.

Agrippa of Nettesheim (1486–1535) was an alchemist 63
and philosopher whose *De occulta philosophia* became a key
reference work throughout the sixteenth century, when it
was read and loved by such important thinkers as Giordano
Bruno. Agrippa insists on the relations between planets and
colours, establishing by means of astrology a connection between colours and the temperaments of individuals. The 62
classical cataloguing of plants, gems and animals for divinatory knowledge starts at this time to become a system
for interpreting human personality. And it is through such
sixteenth-century white magic that we eventually end up,
via the filtering lens of the Enlightenment and the seductive power of advertising, with that notorious question:
what is your favourite colour? This is the old war horse of
our contemporary magazines, placing at the centre of our

AGRIPPA DI NETTESHEIM, 1972

discourse the most important category of modernity: our individual character or personality.

Close to the scientific revolution that is about to be initiated by Galileo, these various theories begin to conflict with each other. The same Giovanni Paolo Lomazzo[11] who was so fond of Egyptian mummy powder begins to realize that there are two aspects to the truth about colour: on the one hand, he knows that if he mixes black and white he will obtain grey, but on the other, he continues to have faith in the authority of the ancients who hold that red is the median between white and black. Artists and philosophers are torn between technical and theoretical mixtures. BURCKHARDT, 1986

It is only the experiment by Isaac Newton, who in 1672 breaks down light through a prism into a spectrum of gradated colours,[12] that succeeds in definitively detaching colour from the concrete materials that exhibit it. From then on, 'purple' becomes a moment in a perceptual spectrum like a rainbow: a point with the same importance as any other, without hierarchy or symbolism, describable in the abstract by means of mathematical coordinates. Today the Queen of England no longer needs to be decked
64 in purple to signify and display her majesty and authority: she can signify privilege and authority by wearing any colour that she likes.

[11] Giovanni Paolo Lomazzo, a key figure in determining the artistic theories of the sixteenth century, and who became blind at thirty-three, wrote the *Idea del tempio della pittura* (1590), a treatise that more than being about art resolves itself into a metaphysics of talent and of artistic invention. The text explains that painting is like a temple, the columns of which are the so-called 'Seven governors of art': Leonardo, Michelangelo, Raphael, Polidoro da Caravaggio, Mantegna, Titian and Gaudenzio Ferrari. Each one is associated with a specific ability, a material, a psychological type, a planet – and a colour.

[12] The year 1672 is the date of its official publication by Newton, in a letter to the Royal Society. The experiments leading up to it, however, had been conducted throughout the whole of the preceding decade.

61

Phlegmatic

Sanguine

Melancholic

Choleric

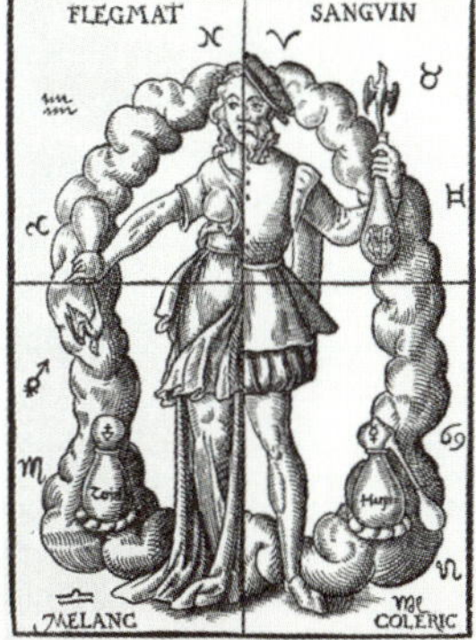

62

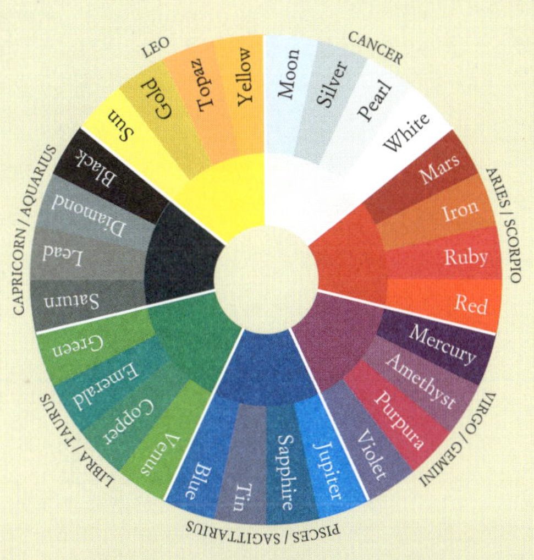

CXX. DE OCCVLTA PHILOSOPHIA.

ptem ordines clericorum, & septem annorũ puer potest ordinari ordine minori, & potest obtinere beneficiũ sine cura. Septem sunt psalmi pœnitẽtiales, & septem mandata secundæ tabulæ, & septem horis Adam & Eua fuerunt in paradiso, & septem sunt uiri per angelum prænũtiati antequam nascerẽtur, uidelicet Ismaël, Isaac, Samson, Hieremias, Ioannes Baptista, Iacobus frater domini, & CHRISTVS IESVS. Denique hic numerus & in bono & in malo

SCALA.

In archetypo	Ararita	אראריתא		
In mũdo intelligibili	צפקיאל Zaphkiel	צדקיאל Zadkiel	כמאל Camael	רפאל Raphael
In mundo cœlesti	שבתאי Saturnus	צדק Iupiter	מאדים Mars	שמש Sol
In mũdo elemẽtali	Vppupa Sepia Talpa Plumbum Onychinus	Aquila Delphinus Ceruus Stannum Sapphirus	Vultur Lucius Lupus Ferrum Adamas	Olor Vitul⁹ marin⁹ Leo Aurum Carbunculus
In minore mundo	Pes dexter Auris dextra	Caput Auris sinistra	Manus dextera Naris dextra	Cor Oculus dexter
In mundo infernali	Gehenna גיהנם	Portæ mortis צל מות	Vmbra mortis שערי מות	Puteus interitus באר שחת

63

64

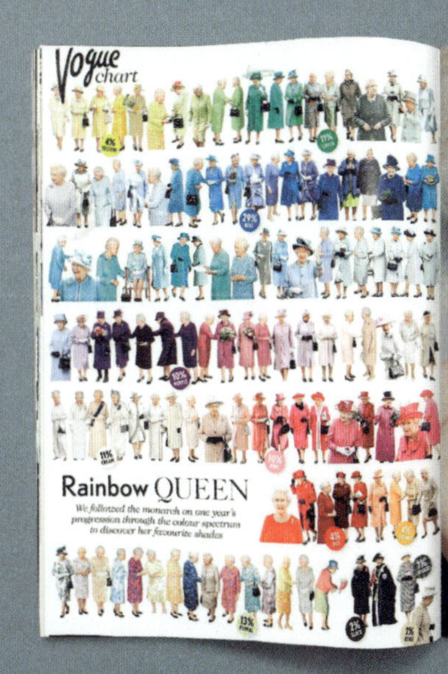

65

IL NEWTONIANISMO
PER LE DAME
OVVERO
DIALOGHI
SOPRA
LA LUCE E I COLORI.

quæ legat ipsa Lycoris.
Virg. Egl. X.

IN NAPOLI
MDCCXXXVII.

66

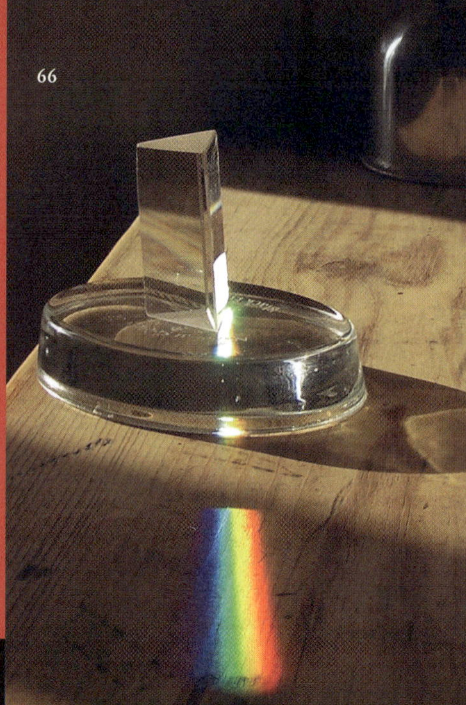

67

68

OPTICKS:
OR, A
TREATISE
OF THE
REFLEXIONS, REFRACTIONS,
INFLEXIONS and COLOURS
OF
LIGHT.
ALSO
Two TREATISES
OF THE
SPECIES and MAGNITUDE
OF
Curvilinear Figures.

LONDON,
Printed for Sam. Smith, and Benj. Walford,
Printers to the Royal Society, at the *Prince's Arms* in
St. *Paul's* Church-yard. MDCCIV.

Spectral Indigo

The Age of Revolutions

Around 1740 it was very fashionable in enlightened salons for ladies to exchange transparent prisms as gifts. These were not precious objects in themselves – they were no more than small glass pyramids – but because of the iridescence they produced, they were much sought after as sources of amazement and discussion. Together with politics and literature, and alongside arguments about history and philosophy, there were salon discussions about the nature of light and colour. It was all part of a remarkable explosion of Newton-mania.

BRUSATIN, 2005

To be able to converse on scientific topics was a sign of being both in step with the times and free from superstition, and a particular book was destined for remarkable success. Francesco Algarotti's *Newtonianism for Ladies* (1737) is a 65
work admired even by Voltaire, and one that inaugurates a line of popular scientific books specifically aimed at women. This putative address to women, however, was mainly rhetorical. Men also read such works with pleasure, and in reality the 'Ladies' of the title encompassed all cultivated but non-specialist readers.

ALGAROTTI, 1737

The book is a summary of the revolutionary concepts expounded at the start of the century by Isaac Newton 68
(1642–1727), which were the fruits of studies begun thirty years previously at Trinity College in Cambridge, where

one of the most important experiments in the history of science took place.

67 In a darkened room, Newton positioned a prism so that
a thin ray of light coming through a window went through
it and was projected onto the opposite wall. Rather than
remaining white, the ray emerging from the prism breaks
66 into bands of colour like a rainbow. And in this way, what
started as a circumscribed study of optics ends up changing the very way we look at matter: if we can *open* light,
if we can split it, break it down and get inside it, then
in principle we can penetrate inside any substance. The
prism becomes a model and a manifesto for the science that
is to come, synonymous with all experimental research.
Metaphorically speaking, it is the light of knowledge that
passes through it, making the invisible visible and available to study. And this is why prisms become fashionable
as a gift: because among the accomplishments that a lady
should not fail to cultivate there is this new, modern and
'masculine' one: scientific curiosity.

Discussion of colour in the salons confers upon it an unprecedented status which is not professional but worldly. Colour is no longer something that we see, use or wear: it is something about which we have an opinion. At the end of the eighteenth century, we begin to see the emergence of what will soon become a general public, or mass audience, though the themes and subjects of its entertainments were fixed at least a century earlier.

From the time of Galileo a period of remarkable experimentation had flourished, the searching nature of which had provoked in Europe a systematization of knowledge that culminated in the publication in 1751 of Diderot and D'Alembert's *Encyclopaedia*. And it is not only the sciences that are being reorganized: everything is passing through the new filter of Reason. Under Louis XIV, in a court that determines the taste of the rest of Europe, both theoretical and artisanal knowledge begins to be regulated, by organizing the production of processes and codifying the styles of everything that it is possible to produce: from porcelain to glass, from fabrics to typographical characters. Skills are honed to perfection while being framed by precise rules and regulations. There are codes and rules established for the production of food and for sport, for working life and for leisure. Cooks lay the foundations of official cuisine, giving names and hierarchies to sauces, and while the arbiters of elegance decide which and how many pieces of cutlery must be used, the court manufacturers create appropriate designs for them, finding a form for every new function. There is scarcely an object that is not invented, or reinvented – from the spoon to the sideboard, from the buttonhole to the stirrup. And together with these material things, behaviour is also regulated and normalized: there is a correct way in which to bow and a right way to stroll; one for trotting and another for dancing. And for women, there are instructions on the many ways of using a fan: now frenetic, now slow; now charming and now caustically and even cruelly snapped shut, as part of an established lexicon of fan gestures.

To each new rule a name is given, and in just a few years this great classifying machine includes everything that is thinkable, producible, usable, and above all saleable. Everything, in other words, that will soon become known as a commodity. It is during that time that rationalism generates the idea of standards, and by organizing the rules of the cosmos establishes the philosophical presuppositions for the future of design in modern society.

In line with such reasoning, Newton carries all before him: colour ceases to be an elusive entity and the rules that govern it can be seen for the first time. It is a revelation that continues to have an impact to this day. But in order to understand its scope and importance, let us describe the Newtonian legacy in more detail.

According to modern science, light is a type of electromagnetic radiation composed of waves capable of arousing
visual sensations in our nervous system. The pyramidal
structure of the prism causes these waves to bend as they
pass through it and to exit at increasing angles, revealing
69 that for each one there is a different corresponding colour. What we see is a luminous, segmented band in which
the colours present themselves to us in an orderly fashion,
like in a rainbow.[1]

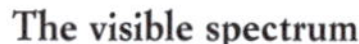

Wavelength expressed in nanometres

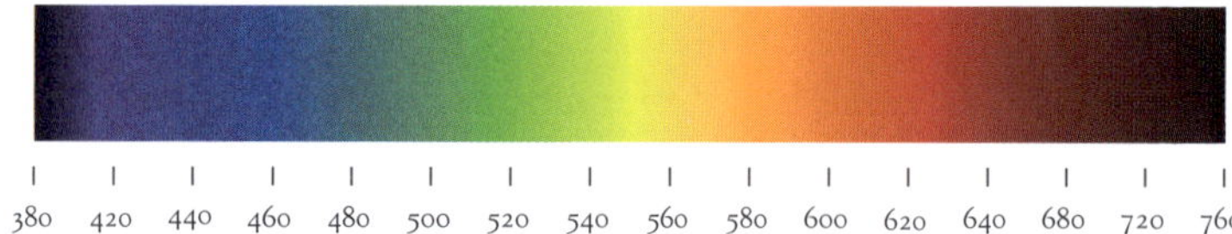

This is given the name 'spectrum', which is to say an apparition, perhaps because phantoms also show themselves as luminous entities in the dark. Spectra, however, were already known before the 1672 experiment. After all, in order to see one it is enough to observe the reflections produced by drinking glasses on tablecloths. At the end of the seventeenth century, due in part to Aristotle's teaching, it was still believed that colour was the product of a mixture of light and shadow, and that prisms acted by 'colouring' the light.

[1] In a rainbow there are small drops of water that bend light waves. These drops behave, in other words, like miniature prisms.

Newton demonstrates that colour is something that is *within* light and not *on* things: it presents itself as a continuous sequence that traverses various colours, from red to violet, without any kind of hierarchy. If in the past there was an enormous economic difference between ultramarine and yellow that conditioned our perceptions of them, thanks to Newton blue and yellow are now on a par.

But this is not all. For the first time ever, black and white are excluded from the roll call of colours – a fact in open contradiction with the age-old pictorial thinking according to which white lead and lampblack are real colours with as much right as any other to belong to the palette. From this moment on, black and white are in scientific terms just forms of darkness and light,[2] and the truths of optics and of art begin to go their separate ways.

NEWTON, 2006

The experiment with the prism also reveals another, perhaps even more audacious idea. If the spectrum is presented as a continuous one composed of indefinite gradations, then individual colours are susceptible to becoming altogether ill-defined. Newton stops short of spelling this out, emphasizing instead that it is possible to detect seven fundamental colours: red, orange, yellow, green, blue, indigo and violet.

FROVA, 2000

According to historians of science, he was influenced to count seven colours by analogy with the seven notes of tonal music.[3] From a perceptual point of view – based on the human eye's capacity to discriminate – there is no doubt that certain main areas are recognized within

GAGE, 2001

[2] The experiment did not finish here. Newton takes the spectrum and projects it through another prism, this time reversed, recomposing it again into a ray of white light, and it is this second phenomenon that is crucially important conceptually. With this it is understood that waves cannot only be broken down – they can also be reassembled.

[3] It was customary to draw parallels between music and painting at the time, to the extent that colour was spoken of by certain writers on art as 'timbre', by analogy with the characteristic sound of a particular instrument (see, p. 174, note 6).

the spectrum, though in truth they appear to be six rather than seven in number. Newton's inclusion of indigo is somewhat forced, and many people would not be able to identify it. It is also possible that its inclusion was due to a linguistic misunderstanding: that he called blue what we call 'cyan', and indigo what we refer to as dark blue. BRUSATIN, 1983

Having got to this point and in order to reaffirm the logical adaptation of colour as a homogeneous entity, Newton draws a diagram destined to become hugely influential, KEMP, 1992
70, 71 especially in the world of art: a disc on the circumference of which the seven colours appear in continuous sequence. A translation of the spectrum, in other words, into a recursive sequence in the shape of a wheel, so that the last segment is joined to the first.

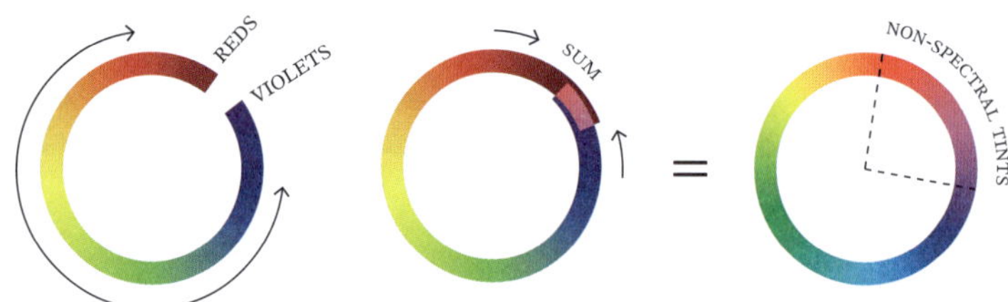

He discovers in fact that by superimposing several coloured rays coming from different prisms, you obtain compound hues that are not present in the rainbow – such as magenta, for instance, which can be generated by adding together the violet and red waves at the two conjoined ends of the spectrum.

The diagram chosen by Newton does not arrive out of nowhere. It is inspired by a drawing from the *Musi-* DESCARTES, 1966
73 *cal Compendium*, a treatise written by Descartes in 1618. Circles and wheels have an illustrious history in the

69

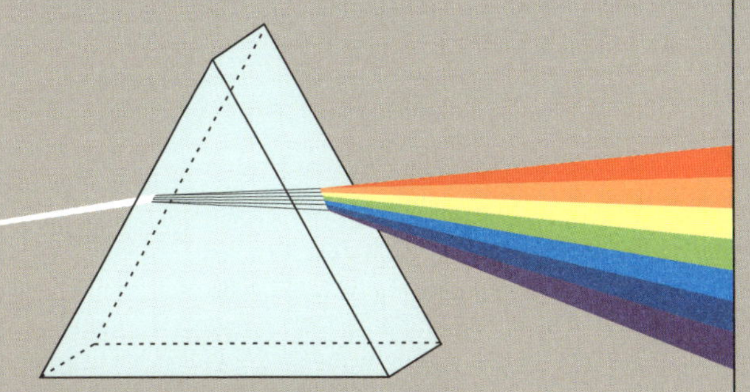

RED
ORANGE
YELLOW
GREEN
BLUE
INDIGO
VIOLET

70

Book I. Part II. Plate III
Fig. 9.
Fig. 10.
Fig. 11.
Fig. 12.

71

Orange
Yellow
Red
Green.
Violet
Indigo
Blew

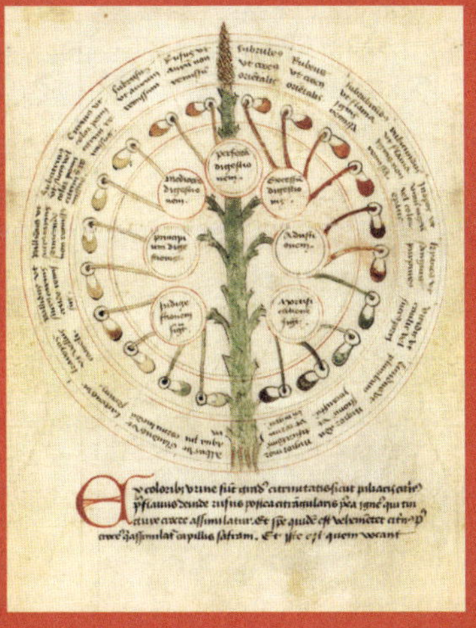

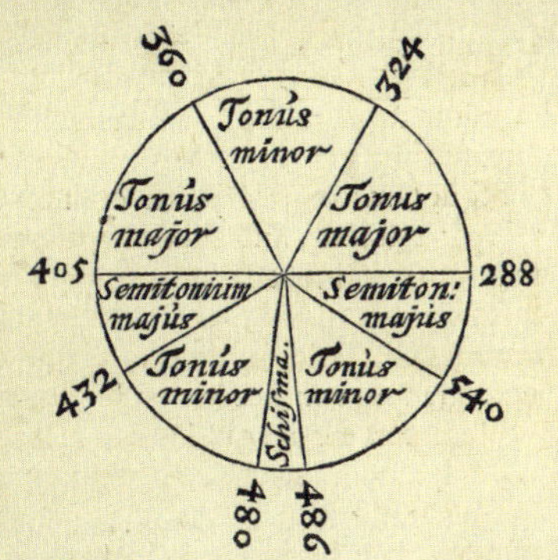

▲ 72
◀ 73

philosophical and scientific domain: they can be found in many medieval manuscripts and were among the favourite tools for reasoning of many thinkers – from Raymond Lully to Giordano Bruno. None of these diagrammatic figures, however, had ever been used before to speak about colour. The oldest example of a colour wheel is in
72 a Latin manuscript from the fifteenth century preserved
in the Bibliothèque Nationale de France. It is a curious GAGE, 2000
and amusing image, in which the colours go from pale yellow to deep brown, and it was designed not to represent the spectrum of colours but as an aide to diagnosing the state of a patient's health on the basis of the particular, nuanced shade of their urine.

What is truly original about Newton's approach is that the circle is not so much a practical or divinatory tool as the graphic embodiment of a scientific concept, that is to say a model for reasoning. Once arranged in a circular spectrum, colours begin to reveal relationships that were previously unthinkable. Each colour, for example, has an opposite on the other side of the circle that turns out be the most distant geometrically but also on a perceptual level: yellow is seen to be furthest from violet, just as red is from green. This is a link that will prove to be central in all theories to come. It is an idea that will change the fate of aesthetics, art and design, thanks in part to the importance given to it in the next century by one of the greatest writers of all time: Johan Wolfgang von Goethe.

In addition to his numerous poetic, dramatic and narrative works, Goethe (1749–1832) writes two books on colour and devotes so much energy to them that he ends up thinking, to the bewilderment of many of his readers, that they are the most important works of his career.[4] Thanks to his remarkable talent as a writer, his *Theory of Colours* lays the foundation for all future science writing. This is the moment that science reveals the extent to which it can be both tangible and passionate.

In contrast to Newton, who focuses upon the essence of light, Goethe investigates the phenomenological aspect of colour, which is to say the way in which we see it in our everyday lives, and in doing so he argues with the Newtonian theory, which he considers too abstract. In many ways, Goethe is as antiscientific as most other Romantics, but he provides fundamental ideas for those who actually work with colour – whether producing paintings, clothes, or objects of design in general. His ideas immediately become popular and the subject of debate, eventually altering many commonly held opinions and beliefs.

GOETHE, 2008

The virtue of his approach, which engages and charms his readers, is its concreteness. Goethe does not begin with an abstract theory and then seek examples and illustrations; he starts from anecdotes and observations, and builds reflective complexity from them. In one famous passage, for instance, he relates how one evening in a hostelry he found himself sitting across from a young
girl with a very white face and black hair, wearing a scar- 74
let dress. She is motionless, he is staring at her, and when she suddenly moves there appears on the white wall behind her an image like that in a negative: a well-defined figure with a dark face and a body of beautiful sea green. Today we would recognize the experience as that of an 'after-image', with the neurons involved in vision – after

[4] The first of these is the *Theory of Colours* (1810), a suggestive text of a conceptual nature; the second, *The History of Colour* (1810), is a notebook of thoughts on colour, from antiquity to the author's own time, which completes the argument begun with the first book.

74

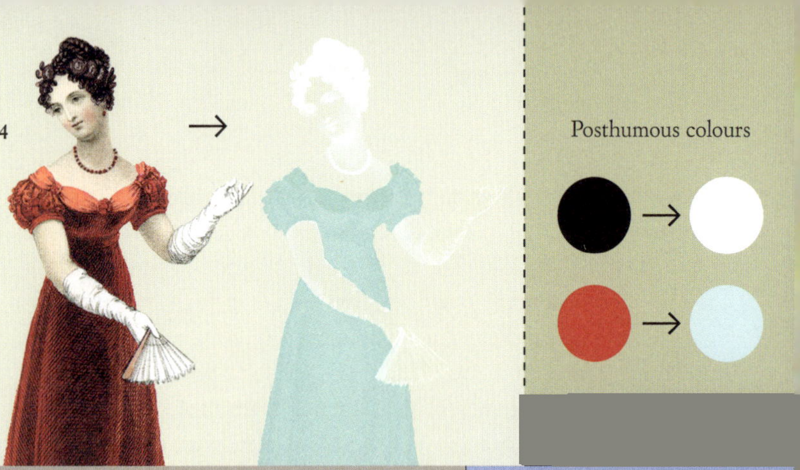

Posthumous colours

75

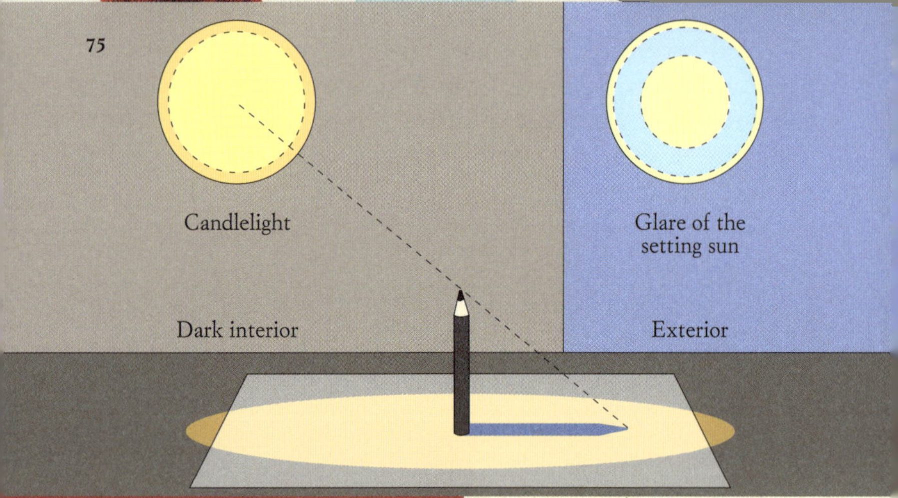

Candlelight

Glare of the setting sun

Dark interior

Exterior

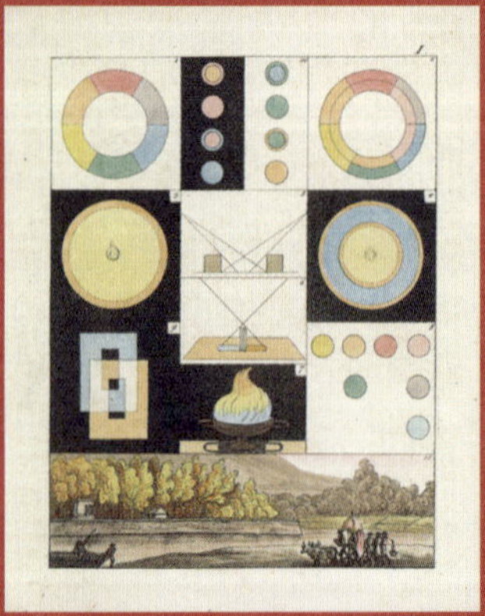

76

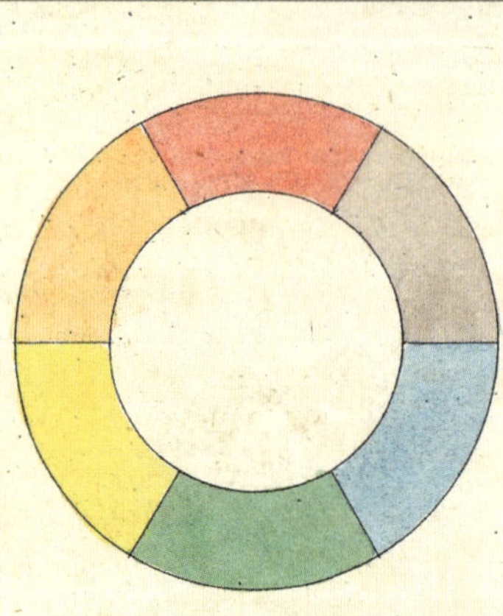

77

being stimulated for a number of seconds by certain colours and a certain quantity of light, in front of a neutral surface (in this case a blank white wall) – constructing a residual and opposite image in compensation.[5]

After a few pages, Goethe recommends an experiment connected to this anecdote. He suggests placing a lit candle on a sheet of white paper at sunset. Between the candlelight and the light of the sun he says we should place a 75
pencil, so that the shadow made by the candle is illuminated but not cancelled by the weak light of the setting sun. The shadow will become a beautiful vivid blue. This effect is possible because the candle, by bathing the white paper with an orange tone, forces the eye to construct a bluish shadow with the help of the colder light that comes from outside.[6] In other words, in the case of Goethe's girl in the hostelry, the mind creates a colour *after* having looked; in the experiment with the pencil, what is formed instead is a psychologically produced colour *next* to the one that has been perceived. The first is a reaction that happens in time, the second in space. But in both cases the colour that we see is created in opposition to the one that's given: the red of the dress generates the sea green, the orange of the paper prompts the blue.

GOETHE, 2008

With great perspicuity, Goethe underlines that what we are dealing with here are colours produced *within* an observer, and not something that exists in reality, thus suggesting that the mind can produce colour even in the absence of external stimuli. This was a highly original, stunning observation at the time – since there had been

[5] For a physiological explanation of such after-images, see Appendix A 5.0.

[6] According to some, the colours of shadows are a physical and not a psychological fact, inasmuch as they are 'photographable'. But this argument does not stand up: if you look at the shadows through a tube, isolated from their context, any colour disappears and becomes greyish instead.

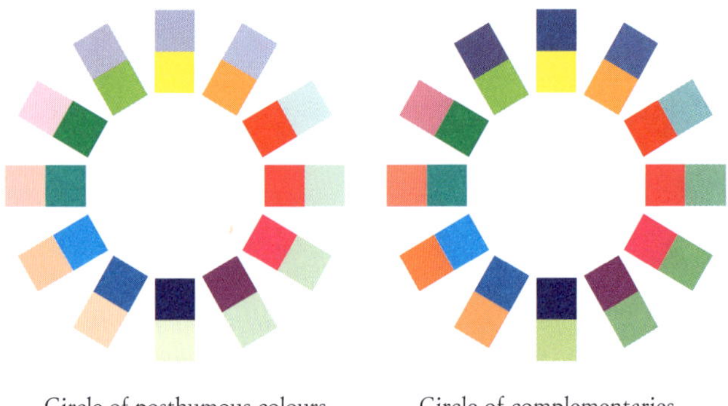

Circle of posthumous colours (the paler on the outside)

Circle of complementaries

no doubt that colours were something that actually existed in the external world.

Starting from these investigations, Goethe builds an entire cosmological model in which colours reveal some of the profound properties of the nature of things. They become the sensible manifestations of forces that govern the universe, and that are either in accordance or in conflict with each other. Red is opposed to green, yellow to blue.
76, 77 Every colour has its 'complementary' one,[7] as we will begin to call it from this moment on, that is to say a colour with which it establishes a relationship of attraction and repulsion, or perhaps an 'elective affinity', to use the title of one of his most famous novels.[8] And this is the salient

[7] For the definitions of *complementary colours*, see Appendix A 5.1.

[8] As is apparent from the anecdote of the girl in the inn, Goethe knows full well that the complementary of red is turquoise and in fact he calls it 'sea green', but in the colour wheel he maintains that the complementary of red is generic green, opening the way to a 'false' opposition that was destined to become extremely successful. All the colour wheels of the eighteenth century place green and not turquoise opposite red. The opposition between red and green thus becomes one of the basics of teaching about colour, despite being unfounded. This does not mean that it can be dismissed: on the contrary, cultural habit and convention often contribute more strongly than scientific fact to the construction of the imaginary. Today, for us, red and green are two poles that are culturally opposed. And if we were to set up a traffic light based on two technically complementary colours it is not at all certain that it would work better (see p. 265, note 4).

factor of the wheel: the two by two opposition of colours divided by equal and symmetrical intervals.[9]

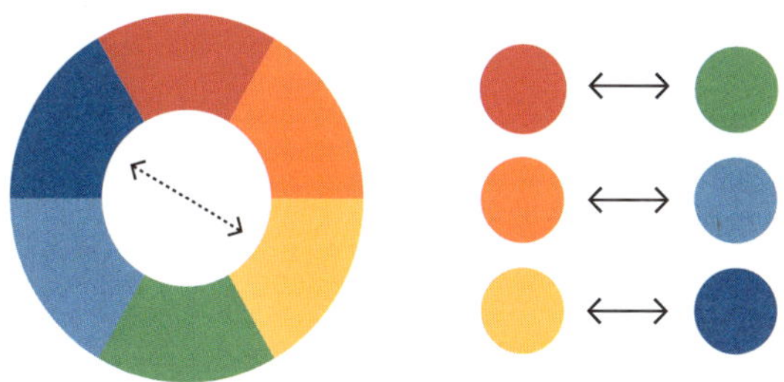

These discoveries provide an extremely rich legacy for artists, but also something fundamental for the psychology of perception: proof that our senses are not limited to just recording the world. The senses provide the brain with the tools with which we construct what we see.

Small children sometimes close their eyes when they are told off, as if by ceasing to see it the world around them would simply disappear. Among the philosophical questions we ask ourselves in our youth is whether or not a thing continues to exist when we are no longer looking at it. Growing up entails abandoning such magical convictions, and yet some questions of this kind re-emerge with all their force when we are dealing with colour. If we shut our eyes, in fact, the things around us continue to exist all right – but their colours do not. If we close our eyes, colour ceases to exist, because colour is not something that exists regardless, separate from the eye that perceives it.

MAFFEI, 1979

In a similar way, it is well known how hot and cold can be decidedly personal sensations: in the same room there can be someone wearing a jumper and someone just as

[9] This is also graphically new: Newton's circle was divided into unequal intervals according to the perceived differences that the colours seem to occupy on the spectrum.

comfortable with the ambient temperature in a T-shirt. Physics can measure the temperature, and notice its increase in the room, but it cannot measure the 'heat', inasmuch as heat, like colour, requires an organism that is experiencing it. There is electromagnetic energy, and physics can study it; there are precise wavelengths, and physics can measure them. But there is no colour, which exists only when someone is able to give it voice and consistency. And it is this voice that interests Goethe.

It should come as no surprise that this way of thinking is in open conflict with Newton's, given that his reflections can seem unhindered by actual experience. Goethe's criticism of Newton, both literary and philosophical, boils down to this: you may have discovered the truth, but it is a truth that fails to capture life as we live it.[10]

It is not a question, for us, of taking sides: these are two points of view on the world, two ways of handling reality. Newton is interested in the causes of colour, Goethe in its effects.

In the nineteenth century, however, there is indecision as to which party to go with. Which is strange, given that a whole century goes by between the two – one that develops in more general terms the different approaches between ourselves and things. Newton becomes the champion of whoever wants to understand reality by establishing its laws and tendencies, Goethe a figurehead for those who want to understand how colour appears in its concrete manifestations, in our eyes.

It is Newton who emerges triumphant, a fact that can be explained historically by the giant steps made by physics, which seemed for decades to be the discipline par excellence with which to investigate vision. Then, at the end of

[10] Goethe even goes so far as to dismiss as nonsensical the idea that the sum of all the colours produces white.

the twentieth century, when neuroscience becomes popular, Goethe is rediscovered as the first to have intuited the psychological aspects of our chromatic experience. So while not taking anything away from the genius of Newton, the position of Goethe turns out today to be more interesting than ever for visual languages, because in its claim that colour is a concrete and subjective phenomenon it offers us a naked and surprising truth: a colour that nobody looks at is a colour that does not exist.

Goethe's ideas were taken up and transformed into something useful to professional practices – not by a physicist or an artist, but by a chemist. His name was Michel Eugène Chevreul (1786–1889) and he came into direct contact with the problems of colour when in 1824 he became director of the Gobelins Manufactory in Paris, renowned 78
throughout the world for its tapestries.

The dyers who worked there at the time could boast of knowing how to distinguish up to 20,000 different shades of colour,[11] though they did not possess a precise system for referencing them – just an incredible number of names, some of them quite improbable-sounding. They included 'man colour', and colours of 'child', 'sage', 'king' and even a colour of 'thought'. Chevreul soon realizes that he will not get very far with this state of affairs, and so he rationalizes and systematizes this quaint nomenclature, replacing it with numbers instead and introducing the use of graduated colour wheels to arrange them in order.[12] This 81
is the basis of all modern classifications. Today, in fact,

[11] In reality, even the most practised human eye cannot manage to distinguish more than 250.

[12] In 1810 it is Otto Runge instead who proposes a three-dimensional model: a 79
sphere that takes into account both the colours and their light and dark values, and this is also crucial for modern theories.

◂ 78

▾ 79

Farbenkugel.

80

1er
CERCLE CHROMATIQUE
DE
Mr CHEVREUL
RENFERMANT
LES COULEURS FRANCHES

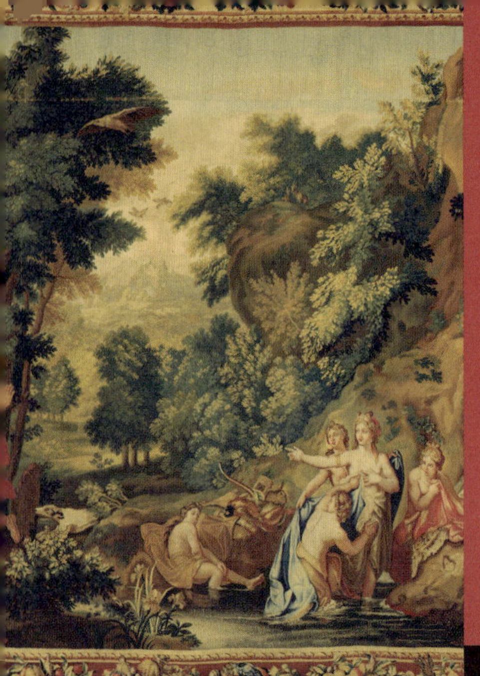

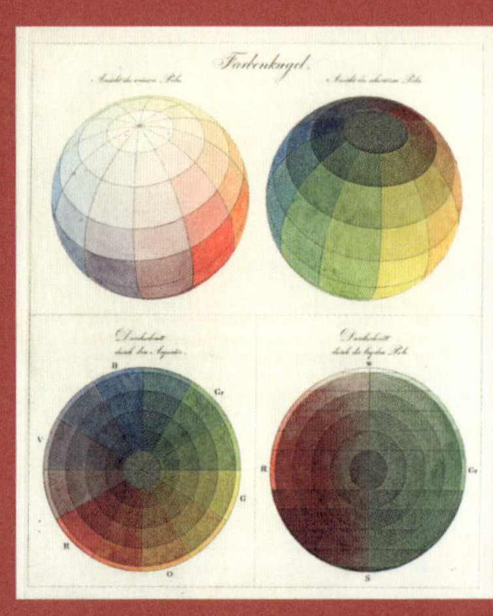

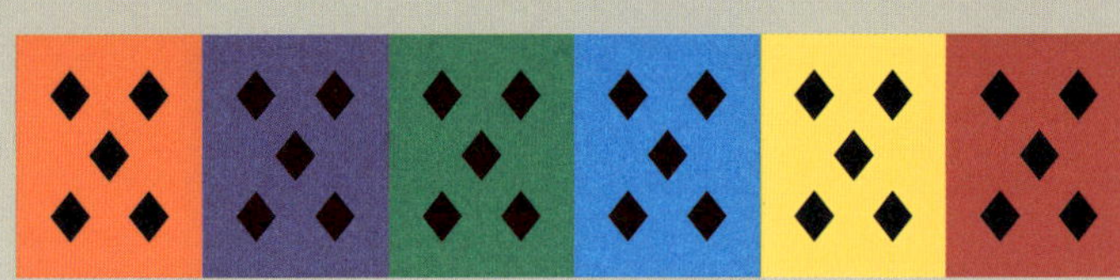

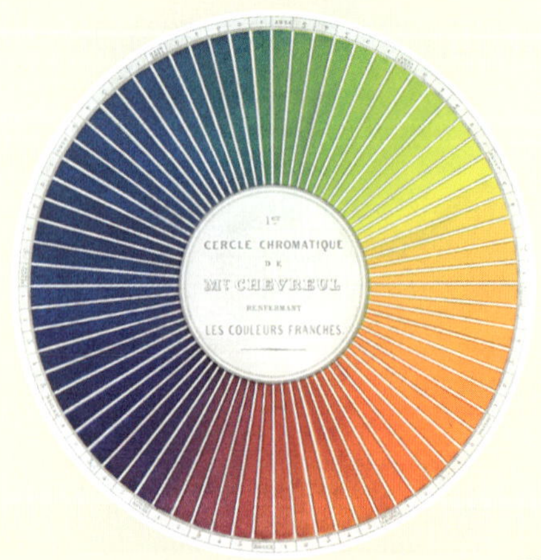

81

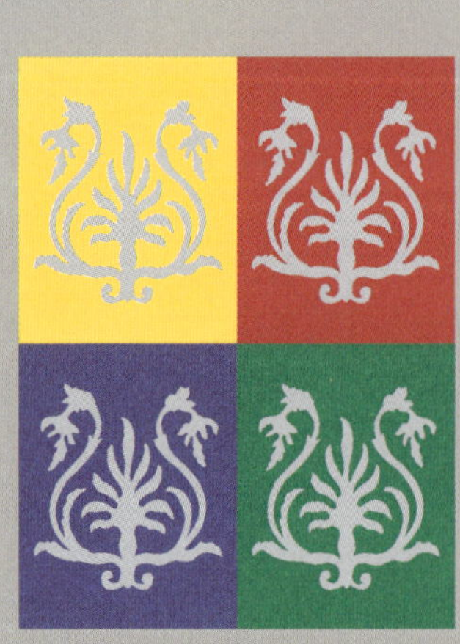

82

the Pantone swatch book refers to colours not by name but only by number.

During this reorganization, Chevreul runs into a problem that has always bedevilled craftsmen working with textiles: namely that the black in designs embroidered on 80
dyed fabrics does not really look black, but changes according to its colour context. It appears greenish against a red background, and yellowish on a blue one.

CHEVREUL, 1987

Inspired by Goethe, Chevreul soon realizes that this effect is not down to the dye, but to the eye of the observer: it is the construction of a psychological complementary, just as in the candle and pencil shadow experiment. He sets out to study all sorts of contrasts and combinations of colours, before concluding that the only way of resolving the problem is to cheat a little. If a grey on top of a red results in something that is too greenish, it will be enough 82
to add to the grey thread a hint of red in order to neutralize it. The colours have to be modified so that they appear as we want them to appear when they are juxtaposed and contrasted with each other.

From this point onwards, the world of art and design takes note of the fact that creating things is not enough: it is necessary to consider how they will be looked at as well, to take into account their representation in the mind of the viewer. It is a crucial development, a new foundation for painting, illustration, cinema and for all visual arts.

CHEVREUL, 1889

Chevreul calls this kind of contrast 'simultaneous', because it occurs *simultaneously* at the sight of the colour and is also its cause – and devotes a whole book to the topic that comes out in 1839, fifteen years after his entry into the royal manufactories. Chevreul says that he has deliberately waited so long because, given that this is a book about colour, he does not want it to be too costly – a preoccupation that reveals the extent to which he belongs to

ITTEN, 1982

a new mass culture. He is no longer the erudite scholar sequestered in his study, but an intellectual preoccupied with the widespread diffusion of his ideas. And he is soon rewarded. The book is an enormous success.

Generations of artists read it, study it and annotate it. DELACROIX, 1994
Among these is the great painter Delacroix, perhaps the
first to apply to painting the theory of simultaneous colour,
employing beautiful purple shadows – shadows enhanced,
that is, with the complementary hue of the warm light of
the sun. It becomes the fashion. Shadows that until now DI NAPOLI, 2006
had been black, grey or brown become multicoloured. The
83 Impressionists are enamoured with them, seduced by a
85 new kind of optical truth exemplified by Monet's depiction of yellow haystacks with vivid and 'unnatural' purple
84 shadows – a choice that will then allow artists such as Gustav Klimt, to the disgruntlement of traditionalists, to use
blue shadows even for the human complexion.

One of the misunderstandings perpetuated in the past by art history books is the belief that the Impressionists depict the world as it looks. The heart of the movement actually lies in a more conceptual approach. The blueness of shadows suggested by Goethe is, as we have seen, a psychological conception: if one were to paint grey shadows, the brain would see them anyway as somewhat bluish. Making them actually blue is a deliberate exaggeration of reality, as well as the most authentic break with tradition devised by painters of the nineteenth century: to depict things not as they are *really* but as they are processed in our minds. It is this liberation of coloured matter – brought about in different ways by a physicist, a man of letters and a chemist – that will be the foundation of all future visual communication. REWALD, 1991 FIORENTINI, 1995

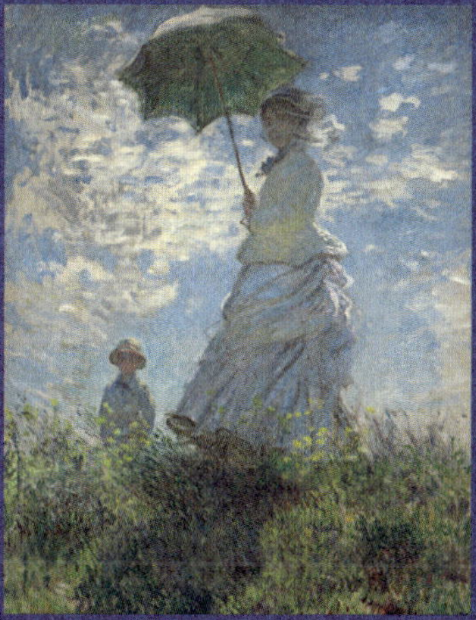

83

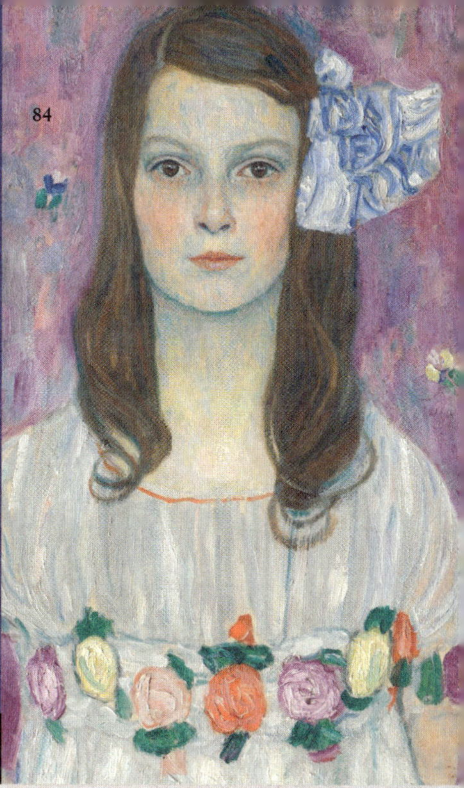

84

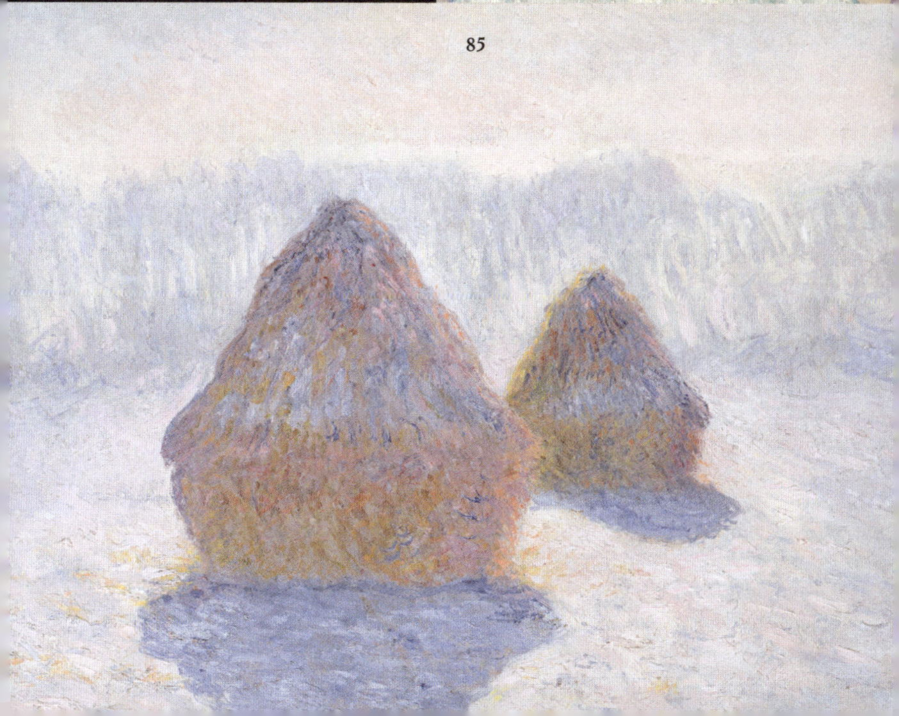

85

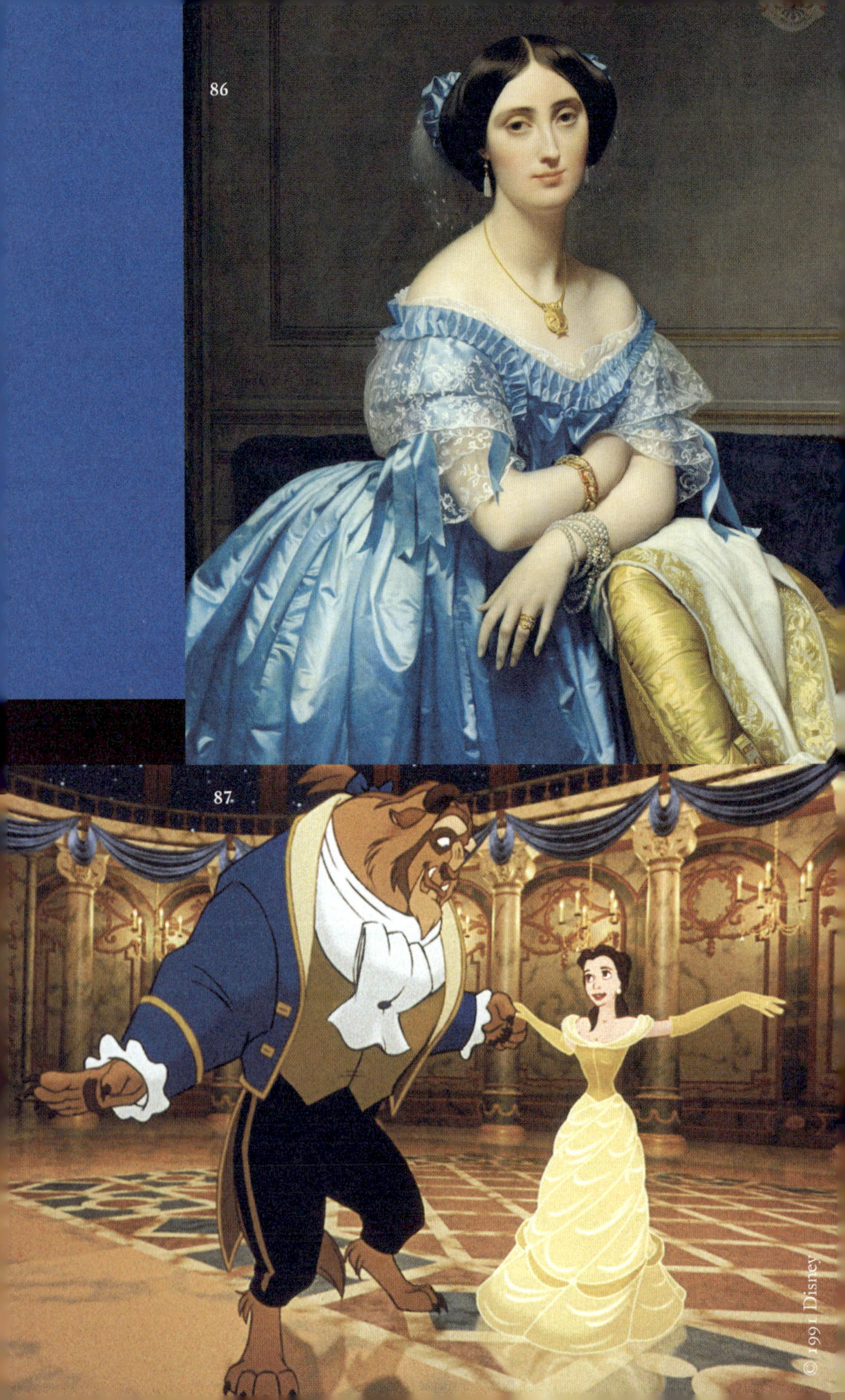
86
87
© 1991 Disney

Blue Bovary

Dressing for Love and to Signify

When a fictional character dresses in a particular colour, it is never 'innocent', never without importance. Or at least not if the author has any concern at all for detail. There are many characters whose identity is quite obviously tied to a precise colour: the green of Robin Hood, the red of Little Red Riding Hood, the black of Audrey Hepburn in *Breakfast at Tiffany's* or the white of Marilyn Monroe's dress in *The Seven Year Itch*. If a narrator tells us that someone is dressed in a particular colour, they are telling us something that goes beyond simple description. Let's try to investigate, then, the destinies of some protagonists – in literature, painting and animated film – who are dressed in a particular colour, in this case blue, starting with the eponymous anti-heroine of that most famous of French nineteenth-century novels, *Madame Bovary* (1856) by Gustave Flaubert.

Having become acquainted during her convent education with the arts, with music and literature, Emma returns to live in a small provincial town where she feels increasingly confined – consumed by boredom and a lack of prospects. Headstrong and egocentric, capable of fainting in the company of nuns merely in order to attract attention, she daydreams of a different, more lively and worldly existence. So when she meets Charles Bovary, the local doctor, she sees in his proposal of marriage the chance to escape from the provincial confines that have strait-jacketed her. But her husband soon reveals himself to be intellectually mediocre and decidedly lacking in ambition. And the more solicitous and thoughtful he is towards her, the more she comes to despise him. 'What a poor excuse for a man,' she is given to repeat to herself – and, when the occasion arises, falls headlong into adultery. At first with Rodolphe, a casually seductive landowner, and then, having been abandoned by her lover, she turns instead to a young lawyer.

Emma seeks in extramarital relationships what she desperately lacks according to those romantic ideals she discovered as a young woman in the pages of other novels. What she seeks above all is relief from boredom – how long the winters are in the countryside! – and this boredom is a very modern feeling, and something quite new in literature, that has a central role to play in the story.

Industrialized society, though not atheistic, is the first to be deprived of the prospect of Paradise, and without the certainty of another life, then to do nothing in this one means wasting the little time that we have and missing the fulfilment of our destiny, or potential. Modern boredom is perhaps just this: the consciousness of a present made anxious by the absence of eternity. All the more reason, then, that meaning should be sought immediately in the here and now, in the things that happen or that may be made to happen. One needs to create days constellated by events and distractions. Better still, by successes. And it is in the first place through reading that, in the new mass society, the emerging classes are entertained by being shown other worlds, other ways of being to which they can aspire. Entertainment is the remedy for boredom – its opposite. From this point of view, even having lovers is a kind of entertainment.

Emma Bovary craves the theatre, horse-riding, illustrated magazines, news of the big city where this or that new shop has opened. She agrees with her second lover, the lawyer Léon, when he says that she should look to art and to poetry to elevate her soul – and yet in her heart she is waiting on an actual, practical event to distract her and give her life meaning. A meaning that is not *other*worldly but worldly and sophisticated.

She keeps small succulents in her bedroom because she has seen the protagonist of a highly fashionable book doing so. It is an important detail, for 1840: from here on we can see the development of what will become, a century later, lifestyle magazines such as *Marie Claire* and *Elle*, and the advice given by home design gurus such as American Martha Stewart, who have brightened the lives of thousands of women by convincing them that there is a kind of salvation in the exercise of taste, even if applied only to découpage.

And so it is that Emma begins to spend beyond her means – both on herself and in order to buy gifts for the men she falls in love with – slipping into a spiral of debt from which she cannot escape and which her husband is ignorant of. In the end, crushed by the weight of her own lies, unable to extricate herself and too proud to submit to ruin before the gaze of those fellow villagers she so despises, she decides to commit suicide by swallowing arsenic.

Rivers of ink have been spilt on what *Madame Bovary* is about: a romantic story that ends badly; a political book on the condition of women; an exploration of the conflict between illusion and reality, between the internal image which everyone constructs of themselves and the inevitable fall into the concreteness of reality. On a chromatic level, it is a novel which scarcely mentions colour – except blue, to which the author insistently returns, in connection with some of the book's crucial elements.

*

The first time that Charles Bovary meets his future wife, Emma is wearing an outfit of blue wool. This is no arbitrary detail. Blue stands out, it is conspicuous, and it speaks of a desire for a different kind of life, rising above the banality of the everyday. On two other occasions, after entering the scene, Flaubert informs us that Emma is wearing this colour – the first time blue cashmere, the second blue satin. As far as her husband is concerned, we learn that at school Charles Bovary had also attracted attention by wearing blue stockings – the sole distinction of an otherwise colourless man, as if some spark in him, if it had ever existed, had died in infancy.

Blue is not something that one wears, it is something that one *is*: Emma has brown eyes, which in full daylight, Flaubert tells us, glow with a dark blue as if they consisted of successive layers of colour. Her hair is parted into two bunches so smooth that they emanate blue reflections.

Blue is therefore a colour-motif, a precise sign that speaks of the ideals of the protagonist. But it is also an ominous and painful colour. When Rodolphe takes his final leave, Emma, suspecting that she will never see him again, stands at her window and watches him as he steps into a blue coach. Then she buys two glass vases – blue ones of course – to embellish the fireplace in her sitting room (perhaps this too has been inspired by books and magazines). And the bottle of arsenic with which she is to kill herself is also naturally made of blue glass. She steals it from the pharmacist, establishing a tragic symmetry between her first appearance in the novel and this final gesture.

Flaubert does not invent all this out of nothing. This desire for blue already had a history.

A century before Emma Bovary there had been another famous literary suicide dressed in blue. The protagonist of

Goethe's *The Sorrows of Young Werther*, published in 1774, 89
the victim of an impossible love for the beautiful Char-
lotte, kills himself with a pistol shot to the temple – and
in a kind of romantic exhibitionism is found dead dressed
as on the night of his first dance with her, in a blue jacket
and a yellow waistcoat.

As we saw in the previous chapter, Goethe is the first to
demonstrate that blue shadows are cast by objects when lit
by yellow light; but unlike the nineteenth-century painters
who will use the novelty as a simple figurative trick, for
Goethe this pairing is a metaphysical fact: the yellow light
and the blue shadow are the poles of a series of oppositions
from which all existence arises. On the one hand, there
is the masculine, the irregular, warmth; on the other, the 90
feminine, evenness, the cold.

MATHIEU, 2002

And so the blue of Werther's jacket is a question of identity, affirming his own special way of being in the world. As
if to say that yes, a nobleman can also die of love. The book
is enormously successful, and this juxtaposition of blue and
yellow – an outlandish one according to contemporary canons
of elegance – explodes into fashion. To such an extent, in
fact, that it almost comes to be the uniform of Sentiment. 91
To dress in the style of Werther is soon considered a sign
of taste, and throughout Europe young men begin to wear
the blue jackets and yellow waistcoats that have quickly become, beyond the book itself, the iconographic signature
of Werther's character – in paintings and illustrations and 92
in theatrical costumes, such as the one used for Massenet's
1892 opera based on Goethe's novel. The unhappy protagonist even appears dressed in this way in China, painted
onto glass and porcelain.

But Werther's case is not an isolated one. For all the
economic challenges that we have already discussed when
it came to ultramarine, from the Renaissance onwards it is

blue, a colour neglected in the palette of antiquity, that becomes both precious and spiritual. By the eighteenth century it already has an illustrious history, and is chosen in cultivated circles as an emblem of distinction in both life and art. One of the key books for this is *Heinrich of Ofterdingen* by Novalis (1772–1801), which recounts the adventures of a *Minnesänger* or medieval singer of courtly love. Accompanied by the shepherdess Cyana, he goes in search of a blue flower that is symbolic of an intuitive capacity to grasp reality, and of the metaphysical heights to which noble souls may aspire.[1] Behind this suggestion there are fashionable botanical theories associating colours with the power to radiate curative energies, but the search for the flower is also a metaphor of the lyrical yearning for the infinite, for the absolute, for the sublime, a yearning that in German is signified with a word untranslatable into other languages: *Sehnsucht*: the feeling for distant things, a kind of nostalgia for something that is physically distant. This blue flower is effectively poetry itself, understood as an existential condition. At the beginning of the nineteenth century blue is a particular way of feeling – and of feeling for – life itself.

In the last forty years or so the covers of paperback editions of *Madame Bovary* have frequently featured portraits by Jean-Auguste-Dominique Ingres (1780–1867), such as
88 those of the *Princess de Broglie* or of *The Countess of Haussonville*, both dressed in shades of blue. Unlike Emma
Bovary, however, both women belong to the aristocracy,
and the expensive elegance that the paintings display is beyond anything that could be aspired to in provincial life.
86 The Princess de Broglie enlivened and adorned some of the

SHELTON, 2010

[1] 'Cyan', as graphic designers and typographers know, is today the colour of blue printing ink. Novalis calls the flower a *Blue Flower*, identified by some as the forget-me-not.

88A

Countess d'Haussonville

88B

Princess de Broglie

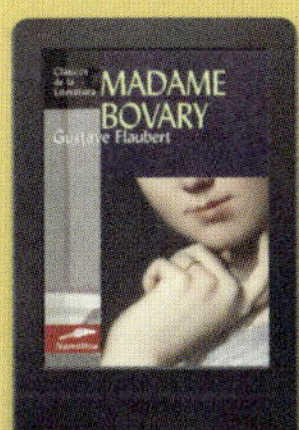

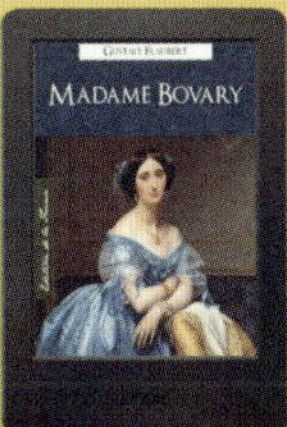

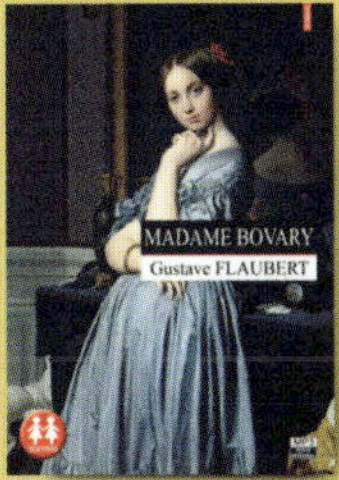

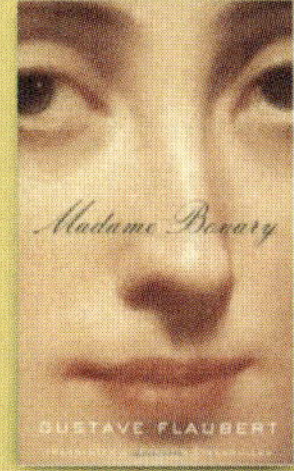

89

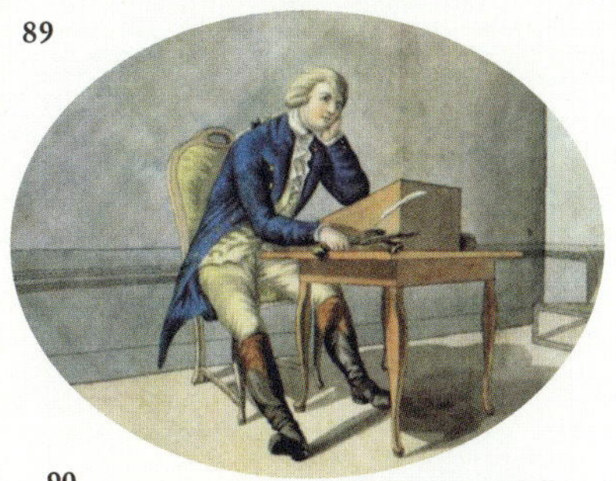

90

Light	Shadow
Clear	Dark
Strong	Weak
Near	Far
Acidic	Alkaline
Repulsion	Attraction
Action	Deprivation

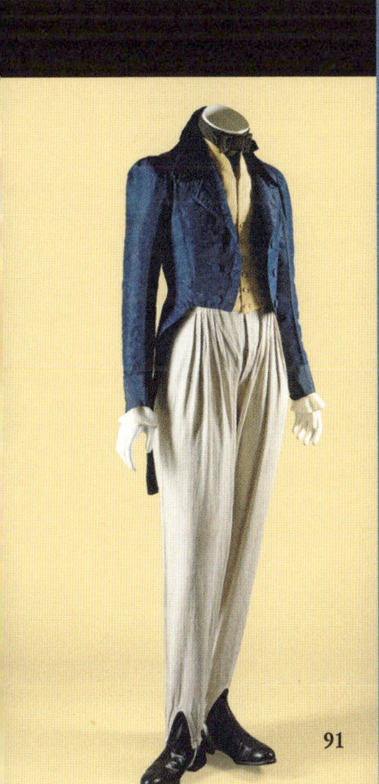

91

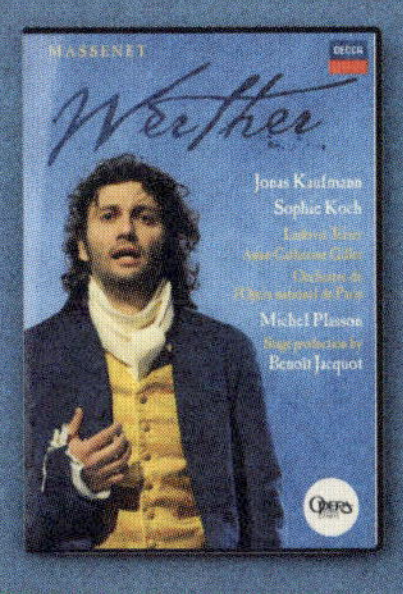

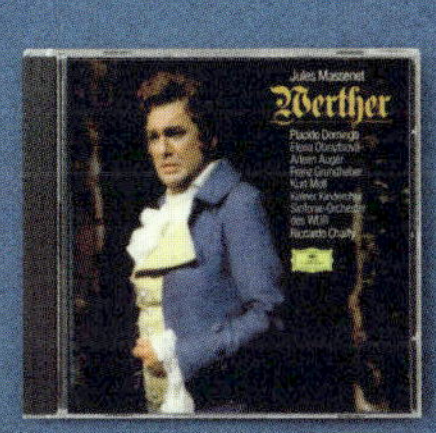

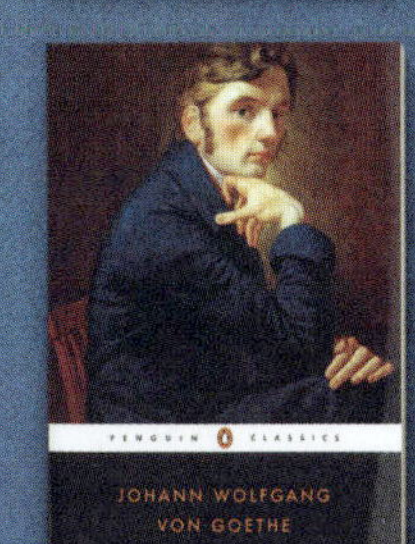

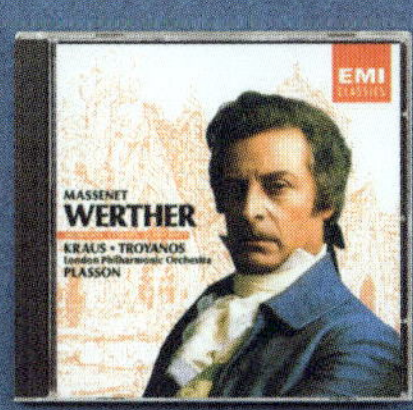

92

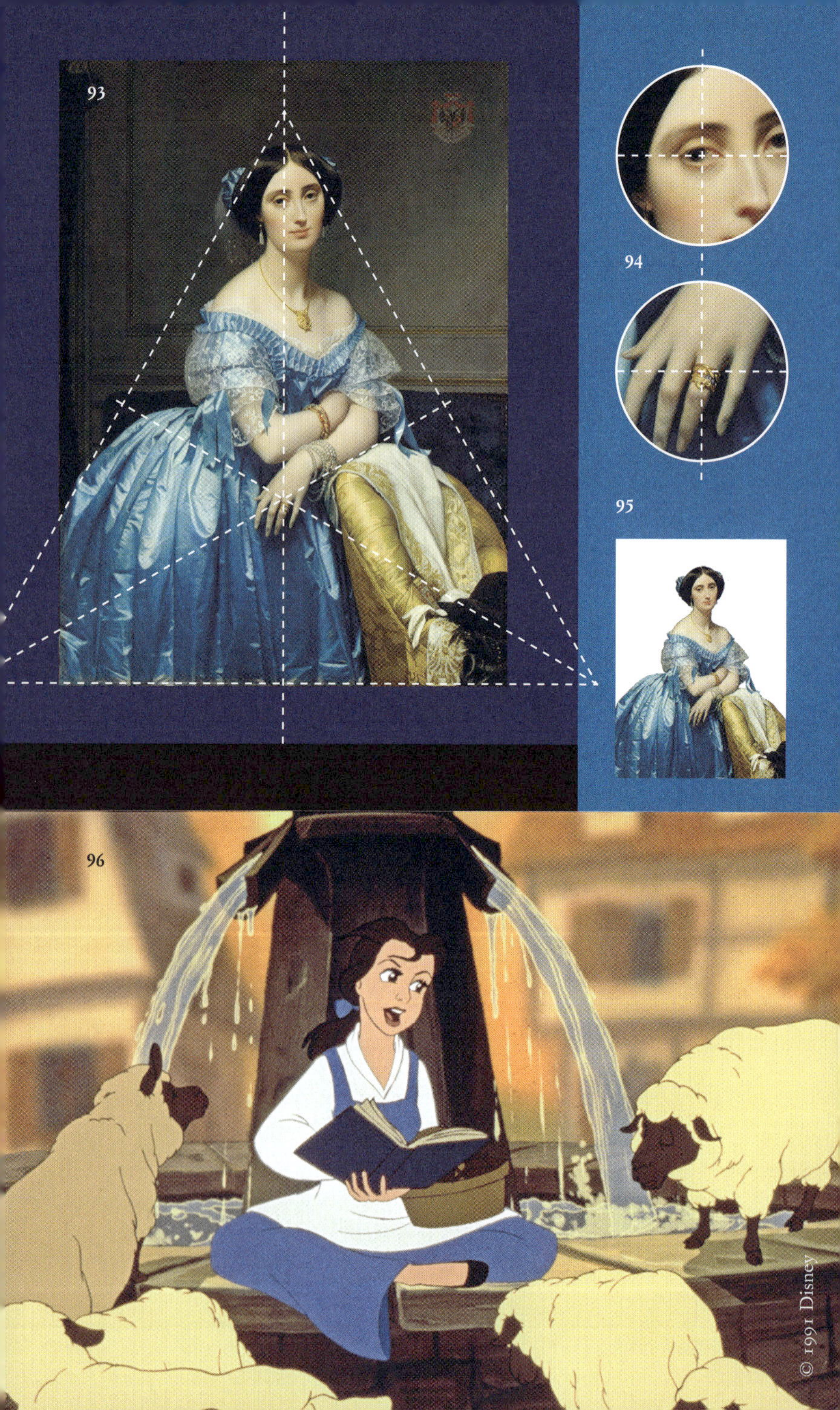
93
94
95
96
© 1991 Disney

most cultivated and refined Parisian circles of the Second Empire and was renowned for her elegance and her reserve, which is to say for that quality habitually preferred by the powerful: understatement. She is therefore a model woman, one who will inspire all of the Emma Bovarys of France. De Broglie is blue by right, it is part of her patrimony; Emma dresses in blue to imitate her, persuading herself that through the acquisition of a colour she might reach a status from which she is in fact excluded.

As is inevitable when dealing with paintings from the past, we cannot see everything that they include, all those things that spoke immediately to their contemporary viewers. Signs of wealth are explicit and in plain sight: sumptuous and gleaming drapery, golden glows, precious stones. Ingres, a romantic classicist, studied the Renaissance masters attentively and introduced esoteric geometry into his painting. The portrait of de Broglie has a classical composition, with the subject at the centre, occupying a
space formed by a pyramid, like in paintings of the Ma- 93
donna as the 'Queen of Heaven'. But what in depictions of the Virgin was hieratic detachment has here become a distinctly profane value: prestige.

RADIUS, 1968

The princess seems to hold out her hand, the focal point for the entire composition. And the ring that she wears, looking very expensive indeed, is located on an axis of
symmetry that connects it with her eyes, as if to say that 94
the gaze of the sitter has profound links with the goods that she possesses. If the eyes are the mirrors of the soul, gemstones are reflections of social status.

These are the most immediately visible things. There are others that require a little knowledge of the customs and fashion of the time. The hand that she shows, for instance, is pale and manicured with perfectly oval and highly polished nails – and her hair, divided into two bunches, is silky and clean. But this is hardly the norm for women of the era. Used as we are to soap and shampoo as everyday elements of the rhetoric of advertising, we have to make a deliberate effort to recognize the privilege inherent in such radiant hair.

The other thing that we do not see is the fact that this is not a simple figure of a woman. Since the invention of photography, portraits are in effect for us almost always psychological reconfigurations of their subjects. The one of de Broglie, however, is also the portrait of a man: namely of the husband who allows her to be as she is, and to possess what is shown to us. Cynically we might say that this is not so much a portrait as a still life, like those paintings showing tables laden with hares and pheasants, in which some wealthy burgher or politician displayed what he was able to afford: a beautiful house, objects, textiles, jewellery . . . And in this case, a superbly elegant woman.

95 If we isolate the figure, detaching it from the background, we become aware that while the backdrop consists only of dull tones and straight lines, her body is all colour and curves. The rigidity of the panelling on the walls contrasts with the fluidity of the figure; the voluminous dress envelops her, like an elaborately fancy cake, like the folds of a meringue or a dollop of whipped cream. The princess is in effect a vaporous mass that inundates the space, reserved but also in control of her role. The figurative idea of Ingres is to depict power by subjecting us to it; we look at the painting but our gaze is not reciprocated. She is looking elsewhere, beyond and through us. A brilliantly original invention for the era, this is a look that will eventually become standard for fashion photography, in which it is de rigueur for models to be lofty and detached. But what in the pages of *Vogue* is just an act in this painting represents inevitable and substantial authority.

BERGER, 2009

To see a woman in a blue dress today hardly signifies what it used to. De Broglie's dress is made from metres of radiant fabric, perhaps satin, and while it communicates even to us an ostentatious grandeur, we cannot see it through the eyes of 1853, when dyeing a textile such a blue would have been a difficult and expensive process. Ingres' public would undoubtedly have known this. In this way colour is not reduced to its perceptual level. It signifies and communicates; it distinguishes and hierarchizes. If the dress is blue, the armchair against which it lies is yellow, in fashionable Goethean contrast.

Let's return now to Flaubert's novel to underline an important aspect of it and to try to connect the threads. Emma Bovary does not dream about Paris but about a closer, more accessible city – Rouen, in upper Normandy. It is in Rouen that she meets with her second lover, and it is in Rouen that she attends an opera, *Lucia de Lammermoor*, in a scene that is very important for the economy depicted in the novel. When she enters the gallery, before the curtain rises, Flaubert mentions that in the stalls some of the spectators are talking about 'indigo'. Not out of any abstract scientific interest but in connection with work. Rouen is one of the most important centres for dyeing fabrics indigo and blue, with a huge volume of production in the trade. Here, then, is the other side of 'romantic' blue: its place in fashion and the significant role it plays in the prosperity of the town's bourgeoisie. To dress in blue is not only a statement of a lyrical sensibility or of taste, as when we ask today for a shirt in blue simply because it looks better; at the time it meant above all that you were able to afford such luxury. This is why Emma's entry wearing a blue dress is so deliberate and eloquent: Bovary blue may be both spiritual and anti-conformist, but it is also (and always) a colour belonging to a particular class.

When a colour has begun its story, to accumulate meaning, it quickly becomes a part of the collective imagination, often without the public being conscious of it. To see how this works we need only look at how, 150 years later, the chromatic values of romantic blue are redeployed in Disney's animated feature film *Beauty and the Beast* (1991).

The film is an adaptation of an eighteenth-century French text by Madame Leprince de Beaumont, which was inspired in turn by variations on stories that go back in time until they reach all the way to *Cupid and Psyche* by Apuleius. Its theme is the opposition between intellectual and passionate love, mind and body. But for Madame Leprince de Beaumont it also becomes an edifying tale, a lesson for young girls in an era of arranged marriages. My dear girls, it clearly advises, do not rebel if you are required to marry old and decrepit men, because in time you will learn to look on these 'beasts' with loving eyes, and in those eyes they will be utterly transfigured.

Belle, the protagonist, is ultimately the reversed double of Emma Bovary: the provincial French girl who accepts her lot and sees the good in her husband, leading to his transformation into a prince dressed in blue. Nothing less than a representative of the colour itself.

The film does not follow the eighteenth-century plot, but puts the emphasis instead on a very different – very Anglo-Saxon and Disneyan – opposition between nature and culture.

Just as Snow White's first thought is to clean the dwarves' cottage and force them to wash, so Belle is the bearer of urban ideals that are counterposed to both the rusticity of the village in which she is born and to the wildness of the Beast. In the opening sequence, as she strolls, singing, through the village, everything from the houses to the other villagers is depicted in brown, ochre and burgundy.

Everything, that is, except for her. Belle, like Emma, enters the scene dressed in blue. 96

This citation of the romantic model is no accident (even the book she holds is blue), but this time it does not convey the aspirations of a sublime soul: dressing in blue is above all a mark of diversity of which one should be proud. Throughout the 1990s, the signature imperative for Disney is to *be oneself*.

Later on, the Beast invites Belle to dinner. The Beast has groomed himself and dressed elegantly for the occasion: like Werther he wears a blue jacket and yellow waistcoat. 87
Belle, divested of blue, now appears in a yellow dress that is all flounces and crinoline, revealing her new nature. This luminous, illusionistic yellow is rational and civilizing. For Belle, it is not just a question of dominating the Beast. She must also learn to stem the romantic impulses that hold her back from life itself. Her development consists of transforming literary illusion into pragmatism – mitigating Bovary blue with the yellow of concreteness, reconciling rationality and sentiment.[2] The Beast will become human only after the true transformation, the internal one, has occurred for Belle.

Werther, Emma, the Princess de Broglie, the Countess of Haussonville, Belle and the Beast: six protagonists dressed in blue (and often in relation with yellow). If in everyday life we happen to wear blue, it is ultimately because it forms part of our wardrobe. The palette of our

[2] Habituated as we are to an idea of entertainment in which everything is explicit, we might ask ourselves what the point is of introducing more difficult, less obvious elements – even a hidden reference to Goethe – into an animated film. Disney films, in reality, unlike cartoons made for TV or games, are aimed at a public which is both vast and diverse – and hence they are invariably constructed like multi-layered works with different levels of address and access: from simple participation in the plot to aesthetic pleasure gained from appreciation of how they are made.

wardrobe was constructed over the years according to precise and personal parameters: to get noticed or to disappear, depending on the occasion; these are colours that reveal us, that we feel define us, that we love and that we like wearing. And then there are those concessions to fashion that after initial enthusiasm sink to the bottom of a drawer. But when a fictional character (or the subject of a portrait) dresses in a given colour, it is the author who is indirectly revealing an aspect of that character to us.

Someone might object that Goethe, Ingres, Flaubert and Disney are all utilizing different kinds of blue. De Broglie's outfit is undoubtedly azure; that of Haussonville is cerulean; whereas Belle's is cobalt, and we have no proof that Bovary's was not navy blue or sapphire. Nothing in the text itself guarantees that Emma's dress and the bottle of arsenic are of the same blue, and that Flaubert deliberately contrived a link between the two signifying 'destiny'. But the point here is quite different. If we understand that azure, cerulean and cobalt belong in our culture to the category of 'blueness', it is Flaubert's characteristic linguistic self-awareness that leads him deliberately to use only a single, generic word. 'Blue' is above all a word. And the truth of words is something different from the reality of perception or of physics. Put simply, we are dealing here not with a wavelength so much as with a cultural category.[3]

Werther dresses in blue as a spiritual metaphor. De Broglie's blue stages the pomp of privilege. Emma's is that

[3] In French the term *bleu* covers a chromatic range that goes from navy (that dark and almost black hue), to Prussian blue, to ultramarine, and ultimately to sky blue, which in Italian (*azzurro*) indicates a colour in which we do not *feel* the addition of white (as happens with *celeste*, or 'light blue'). It is difficult to say exactly what kind of 'bleu' Flaubert had in mind when he used the word. The only definite element is the bottle of arsenic, since we have contemporary evidence concerning the precise blue of 'pharmacy glass': it is just like the colour used in imitation of it today for bottles, albeit plastic ones, containing Roberts Rose Water. What's interesting is Flaubert's decision to return to a word-colour so central to romantic culture.

of the petit bourgeois who aspires to and imitates such privilege, but this blue is disorienting, and with perfect romanticism confuses her social inferiority with an emptiness of soul. Belle dresses in blue out of an eccentricity of which she is proud; the Beast because he cultivates a Werther-like soulfulness, or because he happens to be, after all, an incognito blue-blooded prince. Blue unites them: it is a way of being in the world, and of occupying an iconographic space. In their different ways, they are all bourgeois portraits – of characters embodying bourgeois conflicts. To dress in blue is more or less *not* to be submerged in grey: it counters the modern fear of being invisible, of leaving no trace.

From the few dates that Flaubert gives us, we know that Emma Bovary dies on 24 March 1846. As we shall see in the following chapter, the first artificial colour will be invented in 1859, just thirteen years later. Emma could not have suspected that in the world to come anyone could be dressed in blue. Even by wearing jeans. Even to go to the pub.

97

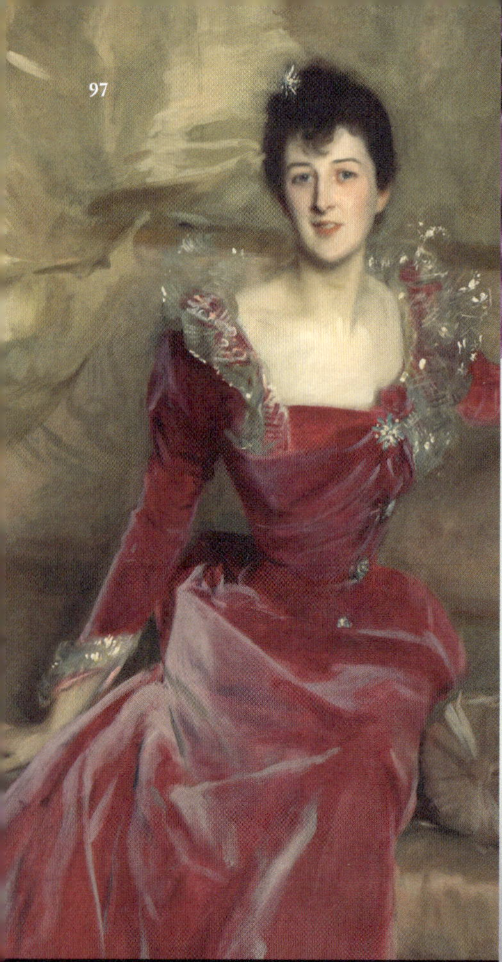

98

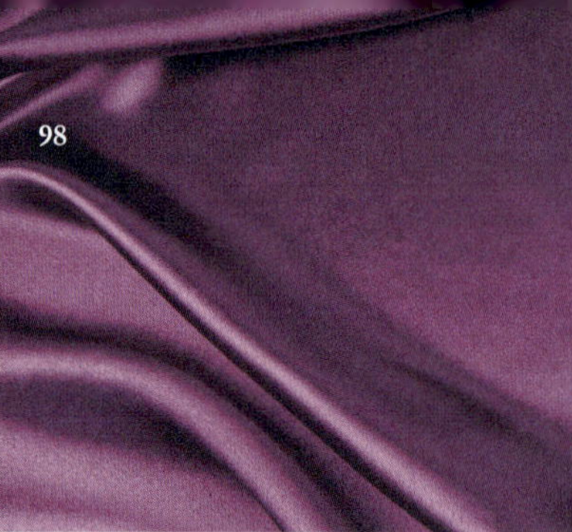

99

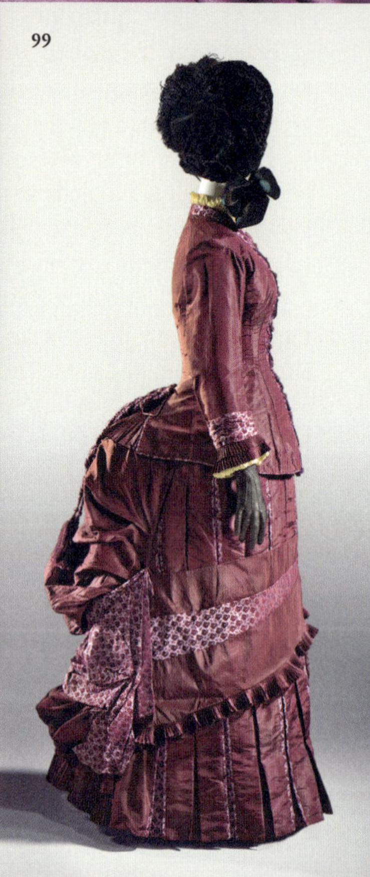

100

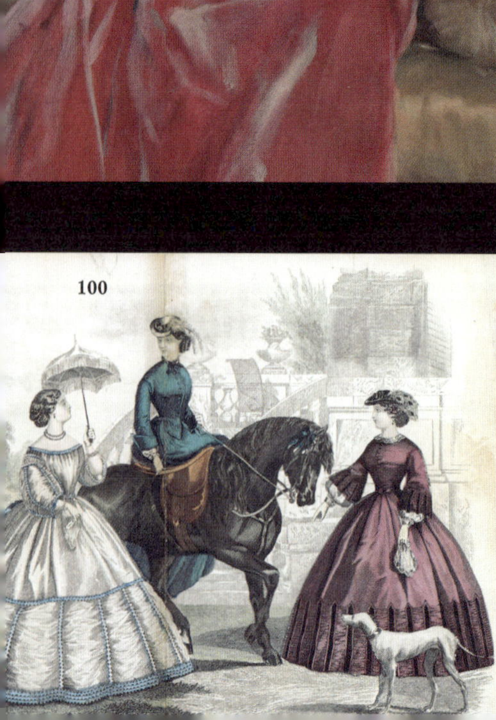

101

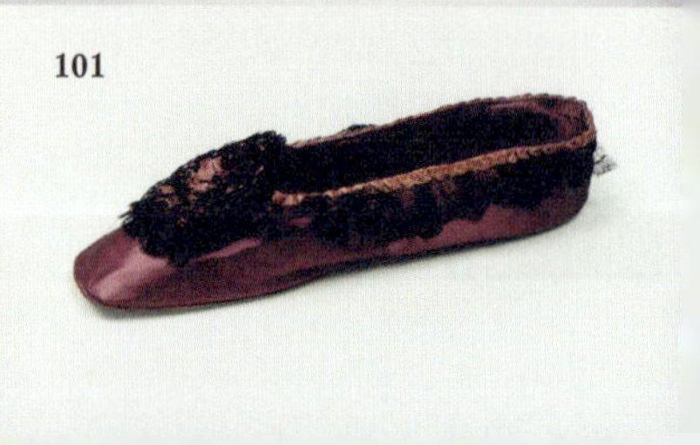

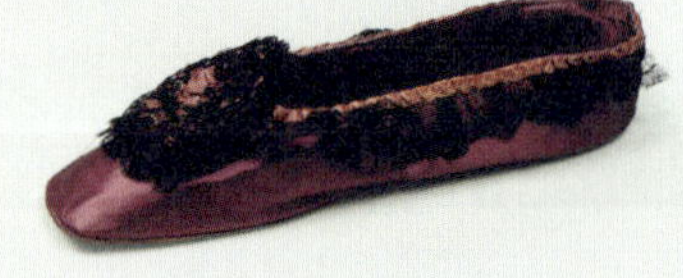

Mauve Modernity

The Birth of Consumerism and Stardom

In 1793, with the memory of the guillotine still fresh in everyone's mind, there was another revolution that is not often studied at school: the advent of the freedom to dress as one chooses.

Prior to this date, inflexible sumptuary laws established which clothing was to be worn – on the basis of class, role, trade, profession. Now, for the first time in human history, there were no longer mere subjects but citizens instead, free to choose and to dress as they wished. Free, that is, to become consumers. This is not to say that everyone suddenly knew how to do it. And as a result, advertising was also born. The most cynical will say that we moved from one form of slavery to another. Be that as it may, in the new world advertisements suggest to everyone how they can finally become themselves.

Together with fashion, the concept of taste is established, and the success of whoever exercises it is proclaimed. Certain individuals soon become the arbiters of elegance, and the more famous they become, the more authority and influence they acquire. Today we would call them trendsetters, or most recently simply influencers. There are still no supermodels or rock stars, but there are queens to be admired and followed – and women, especially bourgeois women, use them as a point of reference. Princess Eugenie of France and Queen Victoria of England become unparalleled models of style. The press chronicles every ball, every opening, every event that they attend. They linger over the details of fabrics, hairstyles, accessories sported by VIPs whose choices can determine the success or failure of a product. A sign from them directs spending. Taste becomes finance conducted by other means.

108 And it is Queen Victoria herself who initiates an epochal transition in the history of colour, by arriving at her
daughter's wedding dressed in an outfit of bright, brilliant,
almost electric violet. This seldom seen colour is a fashion
98 sensation. Everybody wants mauve (as it is called), both
to wear and for home furnishings. This is not merely an aesthetic pivot, it is also a technical one. Queen Victoria's outfit is dyed with 'mauveine', the first synthetic colourant in history, which is to say the first created by artificial processes in a laboratory, without recourse to any vegetable or animal matter whatsoever. It is a chemical novelty and has immediate, unprecedented commercial success. It is significant that the great chemical and pharmaceutical companies of today, from Bayer to Ciba-Geigy and BASF, all began their activities in the nineteenth century as manufacturers of synthetic colours.[1] From this moment on, there is no turning back. The world of colour has been changed for ever.

The invention that changes the fate of clothing is the work of a young student at the Royal College of Chemistry called William Henry Perkin (1838–1907). In March 1856, at the age of just eighteen, while attempting to synthesize GARFIELD, 2002

[1] The chemistry of dyeing is among the major costs of industrial society. The bible on the subject, *Colour Index International*, is a list of all artificial dyes that runs to some 9,000 pages in nine volumes. Yet despite the feeling it gives us of living in such a colourful world, today the most commonly produced dye is white.

the quinine that was used as an anti-malarial drug, Perkin
obtains a dark-coloured substance. It is one of those by-
products of failure that occur frequently in labs, and that
usually end up in the bin. But Perkin realizes that this
unlooked-for residue, when dissolved in alcohol, produces
a purplish effect – and has the idea that it might be turned
into a dye for textiles. He tests it on silk, which immediately confirms its stability: it withstands direct light, rubbing
and washing. Thanks to this new colouring agent it is possible to dye wool, cotton and various other materials in
an even, easily repeatable way and to produce many var- **101**
iations in hue – from lilac to deep purple – depending on **97, 99**
the process used.

This new discovery did not arrive out of nowhere. With
the widespread use of gas lighting there was a lot of interest
in finding uses for and commercially exploiting tar residues.
It was already known that such residues were often coloured,
though their potential as dyes had not yet received particular
attention. Perkin's talent – and this is frequently how great
ideas originate – lay not so much in what he discovered as
in the use he found for it. He immediately patents the new
substance and begins large-scale production, calling it 'ani-
BALL, 2004 line purple', a name that two years later he seeks to change.
The marketing people propose a much more captivating, original and durable name: *mauve* – the French for purple – in
order to subconsciously suggest a conncction with the cap-
ital of fashion. It is a tremendous success, and in no time **100**
at all Perkin acquires fame, glory and wealth. The chemist
becomes an entrepreneur, organizing for himself all of the
processes necessary for mass production. And this too is historically unprecedented.

To show how significant a discovery this was, it is worth considering how things had been dyed up until then. In a

dyeing manual of 1817 there is a list of the ten-stage process
used to obtain red cloth. First, woody impurities were re- BRUSATIN, 1983
moved from the cotton, and the fabric was then soaked in
dung to render it manageable. Then came the processes of
oiling and leaching, degreasing with soda and tanning with
oak gall – followed by aluminization, softening, a rinse to
remove the alum, and the fixing of the caustic. And only
then, finally, did the actual dyeing take place, with madder. PASTOUREAU, 2016
For centuries, making colour had been a laborious process
requiring long, slow, malodorous and even degrading processes. With Perkin, colour becomes orderly and matter of
fact, clean and virtually odourless. These are years of exceptional industrial liveliness, of the kind that we will perhaps
not see again. In the nineteenth century, in fact, the world
of textiles is characterized by continuous technological innovation, similar to what is happening now with electronics.

As we have already seen, artists had known for a long
time about the possibility of artificially making some colours, such as white lead or Egyptian blue. This process ZECCHINA, 2012
was accelerated in the eighteenth century by advances in
chemistry – a new, brilliant science that between 1700 and
1820 changes the face of the world, by allowing us not just
to colour but to modify and transform things, and to treat
illness effectively. During this period, new and seductive
104 colours are created: Prussian blue, as used by Hokusai for
105 his famous wave, arrives in 1704, cobalt blue in 1802, soon BALL, 2013
followed by chrome orange and cadmium yellow. Neither
Prussian blue nor cadmium yellow, however, was used to
dye fabrics. Perkin's originality is to have synthesized not
a pigment for art but a dye for textiles – through a process
that does not exist in nature and that opens the door to one
of the biggest modern businesses: fashion. But in order for
this to be possible, there needed to be a new society as well.

*

Between 1823 and 1828 the architect Karl Friedrich Schinkel designed two buildings in Berlin that represent spatially the conceptual premise of this new era. The Altes Museum is 102
the first public museum where you must buy a ticket to enter, and the Kaufhaus is a commercial centre where you can go to shop. Although performing apparently distant roles, the two buildings are in keeping with each other: Schinkel designs them both in a neoclassical style. It is not just taste or their formal aspect that brings them together, there is something much more profound: both are walkable spaces where it is possible to spend time, looking at things and spending money. Today it is commonly felt, with a degree of snobbery, that the two experiences are completely distinct: to look at a shoe while shopping seems like a purely practical activity that has nothing to do with the contemplation, say, of a Greek sculpture. The first is a necessity, the second poetry. And yet there is more in common between the two than we would like to admit, and this is something that Schinkel's clients were very clear about.

In nascent mass society, people find themselves with something very new at their disposal: free time that needs to be filled with recreational activities. It is this free time that makes Myron's *Discus Thrower* and a gym shoe similar, because contemplation and shopping have both become forms of entertainment, that is to say symbolic fillers of that freedom, that free time.

BENJAMIN, 2010

These are the years when, in parallel to the maturing features of capitalism, the social characteristics of modernity are also defined – the urbanization of the peasant classes as a consequence of industrialization, the literacy of the masses, the establishment of offices for registry (recording personal data) and of organs of control (schools, hospitals, prisons), the use of science as a legitimation of social conventions, and obviously the birth of advertising,

102

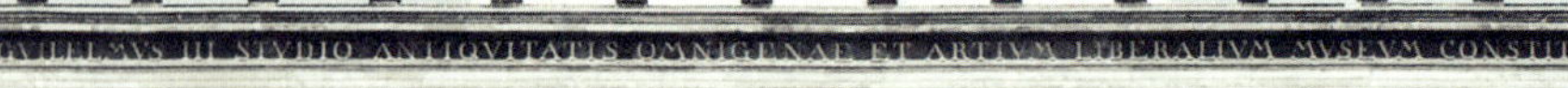

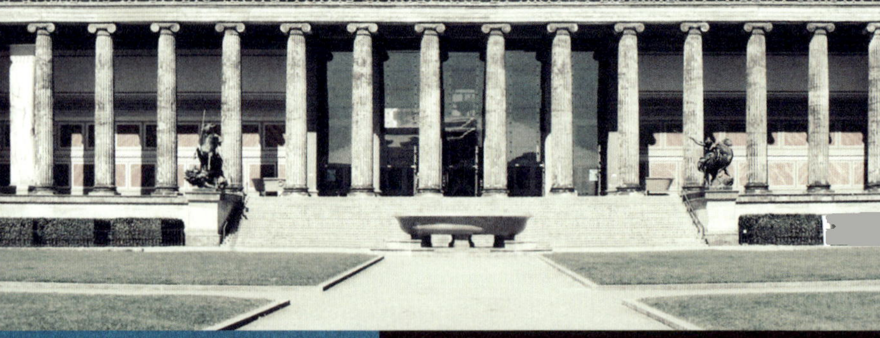

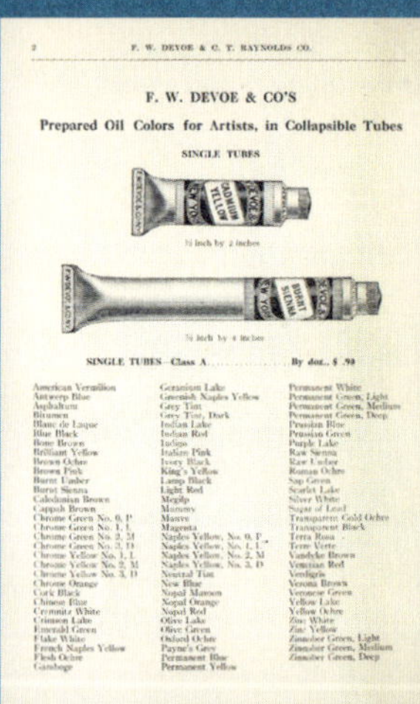

2 F. W. DEVOE & C. T. RAYNOLDS CO.

F. W. DEVOE & CO'S

Prepared Oil Colors for Artists, in Collapsible Tubes

SINGLE TUBES

½ inch by 2 inches

½ inch by 4 inches

SINGLE TUBES—Class A.................By doz., $ .90

American Vermilion
Antwerp Blue
Asphaltum
Bitumen
Blanc de Laque
Blue Black
Bone Brown
Brilliant Yellow
Brown Ochre
Brown Pink
Burnt Umber
Burnt Sienna
Caledonian Brown
Cappah Brown
Chrome Green No. 0, P
Chrome Green No. 1, L
Chrome Green No. 2, M
Chrome Green No. 3, D
Chrome Yellow No. 1, L
Chrome Yellow No. 2, M
Chrome Yellow No. 3, D
Chrome Orange
Cork Black
Chinese Blue
Cremnitz White
Crimson Lake
Emerald Green
Flake White
French Naples Yellow
Flesh Ochre
Gamboge
Geranium Lake
Greenish Naples Yellow
Grey Tint
Grey Tint, Dark
Indian Lake
Indian Red
Indigo
Italian Pink
Ivory Black
King's Yellow
Lamp Black
Light Red
Megilp
Mummy
Mauve
Magenta
Naples Yellow, No. 0, P
Naples Yellow, No. 1, L
Naples Yellow, No. 2, M
Naples Yellow, No. 3, D
Neutral Tint
New Blue
Nopal Maroon
Nopal Orange
Nopal Red
Olive Lake
Olive Green
Oxford Ochre
Payne's Grey
Permanent Blue
Permanent Yellow
Permanent White
Permanent Green, Light
Permanent Green, Medium
Permanent Green, Deep
Prussian Blue
Prussian Green
Purple Lake
Raw Sienna
Raw Umber
Roman Ochre
Sap Green
Scarlet Lake
Silver White
Sugar of Lead
Transparent Gold Ochre
Transparent Black
Terra Rosa
Terre Verte
Vandyke Brown
Venetian Red
Verdigris
Verona Brown
Veronese Green
Yellow Lake
Yellow Ochre
Zinc White
Zinc Yellow
Zinnober Green, Light
Zinnober Green, Medium
Zinnober Green, Deep

103

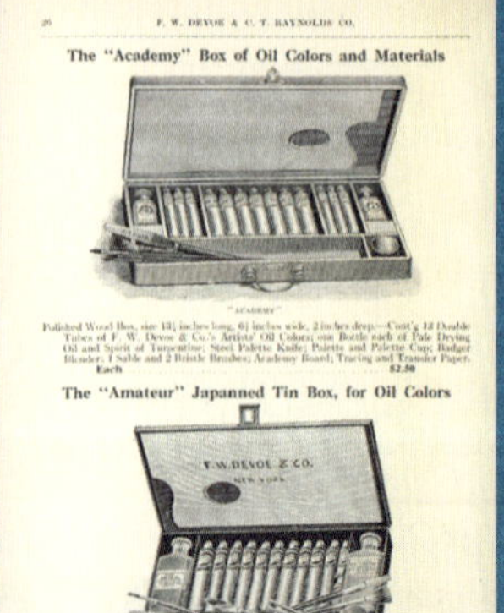

26 F. W. DEVOE & C. T. RAYNOLDS CO.

The "Academy" Box of Oil Colors and Materials

"ACADEMY"

Polished Wood Box, size 13½ inches long, 6½ inches wide, 2 inches deep.—Cont'g 12 Double Tubes of F. W. Devoe & Co.'s Artists' Oil Colors; one Bottle each of Pale Drying Oil and Spirit of Turpentine; Steel Palette Knife; Palette and Palette Cup; Badger Blender; 1 Sable and 2 Bristle Brushes; Academy Board; Tracing and Transfer Paper. Each.................................$2.50

The "Amateur" Japanned Tin Box, for Oil Colors

F. W. DEVOE & CO.
NEW YORK

104

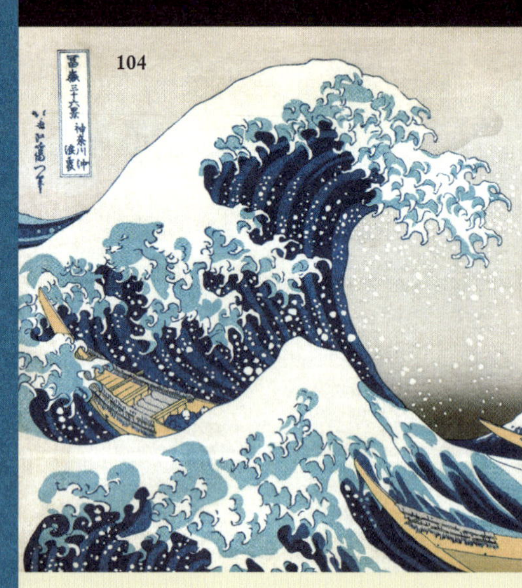

105 THE FIRST SYNTHETIC MODERN PIGMENTS

1704	*Prussian Blue*	1782	*Zinc white*
1802	*Cobalt blue*	1809	*Chrome orange*
1817	*Cadmium yellow*	1838	*Veronese green*

of commercial entertainment, together with the official emergence of the public understood not as a mere group of spectators but as an audience paying for events, works and talks.

BENJAMIN, 2010

To *look* is the principal condition of such unprecedented social practices. And this looking must be directed with a good deal of care. This is the official birthdate of visual design, which educates the public by charming them, informing them or telling a story. Display cases are designed for art and for goods; newspapers are launched and magazines illustrated; boulevards, grand arcades and small covered passageways are built to house shops, exhibitions, shows. It is no accident that glass cabinets in both museums and in shops are called 'display cases'. In the nineteenth century, everything is a display case or *vitrine*, that is to say a transparent screen with which visions of the world and of history are proposed – of the present and of the past, of ways of being, of doing and of dressing.

COCCIA, 2014

Things are no longer inanimate and inert, they become vehicles for the construction of the self, entities with which we entertain dense and significant relationships. The main audience for these representations are precisely the emerging classes, who are willing to spend in order to affirm themselves. Everything is about identity and lifestyle: the exhibition that is seen, the wine that is drunk, the book that is read, the political ideas that one cultivates. It is already, in other words, the world with which we are familiar.

VITTA, 2011

This process is epitomized in the middle of the century by the opening of the first great International Exhibition, in which new objects are put on display – today we would say design objects – from the four corners of the world: from shoes to locomotives, and from wooden chairs to cast-iron stoves. They are exhibited so that the public can discuss, take part, have an opinion. The best way of imposing new values is to talk about them. From this perspective, museums and supermarkets have one thing in common: they are walkable displays. You can move within them, going from thing to another. Observing, daydreaming, choosing. Never have browsing and strolling been such similar verbs as during these years. The great department stores, especially in Paris, become regulatory models which inspire us with things from every part of the world, reigning over clothing and also, inevitably, over colour – as when Le Bon Marché in Paris, at the end of century, puts on a sale of linen that it christens a 'festival of whites', a formula destined to succeed in linking the colour for ever with the idea of cleanness. And appropriate catalogues of everything are put together and published: of artefacts in the museums, and of products in shops. Social and economic modernity, at least in the West, consists of a short circuit between the encyclopaedia and the marketplace.

BRIGGS, 2010

It is a widespread and common idea that the public is just out there waiting for things to look at, to listen to or to read: it is a given. This theory is so ingrained that the demagogues of entertainment, in order to justify the inferior quality of their products, frequently claim to be giving us 'what the public wants'. In truth, things are rather more complex: the public does not always know what it wants, and above all the public needs to be created.

Or rather if, as happened in the nineteenth century, music is taught to a large number of individuals, and becomes a recreational activity; if to play the piano is a social distinction and singing attracts the admiration of friends and relatives – then in a couple of decades concert halls will be packed and tickets for opera performances and the symphonic season sold out. You *build* a public by enabling it to participate and by educating it so it can acquire an understanding of complex languages.

In painting too we find the invention of something that is destined to construct a new public and to cause a fundamental shift in art. In 1841 a modest American painter, John Rand, decides to commercialize already mixed oil paint packaged inside a lead tube with a closable top. Nobody had ever thought of doing this before: it was the advent of colour on tap, or at any rate in a tube. 103

This invention also marked an end to the effort of all that grinding and mixing: it was enough now to just open the tube and paint. Without this invention, according to Renoir, there would have been no Impressionism, or at least not as we know it. Slender and portable tubes of paint make it possible to paint outdoors, *en plein air*, as it has been called ever since.

Actually, this is not quite right. Several decades pri-
SCHAPIRO, 2008 or to this, Turner had gone outside to paint using small
blocks of watercolour, and the Impressionists painted more
frequently in their studios than the rhetoric of new-found
freedom would have us believe. The real transformation is
not so much for the professionals as for everyone else. The
extraordinary practicality of the new product leads to an
BORDINI, 2013 explosion in amateur painting that is a new and truly epochal phenomenon. Everyone begins to paint. Art becomes
fashionable as a pastime, especially with the daughters of
good families, where a watercolour or a small painting in
oil becomes, together with playing the piano and reading
books, a way of cultivating one's soul. The tube of paint
contributes to the construction of the public for exhibitions and museums, just as more recently the availability
of cameras has created interest in photo reportage. The
35mm Leica allowed photographers such as Robert Capa and Henri Cartier-Bresson to take their photos, but it
also made it possible for thousands of people to become

familiar with the medium – and to subsequently become the public for the photographs of Capa and Cartier-Bresson. And the same could be said for comics and graphic books whose readers often draw their favourite characters; or for the success of football, the most followed sport because it is also the one that is most widely and commonly played.

The paint tube, like all mass phenomena, brings with it a decline in the quality of materials when compared to their traditional refinement. After all, to have art as a pastime, to become a 'Sunday Painter' (as it begins be referred to at this time, somewhat patronizingly), one does not want to spend exorbitant sums on the finest lapis lazuli. Accordingly the producers of fine art materials begin to cut colours with wax and with copious amounts of oil to keep down the cost – as well as, since they are pre-mixed, to prevent them drying up they should they remain on the shop shelf for a long time. The new colours turn out to be more unstable, because wax makes them adhere less well and the excess of oil makes them yellowish sooner. This is why many masterpieces from these years have aged more quickly than paintings by Michelangelo or Titian.

MALTESE, 1991

Economy also brought about a stylistic change: anyone who has looked at a painting by Monet or Renoir will have noticed that they have consistently thicker surfaces when compared to the thinner, smoother painting surfaces of old, and if the new colours had not been inexpensive, then the artists could not have been so free with them. Impressionism is the first art movement made with materials intended for the mass market. Between these professional artists and the public there is a new, unexpected closeness. And it is perhaps for this reason that the public has never stopped loving them.

SCHAPIRO, 2008

*

FREUND, 2007

GILARDI, 2000

It would take photography to seal a definitive pact with these cultural models. It is also thanks to photography that celebrity, fashion and the military conscription of the masses are born, all practices that propose prototypes to which we are meant to adhere. The nineteenth century is avid for photographs of every kind, especially for portraits – of the faces of millions of people scattered throughout the world that are reflected in this mirror. It has been estimated that four fifths of all the photos taken in the 1900s were portraits. And it is precisely during these years that portraits of the powerful and of the famous stop functioning as symbols and come to be recognized as images of real people to be inspired by. Celebrity shapes the tastes of the public, legitimizes them, causes them to aspire to their style. The same thing happens to colour, which is no longer just something to buy but to imitate. The social importance of Perkin's mauve is all here: a colour made in a laboratory is quickly harnessed and therefore economical, so theoretically infinite quantities of it can be produced. It stops being a luxury good and becomes a consumer good instead.

Queens have always been dressed in the most splendid colours. But whereas in the Roman era wearing purple established a distance between the regal and the vulgar, when Queen Victoria dresses in mauve she proposes a certain closeness instead. She is saying to her subjects: do as I do. The ancient colour is one that, by ostentatiously drawing attention to itself, is intended to inspire awe and reverence. The modern one asks to be copied instead. The fuel of mass society is consensus: one does not reign by crushing but by befriending, at least superficially.

WARHOL, 2009

To paraphrase Andy Warhol: I drink Coke, you drink Coke, the Queen drinks Coke and nobody, not even the richest, can drink a Coke that's better than mine or yours.

VIPs do not flaunt only the unattainable, but the incredibly commonplace as well.

During Barack Obama's presidency it became news –
106 front-page news – that his wife Michelle chose to attend
107 an official function in a yellow sleeveless dress. It was not
only the brilliant colour that was news: the First Lady's
bare arms expressed a friendlier, more familiar attitude
to the public. That yellow, usually part of the chromatic
realm of free time and leisure activities, underwent a shift
in meaning to newly apply to a kind of noblesse, thanks to
this apparently casual gesture by the First Lady.

Today any colour goes, if it is seen to be the choice of
whoever has the authority to dictate taste. In this sense
colour is design, that is to say the copy of an original reproduced in a series for the masses. When we comb our
hair or dress in a certain way we are repeating something
that we have seen done by someone else, through a sugges-
109 tion given via the mass media. And the same could be said
for exercises needed to have a six-pack like the model in
an advertisement, and the plastic surgery which we apply
to our bodies to conform to a certain iconographic type.

FALCINELLI, 2014

Imitation is an industrial process translated to the level of behaviour. Only this time, by imitating a model, it is *we ourselves* who produce the copy: we are the ones serving industry, consuming an idea of ourselves. In the end, whether she is called Eugenie, Victoria or Michelle, what is a modern queen if not a prototype?

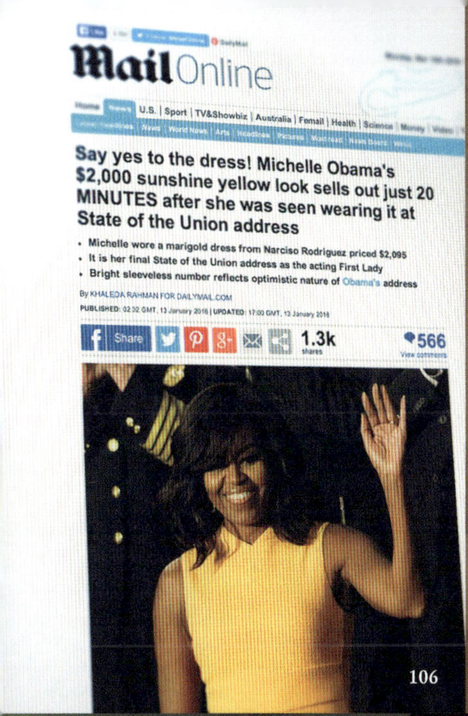

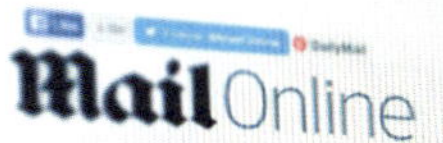

U.S. | Sport | TV&Showbiz | Australia | Femail | Health | Science | Money | Video

Say yes to the dress! Michelle Obama's $2,000 sunshine yellow look sells out just 20 MINUTES after she was seen wearing it at State of the Union address

- Michelle wore a marigold dress from Narciso Rodriguez priced $2,095
- It is her final State of the Union address as the acting First Lady
- Bright sleeveless number reflects optimistic nature of Obama's address

By KHALEDA RAHMAN FOR DAILYMAIL.COM

PUBLISHED: 02:32 GMT, 13 January 2016 | UPDATED: 17:00 GMT, 13 January 2016

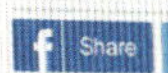

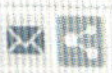

1.3k shares 566 View comments

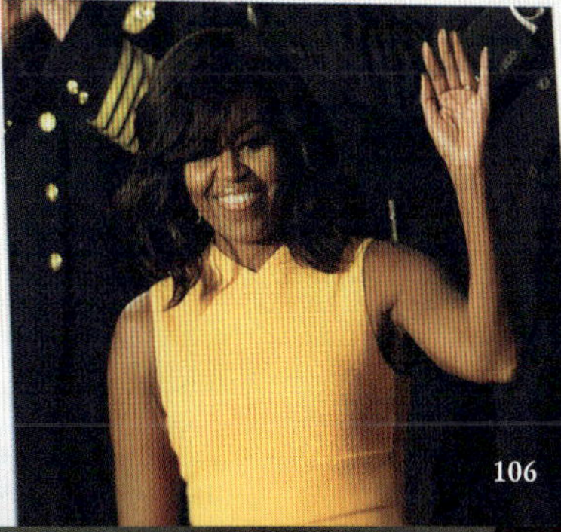

106

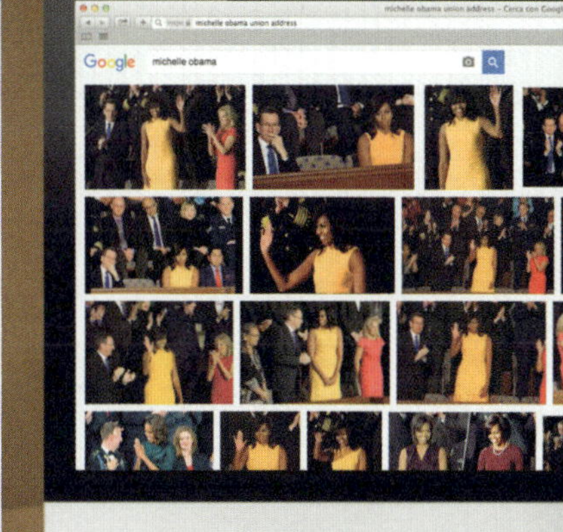

107

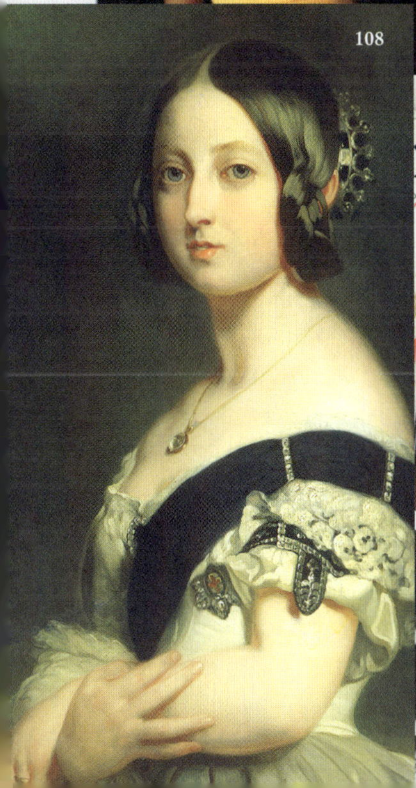

108

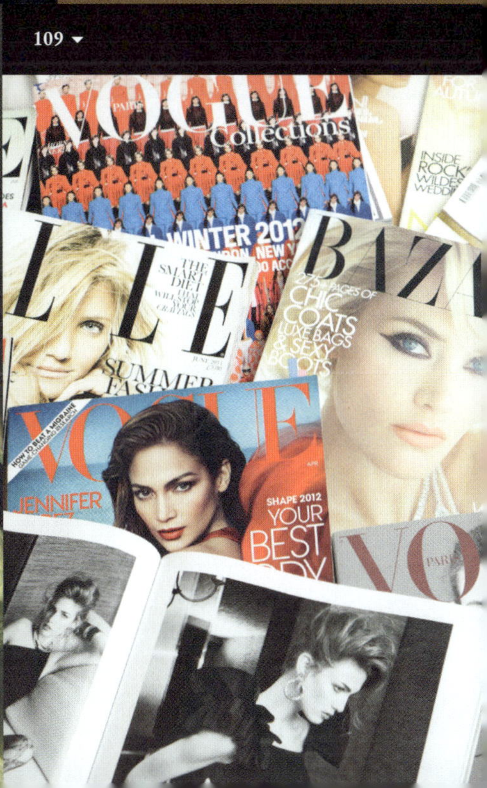

109 ▾

110

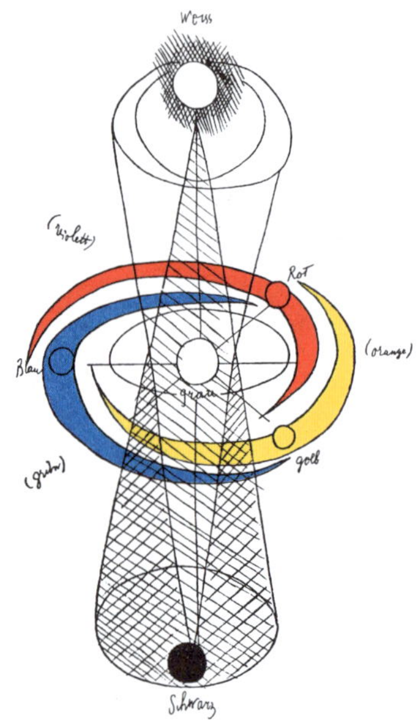

111

F. W. DEVOE & CO.'S

"THREE-COLOR"

WATER COLOR OUTFIT

— FOR — SCIENTIFIC INSTRUCTION — IN — COLOR WORK

Containing the THREE PRIMARY COLORS, YELLOW, BLUE and RED which form, when mixed in proper proportions, the SECONDARY COLORS, GREEN, ORANGE and VIOLET, and with these are formed the TERTIARY: CITRINE, OLIVE and RUSSET.

FOR THE MOST PRACTICAL SYSTEM OF COLOR INSTRUCTION

ADOPTED BY THE MOST PROMINENT INSTRUCTORS THROUGHOUT THE UNITED STATES

GREENS GREENS YELLOW BLUE ORANGES VIOLETS
A B C D E F G H I
ORANGES RED VIOLETS

MANUFACTURED BY

NEW YORK F. W. DEVOE & CO. CHICAGO

THE LARGEST AND OLDEST MANUFACTURERS OF COLORS AND BRUSHES IN THE UNITED STATES

112

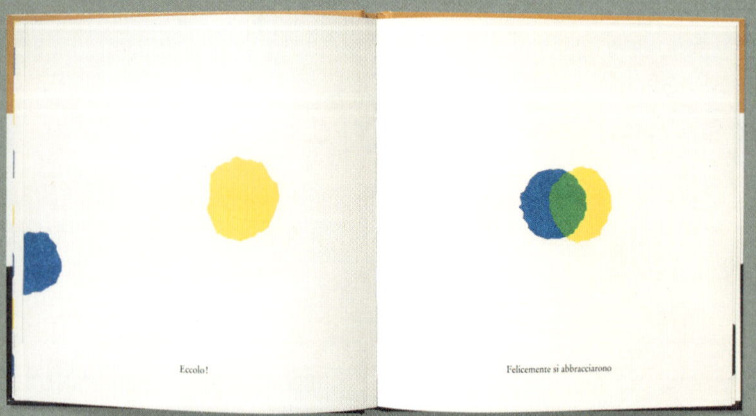

Illegal Green

The Fable of the Primaries

One day in January 1386 the dye-maker Hans Töllner of Nuremberg is arrested and embroiled in a trial which leaves him financially ruined. After being convicted and handed an enormous fine, he is temporarily exiled – and then barred altogether from practising the dyer's art. The crime is infamous, the scandal on everyone's lips. Such a drastic punishment is perhaps in keeping with the gravity of the case.

PASTOUREAU, 2013

Throughout Europe at this time, artisanal activities are governed by laws of a very precise kind. Corporations – also known as 'guilds' – oversee and regulate everything that is produced. In the field of dyeing, for instance, licences are granted determining which material may be dyed and what colour. The laws are rigid, and woe betide anyone who breaks them. Anyone licensed to dye blue cannot dye yellow, and so on.[1] It is a system that is perfect for regulating the market and keeping it under control.

Which brings us to our Hans. He has a licence to dye wool blue and black, and is in effect specializing in the 'dark'. At

[1] In pre-industrial culture the substances used for dyeing something red can be very different from those used for blue (for example, one is animal, the other vegetable), hence they involve different processes and even different professions. The *Aulularia* by Plautus testifies to the fact that in the second century BC colour merchants were divided according to the colours they sold, into *purpurarii* (red), *flammarii* (orange) and *crocearii* (yellow).

a certain point, however, perhaps as a result of a tip-off by a rival jealous of his success, a number of tubs full of yellow dye are uncovered in his workshop. He is selling yellow cloth under the counter, we might think. But no, his sin is actually much greater than this. With double dyeing, by first immersing the cloth in woad (blue) and then in luteola (weld yellow), he is illegally producing a *green* wool that was very much in fashion at the time, especially in northern Europe. The gravity of this is emphasized by the judges precisely with regard to this double process: to dye by mixing two substances in order to obtain a third colour – something that seems perfectly normal to us – is strictly forbidden.

Outside of the circles of painters and dyers, the fact that yellow combined with blue makes green is not common knowledge. It is actually a rare kind of knowledge, so much so that the first official mention of this double-dyeing process only occurs two centuries later, in a manual published in 1540. There are many ancient moral condemnations of such practices that construe the very idea of mixing substances as a kind of diabolical activity. At the origin of this taboo are those passages in the Old Testament in which men and women of different races are prohibited from joining together, and from procreating. Making fabric by combining linen with wool – combining, that is, a vegetable material with an animal one,[2] is also considered to be strictly beyond the pale. Using two dyes to produce a third falls under the same category, and is therefore to be condemned: it is both literally and metaphorically an 'impure' act.

As frequently happens, symbolic reasoning has become absurdly entangled with the everyday. In truth, at least with regard to colour, there is very little mixing in antiquity, because the results are so modest or null: the impurities

[2] Leviticus 19:19; Deuteronomy 22:11.

contained in single pigments react with each other, tending to degrade the final colour and render it greyish. Writing in the third century AD, Alexander of Aphrodisias says that even though one can make green from yellow and blue, he would not recommend doing so, since the result will hardly compare to a true green, such as that of malachite.[3]

Today, we simply take it for granted that a mixture of
DE GRANDIS, 1984 yellow and blue produces green. It is child's play – a game
for infants, in fact – among the things first learned at nur-
sery school when playing with poster paints, without needing
to really think about how colours react with each other. It
is such a familiar fact that the children's author and illustrator Leo Lionni (1910–99) is able to build his *Little Blue* 112
and Little Yellow upon it – a fable about two eponymous
characters who become green by embracing closely, making
themselves unrecognizable to their own parents. If Lionni's
fable is comprehensible even for the youngest children, it
is because modern industry has during the course of many
years stabilized pigments, making it quite predictable that
they will produce certain results when combined.

ZECCHINA, 2012 It is no wonder that children today show such astonishment during chemistry lessons, on seeing two substances react in an extravagant manner in relation to what they expected: iron chloride, for instance (which is yellow brown) mixed with ferrocyanide (which is clear yellow) produces an intense Prussian blue.

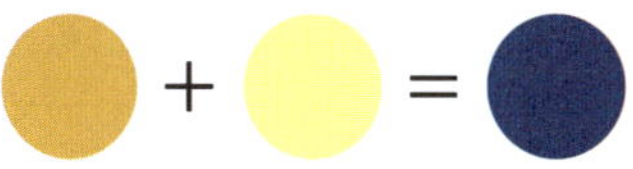

[3] For Cennino Cennini, verdigris and white lead are 'mortal enemies' because the copper in the one reacts with the sulphur in the other to produce copper sulphide – which is black rather than dark green.

This is a phenomenon that seems miraculous (a yellow plus another yellow making blue), but the real wonder is the fact that modern paints always behave in a predictable way.

Our society is so remote from the moral universe that
condemned Hans Töllner that it can even be defined as a
'mixed society', and the majority of the colours that we
have are produced by combining just a few basic ones. The
millions of computers, telephones and TVs that we use DEL MORO, 2004
every day rely upon a technology based on three primary
118 colours: those miniscule red, green and blue lights that
can be observed by looking at a screen very close up. It is
according to the intensity with which they light up that
they produce all the other colours. The result is a so-called
'optical blend', which is to say that the coloured dots are
so small that, at a distance, our eye fuses them together in-
117 to a unifying effect.[4] The same thing happens with colour
printing, which is also based on four colours combining.
And even the Pantone sample book, which seems endless
to us, is in reality built upon a mixture of just eighteen
basic colours of ink. No doubt the Old Testament would
have condemned Pantone, though it probably would have
spared the TV monitor, given that its mixture of lights is
more impalpably optical than material.

It took centuries and the contribution of factors of various kinds for mixtures to become acceptable. On the one hand, Newton's discoveries suggested that perhaps materials, like light, may be combined in a structured way; on the other, with the advent of industry the market sought different systems to produce more colours at an ever-reduced cost. In the end, however, the necessary condition is a change of mentality that occurs in the

GAGE, 2000

[4] On optical or partitive blending, see Appendix A 6.3.

fifteenth century. It might appear at first to be insignificant and unconnected to the market, to industry and to science. I am referring to a change in pictorial technique that will lead, 500 years later, to the invention of three-colour monitors. But in order to establish this link, we must take a step backwards.

Until the fifteenth century, the majority of the paints used by artists were water-based. Fresco and tempera – the medieval painting techniques par excellence – are good examples. At a certain point, however, at first in Flanders and then in Italy and throughout Europe, a technique that has been known since antiquity but always been undervalued begins to catch on: painting in oil.

Unlike water, in which colour is dissolved, oil incorporates the pigment, sealing it into its greasy state so that it can be transformed into a skin which is durable and stable when it dries.[5] Being fluid, it facilitates shading and blending, and diminishes unexpected reactions and results. One rather suggestive and credible theory is that it was precisely the success of oil paints that legitimized mixtures of colour, making them not just durable but eventually legal as well.

It was in Venice that the fashion first exploded – here more than in other parts of Italy, for atmospheric reasons: the humid climate of the lagoon makes it impossible to work with frescoes, which in these conditions tend to crack and create deposits of salt. And so oil is chosen for its stability, and gigantic canvases are affixed to walls. They are called 'panels' and can reach from floor to ceiling – like the celebrated and striking ones painted by Tintoretto. In

[5] Linseed oil, which is used most by painters, belongs to the family of so-called 'siccative' oils that do not remain liquid for long, and that on contact with air and light *polymerize*, forming a hard-wearing skin.

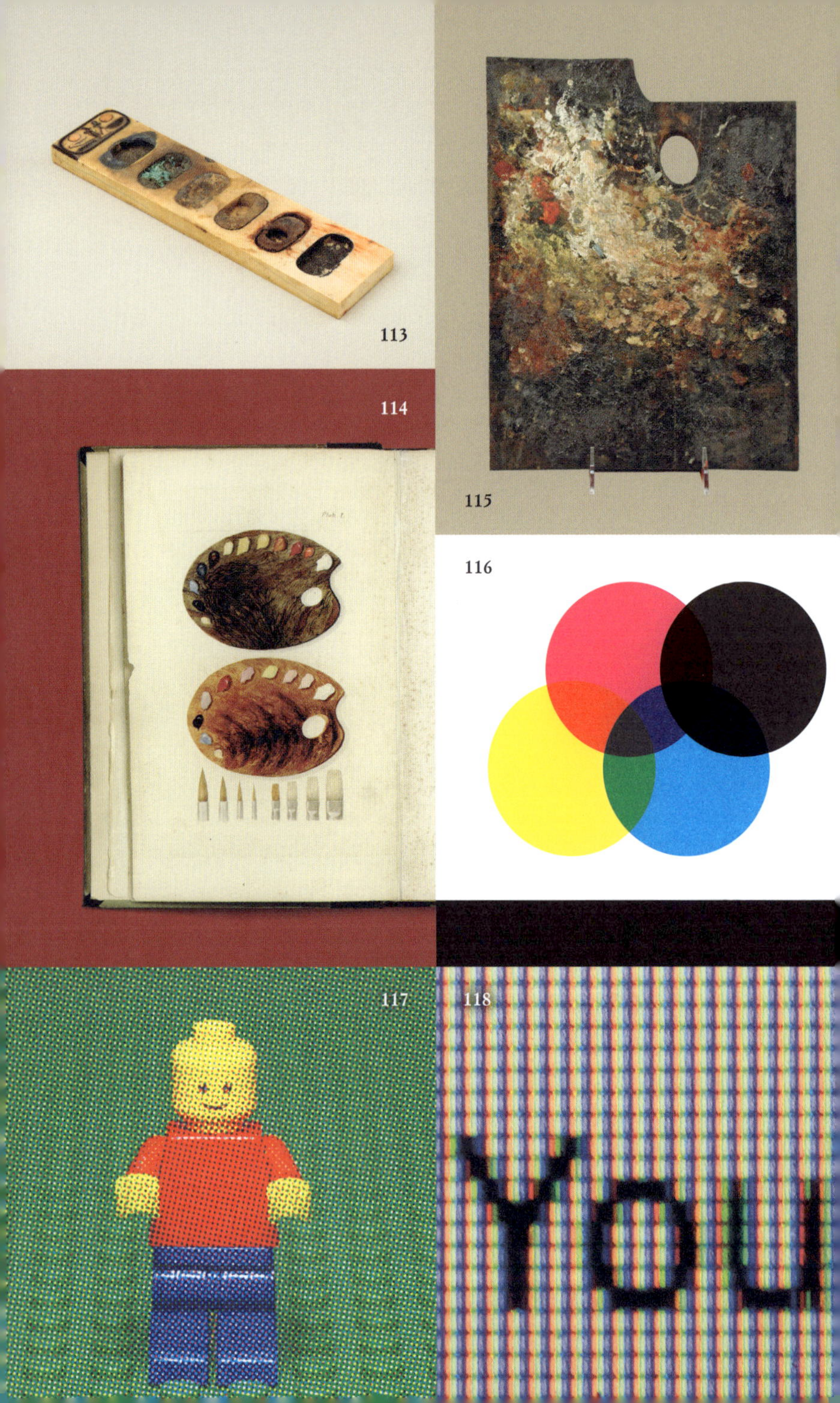
113
114
115
116
117
118
You

Venice, such work is soon facilitated by the city's flour-
ishing naval industry, which furnishes its painters with
copious amounts of strong canvas that could not be easily
sourced elsewhere in Europe. And from there, in just a few
years, precisely because of the need to mix colours, a new
object is also born: the palette, that piece of equipment 114
that has become virtually a synecdoche of the painter, but
of which there is no trace before the sixteenth century.

Of this palette, on which clumps of colour are arranged 115
in order – usually from light to dark, though every artist has
their own preference – there is no evidence in antiquity:
representations of Greek, Roman and medieval painters
always show them dipping brushes into single shells or sau-
cers placed side by side, one for each paint, thus showing 113
that colours were only mixed on the painting itself.

Today, when less painting is done than in the past, *palette* has become an abstraction, synonymous with a type and number of colours that distinguish a certain kind of work, as in software where it refers to a chromatic menu, or when we talk of Armani's or of Ikea's 'palette' to refer to the brand's signature traits. Historically, however, the role of this object is not to exhibit, enumerate or arrange colours but to facilitate mixing them together.

In the middle of the sixteenth century the revolution in colour mixing poses a question that would have made no sense before: if colours can be mixed together to make other colours, which ones should we start with? It is a question asked by artists, apothecaries, physicists, chemists and dyers. In the most varied contexts, people begin to ask what the truly necessary colours are, and how they may be classified and combined. And above all, they ask how many there should be. Should it be thirty, ten, or perhaps just three?

GAGE, 2001

Suddenly we are dealing with an unprecedented idea: that there may be certain colours that are more important than others for theoretical rather than simply economic reasons. Colours, in other words, that today we would call 'primary'.

Lists of fundamental colours already appear in the ancient world, such as those in Pseudo-Aristotle and in Pliny the Elder. However, they are concerned mostly with metaphysical colours, general principles on a par with the four elements that compose the universe.[6] It is only in the seventeenth century that the problem becomes a practical question in the modern sense. Numerous, varied names are suggested for these colours: 'simple', 'first', 'principal', 'elementary', even 'natural', a slippery term that anticipates the positivist belief that the categories of thought exist regardless of culture.[7] The scientific world becomes heatedly involved in this dilemma. The physicist and botanist Edme Mariotte (1620–84) maintains that all colours can be derived by mixing five 'principal' pigments: red, yellow, blue, white and black,[8] while Moses Harris (1730–88), an entomologist

TEOFRASTO, 1999 GUALANDI, 2014

KEMP, 1992

[6] Pliny the Elder (23–79) – the most important source in antiquity for Graeco-Roman art – maintains that there are four basic colours: black, red, white and yellow; but he is referring mostly to aesthetic principles; that is, to colours that determine style, and on which compositions agree. Pliny is a chronicler: he wants to give the state of the art, of norms and customs, and so his is a list of 'cultural' colours reputed to be at the basis of civilization. It is not by chance that despite knowing of green and blue pigments he does not list them (in Roman painting we have many examples, as in the 'Stanza di Livia' frescoes with their plants and birds in the Museo Nazionale Romano), preferring instead to record the classical Greek palette considered to be the model for art par excellence. A primary colour in the modern sense is really an operative colour that may not even be exhibited in a painting, serving only as a base for mixing. If the screen of a monitor is orange, for instance, none of the three primaries are visible in themselves.

PLINIO IL VECCHIO, 2000

[7] In the Latin text the most common expressions are *simplices* (simple) and *principales* (principal); then among the many terms used one appears that is destined to have a significant future, but that will only become dominant in the eighteenth century: 'primary'. A 'secondary' results from the mixture of two primaries, but this a now obsolete usage.

[8] Edme Mariotte speaks of this in his *De la nature des couleurs* (1681), echoed in English by Richard Waller's *A Catalogue of Simple and Mixed Colours* (1686), which once again names red, yellow and blue as 'simple' colours. Among the champions of the theory of primaries there is the revolutionary Jean-Paul Marat, who cites it enthusiastically in his *Notions élémentaires d'optique* (1784).

and engraver, devises the first colour wheel based on just 123
three colours from which it is possible to generate all of the others, a model that was destined to become a successful one for artists of the future.

This mania for cataloguing and simplifying has a twofold motivation: on the one hand, it is an extension of a spirit of critical inquiry, an indication of things to come in the scientific revolution; on the other, it is impossible not to see in it the early signs of those rationalist exigencies from which industry will soon benefit. In short, the ground has been prepared to furnish new weapons to the nascent illustration industry.

At the beginning of the eighteenth century all of these investigations find an empirical confirmation in the work of a painter who is almost forgotten today, and yet to whom our visual society owes a great deal. His name was Jacob Christofph Le Blon (1667–1741), and he is the first to use colour printing, starting from three engraved copper plates, one for each 'primitive' colour: red, yellow and
blue. The results are perhaps crude and imperfect – he 121
uses Prussian blue, for instance, which leads to the imag- 120
es being dominated by a dark, greenish tinge – but it is a monumental turning point. The way in which we print today derives from it.

LE BLON, 1725

Le Blon describes his invention in 1725, in a small booklet
entitled *Coloritto*, a term he uses to refer to skin colour. While 119
the title is bizarre, the subtitle is prophetic: The 'Harmony of Colouring in Painting: Reduced to Mechanical Practice', an expression that would no doubt have got Walter Benjamin's attention. In these pages there is a blueprint of the mechanical reproduction of images, and with their publication it becomes official that yellow plus red makes orange, red plus blue makes violet, and blue plus yellow gives green.

It is particularly relevant that the first appearance of this idea occurs not in a treatise on painting but in a printing manual: this is proof that mixing colours requires precisely such a technical and proto-industrial necessity, one that will soon become the cornerstone of a nascent mass media.[9] It is from this moment onwards that the fact of yellow and blue producing green becomes common knowledge, influencing as it does so areas as distant from art as science.

In 1801 the physicist Thomas Young (1773–1829), one of the most brilliant minds of his generation, asks himself whether it is possible that human vision itself works through blending. Or rather, since it seems improbable that at the back of the eye infinite particles vibrate together with all possible colours, Young suspects that these are limited in number, perhaps to just three, like the basic colours for painters: red, yellow and blue.

GAGE, 2001

This is only a supposition, like an idea thrown up by chance at a conference, though it is one that will be confirmed a century and a half later with the discovery of three types of receptors at the back of the eye, each one sensitive to a part of the spectrum. And it is striking in the wider context of the story we are telling that Young should have effectively laid the foundations of a biological discovery with a suggestion for a printing technique.

At this point, on the wave created by Le Blon's invention and with the official endorsement of science, enthusiasm

[9] Le Blon, inspired by Newton, understands that material colours, that is to say pigments, behave in a different way from light (which he calls impalpable colour), and tries to find a law that governs them. Newton is a powerful influence at this time, but that influence is also turning out to be something of a boomerang: on the one hand, it suggests that colour blending follows scientific rules, on the other hand, this is misleading, because pigments and other colourings are subject to many variables, including the limits of matter. In theory, the sum of the three primaries should be black, but in practice at most we obtain from it a dark grey. Le Blon only digests this fact with difficulty, convinced that the perfecting of the technique and the purification of inks will sooner or later lead to the elimination of any need for a fourth colour plate. But this did not happen: today all printing, including that done by home printers, works by adding black – and is therefore known as the four-colour process.

119

COLORITTO;

OR THE

Harmony of Colouring

IN

PAINTING:

Reduced to

MECHANICAL PRACTICE,

UNDER

Eaſy Precepts, and *Infallible Rules*;

Together with ſome

COLOUR'D FIGURES,

In order to render the ſaid PRECEPTS and RULES intelligible, not only to PAINTERS, but even to *all Lovers of* PAINTING.

By *J. C.* le BLON.

6

I.

Of *Preliminaries*.

COLORITTO, or the *Harmony* of Colouring, is the *Art* of *Mixing* COLOURS, in order to repreſent naturally, in all Degrees of *painted* Light and Shade, the ſame FLESH, or the Colour of any other Object, that is repreſented in the true or *pure* Light.

PAINTING can repreſent all *viſible* Objects with three Colours, *Yellow*, *Red*, and *Blue*; for all other Colours can be compos'd of theſe *Three*, which I call *Primitive*; for Example,

Yellow and *Red* } make an *Orange Colour*.

Red and *Blue* } make a *Purple* and *Violet Colour*.

Blue and *Yellow* } make a *Green Colour*.

And a *Mixture* of thoſe *Three* Original Colours makes a *Black*, and all *other* Colours whatſoever; as I have demonſtrated by my Invention of *Printing* Pictures *and* Figures *with their* natural *Colours*.

I am only ſpeaking of *Material* Colours, or thoſe uſed by *Painters*; for a *Mixture* of *all* the primitive *impalpable* Colours, that cannot be felt, will not produce *Black*, but the very Contrary, *White*; as the Great Sir ISAAC NEWTON has demonſtrated in his Opticks.

White, is a Concentering, or an *Exceſs* of Lights.
Black, is a deep Hiding, or *Privation* of Lights.

But

…d and *Blue* } make a *Purp*…

Blue and *Yellow* } make a *Green*

Mixture of thoſe *Three* C…
…r Colours whatſoever; …
…inting Pictures *and* …
…king of *M*…

120

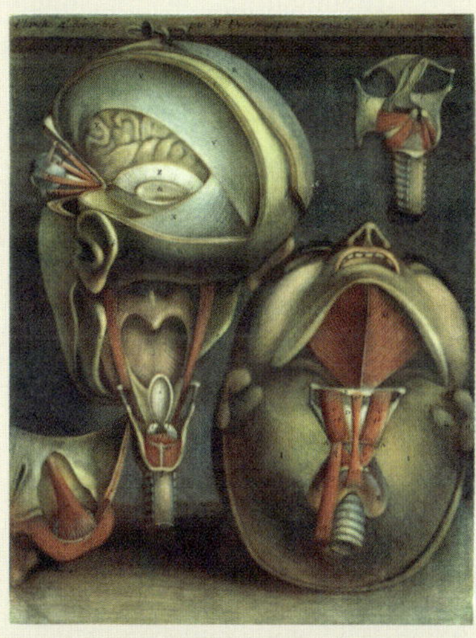

121

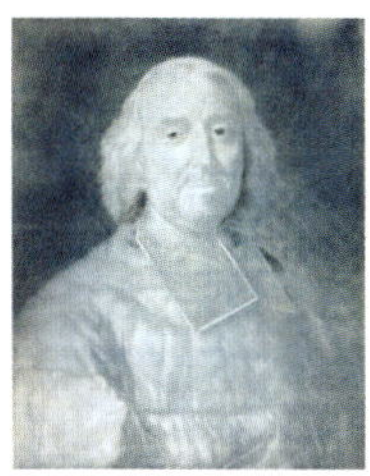

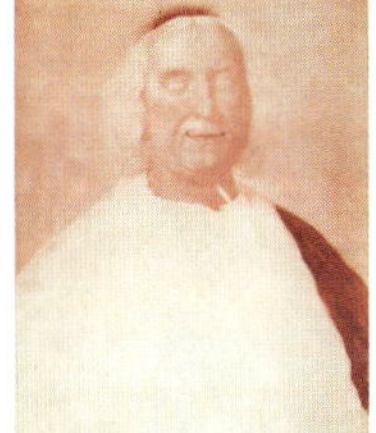

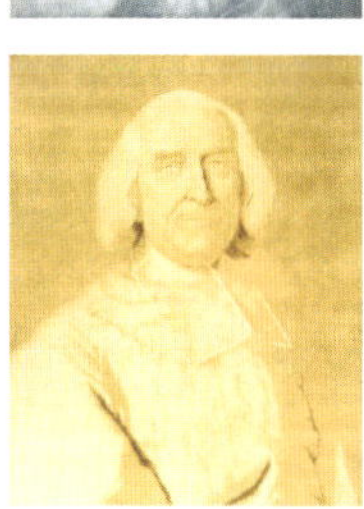

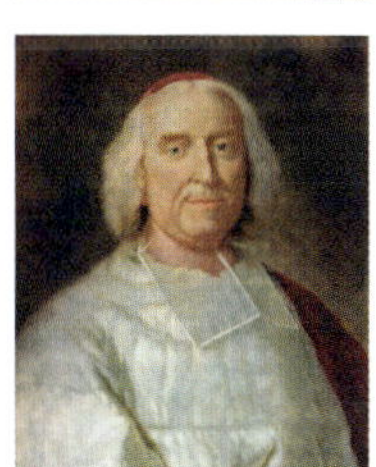

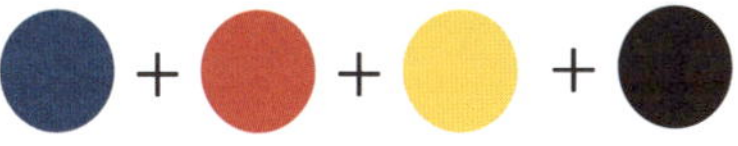

THE FIRST SIX BOOKS OF

THE ELEMENTS OF EUCLID

IN WHICH COLOURED DIAGRAMS AND SYMBOLS
ARE USED INSTEAD OF LETTERS FOR THE
GREATER EASE OF LEARNERS

BY OLIVER BYRNE

SURVEYOR OF HER MAJESTY'S SETTLEMENTS IN THE FALKLAND ISLANDS
AND AUTHOR OF NUMEROUS MATHEMATICAL WORKS

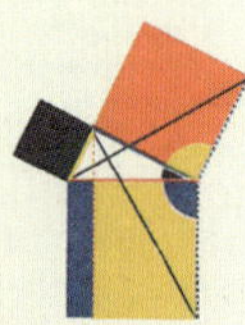

LONDON
WILLIAM PICKERING
1847

4 *BOOK I. PROP. IV. THEOR.*

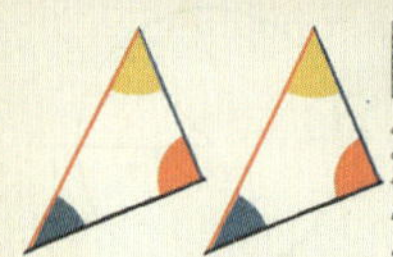

If two triangles have two sides of the one respectively equal to two sides of the other, (to and to) and the angles (and) contained by those equal sides also equal; then their bases or their sides (and) are also equal: and the remaining and their remaining angles opposite to equal sides are respectively equal (= and =): and the triangles are equal in every respect.

Let the two triangles be conceived, to be so placed, that the vertex of the one of the equal angles, or ; shall fall upon that of the other, and to coincide with , then will coincide with if applied: consequently will coincide with , or two straight lines will enclose a space, which is impossible (ax. 10), therefore = , = and = , and as the triangles and coincide, when applied, they are equal in every respect.

Q. E. D.

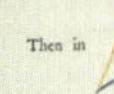

122

123

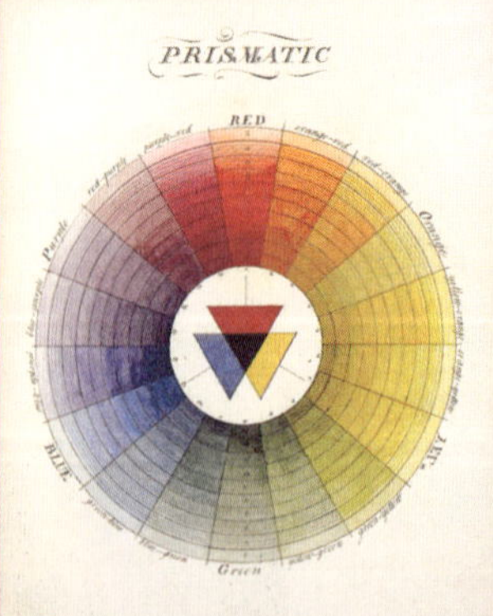

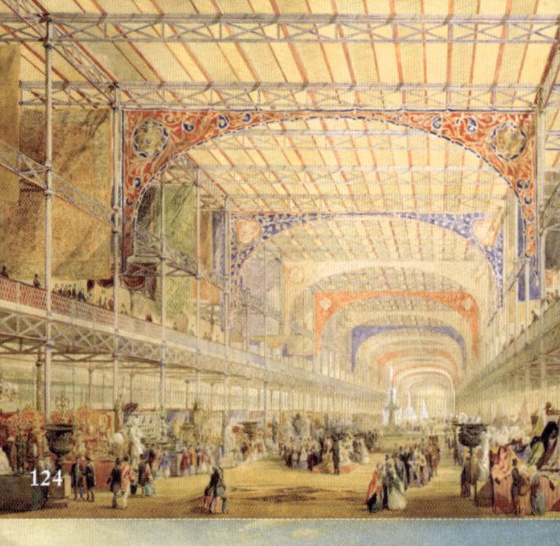

124

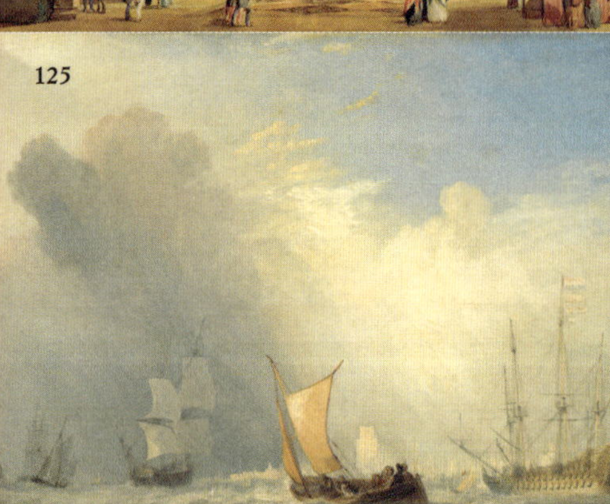

125

for the three primaries knows no bounds. By the mid-
eighteenth century, yellow, red and blue have the status
of law, and tri-chromatism has become an incredibly fashionable concept. When Owen Jones (1809–74), an architect
who is among the most influential design theorists of the
nineteenth century, is called upon to arrange the decor-
ation of the Crystal Palace, the purpose-built venue of the
Great Universal Exhibition of London in 1851, he chooses yellow, red and blue as cardinal colours for the entire 124
design. When Oliver Byrne (1810–80) illustrates Euclid's
Elements in 1847, he uses the trio of colours to make its ax- 122
ioms and reasoning clearer. It is revealing that this should
happen precisely with Euclid, the father of fundamental
theorems of plane geometry, as if positing an equivalence
between the basis of mathematics and that of perception
itself. In the text, in fact, colours were not used to make
blends, but in order to stand out single, pure and solid – as
if they were the fundamental building blocks of reasoning.

While continuing to use numerous pigments, artists
are enthusiastic in theory at least about the fable of pri-
DI NAPOLI, 2006
maries. Turner is seduced by its cosmological aspect, and
maintains poetically that yellow is light, matter is red and
blue distance. But this is only true in his own paintings,
where the air is suffused with unfurling yellow light and 125
material things have the consistency of red ochre. If we
go to see his palette at Tate Britain in London, we notice that the colours from which he started were hardly
just three. And yet, however much it is contradicted in
practice, the concept of the primaries gathers ever more
momentum.

KEPES, 1995
Today all the didactic models with which the theory
of colour is codified and taught are based upon this concept, almost as if nobody has the courage of calling it into

question. But everyone knows that you get nowhere with
111 only three tubes of colour, and shops selling artists' materials obviously offer dozens of variations. This shows how great the gulf is between theory and practice, and why there is such suspicion of theorists.

This idea became popular in academic circles thanks
129 to Piet Mondrian, Theo van Doesburg and other artists associated with the review *De Stijl*, who were also close to the Bauhaus, the most influential school of design of the twentieth century. In Mondrian's famous grids there is yellow, red and blue – but no green, a colour deemed to be secondary and therefore inessential. GAGE, 2006
We are dealing here with an ideological position, devoid of any residual scientific or social input: green is statistically a well-loved and -used colour, the most widespread on the planet and the one that we see in the greatest number of shades. But Mondrian is interested in something else. The mission of the new art is to eliminate the tragic, he writes in the pages of *De Stijl*, restoring an aesthetic in which the search for primordial values is central.[10] The ambition of reducing everything to orthogonal lines, and the obsession with primary colours, reveal a radical simplism that is very attractive to subsequent teaching. MONDRIAN, 1975
Mondrian speaks of colour in terms of good and bad, of what is right and wrong, and like many moralists gets credit and approval for doing so. He is not alone.

[10] A determining influence upon this entire generation of artists comes from the chemist Wilhelm Ostwald, a Nobel Prize winner in 1909 and a brilliant scientist, but one with overbearing ideas that led him to grotesque extremes such as criticizing Titian for having painted the Madonna's mantle two tones too light. Ostwald provides the 'scientific' evidence to support such views. OSTWALD, 1969
Generally disliked (especially by Itten and by Klee, who found him insufferably reductive), he is nevertheless among the few to oppose the dogma of the three primaries, basing his ideas on those of Goethe and of Hering (see p.194 and Appendix A 3.0) in order to devise a 'physiological' colour wheel with more room for greens. Ostwald is also the first to speak of colour by using cut coloured card, the idea behind the theoretical turning point with which Josef Albers overcomes the limitations of the Bauhaus (see p. 202).

126

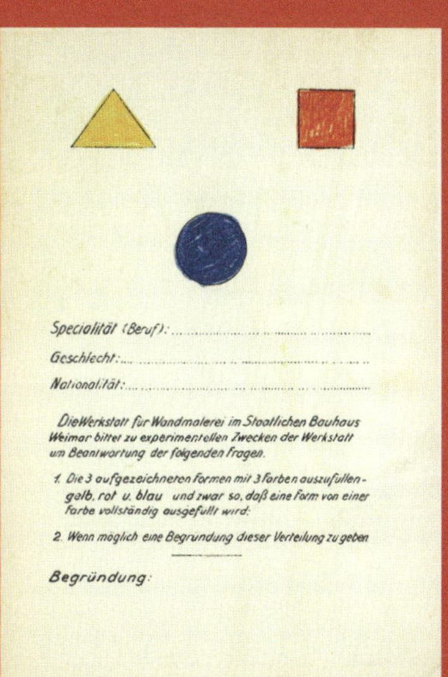

Specialität (Beruf): ....

Geschlecht: ....

Nationalität: ....

Die Werkstatt für Wandmalerei im Staatlichen Bauhaus Weimar bittet zu experimentellen Zwecken der Werkstatt um Beantwortung der folgenden Fragen.

1. Die 3 aufgezeichneten Formen mit 3 Farben auszufüllen – gelb, rot u. blau und zwar so, daß eine Form von einer Farbe vollständig ausgefüllt wird:

2. Wenn möglich eine Begründung dieser Verteilung zu geben

Begründung:

127

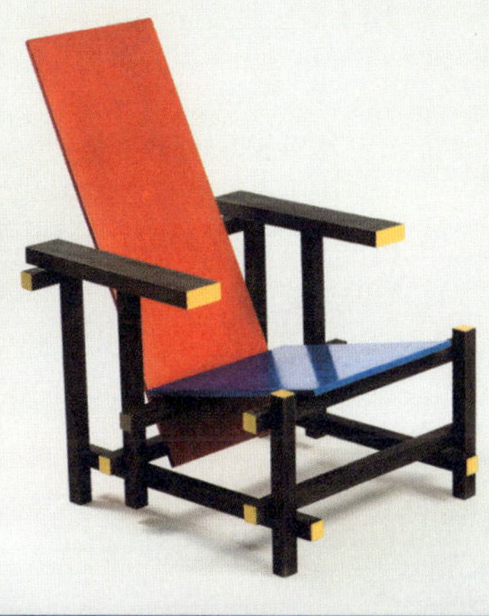

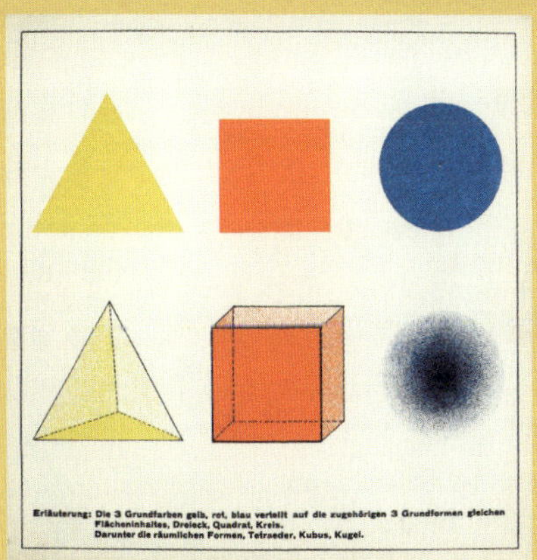

Erläuterung: Die 3 Grundfarben gelb, rot, blau verteilt auf die zugehörigen 3 Grundformen gleichen Flächeninhaltes, Dreieck, Quadrat, Kreis.
Darunter die räumlichen Formen, Tetraeder, Kubus, Kugel.

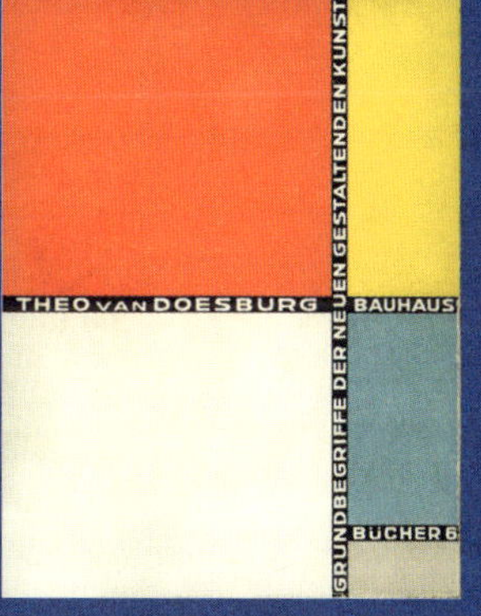

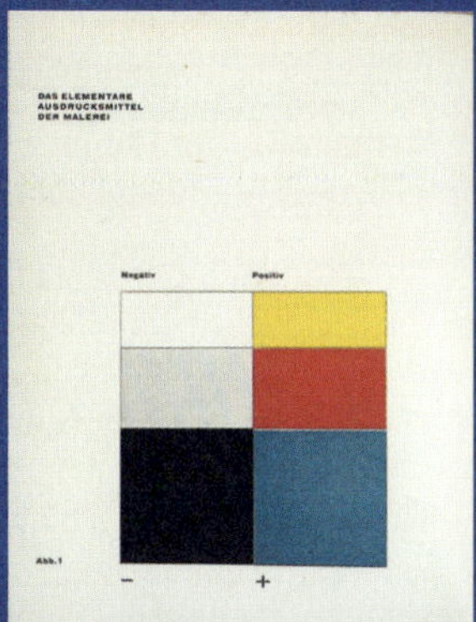

128

129

127 Gerrit Rietveld (1888–1964) designs a chair – now iconic
in the history of design – that is a manifesto of the grammar of primaries. Paul Klee (1879–1940) places the trio at
110 the centre of a dynamic structure that he calls, with abso-
126 lute emphasis, the 'canon of totality'. Wassily Kandinsky KLEE, 2002
puts together a questionnaire in which he asks for an association between the three colours and the three basic
128 shapes – square, circle, triangle – as if no other shapes or
perceptions existed;[11] and Johannes Itten, who taught the KANDINSKIJ, 1989
preparatory course at the Bauhaus, elevates the trio to an
object of veneration, as if it were an ontological if not to
say metaphysical matter.

[11] From the questionnaire issued in 1923, as was to be expected, Kandinsky received the most varied answers but he continued to maintain that the triangle is by nature yellow, the circle blue and the square red. These are synaesthetic associations, and as such quite arbitrary. But what is the point of knowing that the circle is intrinsically blue? During the academic year 2015–16, on my course on the psychology of perception at Isia Roma Design, the test was carried out again by the student Enrica Tartaglione (b. 1995), with 300 people between the ages of twenty and sixty of diverse social and educational backgrounds. Once again, the answers were extremely varied, with a prevalence of 22 per cent for red square, blue circle and green triangle. The diagram below represents a reconstruction of the dynamic between the primaries as suggested by Kandinsky in his key text *The Spiritual in Art*.

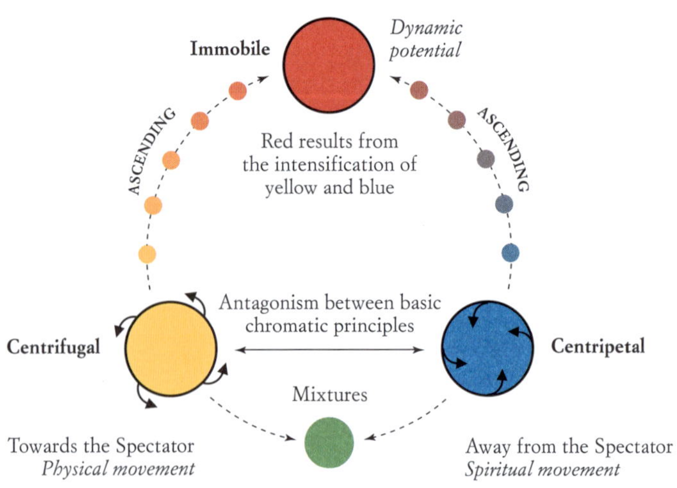

KANDINSKIJ, 2005 MANCHIA, 2004

LUPTON, 1991 It is no exaggeration to speak in this regard of a cult, and one that is much less lucid and enlightened than they are often thought to be. All of the artists involved are in fact acquainted with mystical and irrational influences: from the salon of Alma Mahler (the wife of Walter Gropius, the founder of the Bauhaus) to Theosophy and esoteric thinking – from clairvoyance to numerology – such ideas are all greeted with curiosity. The primary colours are basically shrouded in what we would now think of as a kind of New Age vibe.

The culture of the Bauhaus is usually presented in terms of
WINGLER, 1972 its modern and rational merits, but these esoteric offshoots of Romanticism are equally important and suggestive: above all the utopian attempt to grasp the essence of life and of art by uncovering their foundations. What we are dealing with here is effectively a stubborn obsession.

In fact 'primaries' do not exist. A primary colour is such only because it comes to be used to blend and make secondary colours. Nothing more. Therefore there are many primaries, as many as are needed by every precise industrial system to reduce expenditure. There are no primaries
as such, they are not natural values, merely conventions 131
of a technological and cultural kind.

The illustration in Figure 131, for example, designed by the great J. C. Leyendecker (1874–1951) as an advertisement for Arrow collars and shirts, was printed using only two inks in order to economize. In this case the primaries are black and orange, and from these two colours a dozen shades are produced, including browns and even some bluish greys visible by simultaneous contrast. Any combination of at least two inks allows the production of images in colour, the use of three being only an excellent idea to enhance this possibility. But not even a trio makes it possible to print everything visible. And the same goes for computer and television screens.

The fact that there are three types of receptors on our retinas has nonetheless caused the popular idea to spread BOSCAROL, 2005 that the tri-chromaticism of monitors, known as the RGB system, has the most affinity with the way the human eye works. But this too is a misunderstanding. Tri-chromaticism is not a law, and if we could construct screens with five colours the visible spectrum would be even wider than we are used to, and closer to what we are aware of.[12] The reason why there are still no new technologies of this kind is that few would know how to appreciate any improvement: for the most part monitors are used for accounting, to chat, for gaming or for watching sport and reality TV shows. These are all activities for which the current system is perfectly adequate. So even the age of tri-colour electronics is only a stage in the history of technology. It does not embody any fundamental truth about perception.

Besides, printing has already gone some way beyond the
130 tri-colour process. It is no accident that the exaltation of
the Bauhaus receives a significant blow in 1935 when cop-
116 per phthalocyanine is synthesized, and cyan ink appears
for the first time, providing a very wide spectrum of colour GERRITSEN, 1983
never seen before in blending. From this moment on, red
stops being used in industry and is replaced by magenta,
a sort of deep pink that would have made the members of
the De Stijl movement shudder.[13] In the end, Mondrian
and his peers played with fire, having mistaken a technical
necessity for a natural reality, and the production system
has not forgiven them. Just as it did not forgive poor Hans
Töllner, five centuries earlier.

[12] On the mistake of treating the retina like an RGB system, see Appendix A 2.3.

[13] The same Kandinsky of the lithography for the *Kleine Welten* series that we have seen on p. 35, makes a full red by layering pink upon yellow – and does not begin with a vermilion red as theorized in his writings.

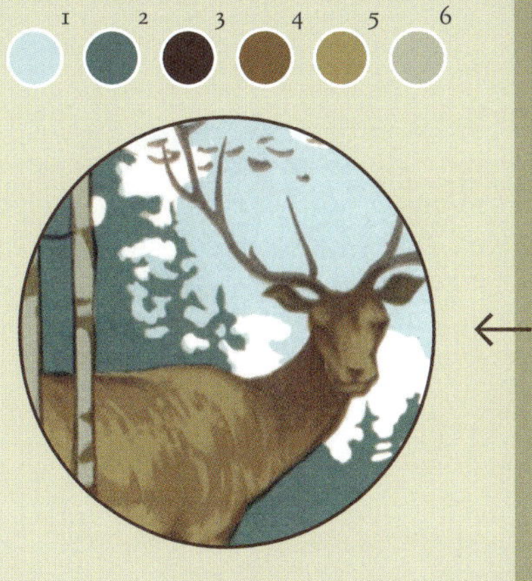

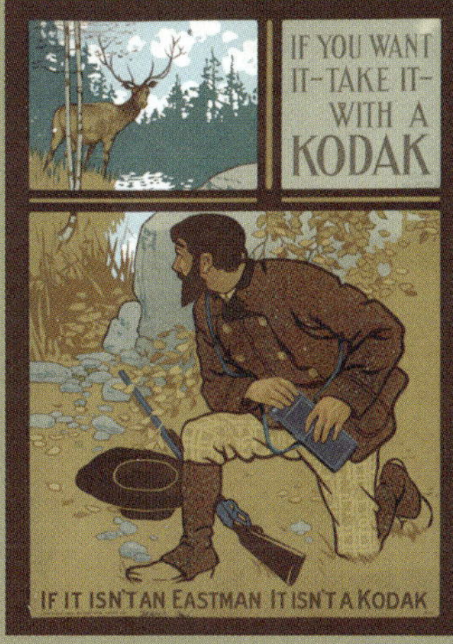

SIX-COLOUR PRINT **130**

TWO-COLOUR PRINT **131**

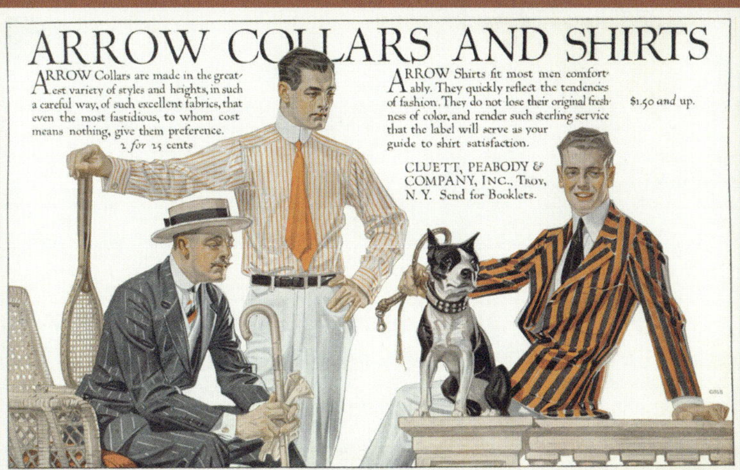

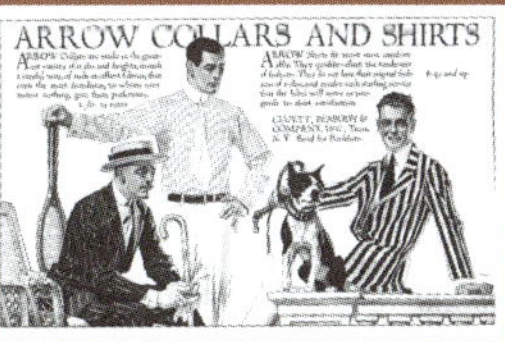

BLACK PLATE

ORANGE PLATE

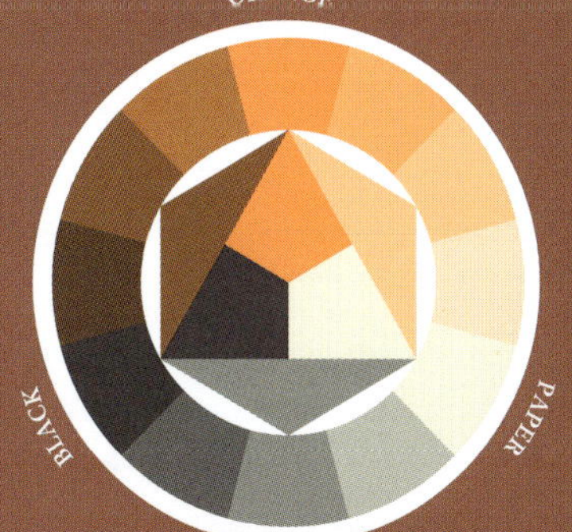

◂ 132

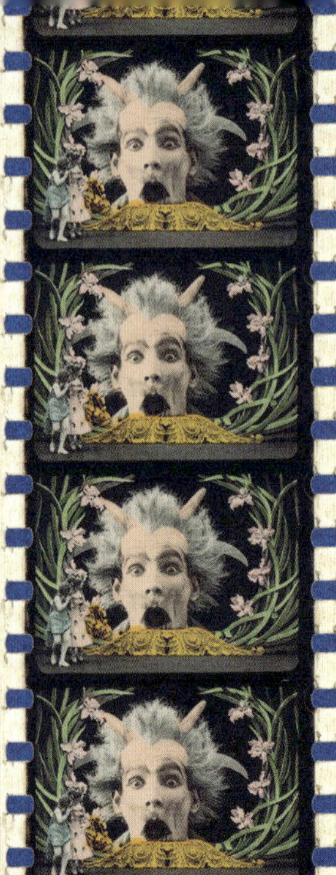

▾ 133

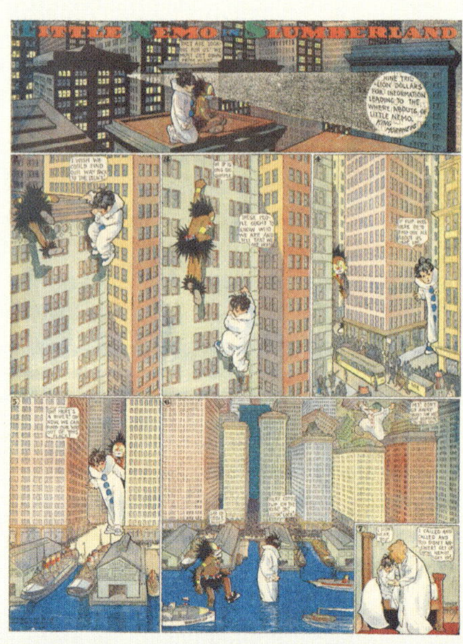

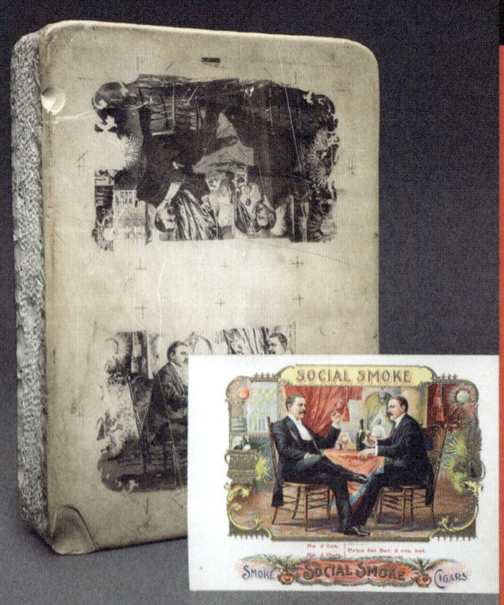

134

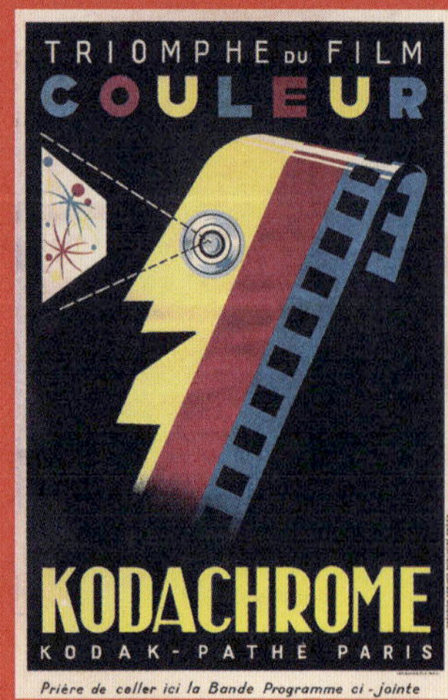

135

Lithographic Cyan

A Brief History of Chromatic Technologies

Destiny can take many forms. It can even take the shape of a piece of limestone. As it did for Alois Senefelder.

It is 1796 and we are in Offenbach in Bavaria. Having been orphaned, our protagonist is earning a living by engraving sheet music on copper plates, in order to support himself and his younger brothers. But the work is meagre and does not bring in enough to feed all those hungry mouths. Driven to despair by poverty, Alois decides to end it all by throwing himself into the waters of the Isar. When he reaches the bank of the river, however, something stops him from carrying out his desperate plan: he notices a piece of limestone that looks different from any he has seen before. It occurs to him that it might be perfect for polishing his musical plates, and he decides not to kill himself after all but to go home. Some might say that his intention to commit suicide cannot have been very serious if a piece of stone was enough to make him change his mind. Maybe so. Or maybe he was waiting precisely for a sign such as this that would save him from death. He can hardly have had any idea at the time that this particular object would transform his life – and society – for ever.

When he gets home he makes a discovery. When it is dry, the stone absorbs any liquid, but if it is soaked first it becomes resistant to greasy substances, since water and

oil do not mix. To anyone else this would have seemed nothing more than an interesting curiosity, but thanks to his expertise in printing, Senefelder has a dizzying idea. He takes the limestone and polishes it, then draws on it with a greasy pencil and finally douses it with water. The stone, as he predicted, is soon completely soaked except for the traces of the drawing that remain greasy, which is to say dry. At this point he dabs the surface with printing ink, and because it is oily it is not prone to adhering to the damp stone but does adhere instead to the marks made by the drawing, to such an extent that by pressing a sheet of paper on it a perfect copy can be obtained. The stone has effectively become a printing press, even though
134 it is not in relief.

Almost all the printed material that we deal with every day – from bus tickets to the packaging of frozen food,
133 from comic books to the instruction leaflets that come
with medicines– is printed as a result of this crucial idea. Even the pages of this book come from a slab that reproduces, in ultra-technological form, that first intuition of Senefelder's. The modern system, called offset, replaces the stone with an aluminium plate onto which the image is transferred by computer. Apart from this, the procedure is the same: the aluminium is washed with water, and it retains the ink only in the lines marked on it, just like the limestone found on a bank of the River Isar.[1]

The story I have just told – readers will not like this – is not true. It is invented. Senefelder never sought to commit suicide, nor was the discovery of limestone the chance

[1] Unlike traditional printing – in which the text is composed with movable type and images with plates, both in relief – the new invention allows us to have one slab for both text and image. At the beginning of the twentieth century, the incision was done by photomechanical means, and is done today by computers.

result of destiny. But this is how people loved to tell it at the beginning of the nineteenth century, or rather this is one of the many versions that circulated at the time. In reality, Alois – who was also a dramatist – had been working for some time on a method that would allow him to print his works without depending on and incurring the cost of an official publisher, and the idea came to him after multiple attempts with Solnhofen limestone (of which Bavaria is full), which had already been used for some time for printing in relief.

Still, this hardly detracts from his achievement: he was actually the first to use the enmity between water and ink in order to print from a flat plate. He is the inventor of lithography (the term means precisely 'stone writing'), which when later combined with Le Blon's tri-colour ideas will facilitate the development of colour printing, which will prove such a turning point for artists, as well as the publishing, packaging and advertising industries. Thanks to this new process, thousands of copies can be produced, crowning years of research into colour reproduction.

It is perhaps not surprising that Senefelder's biography provided an occasion for an elaboration of the truth. His invention is so revolutionary that the collective imagination of the era, as often happens, prefers to tell its story as a poignant fable of genius struck by inspiration rather than the more prosaic one of stubbornness, study and work. If Werther commits suicide for love, the young Alois renounces suicide for his art and the visual society to come. The Romantic and industrialized nineteenth century could hardly have found a better hero.

BRIGGS, 2010

By the time Senefelder launched his invention, the colour printing of images already had four centuries of

experimentation behind it. Ever since the days of late-medieval woodblock books, there had been a variety of methods: from hand-colouring individual copies in an assembly line to filling in areas with the help of stencils. Theoretically the idea is quite clear from the start: you need to make as many plates as there are colours necessary. But it is difficult to make the different proofs of the print fit together. There are times when precision in serial reproduction is still chimerical. In Figures 136 and 137 we can see two copies of *Fasciculus medicinae*, by Johannes de Ketham. Published in Venice in 1494, one is printed
136 in monochrome, the other has had colour added to it with
137 four distinct impressions that are not properly aligned and reveal perhaps inevitable smudging.

To find results that are of modern quality, we must wait until the start of the sixteenth century when Ugo da Carpi (1480–1532) manages to superimpose different impressions with admirable accuracy. In 1516, he obtains from the Venetian senate an exclusive patent for what is reputed to be the first colour printing to use superimposed impressions. The patent is significant, showing how closely the birth of technical reproducibility is bound up with the history of copyright and of industry: ideas are no longer just part of our cultural patrimony, they are the property MASSARI, 2008
138 of an individual.[2] In *Diogenes*, printed in 1527, we can see how Da Carpi used four colours in order to construct the image, including a mid-brown for the base, a dark tone for the shadows and an opaque white for the highlights. It is a 'polychrome' used to make a monochrome. The idea of two colours being superimposed to produce a third has

[2] Da Carpi's method is long and laborious, hence for practical reasons until the nineteenth century it was often preferable to hand colour monochrome prints using stencils or templates: a method, known as *pochoir* colouring, that survived until the First World War, becoming increasingly refined.

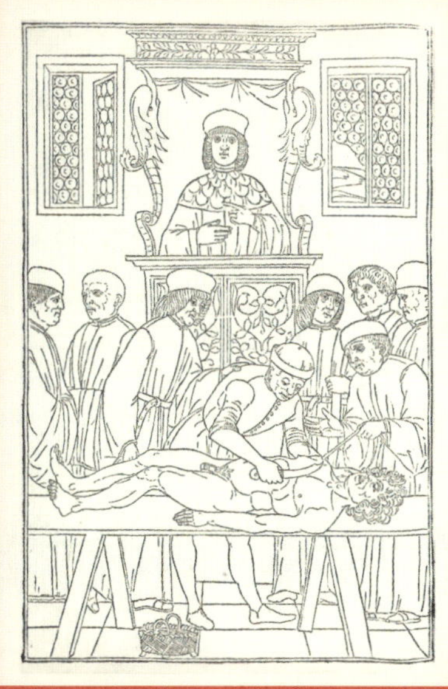

136

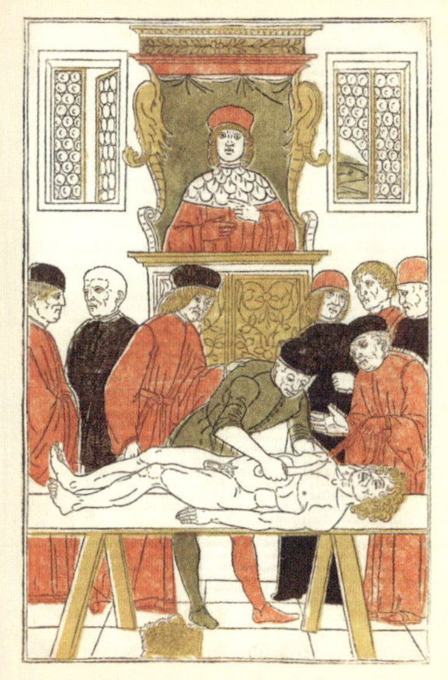

137

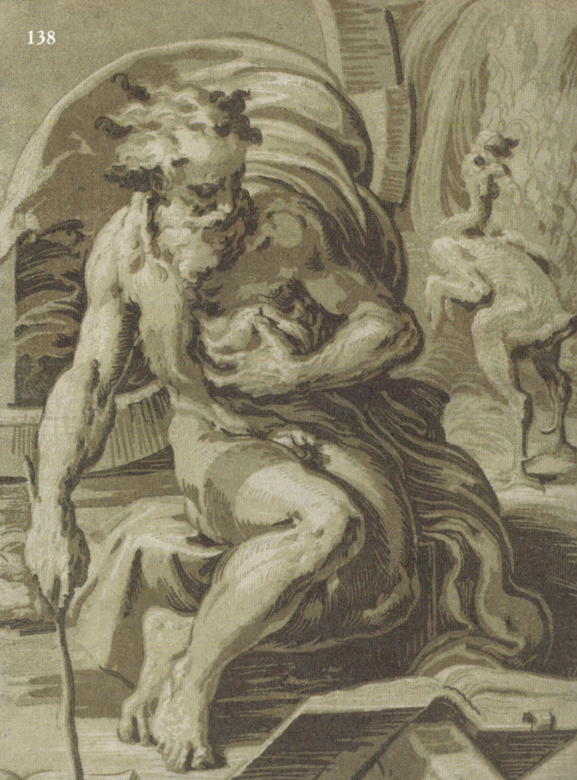

138

139

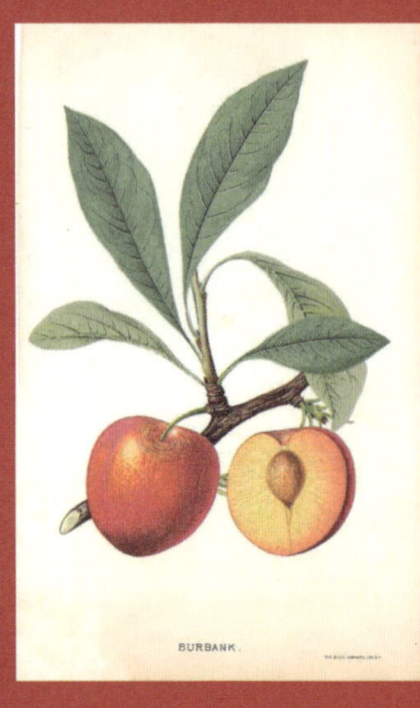

140

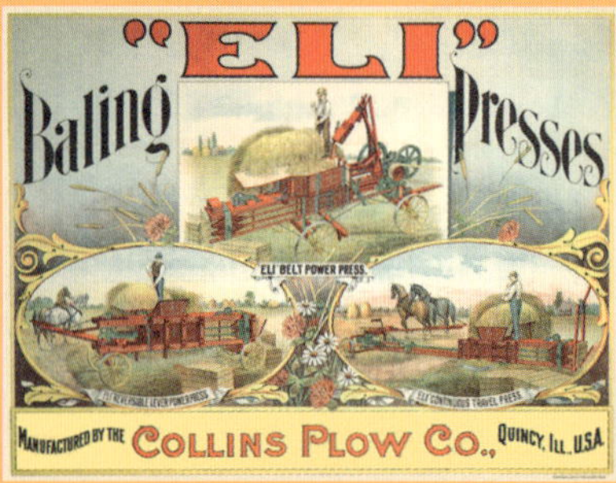

141

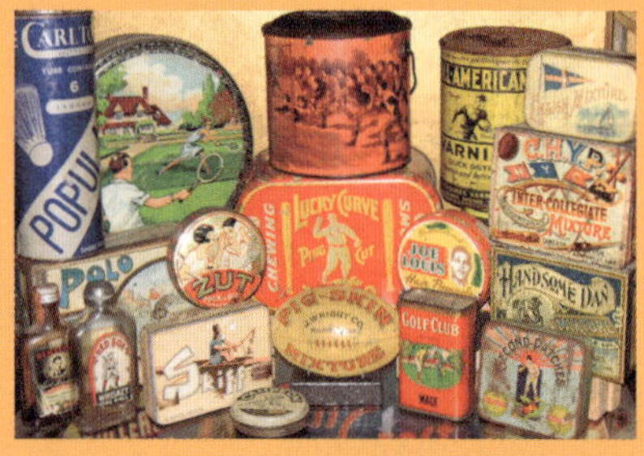

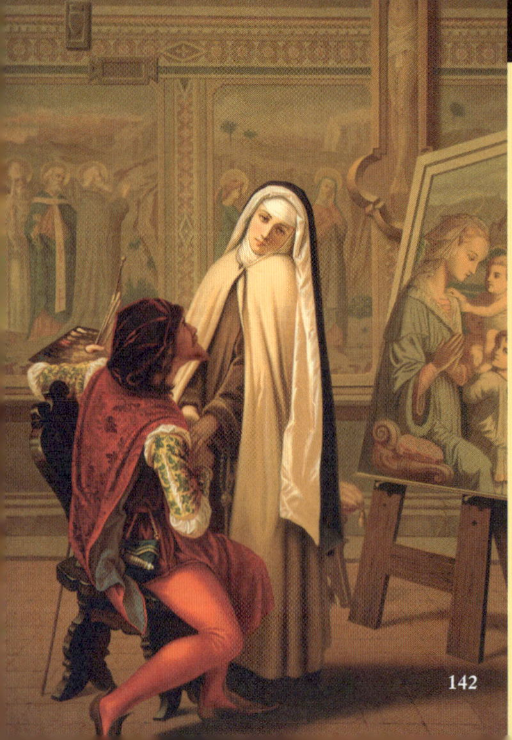

142

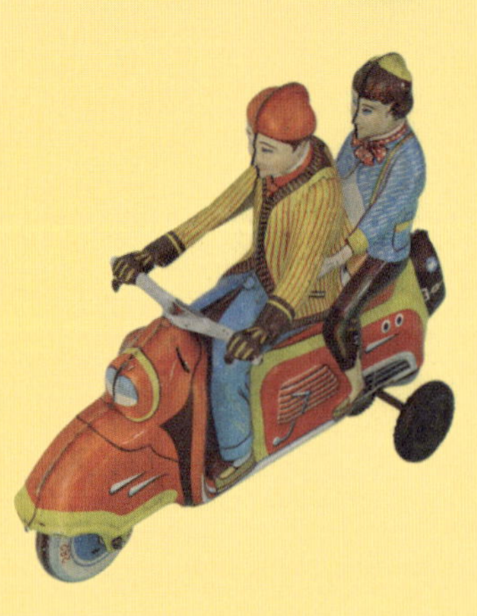

143

not yet appeared, and the benefits of blending are yet to
be understood.

Things continue along these lines until Le Blon's and
JOBLING, 1996
Senefelder's ideas emerge. Once they are combined, they
reach a crowning glory in 1837 with the birth of chromolithography, making it possible to colour-print on the most
diverse materials, even on metal. 143

Victorian packaging is a veritable riot of colour-printed 141
tins – so much so that even today biscuits and conserves use
this method to signify quality and tradition. But it is also
the triumph of a plethora of printed materials produced to
an extremely high quality as well as in large volume, from 139
holy pictures to postcards and illustrated books. Chromo- 142
lithography is the true forerunner of modern offset printing,
and it is the best that the world of commerce could have
wished for. 140

On the creative front, there are many who benefit from this new invention – all of those artists who begin to think again about the virtues and limitations of industrial art, discovering that technology can be tamed and utilized with often surprising outcomes. Fine art lithography soon reveals a reproducible picture-making system enhanced by
MASSARI, 2008
copies that allows drawing with pen and pencil directly onto stone – unlike with the old methods of engraving, etching and aquatint – thus enabling a greater variety of expressive modulation. The copies retain the spontaneity of drawing by hand, without mediation between the artist and the manufacture of multiples. Among the most outstanding results are works by Honoré Daumier, Jules
Chéret, Alphonse Mucha and Henri de Toulouse-Lautrec, 145, 146
whose posters are made by drawing on a separate stone
for each colour used. In the latter's famous *Aristide Bruant at the Ambassadors*, for instance, there are six separate 144
stages of colour.

One of the peaks of this kind of printing is the publica-
151 tion in 1856 of Owen Jones's *The Grammar of Ornament*, the first atlas of modern graphic art: 600 pages, all in colour and with Francis Bedford's splendid drawings, display the principal styles developed throughout human history:
Assyrian, Egyptian, Roman and Renaissance. The meaning GOMBRICH, 1979
and the success of the project lie precisely in wanting to speak to a new, large public that was hungry for images: not to the cultivated or the erudite, but to artisans, artists and designers who could find inspiration and suggestions in its pages. This is not only the forerunner of the great illustrated books, it is the prototype for an unprecedented culture industry, of objects that are not just to be read but to be consulted, leafed through, or even displayed in a sitting room. It is from this new type of work that the 'coffee-table book' will descend, as well as the Taschen model offering hundreds of images to admire or consult in order to get new ideas.

Multiplication means popularity, and among the images that chromolithography brought success to there is a work that has become the visual emblem of a commercial icon. In 1886 the Pre-Raphaelite John Everett Millais paints his *Child's Play*, a somewhat sentimental work in which
a curly-haired child is shown blowing soap bubbles. Its TWYMAN, 1998
oleographic and openly 'poetic' aspect is appealing to less demanding palates: it is a straightforward image devoid of symbolism and one that seems to speak to everyone. On becoming aware of it, the owners of a well-known brand of soap, Pears, ask Millais's permission to use it for the
147 packaging of their flagship product 'Bubbles'. This is one of the first instances of art being used for product packaging, something inconceivable before colour printing. It is enormously successful, and the commercial figures demonstrate the power of such advertising and packaging:

AMBASSADEURS
aristide
BRUANT
dans
son cabaret
H Lautrec

144

145

TRAGIQUE HISTOIRE D'HAMLET
PRINCE DE DANEMARK
SARAH BERNHARDT
Mucha
THÉÂTRE SARAH BERNHARDT

PANTOMIMES LUMINEUSES
Théâtre
Optique
DE
E. REYNAUD
Musique de
GASTON PAULIN
TOUS LES JOURS
DE 3 A 6H & DE 8H A 11H

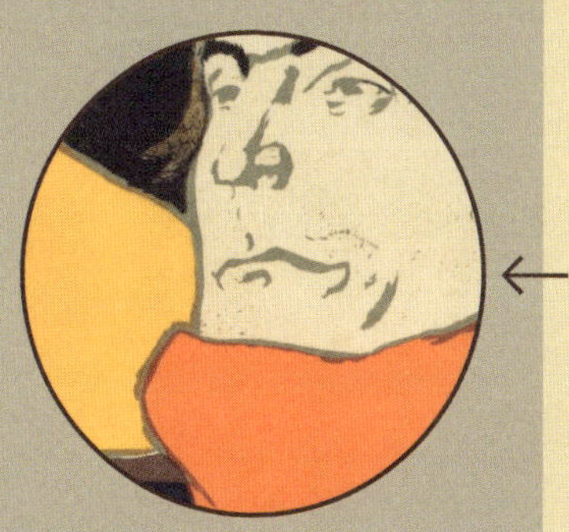

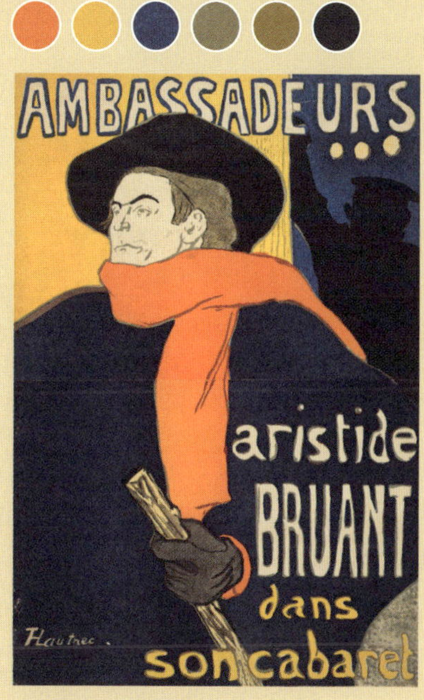

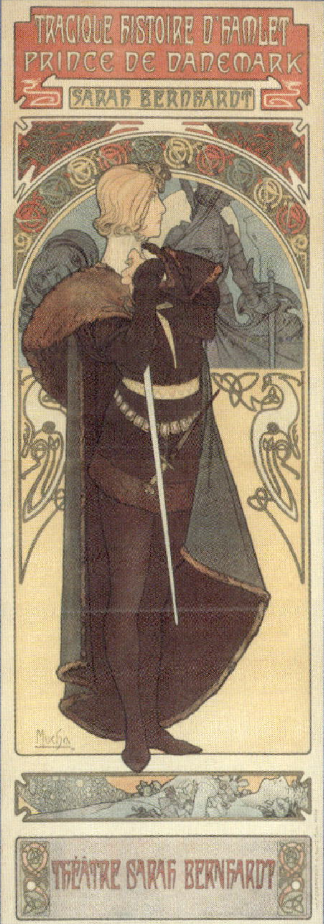

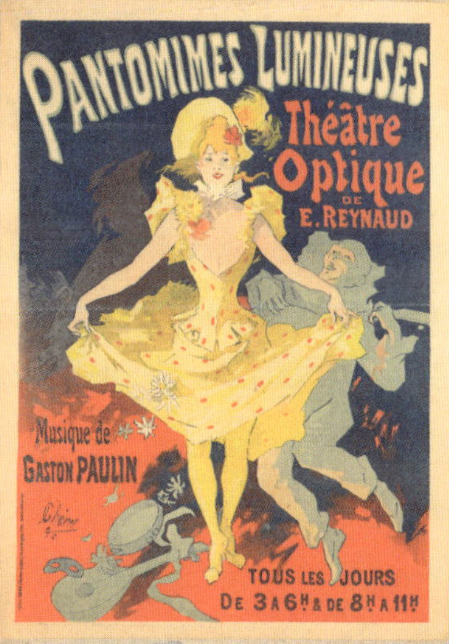

146

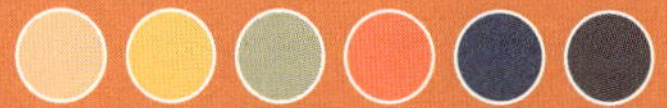

148 ▸

147 ▾

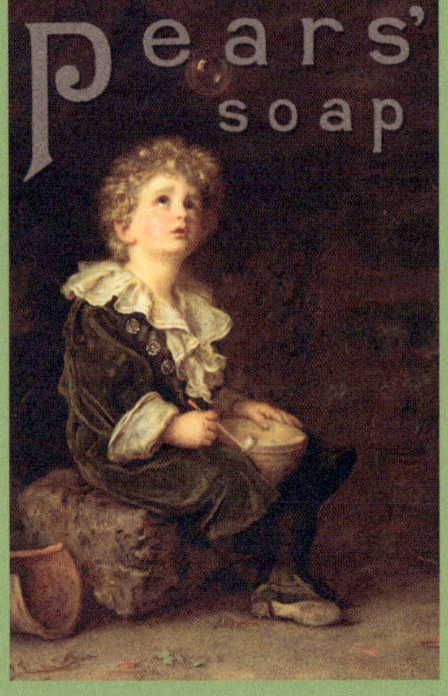

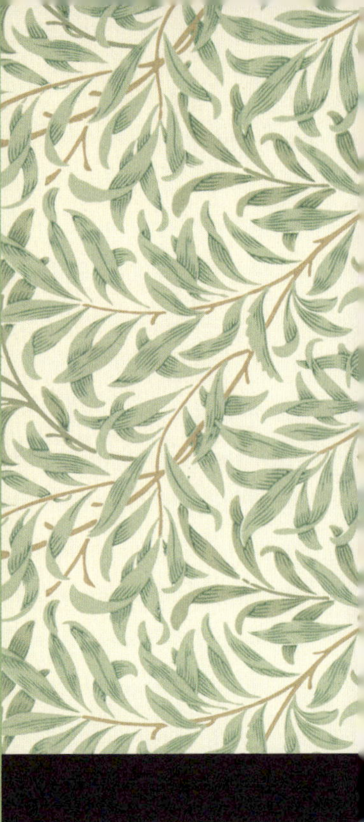

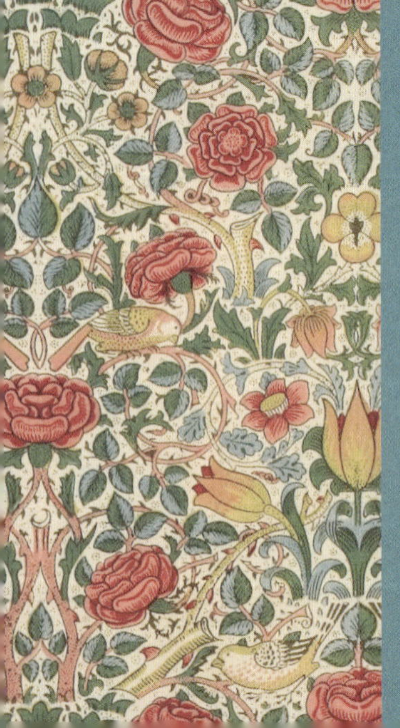

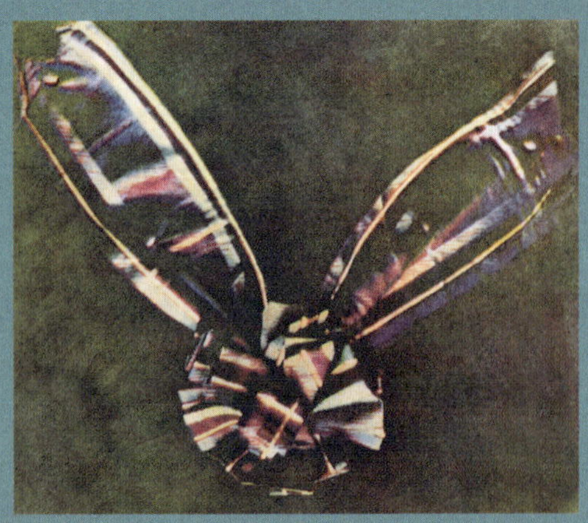

▴ 150

◂ 149

their capacity to go beyond anything previously imagined. From this moment on, Millais's child is synonymous with Pears' Bubbles, which is to say it becomes the mascot for a bar of soap. It would seem that Millais was not particularly pleased, perhaps having underestimated the persuasive power of advertising, or perhaps because he was so tied to the Academy that he felt his work had been somewhat belittled. But the world had changed, and he would just have to deal with the fact.

As packaging was making this giant leap forward,
other commercial sectors were not standing idly by. In
JOBLING, 1996 textiles, there is the crucial invention in 1834 of the
perrotine, a machine capable of directly printing five 148
colours onto fabric at the same time. It provides the basis
for the design of modern upholstery, permitting the
DRUCKER, 2009 combination of different elements in a pattern, without
imprecision and with extremely high-quality results that
open the way for the famous floral patterns of William
Morris. It is Morris who puts printed chintz in compe- 149
tition with much more costly damask, transforming the
appearance of the domestic interior. If damask and em-
BENJAMIN, 2000 broidery had been the languages of the aristocratic big
house, printing becomes that of the bourgeois home,
and technical reproducibility becomes an emblem of the
emerging classes.

The rapid progress of colour printing also determines advances in other technologies, albeit indirectly. The other great invention of the century is of course photography, and from its very beginnings the search had been on to make it possible in colour.

FROVA, 2000 In 1861 James Clerk Maxwell – the physicist who demonstrated that electricity, magnetism and light are all manifestations of the same phenomenon – produces the first ever colour photograph, inspired by Le Blon and

Young's tri-colour ideas. What he achieves is not yet a
photograph that he can hold in his hand but a projected
image instead, a slide of sorts. The subject of the photo-
150 graph is a Scottish cockade, a perfect one for showing
contrasting colours. In order to do this he comes up with
an ingenious technique: he photographs the cockade three
times with a normal black and white plate, each time
placing the object behind a transparent filter, each filter complementary to the colour needed: a green filter,
a red one and then a blue. Then he combines the three
images by projecting them superimposed, in a process GAGE, 2001
wholly inspired by the logic of letterpress printing.[3]

To achieve this he makes use of three magic lanterns (the progenitor of our modern projector) and glass containers filled with coloured solutions. From then on, every colour reproduction process repeats these two actions: to separate and to recompose. Even our own recent software, such as Photoshop, behaves in a similar fashion, dividing chromatic components by means of an algorithm.[4]

A century of research culminates in the union of lithography with photographic processes, which makes it possible to put any type of image on a printing plate. JOBLING, 1996 It is at this point that the society of the image is truly unleashed.

The first to benefit are fashion editors, who can now
show the colours of clothes in magazines and advertisements, increasing the seductive power of their work. The
154 English edition of *Vogue* first appears in 1916, and it is already in large part a colour magazine, phenomenally ahead

[3] The first real three-colour separation process occurs in 1869, achieved in parallel by Louis Duco du Hauron and Charles Cros, who invent the orange, violet and green negative, that is in the complementary colours to be obtained in print.

[4] In 1856 Maxwell formulates the idea that colour can be blended according to two distinct logics: one involving addition (adding coloured lights) and one subtraction (subtracting light through physical mixtures, such as tempera). See Appendix A 6.1 and 6.2.

THE

GRAMMAR OF ORNAMENT

BY

OWEN JONES.

ILLUSTRATED BY EXAMPLES
FROM VARIOUS STYLES OF ORNAMENT.

ONE HUNDRED FOLIO PLATES,
DRAWN ON STONE BY
F. BEDFORD,
AND PRINTED IN COLOURS BY
DAY AND SON.

LONDON:
PUBLISHED BY DAY AND SON, LITHOGRAPHERS TO THE QUEEN,
GATE STREET, LINCOLN'S INN FIELDS.
MDCCCLVI.

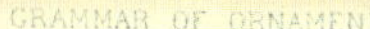

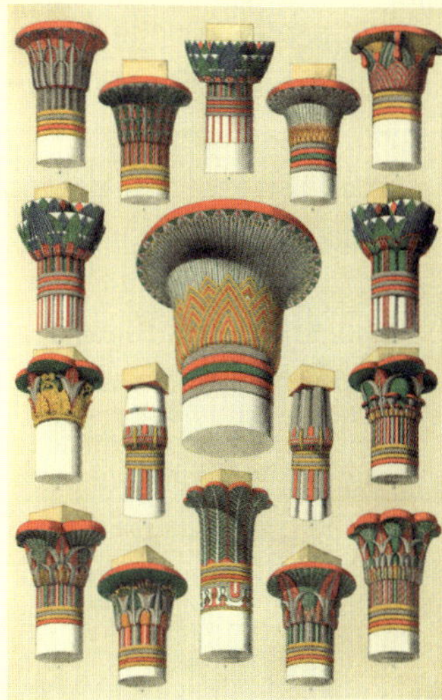

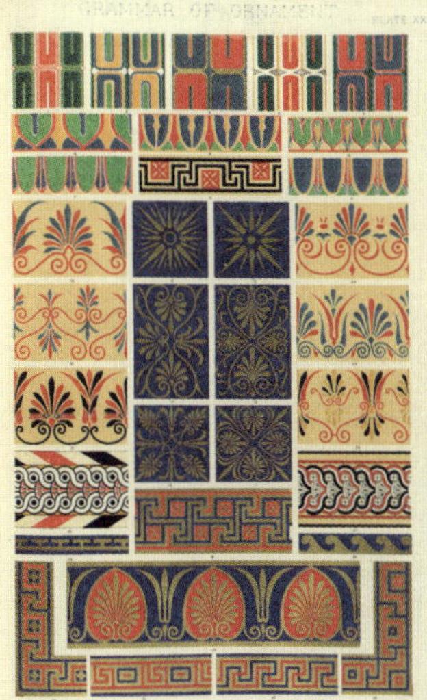

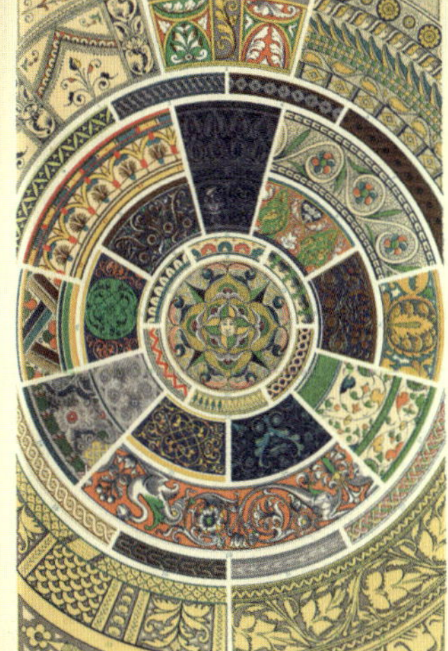

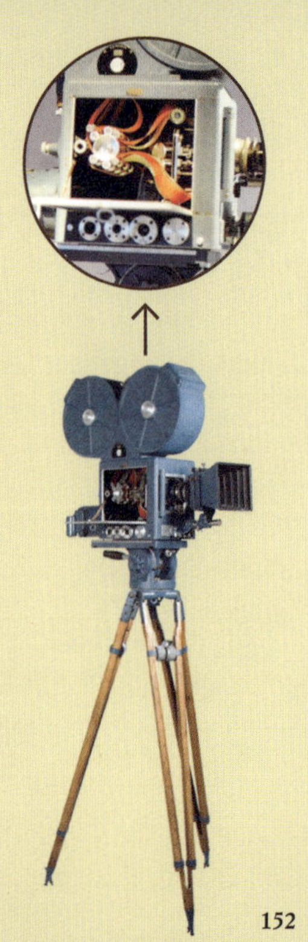

152

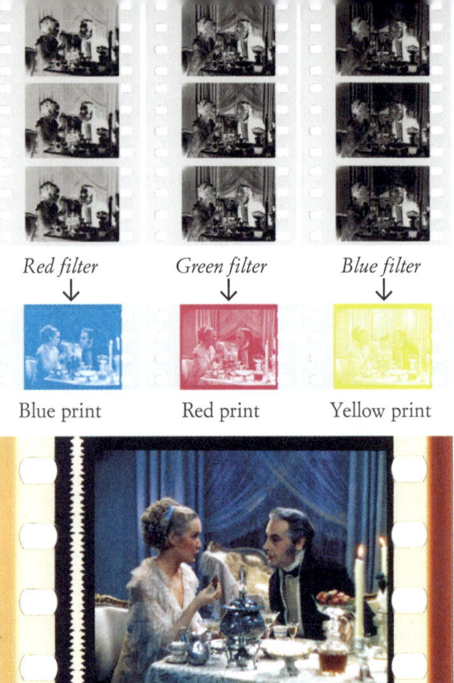

153 ▲

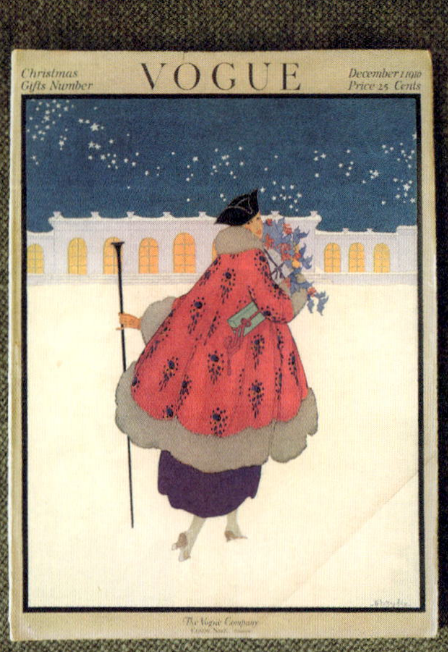

154

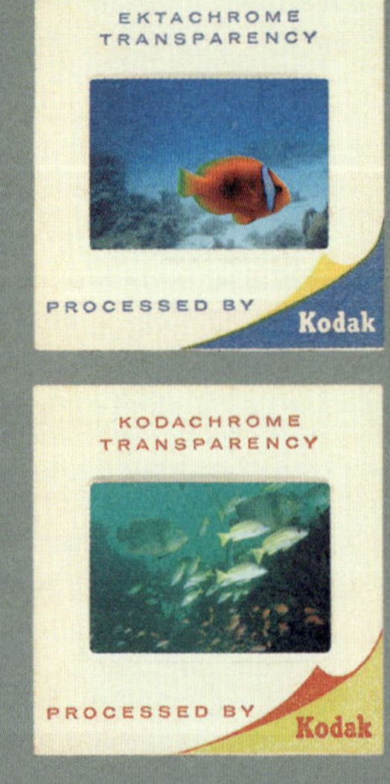

155

of its competitors. No mean feat if we consider that all newspapers at the time were monochrome, and that it was in the middle of a world war.

The most decisive year for colour technology is 1935: in the course of just a few months cyan ink is introduced, the standard for all four-colour printing processes is set, Kodachrome is first used, the first transparency destined
to be consumed by the masses is launched and *Becky Sharp*, 135
the first real colour film, is screened[5] – made thanks to Technicolor, a process invented by three MIT engineers that will go on to shape the experience of at least three generations of cinema-goers.

Technicolor is in many ways *the* ultimate culmination of Le Blon's and Maxwell's ideas. The camera provides three
identical black and white films that reprise the scene simul- 152
taneously, each one filtered by one of the three primary
colours.[6] In the end the three strands are recombined onto 153
a single positive celluloid, with black added for contrast. Technicolor is different inasmuch as it is not a film that is developed but one that is printed, in a similar manner to four-colour processes. And it is precisely its nature as a 'printed' image that provides such distinctively saturated and oleographic colour to mainstream cinema of the 1930s, 40s and 50s.

PIEROTTI, 2012

Seen in this perspective, it is fascinating that the success of Hollywood classics such as *The Wizard of Oz* or *Snow White and the Seven Dwarfs* was the fruit of an idea

[5] Silent cinema was not always grey, as we are accustomed to thinking of and seeing it today. Often the film was coloured with toning baths: certain scenes might be pinkish, others green, still others blue, with different dominant colours linked to narrative ends. Films might also be hand-coloured using the *pochoir* technique, which is to 132
say using stencils (see p. 152, note 2).

[6] The filters were red, green and violet – used to obtain the three positives cyan, magenta and yellow for the print.

born two centuries previously within the culture of the Enlightenment.

It was a very laborious and costly process, managed exclusively by Technicolor with absolute control of every phase of production. The special film cameras that were required belonged exclusively to the company and were rented out for productions together with the technicians needed to operate them. It is said that in order to make the famous scene of the burning of Atlanta in *Gone with the Wind* (1939), thirty-two were hired, or rather *all* of the equipment and expertise that existed in Los Angeles at the time. So what became for decades synonymous with colour cinema was the monopoly of a single company: on the one hand, due to the quality of results that so outstripped its competitors; on the other, because alternative processes such as Kodachrome or Agfacolor consisted of film negatives, that is to say single rolls that can be developed but that do not allow copies to be made: perfect for filming 8mm home movies but not for cinematographic distribution.[7]

PIEROTTI, 2012

Colour film so grips cinema-goers that producers are soon competing to come up with stories that will show its potential to the full. Technicolor is effectively seen in the beginning as a kind of special effect. A recurring gag in early Disney films, for example, sees a character suddenly change colour: an angry Donald Duck goes red in the face; Pinocchio's face turns green after smoking a cigar; embarrassed by Snow White, Bashful blushes; and when the grasshopper gets cold he freezes and literally turns

JOHNSTON, 1981

[7] The game changes in 1951, when Eastmancolor appears, a color negative from which it is possible to produce multiple copies. From this moment on, Technicolor loses its monopoly on colour film and becomes important only for the final prints of films. The results, however, continue to be extraordinary and without compare, as we can see and admire in Bertolucci's *The Conformist* (1970), photographed by Vittorio Storaro; or in Dario Argento's *Suspira*, photographed by Luciano Tovoli.

blue. Such moments amused audiences with their comedy but also on account of their technical innovation: it may seem banal now, but until 1935 nobody had ever seen a drawing change colour before.

PINOTTI, 2016

CASTAGNOLA, 1964

LAMB, 1995

Today colour is intrinsic to the technologies that enable reproduction of things on a large scale, to distribute them and make them widely known. Technology determines what it is possible to see, and therefore conditions how we are able to think about things. The *National Geo-* 155
graphic, for instance, the mass medium that more than any other has formed our view of the natural world, for decades used the Ektachrome camera film that allowed the high shutter speeds perfect for naturalistic reportage. At the time, the most popular film was Kodachrome, which was slower but had fuller reds, making it perfect for holiday snaps. The main difference between the two is that whereas Ektachrome has colder tones tending towards blue, Kodachrome leans towards a greenish tone. This is a technical fact that contributed to a specific imaginary world – namely the idea that all exotic, far-off seas are a deep and brilliant blue. In reality, of course, the sea has many colours: it is blue, green, grey, turquoise, depending on the latitude, conditions and time of year: it was Ektachrome that gave it to us so marvellously, monolithically blue. Technology is never neutral. It always entails and suggests a particular point of view.

For similar reasons, it is thanks to photography that today the works of art of the past are widely disseminated. Among the great painters, the most popular in this regard are the Impressionists, together with Van Gogh, Gustav Klimt and Henri Matisse. Their popularity can be explained partly by the immediacy of the themes treated in their work: quotidian figures and places, brightly coloured landscapes, suffused eroticism. It is all very accessible and good for furnishing home interiors. But there is another reason contributing to the success of these artists, and one that goes unremarked: their paintings are the easiest to reproduce because the gaudily brilliant colours of the originals are not compromised by what can be obtained through printing. The most widespread and economic kind of colour reproduction is of course the four-colour process, in which a decent chromatic spectrum of colours can be had by combining just four inks. This system does not make it possible, however, to reproduce bright pastel shades: based on a combination of percentages of ink, the more the colours are mixed in this process, the darker they become.[8] The earthy and livid tones of Baroque art do not fare well in four-colour, compared to the palettes of a Matisse or a Monet, which are highly consistent with the technology that promotes them through posters, books and postcards. Printing then becomes a selection process, contributing to the success of art that passes most easily through its filter. So much so that the habit of reproduction has ended up normalizing even our perception, making us prefer certain chromatic combinations and conditioning our gaze.

GILARDI, 2000

In the eighteenth century vermilion came to be considered the red par excellence, a hue that tends towards orange and that, following Newton, we find at the edge of the rainbow spectrum. Today, in the West, true red is carmine, that is to say a cooler tone somewhere between

[8] The effect obtained is via a 'screen', the set of regular dots that we see in all printed products and that we see writ large in the paintings of Roy Lichtenstein, in imitation of the grainy colour printing in the comics of a certain period. To lighten a colour the number of dots is reduced, creating an optical blend with the white of the paper (see Appendix A 6.3).

that of a strawberry and a Coca-Cola can. Of this red there is no trace at all in the rainbow; what we are dealing with is in fact a compound of violet and orange light at the extremes of the spectrum. Newton would probably not have recognized it as a primary colour, and Goethe would have thought of it as more purple than red. The change in this psychological category was brought about precisely by the influence of the lithographic printing that produces its best and cheapest red by combining magenta with yellow ink. Coke red becomes the *real* red because it is easier to print and distribute.

It is no surprise Senefelder's biography led to Romantic myths. In the nineteenth century they turned him into a hero; today he should be made the patron saint of the colours used in all mass media.

156

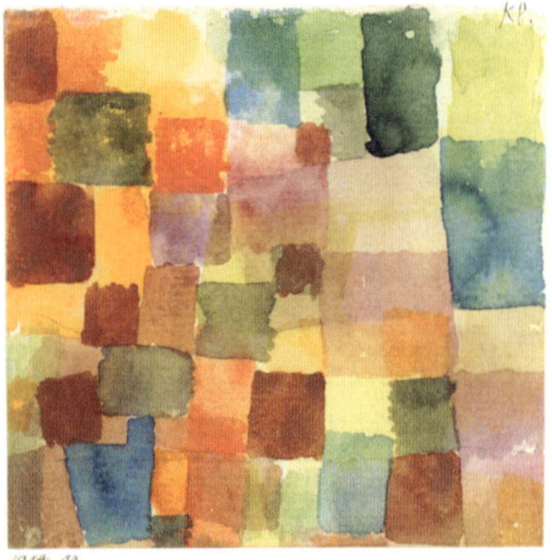

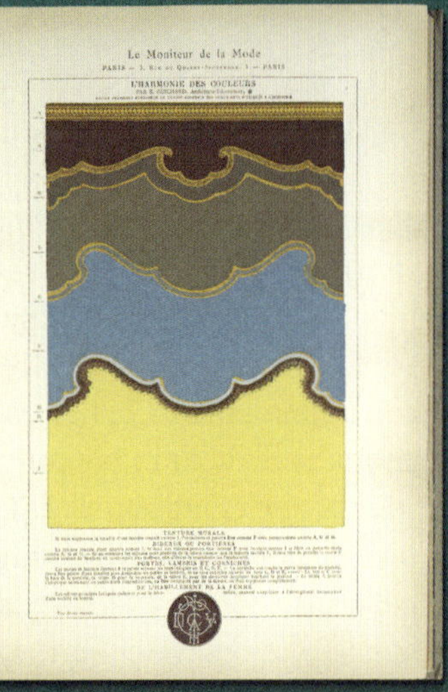
Le Moniteur de la Mode

PARIS — 3, Rue du Quatre-Septembre, 3 — PARIS

L'HARMONIE DES COULEURS

▲157 ▼158

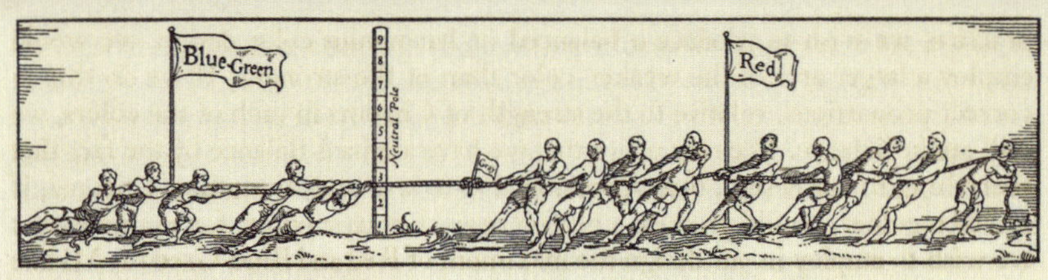

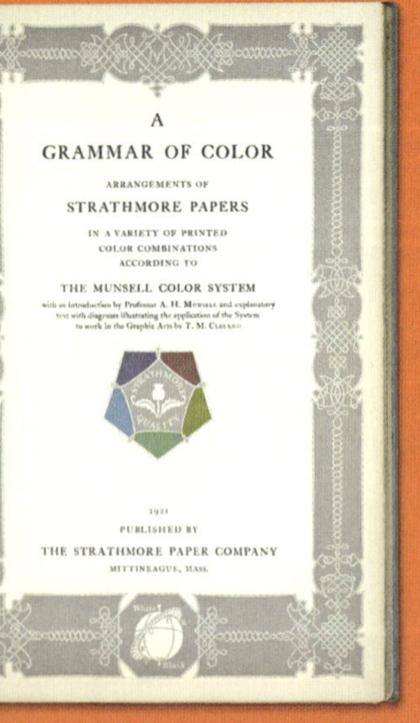
A

GRAMMAR OF COLOR

ARRANGEMENTS OF

STRATHMORE PAPERS

IN A VARIETY OF PRINTED
COLOR COMBINATIONS
ACCORDING TO

THE MUNSELL COLOR SYSTEM

with an introduction by Professor A. H. Munsell and explanatory text with diagrams illustrating the application of the System to work in the Graphic Arts by T. M. Cleland

1921

PUBLISHED BY

THE STRATHMORE PAPER COMPANY

MITTINEAGUE, MASS.

159

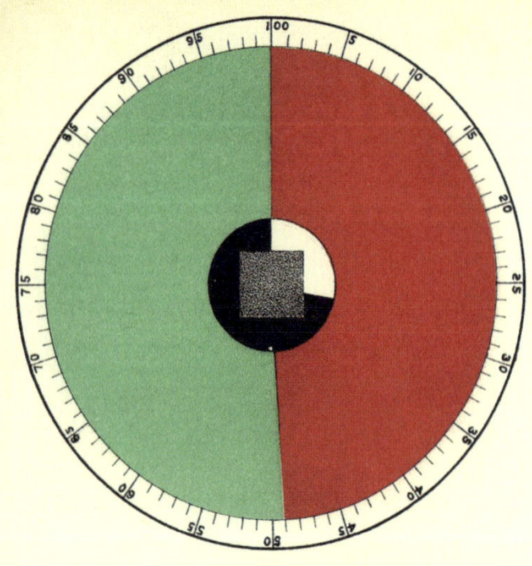

160

Harmonious Grey

Great Ideals for Everyday Life

'Of the two, I would go for the first one as the colours are more harmonious,' I am told by the shop assistant, pointing to the tie on the right. 'It seems to suit you more. You have light eyes, it's more you.'

This prosaic conversation, which occurred in Rome a few days ago – and is no different from so many others which occur in clothes shops all over the world – contains two ideas that are as widespread as they are obvious. Namely, that there is a harmony between certain colours, and that some of these harmonies are better suited to certain people.

We are talking about powerful myths that are popular thanks to certain influential theorists at the beginning of the twentieth century, reinforced by journalism dealing with fashion, design and interior design – and still echoed today in widely differing contexts. Whether in textiles or tailoring, from the hairdressing salon to the photographer's studio, we speak of chromatic harmony or of 'matching' colours. And yet this is not an altogether harmless term, or one without significant pitfalls.

BIRREN, 1969

'Harmony' is a word that comes from the musical lexicon: it refers to the simultaneous combination of two or more sounds – a combination that we take for granted must be pleasurable – at the heart of a musical tradition that runs from Monteverdi to Wagner and beyond. Translated into the context of painting and design, harmony is synonymous with equilibrium, order, coherence, consonance. All positive virtues, in other words. But what does it mean to speak of the *harmony* of colours? And why are some combinations thought to be pleasing and others not?

In the last two centuries scientists, artists and philosophers have tried to answer these questions. In fact, most recent theories concentrate precisely upon the search for some hypothetical perfection. The problem of modernity was the rationalization of colour, that is to say the establishment of universal laws concerning the number of colours and their best combinations. This led to a grammar of the visual in which the idea of harmony – precisely the agreement between two or more colours – became in many respects an unavoidable consequence: if you try to find the correct ordering of colours, sooner or later you end up asking if there are some principles better than others with which to combine them. It's an idea, like so many others, that comes down to us from a long way off.

BOERI, 2010 KOYRÉ, 1967 ARNHEIM, 1987

In October 1919 an eccentric figure arrives at the Bauhaus and proceeds to makes a lasting mark on the imaginations of the students there. He is a follower of the Mazdaznan sect, inspired by Zoroastrianism. He is a vegetarian, has a shaven head at a time when it is far from commonplace, wears loose-fitting 'priestly' garments and brings with him concentration and breathing exercises. He also teaches meditation, gymnastics – and colour theory. His name is Johannes Itten (1888–1967),[1] and his ideas are destined to

WINGLER, 1972

[1] Itten soon comes into conflict with Walter Gropius, the director of the Bauhaus, who in 1923 replaces him with a chemist in order to establish a more rational approach to colour; a somewhat contradictory move given that Itten had joined via the group frequenting the theosophical salon of Gropius's wife, Alma Mahler.

EDWARDS, 2006

be enormously successful: so much so in fact that there is hardly a manual of art, of graphic design or of fashion that does not refer to them.[2] Before Itten, colour theories proposed for the most part models based on isolated colours, such as the famous colour wheel, systematized and arranged without analysing the rapport between one colour and another.

GERRITSEN, 1988

Goethe was interested in the opposition of complementaries, but did not go further than this; and Chevreul with his circles shows the sequence of colours but not the logical or aesthetic links that may be established between them. Itten, on the other hand, is interested in what happens within the circle, concentrating on the relations that are created in passing from one colour to another.[3]

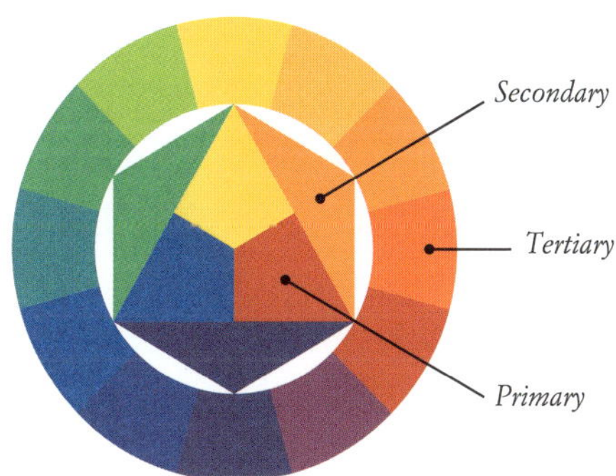

After showing how secondary and tertiary colours are generated from the three primaries (and up to here we can

[2] Itten's fundamental text is *The Art of Colour*, first published in 1961 and in print ever since.

[3] Itten's circle is structurally indebted to Goethe's ideas as filtered by Adolf Hölzel (1853–1934), a now forgotten teacher of painting whose influence extended to at least two generations of artists (see Appendix B 16). Its conceptual core comes from Moses Harris (see p. 136 and Figure 123), the first who, inspired by Le Blon's typographical ideas, proposes a circular sequence derived from the mixing of just the three primary colours.

feel the full force of the legacy of the nineteenth century), he uses this structure to highlight some 'harmonious' combinations, which is to say ones that are more sensible and pleasing than others, taking the colours that lie on the circumference in groups of two or three according to relations of quadrature or triangulation.

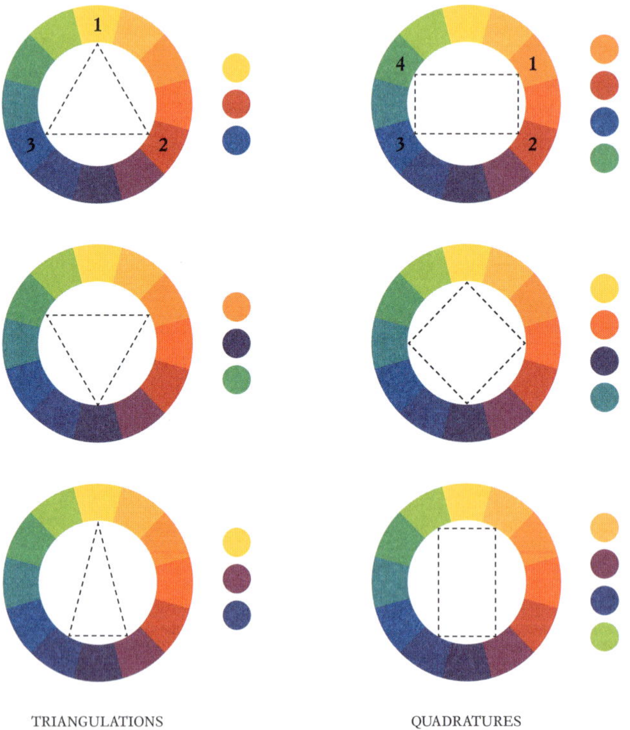

TRIANGULATIONS QUADRATURES

At this point, Itten emphasizes the expressive relationships created between colours: he identifies seven of them, and baptizes them 'fundamental chromatic contrasts',[4]

[4] 'Contrast' is a term that refers to a tension, an argument or a conflict: a curious choice given that the consequence of right contrast is precisely harmony.

recognizing that each one has the capacity to evoke precise and distinctive registers. There is the relationship between light and dark; the opposition between pure colours; of complementary ones; or the play between more or less solid colours. Above all, he pays most attention to the so-called 'quantity contrasts': what happens when the chromatic surface coverage within a work is markedly unequal, with a great deal of blue and a little orange, for example.

ITTEN, 1982

With this in mind he designs another circle in which the space dedicated to the six principal colours is divided into segments in inverse proportion to the quantity of light they reflect.

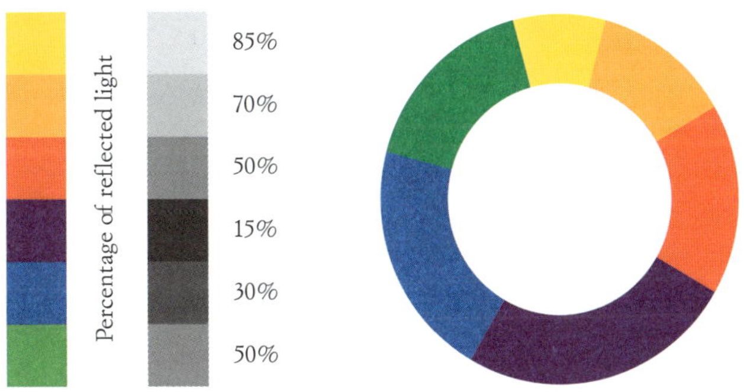

So if there is a true brightness value characteristic of every colour, Itten argues, then in a well-made composition these different quantities of light should be properly balanced. And if this happens, then we have harmony.

In other words, red and green, which have the same luminosity, should appear on the canvas in equal amounts, 158, 160
whereas yellow, which is three times more luminous than violet, should occupy a surface three times smaller. Colours are reconfigured according to their intrinsic brilliance, into

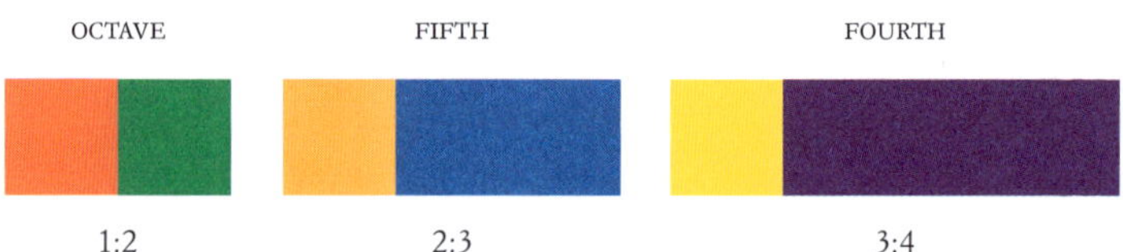

fifth, fourth and octave relations or chords, in a similar way to what happens between notes in the tonal harmonic system.[5]

And it is here that Itten gets into something of a muddle.

If a parallel can be established between colour and music, and if we can speak of a 'scale' when referring to the luminosity of colour – establishing a similarity between the pitch of a sound and a colour's brightness – it is nevertheless impossible to find ordering criteria of a more general kind, given that colours in the spectrum do not follow each other with a logic comparable to that of notes on a stave.[6]

[5] The comparison between music and painting, a classic one in aesthetic theory, becomes popular in the eighteenth century, as artistic knowledge is systematized, and with the analogy between sound and colour assuming an unprecedented centrality. It is at this time that the idea appears of structuring the palette of colours from the lightest to the darkest, in a progression similar to that between notes in a scale.

[6] One of the most significant instances of relations between sound and colour is that suggested by the 'ocular harpsichord' devised by the French Jesuit Louis Bertrand Castel (1688–1757). Pressing the keys of this ocular, which is to say visual, instrument would trigger colours to light up – probably via a series of lanterns and coloured glass. The idea was inspired by some reflections of Athanasius Kircher's, who had already seen possible relations between musical and chromatic intervals. For Castel, there are three primary colours (blue, yellow and red) and they are perfectly comparable to Do-Mi-So. The theme is so fashionable that Algarotti, in the already cited *Newtonianism for Ladies* (see p. 79), suggests the use of the harpsichord above all by ladies in order to match the colours of their clothes harmoniously.

SAGLIETTI, 2002

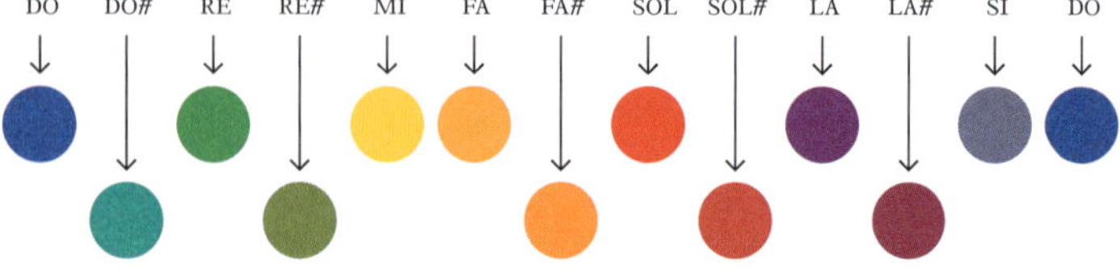

The nervous system codifies sounds and colours in completely different ways. The eye, for example, is not able to see the different constituents of a chromatic sensation: when yellow and blue are combined I see green, and the yellow and blue disappear. But for the ear, a Do and a Mi sounded together do not produce the sensation of Re (intermediate between the two) but actually a harmony in which both sounds are still distinct and recognizable. In effect colour harmonies can only be of a spatial kind, between adjacent areas of colour.

And it is precisely with regard to these combinations that Itten says there would be harmony in a painting if the result of combining its colours would be a medium grey: that is to say what happens in the encounter between half red and half green, or three parts violet and one yellow.

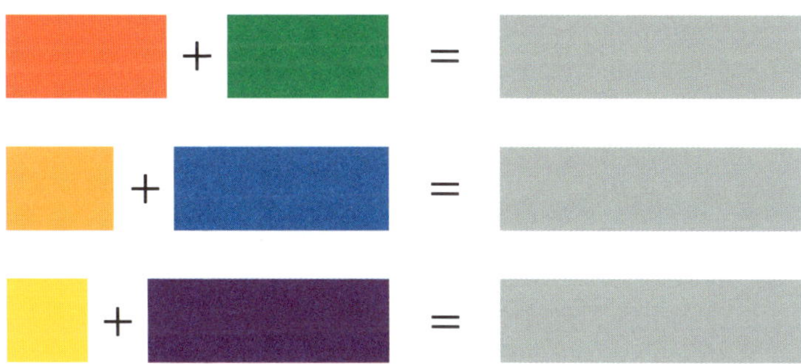

EDWARDS, 2006

This is not a visible grey, however, but a mathematical one: it is what would result if the colours were mixed rather than being placed side by side. It is a question in the end of balancing colours like weights in the two pans of a scale. And Itten is not the only one to have thought along these lines.

A few years before Itten arrives at the Bauhaus, on the other side of the Atlantic in Boston, there is already a professor of the theory of colour proposing a fundamental model for the coming century. His name is Albert Munsell (1858–1918), and he is the father of the system that is most used today in many industrial and scientific contexts. He also ends up talking about harmony, even if his own purposes are quite different from those of Itten.

Since different hues exhibit different brightness at maximum saturation (solid yellow is intrinsically much more luminous than solid blue), Munsell is convinced that it is not possible to contain colours within a rigid scheme. He gets rid of many chromatic models which are too regular – such as circles, spheres and triangles – and
162, 164 proposes instead a three-dimensional shape, similar to MUNSELL, 1915
that of a tree with branches of different lengths and com-
163 posed of progressively arranged tiles of colour. The trunk
indicates luminosity, going from darkest at the bottom to lightest at the top. Around the trunk the colours are arranged in a circle, while the branches represent the various degrees of saturation or depth of colour: the further you go along the branch from the trunk, the darker the tone becomes.

At this point Munsell, like Itten, maintains that a harmonious composition of light and solid colours will
produce a neutral grey. The task of the artist, according MUNSELL, 1921
to Munsell, is to balance the three parameters, and in
159 order to demonstrate it in *A Grammar of Colour*, pub-
165 lished in 1921, he includes two illustrations: one that is
'wrong', the other in which the colours are 'corrected' according to his idea of harmony. Beneath the illustrations, using Maxwell's spinning top,[7] he explains how

[7] A disc divided into segments, each one representing the percentage of that colour included in the composition. When spun, the disc gives the optical interplay or blending of the various shades (see Appendix A 6.3).

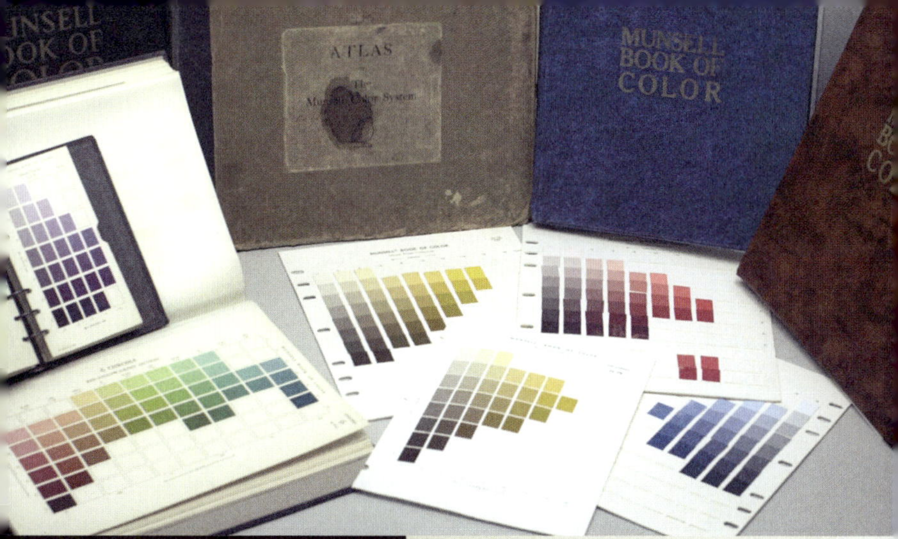

▲ 161

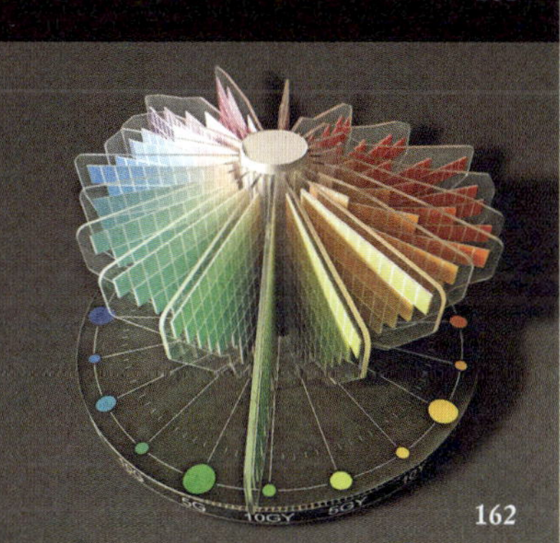

162

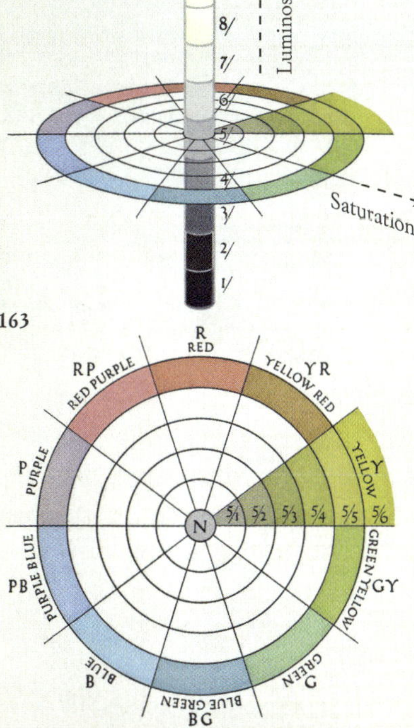

163

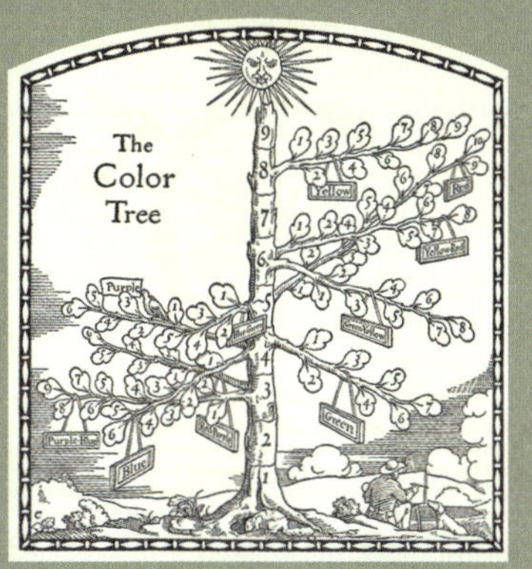

164

Colours arranged circularly
The complementaries are based upon reciprocal posthumous tints

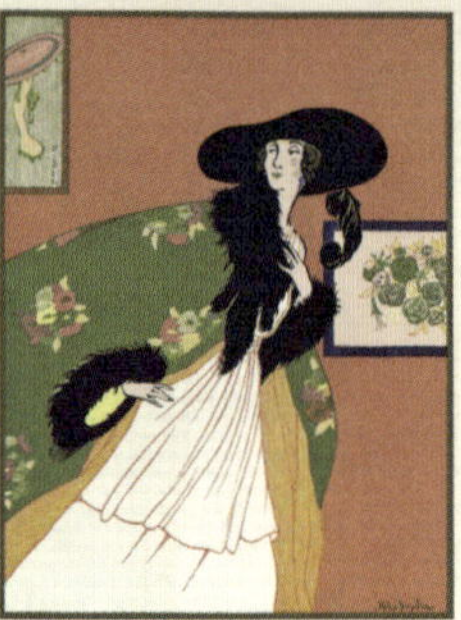

UNBALANCED COLOR

THE colors in this proof are poorly related and do not balance in neutral gray. In the first circle these colors are shown in approximately the same proportions of area that they occupy in the picture. If this circle were rapidly revolved, the resulting mixture would be as shown in the solid circle.

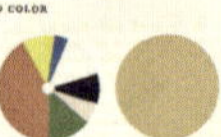

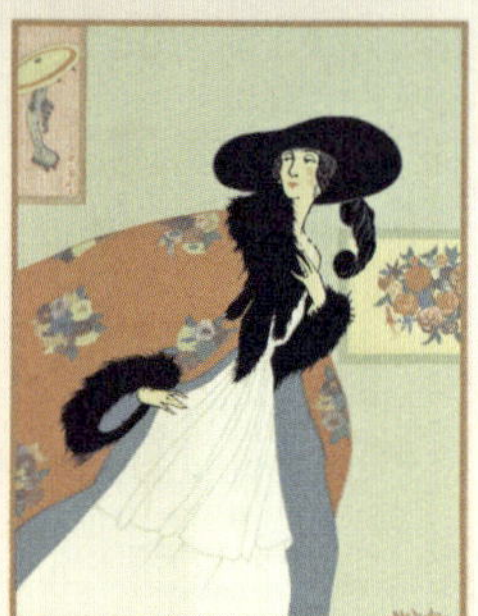

BALANCED COLOR

IN this proof, made from the same plates as the one on the opposite page, the colors are correctly related. The approximate proportion of area of each color to the whole is shown in the first circle. The neutral gray, which would result from an admixture of these colors in these same proportions, is shown in the solid circle.

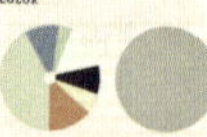

165

166

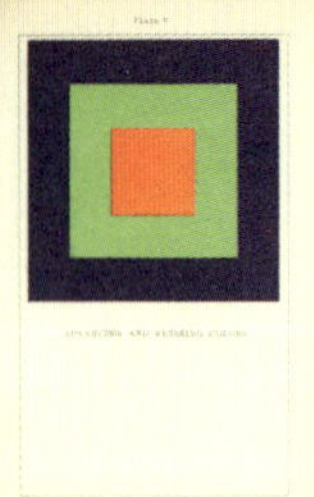

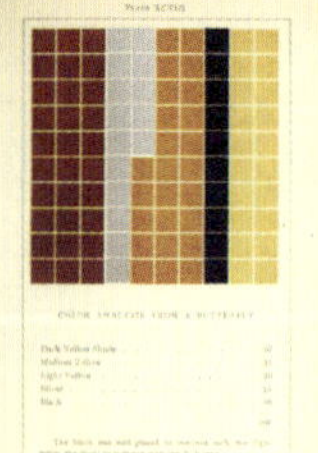

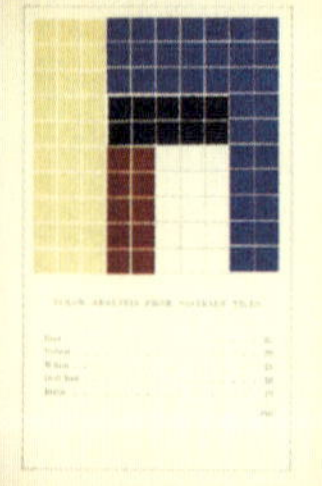

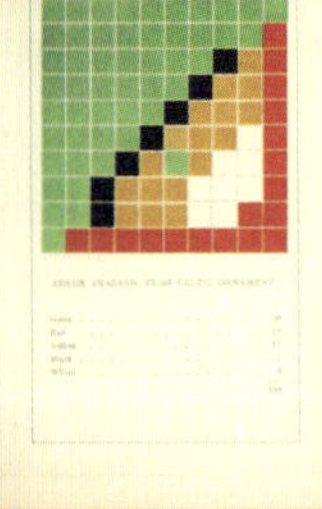

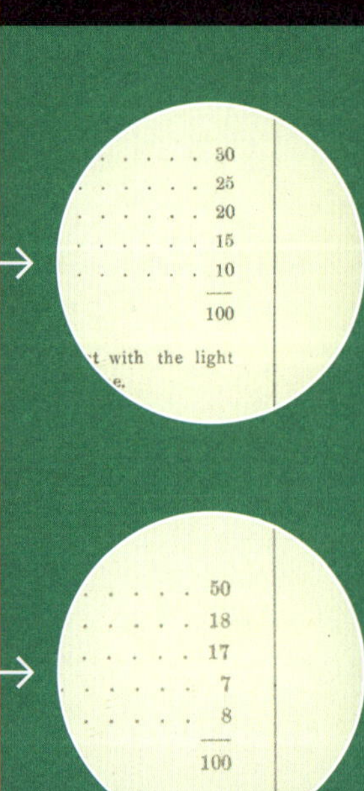

only the second mixture is correct, because it produces the famous medium grey.

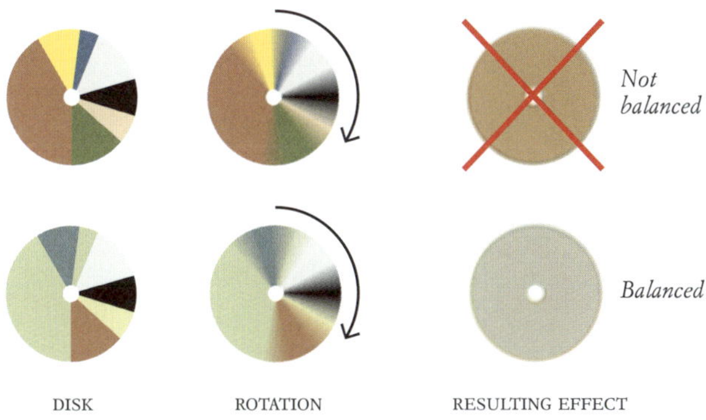

If this reminds us of the kind of 'before and after' advertising logic with which the power of detergents is demonstrated, the benefit produced in this case is not astonishing whites but a putative perceptual equilibrium.

OSTWALD, 1965

At the same time, even the Nobel Prize winner for chemistry Wilhelm Ostwald (1853–1932) supports the idea that the pleasing effect of colours is a result of their precise and regulated rapports, positing as an ideal a eurhythmy in which all colours have the same darkness or lightness.
We are dealing here with the kind of widespread and per- 157
vasive beliefs that crop up in the most diverse fields. So much so, to give one example among hundreds, that in a manual published in New York as early as 1902 we find
multiple readings of works of art based upon the geomet- 160, 166
rical sums of colour percentages.[8] In short, for each of these thinkers the physiological balancing of complementaries and luminous quantities, mathematically arranged, is nothing less than the cornerstone of beauty.

[8] *Color Problems* by E. Noyes Vanderpoel.

For all their success, these ideas are imbued with a rather facile kind of reductionism, and many were sceptical: Paul
156 Klee, for one, pointed out that by following such a rule to arrive at artistic ends we end up renouncing all psychic and creative richness. But the limitations of Itten and those with similar views are above all ideological: their positions are completely disconnected from the real social practices of the world in which they live. They do not take into account, that is, the actual languages in play – first and foremost that of mass communication.

It is no accident that Munsell connects advertising and the circus by asserting that both can afford to indulge in inharmonious combinations as they are designed to instantly seduce and not to last – whereas *true* harmony looks towards the eternal and aims for the sublime. Behind the pseudoscientific facade lurks the infamous Romantic separation of poetry and the fine arts from all commercial art. One wants to find in the physiology of perception, in other words, a way of indirectly condemning consumer society: by arguing that our eye by its very nature 'desires equilibrium', one ends up by condemning advertising as 'unnatural'.

Looking back on it now, such a conception of harmony seems in fact to be an essentially moralizing project, and these theorists are really speaking about something else: they are forcing colour into a system of a distinctly 'hygienic' type.

In order to provide cultural authority for his discourse, Itten claims that he has taken his inspiration from Goethe's theories. But he is either mistaken or confused. Goethe never spoke of anything like Itten's harmony. It is actually an idea that can be traced – and this is significant – to Arthur Schopenhauer instead. Schopenhauer is the first to maintain, at the beginning of nineteenth century, that in order to obtain chromatic consonance it is necessary to counterbalance the amounts of light reflected by colours, which he codifies in the following way:[9]

SCHOPENHAUER, 2002

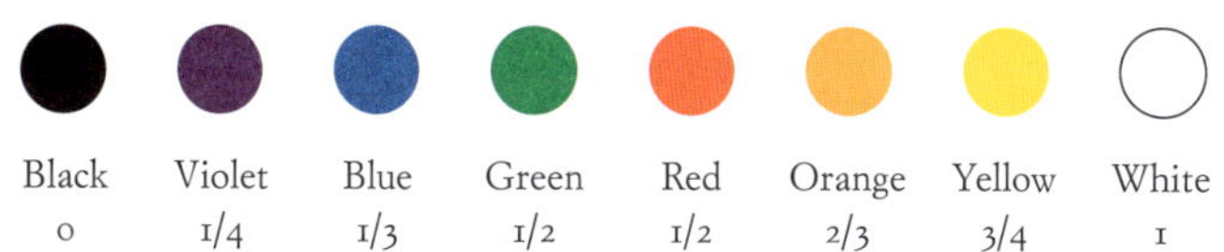

A similar idea develops as part of much deeper and more complex philosophical vision.

According to the philosophical pessimism of Schopenhauer – who is fascinated by Hindu and Buddhist doctrines, among other things – the phenomenal world is the source of all illusion and sorrow; it is constitutive of human existence and therefore unavoidable. Unlike in oriental religions, however, salvation cannot be found through asceticism or by renouncing material goods – but through art or morality instead. It follows that chromatically harmonious compositions have the power to comfort us in our state of existential suffering, restoring to their viewers a degree of equilibrium and peace.

Itten's purifying agenda also seems to respond to a similar imperative: the search for equilibrium, and an obsession with balancing energies that is typical of eastern philosophy. Think of the two cornerstones of Zen, the yin and the yang, that result in wellbeing when in symmetry and generate illness when out of kilter. Even Kandinsky says as much; colour harmony is based on a single principle: effective contact with the soul.[10] Behind

KANDINSKIJ, 1989

[9] The theory in question is laid out in *Colours and Sight*, published by Schopenhauer in 1816; the majority of manuals on the market today, following Itten, continue to attribute it to Goethe.

[10] Already Marcel Herbert – reviewing *The Spiritual in Art* in the March 1914 issue of *La Société Nouvelle* – claims that Kandinsky's book has the defects of all books written by artists and is full of pseudoscience.

the idea of chromatic harmony there are assumptions that colour really has little or nothing to do with.

If it is not Goethe who comes up with the idea of mathematical harmony that Itten has in mind, it is nevertheless the final part of his *Theory of Colours* that influences many health-related approaches to the question that end up seducing certain artists: Goethe is the first to suggest an intrinsic spiritual significance for colours, opening the way to hypothetical medications, often of a decidedly irrational kind.

GOETHE, 2008 BRUSATIN, 1983

Already at the end of the nineteenth century – in parallel with artistic and scientific knowledge – doctrines in which the boundary between medicine and esotericism is blurred begin to get a foothold. In 1890 the physiologist Charles Féré, for instance, begins to cure hysterical attacks by subjecting patients to flashes of coloured light, inaugurating the practice of chromotherapy, according to which the radiant power of light can re-establish mental equilibrium and peace. The idea was that if some wavelengths are clearly beneficial – ultraviolet light, for instance, that can tan and improve the health of our skin – then it was conceivable that every wavelength might bring with it a specific benefit. Today, however, there is no proof of this.

BIRREN, 1978

From Bach's flowers to the practice of meditation, from Jungian therapy to the teachings of Rudolf Steiner, from Rorschach tests to the chromatic ones devised by Lüscher, today there is hardly a field in which somebody will not have something to say about colours and their therapeutic power. We are talking about a range of very different practices of varying credibility – but they are united by a mythic idea of colour that almost always entails superficial generalizations. To give a single instance among many, by linking choices of colour to some deep psychological truth, as happens in Lüscher tests

LUZZATTO, 2009

LÜSCHER, 1976 (one of the best-known practices of this kind), a patient's emotional state is mapped using predictable formulas, with the additional pretence that they have a supra-cultural value. Blue, according to Lüscher, signifies a sense of belonging, yellow means change and green, self-esteem, SAMBURSKY, 1990 and he maintains that every colour is a sign that can be *precisely* defined. In his words we can hear the echo of magical approaches to colours that would like to anchor them to universal significance. The problem here is not just the irrational aspect of such theories but their implicit refusal of one of the great achievements of modern thought: cultural specificity and relativism.

It is no accident that Itten's work leaves behind another
suggestive but elusive legacy: he is the first to associate colour preferences with human types, arguing that the colours
ITTEN, 1982 an artist selects correspond to his physical traits and characteristics: blondes with blue eyes will gravitate towards 168
bright colours; 'Moors' towards gloomy ones, and so on.
These ideas are a disturbing reminder of how much interest there was in physiognomy and its uses in the Germany
of the 1930s. If Nazism made this part of the tragedy of
twentieth-century history, Itten influenced those rather
more innocuous currents, in the first place in fashion and
furnishings, that explain how to match colours to physical
appearance and personality. One example among many: for
WRIGHT, 1995 almost forty years in the United States, the books in the
'Color Me' series explained how to dress in and use make- 169
up of the right colour. Not to mention the plethora of texts
on furnishings, such as those by Laura Ashley, that have
become perennial bestsellers. An indication, too, that the
influence of the Bauhaus was far from being confined to
architecture, and has germinated in widely disparate areas.

*

It is fascinating how decidedly transcendental ideas are now commonplace in books on design or marketing (even the practical manuals) that aim at teaching us how to construct a balanced composition, be it that of a picture, a brand, or the interior design of a room. But beyond the question of the validity of these theories, do they not embody a quite sterile objective? If artistic activity and expression are by definition creative, why seek to impose rules? Why make a fetish of harmony in particular? It is, after all, often precisely their lack of balance (and this seems to be the case throughout human history) that distinguishes the most interesting works.

HORNUNG, 2005

There is no doubt that certain combinations seem more pleasing to us than others, more significant, more emotional – not just more 'decorative'. But it is not so easy to establish which ones. And very frequently we happen to find brilliant combinations that have nothing to do with any rules. What works for a dress will not necessarily work for a sofa; and what functions in a painting cannot follow the same rules as a videogame. Besides, the combination of red and fuchsia thought to be so harmonious in Indian clothing does not seem so to an Anglo-Saxon sensibility. The idea that there can be such a thing as *a priori* harmony is patently false. And all claims to have circumscribed it result only in a handful of little formulas or common-sense advice. Fortunately, colour escapes all such recipes and prescriptions.

GARAU, 1999

While we can say that the combination of red and black is undoubtedly more striking and attractive than that of green and beige, and that this will be the case ninety-nine times out of 100, there will nevertheless always be an occasion on which a combination of green and beige will reveal itself to be a tremendous, even perfect one. It is a question of talent and of sensibility. When working with colour, harmony matters less than having a story to tell.

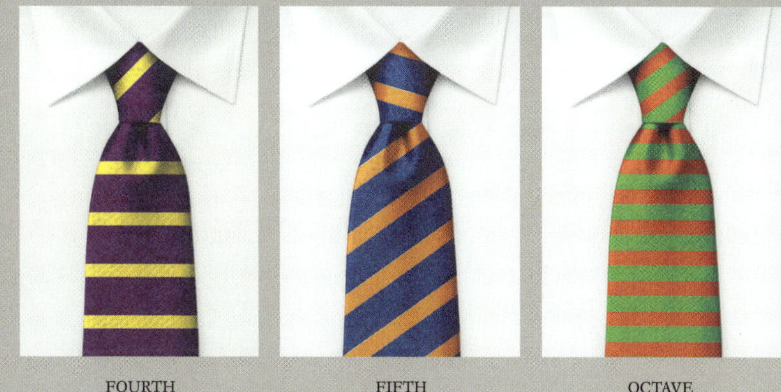

FOURTH FIFTH OCTAVE

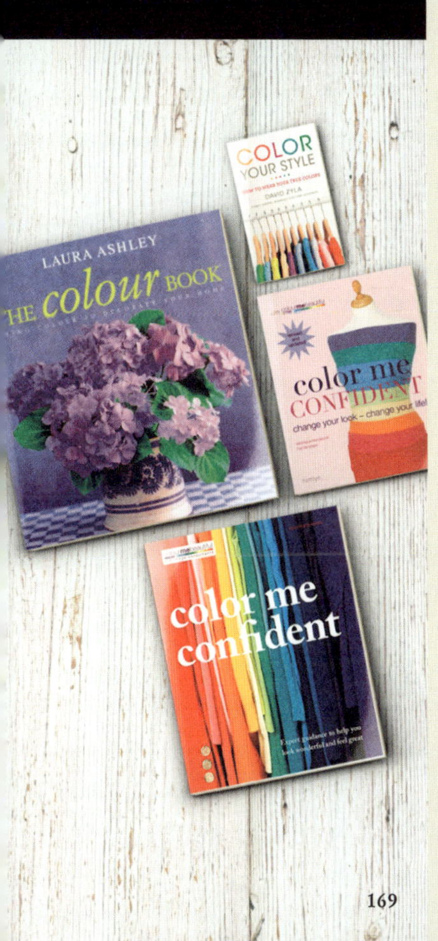

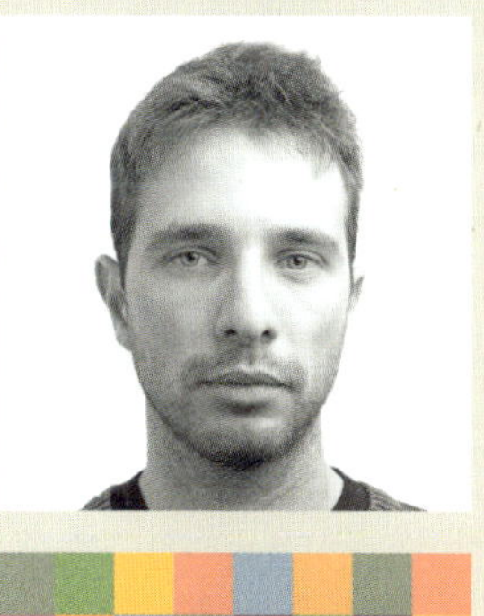

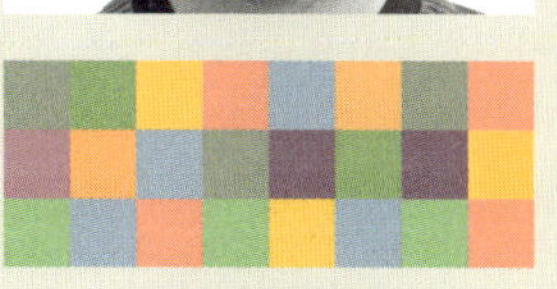

← Palette chosen for a blonde with light eyes

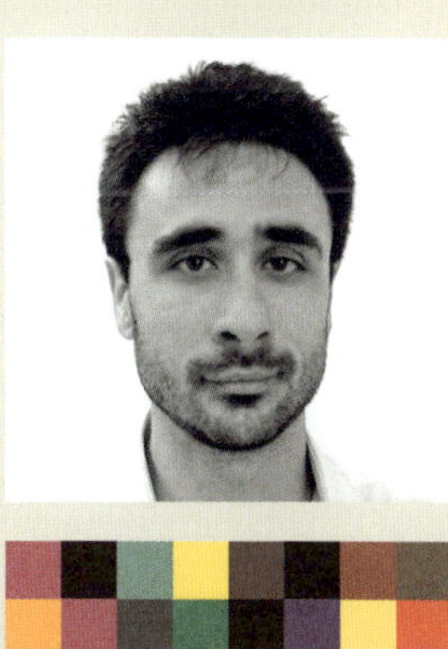

← Palette chosen for someone with dark hair and eyes

The theories we have looked at seem to us today to be far too isolated and abstract, as if colour had its own internal functioning and logic. And yet all of these ideas, whether esoteric, practical or scientific, have been formulated by particular people in precise historical, technological and social conditions. Itten operates within the Germanic philosophical tradition. It is no accident that he inherits the legacy of Goethe and Schopenhauer, and that to be preoccupied with colour is not just a profession but involves a vision of the world, a way of experiencing life itself. Munsell manifests instead the typical pragmatism of American culture: he is more interested in the possibility of specifying with exactitude the relationships between colours than he is in their meaning. It is Munsell who publishes not so much a treatise
161 as an atlas, composed of numerous coloured and numbered tiles – a new tool that prefigures Pantone's more recent system.[11] If we fail to take these contexts into account, we are likely to confuse perception and ideology, and to underestimate the fact that an idea about colour is always and inevitably an ideology, perhaps even a political one.

To conclude, and for the fun of it, let's try to apply to the letter the harmonic theory of Schopenhauer as suggested by Itten, and create three neckties based on fifth, fourth and
167 octave musical chords. As can be seen in Figure 167, the result is not that attractive. In fact, to tell the truth, the three

[11] It is exactly the lexicon that we use today in graphics software. Munsell produced in fact not a theory in the classic sense but a descriptive system for communication in professional contexts, and one used, among other things, to catalogue and compare various types of materials: archaeologists compare soil samples to register work done, for instance. The Munsell 'chip', however, precisely because it is a sample of three qualities (hue, tone, saturation), is not able to take account of everything. For example, if it is put next to a leaf, it can get near to the colour but it cannot account for its volumetric complexity. In general, the limit of twentieth-century classification is that it cannot name the colours that aren't solid colours. There is no RGB capable of showing the colour of human skin, just as there is no Pantone that can identify blonde or brunette (see Appendix A 11.0).

resulting ties are quite eccentric and scarcely commercial. With their clashing contrasts, they are almost certainly too garish for current taste. But perhaps my father would have liked them, since they seem very redolent of the 1970s. I do not need Schopenhauer, whose reflections on colour are gorgeous and imaginative, in order to be able to see this. Design is always a practical, historical matter that cannot rely on universal laws.

In the end, when the shop assistant alleges that one tie is more harmonious than another, they are simply saying that at that moment, according to current fashion, it happens to create a pleasant enough match. And for this reason it is just as foolish to reject theory altogether. It may not seem like it, but to say that a tie is harmonious is itself a theory. There are theories of colour that we carry around with us every day, without realizing it, perhaps in the form of a myth or superstition. Even when buying a tie.

PART THREE

Artefacts

170 ▸

171 ▾

NEWPORT JAZZ FESTIVAL / NEW YORK
1954-1978 / 25 SUMMERS OF JAZZ
JUNE 23-JULY 2

172

PANTONE®
456

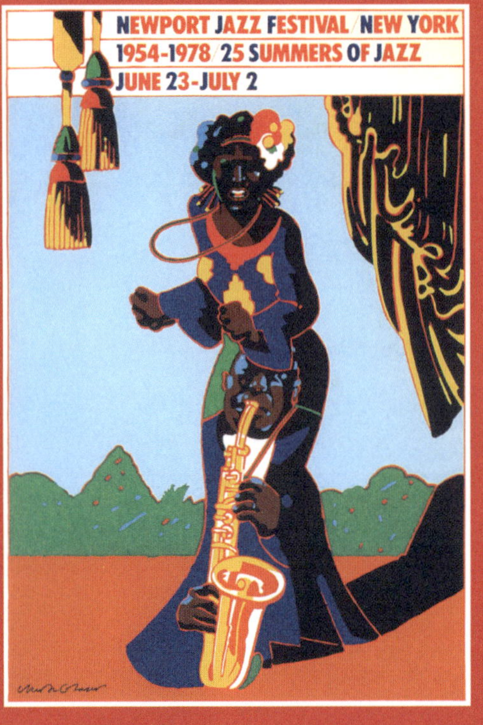

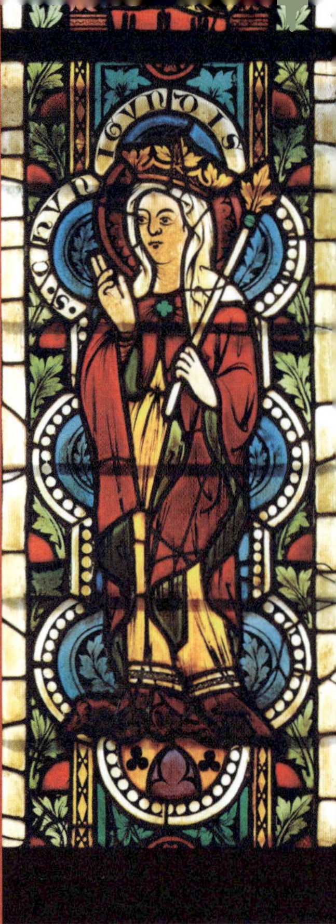

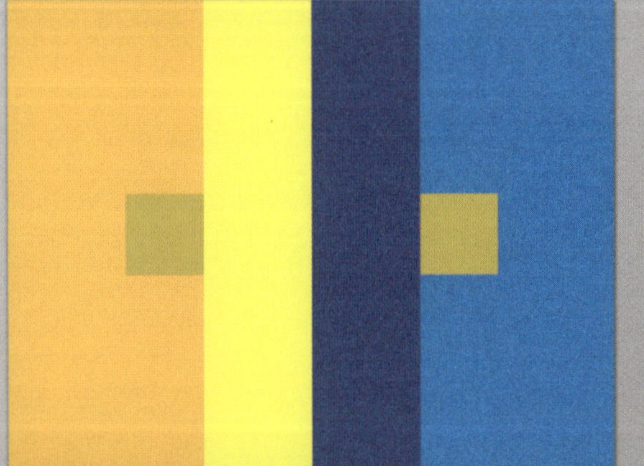

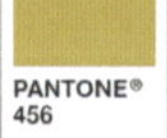

Neuronal Brown

How the Brain Constructs Colour

It is 1959, and it is a day like any other at Johns Hopkins School of Medicine in Baltimore. David Hubel and Torsten Wiesel, two brilliant young neurobiologists, are conducting research on vision; they implanted an electrode in a cat's brain in order to understand what happens when it looks at something. It appears to be a routine experiment, and they have no idea that what is about to happen will change the course of cognitive science and transform their lives, eventually winning them a Nobel Prize. Much of what we know about the psychological elaboration of colour we owe to their research. And to this cat.

BEAR, 2002

The feline brain, like the human one, is composed of neurons in communication with each other through channels – the 'nerves' – that deliver an electrical signal when they encounter a situation that demands it. Hubel and Wiesel set out to find out exactly what it is in a visual scenario that excites a particular neuron, and in order to answer this question they subject the immobilized and anesthetized cat to a projection of simple images on slides (a black dot on a white background, for instance) and measure the cellular response.

The behaviour of the cell turns out to be quite obscure. The neuron is unresponsive. It seems as if the black dot is of no interest. Then, without apparent reason, every so often it *fires*, which is to say it makes an electric response. Hubel and Wiesel change the slide: the neuron responds, and then is still again. They change to another: once again, the neuron makes its response and then goes quiet. The two scientists cannot grasp what is going on: it seems to obey no known rules. Then suddenly they understand.

The neuron is not excited by the drawing *on* the slide, but by the slide itself as a whole: its outline, in fact, when it is inserted into the projector, throws onto the screen a faint vertical shadow, and it is this moving line that the cat's cell likes. The consequences are enormous: Hubel and Wiesel have just discovered a neuron that is sensitive to vertical lines that move towards the right.

That the brain recognizes lines with a precise orientation should not astonish us: registering the contours of things is one of the most important factors in understanding reality. Until the 1950s, however, it was thought that visual neurons were all similar and that images would form in the mind after some mysterious overall process. Hubel and Wiesel demonstrate instead that the cells of the cortex are specialized: there are those that like vertical lines; others that respond to diagonal ones; some that are sensitive to subtle lines while others register bolder and more definite ones. Some love movement and ignore what is stationary; others react only to the colour red, while others still react to red only when placed on a green background. The two scientists have effectively discovered the elementary building blocks of vision.

HUBEL, 1989

By saying that the cell 'likes' a specific shape, that it either 'responds' or 'keeps quiet', we are of course using metaphors. The neuron does not have, in itself, a brain with which to think; it is simply excited or not when encountering

RAMACHANDRAN, 2004

a certain stimulus that corresponds to the task for which it has evolved. It is an incredible fact: a gelatinous mass of cells generates thought, actions and movement. A material substance produces something immaterial: the sensation of actually existing. But how this is possible is still a mystery. The analogy with the computer, which works according to a binary system, may help us to imagine this dense network of communication, but with the difference that our brain can also change: neurons are not limited to 'excitement' and 'inhibition' like an open or shut circuit. On the contrary, they are born and die – and their links, the so-called synapses, can come and go, be made and unmade.

PURGHÉ, 1999

The main lesson to be learned from this research is that the brain is interested not so much in *things* as in the *discontinuity* present within a scene: that is to say in edges, at boundaries, in every point at which there is light or colour contrasts. By virtue of containing more information than homogeneous surfaces, these liminal areas help us to decipher shapes and space.

But Hubel and Wiesel also open the field to a new conception of colour that changes the rules of the game. The most recent colour theories have been formulated in fact not by physics or art but by neurobiology.

BRUCE, 2003

According to current science, perceptions begin when light energy – having been reflected or transmitted from things – reaches the back of the eye, ending up in the retina, a membrane covered in cells whose role is to transform light into a nerve signal.[1] In 1959, following the intuition formulated by Thomas Young 150 years previously, there was the first confirmation that these cells, called 'cones', are of three different types, each one sensitive to a particular band of

[1] On the composition of the retina, see Appendix A 2.0.

INGS, 2008

wavelengths. Some are more involved with gradations of red, others with green and still others with blue. A cone, though sensitive to a determined zone of the spectrum, knows nothing about colour. Its task is merely to count the photons it is struck by, that is to say the particles that compose light: it measures in effect only the quantity of luminosity in the scene, as if thinking in black and white, before superior cells reconstruct the precise wavelength by making a comparison between the data from the three types of cone.

According to the classic model of Thomas Young – developed subsequently by Hermann von Helmholtz (1821–94) – colour vision is the product of a mixture of information from the three primary receptors. By the end of the nineteenth century, however, this theory was being challenged. If the cones are primarily sensitive to red, green and blue, how is it that yellow appears as a distinct and primary colour, and does not seem to be the fruit of a mixture of other colours?

FIORENTINI, 1995

This is the question raised by Ewald Hering (1834–1918). Hering, like Helmholtz, was a physiologist. Yellow, he tells us, is an elementary sensation and not one that is constructed: who on seeing yellow ever thinks that it consists of a mixture of green and red? It is therefore possible from a psychological point of view that there are actually four primaries rather than three, if by 'primary' we mean an elementary sensation in which we do not perceive the presence of other colours.

Hering arrives at this hypothesis fascinated by the way in which certain colours relate to each other: by the fact, for instance, that yellow can tend towards red or green, but that it is unthinkable for yellow to tend towards blue. He begins to suspect that the colours which are most distant from each other perceptually are in fact reciprocally antagonistic: yellow against blue, green against red.

RUNGE, 2008

It is an observation with some illustrious precedents.
Even Otto Runge, the first to have proposed a three-
dimensional chromatic model, in a letter to Goethe 79
maintains that to conceive of an orange that tends towards blue is like imagining a north wind blowing from the south-west. It simply makes no sense and it cannot happen. But unlike those Romantic thinkers who see in such an opposition a struggle between the principles of the universe, as a scientist Hering assumes instead that this is a typical characteristic of our nervous system.

In order to try to explain it, he imagines that the retina sends to the brain not the raw data from the three cones but a signal which has already been interpreted, and that in some way may restore to yellow its autonomy and primacy. Rather disappointingly for defenders of the tri-colour model, recent research in neuroscience would seem to confirm this. The retina, in fact, does not say to the brain 'here is yellow' but compares the data from the cones and provides a *binary* kind of information: 'since there is yellow here, there cannot be blue'. A chromatic sensation, in short, would always be communicated as a pair of opposites. But what is the point of such a cumbersome system as this?

The reason for this counterintuitive and apparently redundant condition is connected with the way in which nerve fibres function. In order to conserve metabolic energy, it is more efficient for cells to divide themselves into two groups: one that responds to the diminishing of a stimulus, and the other to its increase. There is a similar process behind our perception of heat or cold. We have two types of cutaneous receptors that respond to the increase or the reduction of temperature. And the mechanics of the body function in a basically similar manner. To move an arm we use two muscles: the biceps to flex and the triceps to extend it, and we cannot do these two things equally at once:

increasing the force of one requires a reduction of the other. This 'opposition' and contrast would therefore be the same language with which the nervous system allows us to think about the world. Just like heat and cold, the colours would be sensations always given to us in pairs[2] that cancel each other out. BILLOCK, 2010

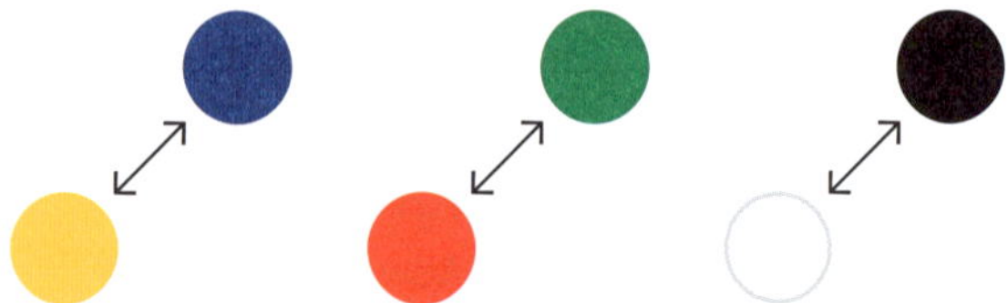

It is impossible to see a yellow that tends towards blue, above all because for the brain it would be a technical contradiction. While at the level of the retina the presence of the three types of cone lends support to the model of Young and Helmholtz, going up the scale of the organization of vision to signals involving opposites favours that of Hering. So for the mind the primary colours turn out to be six in number, organized into three pairs of opposites: yellow and blue, green and red, black and white. ZEKI, 2003

[2] Half a century after Hering, the Austrian philosopher Ludwig Wittgenstein addresses the question of colour opposites as a problem of relationships between logic and experience. Or rather, as Wittgenstein says, language allows us to formulate phrases such as 'red that tends towards yellow' and 'red that tends towards green', which are formally similar but have dissimilar relations with reality: the second speaks in fact of something that cannot be thought. If we turn from the logic of Wittgenstein to that of painting, this phrase can reveal an unexpected meaning. For example, among the tasks Paul Klee often gave to his students at the Bauhaus was that of constructing a chromatic scale, consisting of separate successive steps, that would go from red to green. WITTGENSTEIN, 1981

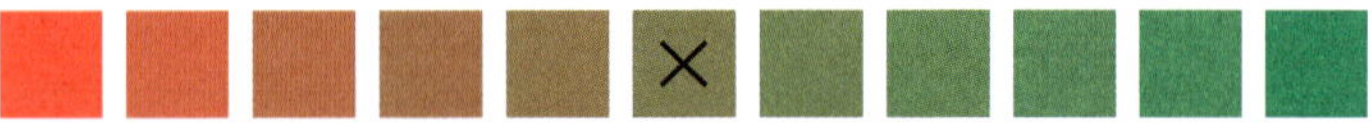

At the midpoint of this progression a median tint appears, called 'military green' (or khaki) and not 'military red', because we feel it is more akin to green – which is why it is also linked to camouflage. With this scale the phrase 'green that tends towards red' therefore has meaning: even if it does not signify what we are able to see we can think of it as part of a sequence/process.

To be clear, when we call red a 'psychological primary', we are not talking about a precise red such as the one that comes out of a tube of paint. And when we talk of an 'opposed signal' for green–red or for yellow–blue, we are not referring to circumscribed colours but to ranges that belong to what for the brain is the idea of yellowness or blueness.

ONIANS, 2008

On the level of visual communication, the system of signals of opposites explains why colour contrasts are so significant, and why artists have always been fascinated by complementarity between colours. After two centuries in which the domination of physics had pushed Goethe into a corner, we find that neuroscience is now redeeming his approach to colour: the yellow and blue worn by the young Werther is not a scientifically unfounded metaphor. It represents, on the contrary and ahead of its time, an image that synthesizes in a narrative mode the way our brains actually process colour. In the end, this is not such an astonishing outcome, given that metaphors are also products of the human mind and so cannot fail to reflect it in some way.

BERTAGNA, 2013

Seeing colour is not a mere registration of physical data. It is also a construction. Colour occurs only in our heads,[3] so much so that many of the creatures that live alongside us do not share our most familiar sensations: for them they do not even exist. Cats and dogs do not have the faintest idea of what red is. Where I see red, my cat sees something else, perhaps something more similar to our yellow. To say nothing of bees, which see ultraviolet rays – wavelengths that are invisible to us. It is the brain that constructs, starting from the same physical data, the experience of colour as we know it.

[3] For the same reasons physics can measure temperature but not the heat which is the psychological way in which an organism internally represents and experiences an external condition.

It is probable that the primordial creatures we have descended from had only one kind of receptor, allowing them
to distinguish light from dark. Then, at a certain point,
a differentiation occurred that gave us the ability to tell
first blue from yellow and then green from red. One of the BRESSAN, 2007
possible explanations for this is that it would have been
advantageous to distinguish ripe, red fruits among green
undergrowth, and it is clear that in a coloured habitat it is
much easier to recognize and find things to eat than in a
173 monochrome one. Looking at an image reflected in water, BERTAGNA, 2013
for example, we see that it is easier to make out what it
represents if there are variations in colour, compared to
seeing it in black and white. It is such a banal concept as
to have been taken for granted, but colour really does represent an efficient way of entering into a relationship with
the world.

This process is also a construction for a different reason:
one of the fundamental peculiarities of the mind is the way FIORENTINI, 1995
in which it perceives the characteristics of things as stable,
even when they are nothing of the sort. On our planet the
light changes constantly: white by day, red at sunset, grey
in bad weather. Yet a white sheet appears white whether it
is noon or it is sunset, when it reflects much more red light.[4]
If vision depended only on wavelengths, the world would
be a difficult place to navigate, and colour would stop being useful to recognize reality by. Instead the sheet is more
or less always white thanks to a mechanism that is one of
the most brilliant that has been put in place by evolution:

[4] It is not true, however, that we are trained to observe the light closely and critically, like a professional photographer. It is no accident that when we look at photographs or films we notice that the light source always has a chromatic dominant: with incandescent lamps, white becomes reddish, whereas with a flash it becomes bluish. After all, to realize how orange the light from lamps is, we only need to look at our rooms at night from the street, in contrast to the cold blues of outside.

'chromatic constancy', the capacity that also allows monkeys to recognize ripe fruit regardless of the light.[5]

ZEKI, 1993

To construct this constancy there is a dedicated area of our cerebral cortex, situated more or less above the nape of the neck and called V4. Processing the data received from 182
the retina, it compares what happens at a given point in a scene with what happens next to it, making up a general idea of the whole freed from variables such as changes of light. The retina, limited to measuring, only sees the sheet of paper at sunset in its exact spectral composition, that is to say as red. The cells of V4, on the other hand, by comparing adjacent points, 'understands' that since the whole scene is illuminated in red, then perhaps the paper (which is the lightest thing there) is white. In other words: whereas the cones are slaves to wavelengths, the neurons of V4 are free to construct that stability or constancy of the real that allows us to use it.[6]

FRISBY, 2010

GREGORY, 1997

In this sense, human perception is always a construction: because we do not limit ourselves to measuring wavelengths but see, or rather constantly process and elaborate, the relations between them. The most fascinating aspect of this is that such *alteration* of physical data is an exquisitely human necessity, given that in reality there is next to nothing that requires it. Paradoxically, we might say that the world does not even suspect that we see it in this way.

The visual cortex does something more besides. The mechanisms of comparing from point to point, as well as guaranteeing

[5] Chromatic constancy requires less than twenty-five milliseconds to be operational: when you turn on an incandescent light, white walls do not appear yellow and then gradually become clearer, they look immediately white, without needing to think about it.

[6] The letter *V* stands for 'vision' and it is the acronym that precedes designations of all areas involved in seeing. The most important studies on the cerebral cortex V4 and its nomenclature have been conducted by Semir Zeki, one of the contemporary neurobiologists most focused upon visual questions (see Appendix A 2.2 and 2.4).

chromatic constancy, also allow us to see some colours that are not contained within the rainbow, such as browns and greys. A little experiment may help to explain how this happens.

174 Let's imagine that we are in a dark room. By means of a projector containing a coloured filter, we project onto the wall a yellow circle using a 100-watt lamp. The space will appear dark except for this disc of lovely vivid yellow. After a few seconds, we turn off the projector and switch on another with the same yellow filter but with a 200-watt lamp, thus doubling the power. Once again everything will be in darkness except for a yellow circle that is a little brighter than the previous one. There is nothing strange about this so far. If we turn on the two projectors at the same time, however, then two discs will appear in different colours – one yellow and the other brown. The less luminous one is interpreted by the brain as a different, much darker colour, even though they are both of the same wavelength.

LAND, 1971

Brown is ultimately nothing more than a yellow seen next to surfaces that are brighter than it is. It is no coincidence that Young's tri-colour theory was unable to explain how it was formed, because brown is not a colour that depends on measurements from the retina, it is a kind of spatial contrast elaborated by the cortex. For the eye, brown does not even exist. It is a construction that takes place only in the brain. It is therefore impossible to project a brown disc in complete darkness: its light, however weak, will always seem yellow to us.[7] But in life we rarely find ourselves dealing with isolated colours: what we almost always see are chromatic neighbours.[8]

BRESSAN, 2007

[7] The same goes for grey, which is a white less luminous than the one it is next to.

[8] If we look at a homogeneous brown background on a monitor in a dark room it

173

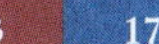

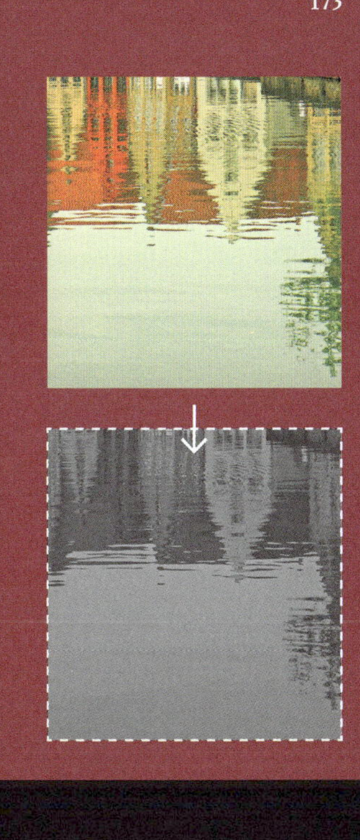

174

PHASE I
ONE PROJECTOR TURNED ON

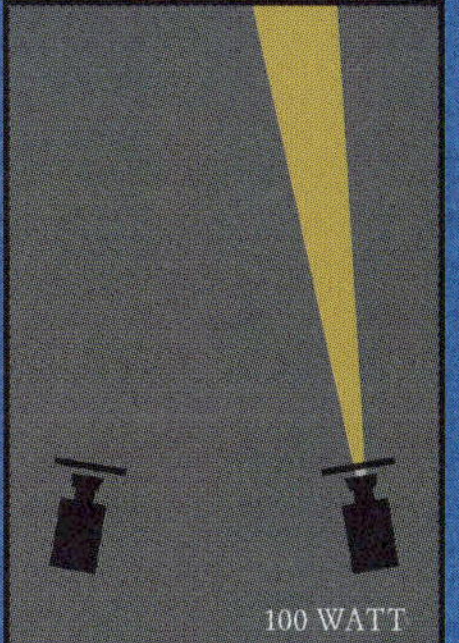

PHASE II
TWO PROJECTORS TURNED ON

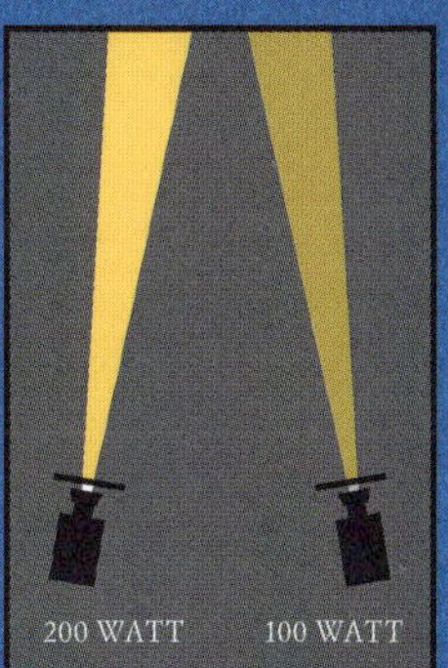

PERCEPTION

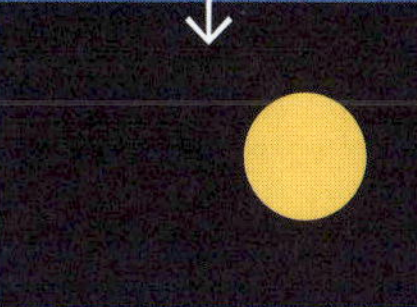

A yellow disc on the right

PERCEPTION

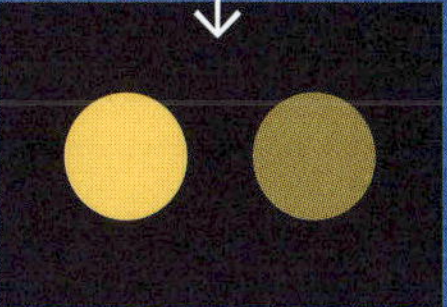

By contrast the disc now appears brown

175

Munkler-White Effect

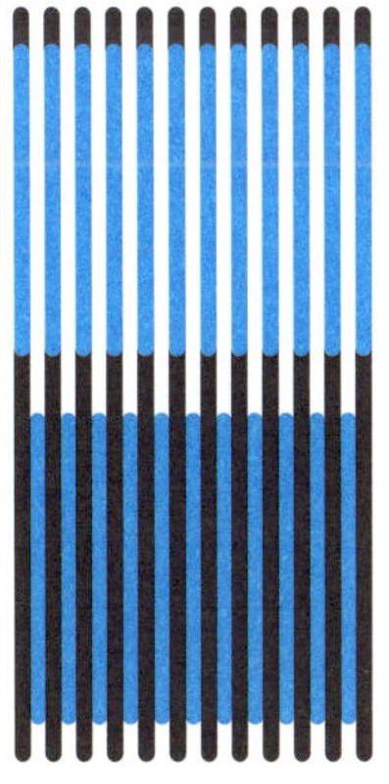

176

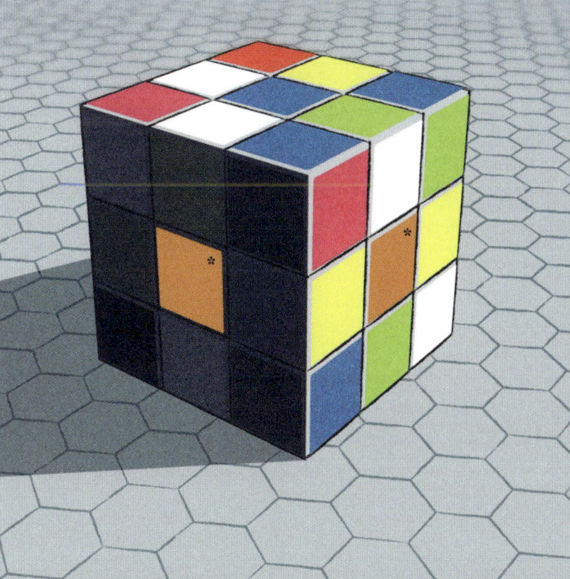

HORNUNG, 2005

The interpretation of the world through such comparisons implies that colours never count as things in themselves: they exist only relative to their context. In
176 the Rubik's cube in Figure 176, for example, the two small squares indicated with an asterisk are of exactly the same colour, but since they are surrounded by tones which are respectively darker or lighter than they are, this causes them to appear orange in the first case and in the other brown. It is an extreme example of that simultaneous contrast that Chevreul discovered during his time at the Gobelins factory, and from which he learned that the influence of colours upon each other is a basic condition of visual languages. The two squares, which to a spectrophotometer are identical, appear astonishingly dissimilar to
our eye. In common parlance, phenomena of this type are called 'optical illusions', yet, as we have shown, it is clear how imprecise a definition this is, given that we are not talking about exceptions to the rule but examples of the usual way in which our mind works.

GREGORY, 1980

The game of making the same colour appear as if it were two different ones became a classic teaching aid for Josef Albers (1888–1976), first at the Bauhaus, then at Yale, during a lecturing career spanning three decades. Born in Germany but settled in the United States, Albers proposes a logic and a didactics of colour that are among the most original of the twentieth century.[9] He rejects all geometrical models,

very soon appears to be yellow. Only the colours of the spectrum and the violets can be seen in isolation, the other colours can only be seen in a context (see Appendix A 4.0 and 4.1).

[9] Albers enters the Weimar Bauhaus in 1920 and studies under Itten's guidance, but already in 1923 Walter Gropius, the director of the school, entrusts him with the preparatory craftsmanship workshop, promoting him to a lectureship in 1925. Here he finds himself collaborating with the likes of Oskar Schlemmer, Wassily Kandinsky and Paul Klee. With the closure of the Bauhaus by the Nazis in 1933, Albers emigrates to the United States and works first at Black Mountain College and finally at Yale. The

circles, diagrams and laws of mixing, deeming them to be far too abstract. He is convinced that colour should be used, looked at and compared if it is to be truly understood. This is why he proposes the use of coloured cards to see how they react with each other in concrete terms. He reacts, in other words, to the position of his teachers, including Itten, with rigorous empiricism.

In Figure 172 we can see a reconstruction of one of 172
his now classic exercises: a strip of ochre card placed against a background that is half blue and half orange (and covered by two bands, one yellow and one blue) results in a yellowish or brownish tone to the ochre, according to context, like we saw with the Rubik's cube. Albers' work is based around exercises aimed at training the eye. In this way, in advance of neuroscience, he shows there are no isolated colours in our perception, only interactions between them. The concepts of hue, tone and saturation, or the laws of harmony that are so dear to classic colour theory and teaching, seem useful for naming colours but not for actually seeing them in context. So the presumed accuracies of Munsell's and Pantone's systems crumble before the phenomenon of simultaneous contrast. As our preceding example elegantly proves, Pantone 456 lets us see two colours that are different according to what we place around them, meaning that this label is always a little detached from actual experience.[10]

ALBERS, 2005

fruit of these years of teaching is *Interaction of Color* (1963), a book destined to be enormously successful – and as influential as Itten's, though very different in conception.

[10] Certain considerations pose a more general question that cannot be answered within a unified theory of colour because every system only takes account of one of the many possible ways in which we can think about or use colour: Pantone is useful in graphic design but not in cosmetics, which is based exclusively on simultaneous contrasts. In the same way Itten can be illuminating with regard to paintings but makes no sense for digital systems. It is therefore a question of asking ourselves what the various theories can be useful for, not of selecting the one that is 'true'. Itten allows us to reason about colour, Munsell to name it – but we need to recognize that only Albers has allowed us to really see it.

We need only look at the examples in the figure below to see how obvious this is: FEISNER, 2001

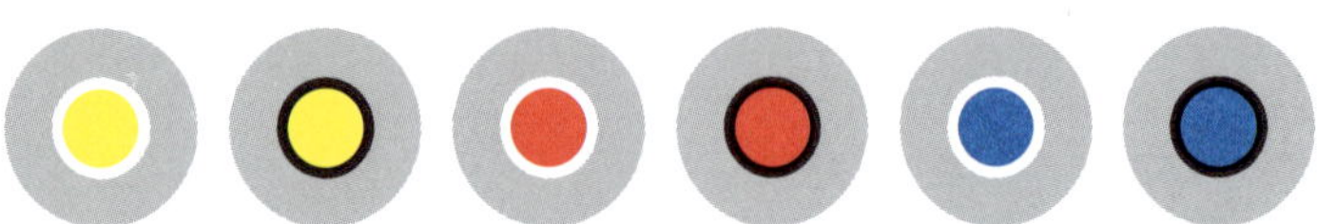

the colours ringed with black appear darker and more intense than those outlined in white, as happens with the
175 so-called Munker–White illusion, in which blue lines appear GREGORY, 2010
darker or lighter depending on the grid that frames them.

Effects of this type have always determined precise aesthetic qualities in art and design. The black outline, for
170 instance, is a stylistic given for all Gothic windows: a structural condition, a necessary technique that brings with it
perceptual consequences that are specific and characteristic, and not found in other visual languages. Without that
black line, the windows would appear pale, washed out,
devoid of the decisive prominence that makes the colours
shine, each one in its own absolute and potent universe.

A device of this kind can also be used in an even more
sophisticated and unusual way. In a famous poster designed
171 by Milton Glaser (b. 1929) for the Newport Jazz Festival,
the entire drawing uses a red outline that intermittently alters our perception of the colours, as if the lead of a
hypothetical window had become incandescent. The result,
partly in line with the taste for psychedelic colours, is that
the image is made vibrant, unstable, and the rhythmical
and musical aspect of the subject amplified. It is thanks
to this treatment that the central figure seems to move,
dance, stand out from the poster as if she were alive. It is
no accident that images such as this should appear in the
1970s, an era in which there is a fashion for psychotropic

drugs, and studies of perception attract unprecedented popular interest.

Yet artists have always been aware of colour effects similar to these. Legend has it that in the studio of Titian, in order to demonstrate skill as a colourist, it was necessary to make Venetian red appear to be vermillion, applying what would three centuries later become known as simultaneous contrast. Already in the sixteenth century, one had to be preoccupied not by colours in themselves so much as how they were perceived. Three centuries later, Delacroix boasts that he can paint the skin of a nymph even with mud, as long as he can place around it all of the colours that he likes. And even Turner seems to suggest to the canvas: 'Be still, yellow stain, until I let you appear white'. But it took years, and the sacrifice of that poor cat, to begin to understand why things were really like this.

DI NAPOLI, 2006

GAGE, 2006

INDIANA JONES
HARRISON FORD
"INDIANA JONES AND THE TEMPLE OF DOOM"
KATE CAPSHAW · AMRISH PURI
ROSHAN SETH · PHILIP STONE · KE HUY QUAN
GEORGE LUCAS · FRANK MARSHALL
KATHLEEN KENNEDY · JOHN WILLIAMS
WILLARD HUYCK & GLORIA KATZ
GEORGE LUCAS · ROBERT WATTS
STEVEN SPIELBERG
Novela publicada por Editorial Planeta
Banda Sonora en Discos y Cassettes POLYDOR
UNA PELICULA PARAMOUNT
177

178

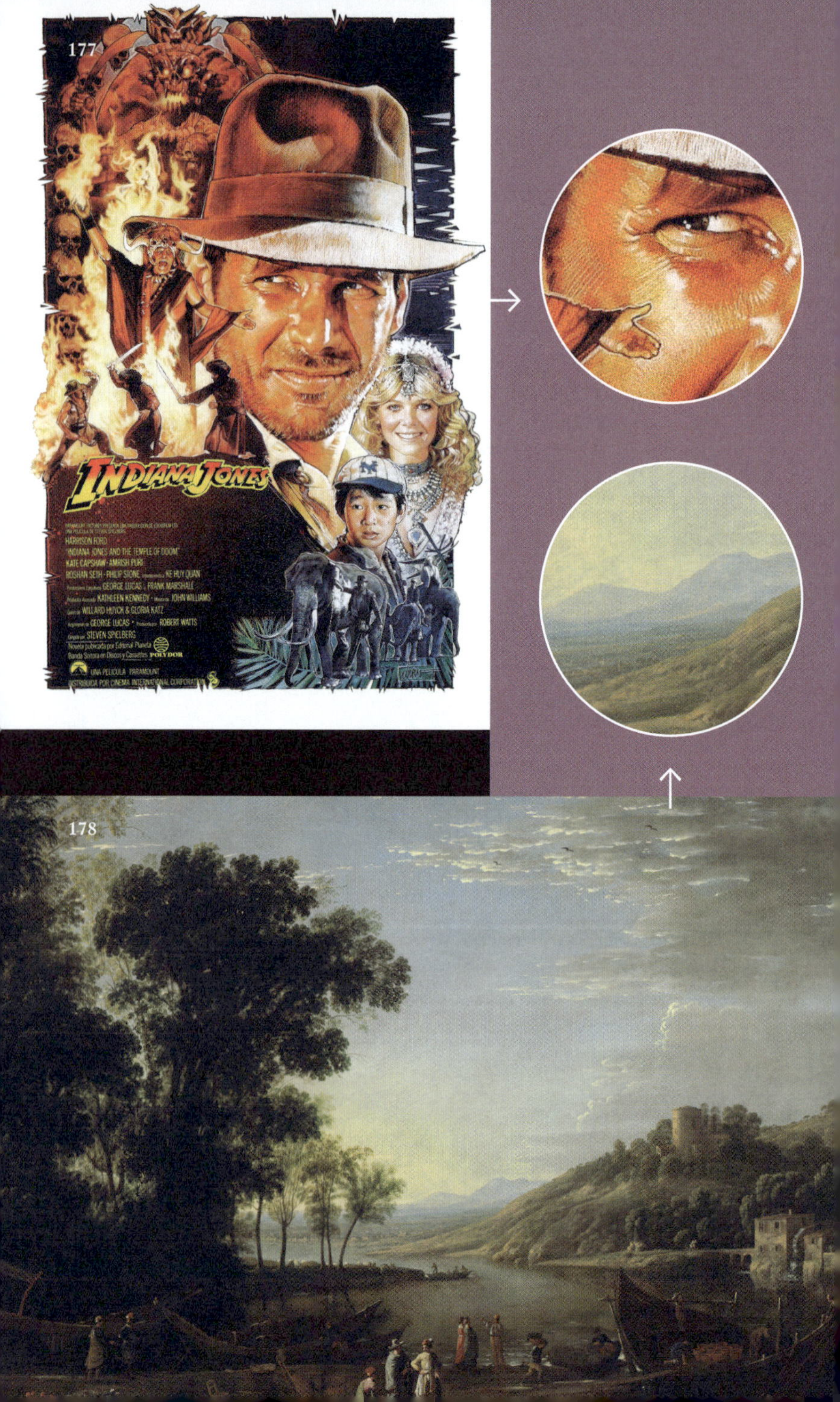

Split Purple

Luminosity and Colour

In the spring of 1900, while the great and the good gathered in Paris for the Universal Exhibition, my great-grandfather moved to Rome from a small village in Abruzzo. He had been appointed as a medical officer in the nascent working-class district bordering Aventino, thanks to the considerable fame he had achieved in his native village. It was said, in fact, that he was the first person from Abruzzo to have carried out an operation on the brain (although nobody ever ventured to ask if the patient had survived). One of my great-grandfather's many stories was about his friend who could not see colours – to him, the world appeared in black and white, like 'the pictures at the cinema'.

I have always attributed these stories to the romantic bent of my mother's side of the family, and I never really believed them. Until some years ago I came across a book by Oliver Sacks and started reading about the case of Jonathan I., a man who could not see colours.[1] The medical term for such a condition is achromatopsia, and in the case of Sacks's patient the cause was not so much a congenital defect as the consequence of carbon monoxide poisoning.

SACKS, 1998

[1] 'The Case of the Colour-Blind Painter', in Oliver Sacks, *An Anthropologist on Mars: Seven Paradoxical Tales*.

Having previously experienced colour, Jonathan lived in a state of perpetual regret and prostration, so much so that he was forced to eat and drink only white or black foodstuffs and beverages – such as coffee, yoghurt, rice and olives – since everything else appeared greyish and repellent. Even sexual intercourse had become peculiarly unpleasant, since he seemed to be touching dead, clay-like flesh. Until finally, after a few years, he realized that he was no longer able to even think about colour.

SACKS, 2004

Cases of sensory deprivation have been a poignant but invaluable resource for understanding the functioning of the mind. Jonathan's story shows how the brain works in modules, and how perception does not cease even if one of these stops working. But it also tells us that information about light and colour travels on parallel tracks, even if we experience them as a single thing. Everyone evaluates the world in black and white in a manner similar to Sacks's patient, except that we do not realize it. This is why black and white movies are comprehensible, because even the healthy brain reasons in black and white, at least in part.[2]

ZEKI, 1993

ZEKI, 2003

According to neurobiologists, achromatopsia, a kind of suppression of an aspect of vision but not of sight itself, would depend on cortical and not retinal damage. And given that, as we have already seen, the construction of colour appears in a designated area, it is plausible that the visual information processed by the brain uses at least two channels: this is why the interruption of the functioning of one does not prevent the other from continuing to 'see'. These two paths were named by neuroscientists the way of 'what' and the way of 'where': the first would provide

[2] All mammals have an area that processes luminosity, but only the primates have an area for colour.

LIVINGSTONE, 2002

information regarding shape, the identity of objects and colour, while the other would process space and our movement in an environment based only on the quantity of light, which is to say thinking in greyscale.

The reason why we have two distinct channels is due to an evolutionary necessity: a colour system would have been added to a much more ancient brain that was exclusively sensitive to luminosity and to movement, since in general it is easier for biology to construct new structures upon already existing ones.[3] This results in the fact that if I place two colours of the same luminosity one on top of the other – such as a red text on a green background – I obtain a flickering effect:

HUBEL, 1988

Images in colour	Equivalent in black and white
Flickering	
Stability	Stability

This happens because, whereas the 'what' channel identifies the writing, the 'where', being blind to colour, sees only a homogeneous surface all of the same grey. In other words, the 'what' identifies the what, but the 'where' does

[3] The study of the chromatic tasks of the two channels was advanced by David Hubel and Margaret Livingstone. This theory has provoked a debate, and many scientists have deemed it to be excessively simplistic. An alternative was proposed by Mel Goodale and David Milner in 1995: the 'recent' channel would be occupied with representation of the world with regard to things and to space, whilst the 'ancient' one would be tasked with analysing our position moment by moment, on the basis of the visual input received from outside.

not know where it is. The flickering effect is the brain's reply to signals that are apparently in contradiction with each other.

This condition leads to significant consequences in the perception of art and design. An artistic use of colours of the same luminosity can be found in psychedelic graphics of the sixties and seventies, where the fluctuating juxtaposition of throbbing, harsh colours mimics HUXLEY, 1986
the effects produced by psychotropic drugs, according to the idea that taking mescaline or LSD produces in some subjects the sensation of seeing new and amazing colours.

179 Claude Monet's *Impression, Sunrise* (1872), the painting that gave us the word Impressionism, uses this effect
differently. The orange sun on a blue-grey background LIVINGSTONE, 2002
is painted with a vibrant but dark hue, of the same luminosity as the sky. In this case too, this characteristic deceives the brain: not being able to establish the exact spatial position of the sun, it ends up seeing it shine with an oscillating shimmer. Before two fields of equal luminosity, the depth disappears, though this time the break between the 'what' and the 'where' serves to create not an hallucinatory effect but a realistic one.

With a few exceptions, the value of luminosity for a SOLSO, 1996
scene is always more important for the brain than colour. Chiaroscuro is the element that before anything else helps us to understand reality. This is why bright contrasts appear more pleasant to us even in geometric
181A,B or abstract designs: if we look at Figures 181A and 181B,
we notice that the first, in which every leaf has a tonal GREGORY, 1980
value different from the others, is more pleasing inasmuch as it is easier to decipher. After all, we have not evolved in order to appreciate art but to use the world,

179

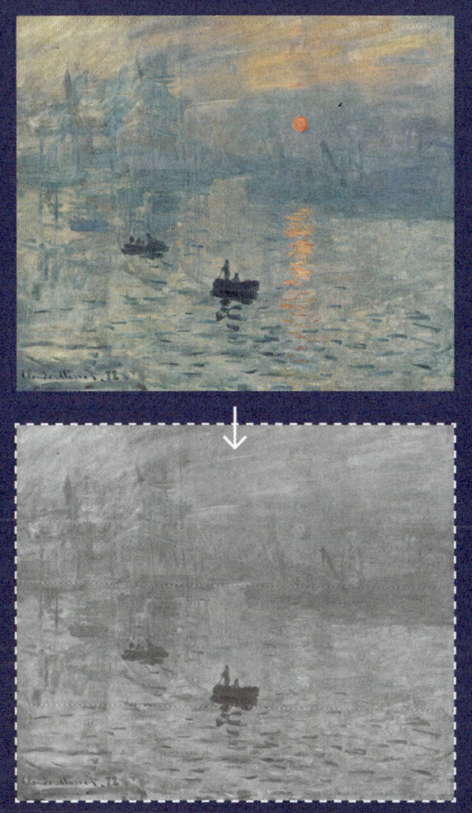

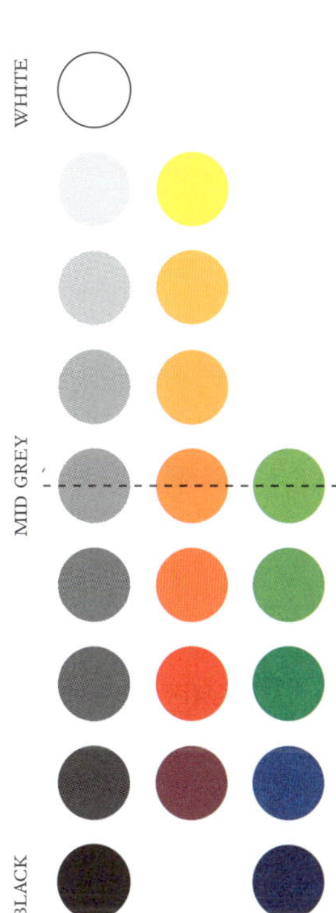

180 Luminosity values of shades

181A

181B

182 Cross-section of the brain

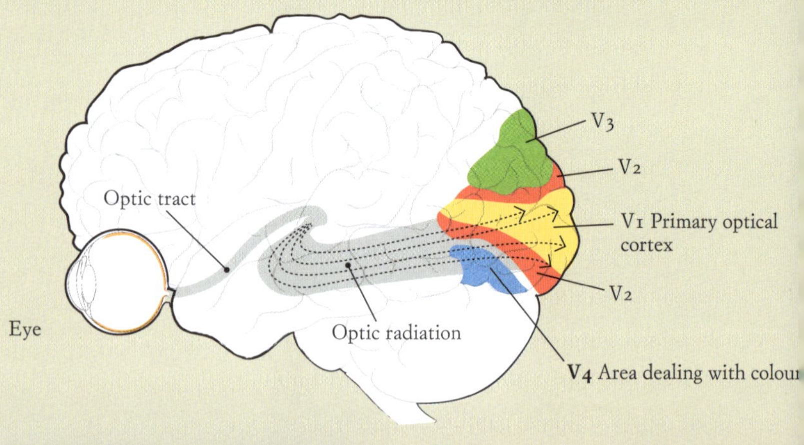

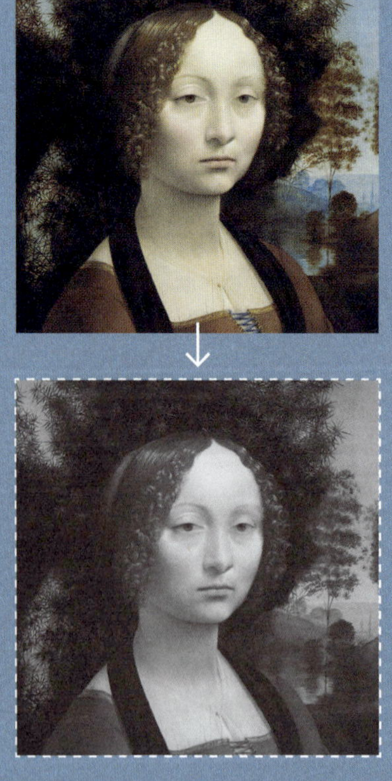

183

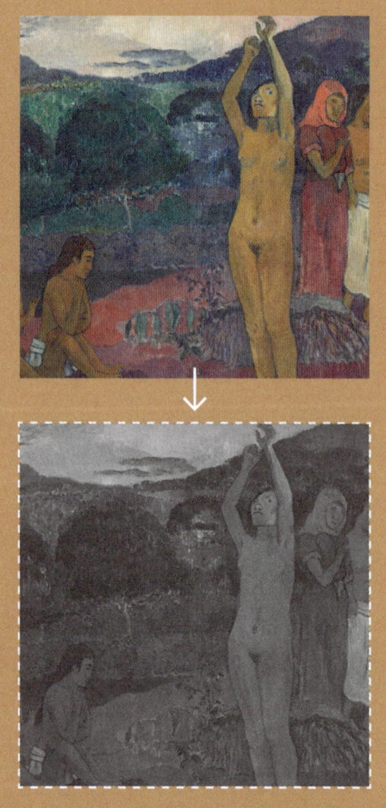

184

KANIZSA, 1985 and hence it is normal that what we find most attractive in artificial images is what is less ambiguous in real life.[4]

In the visual arts, luminosity and colour have always been the pillars of figurative composition, and images
HORNUNG, 2005 present different degrees of realism according to which of these two aspects is dominant. There are works, such as those of Caravaggio, in which light is a 'quality of space'; others in which the representation appears solid and credible thanks to chiaroscuro; still others in which the light is a 'quality of colour', as in Byzantine mosaics, the vi-
STOICHITA, 2000 vacity of Fauvism, Gothic windows or flat colour comics. Here colours may be more or less bright, but there is no chiaroscuro or relief, the light is not used to confer three-dimensionality or illusionism.

In order to understand these mechanisms, which are as
expressive as they are structural, we can conduct a simple
experiment. If we convert a portrait by Leonardo da Vinci 183
into black and white, the plastic masses remain legible and
space remains intact in its dimensions. If we do the same
with a Gauguin painting, there is an implosion and we strug- 184
gle to make out the shapes. This game reveals how different
types of figurative style frequently involve different modes
of perception. When the Fauves declare that they want the
ZEKI, 2003 liberation of colour, they are saying something which is extremely precise in neuroscientific terms, even if they are not aware of it. The liberation of which they speak is the privileging of chromatic aspects over spatial ones, the mental separation of the 'what' from the 'where', of the type of colour from the amount of light it reflects.

The split between chromatic and tonal qualities is in fact something that painters have always had to consider when

[4] This is what the Gestalt school of psychology calls 'good form' – always the easiest, most decipherable, immediately apparent one.

depicting the realistic aspects of the world, or negating them. If you watch an artist or designer drawing from life, you will notice that every so often they will squint, as if trying to concentrate harder. What would look to an external observer like a tic is in reality a very useful tactic, because it allows the partial suppression of chromatic information in order to concentrate only on the luminous aspects of a subject. It is an old trick of the trade, but anyone who tries to draw from life will find themselves doing it naturally. To divide tone and colour is basically a highly useful verification tool: if an image continues to work when the chromatic information is suppressed, it is a good sign that the composition will be sound.

FALCINELLI, 2011

DI NAPOLI, 2004

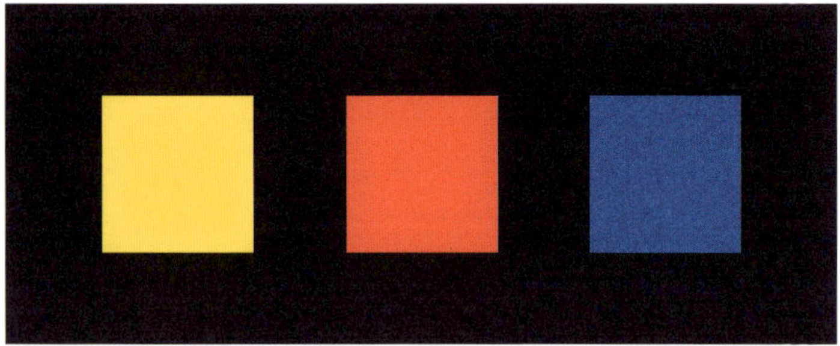

There are other aspects of coloured surfaces, however, that have to do broadly with spatial perception: some colours that seem to come forward, while others seem to recede, even if they are not representing things that are actually in front or behind, and even if they are just patches of colour. This effect depends in the first place upon the difference in brightness between colours and the background on which they are placed – with yellow seeming to advance, for instance, when placed against a black background, more than blue does on the same background because the difference

ARNHEIM, 1997

PURGHÉ, 1999

in light between yellow and black is greater than that between black and blue.

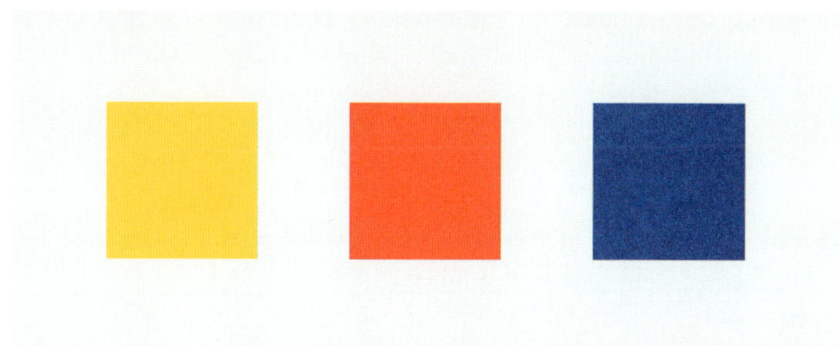

And vice versa, it is blue that 'comes towards us' if placed on a light background.[5] There is more. Even the intensity of the colours, their luminosity and solidity, suggests precise spatial qualities. In the figure below for example:

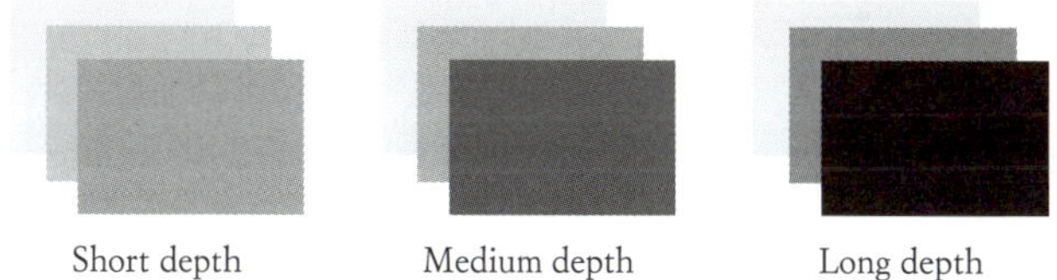

we notice how by increasing the differencc in luminosity between rectangles we also increase the perceived depth, even if the distance used between them is the same.

The same thing can be seen happening, and for similar reasons, in this other figure:

[5] To this we can add that, since our green and red cones are more numerous than those of blue, then red, green and yellow seem to come more readily towards us – because we have more receptors involved in processing them (see Appendix A 8.0).

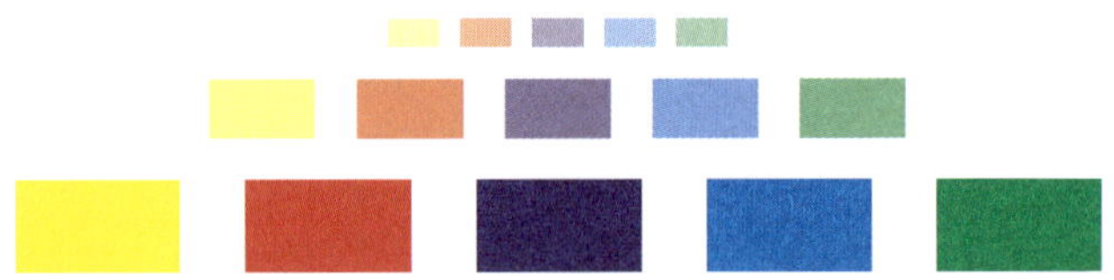

We can see how reducing the strength (saturation) of a colour seems to increase the distance between the pieces. Our mind immediately interprets the tonal difference in spatial terms, since it knows (it has already learned) that things get paler with distance – less defined and less colourful due to the interposition of atmospheric dust.

GOMBRICH, 2008

These diagrams very effectively demonstrate the mechanism that makes a great deal of landscape painting work. We are talking about an effect already known about in the ancient world, to the extent that Ptolemy in the second century AD affirms that when painters of architecture want to show the colours of distant things they use 'veils of air'. Sixteen centuries later, Leonardo da Vinci names this artifice 'atmospheric perspective' and far prefers it to geometric perspective, in which the lines of the drawing are visible and delineated as in the work of Piero della Francesca or Paolo Uccello. There is a marvellous example of this in the countryside depicted behind the Mona Lisa: the background darkens by degrees as it gets gradually further from us, whereas in medieval landscapes everything is in focus, sharply defined and saturated with colour.

TOLOMEO, 1885

ARGAN, 1961

In our experience, however, distant things appear to be not only 'veiled' but bluer as well, because the atmospheric diffusion of short wavelengths of blues and violets is greater compared to the long ones of reds. This is an observation that seventeenth-century painting – especially Flemish painting – took to extreme stylistic lengths.

Claude Lorrain (1600–1682), a master of this technique, 178
paints mountains a definite blue. By sublimating it in this 185
way, art turns a physical fact into an autonomous and expressive sign.[6]

TORNQUIST, 2001

Luminosity is, more generally, a precise quality that we
associate with some colours. Certain colours inevitably
seem much clearer than others: yellow is always luminous 180
and violet is always darker. A non-luminous yellow is unthinkable; it would immediately become brown, which is to say something different altogether.[7]

As we have already seen, Girolamo Cardano was the first to maintain that every colour has an intrinsic brightness that can be numerically defined. This idea will become ever more central in the discourse of those artists, especially from the beginning of the sixteenth century, who begin to study the relations that each colour establishes with the others next to it, precisely on the basis of their apparent luminosity. In the eighteenth century, Giambattista Tiepolo (1696–1770), an artist supersensitive to the modulation of colours, brings this principle to maturity, proposing a new way of conceiving colour that will have an important influence on modern illustration. Given that the illusion of volume depends on chiaroscuro and not on colour, Tiepolo argues, it is not necessary to make black or brown shadows as Leonardo does – you can use any colour, even orange, blue or green, just as long as it is darker than the parts

[6] Outside of pictures as well, aerial perspective provides information on distances: with a clear sky the trees in a landscape appear closer than when there is haze, and in fact in the mountains where the air is clear the space seems much more compressed and close compared to in the city where the air is polluted.

[7] See Appendix A 8.0.

in light. Look, for instance, at the three cubes represented below:

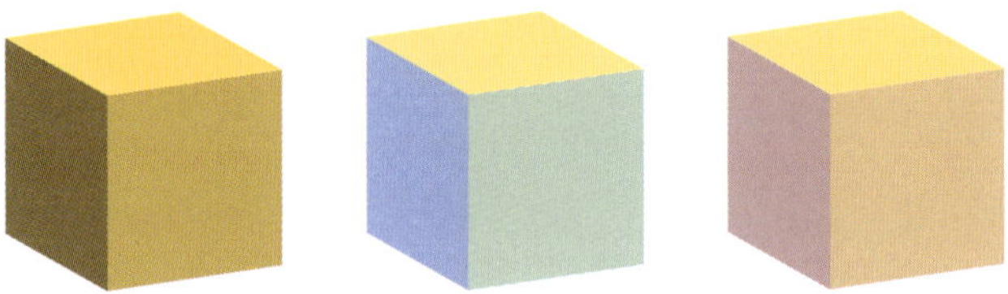

They all appear credible from a volumetric point of view because the contrast between light and dark is realistic, even if the second and third use less traditional colours.

Tiepolo achieves his most fascinating effect by lighten- CALASSO, 2006
186 ing shadows to the maximum, until they are filled with
echoes of the colours around them – an innovation that
was enthusiastically received by his contemporaries, who
named it 'split colour', in reference to the fact that a white ALPERS, 1996
object next to a red one ends up being reddish because red
'splits' across what happens to be next to it.

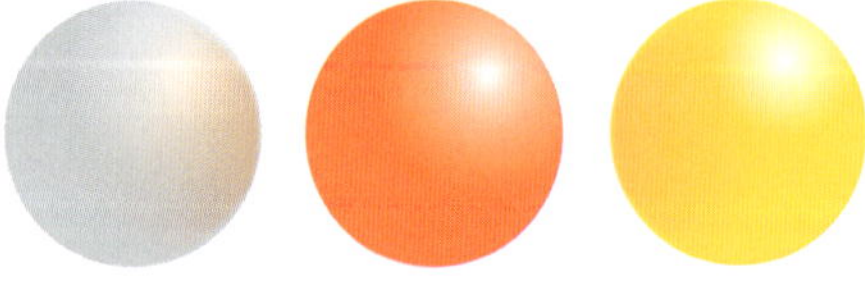

It's an unremarkable fact for those, like us, who are used to photography, but one which nobody had ever painted before the eighteenth century.

This insight is readily appropriated by artists of the nineteenth century, and becomes the pillar of twentieth-century American figurative painting, from Edward Hopper to Norman Rockwell. It is no accident that we encounter

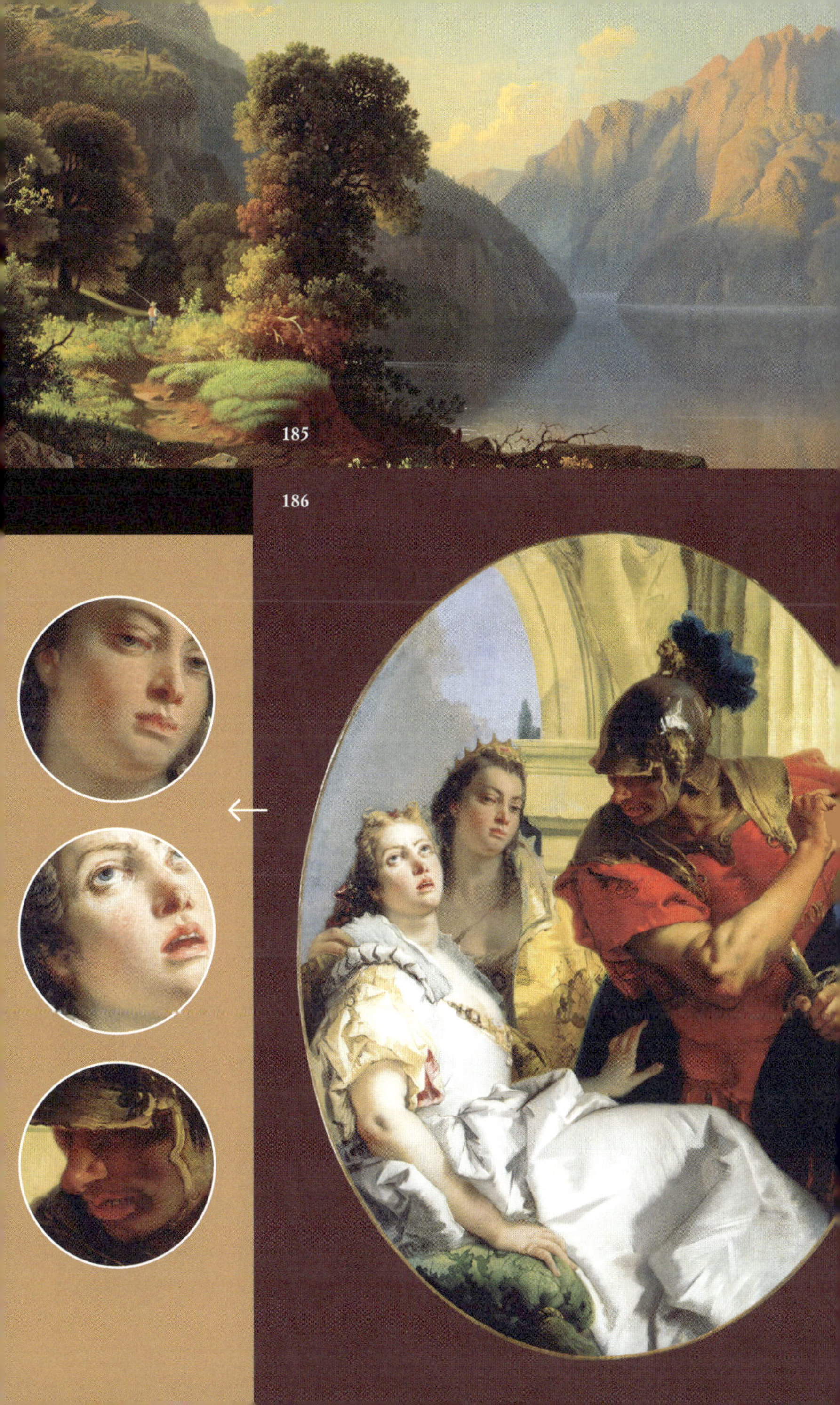
185
186

187

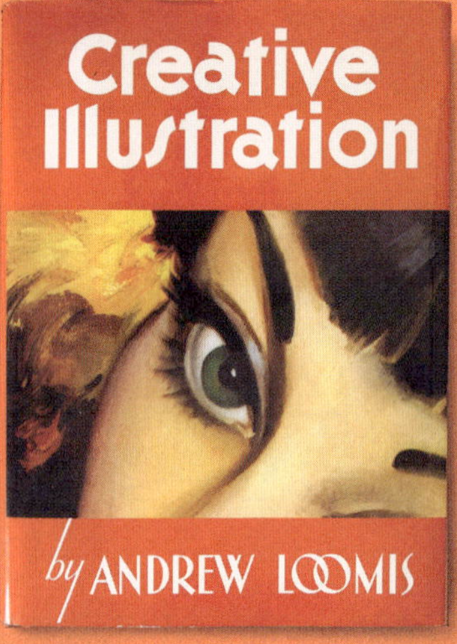

186

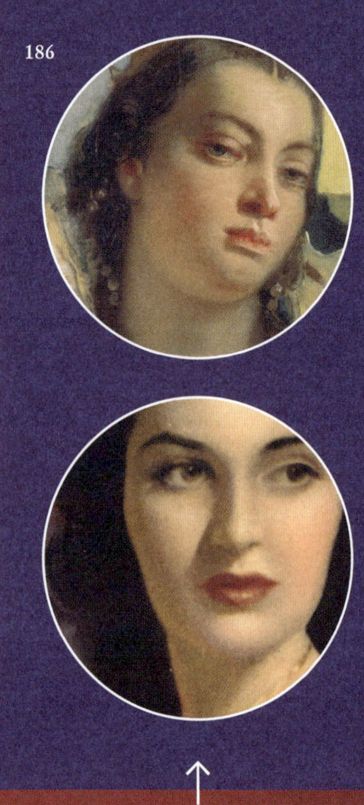

188

TONING THE SPECTRUM OR PALETTE

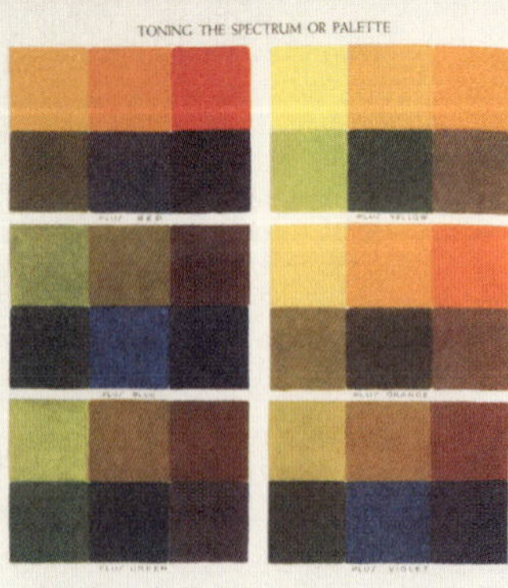

Here is another way to relate all the colors of your palette. Choose one color of the spectrum. Mix some of it into every other color. You can make a very delicate mixture, or up to about one-third. The more you add, the more you are cutting down the brilliancy of all the colors which normally contain none of the color you are adding. But your color will all retain its "identity," though brought into closer harmony. The above are about the limit of mixture. Note in each group one color stays pure, and so will the colors which contain the toning color. The opposite colors change. I have painted four heads in four schemes to show that it is possible to paint flesh in any influence. Stick to your scheme when you start it. When it's all done, you may add a touch or two of pure color outside the scheme if you are so tempted. But more often you will like it better as it was. Very beautiful color may be arrived at in this manner. My examples are only a hint of its possibilities.

156

FOUR SUBJECTS IN "TONED COLOR"

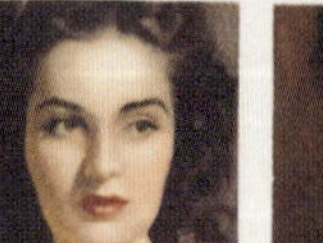

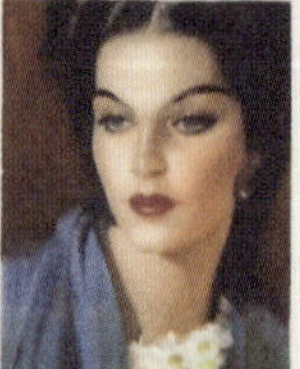

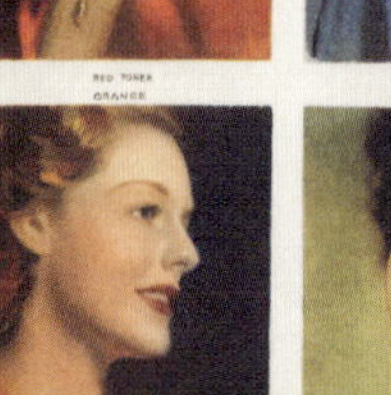

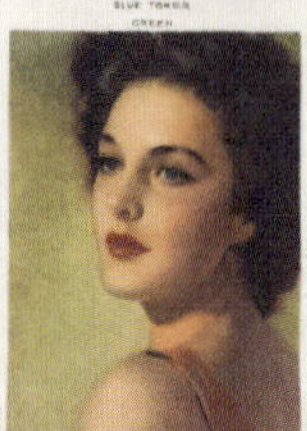

157

a version of Tiepolo's chromatism in much fantasy illustration, in animated cartoons, on the covers of books, on
film posters and in the well-known postwar advertising for
Coca-Cola. A modern theorization of his approach appears
LOOMIS, 2012 in Andrew Loomis's (1892–1959) *Creative Illustration*, one 187
of the best-selling manuals of the 1950s and the era's bible
of 'commercial' illustration. Chromatically, Loomis has 186, 188
many points in common with Tiepolo, adapted of course
to the exigencies of industrial printing. One of the reasons
for this inheritance, less improbable than it appears, is to
DRUCKER, 2009 be found perhaps in the brightness of eighteenth-century
shadowing. American illustration depended – for commercial as well as ideological reasons– upon an optimistic
vision of the world, and would hardly know what to do
with a Baroque chiaroscuro too gloomy for its propagan-
distic purposes. You cannot sell soaps or soda in the style
of Caravaggio. But the language of Tiepolo is radiant, and
therefore aesthetically suitable to be adapted to commercial
seductions. In the superb poster designed by Drew
Struzan (b. 1947) for *Indiana Jones and the Temple of Doom*, 177
for instance, the shadows on the faces of the protagonists
are emphatically red, partly in order to imitate the reflection of flames, as if it were a tracing of a still from the
film, and partly to convey, through a super-saturated colour, the tremendous vivacity of the adventures of our
archaeologist superhero. It is Tiepolo's split colour, adapted
for the age of mechanical reproduction.

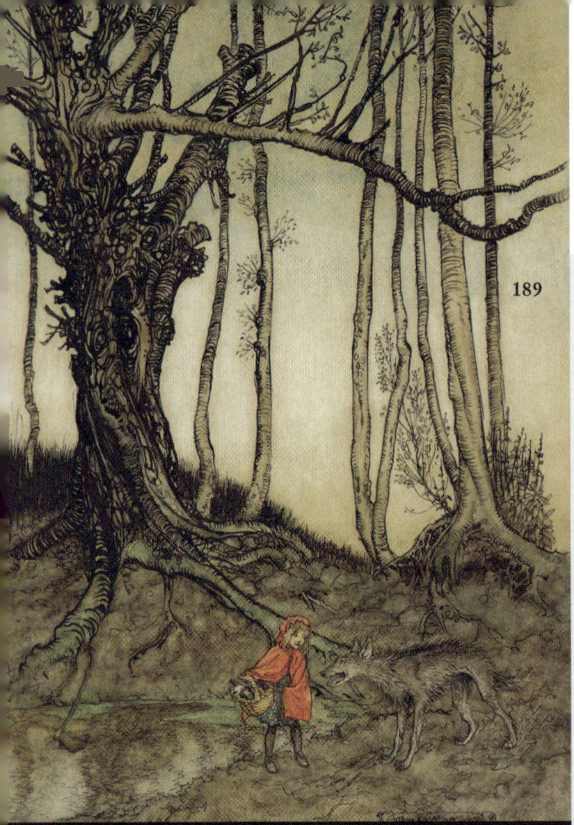

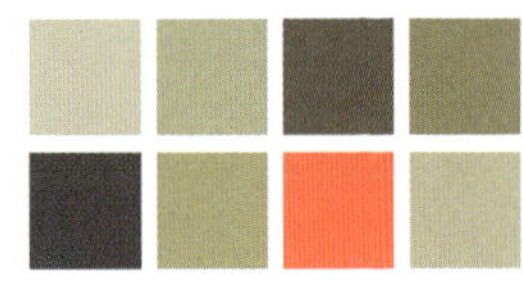

← RACKHAM

189

CONTRAST OF EXTENSION

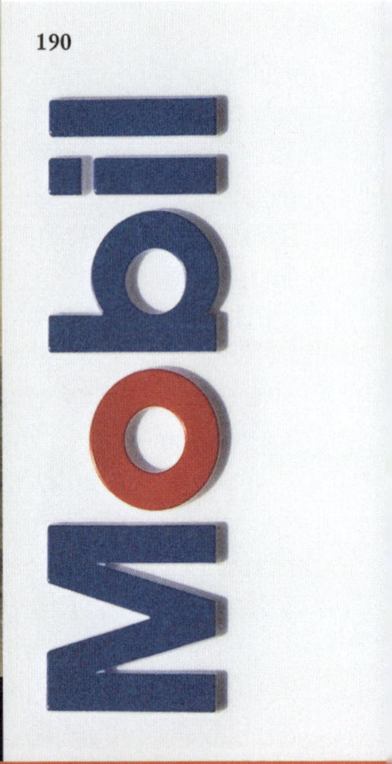

190

Mobil

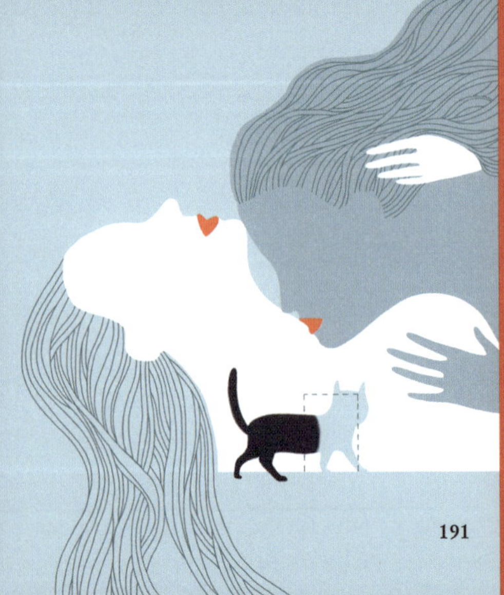

191

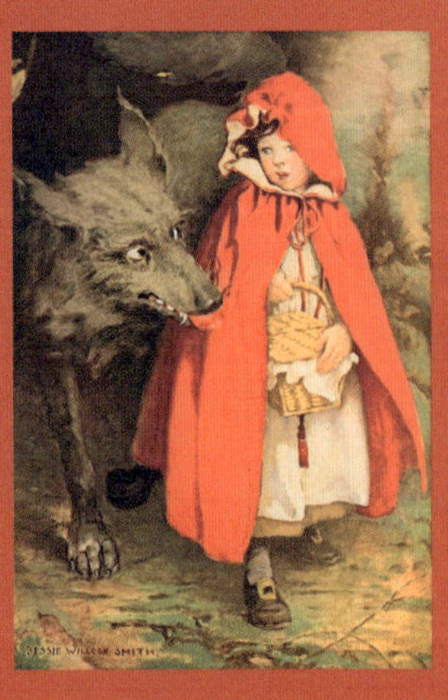

192

Simultaneous Celeste

Fundamental Colour Contrasts

Sooner or later, every child hears the story of Little Red Riding Hood. But why exactly is her cape *red*? According to an anthropological interpretation, this might be an allusion to the blood of first menstruation, as in many tales with female protagonists. From Rapunzel to Sleeping Beauty, fairy-tale heroines are often trapped in a tower or abandoned in a wood, a memory of those ancestral practices that imposed, during the first menstrual cycle, the isolation of girls because they were now deemed to be 'impure', and they would rejoin the community as self-conscious women. Others have argued that the story takes place during Pentecost, the liturgical colour of which is red; still others that children were often dressed in red simply to make them more visible, to keep an eye on them.

Visual artists havc had a lot to say about thc mcaning of the red in Little Red Riding Hood too. Let's look at the work of two of its illustrators at the start of the twentieth century: Arthur Rackham (1867–1939) and Jessie Willcox Smith (1863–1935).

Rackham's compositional choices immediately cast light on the whole story. The wood dominates the scene and is vast, imposing, yet monotone: a succession of beiges and browns, now lighter, now darker – and against everything

Little Red Riding Hood stands out, just a small speck but a highly visible one. The touch of red is a psychological notation: it is the vivacity of the protagonist counterpointed with a menacing and gloomy world. HARTHAN, 1997

We find a completely different version of the story in
192 Smith's work: this time Little Red Riding Hood fills the whole frame, and the red cloak spreads over a great deal of the pictorial surface. The difference is significant: Rackham is illustrating a moment in the tale, Smith is making a portrait. But this is not all. Rackham is completely inside the story: he suggests through the withered wood an atmosphere which is harsh and frightening, something mournful and even infernal that makes Little Red Riding Hood resemble Dante in the dark wood, as illustrated by Gustave Doré. Smith, on the other hand, is designing a postcard. She is not interested in evoking or suggesting dramatic themes. Little Red Riding Hood is the pretext for depicting a lovely girl dressed in red, an attractive colour, festive and perfect for Christmas. Rackham's Little Red Riding Hood is red because she is in grave danger, Smith's because she is a version of Father Christmas.

The chromatic construction used by Rackham is known as 'contrast of extension', one of seven possible contrasts, according to a formula coined by Johannes Itten and now a classic part of artistic vocabulary. It is an easy and clear way of describing a composition constructed by placing a large amount of a certain colour and a small quantity of another in contrast with each other. In this case: a good deal of brown and very little red. It's a relationship that is always effective as the small amount of colour surrounded by the large immediately grabs our attention. It has numerous uses, and almost endless expressive possibilities. ITTEN, 1982

Consider, for instance, the logo designed by Ivan Chermayeff (b. 1932) for the petroleum company Mobil, which 190
is blue except for one red letter. In Rackham the contrast serves to evoke the tremulous disorientation of a protagonist, whereas here it helps to memorize a brand of fuel. And yet the visual logic is the same.

Examples of masterly use of quantity contrast can be found in the work of the French painter Jean-Baptiste-Siméon Chardin (1699–1779), who above all makes compositional use of the technique: he does not employ it to tell us something of an explicit nature but rather to give rhythm to geometric arrangements, as in the *Still Life* 193
in Figure 193. Objects emerge from a muddy semi-darkness, and the painting is governed by dull tones against which the red skin of the fruit and white surfaces of the ceramic cup ring out brilliantly. The contrast is also allegorical: even these lovely apples, so brilliantly vital, will soon fade, becoming as brown as the background of the picture. Often the theme of still life is precisely this transience of material things, and yet if that was all that was involved here, Chardin would be just another painter among many. Instead, his painting is so outstanding because he transforms the moral argument into a counterpoint between brushstrokes. In order to appreciate what he achieves we need to look at his work as if it were an abstract painting, or as if we were listening to a fugue by Bach: by trying, that is, not to focus on or even recognize the natural forms but to enjoy the interplay of clear and dark tones, the rhythmic repetition of the same touches of colour, as if we were following the movement of a melody. In Chardin, quantity contrast is effectively musical, almost contemplative, allowing the spiritual to emerge from the geometric.

An altogether different and very modern use of contrast can be found in an illustration by Valeria Petrone 191

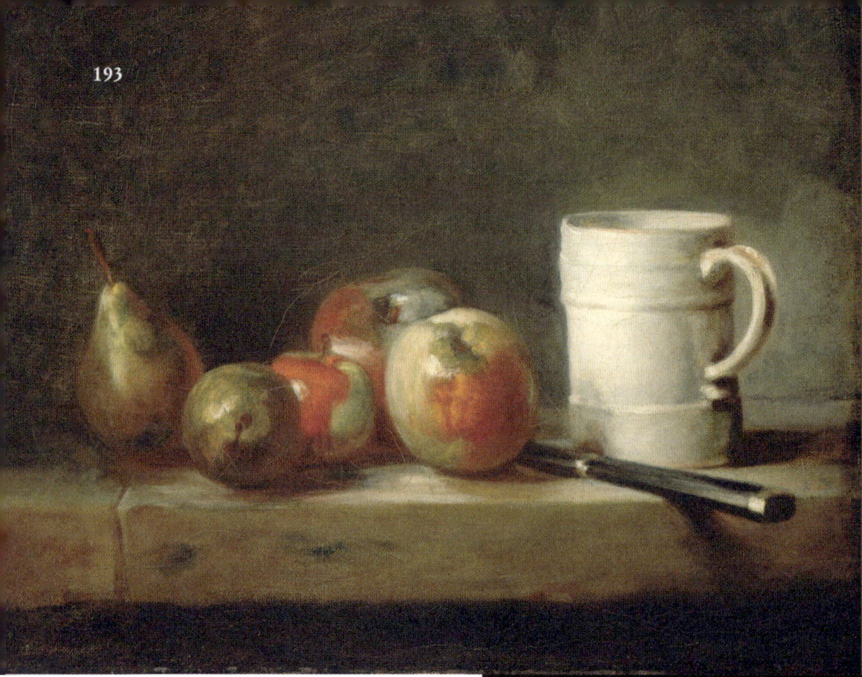

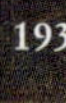

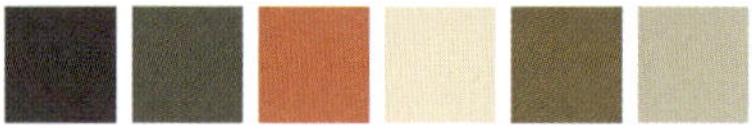

193

CHARDIN

GIPI

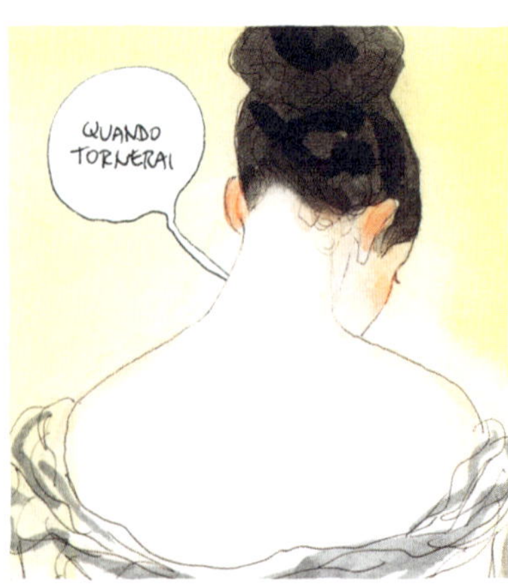

CONTRAST OF EXTENSION

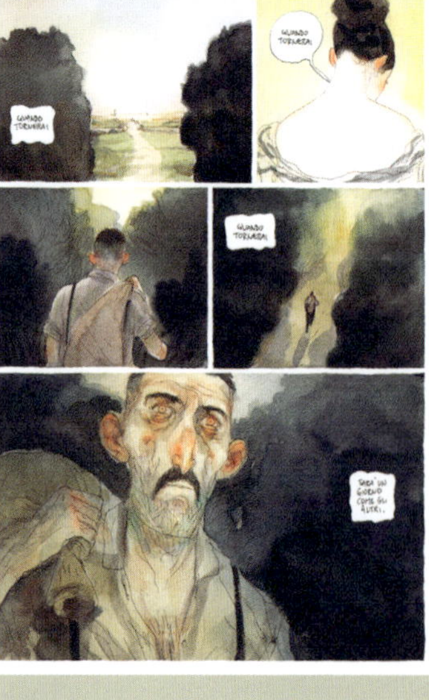

194

(b. 1965): it uses the technique to suggest the twinning of two feminine figures, in the form of a small red stain repeated twice for the two pairs of lips. The image could represent a sexual embrace between the two figures, or the doubling of a single figure: it is deliberately and ambiguously poised between these possibilities. The contrast of extension insinuates that there is a lot in common between the two pairs of lips, leaving the image suspended in a dreamy, somewhat mysterious state, like the black cat that enters the body of the white woman, not as a sign of bad luck but as the poetic correlative of a fluctuating soul.

Among other contemporaries it is worth mentioning the admirable use of the contrast of extension in the work of Gipi (b. 1963), whose watercolour figures frequently have their ears highlighted with a small reddish touch. This is partly a realistic notation: in humans the erogenous zones are often redder than the rest of the body. But the knuckles of those who work with their hands are also red; the noses of those who are cold; the eyes of anyone crying, and the knees of a child who has fallen down. These touches of red are life itself, which always concentrates in certain sensitive points. And Gipi knows this. In a frame of his graphic
novel *unastoria*, the great-grandfather of the protagonist 194
finds that his only respite in the trenches is to think about and write to his beloved wife. She is depicted from behind, as if on returning he had caught her unawares. All white, she fills the frame: her back is a white background, her neck is almost blinding in its whiteness, and crowned by chestnut hair. In this white silence two small red ears ring out. Who would fail to want to kiss this neck? This is contrast of extension not as corporate language but as a universal metaphor for memory and desire.

Rackham, Chermayeff, Chardin, Petrone, Gipi. Comparing such diverse works demonstrates one thing: that great authors, be they artists, designers or both, use colour to say something and not to decorate. The contrast can be implemented naturally with any colour: deep black with a small white dot, yellow with a little blue. The skill lies not in having chosen the red but in having used very little to say precise things.

The first type of contrast on Itten's list is that of light
197 and dark. In this case the type of colour is irrelevant, what counts is the modulation of dark and light, as when you work with India ink, now dense, now diluted, or with a pencil pressing hard or moving lightly on the paper. A for-
195 midable example is provided by Nadar's *Portrait of Émile Zola*, photographed around 1880. It might be objected that the contrast of light and dark in this case is a technical condition and not a choice, given that colour photography did not exist. But the point here is different. The meaning of this type of contrast lies in the movement between a maximum dark and a maximum light, using light contrasts in an expressive way. Not all black and white photos behave like this. It is enough to notice the highlight to the right of Zola's beard that is crucial to framing the psychology here. That light is like an aura, not of sanctity but of culture: it outlines the face and underlines its interiority. Nadar's portraits are not just of faces, they are always intellectual biographies.

To understand this, let's turn to one of the most fam-
196 ous self-portraits in the history of painting, by Rembrandt (1606–69), painted when he was already well advanced in age. This painting was no doubt one of the models that Nadar had in mind, and here too the contrast of light and dark serves to tell a story. There are colours, but it is certainly not a colourful painting – and to the modern eye accustomed to seeing photographs, Rembrandt's picture seems like monochrome

195

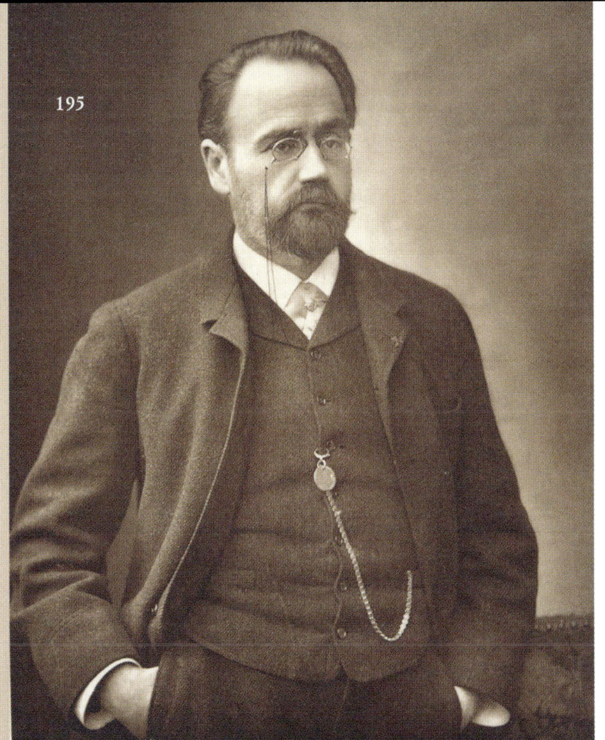

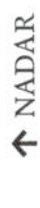

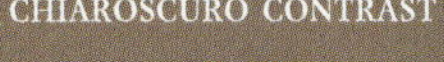

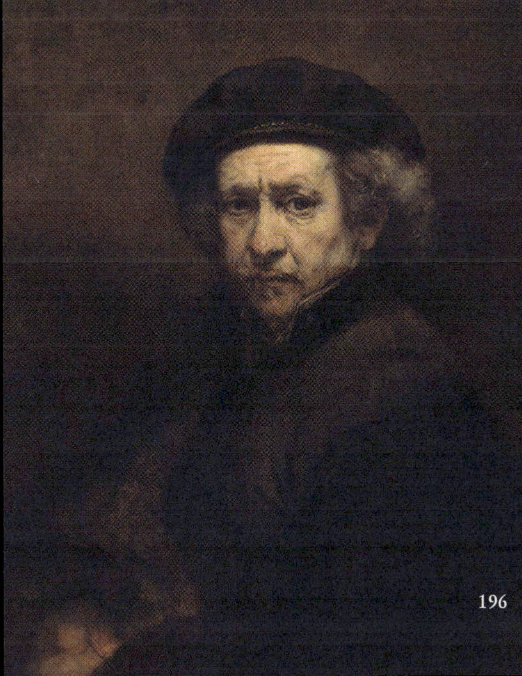

196

197

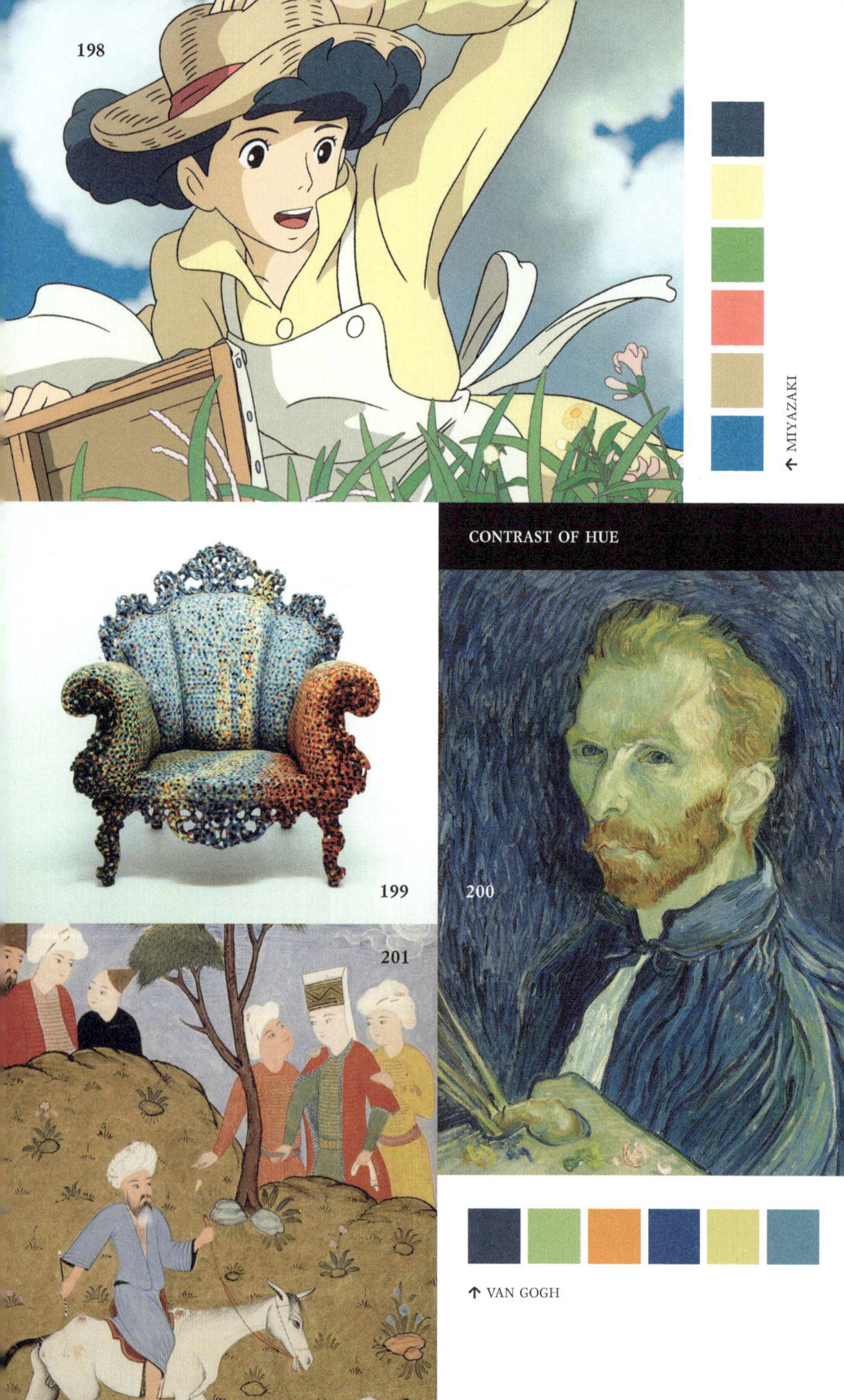

198

↑ MIYAZAKI

CONTRAST OF HUE

199

200

201

↑ VAN GOGH

in sepia. The way the light falls onto his face is analogous to a spotlight, a metaphor for the reflexive self-regard of the artist looking at himself and realizing that he is no longer young. That light brings forth shapes from the dark and indistinct background, or perhaps it is the darkness that will soon swallow them instead: life is what happens between these two poles of darkness and light.

After this comes the 'contrast of hue': that is to say, when solid colours are juxtaposed, without halftones, without obvious shading. What matters here is the relationship 201
between hues and not tonal progression, or luminosity. A perfect example of this is provided by medieval stained
glass: tesserae of absolute, saturated colour placed next to 170
each other. But this is also the language of traditional comic book art and of many animated cartoons, in which hues are juxtaposed in a clean-cut way, as happens in the films
of Hayao Miyazaki (b. 1941). We can also think here of 198
many works by Vincent van Gogh (1853–90) such as *Self-
Portrait with a Blue Background*. It is not that there is no 200
shading, but it is not central to what is being said. The artist is speaking through the juxtaposition of hues, not through a modulated scale, and in fact a pure colour contrast is often a choice that places itself in open argument with the contrast of light and dark: if the latter values shape and volume, the former annuls them and transforms space into an exclusively chromatic fact, at times dematerializing it.

An admirable instance of this can be seen in *Proust Chair* 199
by Alessandro Mendini (b. 1931), a totem for design from the last forty years: the colour makes a virtual presence of the chair, upholstered in an otherworldly and hallucinatory way that idealizes it. It is a super-chair, or the nineteenth-century armchair par excellence.

The contrast of hue can also have a more functional use, as in the famous map of the London Underground designed by Harry Beck (1902–1974), where the contrasts between hues serve to distinguish the different rail lines. It is a crucial factor: if the lines were done with variations on a single colour such as blue or green, the play between similar shades would be an obstacle to understanding the map, and some lines would look visually more important than others. The juxtaposition of hues avoids perceptual prevarication, and the lines appear equal.

WARE, 2004

The fourth type on the list is 'contrast of saturation'. The term refers to the degree of saturation of a colour in relation to other, similar colours. 'Saturation', that is, in the sense of the intensity of colour perceived: how a point in the composition seems *colourful* in relation to another that seems duller. To make this concept clearer we can compare the self-portrait of Van Gogh that we encountered on the
204 preceding page with a copy done by an imitator, similar in design but with chromatic differences. The original hinges on strong colour opposition: the brilliant yellows and oranges standing against the equally intense blues. The painting in Figure 204, though still using yellow and blue, diminishes the contrast: we might define it as a variation in yellow in which reddish and blue reflections are cautiously hinted at.
202 It is an effect that we also find in Polaroids of the 1970s, where everything is imbued with a pallid, pink or yellowish tone. And we can also find it in a darker key in *Madame*
203 *Camus* by Edgar Degas (1834–1917), where the brick-red timbre has multiple variations, now more and now less emphatic. In saturation contrast, the extremes of light and dark are usually avoided, with the image appearing to germinate somewhere in the middle, in the interplay between different degrees of saturation of similar colours.

202

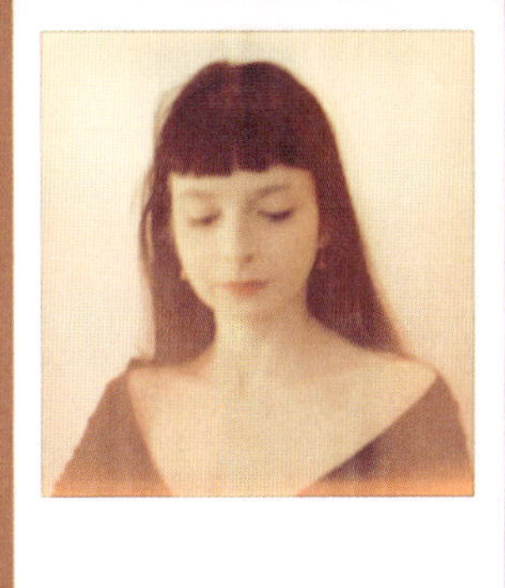

203

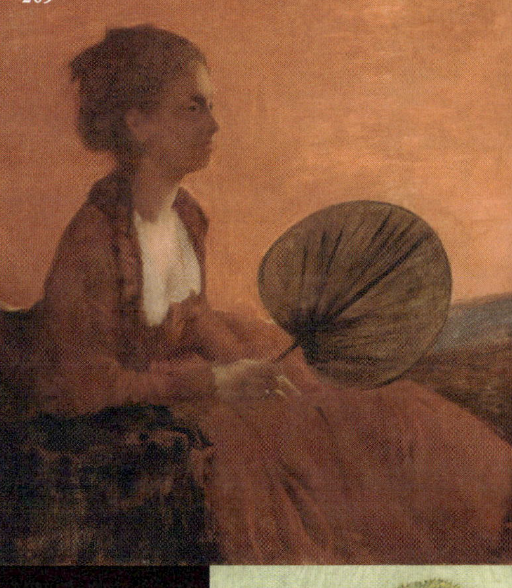

204

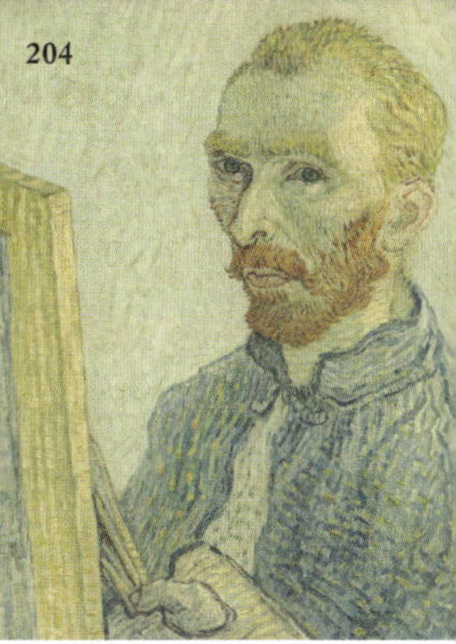

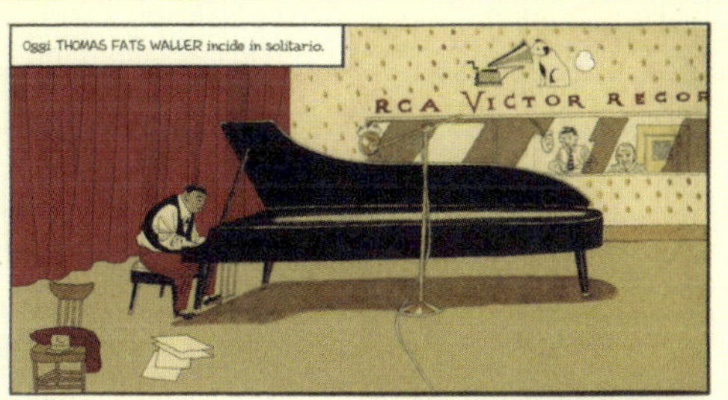

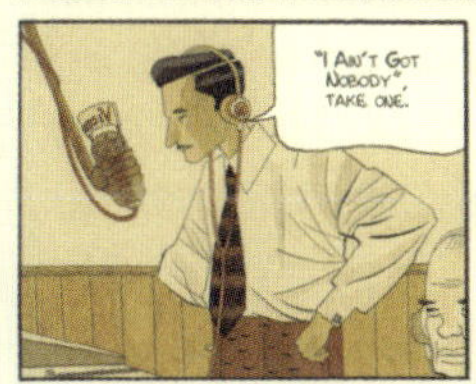

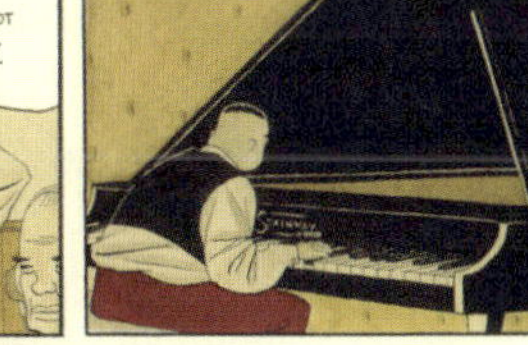

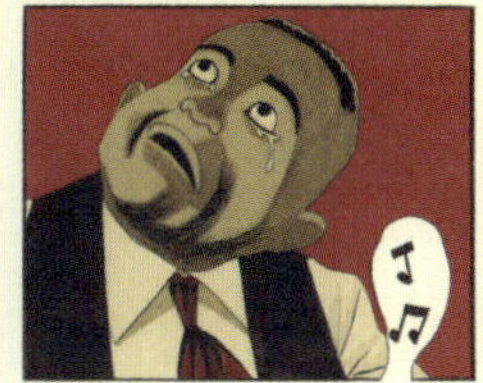

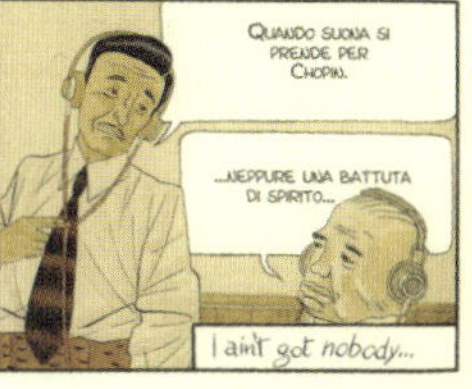

205

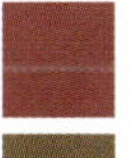

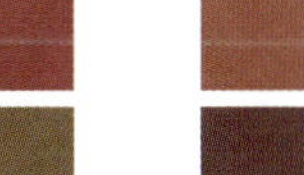

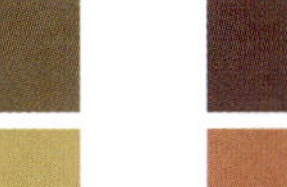

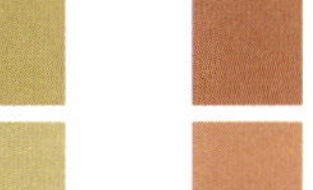

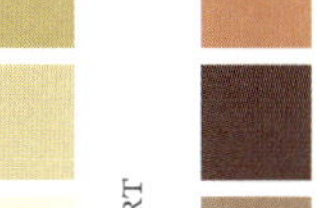

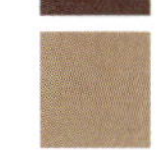

← IGORT

← DEGAS

205 In the graphic novel *Fats Waller* by Igort (b. 1958), something similar is achieved with a palette of heavy warm browns, beiges and greys, now washed out now fully solid. Brown is not just any colour: it has an important history in association with the book's black protagonist. Everything is counterpointed with touches of a red that occupies the highest range of the scale. It's a superbly elegant choice. By choosing any kind of red the artist would have been working a classic contrast in quantity, but the one chosen comes across as the most intense kind of hyper-saturated brown. Red is not external to the palette of the story, it is not a touch of red on a dark background: it stands out, but in a way that is coherent with Waller's world. And therein lies its narrative function: the choice of a palette of browns evokes a distant time, as if we were looking at this world in an old photograph. Once this rule has been established, colour becomes autonomous, it does not imitate the monochrome of a photograph. We forget about it. Things are beige or red because these are the realities of the world of *Fats Waller*, their character.

Then there is 'complementary' and 'simultaneous' contrast, two relationships that depend on the brain's capacity to see colours in different ways according to their context. In the first of these, the contrast between two antagonistic colours causes both to be enhanced by their proximity. A prime example of this is the famous
206 portrait *Afghan Girl* by Steve McCurry (b. 1950): her skin and hair have reddish dominants, like the red fabric in which she is swathed, causing her to stand out from the background green. It is a green which rhymes with the colour of her eyes, surprising the viewer. On the one hand, the subject stands out strongly against this green, but, on the other, she is absorbed precisely by this chromatic

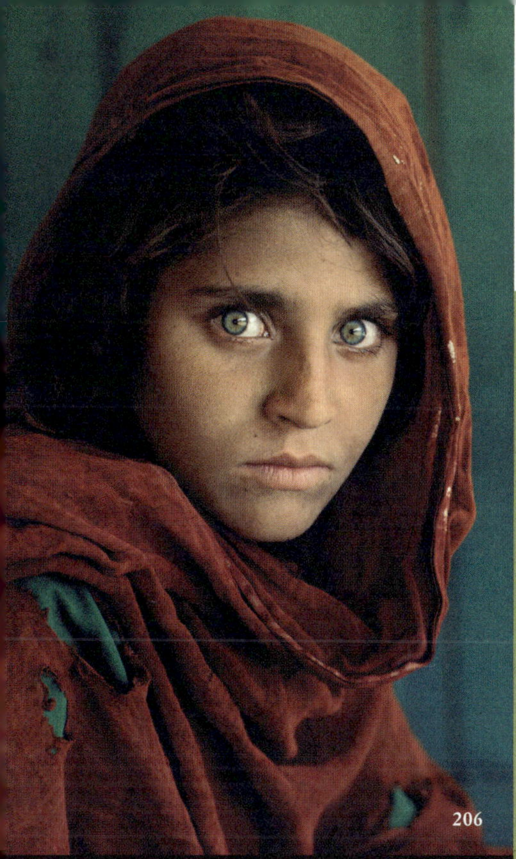

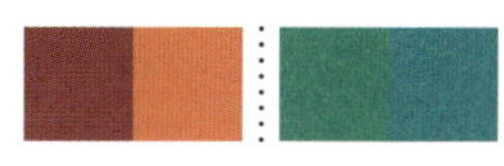

← MCCURRY

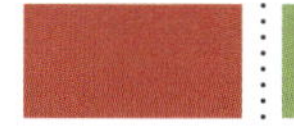

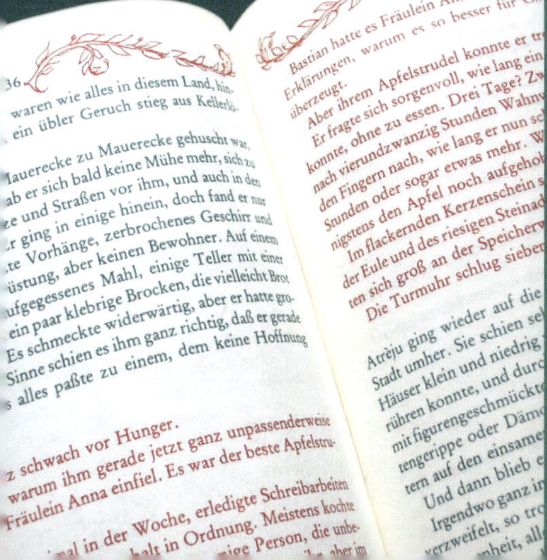

↓ SHOUT

206

207

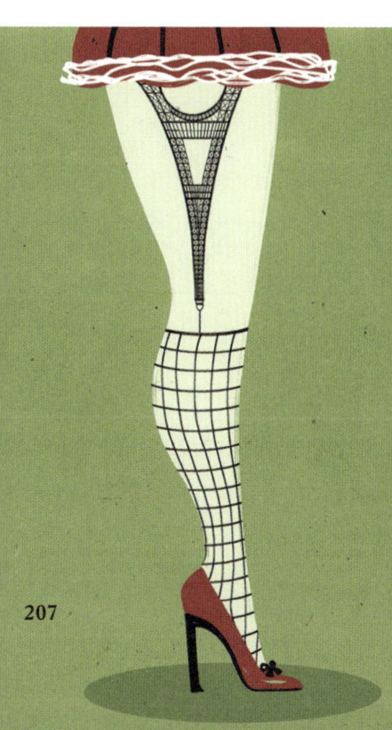

COMPLEMENTARY CONTRAST

208

209

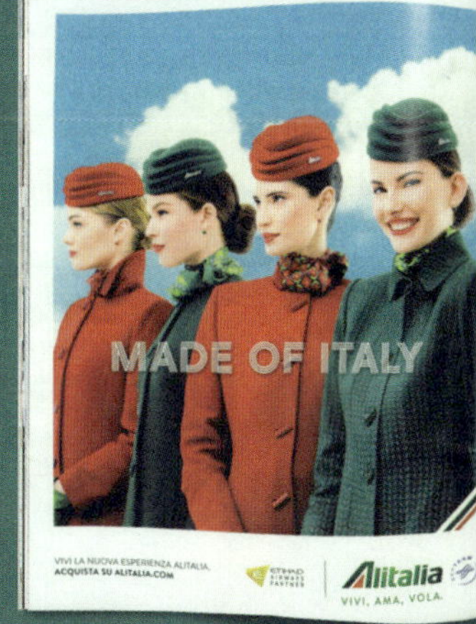

210

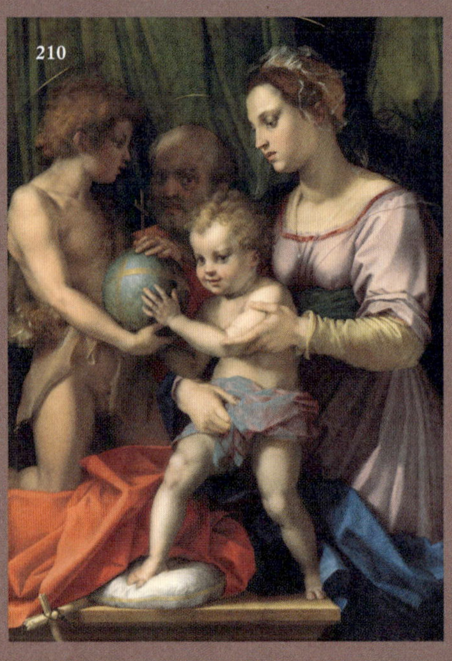

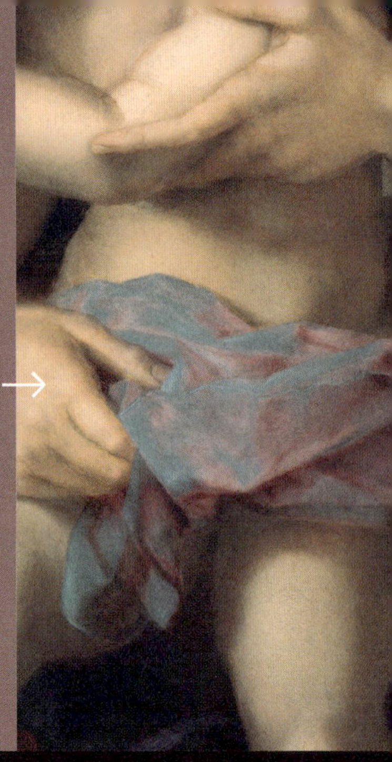

211

CANGIANTISMO AND CROSS PROCESSING

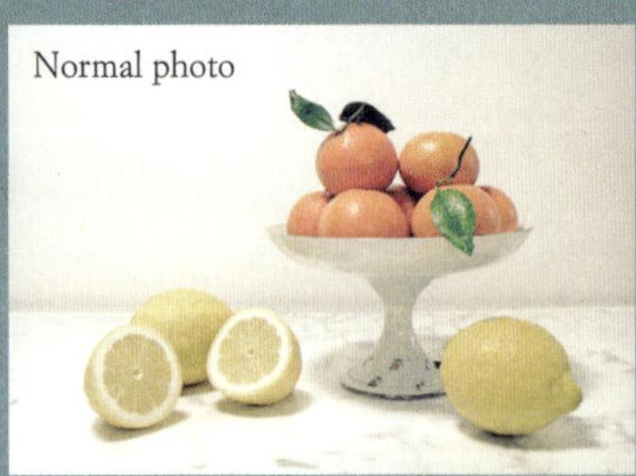

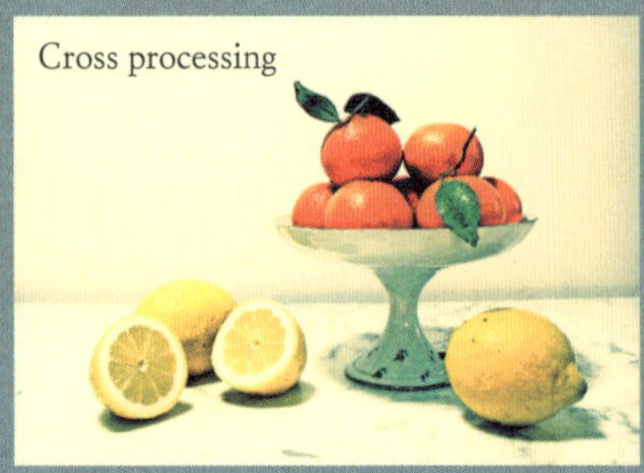

212

twinning with the background, generating a ceaseless back and forth movement that contributes to the portrait's hypnotic effect.

An example of the other type can be found in the illustration *Beautiful Old World* (2003) by Shout, in which a 207
simultaneous contrast serves to frame a woman's leg: the
red of her skirt and shoe funnel the perspective, causing
us to focus upon the centre, from which the garter stands
out in the shape of the Eiffel Tower. Here the use of
colour is not emotive but structural: it serves, that is, to
direct our gaze.

A remarkable *literary* use of complementary contrast can
be found in Michael Ende's novel *The Neverending Story* 208
(1979), where the design of the book is intrinsic to the experience of reading it. The text is printed in two colours,
brick red and emerald green, to indicate to the reader the
two levels of the story: one which narrates the life of the
protagonist, Bastian, in the real world – and the other,
side by side with it, which conveys a parallel world of the
imagination that Bastian discovers in a book he is reading
called *The Neverending Story*. It is a game of Chinese boxes
that questions the very idea of reality. The choice of colours is effective inasmuch as they have equal luminosity,
so from a perceptual point of view they vie for dominance,
wavering and endlessly competing as to which is the most
'real' in our eyes.

A particular kind of complementary contrast can be
found in an effect that was fashionable in the Renaissance:
cangiantismo (hue shifter), when shadows are painted in 210
a cold colour and highlights in a warm one, or vice versa.
This technique appears to first emerge in order to imitate the appearance of silk garments, and since these are 48, 54
costly and come from the East, *cangiantismo* is soon considered an attribute of spiritually superior figures, to the

extent that it becomes recommended above all for the depiction of nymphs and angels. Michelangelo often uses it in the Sistine Chapel, as if it were a kind of chiaroscuro: he paints shadows that are green with orange highlights. As we saw earlier, this is not true chiaroscuro, because the complementaries often have the same brightness, tending to negate volume rather than show it, and causing them to vibrate. At the time, Michelangelo's many imitators began to use it as a mere stylistic device, disconnected from particular fabrics and any attempt at realism, painting shadows with opposite, often acidic colours. This came to be called Mannerism by the Romantics (that is to say, in the *manner* of Michelangelo) and was rediscovered in the twentieth century on account of its almost psychedelic audacity. There is a splendid example in a sacred dialogue painted around 1528 by Andrea del
210 Sarto, in the cloth with which the Virgin has wrapped the infant Jesus.

A contemporary variation can be found in photos us-
212 ing 'cross-processing', a technique very much in fashion in advertising since the early twenty-first century which exploded thanks to the ease of applying it with Insta-
211 gram filters.[1] The image is forced to have blue or greenish shadows and extremely warm highlights, in what amounts to Mannerist *cangiantismo* for the smartphone era.

Whether in *cangiantismo* or cross-processing, there is often a 'contrast of warm and cool', the fifth of the relationships formulated by Itten. We see this in action in
213 a still taken from *Eyes Wide Shut* (1999), the last film directed by Stanley Kubrick, with Nicole Kidman and Tom

1 The cross-processing effect imitates, through contrasting and complementary colours, the result of a film gone wrong (misprocessed) in the developing tray, an effect now also linked to photos made with Lomo cameras.

Cruise in the lead roles. If we look at it as if it were an abstract composition, we notice that it is divided into two fields: the principal one is dominated by orange tones, the other by blue.

The protagonists are in a bedroom, the room is illuminated by a soft, golden electric light. Behind them we can glimpse the bathroom, dark but faintly lit by a blue reflection from the street. With this image Kubrick encapsulates the theme of the story, the conflict between the reassuring comfort of marriage and the temptation of putting it all at risk. The film superimposes two worlds: the orange one of bourgeois interiors, of apartments, of prudence – and the blue one of the outside, of the night, of risk. In the still, the colour is a property not of things but of light. The houses are warm because the lamplight is a metaphor of a universe which is closed and protected, underpinned by economic prosperity. Tom and Nicole embrace in their bedroom. In a little while a new adventure will begin that will put their relationship at risk. In the background of the scene the blueish dark is already there, presaging what is to come.

With cruel irony, the story takes place at Christmas, when New York is studded with coloured lights. These multicoloured strings of lights are everywhere: on the large decorated trees of the well-off, on shop signs, even in alleyways where prostitutes ply their trade. They shine out in the night but fail to convey anything festive, serving on the contrary to emphasize the loneliness everyone feels. If colour is a quality of light, here it is less to do with electromagnetic waves than with the restless oscillation of souls. There is no love, however solid, Kubrick seems to say, that can make it seem that there is nothing outside of it – no relationship, however happy, that is not placed in doubt by our fickle human nature. There is no orange that does not, in the end, desire a little blue.

In the wake of Kubrick's mastery, the use of this contrast as an analogue for relations between interior and exterior has become a classic trope of American cinematography,
214 especially in film noir and thrillers. In Figure 214, a still from the TV series *Dexter*, we are in a bedroom and notice a cold light, in this case a greenish one, that infiltrates from outside. The figure in the armchair is an apparition of the dead father to whom the protagonist speaks. In this instance the conflict between interior and exterior is a metaphor of psychological conflict, a manifestation of a divided self and a double life. The green is the opposite of orange, its darker half.

There is another example of a New York depicted through the contrast of warm and cool in *The Journey of*
215 *the Penguin* by Emiliano Ponzi (b. 1978), a book produced to celebrate eighty years of the publishing house that famously bears the name of the bird. It is the story of a penguin who leaves his native land to seek his fortune in the Big Apple.

The city is bathed in an orange dawn light that makes the shadows on the skyscrapers seem blue. It is a soft, gentle contrast that suggests the protagonist's disorientation, making us see through colour what he is feeling: the warmth of a day about to start. The orange glimmer warms the air and presages a promising day – an air that is charged with the cold of the night, of that which is still foreign and frighteningly large. Orange is historically the colour of the first Penguin paperback novels. Ponzi's elegance depends not on the counterpoint between orange and blue but between this pair of colours and another, entirely different one: the black and white of the penguin.

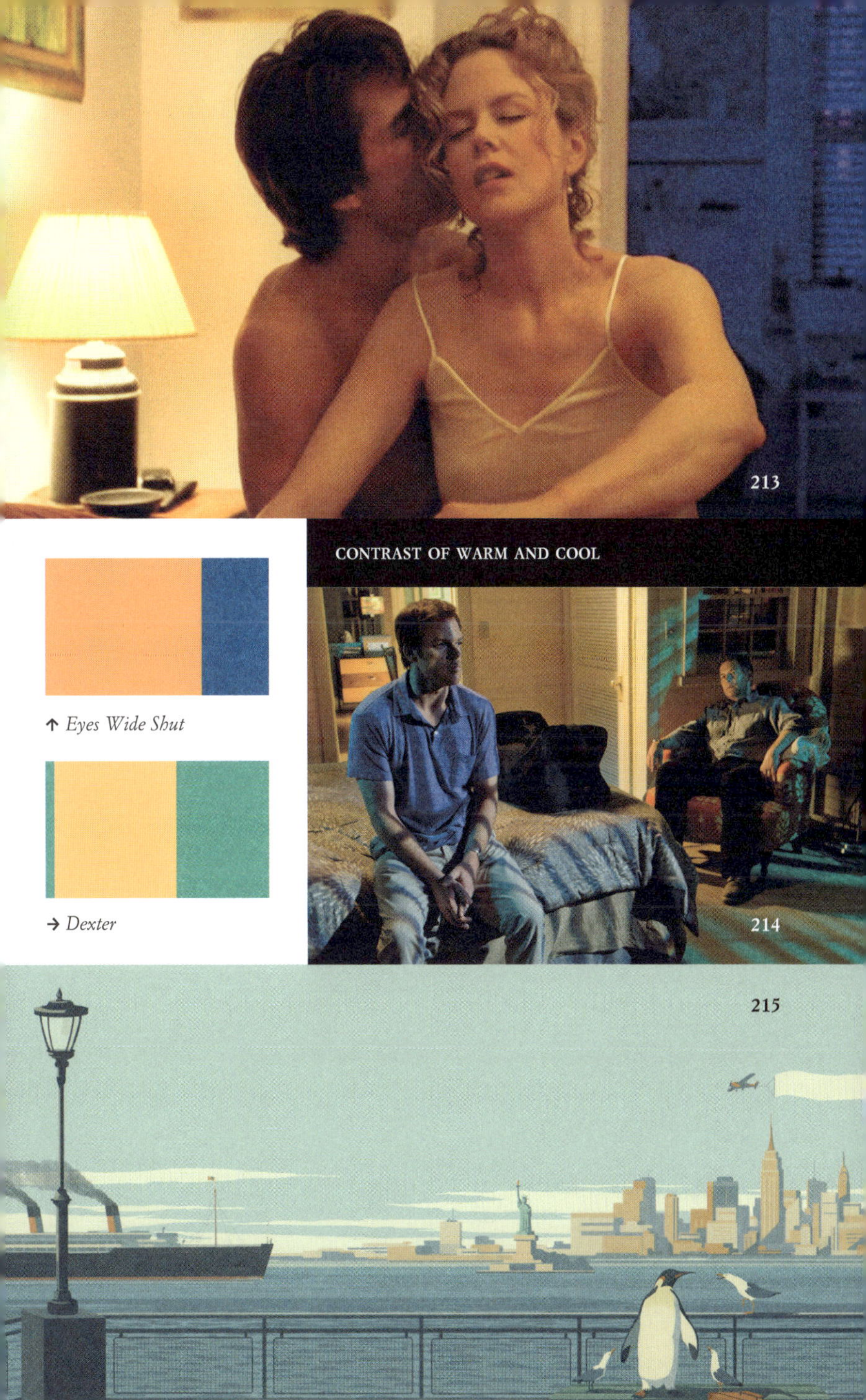

↑ *Eyes Wide Shut*

→ *Dexter*

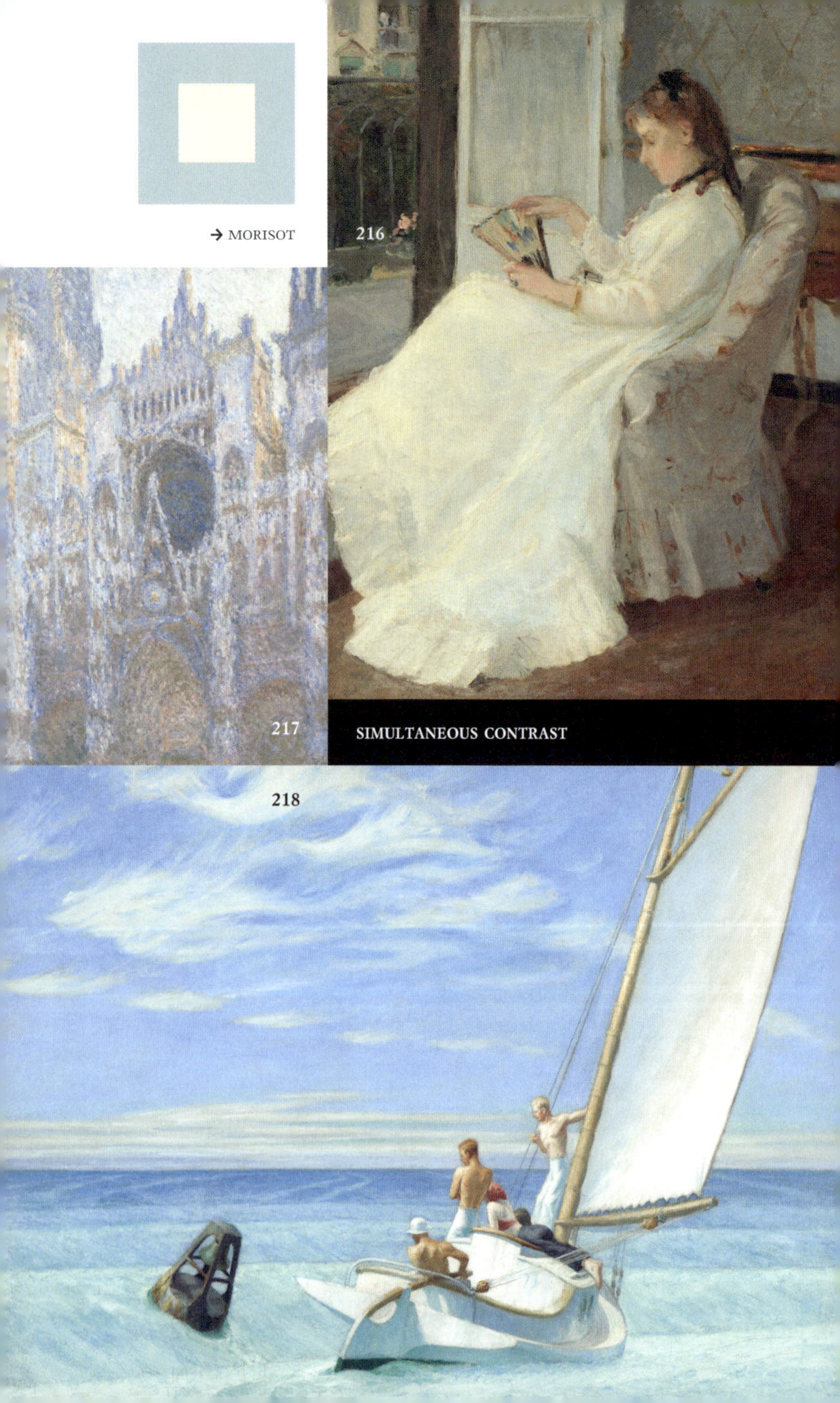
→ MORISOT
216
217
218
SIMULTANEOUS CONTRAST

The most sophisticated contrast, and the one most loved by the Impressionists, is that of 'simultaneity'. It occurs when a colour tends towards the complementary of the one next to it: like a grey that seems greenish when set against a reddish background, or a white that seems yellowish if placed against an azure one.

There is a well-known anecdote in the world of interior design. It concerns a gentleman who wants a grey carpet for his lounge, but when the designer incorporates it into a room with terracotta colour walls the carpet instantly becomes blue, to the great disappointment of his client. Simultaneous contrast can be thought of as a sort of reflex contradiction: when a colour is placed next to a certain other colour, it must automatically assume a bias against it. I don't know if the story of the disappointed client is true or not, but it certainly illustrates how in design the effect of simultaneity is always lurking in wait. Designers of textiles know full well, for instance – and this is a lesson that emerges from Chevreul's *Principles* – that if they wish to supply a fabric with green stripes on a white background, then a little light green must be added to the white. Otherwise, if you use pure white, you will end up with pinkish reflections on account of the compensation that operates in our brains.

CHEVREUL, 1987

There is a suggestive demonstration of how this works in painting, in *The Artist's Sister at the Window* by Berthe
Morisot (1841–95), a composition centred upon its 216
subject's ample dress. Morisot constructs halftones using a greyish blue, and in highlighted areas uses a very light grey and a little yellow, which is to say she second guesses the natural propensity of the eye to construct a warm, simultaneous tint as a counterpart to the cold ones of

the shadows. The result is that the dress appears to be vaporous and saturated with light.

Another, emphatically vibrant variation on this tech-
217 nique can be found in one of the versions of *Rouen Cathedral* by Monet: the mauve rendering of the architecture in shadow is lacerated by orange-yellow flickers of sunlight coming from one side: so the less saturated and greyish brushstrokes appear, intermittently, as cold and warm.

It was Edward Hopper (1882–1967), who must have studied the Impressionists in his turn, who would take
218 this technique to its extreme. In *Ground Swell* he paints the shadows of the yacht blue, simulating the reflection of the sea water so that the light areas of the vessel, although extremely white, tend perceptually to yellow – making us feel, without actually painting it, the warmth of the morning on which the scene is taking place. This is Hopper's great strength, and the strength of simultaneous contrast: there is no yellow in the air, but we feel it.

So far, I have listed the chromatic formulas hypothesized by Itten at the Bauhaus, but, in the eighty years since, things have changed quite a bit. I would like to add two other contrasts that have had tremendous success – especially in the world of design in general and graphic design in particular in the last century. The first is stylistic and has great evocative power: a single colour
219 contrasts with black and white, the colour standing out from a greyscale composition. I would call it 'contrast *with* colour'. A celebrated example is provided by the
221 graphic design of the cover of the magazine *Life*, where full-page black and white photograph is enlivened by the red of the box in which its title appears. Or we might recall the famous scene in Steven Spielberg's *Schindler's List* (1993) in which a child in a red coat stands out against

219

↓ RED TAPE

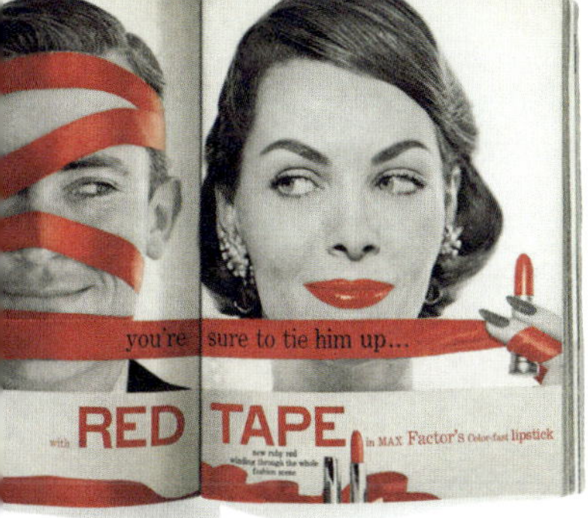

220

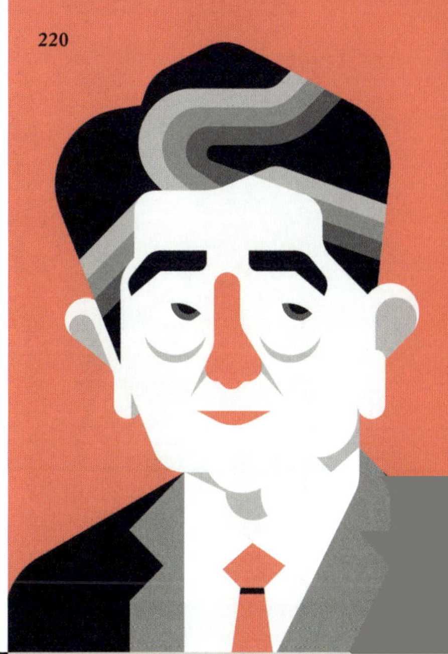

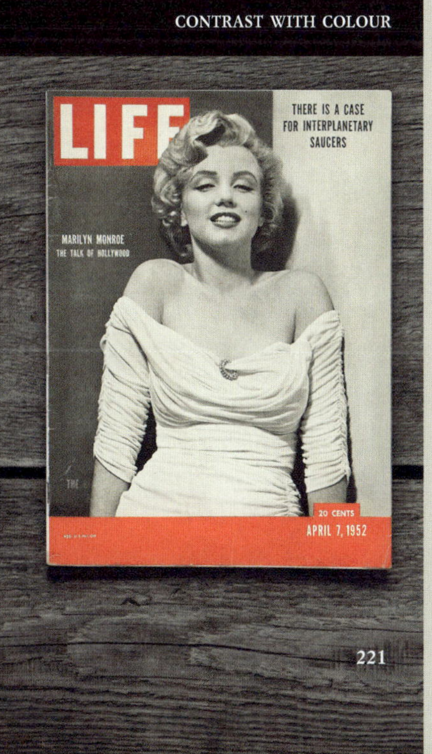

221

222

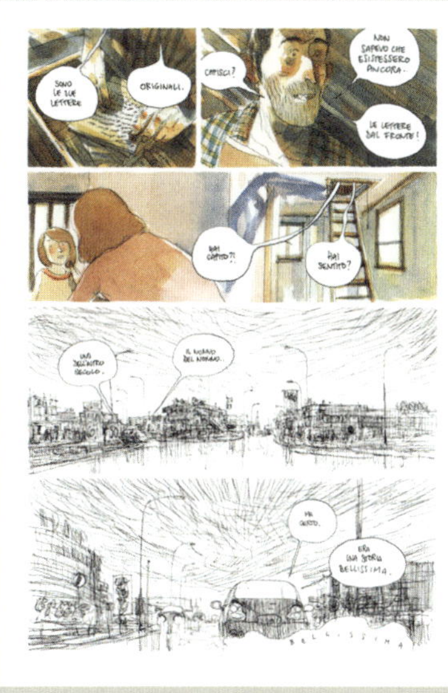

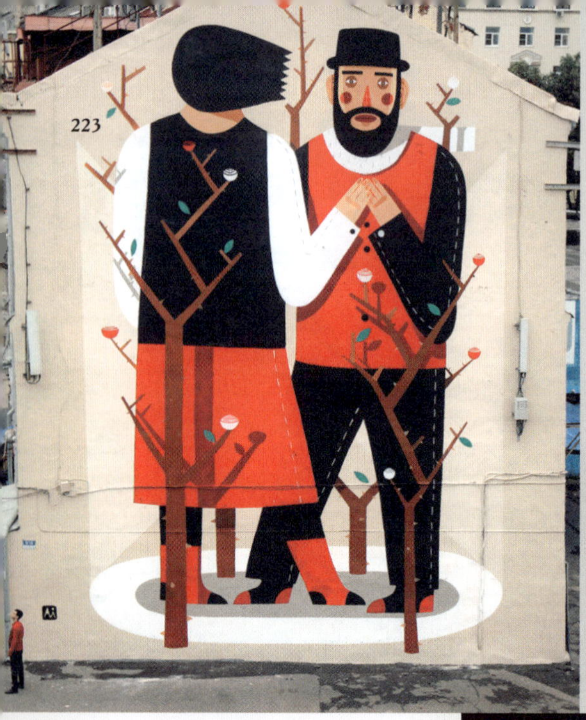

223

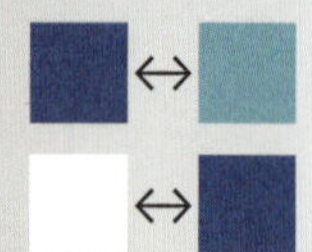

↓ Frieze from the mausoleum of Oljeitu

224

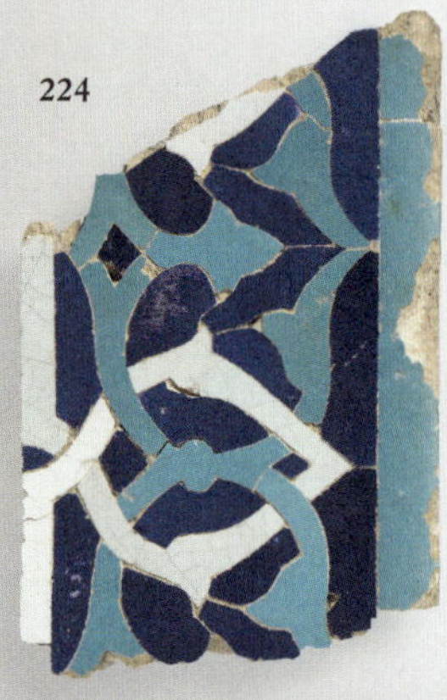

225

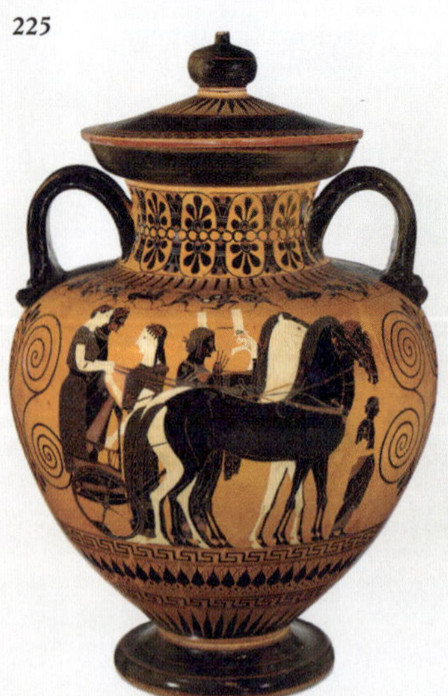

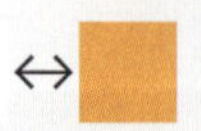

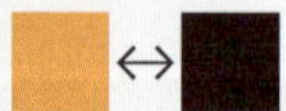

↑ Terracotta vase

COUPLE CONTRAST

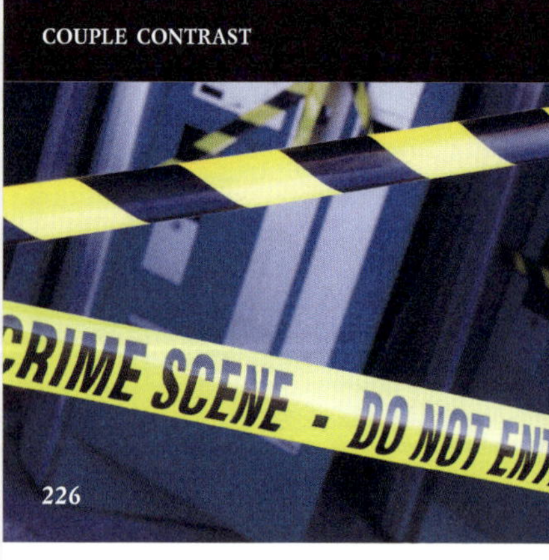

226

227

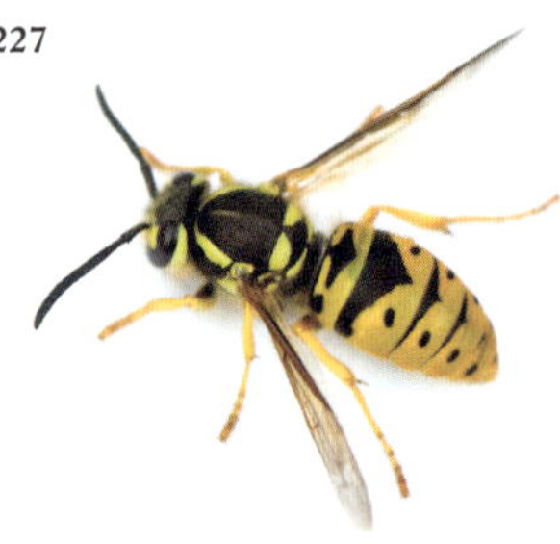

the black and white – as raw as a period newsreel's – of the rest of the film, in a synecdoche of the destiny of individuals caught up in history.

But the scheme can also be reversed, as in some portraits by Marco Goran Romano (b. 1986), in which the 220
overall layout is governed by a principal colour, and
it is the features of the subject that are constructed in
shades of grey. This stratagem is due largely to the fact
that twentieth-century graphic art has often been printed with two inks (for example, black with one other
colour) in order to save on the cost of a four-colour process: a practical necessity that has been converted into
an expressive form. Romano's portraits are sophisticated
because they incorporate into their style the visual legacy of a century of graphic art.

In the graphic novel *unastoria*, Gipi uses this type of con- 222
trast in order to contradistinguish the two temporal levels
of the narrative, giving radical emphasis to the choice: the
black and white is not merely greyscale, and is rendered
even more harsh by insistent and nervous strokes of a
black marker pen. These stylistic contrasts suggest parallel narrative registers.

The final type of contrast is what you get when you
combine two flat and homogeneous solid colours, competing for the field on an equal footing. I suggest that wc 224, 228
call this 'couple contrast'. A frequently resorted to version of this involves the combination of solid black with
a vibrant colour, as in the famous *Hit the Whites with*
the Red Wedge by El Lissitzky (1890–1941), or in Greek 230
vases with black figures painted on a red background. 225
The contemporary illustrator and muralist Agostino
Iacurci (b. 1986) makes masterful use of the technique in 223

a recent mural in Moscow. Red, white and black form a dynamic triad and are opposed to each other in pairs: black with white (used as colours rather than tones) and red with black. The effect is powerful thanks to the addition of a further contrast – with the ambience of the city – because the colours used in the design appear all the more intense against the expected greyish appearance of the city. Perhaps the real conflict chosen by Iacurci is this: while advertising billboards can be as colourful, they become invisible and obvious – whereas such a mural asserts and imposes its exceptional presence, and with the power of art makes us notice the duller everyday tones of our life.

We experience this couple contrast more generally with
all striped fabrics: upholstery, shirts, ties. It is a commonly
used technique, not least for its strong visibility, espe-
226 cially when it is crucial to grab attention: we need only
think of the yellow and black police tape that demarcates
crime scenes. The same thing goes for signs warning us of
danger – electrical or nuclear ones, for instance. Perhaps
such symbolic signalling of danger was inspired by the col-
227 ours of certain noxious insects such as wasps, and certain
species of spiders and snakes.

PASTOUREAU, 2007

It is clear that what attracts our attention is above all visual *difference*. Successful artefacts – whether aesthetic, functional or commercial – are invariably based on the effectiveness of some kind of contrast. If in our world, so filled with visual images, we look around and encounter compositions that we consider to be ugly – whether on television, in graphic art, photography or on the internet – we soon realize that what we call 'ugly' is above all a lack of visual hierarchy: either there is too much included, or too little, or it is too disorderly. Our eye does not know what to pay attention to, and is therefore distracted or bored. We need to focus on a single aspect – and this is how graphic art becomes narrative.

FALCINELLI, 2011

Itten's reasoning on chromatic contrasts remains fresh and relevant because it is a wide-ranging meditation on visual culture. All of the artefacts that we have used as examples, from Monet's painting to Gipi's comic art, from multinational logos to Greek vases, are narratives constructed through a specific use of colour. The underlying question is the same: what are we talking about here? What is it saying? By choosing the most suitable contrast for our story, we are ultimately asking what is the most precise or expressive way of narrating it.

We should not come away with the idea, however,
that contrasts always work one at a time. As we have
seen, the Parisian illustration of Shout in Figure 207 is 207
based on complementaries but also on quantities. And 218
in Hopper's seascape there is simultaneous contrast
and one of quantity as well in the small warm tones of
tanned bodies.

Let's conclude then with a superb and moving example,
an unexpected one from the Russian film director Sergei
Eisenstein (1898–1948), in a key scene of his 1925 black
and white film *Battleship Potemkin*. When the ship's crew 229
mutinies against the powers that be, amid the enthusiasm and applause of the crowd a flag is raised. It goes up the flagpole unfurling – and as it does so it is suddenly, actually, *red*!. At the time such effects could be achieved by hand-colouring the film frame by frame. Contrasting with a grey background, the flag creates an unexpected

chromatic dissonance, all the more revolutionary for breaking down the standard technical and linguistic framework. This narrative choice becomes, immediately and without intellectual mediation, a way of poetically involving the audience.

228

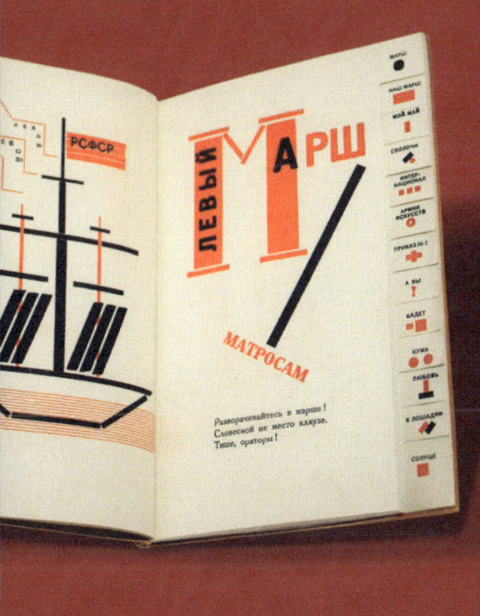
РСФСР
ЛЕВЫЙ МАРШ
МАТРОСАМ
Разворачивайтесь в марше!
Словесной не место кляузе.
Тише, ораторы!

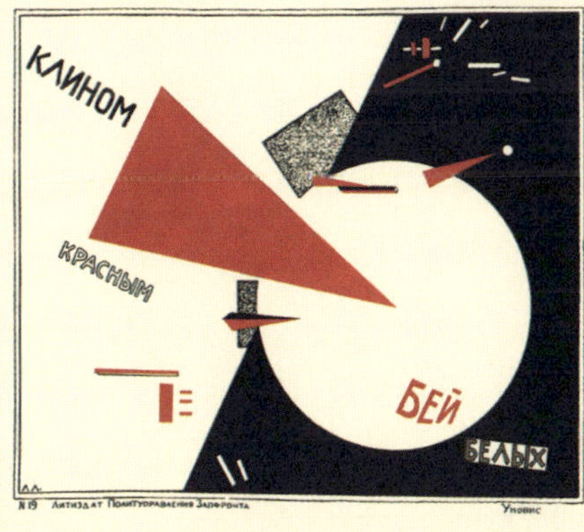
КЛИНОМ
КРАСНЫМ
БЕЙ
БЕЛЫХ

230

229

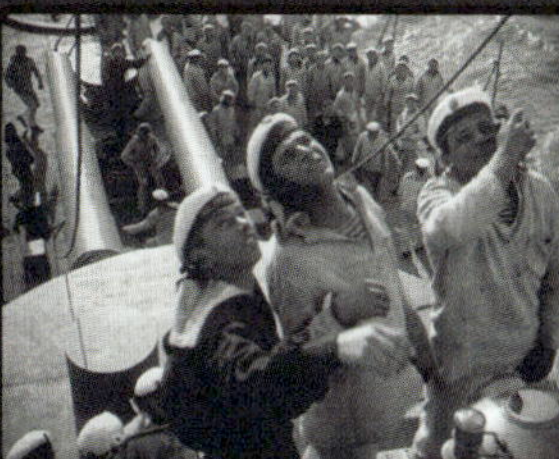

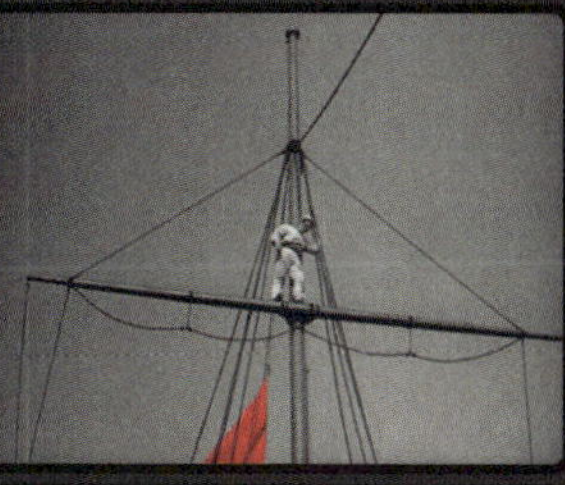

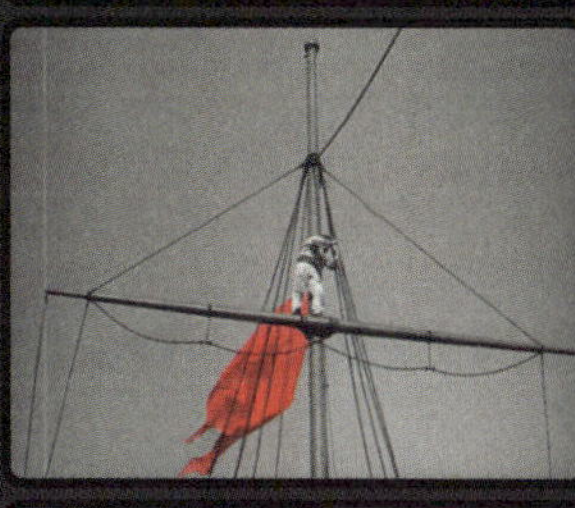

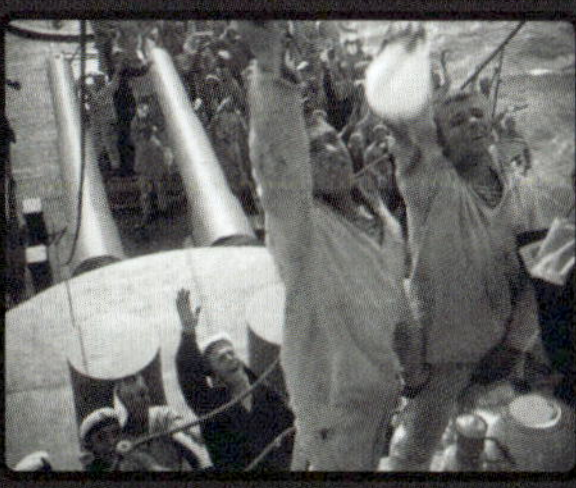

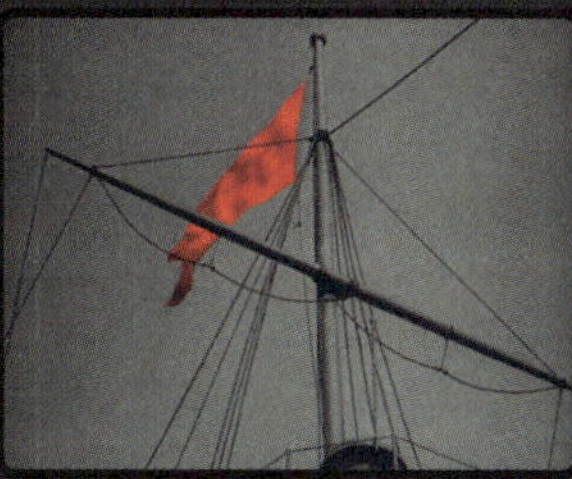

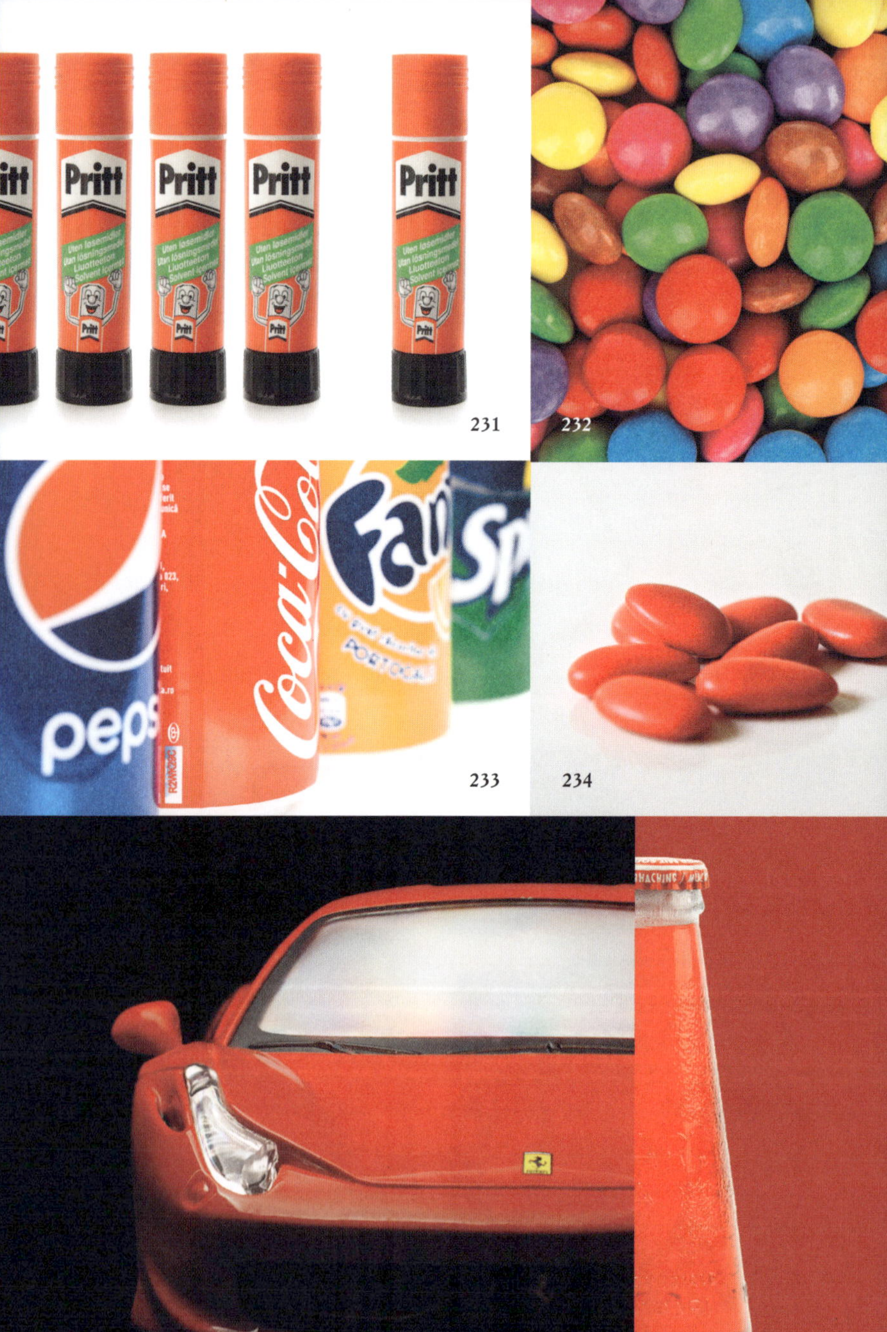

231

232

233

234

235

236

Significant Red

The Colour of Things

In 1937, Smarties made their appearance in Great 232
Britain – sugar-coated chocolate sweets that were destined
to be an enormous success. They introduced a chromatic novelty into the world of confectionery. Smarties come
in eight different colours, but the differently coloured
sweets in every packet all taste the same. The red ones do
not taste of strawberry, or the green of pistachio. They all
taste only of chocolate.[1]

Smarties were not invented from nothing: they are a
simplified and industrialized version of Italian *confetti*,
or French *dragées*, the traditional sugared almonds that
Italian godmothers offer to guests at a baptism. If confectionery originates in the practice of conserving fruit, in
the case of sugared almonds their colour soon turns them
into something symbolic. *Confetti* soon becomes pink or
pale blue to celebrate a birth; white for confirmations; red 234
for graduations; and silver or gold to celebrate twenty-five
or fifty years of marriage.

With Smarties the colours have no symbolic value: what matters is that the mixture is variegated and playful, like

[1] In 2001 Smarties made 56 million pounds for the company that manufactures them – not bad for little coloured sweets. There were eight colours chosen when they were launched, but in 1989 the light brown was replaced by a blue, perhaps because brown is too banal a colour for a chocolate sweet. Recent research has confirmed that, statistically at least, children's favourite colour Smartie is orange.

a box of pastels or Lego. A Smartie and a sugared almond are only superficially similar objects, given that on the level of significant colour they say such different things. The red of a sugared almond is symbolic, that of a Smartie is more a role or an assignment. A symbol is something that *stands for* something else (such as black for mourning, or red for graduation), while a role is something that signifies because it occupies a certain position within a system of signs.

A salient feature of Smarties in being multicoloured is the suggestion of something designed specifically for children. Their colour relates to their positioning as a commercial product, something that is absent in the case of *confetti*. So to understand what colours signify commercially, we need look no further than the target audience (or recipient) of any visual communication and the context in which that communication occurs. SCARZELLA, 2008

Let us begin with an object that embodies better than any other a key shift in chromatic habits, so much so that it transformed the electronics market. I am talking of course
238 about Apple's iMac, designed by Jonathan Ive (b. 1967), a computer that was in the avant-garde or at the cutting edge of design when it was launched in 1999. Translucent and vivacious, the iMacs looked stunning above all because of their sophisticated colours, glassy and changeable as those of a gemstone: brilliant mandarin orange, enamelled green and a deep blue that Apple calls Bondi blue after an Australian beach famous for the intense blue of its ocean and its popularity with surfers. According to some, given that the iMac was first promoted for using the internet, the name of this blue alludes to the expression 'surfing the web'. One thing is clear: the Apple iMac is the first computer that promotes itself like a sports product: it has to do with free time and

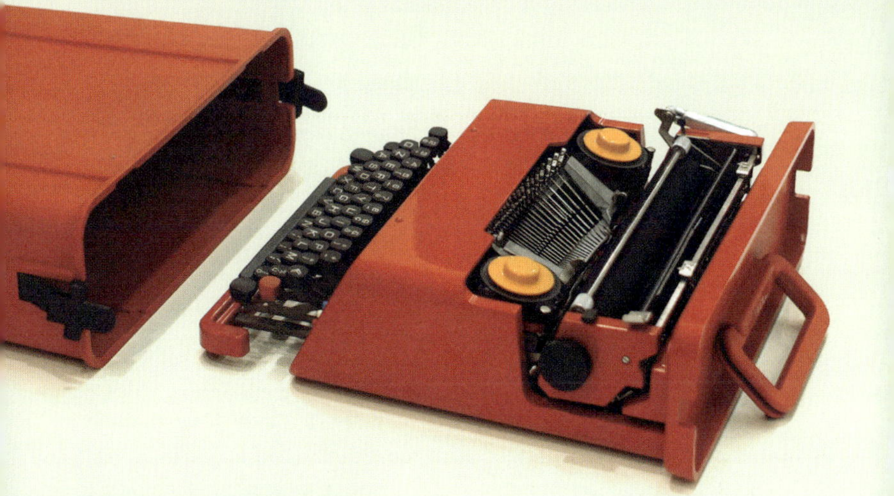

237

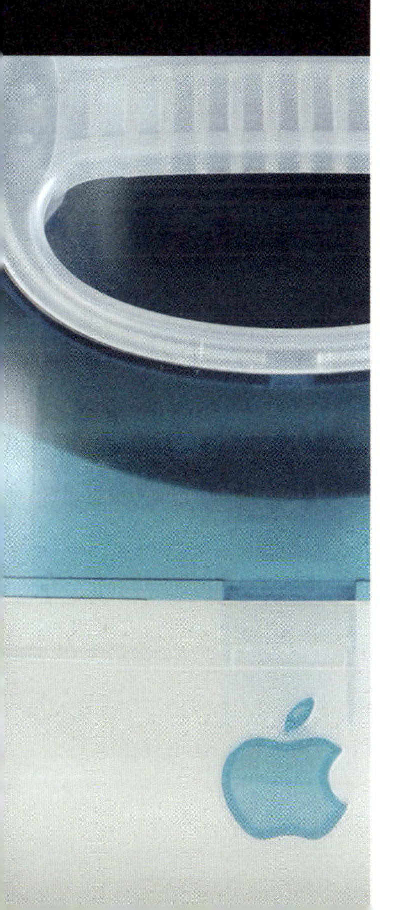

238

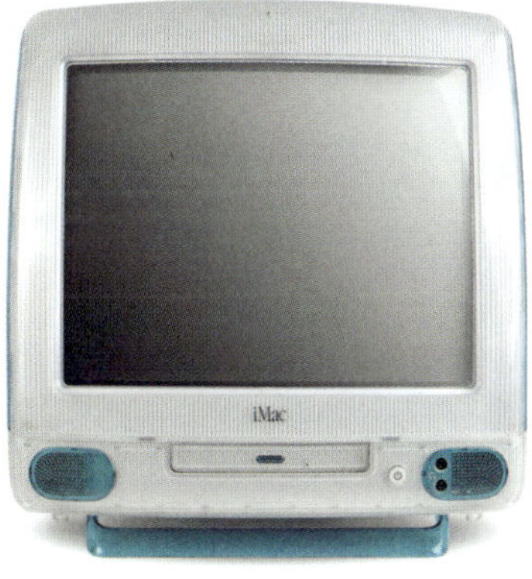

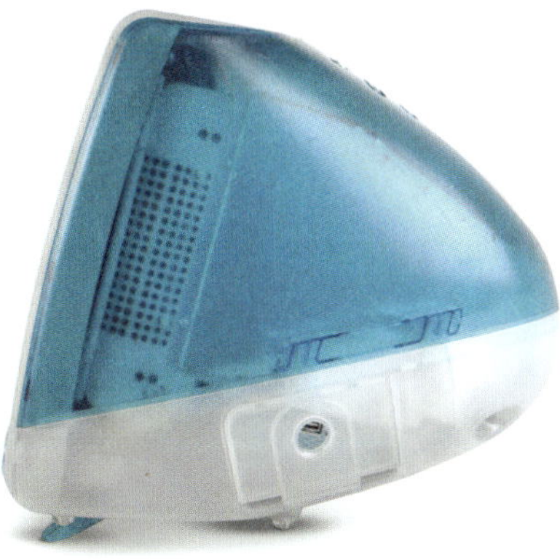

with entertainment; it is a truly *personal* computer – like an item of clothing or, indeed, a surfboard.

Up until this moment, PCs had been grey, white or black, all right angles and straight lines, signifying efficiency and seriousness. These were objects of a distinctly technological or bureaucratic kind, useful for professional reasons such as writing, calculating or designing.

With the birth of the internet, electronic products change status, starting to become instead a part of our personal identity, especially when the realities that we encounter through the computer – via the explosion of social networks, for instance – are no longer work-related.

Apple anticipates these new rituals and uses, and suddenly changes the commercial and iconographic codes with which these 'calculating machines' are designed and marketed. The iMac is rounded, soft, almost rubbery in appearance; its strikingly vivid colours inaugurate an era, from which we have yet to exit, in which style is of crucial importance. The imperative is to be 'smart', to show off, but with a certain nonchalance. 'Think different!', as one of the most successful publicity slogans of the time has it. To think in a new way is central to Apple's 'philosophy', and the iMacs, especially the laptops, as well as being functional embody a vision of the world. It was a revolution that continued with the invention of the iPod and iPhone, in one of the most successful marketing strategies of the last thirty years. Apple were not just selling an object but a social practice, a lifestyle and a way of being, corresponding precisely with a particular sector of the market.

So colour is opposed to the colourlessness of machines such as the IBM, above all in moral terms and following a company tradition. As early as 1984, for example, with the first Macintosh computer to be launched, Apple had chosen this characteristic contrast in colour. Its commercials at the time were set in a black and white dictatorship where behaviour is repetitive and oppressive – like in George Orwell's dystopian *1984*.

Into this drearily monochrome scenario a girl appears and breaks the screen on which Big Brother is speaking, shattering it in order to reveal the company logo: a vivid, rainbow-coloured apple. Playing upon Orwell's title, a voiceover intones: 'Soon you'll discover why 1984 will not be like *1984*.'

FLOCH, 2015

Black and white is associated with the essentially retrograde, and the launch fifteen years later of extremely colourful computers is the logical outcome of this advertising strategy. If the black or metallic cases of traditional electronics speak of an old-fashioned way of being in an office – one that wants us to wear a suit and tie and to dully conform, as in a dictatorship – with Apple you can finally be colourful and spontaneous. You can be yourself, whatever that happens to be.

The iMac is ultimately the first computer to be used anywhere *except* in the office, and metaphorically introduces into professional routines the spirit of *casual Friday*, that day of the week when you can go to work dressed as you like, even in bright colours. The product's success, especially among so-called creatives, is immediate. Designers, writers, stylists, photographers – everyone buys and uses an iMac. It still remains to be seen, of course, whether or not going to the office wearing a sweatshirt rather than a collar and tie makes us better or happier people.

Although it seems utterly original, the iMac does not appear out of nowhere. The philosophical and design ideas that underpin it have an illustrious forebear in one
of the landmarks of twentieth-century design: the Val- 237
entine typewriter, designed in 1969 for Olivetti by Ettore

Sottsass (1917–2007). The seeds of all future invitations to 'think different' had in fact been sown thirty years previously in those liberation movements – from May 1968 to Woodstock – that together with real political consequences introduced a stylistic and lifestyle revolution: in clothing, outlook, sexual mores. And it is at the height of all this that Sottsass comes up with a compact, light and vividly coloured machine that provides the conceptual premise for iMac laptops.

DE FUSCO, 2017

The Valentine, as it was called, is the first such piece of equipment designed to be used outside of the office. The key word in its design is 'portability'. In order to reduce its weight, Olivetti even produces a version without uppercase letters. But unlike those of the iMac, its approval ratings are modest. The time is not yet right.

Despite the real continuity here, there are also substantial differences. Whereas the philosophy of Steve Jobs is more American than Greek – something practical, located halfway between a self-help manual and a cult – that of Sottsass is a poetics, an aesthetic way of rethinking everyday things. From this point of view, the red of the Valentine has a specific historical significance: it is not produced by lacquering or painting; it is not a patina of any kind. Red is the colour of the very plastic from which it is made.

SPARKE, 2013

The postwar design renaissance in Italy, which became famous around the world, is the story of entrepreneurs who begin to specialize in investing in products made from innovative materials. Washable, stackable, modular, flexible – these new objects differentiate themselves from everything that has gone before. On the one hand, there are novel technological possibilities thanks to substances such as polyvinyl chloride, which is injection-moulded and allows production of the most audacious forms and shapes; on the other, such compounds can be colour-dyed when

DESIGN IN 1000 OGGETTI, 2008

in liquid form rather than painted on the outside. The design classics that furnished houses during that period are distinguished precisely by this quality: they have not been coloured, they are *made from* coloured material. Think of the Brionvega TV, designed by Marco Zanuso and Richard Sapper, of Joe Colombo's universal chair, or of Enzo Mari's perpetual calendar, to mention just three of the most famous examples.

FRANCALANCI, 2006

The material from which the Valentine typewriter is made, known as ABS, is a thermoplastic polymer that allows objects to be both rigid and very light. Lego bricks are made from ABS, and the Valentine is as visually vivacious as such toys: it is emphatically not decked out in the dull colours of old office equipment. If in the nineteenth century there is between a typewriter and a kitchen jar the gulf of two non-communicating systems – the first technological, the second culinary – with plastic everything
changes: a Valentine and a Tupperware container share 263
an essential, existential status. So Sottsass stands as the inevitable forerunner of the revolution instituted by Apple. The red of the Valentine itself alludes only in part to the colour of revolution: more than anything, it is a way of being in space.[2]

Colour's narrative aspects go well beyond objects created by great designers; they also involve everyday, common or 'battle-hardened' things. Let's look at two utensils commonly found in our homes: the electric drill and the food blender. Here colour is both functional and part of a commercial decision. In the case of domestic appliances, coloured plastic always serves to protect the working

[2] We could say that in the contemporary world, by standing out insistently against its background, red is above all a way of occupying space, an egocentric and wilful presence. More than a signifier, it is a character trait. Ferrari, Campari, Coca-Cola and fire
extinguishers are red because their role is to stand out strongly. 235, 236

mechanism of electrical goods, and at the same time renders the brand distinctive and memorable. If we take the range of DIY tools produced by Bosch, for instance, the combination of black and green confers personality upon
240 its electric drill while at the same time distinguishing it from a Black & Decker, which is orange and black. Without such colour differences, the products would look scarcely different from each other.

Creating stand-out recognizability with a combination of two colours is hardly an invention of modern design and marketing. Already in Ancient Rome, chariot races divided crowds into opposing groups of fans, each represented by a distinctive pair of colours – a system that is still today the basic model for all team sports. A few centuries later, it is an important aspect of Byzantine sartorial convention to dress in the colours of one's neighbourhood; the same convention we find in the colours representing the different 'quarters' competing in the Palio di Siena. And colour use of this kind is at the heart of one of the most important graphic systems of the medieval period: heraldry.

DI MONTAUTO, 1999

The reason why such 'team' strips always use a combination of two colours is that a system of single colours is not as easy to remember. If we want to buy a blue jacket to wear with blue trousers, we need to physically take the trousers into the shop: it is impossible to choose the right blue from memory. A single, isolated colour is psychologically changeable, and can be easily substituted with another, whereas combining two colours cements the relationship between them in our memory. Modern commercial branding continues to function according to a similar system.

Bosch's decision to combine green and black is a heraldic use of marketing logic. In this field, black often reminds us of firearms: the addition of green, especially dark green, evokes mountain landscapes too. So Bosch

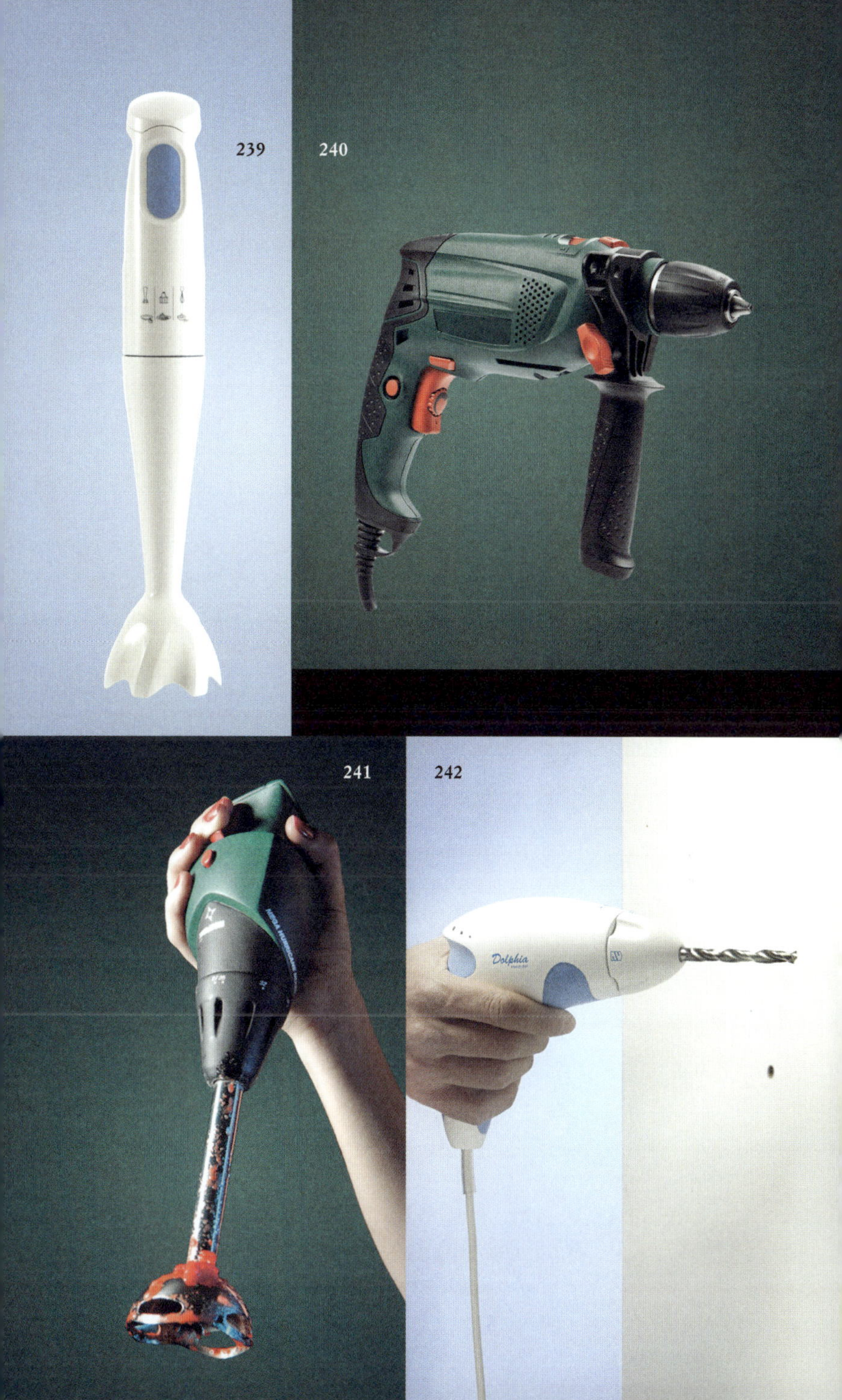
239
240
241
242
Dolphia

adds a sylvan note to the military one, thus appealing also to the lumberjack spirit of DIY.

To better understand the significance of these chromatic choices, let's put next to the drill an apparently quite
dissimilar object: a kitchen blender such as Braun's fam-
239 ous Minipimer. In essence, both the drill and the blender
are small electric motors that turn an interchangeable accessory: one of them, of course, is much more powerful
than the other – but what makes them seem so different
is above all their design and colour.

Comparing them, what immediately strikes us is a contrast between light and dark: while the drill is dark, severe and even brutal-looking, the blender is white and looks designed for gentle, almost sanitary use. The drill has a markedly masculine ethos, not because it mimics a phallocentric shape but because it apes that of a pistol or other firearm: even the switch is placed exactly where a trigger would be, in a red plastic that stands out against its green background to signal that, if squeezed, anything might happen.

In reality the Minipimer too is 'violent': it can reduce vegetables to puree in under ten seconds. But its design conceals that fact: the blade is hidden from view, enveloped by a crenellated cup resembling a tutu. The point of the drill is exhibited, like the sex of a male body, but the blade of the Minipimer is hidden, like that of a female.

These differences are reiterated by marked synaesthetic peculiarities. As dozens of tests conducted in the last century revealed, a black suitcase is perceived to be heavier than a white one of exactly the same weight. Dark things seem, albeit unconsciously, to always require more effort from us. Perhaps this is why in gyms the weights designed for women are made in pastel colours, while those of body

BRESSAN, 2007 RICCÒ, 2008

builders are black and menacing: to reassure the former and bring out the strength of the latter.

Developing this parallel, we can say that if we are macho – like a soldier or a hunter – when we are shooting, then the drill restores this testosterone-driven thrill, even to those merely making holes in a false ceiling. And if we are more feminine and move with measured elegance, then the blender guarantees that we can dive into the soup with all the elegance of a trained dancer. Reinforcing such strongly ingrained stereotypes reiterates the idea of gender difference not so much between people as between spaces: on the one hand the workshop, on the other the kitchen. Spaces, in other words, where the roles of men and women have been historically separated.

In order to graphically reveal the conventional nature of these chromatic choices, the Swedish researcher Karin
Ehrnberger (b. 1977) has designed two new electrical **241, 242**
appliances by swapping the shape and colour of the drill with that of the blender, short-circuiting our conventional product coding.[3]

EHRNBERGER, 2012

We are dealing with two theoretical (and political) objects that reveal how the rhetoric of gender distinction shows up in unexpected places. In Ehrnberger's project, it is now the blender that appears to be a weapon of war – while the drill seems medical, almost gynaecological. And to a large degree these significations are conveyed by colour.

A brand, in the end, is never just the product itself but the psychological idea that we have of it. It is for this reason, as one of the godfathers of Italian design, Andrea Branzi, has noted, that we register the chromatic identity of objects before either their form or function.

[3] The idea of comparing the Bosch drill and the Minipimer was used in Karin Ehrenberger's brilliant study *Visualizing Gender Norms in Design*. It seemed important to me to add some psychological implications to her sociological interpretation.

The relations that we have just talked about would in the parlance of semiotics be a question of the 'pragmatics' of colour: systems in which colours signify because they are used in a certain way within culturally defined worlds. This is a key factor that is always present in mass communication. A certain colour tells us something, in contrast to another which speaks and behaves differently. Pepsi is blue in order to affirm that it is not red (like
233 Coca-Cola). AGNELLO, 2013

A general example may help us in summarizing this concept. Imagine a lit red light bulb.

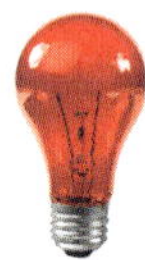

If we saw it at night, as we were walking in a modern city, it might evoke significations linked to sex or pornography, given that 'red light districts' are traditionally contrasted with those lit by white lights. If we saw it instead along with bulbs of other bright colours, we might think of the funfair, the circus, or of Christmas: the sexual aspect disappears and is replaced by a festive, carnivalesque one.

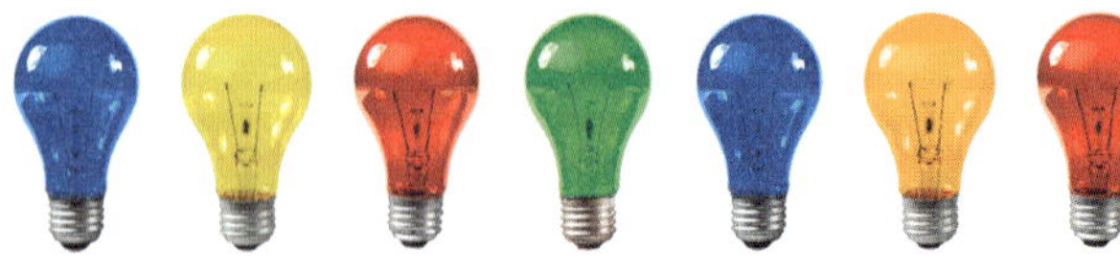

If we come across it next to a green light, however, we immediately recognize that in this context it means 'stop'.

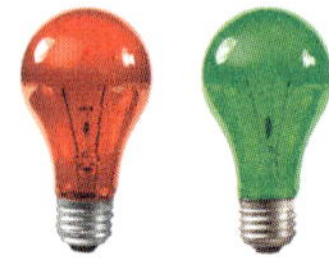

BENSE, 1972

Between the red light of the brothel and that of the traffic light there is no relationship other than a perceptual similarity: it is only in context that they have a 'content'. In the case of the traffic lights, the red is not in itself tied to the concept of prohibition, but together with the green it forms a pairing that *stands for* another one: that of prohibition-permission, or stop-go.[4] And in a different context, of course, such meanings can be reversed: green mould on a red jam, for instance, inverts the significance the colours have on the traffic light, with green becoming a sign of danger and alert.

The traffic light model, with its rigid codification, is a kind of limit case that cannot explain the complex ways in which colour 'speaks'. Colour signification is rarely this cut and dried – not least because while the meaning of the traffic lights was acquired in a prescriptive way, the same is hardly true of the Bosch drill or the thousands of other greens that we encounter every day. When Bosch chooses that particular green for its range of tools, it has certainly thought long and hard about the decision. The consumers at which its products are aimed will have varying responses to the colour: there are those who will be fond of it and recognize it as a brand; those who associate it with woodland colours; others who see through it as a question of fashion, designed to sell a few more units; others still who will use it without

[4] The traffic light is based upon two conventions: that of colour and that of position (the 'stop' light is always above the 'go'). But whereas 'stop' and 'go' are true conceptual opposites, green and red are not really 'opposite' colours, and a traffic light might work equally well with two different colours. The colour psychologically opposed to red, it's so-called complementary, is actually turquoise rather than green. The misunderstanding, as we have already noted, was down to Goethe – the first to support an idea (that green and red were complementary colours) that was destined to find widespread currency. Around this conviction, beginning in the nineteenth century, significations of a positive kind accrued to green (from nature and ecology to free telephone numbers) while red became associated with danger and prohibition.

even being aware that it *has* a colour. At the other end of the spectrum there is the journalist who has to review the product for a DIY magazine, and who is more than a little aware of the significance of that green. Communication is not a set of ideas that pass from an issuer to a recipient; communication is a process, and it is in this process that some pieces may be lost, become misunderstood or even over-interpreted. The chromatic meanings of products encompass all of this.

There are many reasons that can lead to objects acquiring a certain appearance: sometimes it is down to stringent and intentional choices, such as those of Apple; at other times it is merely the result of stylistic habits, which is to say the repetition of something that is liked and has become the norm; in other cases still it may involve merely casual or extemporary associations. In other words, colour does not always have a reason behind it or a precise, intended, rational significance.

If we attempt to use semiotic, symbolic or functional deductions as to why the most successful glue-stick is red, for example, it soon becomes an empty and absurd exercise. To invoke love? Or blood? Because Mr Pritt was a communist? It is one of those instances in which, if we do not know the whole story, it is impossible to guess. We are speaking about a cylindrical tube of solid adhesive with a wheel at the base, which when turned enables the glue-stick to slowly emerge from its plastic case. Legend has it that its creator was inspired while looking at a woman applying her lipstick: Pritt is red, therefore, because it was conceived as an imitation of the classic lipstick
231 holder. This mythical origin is unknown to the product's current customers. And yet this red works. It is now a brand: a precise and recognizable way of dominating the

DESIGN IN 1000 OGGETTI, 2008

shelf in the stationery shop. It has not a meaning but a role: to differentiate itself within the marketing of adhesives. And this applies, perhaps, to all of the products in our world. Tiffany's turquoise, Campari red, Facebook's blue do not signify something precise: they are above all ways of inhabiting our imagination.

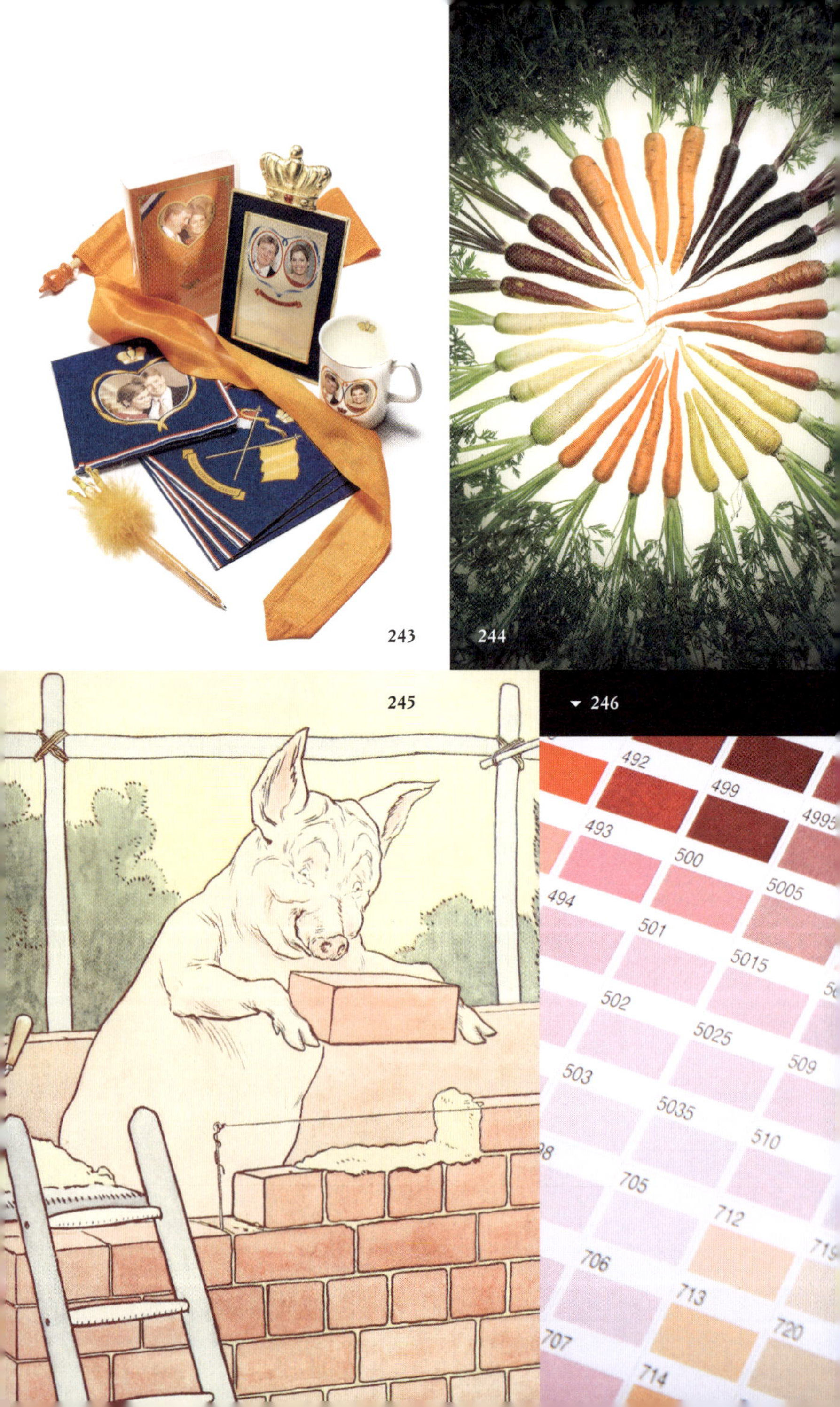

243

244

245

▾ 246

Bitter Green

Colours to Eat and Drink

Once upon a time there was a king, William Alexander
Nicholas George Ferdinand of Orange-Nassau of Holland,
who on 2 February 2002 married the Argentinian Máx-
ima Zorreguieta Cerruti. For the occasion, Amsterdam
went into festive mode, and everything – from decora-
tions to gadgets, from souvenirs to people's clothing in
the street – was orange, the official colour of the brand 243
constructed around the name of the reigning monarchy.
Precisely around, that is, the Oranges.

On seeing this colour, so vivid and brilliant, we might be forgiven for thinking of carrots. In fact, by thinking of them we are on to something. There is a historical connection between these two types of orange, though the story needs to be told the other way around.

The colour of the vegetable is the result of artifice.
The carrot that we know today did not exist in nature. It
did not evolve by itself but was designed and produced
in the seventeenth century, in homage to the Dutch
sovereign, when court agronomists selected for colour 244
in multiple graftings in order to end up with an orange
root. Even though when eating carrots we assume that
they have always been this way, they are only orange in
tribute to the Dutch monarchy.

MONTANARI, 2009

Selective breeding of plants and animals has been a characteristic human activity at least since Neolithic times. Contemporary genetic engineering amazes and frightens us because it intervenes with the origin of life itself; but the ideas on which it is founded are almost as ancient as humankind, the only living beings who think it makes sense to drastically alter the world in order to improve it.

In this process colour has often had an important role.
Pigs, for instance, until medieval times were feral and
black, similar in appearance to wild boar. Today, stereo-
245 typically, from the Three Little ones to Peppa, pigs are
pink – the new breeds being the result of selective breeding designed to make them domesticated, docile, adapted
to being reared, and ultimately to being made into sausages.

Up to this point we are still in the realms of ancestral practices: the gradual union with animals, the grafting and the cross-fertilization of plants. Today, however, foodstuffs are controlled through industrial strategies that we can only describe as *design*.

Think of the many products distributed en masse. For
even the most sophisticated, such as cured ham, Par-
mesan or balsamic vinegar – to name just a few of the
most well-known made in Italy – it is important that
they have a colour that is always consistent with expec-
248 tations: if one cured ham is darker than another of the
same brand, it runs the risk of being taken for a product
that has gone bad.

And yet precisely because they are derived from living matter, foodstuffs are by no means always uniform in colour. To obviate this inconvenience, many procedures have been used in order to standardize them chromatically – from selecting for colour the foodstuffs with which animals are fed to intervening with synthetic colourants. The category 'natural flavourings' that we see listed on many labels

CLYDESDALE, 1991

also includes substances used to correct any variation in the product. In practice it is not just sweets, ice-cream and carbonated drinks that are highly artificial. Today all foodstuffs are rigorously controlled with regard to their taste and appearance.

On the other hand, if we think about it, we realize that it could hardly be otherwise. Every time that we cook, however expert we are, the results are never the same: sometimes the mayonnaise is darker, sometimes lighter. Sometimes it is much yellower. So how could Kraft produce tons of chilli sauce that is always the same without having a protocol and an archetype ensuring that every spoonful is the same?

In all such cases what leads us to recognize the 'right' colour is memory – being reminded of something that we have already encountered, perhaps in a pleasurable way. Thinking about food reveals something more general about our relationship with colour: we always ask ourselves where it was that we previously encountered a given colour. This is why the colour system does not have a rigid semantics, but functions instead through memories and analogies.

GRAZIANI, 2005

A precise shade of colour therefore serves to unmistakeably identify commercial products. The nuanced colour 251
of butter, for instance, has been developed over time and with good reason: if it is too white, it risks being mistaken for lard; if it is too dark it may appear rancid; if it is pale it may be confused with margarine. While it was still being bought in grocery stores that customers trusted, butter could be allowed a certain variability. But with the appearance of bulk selling and distribution, communication between shops and customer had to become very precise. So what is the right yellow for butter? The answer is somewhat tautological: the one which best corresponds to our idea of 'butteriness'. This is largely thanks to supermarkets,

since regardless of nutritional value we now expect food to look a certain way. And these expectations frequently have a strong national character.

This is the case with mayonnaise: commercialized in
250 France it is decidedly yellow, thick and creamy, making
the presence of eggs unashamedly explicit. In complete
249 contrast, in the United States it is almost white and emphasizes (non-fattening) lightness. A yellow mayonnaise
is unsellable in the US, just as a white one would be in
France, where it would be mistaken for an inferior-tasting
product.

Americans also tend to refuse to buy eggs with a dark
247 shell (the norm in Europe) – so much so that American CAUSSE, 2015
farmers have refined their selection of feed to ensure their
birds produce eggs that are almost pure white. The same
goes for poultry, which in Europe is thought best when
dark, sinewy and free-range – whereas in the United States
it must be as white as the inside of a McDonald's cutlet.
Colours do not change from country to country just because the geographical context changes, including that
relating to animals. We are dealing here instead with deliberate interventions designed to make foodstuffs (and
animals) conform to the ideas that specific cultures have
about them.

In nature the potential nuances of foodstuffs are less marked than those we have become accustomed to in industrialized society, where beef must be the reddest of all meat and veal must be pale, which is to say chemically bleached. So whereas in the past food colouring was used to liven up meals, in a festive and theatrical way, today – paradoxically enough – we colour food in order to make it seem more healthy and natural. Of all the concepts we have invented, there is none more artificial than 'nature'.

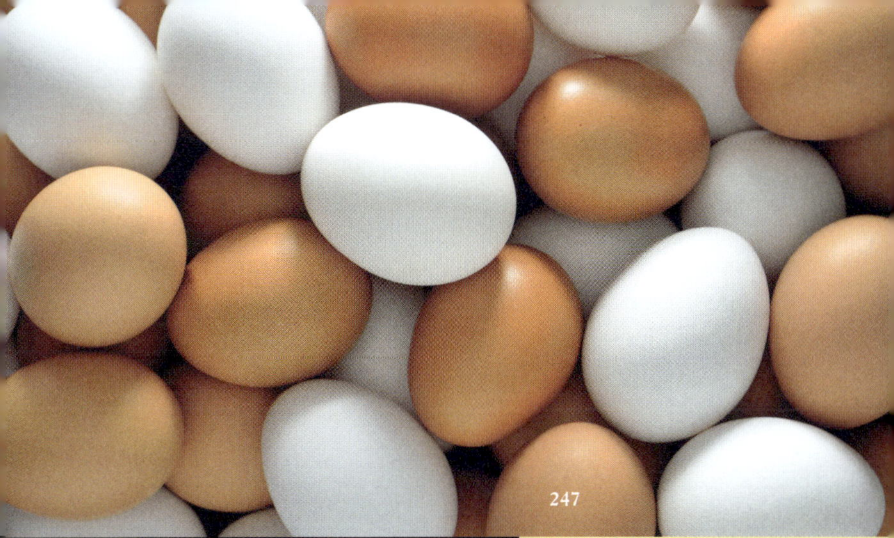

247

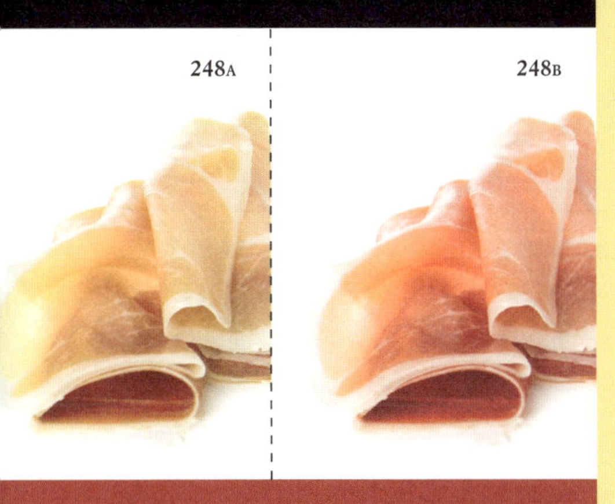

248A

248B

249

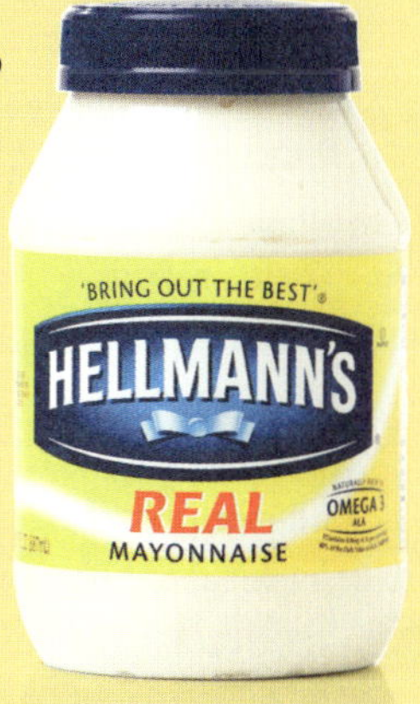

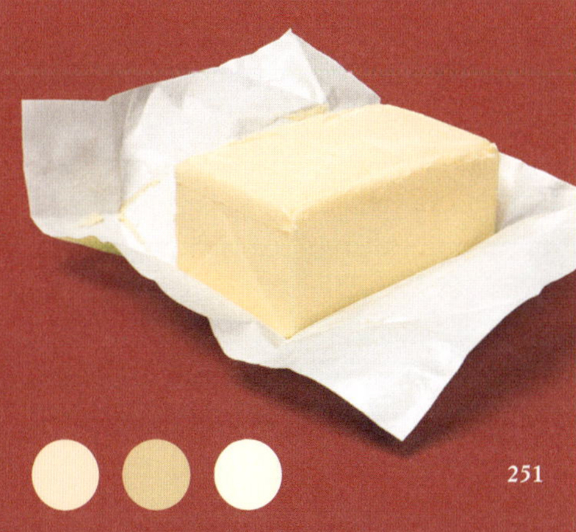

251

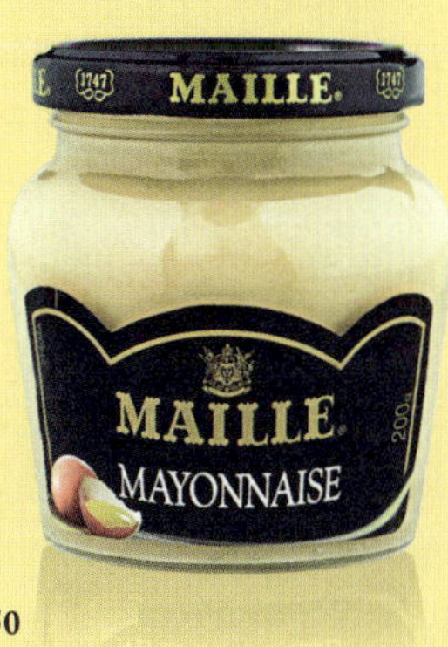

250

It is obvious that colour management in food design is crucial to its success. Icing has been made in literally every colour, to the great approval of the public. The same did not work, however (in fact it flopped completely) with mashed potato and with bread: potatoes are yellowish white and there is no way of finding them appetizing if they are green or blue – and there is even less chance of selling red or blue bread.

Much depends, to be sure, upon the particular historical moment in which certain innovations are tried: it is not impossible that in twenty years' time green bread may end up being very fashionable. After all, blue 'Smurf' ice-cream has recently been popular on the back of the success of an animated movie – but perhaps the reason for this, as with icing, is that we are more inclined to accept a break with rules regarding sweet things, given that we associate them a priori with fun. Otherwise blue in foodstuffs suggests something 'gone off' rather than unconventional – not least because the colour is strongly linked to (potentially toxic) moulds. It is no accident that the food industry invested huge amounts of money over the last century to try to explain what happens in our heads when we are confronted with different foods and their colours, revealing in the process that we always perceive food in a synthetic manner, in relation to our other senses.

The connection between colours and flavours is very ancient; Aristotle reflected on it in his *Sense and Sensibilia*. In the West it is common to associate black with bitterness, grey with saltiness, yellow with fat, warm colours with sweet and green with acidic things. As always, however, there is no rigid code. Red is often sweet, but it can also indicate something hot and spicy, evoking for instance chili peppers that are very far from sweet. These combinations are in reality extremely varied, almost infinitely so.

RICCÒ, 1999

The first to become interested in chromatic synaesthesia was Francis Galton (1822–1911), a cousin of Darwin's who noticed how for some people even *numbers* appeared to have colours. If on a page there was a series of digits written in black ink, for instance, the number 5 might stand out for them in brilliant red. Recent studies have shown that this is not a question of fancifulness or suggestibility: synaesthetics do actually *see* red numbers, perhaps due to the proximity of areas of the brain that process numbers and colours.[1] It would seem to be a mental association of a particularly strong kind. To demonstrate how a similar phenomenon affects everyone, albeit in a less decisive way, there is a simple and quick experiment devised in the 1930s by Wolfgang Kölher, one of the fathers of Gestalt psychology. It presents us with the following two figures:

RAMACHANDRAN, 2004

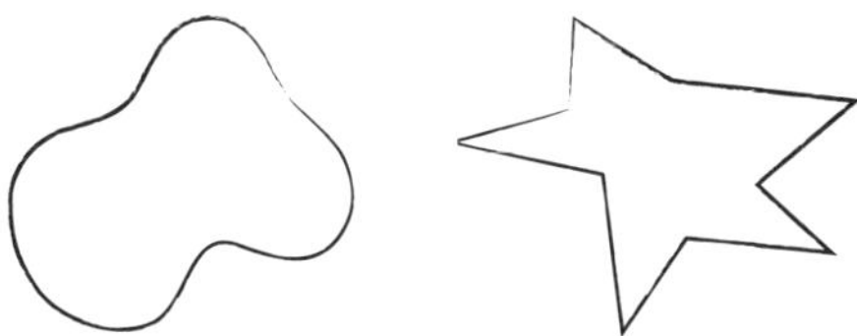

and then asks which one is 'Maluma' and which one is 'Takete'. In the majority of cases, Takete is identified as the spikier figure with acute angles, while the rounded shape is chosen as Maluma.[2] Ernst Gombrich (1909–2001) relates how, when presented with names such as 'Ping' and 'Pong',

[1] The synaesthesia is not triggered if the numbers are written in Roman numerals, indicating that the mechanism works through the shape of the script and not through the concept of ordinality. It is an exemplary case of the vertiginous entanglement of biology and education. Probably the cause is to be found in the area of visual representation of numbers that is contiguous to V4 – that is, the area of colour.

[2] Note that the test works even with populations who do not have the sharply angled *k* in their writing system.

there is not much difficulty in understanding which is the cat and which the elephant – and there is general agreement with the idea that 'u' is *darker* than 'i'.

GOMBRICH, 2008

This is possible because the brain, when confronted with two or more objects, always builds synaesthetic relationships according to which one thing is more similar than another to a term of comparison. The chromatic consequence of this process is that red is almost always sweet and rounded, whilst green is usually sour and pungent.

RICCÒ, 2008

The experience that we have of the world corroborates these associations. If we think of fruit, for example, it is notable that when it is green it tends to have a more bitter taste, while when it tends towards red it is softer and sweeter.[3] It is as if nature provided us with a graduated scale that informs us in advance of what to expect. And it is interesting to note that unripe, unpicked fruit blends in with the foliage: the riper it becomes, the more it stands out against its background. So it is clear that theories of contrasts formulated by Chevreul or by Itten, even though they do not refer to universal meanings, are nevertheless anchored to flagrant qualities of the world.

RAMACHANDRAN, 1999

With this in mind, a classic test – one often repeated and always surprising – has confirmed that the same soft drink served in different colours produces distinctly differ-
252 ent flavours: when red it is perceived as sweeter, if brown
more bitter, and when green it seems to be sourer. The expectation that we place on colours in food and drink is so strong that it ends up influencing how we actually experience taste, providing us in advance with a categorization of flavours. It is further confirmation that perception is not passive, and that our brain projects psychological images

[3] In the case of blackberries, after red there is purple and then black – the degrees of maximum sweetness.

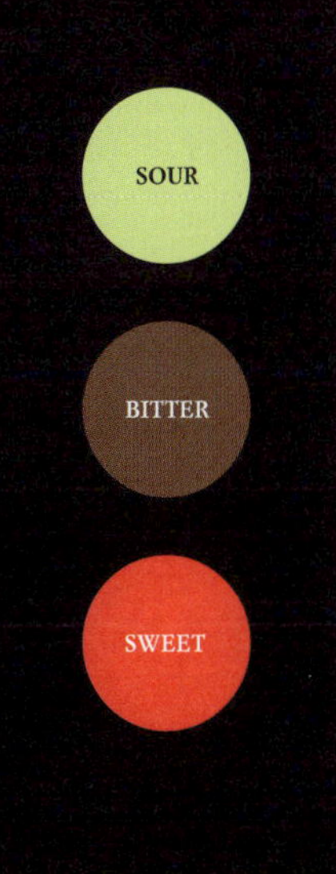

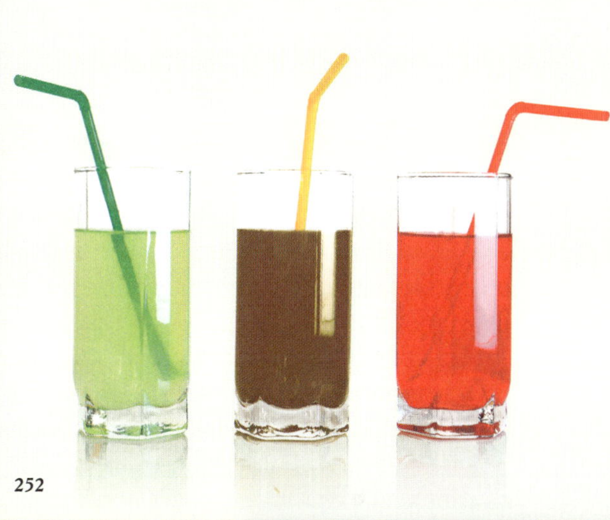

252

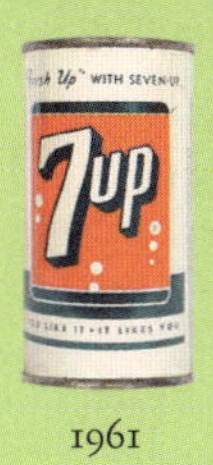
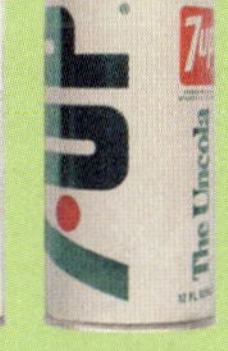
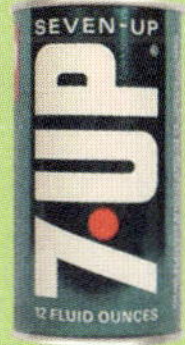

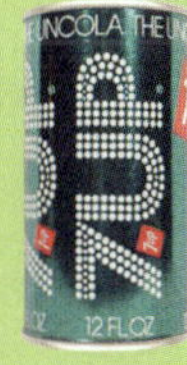
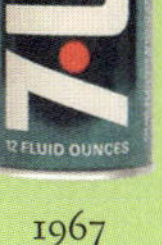
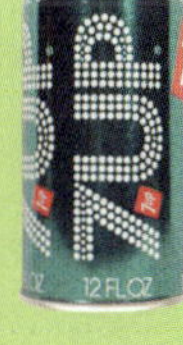

1961 1964 1967 1972

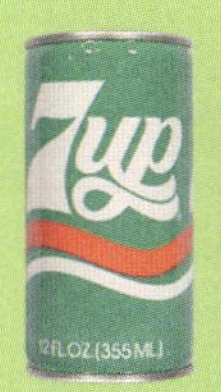
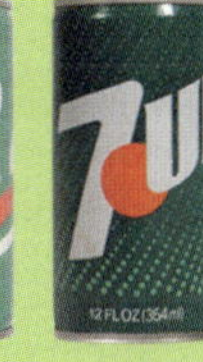
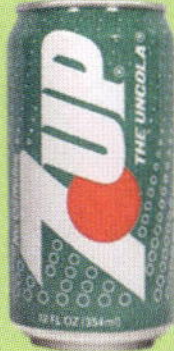
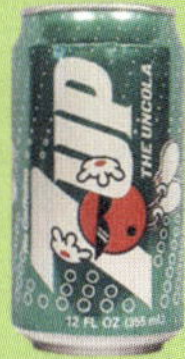
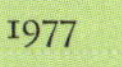

1977 1980 1992 1994

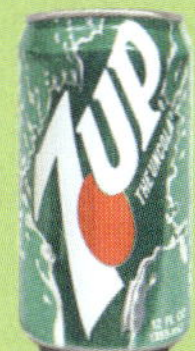
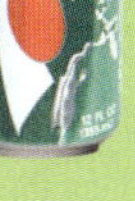
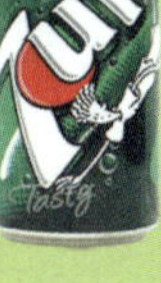
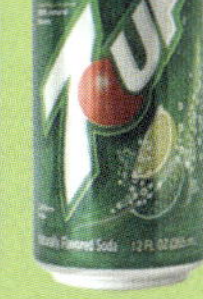
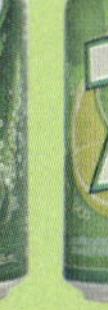

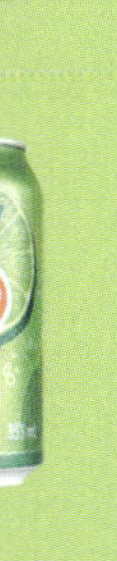

1995 2000 2010 2015

253

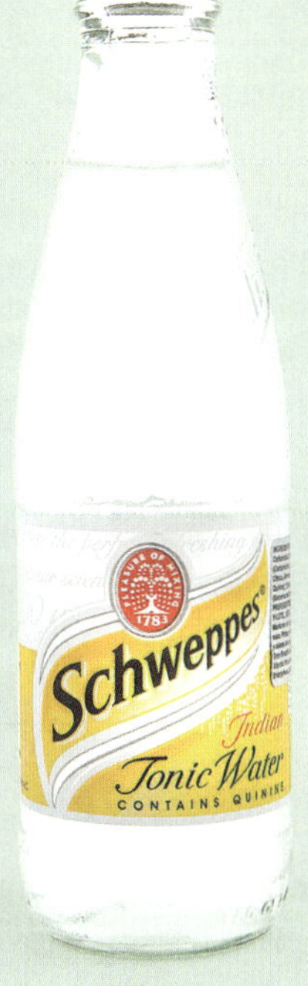

254

onto things that speed up our comprehension. Studies that have tried to explain the reasons for this have come to evolutionary conclusions – sometimes forced, but for the most part convincing. The mind, when confronted with danger (from a predator, say), does not weigh up pros and cons: it recognizes the danger and instructs us to flee. The brain always works like this: formulating rapid assessments that are more adapted to survival. This is why, when confronted with a red drink, it guesses that it will be sweet, and only then finds out. But we need to be cautious: automatic responses apply prejudices to reality, but the association of redness with sweetness is a learned fact. This is confirmed by an amusing and somewhat cruel experiment, in which a glass containing white wine BRESSAN, 2007
coloured red is offered to some sommeliers – and all of them, perhaps needless to say, detect in the concoction an aroma of currants. This is not to say that they are not expert enough; it confirms rather that the brain, even that of the most refined connoisseur, always operates according to culturally structured expectations. So much so that if we offer an orange Coca-Cola to a Western person, not only will they taste it as orange-flavoured, but they will even maintain that it is Fanta, in other words taste the BUCCHETTI, 2012
flavour of a particular brand.

Such gustatory biases have been exploited by industry not just to modify food but to package it. Packaging conserves, protects, displays and narrates – above all through colour. And it constructs the product, guiding how it will taste.

253 One example among many is 7UP, the well-known American soda drink, which added a significant amount of yellow to its packaging, leading customers to say that it tasted more lemony, even though the contents of the tins

had not changed in the slightest. An elegant variation on
this idea is provided by Schweppes, who on their trans- 254
parent bottles of tonic utilize a yellow label and cap that seem to anticipate the slice of lemon with which the refreshment is usually consumed. In this way an accessory element has been incorporated into the design as an indispensable presence in a ritual. Packaging aims to reprise and remake taste at a chromatic level, transforming the synaesthetic mechanism into a narrative formula.

Yet it is not always easy to find the right colour with which to present particular foodstuffs. When margarine was launched – the first alimentary fat derived from plants – it was swathed in yellow to remind consumers of butter. But it was a flop. After several attempts, packaging tends to be mostly golden with some green elements to recall the product's vegetable origin, inventing through the use of colour the story that it is a lighter and healthier fat. In this case the green, which is not the colour of the product, indirectly suggests the concept of naturalness.

Packaging frequently conveys something that is invisible to the eye. Some bottled water, for instance, indicates its degree of effervescence through the colour of its glass: blue for still, red for sparkling. In this case, since we are dealing with water, the international code used in plumbing – blue for cold taps, red for hot – is transposed to the culinary world. The idea of heat and that of effervescence have nothing in common, but they do when they are each paired and opposed to something blue. If the colour for cold indicates water in its natural state therefore pure or still, the red indicates a degree of modification – made sparkling by being carbonated. In cases like this, what counts is the construction of a scale within a system. The colours act as indicators. A classic example is that of herbal, mentholated sweets where the scale often goes from green to

255

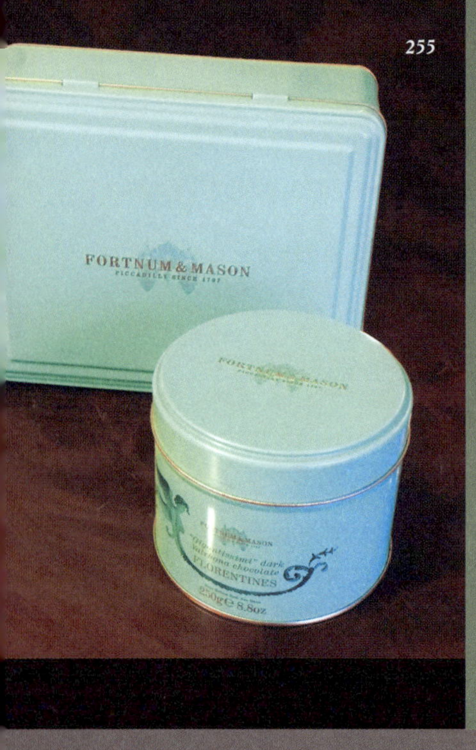

256

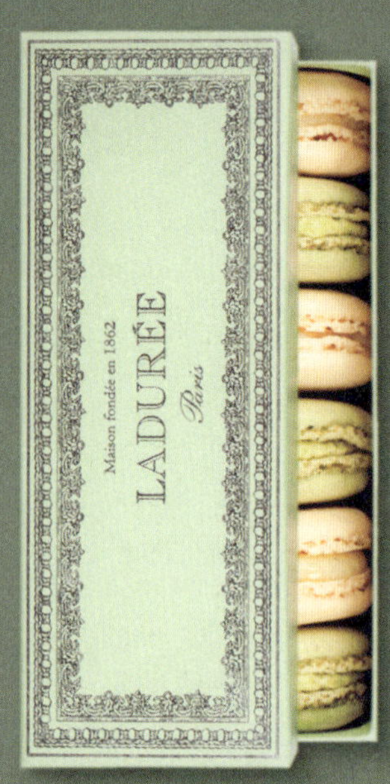

257

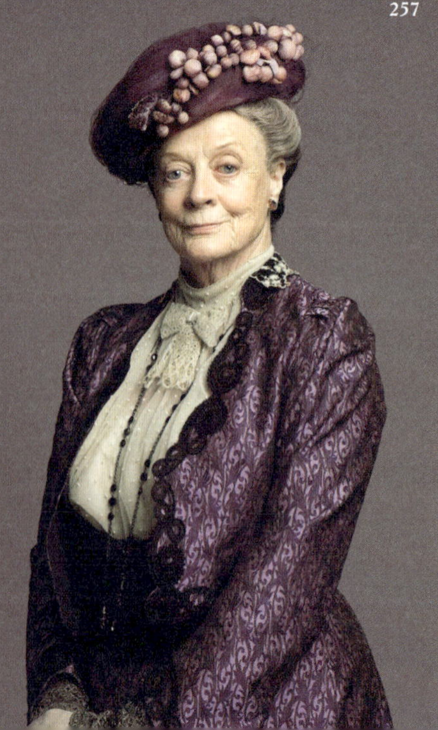

258

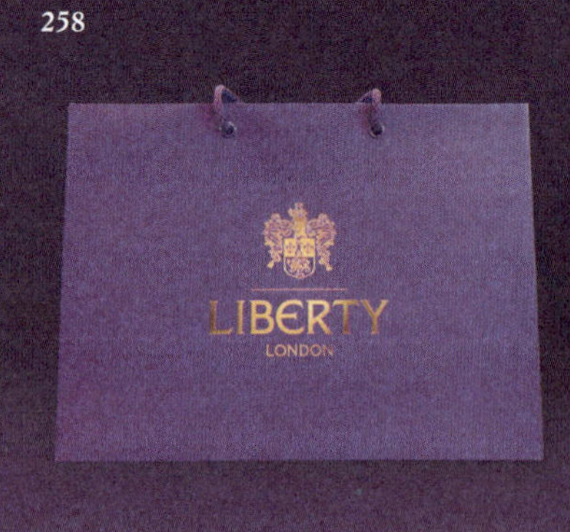

259

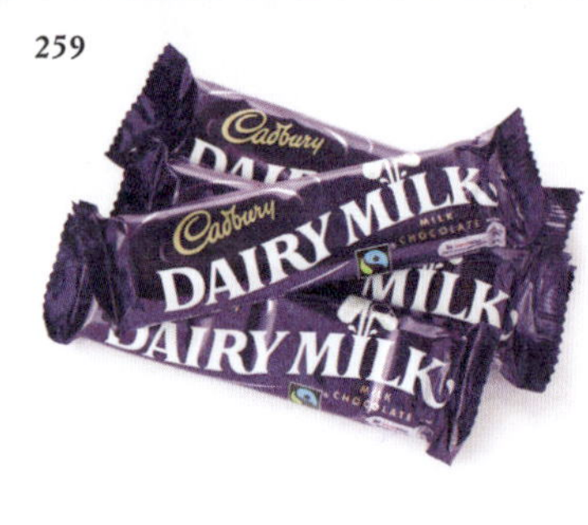

white via blue, following the typical tonalities of mountain landscapes: green in summer, under snow in winter. Moving from the colour of meadows towards the wintry ones, the pastilles become increasingly cold and intense in colour. We scarcely think of this when we pick up some sweets from a supermarket shelf, but this is precisely the power of codes: to function because they are anchored to deeply sedimented visual memories.

Unlike in other product sectors, the colour of food packaging also frequently indicates the price band. Expensive products usually display solid and refined colours, like
the teas and biscuits of Fortnum & Mason that come in 255
aquamarine or burgundy tins; or like Ladurée's famous 256
macarons, represented by a sage so redolent of the eighteenth century that it seems to have issued from the court of Versailles itself. This unique and sophisticated colour conveys luxury, calm and voluptuousness. As in fashion – think of the celebrated style of Marchionne – where the absence of designer labels or branding signifies the acme of privilege. The combination of a number of colours, on the other hand, immediately signals something commercially and economically downmarket or 'popular'. We need only think of the yellow and red of fast food, which on the one hand remind us of ketchup and mayonnaise – standard accompaniments to all such dishes – and on the other communicate a sense of speed, not only of service but of consumption.

Of all the colours used in food packaging, there is one that stands out as being of particular interest: violet. While not being vivid or primary, or anyone's particular favourite, it is a colour that never goes out of fashion and has multiple uses. From the packaging of plums and elderflower sweets to blueberry juices and everything laxative.

In the famous Milka wrapper, the particular pastel shade of lilac underlines the calming qualities of the creamy milk chocolate within – in contrast to the energizing, strenuous ones of pure, dark chocolate. In violet foods, there is always something that is slow, becalmed.

If we had to compare it to a contrasting character trait,
we could say that, unlike red, which is straightforward and
direct, violet is reserved and formal. It bears the name of
a flower, and is the traditional colour of Lent: it is con-
trite and reserved. It is the colour of maturity, in both
positive and negative senses: now signifying wisdom, now
death. In the world of (American) animation, violet is
often associated with severe or wicked adult characters,
such as the Queen in Snow White – so much so that even
their skin can take on this colour, as is the case with the
witch Maleficent in *Sleeping Beauty*, or the wicked Ursu-
la in Disney's *The Little Mermaid*. In these cases violet is
a pink that has been transformed and aged: a symbol of
those who were once desirable but are no longer so. This
is an association with some illustrious precedents: Wassily Kandinsky asserts that there is something unwholesome
about the colour and that it is suitable for elderly women.
But perhaps this redolence of old age is linked to the success the colour had in the nineteenth century, thanks to
Perkin's mauve, which made it the Victorian colour par excellence and something luxurious, elitist. It is no accident
that Maggie Smith is constantly decked out in violet in the
257 hit TV series *Downton Abbey* – with both historical and
psychological accuracy regarding the character she plays.

This Victorian lineage still speaks to us today through
258 the brand of Liberty, the prestigious London store with
its luxury textiles, teas and soaps, as well as in the signa-
259 ture packaging of another classic British firm, Cadbury's.
Regarding the latter, it is interesting to note that whereas

violet is interpreted as chic and high-end throughout the West, when the company decided to expand into the Chinese market this association was completely lost. In China, violet is 'poor' because it is the perceptual opposite of imperial yellow. So in order to signify British elegance to Chinese customers, Cadbury had to change track and incorporate yellow into its packaging.

CAUSSE, 2015

Faced with the full panorama of designs and styles, the question inevitably arises: which is the colour that 'sells' best?

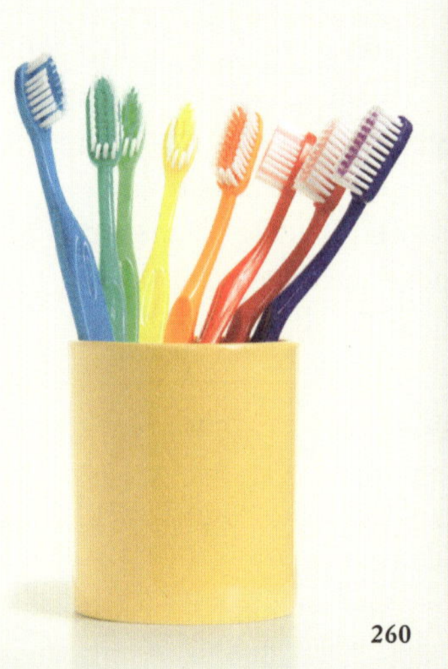

260

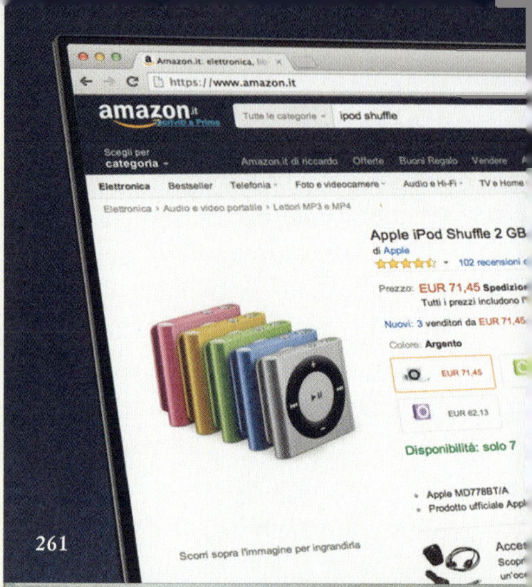

261

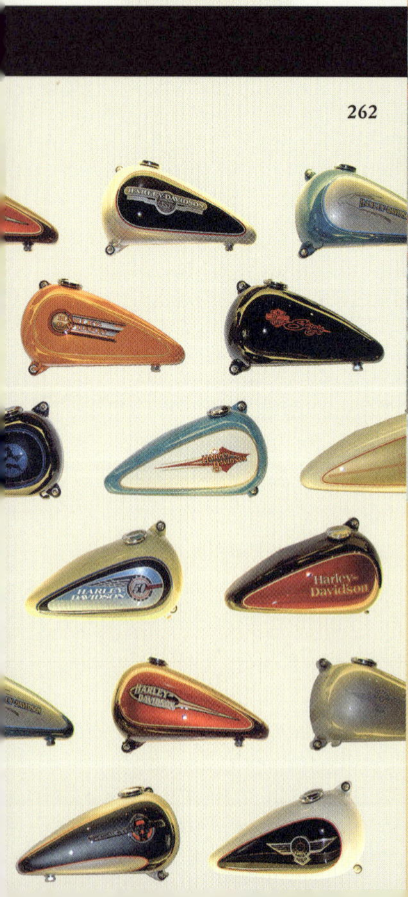

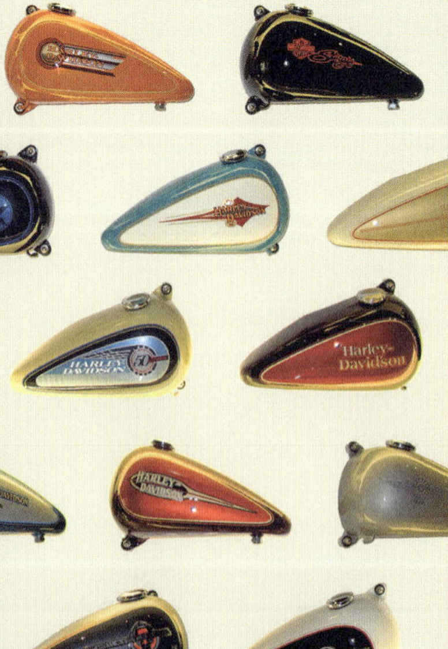

262

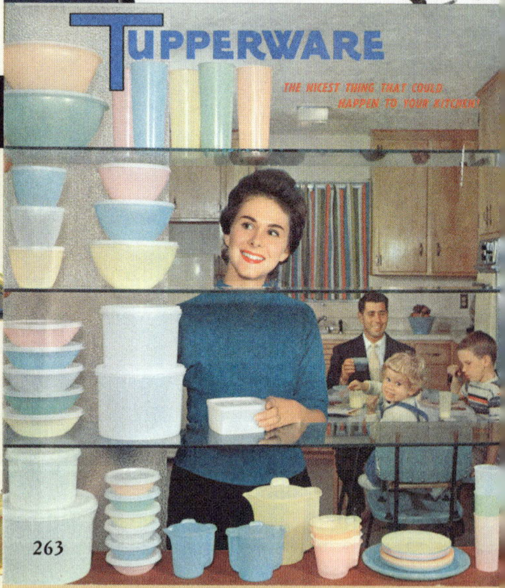

263

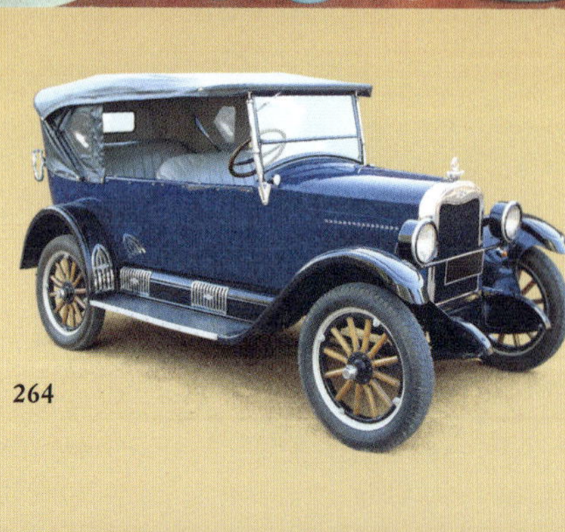

264

Colonial Beige

And Other Marketing Problems

One night, when I was about twenty years old, I was driving my mother's old red car when it broke down in the middle of nowhere. The tow-truck called to rescue it cost more than the car was worth. But at least this meant the time had finally come to buy my own car. And I wanted that car to be white.

When I arrived at the showroom, with the casual air of someone who knows exactly how to do his job the salesman told me that for a *young man* such as myself there was a new highly fashionable colour that was available at no extra cost, and he showed me a car painted improbably in 'metallic papaya'. I politely declined the offer. Slightly annoyed but compassionate, he then explained that white was classed as a special colour, and that if I really wanted it, I would have to pay for it as an optional extra. My poor parents, moved to pity at the prospect of their son driving around in a papaya-coloured car, agreed to pay for it to be white.

It would be fair to say that since a significantly large part of the public prefers white cars (one need only look around to confirm this), to categorize white paint as an optional extra is nothing other than an astute marketing strategy – especially for cars launched, for the purposes of publicity, with a lower price available in a colour that no one actually wants. Cars with metallic papaya paint jobs have been a rare sight on Italy's roads.

So far, I have underlined how the colour of products stages their identity in order to tell a story, or to make the brand memorable; and how the colours of foodstuffs interact on a psychological level with consumer expectations. Colour corresponds not only to the identity of objects but also to that of the public. If a Pritt glue-stick is red in order to render the brand recognizable, I want my car to be white in order to satisfy my own taste. It is clear that the colour of things changes status according to what those things are, and the relationship that we have with them.
A glue-stick is not a car, not least because it does not de- ASLAM, 2011
fine us in any way in the eyes of others. Nobody notices if I write with a fluorescent green marker; it would be different if I drove a car of that colour. And companies have learned how to play on this.

The first products to be offered in various colours were
items of clothing, followed by automobiles. In 1923, with
Ford only producing black cars, General Motors introduced
264 a coloured Chevrolet – thanks to the recent discovery of
Duco,[1] a nitrocellulose paint that manages to keep more
pigmentation on car bodywork in a stable manner. Offering the same car in many different colours will only become the norm after the war.

In 1950, Kenwood, the well-known manufacturer of SPARKE, 2013
electrical kitchen appliances, put on sale a white food
blender that for the first time allowed customers to choose
the colour of a product's details. Soon after that we find
263 Tupperware offering its ultramodern polyethylene food

[1] Duco is also the paint used by Jackson Pollock for his drip paintings. Drip painting is in fact a technique only made possible by the low cost of this new synthetic mixture, which is sold not in tubes but in tins of at least five litres, like standard wall paint.

containers in a variety of colours. A forerunner of these strategies, which were soon to become standard, is to be found not in the kitchens of housewives, but in the world of American motorcyclists.

After the war in the Pacific, soldiers returning from
the front who found themselves back in California discovered that it was possible to acquire army surplus
Harley-Davidsons at a good price. Given that they were
second-hand, these bikes needed to be worked on, and
along with the inevitable desire to get the engines roaring
again, the paintwork on fuel tanks begins to be customized – 262
inspired perhaps by the wartime habit of customising the
noses of combat aircraft. In the end it is motorcyclists who
are the first to flaunt the same product in different colours,
as we see in the cult film *Easy Rider* (1969), in which such
a coloured tank becomes a hiding place for drug money.

The history of this motorcycle is significant in that it testifies to a way of entering into a passionate and intimate relationship with objects: a Harley-Davidson is not only something you ride, it is something that you construct yourself, that is modified by hand, like a bespoke suit. There are those who fit longer forks, and there are those who paint the fuel tank in order to express something of their personality.[2]

In the postwar era many companies understand that there
is a new demand for personalization, and they decide to
systematically cater for it. Today it is the norm. And colour
is the primary means of personalization. If we think about
it, among the thousands of possible products – from iPods
to toothbrushes – it is not by chance that they enter into 261, 260
a relationship of close proximity with our bodies. Their

[2] The Harley-Davidson Museum in Milwaukee has an entire wall of such tanks, the so-called Tank Wall, each one with a unique paint job.

colour is in this sense quite literally personal. Still, compared to passionate owners and their Harley-Davidsons, what we are dealing with here are really pseudo-choices.

Through such practices we encounter the idea that colour is not just an attribute of commodities but also of consumers. I buy a red object because this is my favourite colour, because I like it, because I feel an affinity with it. This is the commercial application of Itten's idea that there is a profound relationship between chromatism and individual psychology. And it shows that when we ask a child what their favourite colour is, we instantly initiate them into their role as consumers.

Given the personal nature with which colour is linked to things, the soap and bath foam industry learned how to use that connection more than any other. If we look at the supermarket shelf – where bottles are arranged in or-
267 derly display – we notice that the logic of classification closely follows that of foodstuffs. Soaps for personal hygiene have 'flavours' and personalities, like yoghurts or fruit juices, with the packaging using the same design in various colours to evoke various fruits and their aromas.

This is possible because washing, especially with long soaks in the bath, has been transformed over time from a hygienic to a recreational activity. We do not merely wash ourselves, we relax – often using fragrance and candles. Soaps enter into contact with our bodies: they touch, envelop and even 'nourish' our skin, as the labelling has it. And it is these psychological affinities that influence the way we are sold a yoghurt and a shower gel: because both are 'to the taste of' individuals. Often in sophisticated ways.

'Taste' is before anything a term linked to flavour, as when we say that a certain food tastes of strawberry or

265

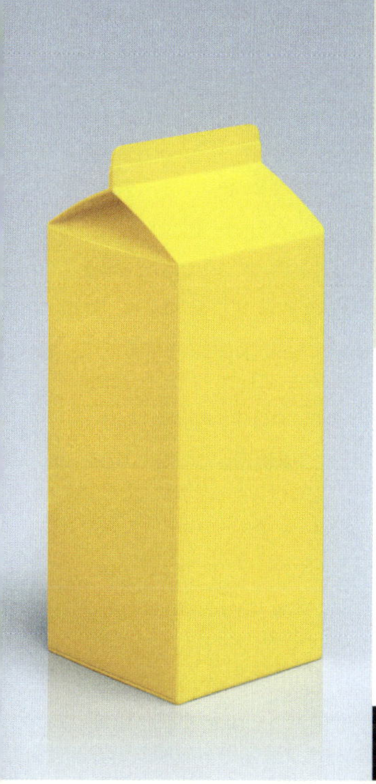

266

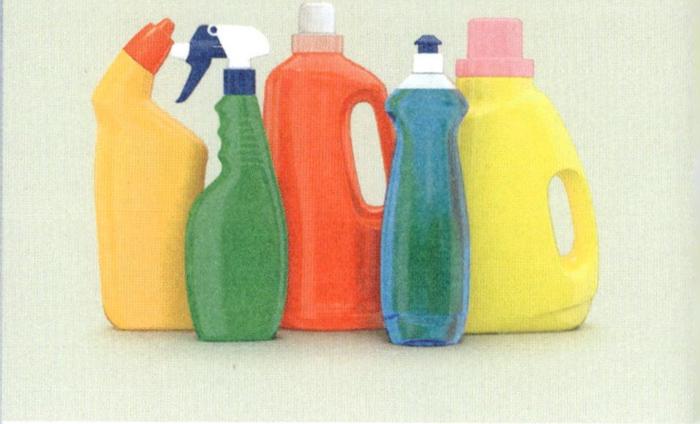

267

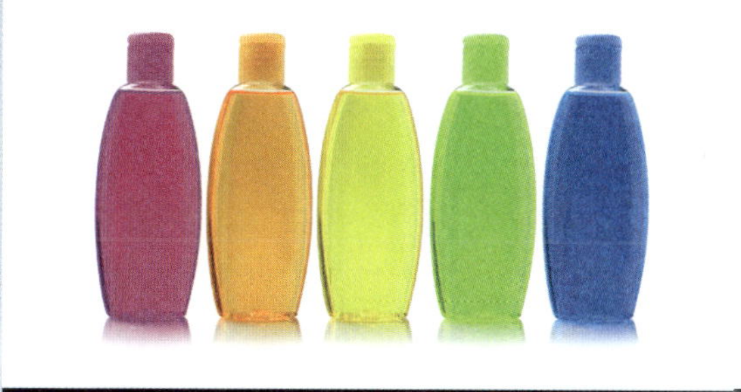

268 Survey of reactions to some generic yellow packaging (1969)

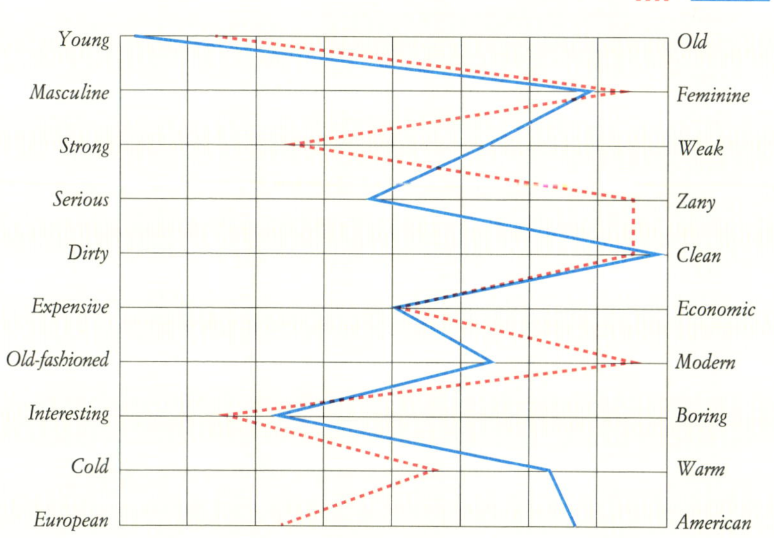

of lemon; but taste is also the capacity to discern and to choose, as when we say that someone *has* it. Exploiting this mechanism, packaging performs an evocative role: changing the fragrance of a shampoo means changing its colour. And that colour is certainly not a given. Soap does not have a colour, and deciding upon which one to lend to it is purely a matter of design, imposing upon it a 'psychological flavour'. It is no accident that when this does not happen the product is described as 'neutral'. In this sense the colour is a rhetorical figure, something that stands for something else. The many nuances refer to plants and to flowers, suggesting links between these and their association with possible curative and medicinal properties: energizing fern, relaxing camomile, soothing sandalwood, refreshing orange and so on. At the root of this is the traditional model of herbal taxonomy, but fancifully transformed into a fictional world. While products aimed at the family or at women continue to have a connection with the natural world, those designed specifically for men, especially sporty ones, quite deliberately avoid this – explicitly declaring the artifice of their manufacture and recalling instead the colours of cars, of chrome plating and sports equipment. In soaps for men, there is no 'flavour' but personality. Only chemistry, with no connection to plants and flowers.

And so any association seems possible – even using beige to give bubble bath a certain 'colonial' redolence, albeit one based on its cinematic stereotypes, suggesting through a dominant note an entire chromatic imaginary: that of exotic landscapes, white linen suits, and wicker mats and armchairs. From films such as *Out of Africa* (1985), featuring a sighing Meryl Streep, to *Indochine* (1992), with the passionate Catherine Deneuve, beige became a synonym of relaxation, of a health cure, of a break from the

AGNELLO, 2013

noise of the contemporary world. But it is, of course, a ridiculously problematic and paradoxical choice: one that identifies only with the worldview of the conquerors. Colonialism involved the subjugation and exploitation of entire peoples – and it is bad taste to use it in marketing toiletries. But, as we know, not all historic facts were reported in the same way to a public whose memory is short-lived and often seems not to recognize such vulgar contradictions. After all, visual design has an enormous, sometimes nefarious power: as when deceiving the consumer to be always on the side of the winners and the privileged. Even when purchasing a bar of soap.

For some years now, this logic has been echoed even in the world of household detergents, products that are usually less amenable to personalization. Bleaches, ammonias **266**
and perborates have begun to exude the 'taste' of lemon, orange and even coal – the latter based on the idea that at one time ashes were used to wash clothing. Even if the possibilities appear infinite, we always have particular expectations for specific products, and it would seem strange to us, at least at the present moment, to buy a detergent in a brown container, even if marketing has managed to get us to accept a black bottle for those intended to be used for dark clothes. This would have been unthinkable thirty years ago, when the cleaning power of soaps was linked exclusively to whiteness.

There are consumers who think that lemon is best for washing plates; those who love the fragrance of 'fern'; and those who prefer the traditional 'Marseille', maintaining that soap should be colourless and should just smell of soap. The only chromatically viable path is therefore differentiation. Like at the movies, where we have westerns and romantic comedies, thrillers and costume dramas, in the society of the image all consumer goods, even soaps, have become narrative genres.

It is not for nothing that corporations have for years been conducting market research in order to understand which is the most suitable colour for detergents. It is an industry worth billions. Nevertheless, a century of market research has only succeeded in confirming that there is no colour, other than white, that is better at signifying cleanliness.

This question about favourite colours (and about the one that sells most) is actually more complex than it seems. If we look at the results of tests conducted by companies fifty years ago, in the golden age of marketing, responses to colour change from country to country, and in some ways are more interesting than those that are emerging today.

In a prescient book from 1969, *Color Sells Your Pack-* FAVRE, 1969
268 *age*, there is a graph comparing differences in chromatic
taste between Holland and the United States, among other
places, showing the maximum distances between what
the public in each regards as important, authoritative or
265 attractive. For the Dutch, yellow is definitely a peculiar, even a non-serious colour; for the Americans it is associated with nothing less than modernity itself. Today, in globalized times, national differences between consumers are less marked and preferences are becoming uniform, partly due to the new supranational imaginaries favoured by the internet.

With this in mind, a few years ago I was asked to design a series of novels to be sold on news-stands, the idea being that they would be divided according to the dominant emotions with which they dealt – love, hate, friendship, and so on – replacing classification by traditional literary genre, and building a library of bestsellers based on emotional atmosphere instead.[3] From the point of view of design, the idea was to link each sentiment with a distinctive colour. Making the first associations was easy: red for love, black for hatred. But the others proved to be somewhat more problematic: would friendship, for instance, be better represented by orange, or by green? Since we are talking about an edition with a large print run and decidedly 'popular' purpose – conceived, that is, in order to speak to readers of different social backgrounds and age groups – some preliminary research was in order. It was in the process of this research that the first surprise occurred. The statistical results, spread across Italy and drawn from the whole social gamut, revealed that for Italians love is violet and hatred is blue. This was data that no one could have second guessed.

This little anecdote speaks volumes about how slippery, difficult to utilize, if not to say altogether useless, market research can be. Those surveyed, in effect, had to link ten colours to ten emotions – proceeding partly by precise choices and partly by exclusion; so that if while linking red to love they preferred to attribute this colour to friendship, in the final result love ended up being violet. This story also shows that there are no intrinsic meanings to colours, not even for a hypothetical 'average person'.

One of the crucial ways in which companies think about colours concerns not just what we think of as attractive now, but what might be fashionable in the future. This is done in what the industry calls 'colour forecasts', a significant term indicating that, like predictions of the weather, they are uncertain – and when long-range are especially subject to chance and guesswork.

[3] This was Benedetta Centovalli's idea, for De Agostini.

The way colours are constructed in fashion is very well portrayed in a memorable scene in the film *The Devil Wears Prada* (2006), a broadly fictionalized but substantially accurate take on the industry. The protagonist, Andrea Sachs, is a young journalist who finds herself in the coveted position of assistant to the infamous Miranda Priestly, the editor of New York's most prestigious fashion magazine. Andrea starts out by looking down on glossy magazines, to the point of laughing at the minute evaluations that go into choosing the precise colour of a belt or other details. Faced with such an attitude, Miranda makes a speech on the true power of design that is as didactic as it is exemplary.

'You think that this world does not concern you,' she says; 'you go to your closet and you select out, oh I don't know, that lumpy blue sweater, for instance, because you're trying to tell the world that you take yourself too seriously to care about what you put on your back. But what you don't know is that that sweater is not just blue, it's not turquoise, it is not lapis, it is actually cerulean. You're also blithely unaware of the fact that in 2002 Oscar de la Renta did a collection of cerulean gowns. And then I think it was Yves Saint Laurent, wasn't it, who showed cerulean military jackets? And then cerulean quickly showed up in the collections of eight different designers. Then it filtered down through department stores and trickled on down into some tragic "casual corner" where you, no doubt, fished it out of some clearance bin. However, that blue represents billions of dollars and countless jobs and so it's sort of comical how you think that you've made a choice that exempts you from the fashion industry, when in fact you're wearing the sweater that was selected for you by the people in this room.'

This lecture highlights two key concepts. On the one hand, it reiterates that colour in fashion is the result of thoroughgoing scrutiny: evaluating what has worked, discarding what is tired, thinking about current and historical trends, as well as even about the political and social values of the moment. On the other hand, it makes clear how the success of a particular colour may well also be determined by chance and inscrutable elements that lead to its survival – inasmuch as it is more adapted in a Darwinian sense to certain prevailing historic conditions.

This implies that the forecasts are the product of both study and chance, and that a good designer is perhaps one who combines cultural flair, the courage to take risks and the power to impose an idea thanks to the influence they have gained over the years. It is important that Miranda underlines how cerulean was first launched by Oscar de la Renta and then copied. It is saying that only when we are authoritative do we become imitated.

The elusive and aleatory aspects of colour that prevent it from ever being dominated by marketing are due to the fact that not everyone is interested or attentive. For many, one colour is as good as any other. So much so that when I asked my mother why she had chosen red for the colour of our old car, she replied simply: 'It was the cheapest.'

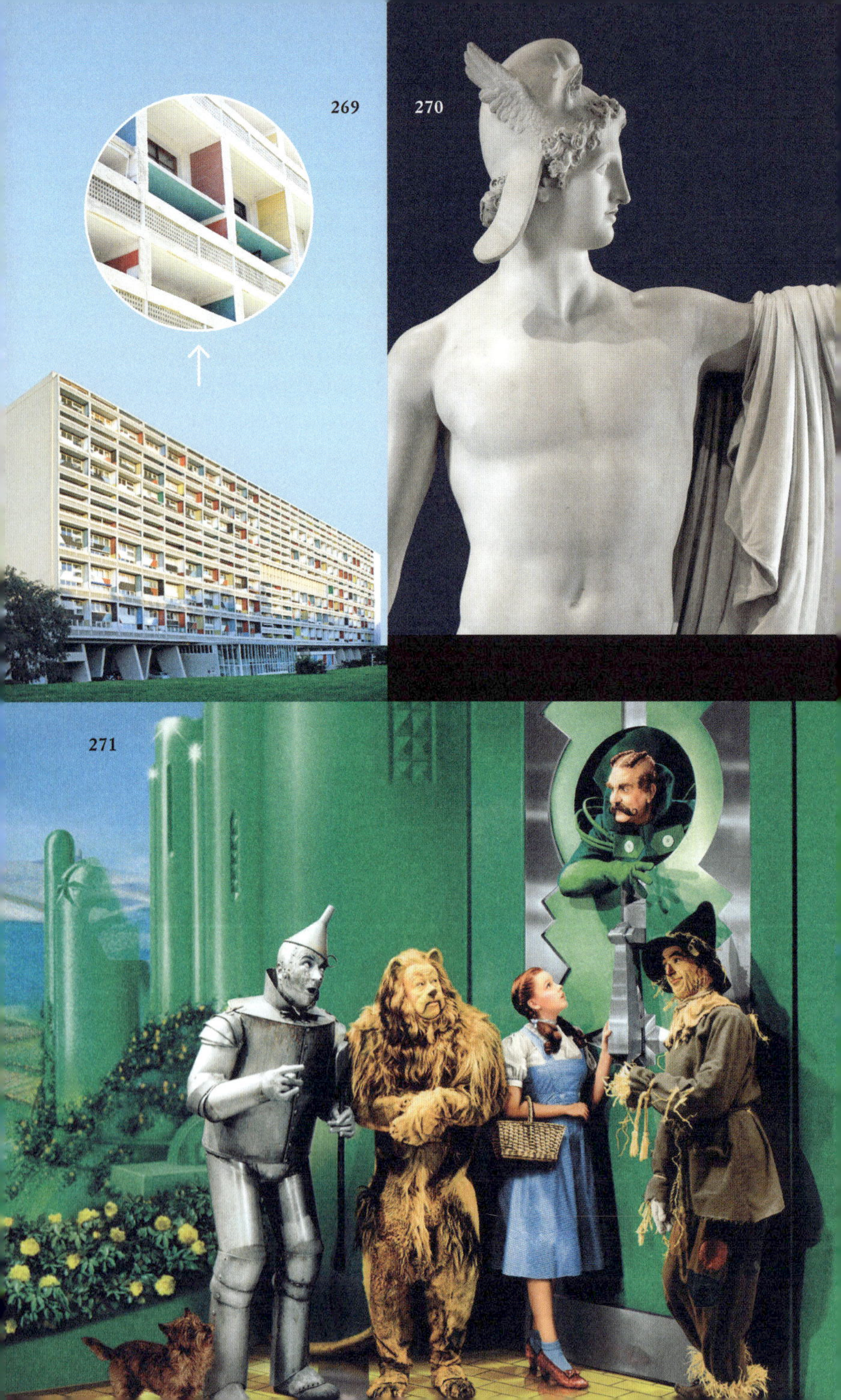

269
270
271

Moral White

Myths of Today, Born Yesterday

Travelling in a parallel world is a classic motif of fantasy fiction, as is the trope in which we eventually find that everything, after all, was 'only a dream'. In the *Wizard of Oz* – that most famous and extremely colourful film from 1939, based upon an almost equally famous novel first published at the beginning of the twentieth century – Dorothy, like Alice in Wonderland, crosses a threshold, passes daringly through perilous adventures, learns a lesson and makes it home, older and wiser, to her relatives' farm in Kansas. Travelling on the *other side* teaches her to appreciate a reality that had previously seemed too straitened. 'There is no place like home,' Dorothy concludes. It is a fairy tale with a moral, in which the heroine learns something fundamental and becomes a better person.

In visual terms the highly imagined and astonishing Land of Oz is contrasted with the reality of a rural Kansas peopled by simple, actual folk. Whereas Oz is extravagant and unreal, Kansas is traditionalist and concrete: in the former we see characters performing a kind of vaudeville who in the latter are working the land. The contrast is pushed to the limit of stereotyping: if Oz is artifice, conspicuous consumption and hyper-civilization, Kansas is inhabited by those who are untutored but in authentic contact with the truths of life. These are themes dear to the American narrative: the contrast between metropolis and province, town mouse and country mouse.

Designed to showcase the new marvels of Technicolor, the film uses a narrative trick which has contributed to its iconic status: the scenes set in Kansas are in black and white, whereas those in Oz are in colour.[1] And what amazing colour it is! We are dealing here with a moral contrast translated into chromatic terms: if the simple peasant protagonists triumph over the seductions of the metropolis, then it means that the austerity of black and white is preferable to the frivolity of the multicoloured because it is more authentic. Paradoxically, and not without irony, it was as if Hollywood was demonstrating the false value of Technicolour.

This is an ancient theme and its echoes are still being felt. For many years *auteur* films were shot in black and white as it was seen as more serious and concrete compared to colour; and there are many young photographers who attribute to compelling artistic reasons their decision to work in black and white. If the fear of images and the desire to destroy them is known as iconoclasm, we are dealing here with a similar phenomenon on a perceptual level: chromophobia.

BARTHES, 2005 BATCHELOR, 2001

The contrast between colour and non-colour is so ingrained that the significance of it is overlooked. This is also a way in which colour speaks and narrates, though in this case rather than talking about meanings in the strict sense we should talk about habits, idiosyncrasies, social uses.

There are multiple instances beyond those provided by cinema and photography in which we think and behave by employing just such a dualism: when we divide the laundry

[1] In the original print of the film the sequences in black and white were actually coloured sepia, in order to suggest a more distant past or bygone era, like nineteenth-century photographs.

into whites and colours before putting them into a washing machine, for instance – for here too, as in film, colour can assume the role of a dangerous antagonist – in the form of a bright red sock that contaminates the pure whiteness of sheets and towels. Or think about how men's dress- and workwear, which is always dark or black, contrasts with the colourful shirts appropriate to leisure and sport.

There are even phrases that reaffirm such moralized colourism: when we speak of 'white' or 'plain' food to indicate a strict diet or penance, or of 'colourful behaviour' to signify behaviour that is excessive or unregulated. The origin of this ideology is probably to be found in sumptuary laws that have set themselves against brashness and 'show'. Colour is baroque and immoderate; monochrome is measured and tastefully correct.

QUONDAM, 2007

In art, design and matters of taste, the myth of plainness has ancient roots – and appears to be an ethical imperative before it is a question of form. It is Protestant culture at the beginning of the sixteenth century that establishes – or imposes – the virtue of understatement. From portraits of the period we can see that the Northern bourgeoisie dresses in black, in open conflict with the 273
bright colours worn by the princes of Italian courts: colourful dress is perceived as disproportionate, excessive, Catholic and Mediterranean in its showiness. By the same token, dressing in black becomes synonymous with moral measure and restraint, with inner composure. It is symbolic of the virtues of nascent capitalism, of people who have prospered through hard work rather than with inherited wealth and privilege.

It should be said, however, that dyeing cloth black at the time was itself a difficult and costly process. This is why it is favoured by the dominant class, who prescribe it as a sober colour par excellence. Until the end of the

nineteenth century, the popular classes dress for funerals SURACE, 2000
in their 'best' clothes of any colour; the choice of the elite
to wear the most costly colour instead becomes a question
of status as much as it is of mourning.

The industrial revolution inherits and develops this
mentality, until it becomes the winning, dominant model: PASTOUREAU, 2008
today, on formal occasions, we cannot *not* dress in black.
274 The dinner suit is the prestigious oxymoron of under-
272 stated glamour. Audrey Hepburn in a black dress is the
epitome of the restrained plainness (non-aristocratic and
non-Catholic) that continues to be considered one of the
most authentic forms of elegance, including in many Mediterranean countries.

Henry Ford once famously joked that his customers could have one of his cars painted 'any colour they like, as long as it is black'. And cars were not the only products subject to this rule. The first telephones were black, as were the first irons and many electrical appliances. White, on the other hand, was used for fridges, in association with the idea of hygiene. Giving impetus to such convictions, there is a fact that seems unconnected and of secondary importance but nevertheless had a profound effect: the circulation, starting from the Renaissance, of printed texts.

Before the fifteenth century books had extremely col-
275 ourful illustrations, and even the paper or parchment from
which they are made would be dyed, providing red pages to
be written on in gold, or black ones with white writing. Bibles, prayer books and other illuminated manuscripts are a
flowering of chromatic expedients and visual seductions. But
the printed book invented by Gutenberg, for both technical EISENSTEIN, 2011
and economic reasons, immediately imposes as standard a
276 black text upon a white background. This quickly becomes
the type of all books, so much so that even today colourful

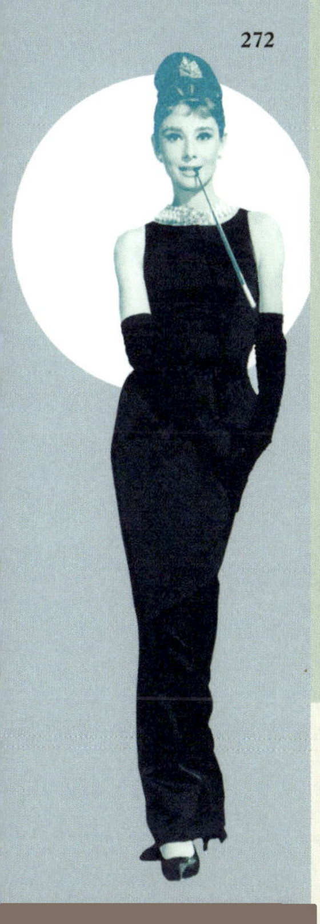
272

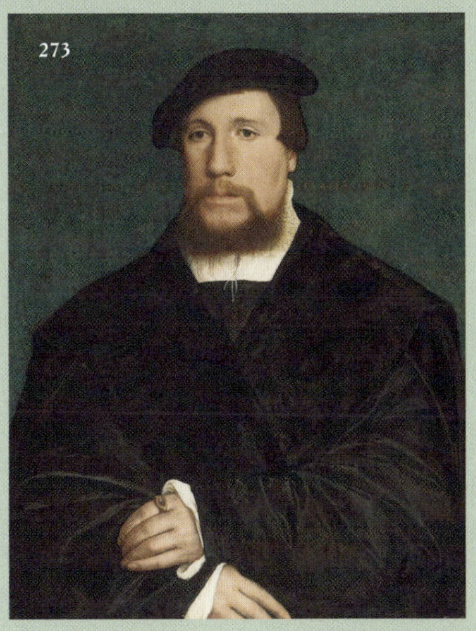
273

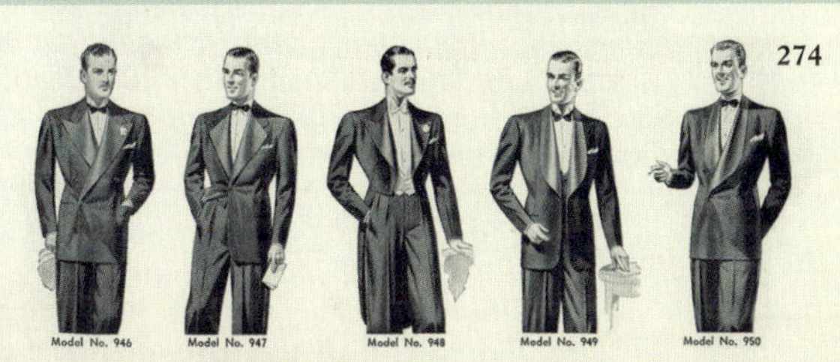

274

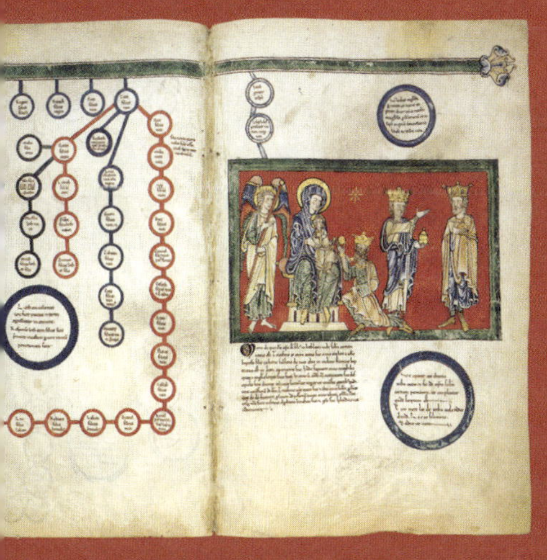
275

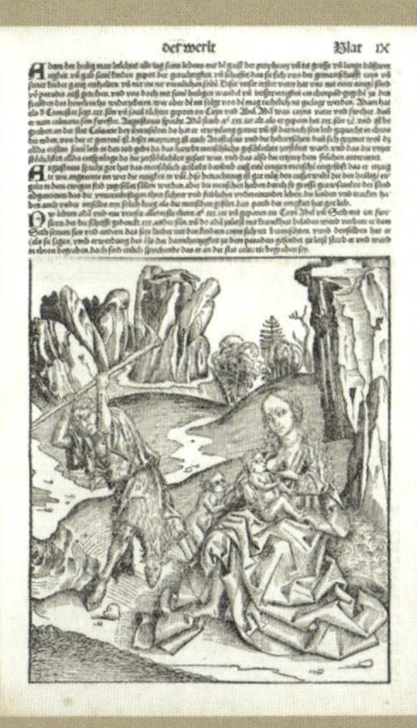

276

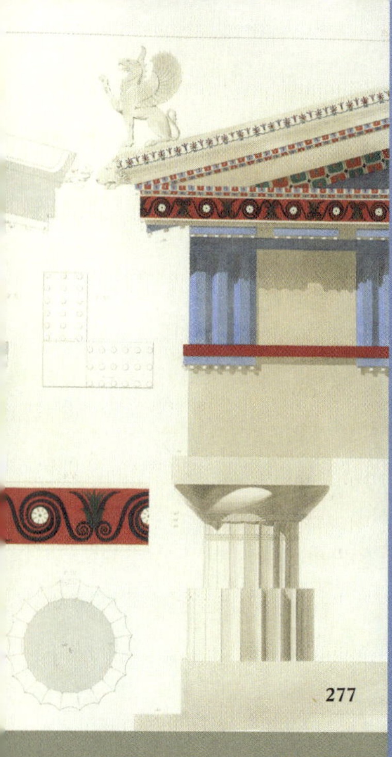
277

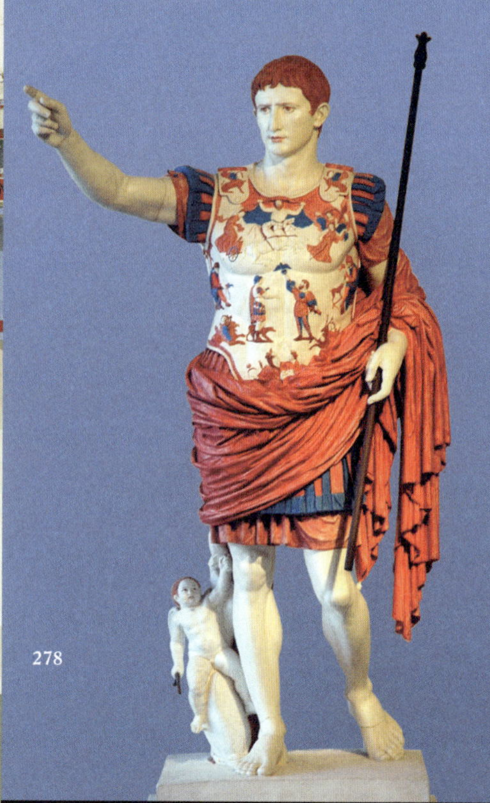
278

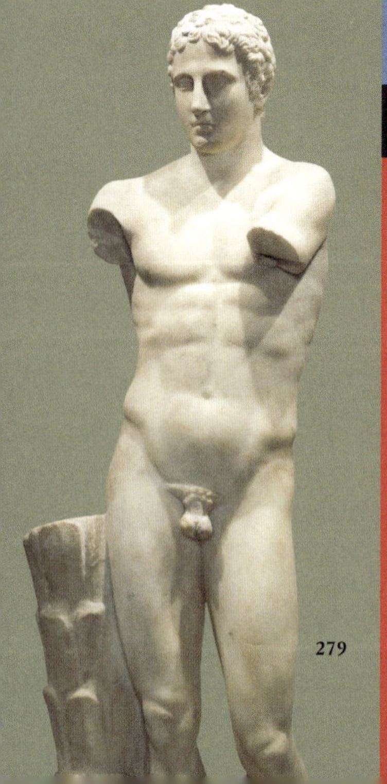
279

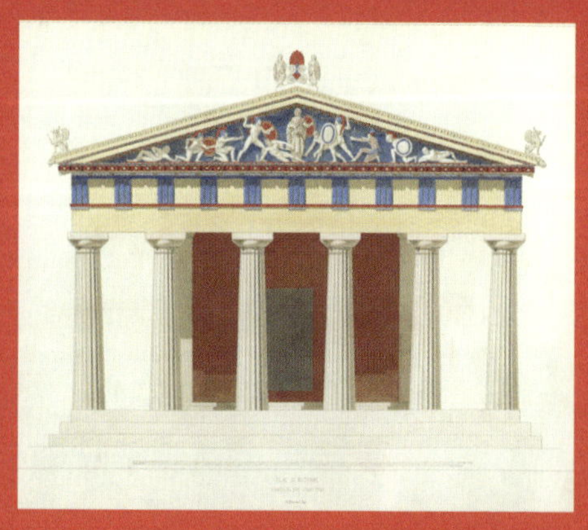
280

PASTOUREAU, 2006

text is experienced by readers as graphic whimsy or something suitable for children. Even e-books and web pages, falling in line with this tradition, for the most part use dark text on a light background. This is hardly a natural phenomenon, it is a matter of pure convention – albeit an efficient one – imposed by the printed texts of the Renaissance.

The book, however, is not an object like any other, especially during those centuries in which literacy was something that belonged to a minuscule elite, and to be able to read meant that you were an educated person and therefore socially superior. In the space of a few decades, the notion emerges – faint and uncertain at first, then increasingly stronger – that colour is for the uncultivated and for children. Before her adventures in Wonderland begin, Alice laments how boring books are when devoid of illustrations, and therefore of colour. On the threshold of industrial modernity, colour is already coded as 'non-serious' and regarded with suspicion.

If black is contrasted favourably with the multicoloured
in terms of its austerity, it is white that is king when it comes
to the values of purity and incorruptibility. Today white is
synonymous with the 'classical': it is the colour of Armani
showrooms, of the latest Apple computers and of the walls
of art galleries. The origins of this can be found in the belief
that whiteness was fundamental to the language of Greek 279
and Roman art – an unquestioned model for many generations of artists. In reality, as twentieth-century research has
demonstrated, statuary in the Greek and Roman worlds was
brightly coloured. The majority of the smooth, shiny sculp- 278
tures that we admire today would originally have been very
colourful indeed, in a manner that would strike us now in
fact – having been educated to admire its marble purity – as
disturbingly kitsch. Such statuary was originally very similar

BANKEL, 2004

to medieval polychrome wooden sculptures with their mimetic painted surfaces and inset, painted eyes like those of dolls. To say nothing of Greek bronzes – the so-called Warriors of Riace, for instance – which were originally highly polished and gilded until they would have shone like the chrome on cars, or like temple Buddhas.

It was only through the action of time and being buried for many years that such marble figures were slowly divested
277, 280 of their colourful painted patina, so that when the neoclassicists rediscovered the ancient world – above all through the excavations of Pompeii and Herculaneum – they were convinced that the world of Phidias and Praxiteles was entirely uncorrupted by barbaric chromatism. And as often happens when we are fond of an idea, the evidence was spun in order to accord with it, perhaps in good faith – but also at the cost of cheating a little. In the mid-eighteenth century the first and most authoritative apologists of the ancients, Johann Winckelmann, sets out together with his followers to wash statues in order to eliminate the last, residual traces of colour; inventing in the process, with the elbow grease of good housewives, the dazzling white classicism which we admire today in museum collections throughout the world. From this moment on, the perfection of antiquity is estab-
270 lished for such artists as Canova, and the white marble nude becomes an absolute.

But why did the Greeks and Romans like coloured statues, whereas to us they seem tacky? As we have already pointed out, colour in the ancient world is a rare thing and not a common feature of everyday life – so that its use is always eye-catching and impressive. Besides, sculptures, especially if we think of those placed outdoors such as those on the Parthenon, which were also brilliantly coloured, are subject to the changing light, becoming whiter in the morning and redder in the evening. It is plausible that painting them would have diminished this mutation, elevating them on the one hand to a more concrete level (in that, painted, they resemble more the things of everyday life) and on the other to a more abstract one (since they would no longer be subjected to mutability by the light, remaining consistent with themselves, like ideas).

We also need to recognize that there was no concept in antiquity of what we call kitsch, which is to say the cheap imitation of great works, partly because art was not held in such exalted esteem as it is today (its production was a type of blue-collar work) and partly because it is only the diffusion of industrial objects that has fed the ranking of – and the gulf between – 'high' and 'low' art.

We could go further and conclude that Winckelmann's predilection for marble whiteness has become influential precisely thanks to the contrast with the noise and clutter of industrialization: the more commercial images become coloured and pervasive, the more the elite juxtaposes to them the white rarefaction of a classical ideal that never really existed. It's a fact, like so many others, that confirms how history is not just something that we discover, but something that we invent.

In Italy in 1977 a big controversy exploded, involving both intellectuals and public opinion, which soon revealed a form of actual chromophobia – and not simply a fear of colour but a radical rejection of it. In defence of the spartan authenticity of black and white television, the moral custodians of the nation went into battle: the introduction of colour must be prevented lest it corrupt our very way of life. The debate, a frankly pathetic one, pivoted upon an equivalence (amply undemonstrated) between chromaticism and moral decadence. It attributed to the new technology a seductive luxuriance that is quite unnecessary in a sound society.

Already, in the second half of the nineteenth century, in the United States a crusade has got underway against chromolithography, which is considered to be a useless yielding to luxury and slackness. It is clear, however, that what is at stake is not colour itself but the seductive power that it confers upon things. Looking back on it now, a polemic such as the one about colour TV seems like the umpteenth variation of an empty moralism that finds an enemy not in substantial facts but in superficial matters. And it will shortly not be colour but the advent of private broadcasting that will radically change the taste and morals of the public.

However paradoxical a story this might seem, it is hardly an isolated case, and the condemnation of colour has some illustrious precedents. The twentieth century is not new to such judgements, behind which lurk wider fears, above all that the spread of consumerism necessarily entails an impoverishment of existence.

COCCIA, 2014

Leaving aside that exceptional philosopher Walter Benjamin, with his unprejudiced curiosity about even commercial forms of modernity, intellectuals are often defensive, looking down on mass products, whether objects or artistic works, and seeking to impose their taste upon all classes, in the first place upon those who are subordinate to them. Colour becomes a victim of the same mentality: if the incredible variety of products leads us to decadence, then a promiscuous variety of colours corrupts our sensibility. Or so it would seem, at least, according to this 'elite'.

Modernist artists and theorists can be cited in support of these positions. Adolf Loos, the father of simplicity in architecture and design, when condemning ornament as a crime does not spare colour; Le Corbusier completely rejects wallpaper in favour of whitewash, since for him colours are savage. He does not, however, preclude certain masterful uses of them, as in his own *Unité d'Habitation* constructed

LOOS, 1972 LE CORBUSIER, 2003

in Berlin in 1957, though, as we can see, these colours are 269
extremely measured additions to a structure that is otherwise pure white.

But between the two there are significant differences: whereas Loos pursues his essentiality in recoil from the tribal and the primitive, Le Corbusier appreciates some forms of primitivism and wants white as a kind of shield against the glare of the contemporary world, that is to say against the noisy mediocrity of the marketplace. Even Mondrian and the movement known as De Stijl reduce the palette to just three colours, imposing principles that before aesthetics relate to the idea of the good. The more colourful advertising and communication becomes, the more the educated class encloses itself within a citadel where colour is barely tolerated.

MONDRIAN, 1975

KRACAUER, 1962

In the world of cinema, an important thinker such as Siegfried Kracauer denigrates colour for its lack of realism: superficially distracting, it ends up being less true than black and white. For Rudolf Arnheim, who introduced perception studies to the world of art, colour in cinema is saccharine, vulgar and characterized by a complete lack of form. While for Michelangelo Antonioni, the problem is an *excess* of realism with colour that destroys the profound artistic nature of the medium.[2]

PIEROTTI, 2012

We should not underestimate the influence of Neorealism, which made an extremely powerful link between black and white film and moral commitment – consigning colour, without explicitly saying so, to frivolity and evasion. And since the nonsense produced by Hollywood was in colour, it was therefore a good and necessary thing that politically engaged films should be shot in monochrome.[3]

[2] It is no accident that when Antonioni decides to use colour in the film *Deserto rosso* (1964), he does so in an openly antirealistic manner.

[3] In photography, the barbs against colour arrive from various fronts: Walker Evans dismisses it as pure vulgarity, and for the entire twentieth century, with the excuse that

If superstition and ignorance seem frequently to be attributes of popular thought, when it comes to colour it is among the educated classes, who should really be more careful and know better, that we find the most retrograde and unfounded positions. Colour is a litmus test from which certain social contradictions emerge.

It is not insignificant that the movement for gay liberation
281 should have chosen a rainbow flag as a symbol of opposition to the subdued reserve of love that is reputed to be 'normal'.[4] What is a brilliant colour, after all, if not something that we wish to stand out? In the flag, the multicoloured element does not signify radiance so much as progressiveness: the varied palette, since multiplicity is inherent in desire, of those who rebel against a single way of framing relationships. This is also why queer icons tend to be outrageously gaudy: think of David Bowie or Lady Gaga; of the sparkling outfits of drag queens and the frenzied colour saturation of the photos of Pierre and Gilles; of David LaChapelle, or of film directors such as Pedro Almodóvar. To say nothing of the rereading of Technicolor melodramas that places a brash chromatism – almost that of an animated cartoon – at their centre; a youthfulness of spirit that does not allow itself to be intimidated by the black and white moralism of traditional culture. By using improbable colours, they pursue a deliberately *artificial* effect in order to demonstrate that the 'natural', fundamentally, does not exist.[5]

colour reproduction is not very reliable, only black and white photographs are generally used in art history departments – as if reducing everything to grey were preferable to the falsity of an imprecise colour. Although during the First World War, the distinguished art historians Aby Warburg and Bernard Berenson were using colour slides for their teaching, very few followed them.

[4] The flag of the peace movement is also multicoloured, in this instance in allusion to the rainbow that appears after the biblical deluge as a symbol of the peace that now exists between God and men.

[5] In the film *Pleasantville* (1998), the protagonist is catapulted back to the black and white of 1950s American TV, immediately becoming a champion of colour as a

The children's book *Barbapapa* is multicoloured for similar reasons. Conceived in the 1970s in France by the architects Annette Tison and Talus Taylor, its characters originate in the ferment of 1968 and the ecological and pacifist movements: they are against hunting and pro the rediscovery of artisanship; they support self-sufficiency and combat bourgeois values. And yet they are never outlandish or ideological: in the ideal society there must be space for the yellow ecologism of Barbazoo; for the red bodybuilding of Barbabravo; for orange intellectuals such as Barbalib, and for the passion for cosmetics of a purple Barbabelle. The head of the family is pink, while the mother is black: metaphors for an alternative kind of family. The colours function partly to signify that everyone has their own personality and their own skin, but partly to show how the virtues and limitations of individuals can constitute the strength of a much richer and cooperative society. In the end, the Barbapapas are not just colourful, their principal virtue is to be able to change shape as they please.

The fear of colour underlines how visual choices invariably speak of social questions, and reaffirms how the first meaning of a colour is often simply how it is used. To see how this works, it is worth looking at how colour is employed in the world around us. The photo in Figure 284
284
was taken recently in an underground railway carriage in Rome. It speaks eloquently of how the most prevalent contemporary colours are dark. Black clothes predominate, in a way that would hardly be the case if the photo had been snapped on a packed beach in August, where coloured bathing suits would be the order of the day.

metaphor for freedom of expression in all its forms – from sex to art – in accordance with the rhetoric that pushes us to seek for inner authenticity and to be ourselves.

Do we choose black in the city so as not be seen? To
become invisible? Or is it only to adhere to that restraint
283 and composure appropriate to urban contexts? Perhaps we
love colour in art and cinema but do not actually want it
on us? It is probably all of these things at the same time. GOETHE, 2013
Even Goethe, who can hardly be said not to have loved
colour, says the refined have a natural aversion to bright
colours; and Munsell adds that measured colours are always indicators of good taste. It seems like the proudest
champions of colour have distanced themselves from it MUNSELL, 1921
when it came to being associated with identity and behavioural or moral values.

What is remarkable is the extent to which we have interiorized certain attitudes: today there are many, at least in the West, who treat chromatic minimalism as an indisputable given. Loud colours are commonly condemned. Black is simply indispensable. Love for white is a law. But these are myths. They are part of the set of meanings, commonplaces, legends, prejudices and idiosyncrasies generated around colour, and it is all these different positions that shape our imagination.

I must confess that even I, despite having devoted no
little amount of time to colour, always choose to wear dark
blue or bottle green – and that I could never wear an orange jacket, because I would feel out of place. And yet I'll
wear a vividly coloured T-shirt on holiday, or a shirt in a
282 solid, bright colour. Nobody is so free as to liberate themselves entirely from social conventions and prejudice. The
photo taken on the metro tells us a lot about the gregari-
ous inclinations of *Homo sapiens*. As we've already seen,
the first complete liberation of dress code was decreed in
1793. From that day forth, anyone can wear what they
like. But 200 years later, we are all wearing more or less
the same uniform.

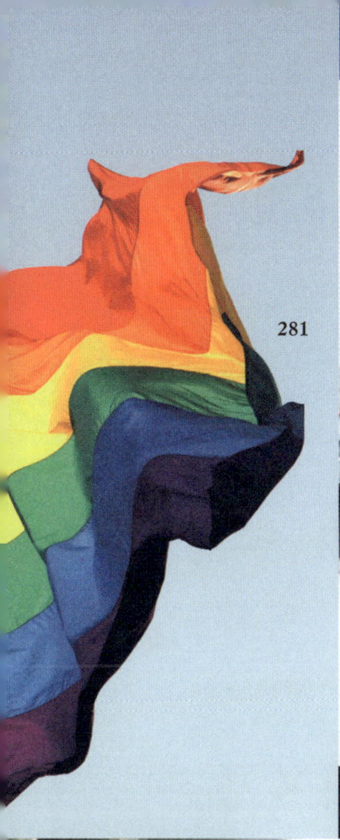

281

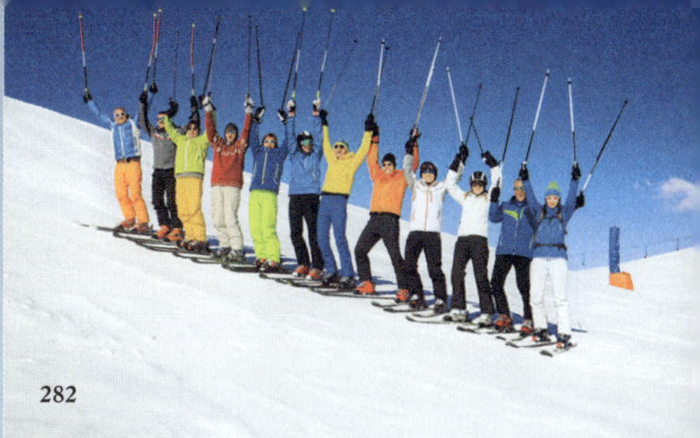

282

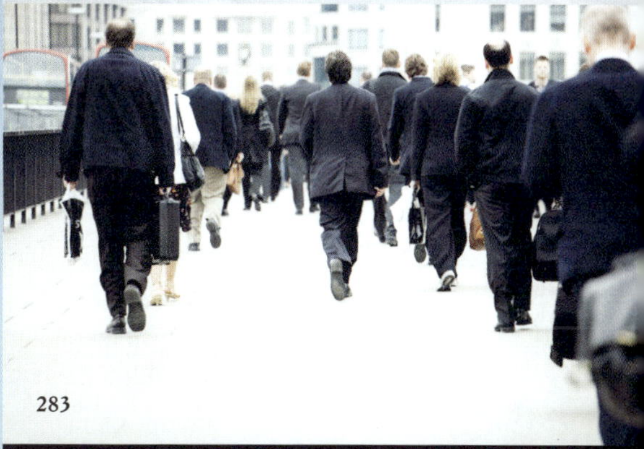

283

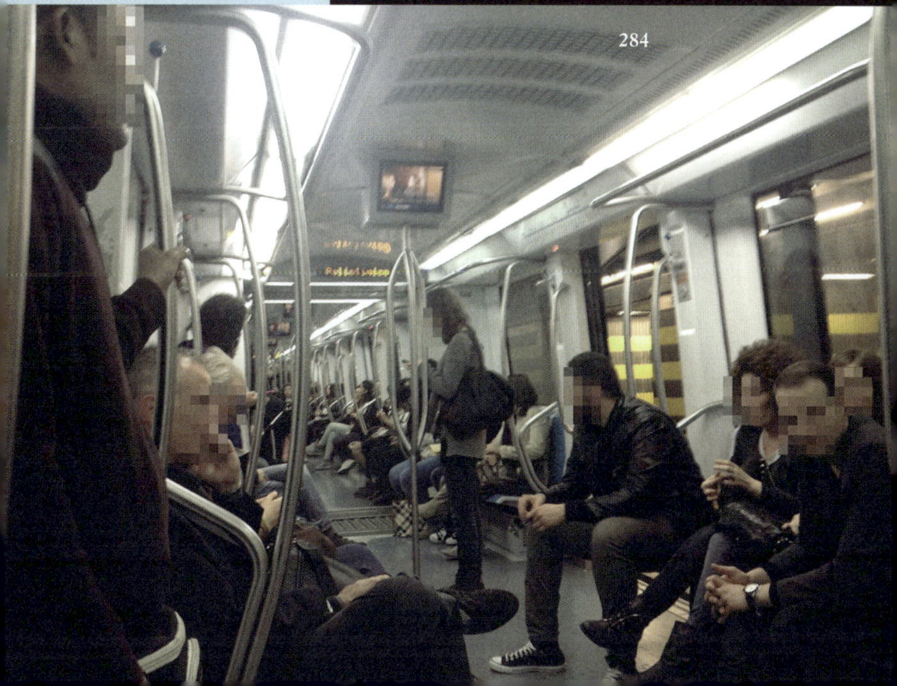

284

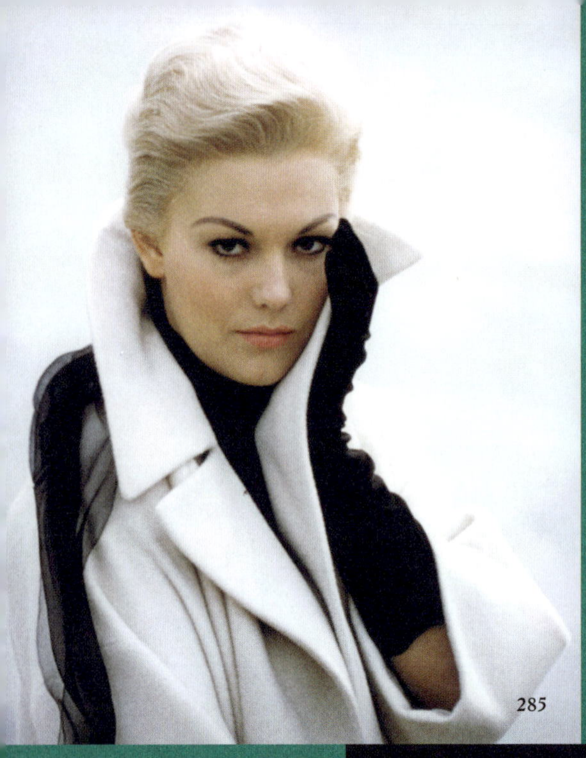

285

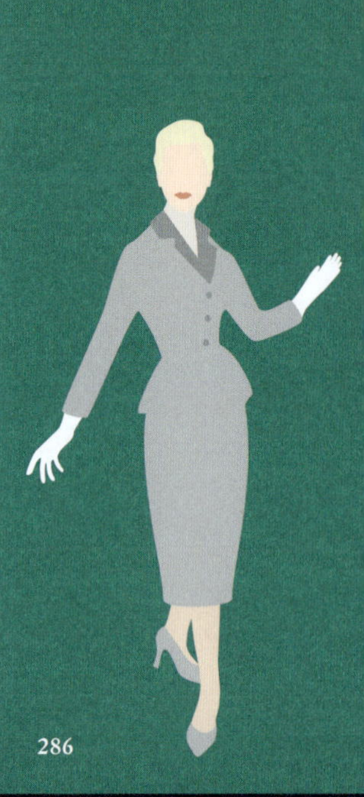

286

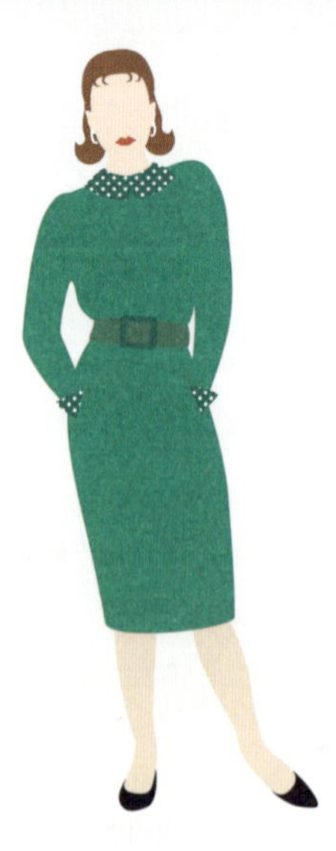

287

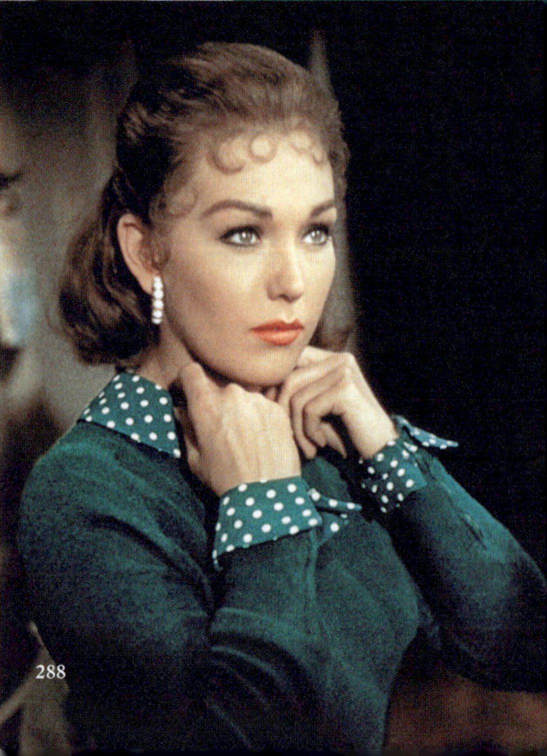

288

Vertigo Green

'The Woman Who Lived Twice'

The scene: San Francisco. The protagonist: a police detective. During a chase John Ferguson – Scottie to his friends – witnesses the tragic death of a colleague who has fallen from a building, and due to the trauma caused by this develops a disabling vertigo that leads him to hand in his badge.

Some time later Elster, an old friend, asks him to trail and keep an eye on his wife, Madeleine, who has become convinced that she is the reincarnation of her great-grandmother who committed suicide aged twenty-six. Icily ethereal, reserved, with white blonde hair brushed tightly back and tied, Madeleine stands out. When Scottie first sees her, he is immediately smitten and accepts the job.

He begins to shadow her as she wanders the city, seemingly under some kind of spell and in a melancholy, trance-like state. One afternoon, while walking by the Golden Gate Bridge, she suddenly throws herself into the waters of the bay. Scottie plunges in and saves her; takes her to his apartment, dries her, takes care of her. By now he is in love with her. He decides to step in, to help her to get well, to try to save her from the demons of a tragic past that she seems condemned to repeat. One of her obsessions involves returning compulsively to a place that has appeared to her in a dream – a place which Scottie recognizes as the Spanish mission of St John the Baptist. So he decides to take her there, convinced that if she is confronted with the reality of the place her morbid fantasies might finally dissolve. Once there, Madeleine collapses. She loses control and runs up the stairs of the tower. Prevented by vertigo from following her, Scottie is powerless once again, and can only look on as she falls from the tower onto the roof below. This time Madeleine has done it: she has committed suicide.

A year passes, and Scottie meets by chance a shop assis-
288 tant called Judy Barton, an attractive brunette with a faint resemblance to Madeleine. He does not know it yet, but there is a good reason for this resemblance. Judy *is* Madeleine. It has all been a very elaborately contrived deception. Elster, Scottie's friend, has carried out a diabolical plan to get rid of his wife (the real Madeleine), who in reality is perfectly sane and living far from San Francisco. He has hired Judy to play the part of a mentally unstable wife in order to anticipate and justify her suicide; and then engaged Scottie as an eyewitness, knowing full well that his vertigo would prevent him from going up the tower, where two accomplices were waiting to throw down Elster's actual wife, having kidnapped and drugged her.

Scottie has no idea what has really happened, but becomes manically preoccupied – as if at some level he suspected something. The memory of Madeleine obsesses him. He courts Judy and insists on getting to know her. He also convinces her to dress, to make herself up and to dye her hair like Madeleine. And she agrees to do this, since in the meantime she has fallen in love with him too, and does not want to have to give him up a second time. From this point on, things begin to move inevitably towards a dramatic conclusion.

One night, just before going out to dinner, Judy asks him to help her with the clasp of a necklace. Scottie recognizes the necklace as one that belonged to Madeleine's great-grandmother, and in doing so realizes that he has been deceived (the jewellery is probably part of the payment given to her for her criminal performance). Furious, Scottie forces Judy to return to the old Spanish mission, to revisit the scene of the crime. Overcoming his vertigo, he pushes her up the staircase of the old bell tower, where she ends up confessing everything. They are about to kiss passionately, but the film has a tragic twist in store that will prevent any such 'happy' ending.

PIEROTTI, 2012

What I have just summarized, and some will of course have recognized it, is the plot of Alfred Hitchcock's masterpiece *Vertigo* (1958). Colour plays an important role in it, on both a narrative and a technical level. Ruby red and emerald green – two of the colours which work most brilliantly in Technicolor – bring into play antinomies connected to the duplicity, doubling and falsehood that characterize the protagonist.[1]

In order to achieve this, Hitchcock draws on two models that were much loved in the postwar period: artistic theories centred on colour contrasts, and psychoanalytic symbolism of the kind that he used in other films, such as *Marnie*. The film's use of colour is consequently quite different from what we have become accustomed to today, when it is more often than not an expressive or atmospheric element. In *Vertigo* colours are in a strict sense symbolic, juxtaposed according to a rigorous and elegant geometry. Here colour is not only to be enjoyed, but deciphered.

So it is worth playing a game where we try to interpret the film with reference to the ideas and superstitions widespread in the culture of the 1950s. This will allow us

[1] The movie was shot with a colour film and only afterwards printed by Technicolor, without the using classic technique involving three rushes (see p. 163) or layers.

to propose an analysis of colour within the work, and to see certain chromatic myths of the time in action, such as the chromophobia that we spoke of in the last chapter, and which plays an important role in relation to Scottie and Judy. What follows is both a possible interpretation of Hitchcock's film and an indirect analysis of interpretative canons in fashion at the time of its release.

According to language historians, at the origin of the word 'colour' (*colore*) there is the verb 'to conceal' (*celare*): the appearance of things seduces our gaze, hiding their real essence. Colour interposes itself between ourselves and knowledge. There is no doubt that of all the possible meanings that can be found in it, this is closest to the most profound significance of Hitchcock's film. Madeleine's blondeness, for instance, is an artificial colour that conceals the brunette woman beneath. It is therefore appropriate to start from this blondeness.

It is an extremely light shade, verging on white, known not by accident as 'platinum blonde', a now outmoded colour that was very much in fashion among actresses in the decade after the Second World War. In their different ways Marilyn Monroe, Jayne Mansfield and Lana Turner all used versions of this colour, which was imitated throughout the world. They all had brown or darker hair, like Judy. They were women who concealed themselves in order to construct a glamorous otherness adapted to the language of the mass media.

The principal characteristic of this particular shade of blonde was the fact that it was openly artificial, synthetic, modern, unknown before industrialization. The relationship between the two women in *Vertigo* is therefore based on a series of oppositions: natural versus artificial, authentic versus constructed, true versus false. But we could also add that, since blondeness is a characteristic of cinema divas, the relation between Judy and Madeleine is one between a common woman and an actress. And this is the case for at least two reasons, one internal to the story, the other external. Madeleine is blonde because she is playing a part; but she is also blonde because all of Hitchcock's leading women had to be blonde. Grace Kelly, Tippi Hedren, Janet Leigh and Kim Novak were actresses with particular, strong personalities – and yet when they worked with the master of suspense they ended up performing the same gestures, in the same atmospheres, with their hair dyed the same platinum blonde. The colour is configured as a psychological category – but above all an erotic one.

COSTA, 2014

In a famous interview, Hitchcock confessed to François Truffaut that he had always had a preference for British rather than American women, given that the US take on sex was too obvious and explicit while being ultimately puritanical, whereas the British usually seem cold and yet as soon as the occasion arises reveal themselves to have uninhibited and passionate natures. Perhaps we are dealing here partly with a quite common fetish: men who like to be dominated, even if only playfully, by icy and detached women. What makes it special in this case is Hitchcock's capacity to transform a private desire into an expressive universal. If brunette hair stands for spontaneity and open sensuality, then platinum blondeness is trammelled eroticism. This blondeness is not just about concealment, it holds back the passion that simmers beneath the visible surface. Platinum blondeness is like a dog muzzle preventing sexuality from attacking. Madeleine's hair is pulled back tight, under rigid control – it does not move in the wind; it is crystallized into a bun twisted upon itself like a spiral. And this spiral is a key image and symbol of the film, a metaphor for vertigo, an infinite vortex that by rotating sucks in anyone who gets too near to it.

TRUFFAUT, 2014

As for her clothing, Madeleine's official uniform is
286 a tight-waisted grey suit. Like her hair, it is restrained yet eloquent; sensual precisely on account of being restrained.

In the erotic imagination, whether Western or Eastern, there is a constant that unites often very different psychologies: the fascination exerted by everything that tightens and confines, suggesting in the process some kind of suffering. Tight dresses, stockings, belts, underwear – as well as 'professional' equipment such as rope, handcuffs and so on. Why is everything that binds exciting? In some cases, we can say that since erotic relations are always power relations of one kind or another, the tying up mirrors and amplifies inequality between participants. On a figurative level, however, and this is the one that ultimately interests us, what is used to do the tying acts as a focus of attention, highlighting something. On the female body the garter is something that by squeezing flesh reaffirms it. It is literally an underlining, a line traced on the thigh to make it more eloquent and memorable – in the same way that a skin-tight fit on a male body will emphasize muscles and make them bulge. From a conceptual point of view, there is little difference between a dress that's tight at the waist – as in the New Look of Christian Dior – and the latex suits of sadomasochism. All that changes is the degree of intensity.

One knows then that the platinum blonde of Madeleine's hair is not just a colour, it is also an article of clothing. It dissembles and contains, feints and imprisons, conceals and envelops. On an erotic level it is not the fire but the smoke. That blondeness and that tight waist are a type of bondage – but spiritualized.

Madeleine, whose hair assumes greyish reflections, and who wears an ample white coat with black detailing, is a

classic cinema diva, and therefore appropriately in black and
white; whereas Judy, in contrast, is not only 'in colour' but
is herself colourful. As much as the one is reservedly com- 288
posed and inaccessible, so the other is emotional and direct.
As much as platinum blonde hair is styled with hairdressing
expertise, so chestnut hair is washed at home and slightly
ruffled. And while the fabrics worn by Madeleine fall with
the geometrical elegance of fine tailoring, Judy wears soft,
elastic, almost felt-like knits. The difference between Ma- 287
deleine and Judy is not just that between different types of
colour but also between degrees of intensity: the suit and
platinum hair have a minimum amount of colour and seem
washed out; the dress Judy wears when we first see her is
on the contrary of an intense emerald green, and her hair is
bright brown, almost tending to red. Judy has more saturated 292
colours than Madeleine, and is made up in a stronger, showy
way: the eyebrows are more pronounced, the eyeshadow
more emphatic. Madeleine is diaphanous, Judy is striking.

In this contrast we encounter again the idea that colour seems to belong to the uncultivated, whereas black and white is a sign of cultural refinement. There are numerous instances of this difference: Madeleine wears minuscule earrings, pearl studs carefully highlighted by Hitchcock in one of the film's first frames; Judy has large earrings that are both showy and inexpensive-looking. Between the two women there is also a difference in social status, something that the film thematizes without making it explicit. Madeleine is bleached or washed out to signify her higher class.

WÖLFFLIN, 2012

We are therefore dealing not so much with two types
of women as with two contrasting forces that regulate the 289
universe: the rigid versus the flexible, the cold versus the
simmeringly hot, the intransigent versus the attainable.

*

Scottie is also dressed throughout film in an outfit that contains him: a traditional men's suit. The colours are downbeat, masculine – brown and blue. For two centuries, dressing in a jacket has been standard for men in a professional context, and it is the design par excellence of urbanization, with a powerful social significance. A jacket and tie is an uncomfortable combination that does not allow the complete mobility of the body afforded by a sweater or a tracksuit. Anyone who has worn a jacket knows that the most difficult movement to make in it is raising one's arms (the Vitruvian man of Leonardo's famous drawing would find it impossible to function in such a suit). This flaw has a symbolic value: whoever wears a jacket is in effect declaring that their occupation does not require physical exertion, and that they belong instead to a class that earns its living sitting at a desk. The jacket makes this quite clear in the eyes of the labouring classes.

What is a tie other than a knot? You tie it to your neck – and, hanging in the centre of the male body, it is a metaphor for the penis, sublimated, in aesthetic form. Jacket and tie are also models of constriction: wearing them one cannot become aggressive, come to blows, or make love.

In Scottie's case things are a little bit more opaque: he is an everyman, the personification of the common man confronting moral conflicts, vices and virtues. He has no original characteristics, other than the vertigo that paralyses him. There are nevertheless some clues that emerge from such rigorous composure: the tie he is wearing at the beginning of the film is red. It is undoubtedly a sign.

Into a neutral-coloured *mise en scène*, and into spaces with common colours, Hitchcock introduces some very striking chromatic notes. If we look at the sequence of still frames as a whole, as if getting a bird's-eye view of
293 the storyboard, we soon realize that there is a chromatic

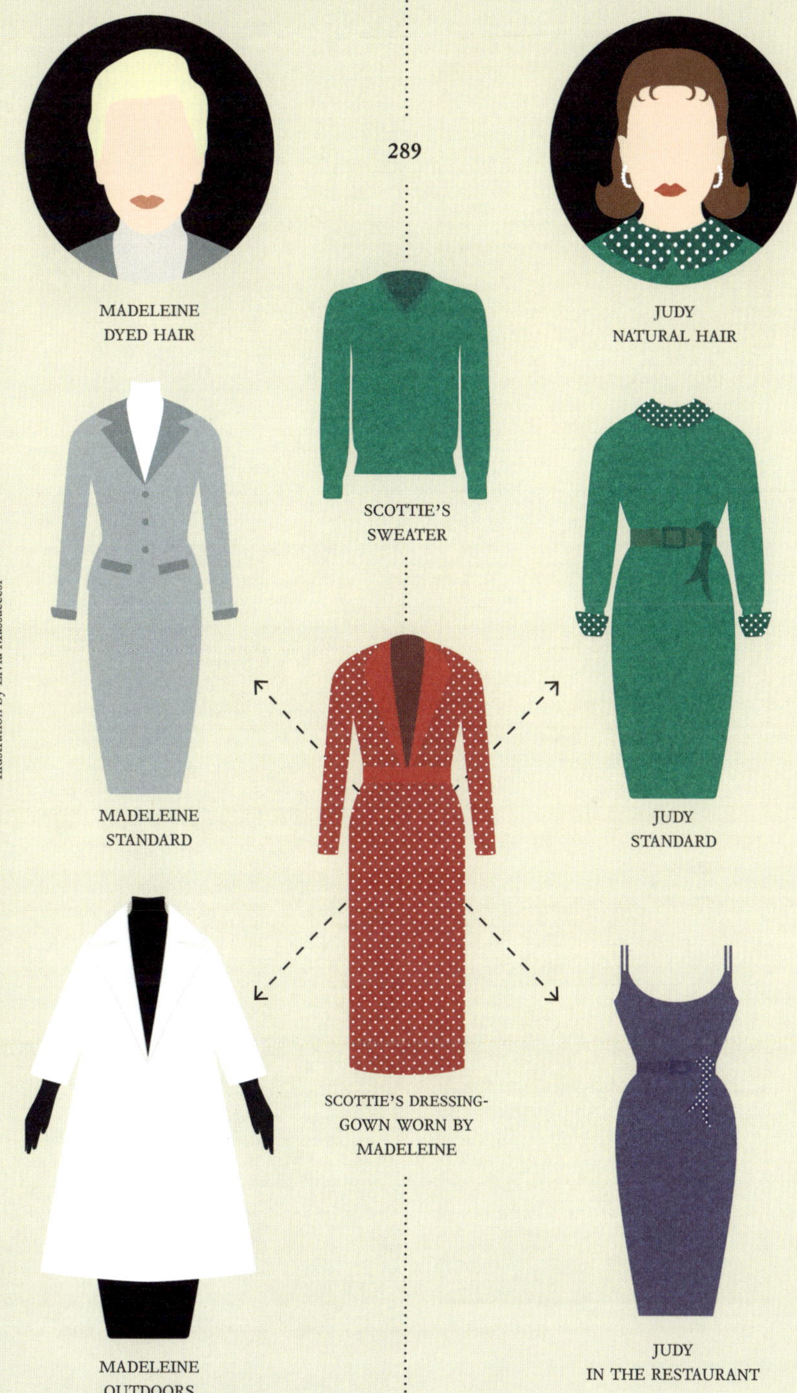

Illustration by Livia Massaccesi

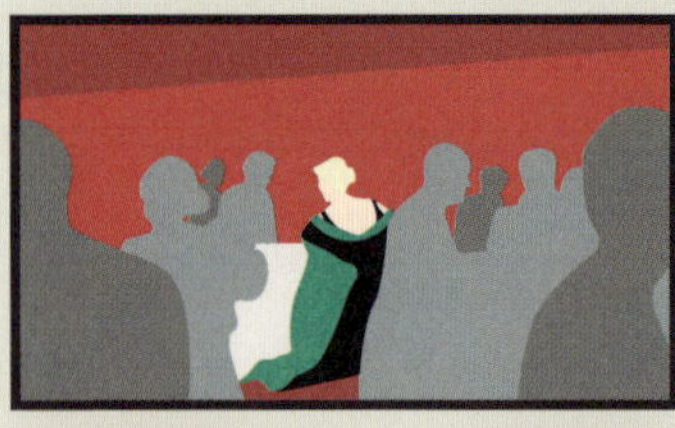

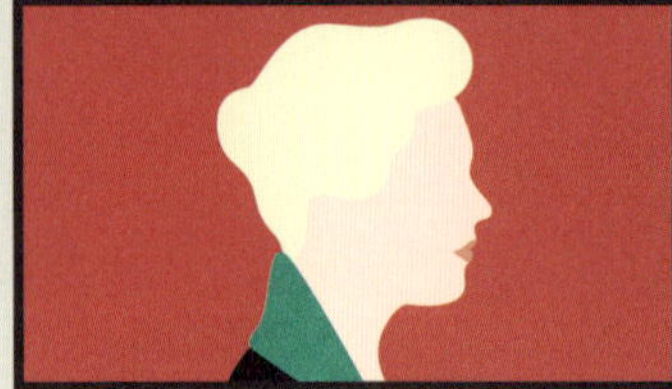

290 Madeleine enters: she is dressed in green

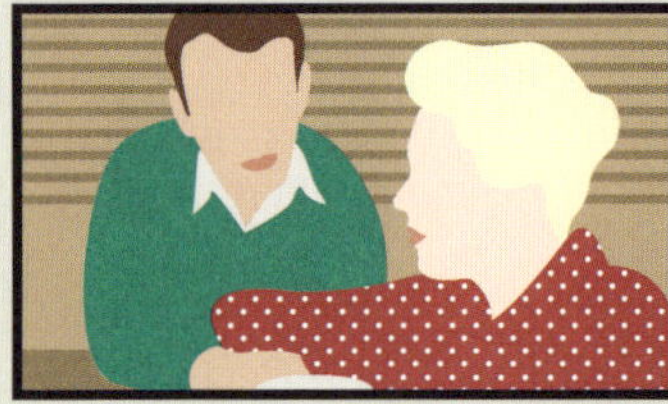

291 Madeleine in Scottie's house. She is wearing his red dressing-gown. He is wearing a green sweater.

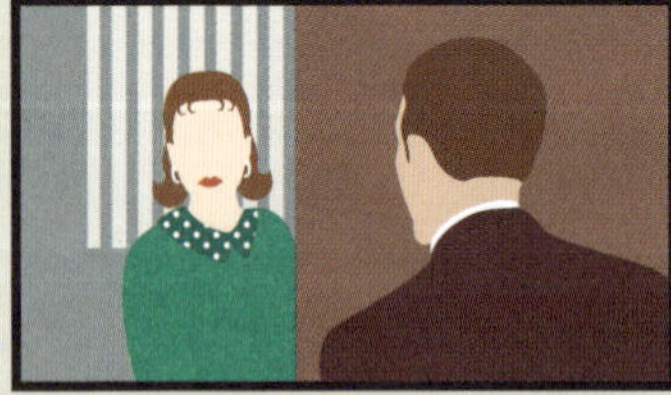

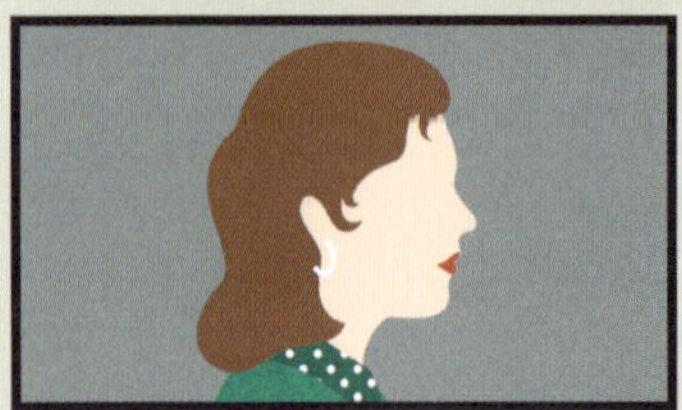

292 First appearance of Judy. She is dressed in green

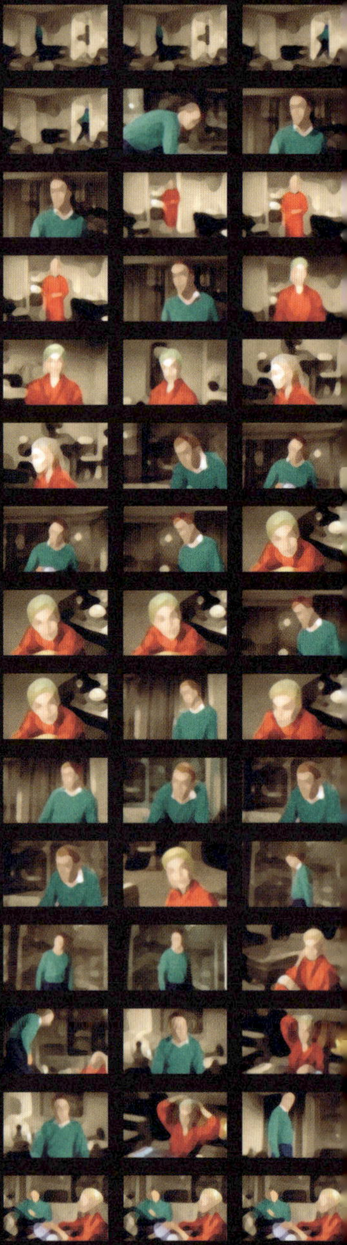

293 Reconstruction of the red-green rhythm in the Madeleine sequence in Scottie's house orchestration that establishes the register of the entire story. In cinema, even more than in photography, the dominant colour in a scene is fundamental, establishing and nuancing the tone of the story; especially in American cinema, where the chromatic aspect of sequences forms the basis of their emotional structure.[2]

The first time that Madeleine appears on screen, she
is wearing a black evening dress with a green satin stole. 290
Hitchcock frames her sitting at the table of an upmarket restaurant with damask red walls, and where the other diners are all dressed in white, black or grey. She is the only blonde, and the only one with colourful clothing, which is juxtaposed with the complementary colour of the scenography. There is a maximum possible contrast.

The first time he sees Juliet, Shakespeare's Romeo asks who this wonderfully beautiful girl is, standing out 'like a snowy dove trooping with crows'. Hitchcock seems to want to construct his frames according to a similar metaphor, translated into purely chromatic terms: who is this extremely beautiful woman who emerges, the only blonde, among so many dark women? And in the framing the effect is reaffirmed by the element of green that is juxtaposed with the intensely red walls. We are presented in this way not so much with an outfit as with a clue. The green is in fact an intruder, out of place: it is Judy's colour, not
Madeleine's. We are being shown a glimpse of the second 287
woman contained in the first: that green is not a sartorial detail, it is an anticipation, a 'teaser' of the kind common

[2] In film animation the first draft of the screenplay is called the 'colour script', and is based solely on elements of colour and light. The sequence of colours and their brightness already shows, even before the appearance of characters and dialogue, the psychological and emotional atmospheres and the outline of the work. Looking at a colour script is therefore like looking at the score of a symphony: it gives an overview of the writer's/director's way of thinking by revealing the deep structures of the language used.

in thrillers. We will not see Madeleine wearing green again, yet from this moment on the contrast of red and green becomes a consistent feature of the film, a chromatic subtext that will seem at times to be itself becoming the main story.

When Scottie saves her from her first attempt at suicide and takes her to his apartment, we notice that Madeleine is
291 wearing a red robe – a colour, in other words, that is alien to her character. It is not very difficult to gather that, since she was soaked having gone into the bay, the robe must belong to Scottie. And this is not all, for Scottie has taken off his jacket and is now wearing a sweater. The sweater is green. The two items of clothing – soft, comfortable, enveloping – speak metaphorically of letting go, of relaxation: if their suits signified constraint and regimentation, the sweater and dressing gown enable spontaneity.

So the two protagonists are comfortable, and above all for the first time lay themselves bare. Red and green, in all their vivacity, represent the passions that are simmering beneath social appearances.

As we have already seen, for our psyche a red that gives way to green, or vice versa, is unthinkable. It is the law of complementaries. Scottie and Madeleine, with their opposed colours, are like two poles that cannot but attract. But be careful: green is the colour of Judy, the second woman, so the fact that Scottie wears it amounts to saying that between Judy and Scottie there are subterranean ties – profound and perhaps irrational ones.

We gradually realize that the film is studded throughout with red and green lights that follow, contrast with and balance one another. They are the ground bass of the film, with which Hitchcock narrates the laws of desire. Madeleine's car, the one that Scottie follows when he is spying on her, is green; Scottie's tie, as we have already noticed, is red; and when in the end Judy, exhausted, agrees to dress exactly like the other woman, we see her moving towards us bathed in the green of a neon light that is coming from the street and that makes her seem spectral. Appropriately so, because now she is nothing other than the ghost of a self that never actually existed.

At the start of every relationship we try to show the best of ourselves. Then, as we gradually get to know each other, we begin to reveal our true nature, warts and all. What often in everyday life resolves itself into comedy – the elegant dresser who begins to leave his socks around the house, the sweet girl who turns out to be a nag – in *Vertigo* is played out as tragedy.

When the two become acquainted, Judy plays the part of Madeleine, designed for his pleasure; when she shows her true self instead, she hits a wall, as if Scottie had said: if this is how you really are, I can no longer love you. It is the worst nightmare of someone who is in love: not feeling worthy of a previous model and suffering in comparison with them.[3] If this happens in real life, the tendency is usually for relations to go into a spiral that exhausts and ultimately destroys the relationship. Hitchcock, with ruthless irony, tells us that this spiral is a kind of vertigo from the experience of which nobody can get out alive.

And it is here, in a vain attempt to save herself, that Judy enters into a very dangerous and ultimately fatal game: she accepts that she must be Madeleine. Scottie forces her to wear the grey suit, then the shoes and finally to cut and dye her hair: the last act is to consent to be *recoloured* like her double, like a dead person who has never actually existed. Scottie's obsession is iconographic. He has fallen in love with a figure made up of certain lines

3 This is also the theme of *Rebecca* (1940), another of Hitchcock's most famous films.

and certain colours, and expects Judy to resemble it – or better still to actually *become* the object of his desire. The saying goes that when someone shows what they are really like, they reveal their 'true colours'. Scottie abuses Judy by imposing upon her colours that are not her own. It's a gesture as cruel as it is abstract. He is not 'reforming' Judy with the excuse of a perceived character flaw but on account of a physical fact – saying to her, in effect, that he will never love her unless she is platinum blonde and dressed in greys, bleached of all other colour.

ATTRACTION BETWEEN CAMOUFLAGED COMPLEMENTARIES

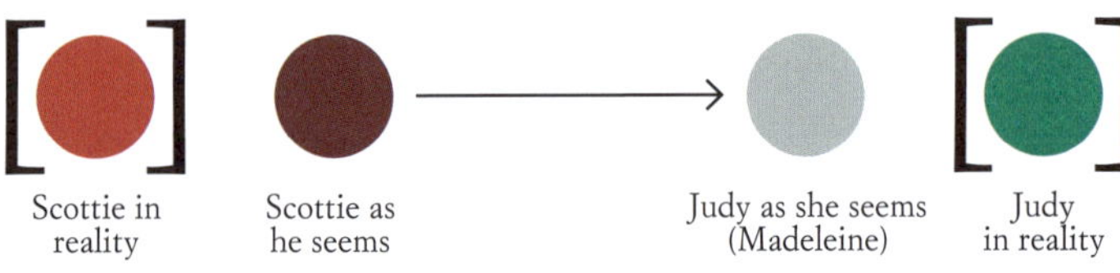

There is a famous quip, attributed to George Bernard Shaw, according to which all operas boil down to stories of how when a tenor and soprano want to make love they are prevented from doing so by a baritone. It's a brilliant witticism, underlining how aesthetic pleasure is often a question of abstract structures: in this case the typology of the voice establishing roles and relations even before the historical or psychological characterization of the protagonists. In *Vertigo*, Hitchcock does something similar in chromatic terms.

We could say that the story is about a man with a red soul – red, in this case, for fear of women – who disguises himself in brown and tails a grey woman (who is actually green) and falls in love with her. But when he is loved back he takes fright and, not being able to stand green, he seeks to change it, to make it grey, achromatic, to control it and to control himself.

In the hands of a great director, colour is not decorative but structural. The phobia that is central to the plot has to do with seeing emptiness, the deepest kind, in green – an ambiguous colour that reminds us of both the natural world and decay. It is at one and the same time the colour of life and of death.

For centuries, we have associated love with red – but this is the masculine version of the story. Judy, on the contrary, is green: the personification of the female principle of giving life, and perhaps of taking it. This is why Scottie fears her. He fears green and wants grey again. Green is analogous to the fear not of emptiness (which is only a pretext), but of the sexual power of women. By subtracting the green from Judy, Scottie refuses to 'couple' with her: he refuses the generative power of nature.

The tragic conclusion of the film seems to eliminate all hope that women and men (and more generally, all lovers) can really come together. It resonates with a melancholy, colour-coded moral: we need to accept the other for what it is in them that attracts us: wanting to change them is disastrous both for ourselves and relationships. You cannot suppress colour without paying a heavy price. Woe betide those who are red but want to pass themselves off as brown. Woe betide anyone who falls for green and would like to make it grey. Inauthenticity in love must be paid for, even with death. Because passion will not be confined. And because, even if the otherness of the complementary risks cancelling our identity, we cannot do without it.

PART FOUR

Perceptions

294 *Last Tango in Paris*, Vittorio Storaro

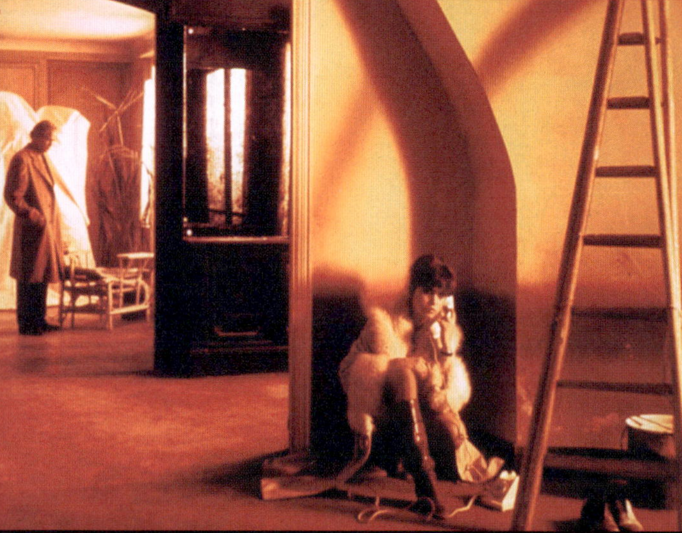

COLOUR TEMPERATURE 295 ▸

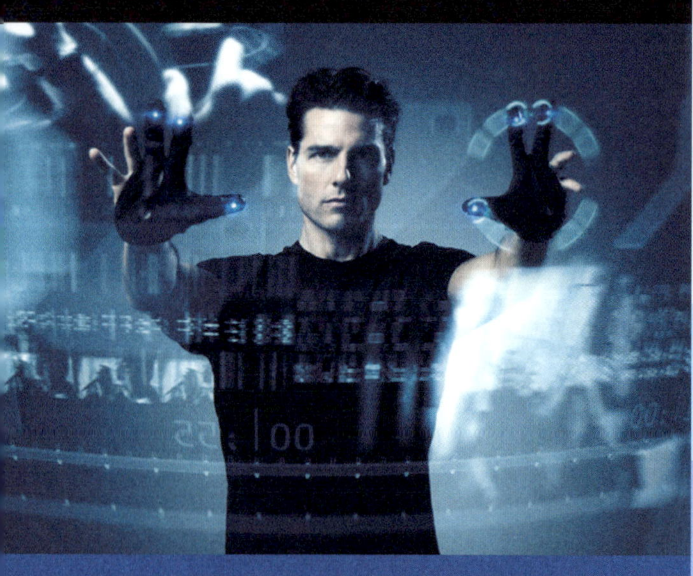

296 *Minority Report*, Janusz Kamiński

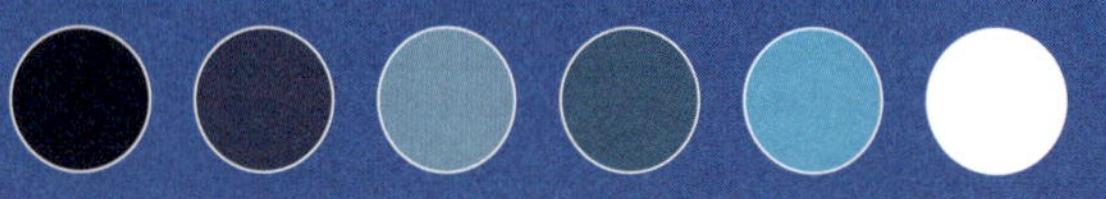

Colour temperature	Light source
1000 K	*Candle*
2000 K	*Sunset*
3000 K	*Lamp*
4000 K	*Neon*
5000 K	*Midday sun*
6000 K	*Flash/Monitor*
7000 K	
8000 K	*Cloudy sky*
9000 K	*Shadow of a blue sky*
10000 K	

Hot Orange

Seeing the Temperature

There has been a trend in science fiction – in graphic novels and comics, video games, cinema and TV – for images dominated by cold colours and tonalities: blues and greys, sometimes dark greens. It is a stylistic choice that conveys at first glance an allegorical coldness: technological, industrial, metropolitan or nocturnal. Influential examples of this can be found in such films as *Alien* (1979) and *Blade Runner* (1982), and among the most successful uses of it is the dominant blue-grey that pervades Steven Spielberg's *Minority* 296
Report (2002) – a colour that enables a vivid contrast with the red that is linked to the solution of the thriller.

The use of a warm key, yellow or orange, creates instead an atmosphere of enveloping melancholy, like a perpetual sunset in which the air itself is impregnated with coloured particles. It's a classic of the cinematography with which Vittorio Storaro constructs situations at once intense and still, suspended in the dust of memories as in many of Bernardo Bertolucci's films, from *Last Tango in Paris* (1972) 294
to *1900* (1976); or in Francis Ford Coppola's *Apocalypse Now* (1979).

STORARO, 2002

In contemporary visual languages, the opposition between hot and cold is among the most widespread and popular of chromatic formulas. In a film or an illustration, an orange or blue keynote suffices to draw us immediately into

NEWHALL, 1984

the story. We are talking about a relatively recent invention that has taken hold since the 1960s, led by a technical development in photography which recovers the dominant radiation in a scene, amplifying it in our eyes. A physical condition becomes transformed into a new stylistic fact; one that painting, in previous eras, had never known. If we
213 look at Tom Cruise in the two stills – in *Eyes Wide Shut* and
296 *Minority Report* – we notice that in the first he has orange
skin and in the second blue, a technique that seems obvious to us today but that has next to no precedent in visual art before Technicolor. In the fifteenth century, a face could only be blue if it belonged to a devil, not for any reasons to do with lighting. Cinema has effectively furnished us with a new form of visual metaphor, in which colour becomes atmosphere and operates at an important level with regard to character and plot. Emotional and chromatic temperatures become one.

If we ask ourselves, in everyday terms, which colours are warm and which are cold, the answers are clear and almost beyond dispute. Reds, oranges and yellows are warm; blues, light blues and some violets are cold. Greens can be more or less warm depending on the presence of yellow. For other colours, however, the question becomes much more slippery and uncertain: we are not sure about turquoise, not to mention khaki. Generally speaking we seem to be dealing with obvious attributes that do not require much thought or discussion. And yet in practice things are much more complicated. So what are we really saying, in fact, when we describe a colour as *warm*?

In the majority of cases we are using a metaphor, or proposing a synaesthetic connection with which to link together a certain colour with things – such as fire or sunlight – that give us an actual sensation of heat. These connections, however, are much more tenuous than they might seem.[1]

If we heat up a piece of iron to a very high temperature it first becomes orange and then, as the temperature increases, it changes to yellow, then to white – and finally to blue. According to physics, blue is actually hotter than red. And it is for this reason that the cold light of a cloudy sky has – in the parlance of photographers – a much higher
'colour temperature' than that of a sunset.[2] 295

The association between colours and warmth would therefore appear to be truely a matter of convention. There are many cases of cold orange and incandescent blue, and ignoring them is a precise choice and the fruit of a particular society and historical moment. To cite just two common
instances: it is well known that the flame of a gas cooker is 299
visually blue and burning hot, and it is obviously possible
to feel cold before a beautifully tawny September sunset. 300
Such experiences, however, tend not to particularly strike us – certainly not enough to become part of our collective imagination, in which flames are stereotypically only hot when they are red, just as all sunsets are fiery, even when we are freezing.

The question we need to ask is why certain associations apply and others do not – to see whether there are some which are particularly favoured, perhaps for some supracultural reason.

In the last century a good deal of energy was expended in order to demonstrate that the warmth or coldness of colours was backed by incontrovertible facts of nature,

[1] The primary colours used in printing – cyan, magenta and yellow – do not seem either warm or cold, yet they appear to many observers to be cold.

[2] The colour temperature of light in photography is measured in kelvin and corresponds precisely to the nuances displayed by a piece of iron as it is heated to different temperatures. The light of an incandescent light bulb is around 3,500 kelvin, whereas that of the midday sun is 6,500 K, also known as 65D where the 'D' stands for 'daylight'.

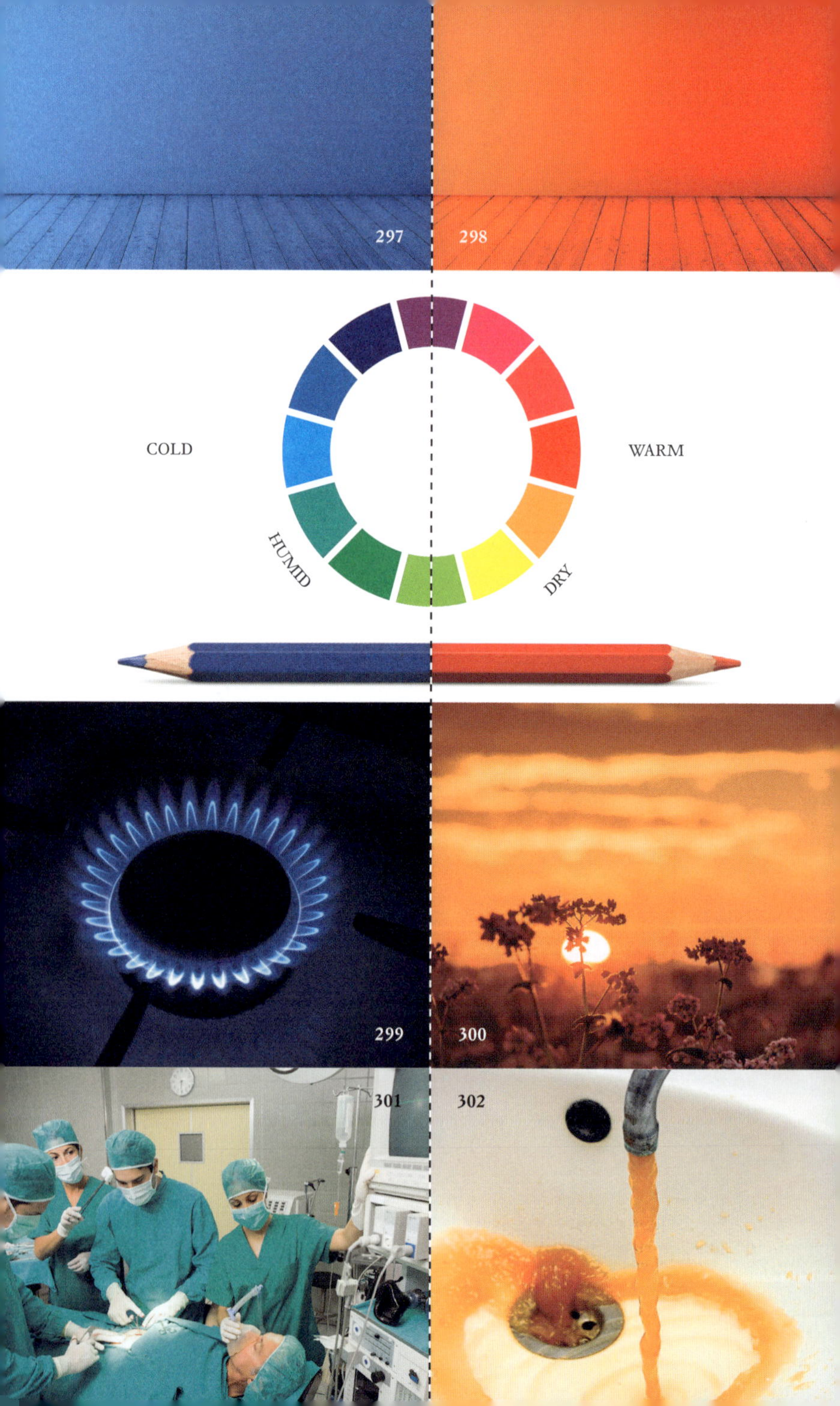

297
298
COLD
WARM
HUMID
DRY
299
300
301
302

with hypotheses supported by experiments based on the
capacity of wavelengths to influence the human metabol-
ism. A classic example, cited by Itten and much repeated,
BIRREN, 1978 maintains that entering a red-painted room will acceler- 298
ate our heartbeat and increase the conductive activity of
our skin more than entering a blue room. 297

It's difficult to say whether this is always true; it depends on the kind of red, and on the kind of blue – but above all it depends on context. What we can observe, in fact, is that the heartbeat does accelerate for a few minutes, but that this only lasts for a very short time before returning to normal. The excitement could be METHA, 2009 due to a change of scene rather than to the colour itself. We cannot overlook the fact that it is not just the colour but the room that is in play, and that perhaps it has affected our metabolic rate by creating a sense of claustrophobia.

We know that some colours such as red give the impression that space is much smaller, whereas blue, especially light blue, seems to expand it. Could it be this effect, and its contrasts, that makes the red room more oppressive? Or vice versa, that allows the blue one, with its association with the sky, to convey a sense of boundlessness and therefore of calm? Whatever the answer, it is clear that even when such explanations are plausible they do not tell us anything that is absolute or always true about the colour itself.

Recently I happened to be walking in a forest, in autumn, where everything from the trees to the carpet of leaves on the ground was dominated by intense reds and oranges. The sensation was one of great relaxation and peacefulness, because the space seemed open and limitless. To be completely surrounded by red, then, can be as restful as being surrounded by the fresh greens of spring. The weakness of such experiments from a scientific point of view lies precisely in considering perception as a set of isolated data, when in fact it is a holistic process that happens within precise psychological, historical and social situations. Let us not forget that rooms covered in red damask have always communicated a sense of solemn repose, and that the aristocracy were not prey in their palaces to perpetual tachycardia. Heart rates can of course sometimes increase – but it depends on who is doing the looking.

Besides, the sensation that a colour suggests is tied to
the context and not to the colour itself. A rust-coloured
302 liquid is repulsive if seen gushing out of a bathroom tap, TRIEDMAN, 2015
even if that colour shares the same wavelength with the
300 most beautiful of sunsets. That is why to say that red is
exciting in itself, in the abstract, is a meaningless generalization. Colour is necessarily always the colour *of* something.

The idea that red is linked to excitement and that cold tones transmit calm has led to the construction of elaborate visual codes beyond the world of the arts. It is behind, for instance, the tradition of using green or blue for operating theatres and doctors' gowns. But there is a technical reason for this as well. On the one hand, the psychological need for a calm atmosphere is being catered for; on the other, there is a deliberate attempt to minimize the disturbance caused by so-called 'posthumous images', or afterimages: after having looked at blood red, if you then look at a neutral field you see complementary greenish stains that can interfere with the ability to focus. Surrounded by green, the stains are subsumed by the context, allowing surgeons to concentrate. But this is quite a recent convention: in the nineteenth century hospitals were rigorously white. Until at a certain point we became fed up with white and it was considered sickly and better avoided. It is only in GERRITSEN, 1983

BIRREN, 1978 DELONG, 2012

1924 in New York that Doctor Paluel Flagg proposes to paint hospital settings with the colour complementary to blood, a shade that soon becomes known as 'eyerest green'.[3] 301
And, as always happens, what began as essentially a specific practical choice soon becomes ubiquitous and taken for granted as part of our image world. Today relaxing medicines and analgesics have blue or green packaging; in advertising for pharmaceutical products, red indicates an inflammation that needs curing, and in many commercials the area highlighted in red turns blue thanks to the salving or curative action of the product.[4]

That certain colours may be more relaxing than others is an idea that goes back to antiquity. Galen, in the second century, tells us of how miniaturists keep grey or black objects to hand, in order to look at to help relax their eyes during long periods of work upon white parchment. And already, in the fourth century, Basil of Caesarea identifies blue and green as 'calming' colours.

In all of these arguments, there is an unexamined element that is simply assumed to be the case, and that has little to do with colour in a strict sense: namely the convention of thinking that warmth is always more 'tiring' than cold. Might this not, however, be an idea typical of someone living in a temperate climate? If the story of colour had been written in Greenland, for instance, can we be sure that orange might not be considered the most relaxing colour instead?

[3] Until the 1920s in America, operating theatres were painted in a range of colours. In order to identify the true complementary of blood red, Flagg used Munsell's system.

[4] Overturning such established codes can be disorienting, even disturbing. In the film *Dead Ringers* (1988) by David Cronenberg, in which Jeremy Irons plays twin gynaecologists in the throes of a disturbing identity crisis, the director suffuses the operating theatres with a fiery red – from the gowns of the doctors to the paint on the walls – indicating a medical intervention that is no longer restorative but a form of violence: no longer Hippocratic but an act of self-destructive omnipotence.

A recent experiment along similar lines tells us that working in a blue room apparently makes us more creative. But this assertion is quite tenuous inasmuch as the researchers, with culpable disingenuousness, do not produce a definition of creativity – as if it were a phenomenon that could be taken for granted. It seems that, as far as they are concerned, being surrounded by blue would enable us to have more ideas. This involves some debatable assumptions, to say the least. In what way is producing 'more' ideas actually more 'creative'? What matters surely is their quality, not their number, and that quality can only be assessed in a social context, which is to say on the basis of the strength of those ideas as they are taken up within a society. Stephen King has written over eighty novels; J. R. R. Tolkien wrote only eight. They are two very different writers, due to both sensibility and craft, and nobody would dream of saying that King is more creative than Tolkien because of the *number* of ideas/books that he has produced. And yet this is what such experiments seem ultimately to imply.[5]

CAUSSE, 2015 METHA, 2009

In certain data passed off as scientific research there is unfortunately the prejudice – very widespread in advanced capitalism – that human actions, including metabolic ones, should always be framed in terms of efficiency. Whereas creativity, if it exists, is made up of subtle, often invisible gestures, and great ideas can be turbulent and manifold as well as silent and rarefied. A room can hardly render you more creative because of a colour chosen for it by someone else. If all blue environments were creative, no one would

5 Another test leads to the conclusion that, when set to work in front of either a blue or a red monitor, the blue creatives would produce twice as many ideas as the reds. In the same vein there are even those who maintain that women are less efficient when working in a beige setting – one that men, on the other hand, tend to like. Here too it is taken for granted, with enormous superficiality, that the category 'women' is constituted by one amorphous thing. The data from such tests are interesting, but in this case a distinctly masculinist assumption leads to suspect conclusions.

METHA, 2009

be creative any more. The only truly creative room would not be red, yellow or green but the one that we have painted ourselves.

BIRREN, 1988

Among the most extravagant experiments conducted to determine the power of red and blue were those carried out by John Ott (1909–2000), the inventor of time-lapse cinematography – the process that allows us to see, within a single shot and a short space of time, a flower blooming, fading and dying before our eyes. In the 1960s, Ott bred mink and divided them into two groups: one group living under a red light, the other under a blue. He concluded that the first became more aggressive and only mated with difficulty, whereas the others had numerous offspring and were quite docile. Up to this point we are dealing with reasonable enough propositions: light controls many biological functions, starting with the rhythms of sleep and wakefulness, and blue light is much more similar in its composition to that of natural environments.

Ott then works with mice and raises the stakes: he divides them into three groups: one raised in white light, another in pink and the third in blue. And what does he discover? That in blue light 70 per cent of the offspring produced are male; in pink light seventy per cent are female, and with white light half those born are male and half female. Ott's results have been cited many timcs by rcputable scientists, but I find the story a little too edifying to be credible. The preference for pink or blue attributed to little females and males respectively is very recent and the most conventional imaginable. So much so that until the end of the nineteenth century exactly the opposite was the case: pink was assigned to males because it was felt to be a softer kind of red, a colour that was symbolically fiery and virile; whereas celestial blue was the colour of little girls in homage to the blue mantle of the Madonna. It was a habit so established, in fact, that in 1914 the American newspaper the *Sunday Sentinel* advises mothers to dress boys in pink and girls in blue if they want to respect tradition. SPARKE, 2010 But the convention is not just about colour, it is really about that thinking through opposition between colours that is characteristic of modernity.[6] In the ancient world, there is no trace of such strong dualism in dress code; not only is clothing often similar (the invention of tights, and hence of trousers, happens only in the medieval period), but a woman can go out wearing her husband's cloak without this being seen as a peculiar or strange way of dressing.

There is, however, a biological fact that has probably contributed to the construction of this myth. ABRAMOV, 2012 Defects in
303 colour vision, which is to say that colour-blindness and its variants are experienced exclusively by males because a deficit of the retina is transmitted via a male chromosome; and it is precisely the wavelengths of reds and of pink that typically cannot be recognized with such defects. We are not talking here about something that affects small numbers of people: it is something experienced by almost 8 per cent of all human males. GREGORY, 1991 It is a fact that must have contributed to the spread of clichés such as that men are less good at combining colours, with everything that entails in relation to clothing, fashion, furnishings and so on. It is no accident that the products aimed at male consumers abound in blue – not because it is their favourite colour
305 but because all males will be able to see it. This is merely a statistical fact: it tells us nothing about any presumed essence of masculinity, or about blue in general. We can

[6] It would seem that the fashion for exhibiting the gender of newborns through colour only really took off when it became possible to know their sex before birth – and therefore buy clothes for them in advance.

303

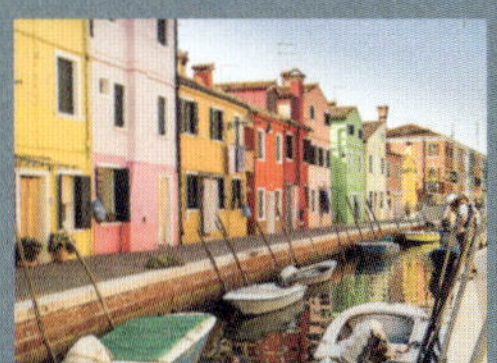

COMMON VISION

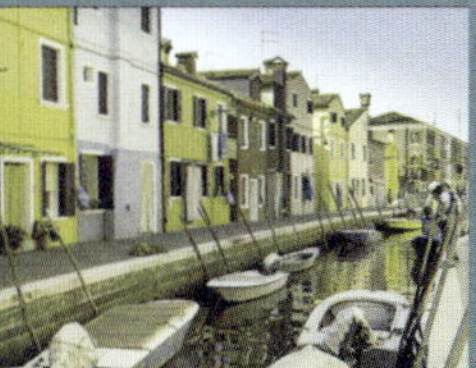

DEUTERANOPIA

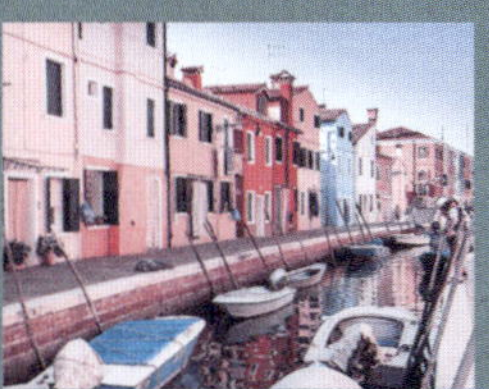

TRITANOPIA

304

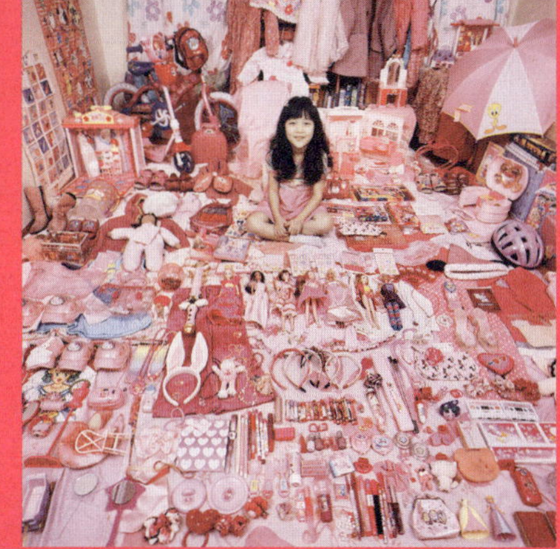

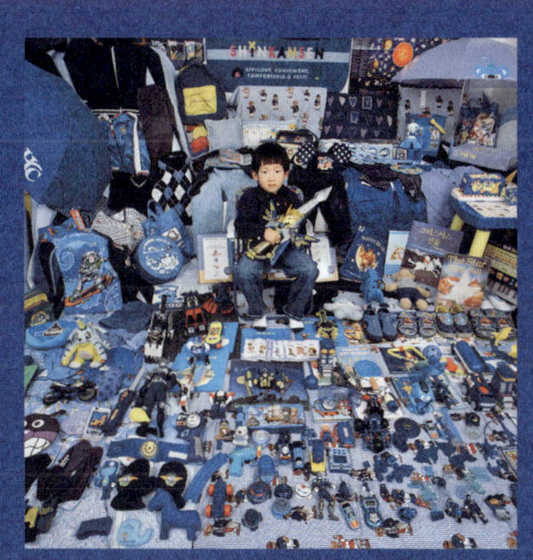

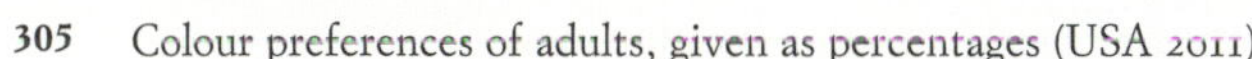

305 Colour preferences of adults, given as percentages (USA 2011)

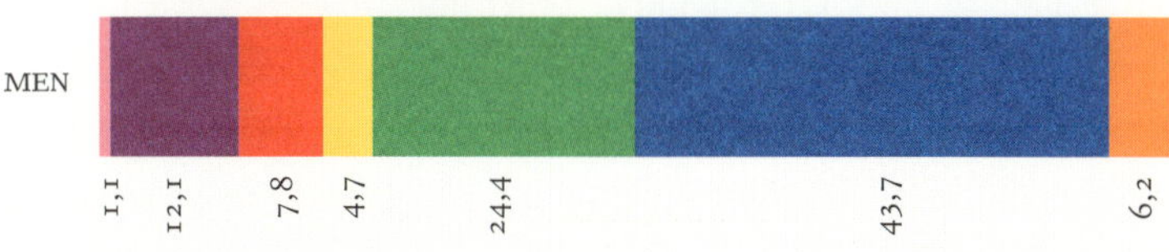

hardly exclude the other 92 per cent, which is to say the overwhelming majority of men, who are able to see red, pink and even fuchsia perfectly well, frequently even finding these colours likeable.

Conventions change, much more quickly than we might think. Today many parents refuse to dress infants in pink or baby blue, a fact that could in the course of a few generations expunge this particular element of our visual code. Nonetheless, the majority of products designed specifically for boys/girls, especially for very young boys and girls, continue for now to perpetuate this stereotype, as is strikingly
304 demonstrated by the works in *The Pink & Blue Project* by the Korean artist JeongMee Yoon (b. 1969), which replay, with great figurative intelligence, the extremely close relationship between consumer goods and the construction of gender stereotypes. The idea was born, according to JeongMee, when she was faced with her five-year-old daughter's desire to own exclusively pink objects – a desire that few children can have formulated before the pervasiveness of characters and products such as Barbie and Hello Kitty.

In reality, behind research on the capacity of colour to influence our psychology there lies a more general, ancient and thorny question: whether or not there are colour meanings that are universal, trans-cultural, and perhaps based upon innate predispositions.

With specific regard to red and its association with warmth and passion, the advocates of potentially innate meaning always point out how this colour characterizes the genitals of many mammals; the crests and wattles, the mouth, tongue, blood – all elements that stand out and have power as signs and signals – so that red is 'naturally' linked to sex, to passion, to impetuosity, to alarm and to danger. And this is the case for all people, regardless of time and place.

Yet even this appears to be too vast a synthesis and generalization. Sex and danger are quite different concepts, and even an orthodox Freudian would be hard-pressed to justify a possible shared signification between a passionate red and that of a no-entry sign.[7] As for genitalia, there are of course various colours: from pink to purple to brown. They are sometimes more reddish than the rest of the body, but certainly not poppy red. Besides, the observation of a connection between blood and the impetuous/spontaneous characteristics of red needs to be treated with some caution, since it takes for granted that blood already has a significance, when in truth the violence, passion and pain that are attributed to it are themselves symbolic elaborations.

Blood is in fact red only if we observe it in small quantities, as when it is smeared or diluted, whereas the experience of violently spilt, copious and free-flowing blood is more often that of a liquid which is dark, brownish, even almost black. If meaning was innate, then brown should make us think of a kind of super-red and of ultra-violence. But this is not the case.[8] Many red things are linked to sex, to danger and to eruption. Many, but not all things – and not always. Between perceptual experience and signification, choices necessarily arise and decisions are made to dwell on some aspects rather than others.

To say that the meanings of colours are culturally constructed is not the same as denying the physiological characteristics with which culture is made, or the power of our emotional response to colour. Such misunderstanding is in reality due

[7] If the no-entry sign is always red, signs indicating a kind of maximum prohibition or warning tend instead to be yellow – as is the case with those warning of danger of death or a radioactive substance.

[8] The idea that red can innately inspire impetuosity or passion has led to the creation of myths such as that bulls are enraged at the sight of cloth of this colour. In reality, bulls see everything in black and white, and it is the movement of the cape that goads them.

to the kind of thinking through opposites, or antinomies, that is typical of our contemporary society; in making, that is, a clear-cut opposition between 'nature' and 'culture', almost as if we were dealing with non-communicative systems. Culture consists, in fact, of all that we have learned from the moment of our birth; indeed it can be said that it is the same way in which our brain works, which in order to develop needs constant interaction with its surroundings. Culture *is* the nature of our brain. This is why the distinction between 'innate' and 'acquired' is too rigid to explain complex phenomena such as cognitive ones.

If, absurdly, we were to raise a child from birth in such a way that they could never get hurt – never experience pain or see blood – and restrict their experience to only the colours of industrially produced products, it is very probable that they would have an idea of red that was free from the set of associations that it immediately brings into play for us. Now, since this is a situation of a highly improbable kind, and since sooner or later as a species we are in contact with blood through intense if not traumatic experiences, there is in fact no one who escapes from these associations.

In this sense, the meanings that link the colour red to blood are always cultural but at the same time simultaneously motivated by unavoidable conditions. But it is the association that is inevitable, not the meaning that follows from it.[9]

SAUSSURE, 1967

In China passionate love is not red; it is represented by delicate, light shades such as pink or celestial blue, and there is therefore no relation – an obvious one in the

[9] At the origin of modern linguistics and semiotics there is an idea of Ferdinand de Saussure's that is still a cornerstone: the connection between signs and concepts is always arbitrary and conventional. If we call a particular animal 'cat', this is arbitrary inasmuch as we have chosen a certain type of sound and sign with no intrinsic connection to the animal; and it is conventional because we have agreed to call it this.

West – between sensual arousal and chromatic saturation.[10] This is a fact not be underestimated by anyone involved with design in a multicultural and global age.

GOODMAN, 2008

It follows that colour can be made to mean anything – as well as its opposite. For example, bright colours can be linked without any forcing to our happier feelings because our psychological response to light is a fundamental aspect of our being in the world – and colours tend in fact to be more vivid when there is most light; in good weather, in the spring and summer. But nothing stops us from doing the opposite, and building positive significance with dull or dark tones, as can be seen in the use of brown or beige in the packaging of natural and organic products.

Experiments that claim to prove the connections between excitability and warm colours are scarcely convincing, and many counterexamples can be found leading to opposite conclusions. Which is not to say that convincing evidence will not be found tomorrow that might lead us in one direction or the other.

HUBEL, 1989

We know that reds, oranges and greens are *seen* better by us than other colours, because we possess a larger number of photoreceptors at the back of our eyes predisposed to processing them. Is it possible that more intense neuronal activity links the colours to greater excitability for complex associated movements? Is this what makes red much hotter than blue?

Scientists put forward hypotheses, often in contradiction with each other, and yet a century of research and experiments has not led to a definitive answer. Perhaps the question itself is badly put; perhaps we need to revisit

[10] In China you get married in red and attend funerals dressed in white, the colour of bones.

and review what we mean by hot in relation to colour. We still do not know the extent to which cultural aspects influence our emotional and metabolic states, and it is probably this area of research that it the most interesting, rather than chasing the phantasm of innate meanings. We need to develop an anthropology of vision, in which biology and culture are no longer in opposition but rather flow into each other.

At the same time we should not overlook how what seems innate, organic or biological is not detached from history, from society and from its practices. Colour-blindness was diagnosed only in 1794, because it was simply overlooked before the widespread diffusion of coloured objects. For almost 2 million years, humankind did not notice that some of us could not see some nuances well, and never thought of it as a defect. Colour-blindness is consequently an 'innate' condition that did not *exist* conceptually before a precise historical moment.

BRUSATIN, 1983

The contemporary scientific view is that colour is a continuum, from red to violet, that passes through every tonality and that can be segmented: we can go on taking pieces of it to talk about, use or give a name to. In this respect every colour is located at a point that is always in some relation of proximity with or distance from other points. That a red may be defined as 'warm' is only possible because we can compare it with another red, in another place on the spectrum that seems less warm because it is more distant from yellow. Without this internal comparison the distinction between hot and cold makes no sense, and is even impossible to conceive of. In fact, in the medieval period, which tended to hierarchize colours and had no idea of their spectrum, both red and blue are reputed

PASTOUREAU, 2010

to be warm because they are brilliant and intense, whereas yellow is cold because it is more akin to metal.

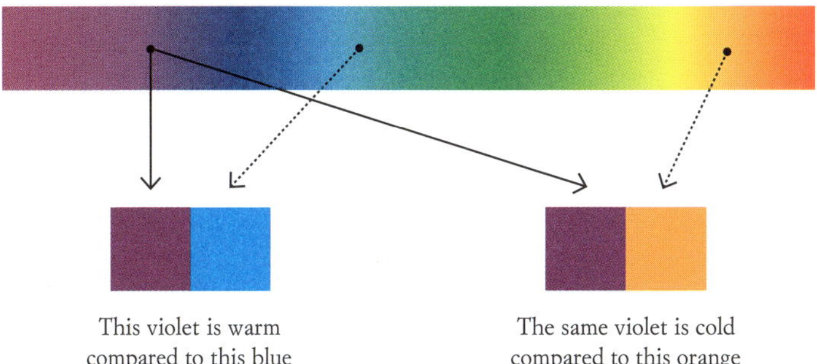

This violet is warm compared to this blue

The same violet is cold compared to this orange

We cannot, in the end, believe that our modern world, however colourful, is radically different from the visual scenario in which we have evolved. A red, purple or blue room provides a definitely post-industrial experience, and it may well be that some reactions are linked precisely to this artificiality even more than to a particular colour. In conclusion, we can say that for many people today red shows itself to be more excitable and aggressive than blue, but that is as far as we can go. Perhaps we are not at the right historical moment to go any further. We are too bound up with artificial colour to be able to make any general claims about *Homo sapiens*.

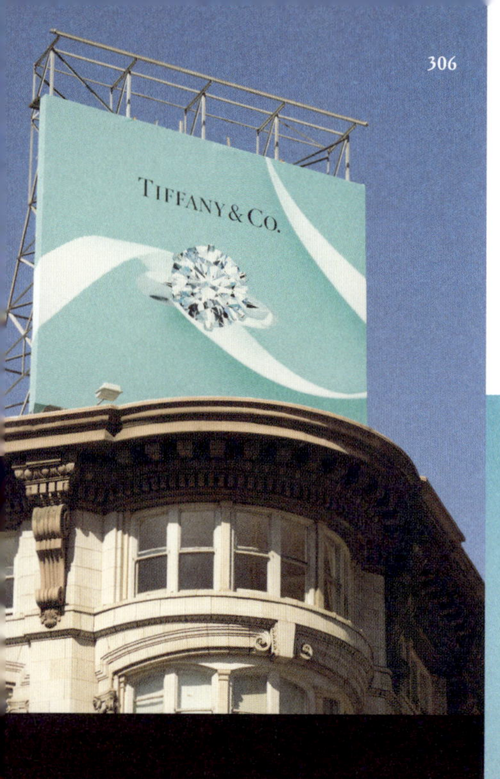

306

307

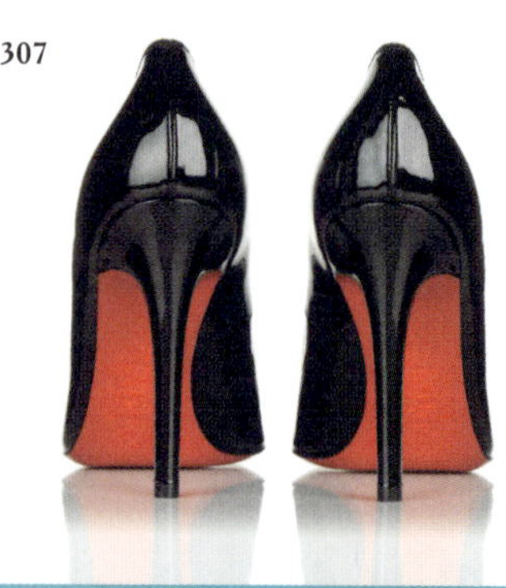

308

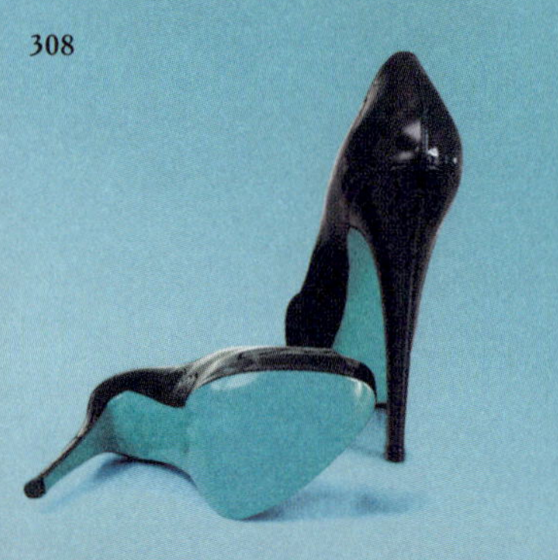

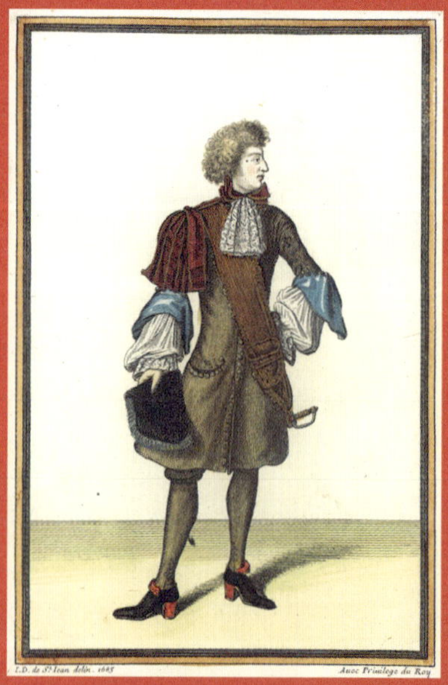

309

310

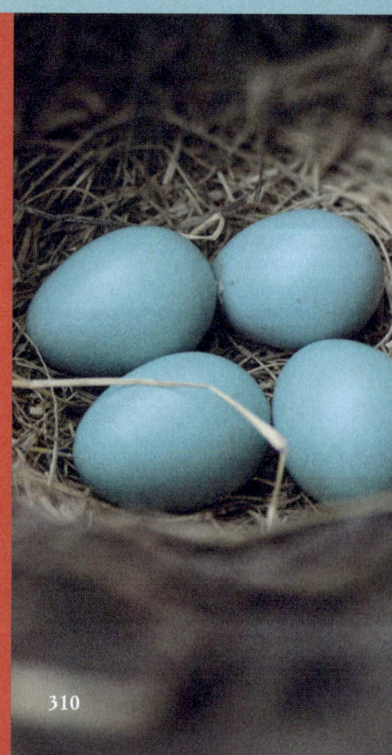

Patented Turquoise

Copyrighting Perception

In 1845 the famous New York jeweller Charles Lewis
Tiffany chooses for the cover of his catalogue a shade of
turquoise which from that moment on becomes the signature of the brand. It is the colour of the eggs of *Turdus* 310
migratorius, better known as the American robin, but the
reason for the choice is to be found not so much in or-
nithology as in the fashion, common among Victorian
brides, to give as a gift to their servants a brooch with a
turquoise stone. All the promotional material of Tiffany & 306
Co. – such as the small boxes and the shopping bags – is
made in this colour.

If in the nineteenth century that tint was hand-crafted by the typographers who printed for Mr Tiffany, today the colour has its own code: Pantone 1837, referencing the year the company was founded. And yet if we look for it in the swatch book, the colour does not appear anywhere. The closest to it is 2226, but it is obvious that this is not really Tiffany turquoise. The reason for this absence is that in some States the 1837 is a registered trademark allowing its use exclusively for jewellery. It's a sophisticated marketing idea: since all design studios have the Pantone sample collection, that particular turquoise shows its prestige by its very absence: it is something exclusive, that definitely exists but cannot be bought or used. At least not by everyone.

This story, which looked at one way has the effervescence of a romantic comedy, in reality conceals a deception and poses a question with which corporations struggle: is it really possible to patent or copyright a *colour*?

Two trials involving disputes over colour copyright have recently been in the news, and not just in the financial sections of newspapers. In the first, the fuel giant BP was seeking to protect from imitation its use of a combination of green and yellow; in the second, the French fashion house Louboutin had accused Yves Saint Laurent, Zara CAUSSE, 2015
and Eden Shoes of having copied its iconic black shoes
307 with red soles. These were landmark cases in which colour played different roles.

In the BP case, the court rejected the company's request as unacceptable and even nonsensical: you cannot patent a combination of two colours (there are many brands that combine yellow and green), even if it is ultimately ill-advised, because it is confusing, for a direct rival in the petroleum industry to use it.

In the Louboutin case, things were a little more complicated, inasmuch as the designer was seeking to protect not a particular red but the way in which it was used. The Louboutin claim was that the chromatic design of the shoe had quickly become an icon of contemporary luxury. By copying it, Zara was not so much reprising a colour combination as appropriating an idea. From a legal point of view, one would only need to find a single shoe with a red sole made *before* Louboutin's in order to demolish any claim to copyright. And to name just one instance: in the era of
309 Louis XIV the so-called 'talon rouge' was fashionable – men's shoes with red-painted heels. For the judges, the use of a coloured sole was deemed to have an affinity with other generic ideas that characterize fashion (you cannot

patent a ‘high waist’, or a certain type of hem), hence the only prohibition placed on competitors for the moment is the use of red soles for black shoes. So it is that particular colour combination that belongs to the French brand, not the colour itself.[1]

It is clear that Louboutin lost the essential part of its claim: if everyone can produce shoes with different coloured soles, for example black shoes with turquoise soles, 308
within a decade the idea will have lost its shine, recognizability and even paternity. Who remembers today (except industry insiders) which brand was responsible for the first yellow Post-it notes?

The claims of commercial giants often demonstrate a good deal of incompetence regarding what is possible or illegal as far as colour is concerned. Or perhaps they are just trying it on, hoping to get away with something. A very rich and powerful client once asked me, somewhat arrogantly, to use a colour that nobody would ever have seen before. I did not begin to explain that if no one had ever seen it, then perhaps that colour did not exist – and presented him instead with an existing pastel green that he nevertheless liked very much.

The heart of the problem is whether it is really possible to protect a colour. If the answer is often sought in legal terms, in reality the only ones who can provide it are scientists and philosophers. Let’s see why.

Imagine two firms that both make shirts – we’ll call them Yellow Co and Yellow Copy. One day Yellow Co, which is

[1] There are illustrious antecedents in fairy tales and films for iconic redness in footwear – such as ‘ruby slippers’ in *The Wizard of Oz*, and the ballet shoes in Powell and Pressburger’s *The Red Shoes*. With its harrowing melodramatic scenes, the latter established an image of classical dance for generations, the protagonist with the red shoes demonstrating how it may be necessary to die for one’s art.

famous for its yellow, becomes aware that the shirts of its rival are identical to its own and decides to officially protect the brand. In order to do so, Yellow Co must address a philosophical question: it must explain what it means that two things have the same colour.[2]

A statement of this kind, so simple to make in everyday life, is difficult to define and pin down in jurisprudence. When we say that two things have the same colour, we are in fact implying that this is true in certain conditions, and not in absolute terms. For instance, if we happen to choose a pair of black socks from the sock drawer – look at them, check that they are the same – we might only realize later, once we are outside in the sunlight, that one is black and one blue. This phenomenon, which can appear socially as
311 carelessness, has a scientific name: 'metamerism', that is, two colours can appear to be the same in one light but different in another. Indoors, with incandescent light, the blue appears indistinguishable from black because the radiation of the bulbs tends towards warm tones, whereas in sunlight, which has a much wider band of wavelengths, the two colours are revealed to be different.[3] This is also why women are advised that make-up which appears right in artificial light may subsequently appear too garish in the light of the sun. GERRITSEN, 1983

With these problems in mind, the American multinational General Electric suggested that if two colours appear identical beneath both a fluorescent light and an incandescent one, only then can they be defined as the

[2] If we compare different materials, the matter becomes a really thorny one. What does it actually mean to say that a piece of glass and a piece of wood are of the same colour? It's something that is easy to assert in common parlance, but in essence it is not something that is exact or measurable.

[3] To complicate matters, there is the fact that the dye used to colour cotton blue has nothing to do with the one used for wool, and that the two chemical substances respond to light in different ways.

same.[4] This is why in industrial procedures colours are usually evaluated in a standard light of 6,500 kelvin, which roughly resembles that of the midday sun; that is, with a wider chromatic range. This is only a useful tactic, for the purposes of verification at a distance, such as when communicating by phone. It solves nothing with regard to the conceptual or philosophical status of the colour.

It is for this reason that assistants in fabric shops often accompany their clients outside so that they can see better, in the sunshine, the exact shade of cloth they are thinking of buying. Never mind that we then use this material to cover cushions and make curtains that will never be seen in full daylight. As a matter of fact, given that many of us are likely to be at work during the day, we spend most of our time in our houses after dark, so that those curtains and cushions will be seen mainly under electric light. However white it may be, that electric light is always yellower than sunlight. Stepping outside of the shop may contribute in the abstract to the appreciation of a textile but is frankly useless, since what matters is how that textile will actually be used and seen.

Behind all this there is a misunderstanding: the idea that there is a 'true' colour that just needs to be placed in the right light to be seen. To consider the light of the sun to be more reliable than that of a lamp is a convention. We live in a world in which light changes continuously and produces different colours according to the time of day and season of the year. To consider 'correct' only the light of midday in good weather because it allows us to see more colours is a specific choice, but it cannot be said to reveal the truth – unless we want to argue

[4] In general it is difficult to find consistent correspondence between the physical and the phenomenal world, because to one-dimensional variations of physical quantities there are corresponding multiple variations in psychological ones.

that we spend most of our lives having to make do with 'false' colours.

Why should an apple become more real in 6,500 kelvin than when seen in the reddish light from a fireplace? In the end, we live in full daylight for less than a quarter of our lives. So the very idea that there is a 'right' colour for things, properly viewed, is itself only a consequence of the industrial revolution.[5]

HOLTZSCHUE, 2011

On the subject of 'true light', an old anecdote from the world of design relates how a New York restaurateur decided in the 1970s to make his restaurant warmer and more romantic by suffusing it in a soft red light. But things did not quite go according to plan. At the opening, the effect was seemingly magnificent: everything was bathed in a warm and intimate atmosphere. Enthusiasm for it evaporated just as soon as the first meals were served. In this light vegetables were no longer green: they appeared in-
312A stead to be black, dirty, almost rotten.

The designer responsible for the restaurant probably did not know much about physics. Instead of choosing red light bulbs (which usually also contain some green and yellow wavelengths) and probably inspired by theatre lighting, he decided to use white bulbs with red filters. The result is that the irradiated light is exclusively red – and the poor greens, having no green radiation to reflect them, remain mute, as black as if there were no light on them at all, as if they were in darkness. Filters and coloured slides are in fact modifiers of wavelength, loved for good reason by cinema and theatre for enhancing some forms and negating

[5] Colorimetry, the discipline concerned with measuring colour, operates in the abstract and is able to talk about colour only under certain conditions. It's an excellent system for industry, but its numbers and formulas, for all their usefulness as design tools, cannot aspire to tell us the truth about colour.

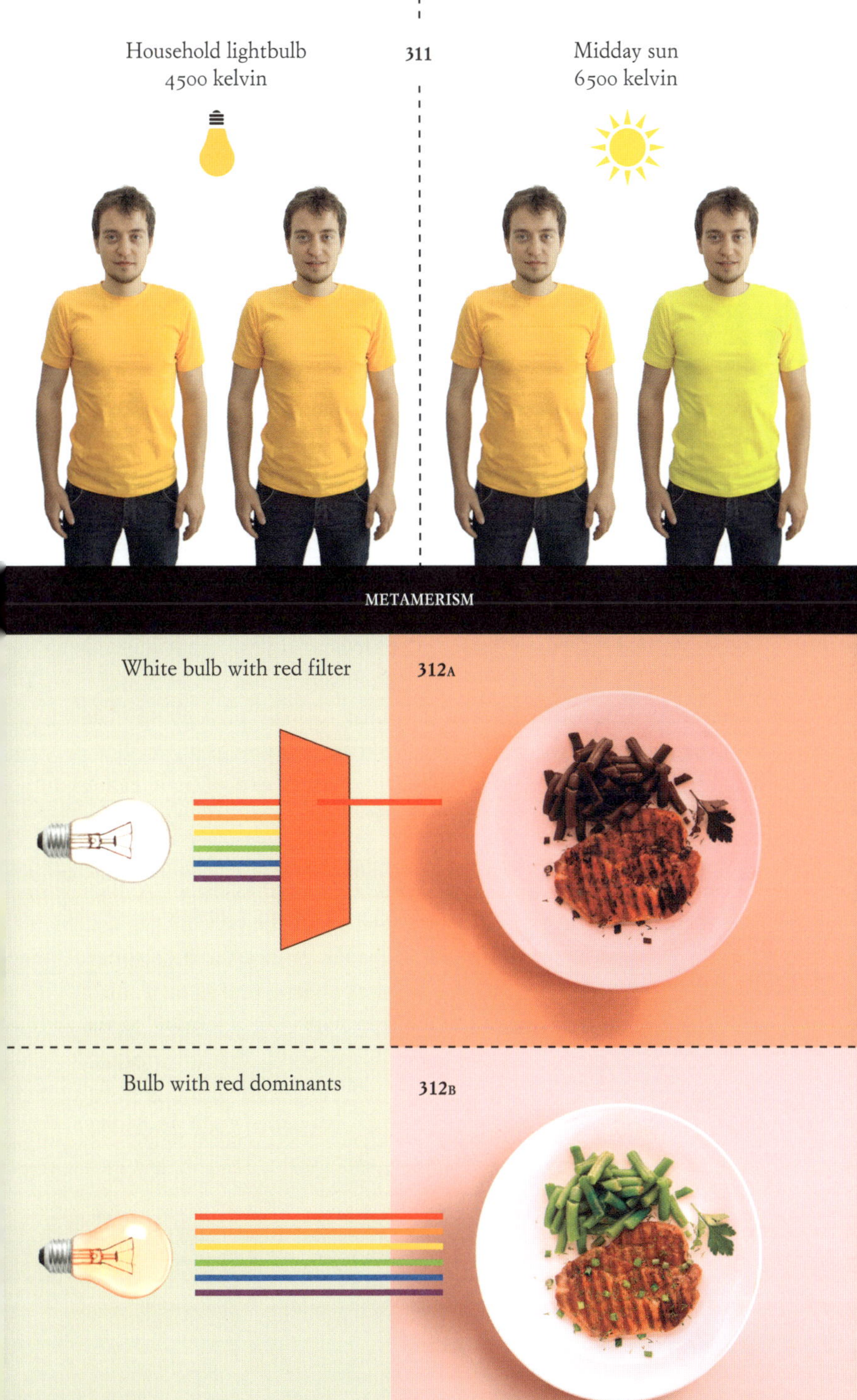
Household lightbulb
4500 kelvin
311
Midday sun
6500 kelvin
METAMERISM
White bulb with red filter
312A
Bulb with red dominants
312B

others. They act, in other words, like sieves: the red glass completely blocks green radiation, something that we never see in the natural world because the light of the sun always contains a mixture of all wavelengths.[6]

This anecdote, as well as explaining the physics of colour, reminds us that we have turned lighting into a communication code: light has become a way of describing and furnishing space. The reason why expensive or 'luxury' places have a preference for warm light, for example, is to appeal to our vanity: the dominant red evens out discoloration; redness and spots blend in to the overall tone and our skin appears clear. Even our teeth seem whiter, and the dark circles under our eyes diminish. There is no better cosmetic foundation than warm light. The proprietors of hotels, restaurants, theatres and fashionable bars know this perfectly well: soft lighting that makes us appear better-looking also makes us want to stay and to spend. And the lower the lights, the higher the prices.

BIRREN, 1988

On the other hand, fast-food outlets are spotlit from above with very cold, white light. Eyes are hollowed out, teeth appear yellowish, hair sparser and skin blotched. The blueish cast amplifies defects. There is nothing like neon for making you look unhealthy. But even this is the result of a precise, deliberate choice: it is an atmosphere more reminiscent of a supermarket than a restaurant, and just as in the supermarket it reminds us that we have come in to buy something and leave. Fast-food lighting implies: 'grab and go'. Or at most: 'eat and be gone'. This is light as a rhetorical device: the squalor of neon in all discount stores deliberately flattens space, because if that light were

WRIGHT, 1995

[6] There was an easy enough solution for the restaurant owner: it would have been
312B enough to choose light bulbs that had a strong predominance of red wavelengths but
that did not lack green radiation. In this way the warm atmosphere would have been
preserved and the greens on customers' plates would have still been recognizable.

more sophisticated they would not be able to convince us that the prices are really so very low.

The light that we have to deal with in our everyday lives has another important characteristic: it is frequently a constant, regular light, available in apparently unlimited amounts. The passage from natural light (sunshine, candles, oil lamps) to electric light has brought with it a paradigm shift in perceptions and in the production of coloured artefacts: it is the quality of light that determines the tone, the style, the aesthetic language of things. One of the most substantial differences between ourselves and pre-industrial humanity, in addition to their lack of artificial dyes, is the absence then of that electric light which has regulated our perception in an unprecedented way. A reflection on the art of the past will help bring this into focus.

There is an aspect of Renaissance painting to which too little attention is given. In the treatment of biblical subjects and narratives, everyone depicted is dressed in contemporary fashion: the Virgin, Joseph and the Magi are wearing clothing that was typical of fifteenth-century taste. If we were to do something comparable, the results would probably appear to us to be more kitsch than Pop – or both, as in the case of *Jesus Christ Superstar*. For contemporaries of Botticelli it was simply the norm, with nothing strange or provocative about it. And this was the case for two reasons: on the one hand, dressing the ancients in modern clothing reflects the notion that the Gospel message is always contemporary; on the other, no one has sufficient reason yet to think that the everyday clothing of the past was so very different from that of the present. This last idea seems inconceivable to us, because of a fact so simple that it is overlooked: we have electric light. Light bulbs, trains, washing machines, to say nothing of computers, remind us every day that we are in a different world; that there has been a break with the past. Becoming habituated to artificial light has in effect brought with it new ways of relating to space, influencing our rhythms of sleeping and waking and our social habits.[7] As well as the way in which we look at art.

Today the paintings of the past are admired in museums, hanging on white walls that transfigure them into isolated and distant concepts: a Byzantine icon next to a seventeenth-century still life and a Jackson Pollock painting, rendered homogeneous, among other things, by the type of lighting used. The painters of such icons designed them rather for spaces that were dark, or lit by naked flames – a light that, unlike electric light, trembles, oscillates and produces sudden changes in intensity. Before the flickering candles, the gold backgrounds would be now dull or almost black, now illuminated by a sudden movement of the flame. We can see how the idea of a 'right' light and of colours that are always the same does not make any sense in such a context: the yellow of a golden background is marvellous because it is *never* 'right' or true but multiple – rather like manifestations of the divine. Electric museum light amplifies the figurative while diminishing the metaphysical aspect of the image.

FLORENSKIJ, 1977

Returning to our original problem, it is clearly only the standardization of light that allows us to speak of objects of the same colour. This was an idea that for the ancients

[7] We use much more light now than in the past. At the beginning of the twentieth century in Germany, Herman Cohn calculated that, in order to read a text printed in 'corpo 8' (around 5mm), an amount of light equivalent to that of one candle (10.7 lux) was needed; at the beginning of the 1970s we began to use 500 candle power for the same job. In the course of less than a century, in other words, industrial progress had increased the average person's need for light five hundredfold.

was decidedly much more elusive. In practical terms, that is, the white light that we encounter in many clothes shops can make the yellow of Yellow Co's shirt look right[8] – if by right we mean consistent with the maker's original idea. Yellow Copy, however, in an absurd version, could exploit metamerism, and poach customers by inventing a colour that appears identical in the shop but changes in sunlight. In the light of the sun, that is, it would be a different colour and therefore a legal one. Making the light of the sun the yardstick of the law clearly guarantees nothing. Would it, in the end, be a legitimate or sensible way of distinguishing between them? Which is the true Yellow Co yellow? Perhaps there isn't one. Because, as the reader will have understood by now, the colour of things is 'true' only in relation to how we decide to think of it.

WITTGENSTEIN, 1981

Still, on 19 May 1960 the artist Yves Klein obtained from the patent office a certification for his International Klein Blue, a brilliant ultramarine pigment that when spread with a roller covers so evenly as to seem almost disembodied. And more recently the British company Surrey NanoSystems created Vantablack, a substance composed of carbon nanotubes that absorbs up to 99.9 per cent of light, resulting in a black that is effectively blacker than anything that has ever been seen before.[9] Beyond what was enthusiastically reported by journalists, in both cases what gets patented is a technical procedure rather than a colour. It is not by chance, sixty years later, that the

BALL, 2004

[8] This white light can at the same time make things/the wearer look pale. In terms of sales, however, whether or not a T-shirt appears in its right shade of yellow is less important than whether we like it when we look at ourselves in the mirror, since we will only buy it if it makes us look good.

[9] Developed for military purposes – to make stealth planes 'invisible' to radar – Vantablack immediately interested artists such as Anish Kapoor, who has patented its exclusive use.

effect of Klein blue can be easily reproduced using synthetic ultramarine and an aerosol fixer obtainable from any shop selling fine art materials. It is also clear, at least in Klein's case, that his copyrighting of a colour is not so much a form of protection as a performative act, a piece of the artistic discourse itself.

How is a patent different from copyright? A patent is a practical matter, it is the registration of a design or of a procedure and may be sold or licensed to third parties. Copyright, on the other hand, implies that an individual is the moral possessor of a certain idea, and that this is inalienable – it cannot be sold, although it may be left as an inheritance. In both cases, we are dealing with ideas, but whereas with a patent the idea is a concrete one that can be described in a technical way – a chemical formula, say, or a mechanism – in the case of an author's or artist's copyright we are dealing with an indefinable value that can only be exhibited, as with works of art. There is some crossover, but for the purposes of simplification we could say a door handle has a patent, while a painting by Mark Rothko is covered by the author/artist's copyright. I can explain the first with technical drawings and with a text defining its characteristics; with the second I actually have to show the work of art.

We realize at this point that Yellow Co cannot protect their shirts in either of these two ways. There can be no author copyright on colour, because if we are talking about the effect that is has on the eye this is not something invented by anyone; there is no moral authorship. As far as the chemical formula is concerned, if Yellow Copy came up with a different formula that produced a yellow indistinguishable from Yellow Co's, there would be no grounds for bringing a lawsuit. This takes us to the philosophical crux of the question. The shirts of Yellow Co and of

Yellow Copy may be chromatically indistinguishable from each other, but if they have been produced using different processes, then for the law they are two different things. Yellow Co is defeated in the end more by the changeability of light than by the rules of the patent office.

This is why there are so many manufacturers of the yellow Post-it note, even though it was invented by 3M. It is why Louboutin will find it difficult to win any future lawsuits; and why Tiffany may register its Pantone as a kind of magical self-promotion but will never be able to prevent anyone from using a similar colour. This is the fundamental misunderstanding behind Yellow Co's idea: treating colour as a 'thing' when it is clearly not. To want to protect a certain type of yellow is like trying to patent warmth or saltiness. It is simply absurd. Colour, when we close our eyes, ceases to exist: it is not a thing but a sensation. And the moral of the tale is that you cannot copyright sensations.

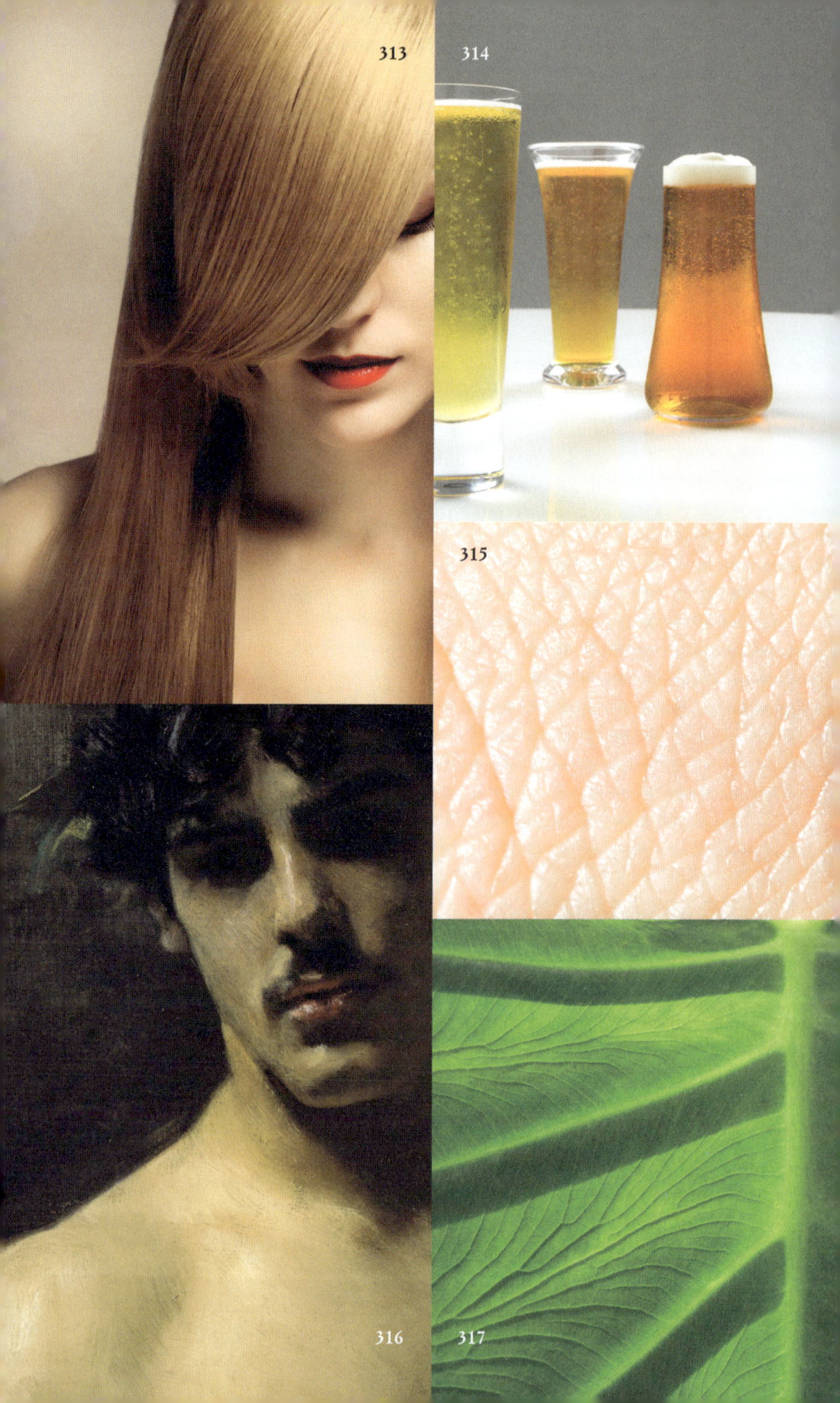
313
314
315
316
317

Peach Pink

Crayola Stands Corrected

According to the conventions of classic European fairy tales, any self-respecting princess must have hair as blonde as gold, or as black as ebony; red-rose lips and skin as white as snow.

This comparison between looks and precious substances is a convention derived from courtly literature: we compare the loved one with the best things in the world, underlining rarity and splendid workmanship, as if describing a piece of jewellery. How can we do otherwise? We cannot say flatly that hair is 'yellow', for instance, without rendering its chromatic complexity banal.

Hair is fluid and shifting, characteristics that are irreducible to the word for a single hue.[1] Blonde hair is often compared to gold because this is not a true colour: to say gold, silver or bronze is to suggest aspects such as lustre, metallic sheen and reflective shine – aspects which add to the perceived colour and change in brilliance as our point of view changes. To say 'gold colour' is in fact always a simile or metaphor.

If thinking in solid colours is among the main consequences of industrialization, we could say that hair and

[1] The opposite is also true: it is not without significance that it is only for the simple, basic, primary colours that we have proper names.

metals are on the contrary examples of variegated, non-uniform, articulated colour. And it is for this reason that recourse to metaphor is not just a poetic choice but a necessity. It is certainly no accident that advertising for hair dyes speaks of 'three-dimensional' colour, promising an effect that enhances the natural shine of hair without reducing it to a flat painted cap.

The colour of things can present itself in at least three FAIRCHILD, 1998
'modes': the 'superficial' one, characteristic of any opaque
object and often corresponding to a uniform colour, where
light is *reflected* from a surface. The 'luminous' one, as in
a lighted lamp or anything else that *emits* light. And the
so-called 'volume mode' that we get when looking through
314 something, such as plate glass, a glass of wine, boiled
sweets, etc., where there is an actual *transmission* of light.
In this case the effect is qualified by continuous changes,
in which the light is felt to be now dark, now bright, according to the varying thickness of the material through
which it passes.[2]

In the natural world the boundary between surface and
volume is often elusive. The freshness of living things is
due in fact to our perception of colours that are not reducible to superficial tints but have depth, as if revealing
317 underlying substructures. Leaves, for instance, especially
when light plays over them, allow their internal reticulation to be seen, and it is precisely these changing reflections
that confer upon them for us their naturalness and organic nature; so much so that if we take a leaf and paint it
uniformly green, what we have instead is a plastic plant,
emphatically deprived of life.

[2] For the 'modes' in which colour presents, see Appendix A 7.2.

Human skin can be considered a good example of intermediate location between surface and volume colour, not
only for the transparency of underlying tones (including 315
those complementary ones of the veins), but also for how
its nuances of colour change with variations in the thickness
of skin; for how it becomes redder or paler, for instance,
in different parts of the body; and its ability to stretch or
pucker, to suddenly lighten or darken. In fact, every time
that artists and designers have to deal with complexion
and with skin, the conflict between articulated and solid
colour rears its head.

To paint human skin in a realistic way you cannot apply a solid layer of paint, you have to combine many small
touches of different colours or many superimposed layers.
Historically it is a procedure that always proved extremely difficult with tempera (which is not fluid); so much so
that Willem de Kooning once remarked brilliantly that
human flesh was perhaps the only reason that oil paint- 316
ing had been developed.[3]

CARRIERA, 2005 BRUSATIN, 2006

No doubt the fluidity of oil allowed for the shading and
nuance required to render human colouring, even though
a peak in this regard was reached by Rosalba Carriera 319
(1673–1757), a portrait painter who worked with pastels.
The technique had enormous success in eighteenth-century
Europe. These are years in which portrait painting begins
to scrutinize the gaze of its subjects, in an attempt to capture their character. This is the first psychological painting
in the modern sense. In fact, for Carriera a highlight on
a cheek is enough to tell us something about power, pride
or hope, and the very fine grains of pastel are inimitable
for this purpose, managing to evoke the palpitation of the

[3] Willem de Kooning, 'The Renaissance and Order', lecture given at Studio 35, 8th Street, New York, in the autumn of 1949.

epidermis in its faintest vibrations. The fashion for face powder greatly helped: everyone wore it, men as well as women, and so we often see immortalized subjects whose skin is already covered by a pigmentation that levels it out – as if face powder and pastels, both being dust, worked together. Between the painted and made-up face there is an equivalence: pastel caresses the contours of faces – and these, veiled by an artificial colour, offer themselves to art already pre-painted.

Representation is only one aspect of the creative problems presented by the complexion of skin. In the last century the market had to figure out how to industrialize its qualities. And it was the manufacturers of cosmetics who were in the forefront of providing an answer.

The various pigments that have succeeded each other over the years have had to take account first and foremost of the ideas that we have about human skin – the fact, for instance, especially in relation to the face, that it reveals at a glance our vitality or fatigue, stress or happiness. It follows that a foundation that is too thick gives an impression of artificiality or fakery, unless this artifice
318 is deliberately pursued. If we look at the actors of the Pe-
320 king Opera, for instance, we notice that the thick, white
foundation transforms the face into an abstract sign. The skin is converted into a mask, so that even men can play the role of women because uniform colour neutralizes the body, signifying character rather than gender.

BARTHES, 2002

Outside of such rigid codes, and beyond the world of theatre and spectacle, foundation is used in everyday life by many women in order to enhance their looks and self-confidence. The ideal colour must smooth out or homogenize the complexion but not too much, since it is necessary to remedy discoloration without flattening

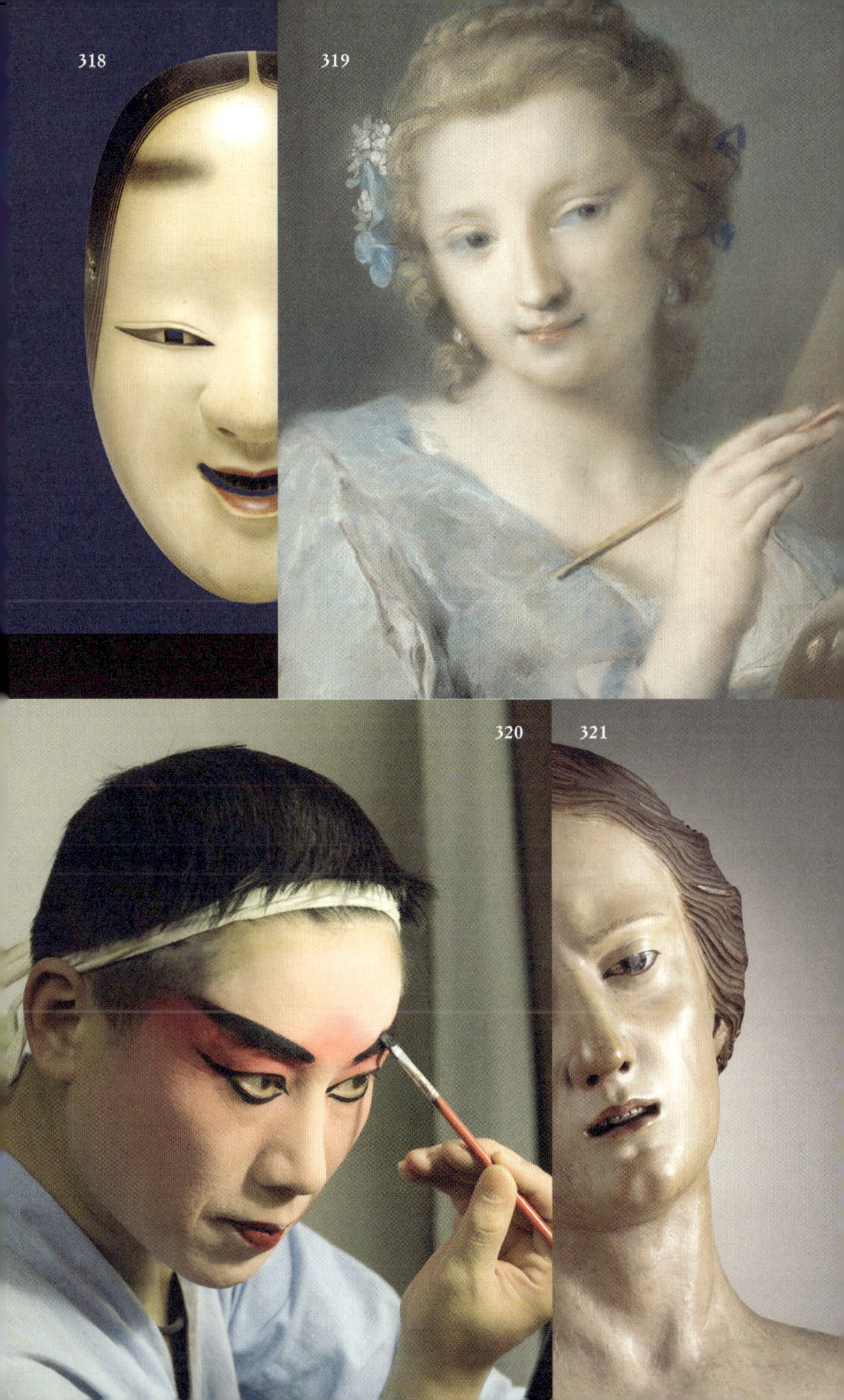

318
319
320
321

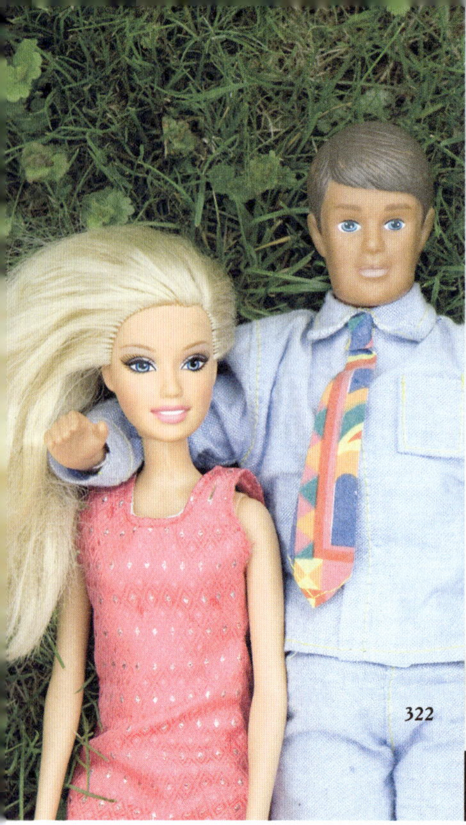

322

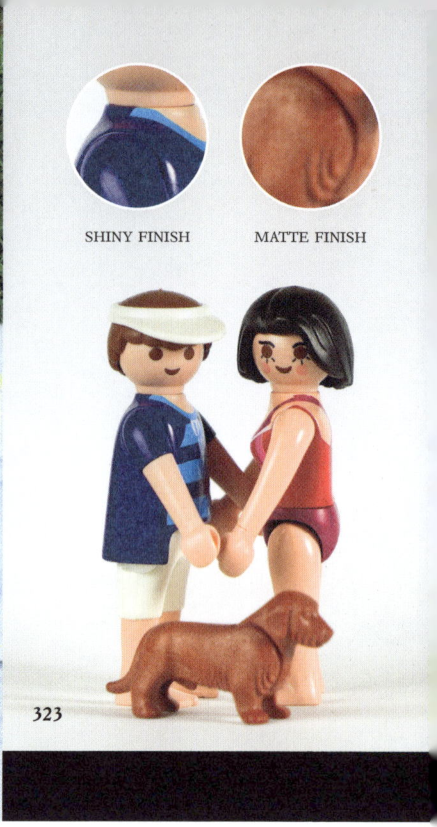

SHINY FINISH

MATTE FINISH

323

324

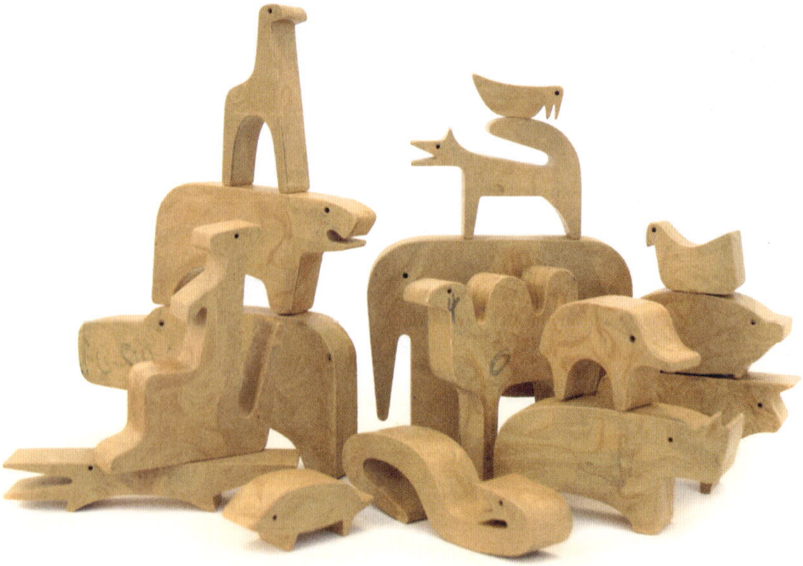

expression. In reality, given that cosmetics use industrial
colours, the only way to obtain a natural effect is by combining them – not so much colouring as interpreting the 325
face, just as a painter would. And people less skilled in the
art of make-up, in fact, tend to worsen skin by making it
more 'painted' than enhanced, spreading colour thickly
across a surface which is meant to have depth and articu-
lation.

There are other contexts in which skin colour has posed some problems for industry – in the world of toys and that of animated cartoons, for instance, where it has inevitably been represented for the most part with a solid colour.

In the case of toys, a ploy to restore a rich and vital effect often involves concentrating on the finish rather than
the colour itself. When Enzo Mari (b. 1932) makes a version in plastic of his *16 Animals*, for example, he chooses
an unusual paste-like resin that is magmatically veined, as
if it were animated, in this way evoking an organic texture 324
which is not homogenized like the usual reds, yellows and
blues that are typical of toys. So that if we were to ask what
colour the Mari animals are, we would have to reply with
an oxymoron: they are made of 'wood-coloured' plastic.[4]

Moving on to the mainstream market, in the incredibly
successful world of Playmobil, the human figures are made 323
of shiny plastic whereas the animals have a rough surface,
signifying the clear distinction between nature and culture
in the civilized world in which these figures dwell. Besides, common experience tells us that shininess or polish
is often the fruit of work, while roughness is an attribute
typical of things before humanity intervenes. A schemat-
ic choice, but one which shows great design sensibility.

[4] The first version of *16 Animals* was made in 1956, of actual wood.

The most famous case of the 'reinvention' of human skin is that undertaken for the decidedly WASP original Barbie doll (launched in 1959), involving considered and original variations upon beige.[5] A maximum degree of illusionism can be achieved, in the case of both dolls and mannequins, when they are modelled in wax, a material that makes the distinction between surface and volume colour ambiguous. Wax, though, has the drawback of often producing macabre and unsettling results, since it can render the features of the face highly realistic and at the same time immobile, like those of the dead. Barbie wisely stops short of this: she is made from a waxy material, a slightly sticky rubber, and is coloured in an even way, producing a sophisticated form of *semi*-realism that has certainly contributed to her success. In such a system the contribution and impact of the colour is not an isolated thing in itself but is related to and interacts with the other
322 toys in the set or series: Ken, for instance, the famous boyfriend, has skin that is much darker in order to indicate that it is masculine. When Mattel takes this decision, it is not imitating nature (not all men are darker than women), it is applying a very ancient iconographic colour code.

In the West, the use of light pink to depict feminine flesh can be traced to Greek and Roman painting, where in all probability it carried a meaning that was more social than biological: in the ancient world, especially among higher classes, women spent a good deal of time at home and therefore ended up having lighter skin than men, who on account of more outdoor activity – from work to warfare – are consequently more tanned. It is a theme reprised and amplified in the literature of courtly love, with

GUALANDI, 2014 CENNINI, 1982

[5] Although there were subsequently several attempts to launch Barbie dolls of colour, some of them controversial, the first official African American and Latina Barbies were not launched until 1980.

its continuous celebration of the whiteness of the faces and hands of beautiful chatelaines, consolidating as a consequence the association between paleness and nobility. Cennino Cennini is prescriptive on this subject: in painting, handsome men should be dark and women white. At the beginnings of the industrial world these courtly ideals re-emerge in fables, so that – complicit with romantic illustrations – the tonal difference becomes a law, and all the princesses in animated films have the palest skin compared to that of the male characters. In the world of Disney, ultimately, the Prince is not only dressed in blue but always 20 per cent darker.

The fact that skin tone can only with considerable difficulty be described with a single colour brings into focus a more general problem connected with the relationship between colours and the ways in which we think about and name them. While it is relatively easy to name a solid colour, the articulated colours are hampered by the insufficiency of language. In these cases, in order to escape such inadequacy, we have had recourse to terms such as blonde, chestnut, pale, sun-tanned or dark that express chromatic properties separated from physical ones: chestnut, for instance, is indeed a colour, but it does not refer to a precise hue – and much less to one that is homogeneous. It is the way in which we refer to the brown of hair, just as 'hazel' can refer to the brown of eyes – according to a now opaque comparison with the skin of an actual nut. We do not speak of chestnut or hazel textiles or glass. Our vocabulary for hair is admitted, in part, into only one other specialist lexicon, when we speak of blonde, red or dark beer – not accidentally since we are also dealing here with 314
'volume colour'. That skin is pink is true, effectively, only in medieval and Renaissance metaphors, in animated

cartoons and in the stereotypes of many children's drawings. Actually, the terms of comparison often work the other way around, as in sets of crayons in which the pink is called 'flesh' (-coloured).

Crayons, coloured pencils and pens play a significant role in the construction of our imagination in the Western world: they are the first tools with which we begin to handle colour, and to propose a matrix of relationships that appears to be free but actually contains within itself certain prescribed decisions. By saying in effect that these *are* 'the colours', we are using a practical tool to suggest to children an abstract idea of reality. Who is it, in fact, who decides which and how many the basic colours are? And who decides on their names?

Among the many possibilities there is one that is worth relating. The forerunners of the crayons we use as children were first launched in 1903 in the United States, by Crayola. The brand is still an institution, so much so that a Yale study has listed the smell of Crayola crayons as among the twenty smells most recognized by adults in America – a fact that is not so surprising, given that paints and glues almost always seem to have highly memorable aromas (all Italians know the hypnotic almond smell of Coccoina glue).

DESIGN IN 1000 OGGETTI, 2008

The first box of Crayolas, sold for a quarter, contained
326 eight colours. At the time the selection contained no pink.[6]

[6] This raises the question as to what colour children would use for human skin, since they were lacking pink and free to decide. The problem persists because we attribute a strongly representational role to school drawing, otherwise skin could be rendered for reasons other than imitating its colour: to indicate character, for instance, based on the personal associations of individual children: red for a father, say; blue for a mother and green for a cat. But if you ask them for a realistic (verisimilar) drawing, the young artist has basically two possibilities: the first is conceptual, that is selecting the colour closest to the luminosity of skin, namely the yellow or white; or else, and this is a more painterly one, the red can be lightly rubbed and spread on the white paper to produce a pink effect.

325

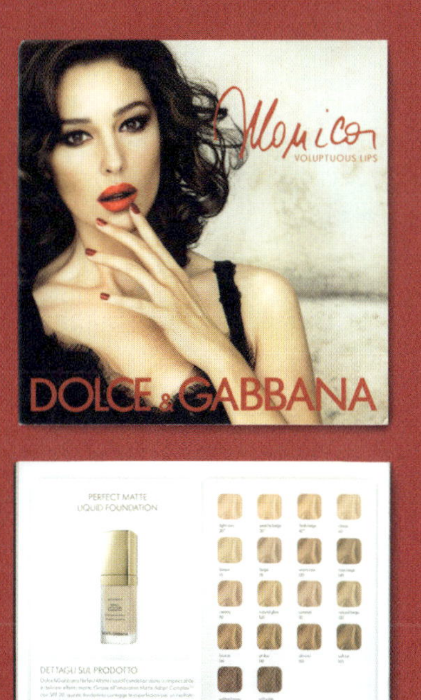

326

Brown Red Blue Orange Green Yellow Black Purple

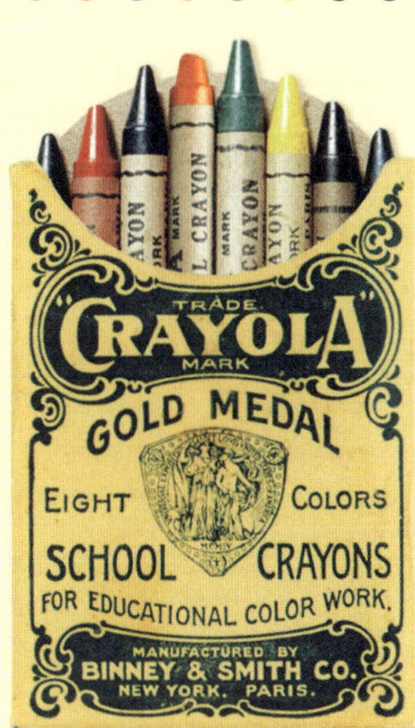

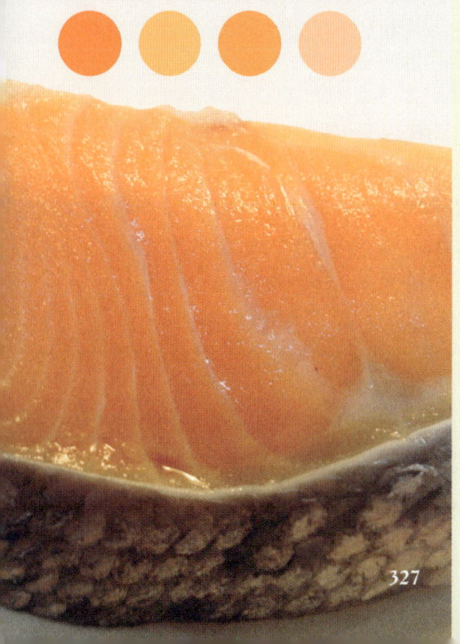

327

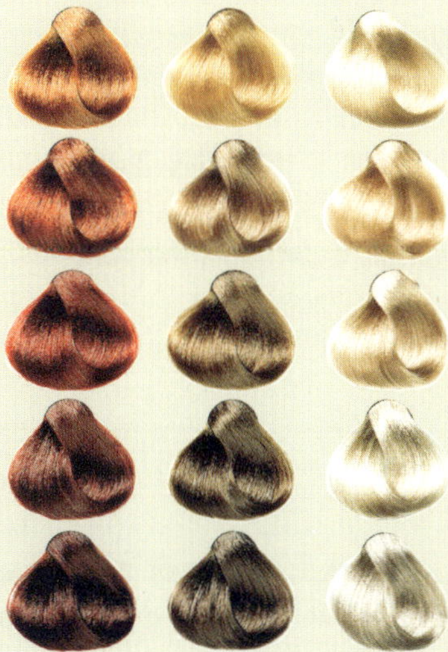

328

As often happens, a conceptual problem soon becomes a question of marketing and Crayola, perhaps pressurized by parents and teachers, perhaps after accurate market research, introduces in the 1910s the coveted pastel pink crayon, naming it 'flesh' colour. This new arrival went on to have more than fifty years of success. Until 1962, when the company had to change the name after someone rightly pointed out that skin can be many colours, from light beige to dark brown to black, and that no wax crayon of a particular colour can presume to have primacy when representing it. At this point one would have expected 'flesh' to be simply renamed 'pink'. Instead Crayola re-named it 'peach'. So did this mean, we might wonder, that the crayon used by three generations of Americans to colour in human skin was not pink after all but peach? And hence that what we call white human skin bears more resemblance to a peach than to a rose?

In reality, whether pink or peach, the choice demonstrates how giving a name to the colour of complex surfaces is never very convincing, and that we must resort to different systems in order to evoke through comparison a surface with similar characteristics.

All cultures have resorted to indirect expressions of this kind. The Mbaye tribe of Chad in Central Africa only use comparative expressions: among their colours are 'like the bush bird' and 'like the nightjar's eggs'. If these names sound outlandish we should remember how in post-industrial societies we use similar indirect formulas: when we say 'salmon pink', 'mouse grey' or 'paper white', we are obviously suggesting quite specific comparisons.

SQUILLACCIOTTI, 2007

Nothing prevents us from inventing our own word: we could call salmon pink 'gebo' and start to speak of a dark gebo dress, or of a vivid gebo sunset. The only limitation is that we must evoke an experience that our interlocutors will recognize, and for this to be possible we would need a context in which they would be familiar with the appearance of salmon flesh. This is hardly a secondary factor: before this fish became globally successful as a food, a name such as this would have been completely useless. The human eye can discern around 200 colours, but every culture and every historic moment only needs words that correspond to their own technical, psychological and social world.

What is the actual colour of the salmon that we are dealing 327 with? At the fishmonger's it is usually light orange; once it is cooked it becomes paler; smoked it is decidedly darker, and when tinned it is more whitish. Salmon does not have a definitive wavelength to be recognized and linguistically certified. A painter would explain that from a practical point of view what we call salmon is in fact an orange in which we detect a hint of white. And perhaps this is the general perception of everyone who uses the phrase, without necessarily having brought it into focus. 'Salmon' has become a mental category, a cognitive typology.

Here we encounter another of the many philosophical problems of visual perception: if my interlocutor has no experience of a particular colour, I have no way of explaining it to them in words; at least, that is, unless we share the same mental models. For instance, designers can use among themselves the system of typographical blends in order to say that a certain tint is composed of 40 per cent magenta and 50 per cent yellow, thus allowing the colour they are talking about to be more or less accurately visualized.

If the conversation involves people who do not share a common language, the colour can only be shown and seen. If I am speaking to someone who does not know what 'periwinkle' is, I cannot provide an encyclopaedic or numerical definition. I can only point to periwinkle-colour objects and say 'the visual quality that they share is what we call periwinkle'. In this case, I need an ostensive gesture, that is to say a pointing towards something which exhibits the characteristics to which I am referring. It is only when that particular colour is recognized and understood by both parties that we can talk about it in its absence, because it has become a cognitive type that we have in common.

WITTGENSTEIN, 1981

In a certain sense, even in our everyday language, every time that we say 'salmon' we are making or implying that ostensive gesture, as if mentally pointing to a stereotype of the fish, with a characteristic colour implicit in the reference. This is why, if we want to indicate a very precise tint, we need to leave words behind and rely instead upon an example, passing from the theoretical to an actual fish.

An extreme example – though one no less legitimate for that – would be to go into a store brandishing an actual salmon and ask for a paint *this* colour. Even if the situation may appear absurd, the number of people who take this kind of approach is greater than we might think: a famous writer once came into my study carrying a cushion from his bedroom, in order to let me know the colour he wanted for the cover of one of his books. The only way of identifying a precise colour is to point to it, to physically show it. The Pantone swatch book was invented expressly to simplify such exchanges, and to oil the wheels of communication.

Today, in fact, all colour is commercialized through the sample system – a system which cannot say everything precisely because it works through examples. The understanding between a buyer and seller is that the sample shows more or less the colour and partly the finish: gloss, matte or satin. A sample only shows some characteristics, and

GOODMAN, 2008

is always a 'practically this', a 'more or less' that.[7] Words and samples are two ways of speaking about colour, each with particular limitations that emerge most when dealing with surfaces with complex and variegated colours.

The sample book as a model belongs to a precise historical moment. It is the system by which in contemporary society we indicate colours that often cannot be identified in words, just as metaphors and other comparisons were the medieval models par excellence. This is why – returning to the hairstyling with which we began – samples of dyes shown by hairdressers do not consist of a little square of colour, but a real shock of hair that has been dyed. Be- 328
cause if we want to do justice to an articulated colour, the sample cannot simply be 'yellow' but, as in the classic fairy tale, must show itself as blonde and luminous. Like gold.

[7] A little square of a few centimetres of pink seems much lighter than a whole room painted this colour, because the amount of surface covered alters the way we perceive it; or, in the case of textiles, the colour sample cannot convey the dynamic effect of the cloth in action as a dress or upholstery.

329

STUDIES ON HOMER

AND

THE HOMERIC AGE.

I. AGORÈ:
POLITIES OF THE HOMERIC AGE.

II. ILIOS:
TROJANS AND GREEKS COMPARED.

III. THALASSA:
THE OUTER GEOGRAPHY.

IV. AOIDOS:
SOME POINTS OF THE POETRY OF HOMER.

BY THE

RIGHT HON. W. E. GLADSTONE, D.C.L.

M. P. FOR THE UNIVERSITY OF OXFORD.

Plenius ac melius Chrysippo et Crantore.—HORACE.

OXFORD:
AT THE UNIVERSITY PRESS.
M.DCCC.LVIII.

[*The right of Translation is reserved.*]

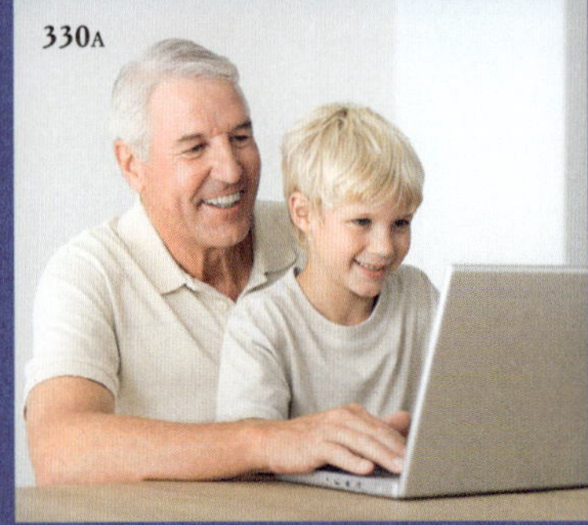

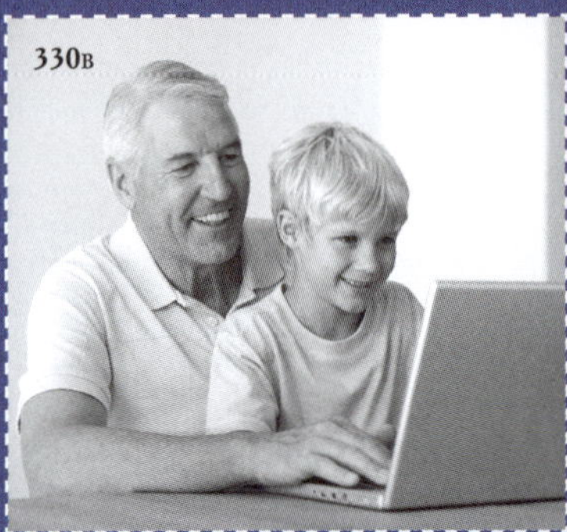

331

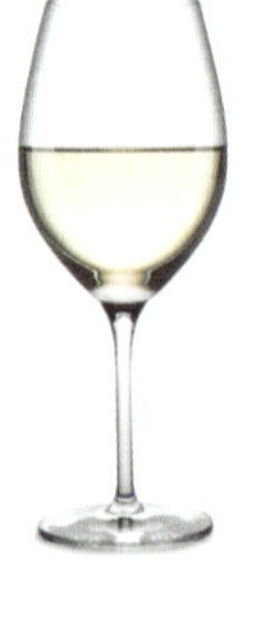

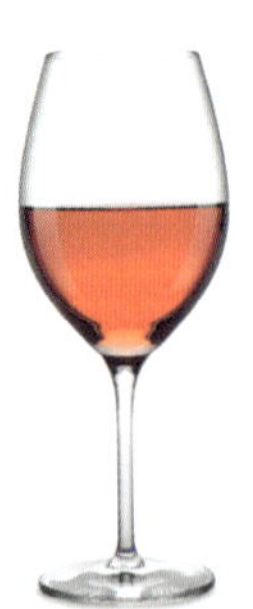

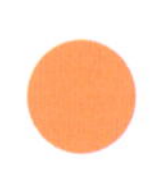

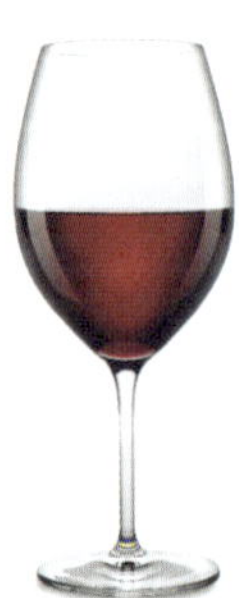

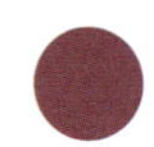

WHITE WINE
Yellow or greenish in our perception of it

ROSÉ WINE
Pinkish or orange in our perception of it

RED WINE
Perceived as purple or brown

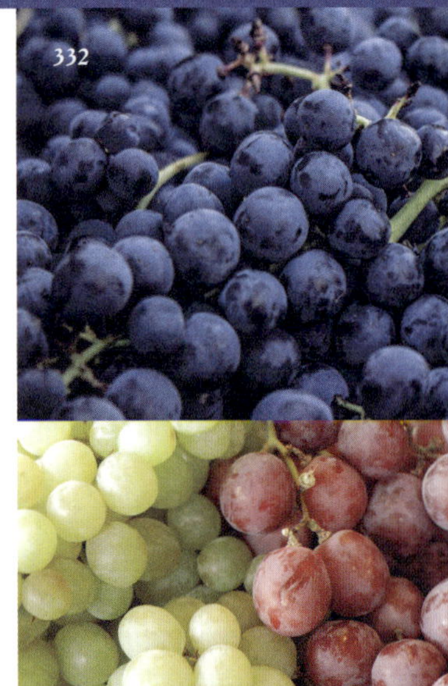

Homeric Blue

A Hypothesis for Perception

London, 1858. William Ewart Gladstone is a politician with a brilliant career: four times Prime Minister, he will be considered by posterity one of the greatest statesmen that Britain has ever had. Everything seems to be going well, and he is held in high esteem by the whole world. But Gladstone has another passion apart from politics, and it obsesses him and makes him the target of ferocious attacks, so much so that on this subject at least he becomes an object of ridicule – for everyone from *The Times* to Karl Marx. This not so secret passion of his is for the work of the Greek poet Homer.

At the time, the Greek epic was considered to be purely fictional. One of humanity's great foundational narratives, no less, but the fruit of fantasy. It is only in 1872 – fourteen years later – that Heinrich Schliemann uncovers the remains of the Palace of Mycenae, proving the historical existence of Troy.

Gladstone, in anticipation of this discovery, had argued for the historical authenticity of the Homeric world, by publishing a book 1,700 pages long, the fruit of his astonishingly vast knowledge of the classical world. He writes in it about a huge range of things: battles and customs, geography and beauty, ethnology and the condition of women. And in the midst of all of this erudition there is a chapter that is destined to be much discussed: 'Homer's Perceptions and Use of Colour'.

GLADSTONE, 1858

Here, after having compared various expressive formulas, Gladstone argues that there were some colours that the Greeks of the heroic age did not see, because of the immaturity of their visual faculties. This is a statement that – due no doubt to the cultural climate of his time – is immediately interpreted in evolutionary terms and harshly critiqued. The distance separating us from the ancient Greeks is too brief an interval, some argue, compared to the whole history of *Homo sapiens*, to allow for the biology of the eye to be substantially altered.[1] And yet Gladstone is not at all naive and, as we shall see, it should not be assumed that by 'visual immaturity' he was referring to a strictly biological question. Indeed, the way in which he focuses on certain linguistic data – from a historian's point of view, not a scientist's – is still fascinating today for what it reveals of the complex nature of the relationships between perception and language.

As far as colour is concerned, Homer is parsimonious with names. Contrasts between black and white, light and dark, are present throughout, but there are very few traces of other colours. In the whole of his work, almost 8,000 hexameters, red is mentioned only thirteen times, compared to 100 references to white and 170 to black. Most strikingly, there is not a single reference to blue. When he comes to describe things that we would call blue, Homer uses periphrases that confuse rather than clarify. He never once says that the sky is blue. He calls it great, star-studded, and sometimes even maintains that it is like copper. But

[1] Charles Darwin's *On the Origin of Species* would be published just a year later, and at this time Lamarck's theory, according to which giraffes lengthened their necks to reach the leaves of the highest trees, was widespread.

never blue. The same goes for the sea, which he famously describes as 'wine-coloured'.[2]

A lot has been written on this subject, and the most improbable hypotheses devised. There are those who support the idea that Homer was talking of the colour of the sea at dawn, when it is dark and opaque. Others have hypothesized the presence of a red algae that would make it seem similar to a glass of Chianti. There are even those who, by swapping the terms of comparison, have tried to maintain that wine, when it is dark, has bluish reflections. It is also possible that we are dealing with a simple case of poetic licence. So it is worth asking how the ancients used the chromatic lexicon more generally.

DEUTSCHER, 2013

In the industrialized world, we are so accustomed to speaking of colours by referring to them literally that we often struggle to imagine other ways of doing so. For us, colours are red, yellow, blue and so on – and yet, as we have seen, for centuries colour was instead the complex appearance of things, the articulated way in which they offer themselves to our perception.

If by colour we mean the set of these phenomenal properties, it no longer seems quite so absurd to declare that the sea is the colour of wine. Both sea and wine are instances of volume colour, that is to say substances whose chromatic effect is not produced by superficial characteristics but by perception of their three-dimensionality. The sea, like wine, has a colour in which density and transparency coincide. So it is possible that Homer was comparing them not for their surfaces but as liquids. Perhaps this is not the solution to our question, but if we want to understand it,

[2] The adjective used by Homer is *oînops*, from *oinos* meaning 'wine' and *op* the root of 'to see'. He defines oxen in the same way. Another apparent incongruity is his use of *chloròs*, 'green', applied to various things including honey, faces pale with fear, and fresh branches/sprays.

333

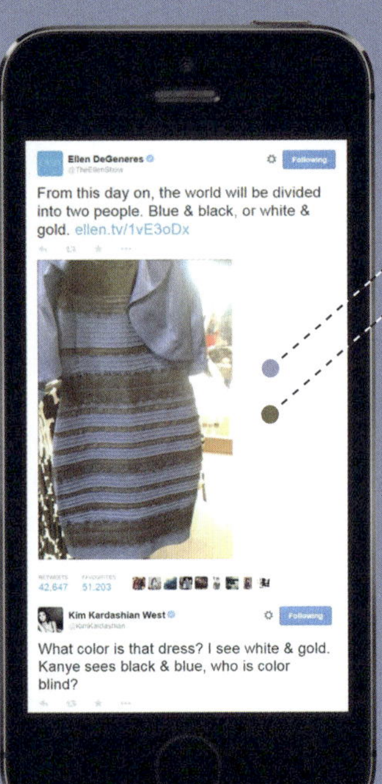

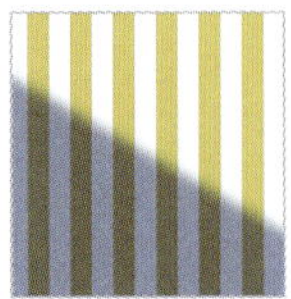

HYPOTHESIS A

The dress is white and gold, but is in partial shadow and therefore the white appears bluish, i.e. darkened

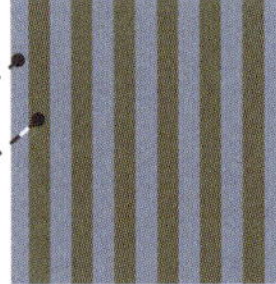

THE DRESS AS IT APPEARS IN THE PHOTO BY SAMPLING THE COLOURS

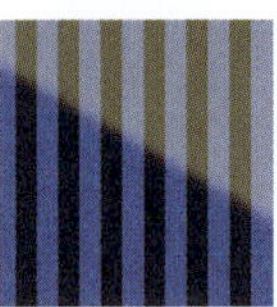

HYPOTHESIS B

The dress is blue and black, but is in a warm and intense light, so the blue appears blueish, i.e., faded

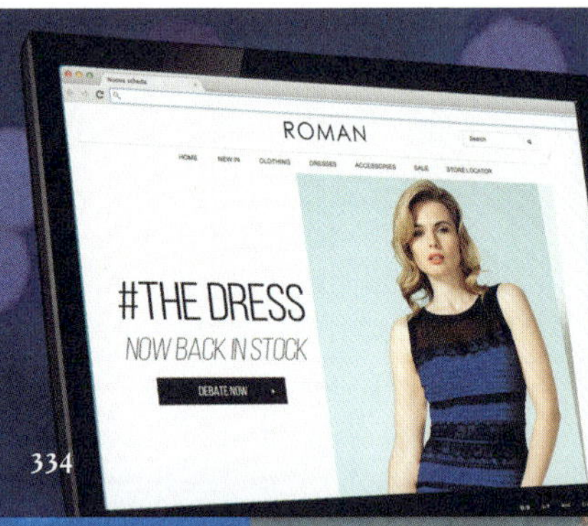

334

335

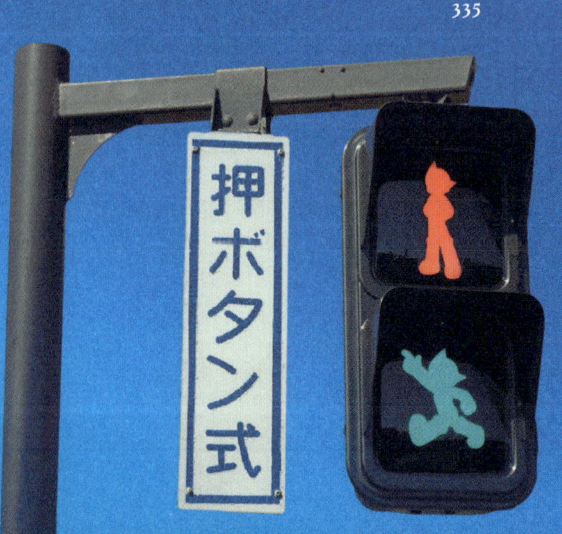

336

we need to distance ourselves from our modern uses, given that the crux of it is still here, in the problematic relationship between what we see and how we choose to name it.

WITTGENSTEIN, 1976

On this subject the philosopher Ludwig Wittgenstein brings to bear a particularly significant proof: looking at a black and white photograph we are always able to say (and to see) if someone has blond hair, even if what we see is *really* only a shade of grey.[3] In the photograph of
the man and boy in Figure 330B, for instance, their hair 330B
colour is of the same tonality if measured with a spectrometer, and yet we have no doubt that one has blond and the other grey hair, because we evaluate what we see according to other information such as age, type of skin and physiognomy that enables us to recognize distinct aspects of reality. The gap between how we perceive things and how we choose to think about them is a fundamental characteristic of all our chromatic experience.

The very use we make of the terms black and white in common parlance is also revealing: we call 'white' the wine that we actually see as yellow, and grapes that we see
in reality as purple we call 'black'. Black and white are 331
consequently concepts more than they are phenomena – 332
concepts with which we refer respectively to a maximum of darkness and a maximum of clarity, within circumscribed systems of reference. In other words, like the ancients we too are rarely referring to an actual colour when we say 'white'.

A few years ago, the internet was taken by storm by a perceptual game or conundrum that everyone seemed captivated by, and about which everyone seemed to have an

[3] In *Philosophical Investigations* and *Remarks on Colour*.

334 opinion. It involved the photograph of a notorious dress that seemed blue and black to some, whereas others saw it as white and gold. It is not so much the mystery of the dress that fascinates, as the fact that, faced with the same image on a screen, people could come to such different conclusions, and it is an enigma that may help us to understand the colour questions thrown up by Homer.

To solve this enigma we must take into account the fact that we are dealing with a somewhat ambiguous photograph in which it is not clear where the light is coming from, and which allows itself to be interpreted in differ-
333 ent ways. If measured, there is a light blue and a brown; we all more or less see them in this way, and if we isolate a detail then the ambiguity disappears. The brain, however, can decide to read this data in context as a white dress in shadow (with the unlit areas light blue), or as a blue dress bleached by too much light. Having made these assumptions, by way of simultaneous contrast the brown could be interpreted as gold in shadow, or as a highly lit black. In a similar way to the famous duck-rabbit figure, in which we see one or the other of the two animals but cannot see both at the same time, here too we either see the dress as blue or we see it as white.

To complicate the relationship between seeing and naming, there is the further fact that the two activities work in radically different ways: whereas for perception colour continues to be a gradual continuum in which the colours blend into each other without edges or breaks, for language it is a question of discrete segments. In reality, the eye does not see interruptions between crimson and carmine, and between the two there are indefinite intermediate perceptions. For language, on the other hand, crimson and carmine are two cleanly separate colours.

GROSSMANN, 1988

Neither should we overlook the fact that every social group speaks of colour in its own way. Anyone brought up in a family that appreciates art or has a sense of fashion may develop a more articulate vocabulary and nuanced perceptions than someone raised in a family with other interests. Not because they see more colours, but because they are accustomed to naming them in a detailed manner. Having parents who are both painters, I always saw clearly the distinction between blue, azure, navy blue, petrol blue, sugar paper and celestial or sky blue. For my grandfather, who worked in a bank, these shades were all just the one generic 'blue'. He found it pointless to name something that he did not use.

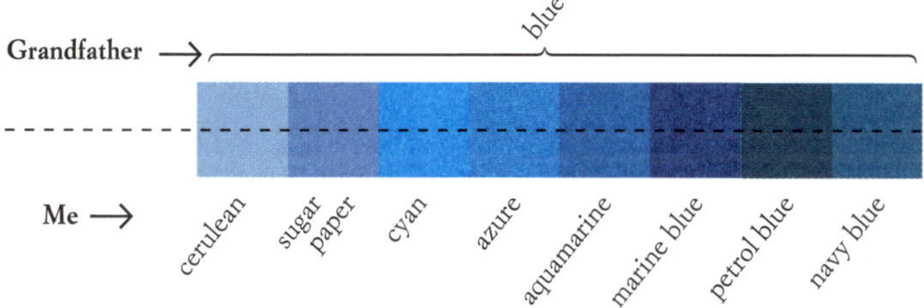

In addition to this, a century ago we owned fewer items of clothing than we do today, so if my grandfather said he would be wearing his blue outfit it is clear what he meant: not the brown one and not the black one. Today I would need to specify whether it is going to be the dark blue, cerulean or petrol blue sweater that I will be wearing.

JARMAN, 1995

Certain telling anecdotes come to mind. For instance, in ancient Japanese there is the word *ao*, which refers to a range on the spectrum that includes both our blue and some green. Then *midori* appears, a term indicating just the section of greens, thus leaving *ao* free to refer solely to blue. The matter becomes a little more complicated when, in the 1930s, the first traffic lights are imported to Japan from the

United States. *Ao* in modern Japanese also means 'free path' (or what we would call 'green light') and therefore seems perfect for signposting, but an international convention forbids the use of blue traffic lights. In the end, after years of hesitation, Japan decides in 1973 that instead of altering the language it will alter reality, and installs traf-
335 fic lights of an ineffable turquoise which is neither green
336 nor blue, bypassing the subdivisions of language with an intermediate perception.[4]

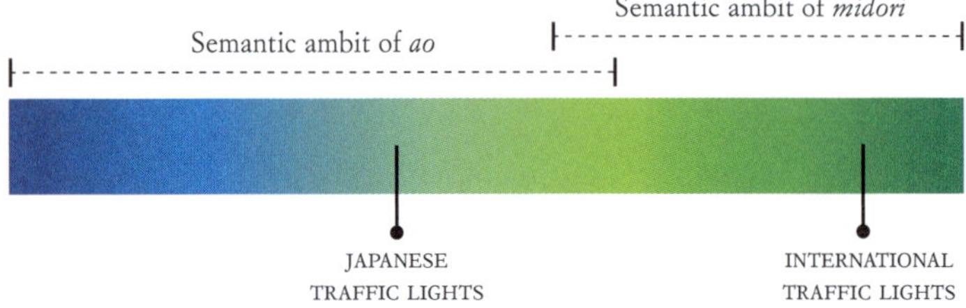

This lack of homogeneity between words and perception is also seen in a historic experiment among the Nubian people of southern Egypt and northern Sudan, during one SAUNDERS, 2007
of the many anthropological investigations conducted in the second half of the nineteenth century. They were asked to identify skeins of wool of various colours and to pair them two by two, a task completed without any errors, demonstrating an acute visual precision. When asked to name each colour, however, the terms were associated in an apparently 'mistaken' way, and the greens and the blues ended up in the same group. When the anthropologist asked why they made this decision, the subjects replied that yes, they could see that they were dealing with different colours, but that it seemed foolish to use two distinct names. There is no doubt that my grandfather would have agreed with the

[4] In recent years, however, traffic lights with decidedly blue glass have been installed.

Nubians. Every language organizes the data of experience in a particular way, as does every family.

In 1969, two anthropologists, Brent Berlin and Paul Kay, published one of the most controversial, discussed and cited studies in the history of colour: *Basic Color Terms*. After having interviewed speakers of ninety-eight different languages, the two scholars came to the same conclusion that among populations that have only two words to indicate colours, these are always white and black. If there are three words, then the third one is red. If there are four or five, then, after red, it is green and yellow.

BERLIN, 1969

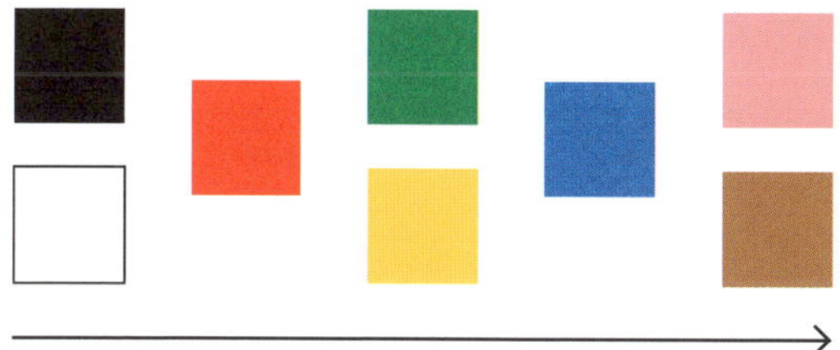

Berlin and Kay are not seeking a perceptual universal – which is assumed to be the same for everyone – but a linguistic one. What is clear is that data of this kind are susceptible to multiple interpretations, and their research was enthusiastically received by some and criticized by others. The first objection is that those interviewed, though speaking different languages, all came from the San Francisco Bay area and were therefore part of a bilingual, highly urbanized community.[5] The second criticism was that in conducting the interviews they had used colour samples taken from Munsell in the form of swatches of isolated tints. From a

[5] The principal languages were: American English, Bulgarian, Cantonese, Catalan, Korean, Hebrew, Japanese, Ibo (Nigeria), Indonesian, Lebanese, Mandarin, Pomo (California), Spanish, Swahili, Tagalog (Philippines), Thai, Tzeltal (Mexico), Hungarian, Urdu and Vietnamese.

system, in other words, that was specialized, Western and the expression of a precise moment in the history of industry, containing within itself an inevitable point of view on things. The presentation of a graduated sequence or the separation of hue from brightness are, as we know, very recent ideas, and to opt for these to speak about colour is only a question of custom and convention. The criticism directed at the two anthropologists is basically that they question different cultures starting from the assumption that naming a colour is a universal given, while it is evident that other populations, distant from each other in time and geographically, do not necessarily make this distinction.

Still, there are aspects of this research that cannot be gainsaid or ignored, such as the fact that tonal evaluation (white–black) precedes the concept of colour, so brightness/luminosity is the characteristic felt to be most important in describing the appearances of the world. After this, the most striking finding is the suggestion of a succession centred upon the anthropological rather than the psychological primacy of red.

There are many words for red – *rouge*, *rot*, the English word 'red' itself – that come from the Sanskrit *rudhira*, meaning 'blood', supporting the idea that it is the deep, universal significance of this substance for humanity that underpins the importance of the colour. The term does not necessarily have everything to do with the specific colour, however: it could be a more general visual quality. That is, if in some contexts it may mean red, in others it might just signify coloured, vivid, alive or vivacious, without referring to anything we call colour.

There is another factor that we should consider, perhaps even the most important one for our argument. From a historical point of view, red is the first colour that humans made. While we had to wait for Egyptian civilization for blue and

BRUNELLO, 1968 green, and for the revolution in chemistry to give us mauve, red pigments are easily extracted from the earth and were used to paint with as early as Prehistoric times. In the frescoes of Lascaux there is red, but there is no green, mauve or blue. It is clear that we invent words for things that we actually use, and it is therefore possible that red was the very first colour to be given a name, since it was the first to have been used in artisanal activities.

With this in mind, Gladstone's argument needs to be revalued, as it no longer seems to be the eccentric fruit of fanatical enthusiasm. There is a striking passage in his Homeric analysis that has been overlooked. In it he underlines how in heroic times the art of dyeing was just
DEUTSCHER, 2013 taking its first steps – and suggests that the reason blue was not named might be directly linked to the impossibility of producing it. It is likely that the eye needs to be familiar with an orderly system of colours to be able to recognize any one of them with precision. This is of fundamental importance. The visual immaturity about which Gladstone speaks would indeed be a matter of psychology but in cultural rather than biological terms. Colour would undoubtedly only assume importance and linguistic currency through objects and artificial pigments: it is not enough to *see* it, for it is only when we ourselves *make* it that it is detached from things and becomes a manageable concept.

Let's for a moment try to imagine ourselves in the position of those ancient men and women. If I look at the sea I see it as blue, but I take this to be a characteristic that I cannot possess, that I cannot detach from that water and that use. The blueness is the very way of being of the sea, and of not much else. But if I have in my hand a red powder with which I can colour cloth, vases, walls or my own face, then this stops being a powder and becomes something else, something more abstract: a general idea of colour.

To understand the psychology of this better, we can resort to a comparison with taste – on the gustatory front, even today we possess instruments that are less organized and calibrated compared to how we deal with colours.

It is common knowledge that metal has a distinctive taste: we all experience that elusive sensation, at the crossroads between sharp and acidic, that we get at the bottom of a spoon, or sometimes in food or certain mineral waters. We still do not have a word for it. We could call this sensation 'metallicness' but would probably not have many occasions to use it – perhaps because it is an infrequent experience, but above all because it is not something that we can actually *use*. In current gastronomic practices, it is not possible to buy 'metallicness' to flavour meat or to make drinks and ice cream. In this way the metal taste remains anchored to metal, and we are not capable of speaking of it as detached from metal. If in the near future such a flavouring was available in ordinary supermarkets, just like vanilla or cinnamon, and we were able to use it for making ravioli, it is likely that only then would we be able to realize that it is a much wider category that does not relate exclusively to metals. After having eaten those ravioli for a few years, we would stop treating it as a characteristic of a specific material. It is even possible that iron itself would end up being only distantly associated with the taste, as merely one among countless other materials that exhibit it. This is more or less what we do today with yellowness and blueness.

The ancients saw the same colours as we do, but they were not always able to insert them into an overall category, just as we undoubtedly perceive 'metallic' tastes but do not have the mental tools to generalize them. Who knows, perhaps there is some metal-ness in roast beef or in strawberries, but at this moment in history we are not able to say so. Because in order to abstract the world we first need to have taken it apart, and concepts are only formulated when they are claimed by concrete practices.

Almost 2,800 years separate us from the *Iliad* and the *Odyssey*. If the retina of our eye has not changed its biology, we have certainly changed the concrete practices with which we fashion and use colour. And if, as the historian Giambattista Vico maintained, we can only truly know what we have actually done, then the acceleration of such *doing* that was produced by industrialization must have surely changed our way of seeing the world. Having so many sensations, being able to synthesize in labs an incredible range of colours, being able to dye the same pair of trousers, or chairs, or forks, any colour we choose, has allowed us to manage perceptions in an unprecedented way. To think of colours, that is, in the abstract, regardless of precise objects. In a certain sense, it is industry that has contributed to the definitive detachment of blue from the sea, given that it is only when blue becomes a thing in itself – like a pigment or a dye, separate from perceptions of blueness – that we can finally name it. It is not our eyes that have changed but the way that we look at things.

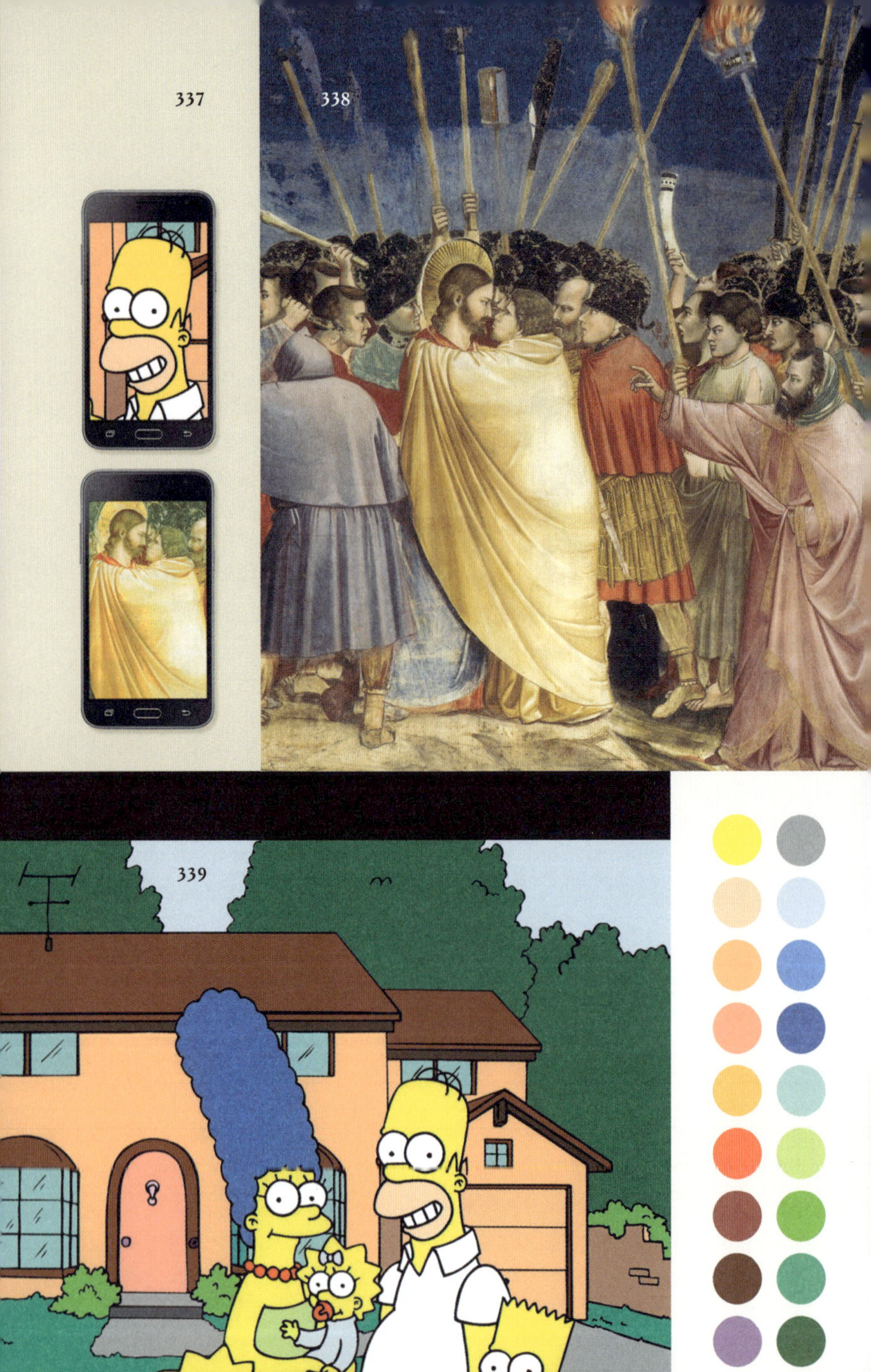
337
338
339

Judas Yellow

Technology and the Gaze

For at least twenty years now, ever since the frequent everyday use of various screens became the norm, the majority of images we deal with emit light. This fact has led us to think that all the images we see on screens must operate in the same way, since looking at them through a single medium flattens out many of their specific characteristics. Viewed on a smartphone, a painted fresco becomes as luminous as a TV programme, assuming some of the qualities of digital images. Even when we try not to give it much importance, technical reproducibility entails a modification of the expressive characteristics of the works of the past. If we limit ourselves to judging the colour on a monitor, then the yellow used by Giotto to depict the robe of Judas in the Scrovegni Chapel in Padua can appear similar to the skin colour of the Simpsons in the eponymous cartoon show. Yet whatever hypothetical wavelength they may have in common, these yellows are of course cogs in extremely different mechanisms.[1]

Attempting to account for their contexts and the conditions that gave life to these two yellows may help us to better

[1] When printing them in this book, Giotto and the Simpsons become reduced to a common chromatic range, the one permitted by four-colour printing, a medium a long way from both TV and frescoes.

understand how no colour is ever really the same as another, and to clarify the specificity of the contemporary gaze.

Comparing Giotto with the Simpsons is pretty much what happens every day when we use the internet. The juxtaposition of disparate languages and codes is standard to all the social networks, from Facebook to Pinterest, visual universes in which syncretism is the norm. We look at Renaissance paintings alongside animated cartoons, paparazzi photos and images of the latest tragedy to make the news. We look at sacred icons and at pornographic ones. It is an appealing kind of hotchpotch that nevertheless risks flattening out the protean nature of the images, rendering them all similar and detached from history, like exhibits in an imaginary museum, endless in number but also perhaps insipid.

These conditions may suggest an idea of colour that is too abstract: as if every object can be produced in any colour, something that is only partially true. In reality, every material and every language allows only certain chromatic effects and not others. Common plastics such as polyvinyl, for instance, that seem to be able to acquire any appearance, fail to capture the hard, dry, chalky colours of frescoes and pastels, or the luminously bright ones of a neon sign.

To understand the authentic value of Giotto's yellow, and that of the Simpsons as well, we have to ask why Judas's robe is that particular yellow and not another, and why Homer's skin is precisely that shade and not darker or lighter. As we have already seen, to understand colour is not just a question of knowing what it *signifies*. More importantly we must know how it *works*, given that it is its material reality, technical or technological, that will determine its appearance.

According to a tradition that goes back to the twelfth century, yellow is synonymous with falsehood, with deceit

PASTOUREAU, 2005

and mendacity, since it was felt to be a degeneration of the luminous and moral qualities of gold. In medieval art it is those considered treacherous – often Muslims or Jews, according to prejudices of that era – who are depicted wearing something yellow. This was an obligatory colour category and unmistakable sign for Judas, required by the commissioners of art and immediately recognized by the illiterate masses frequenting churches. If there is any yellow being worn, it must be Judas.

To paint the clothing of the traitor, artists had at their disposal only certain pigments, none of them actually yellow. At the time, the colours available were lead-tin yellow, weld yellow or orpiment, and as we know we are talking about powders of a precise, limited type, the supply of which was also limited – though even today they can be found among the great variety of colours available in shops selling artists' materials

This fact, an exquisitely technical one, poses a problem of perception which also raises a theological question. If Judas has a colour that is obligatory for our story, this is not the case for Christ, whose iconography does not foreshadow his fate: we recognize Jesus from his beard and vaguely Syriac appearance, not from any colour. The artist's client, perhaps needless to say, requires him to be dressed in the most precious colour, which means, most frequently, the famous lapis lazuli blue. But yellow is brighter than blue and stands out more, especially from a distance. Christ can consequently seem visually less important than Judas. A period eye would certainly be sensitive to the preciousness of ultramarine blue but would hardly be blind to the brilliance of yellow. It is a visual contest between two strong models: that of colour as something with an economic value/cost, and that of colour as a strikingly visual phenomenon. We need to place ourselves within the

BARASCH, 1992

profoundly religious culture of the time in order to recognize that this is a deliberately staged manifestation of a not
insignificant dilemma. The painter essentially finds himself in a double bind. Some artists choose to relegate the
yellow of Judas to a small piece of cloth emerging from a
sleeve, allowing the Redeemer's salvific azure to predominate triumphantly. But Giotto does not do this. He chooses
instead to emphasize and exaggerate the opposite: he cre-
338 ates a dominant Judas, enveloped in an enormous yellow
robe that seems to engulf Christ as well.

So colour needs to come to terms with technical limitations, with theological prescriptions and with the internal rules of artistic systems. Within this complex we have a colour scheme in which something yellow is opposed to something blue, and where something visually brilliant is opposed to something expensive. And it is the interaction between these two systems that gives a meaning and a logic to the colour. Giotto did not choose that particular yellow for purely aesthetic reasons, because he liked it. That yellow is the fruit of complex social dynamics.

339 The Simpsons' yellow is naturally something very different. The characters are born as the protagonists of a TV show first televised on 17 December 1989. Its originality lies in the fact that it is a sitcom but an animated one. In other words, a cartoon within the narrative and technical formats of adult TV.

Comic books and animated cartoons manifest in their style the virtues and limitations of the technology that produced them. Superheroes, for instance, are traditionally dressed in blue and red not only for patriotic reasons but because these are the colours that are easiest to print, including on low-grade paper for which a very reduced palette is available; in fact, they can be produced without

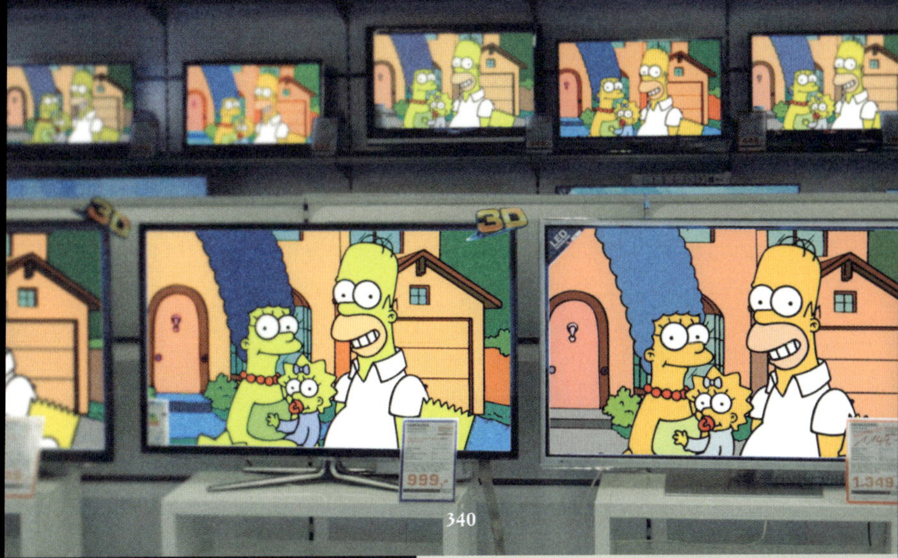

340

341

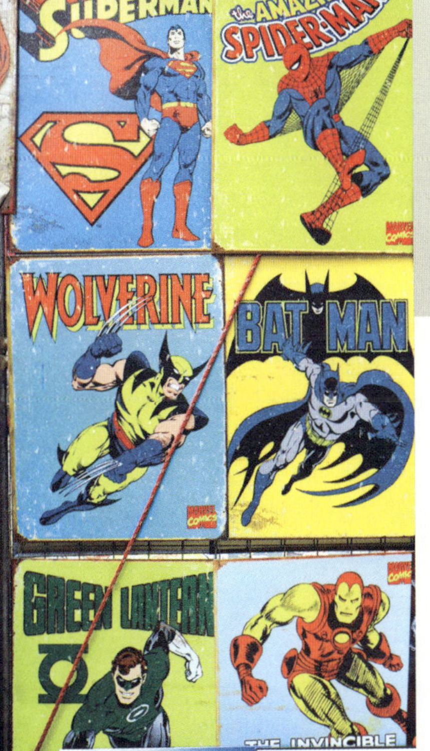

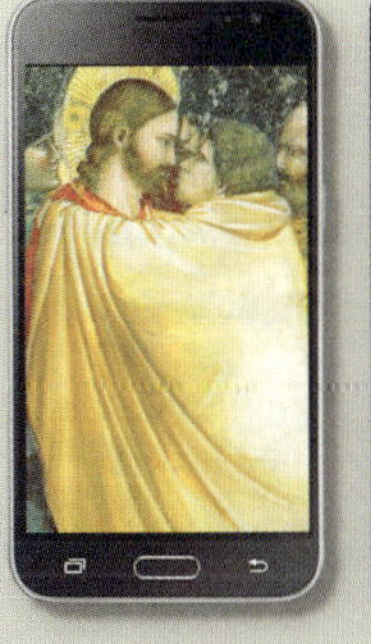

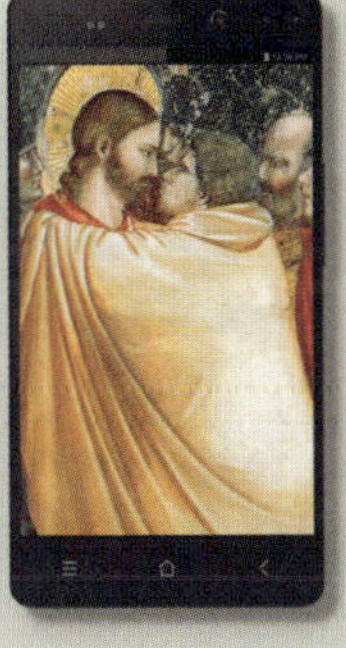

Superman: *Tights*
Spiderman: *Tights*
Donald Duck: *Cap*

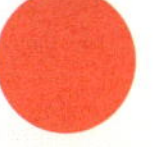

Superman: *Cape*
Scrooge McDuck: *Coat*
Huey: *Cap*

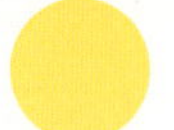

Iron Man: *Tights*
Donald Duck: *Jacket buttons*
Dewey: *Cap*

Green Lantern: *Tights*
Louie: *Cap*

▲ 342
◀ 343

screening and with full inks, with solid and brilliant results.
It is no accident that the look of so many classic cartoon
and comic-book figures has been determined by this. The
343 cyan blue of Superman is the same as the blue of Donald
Duck's beret, and the red of Wonder Woman is the same
as Scrooge McDuck's coat – at least at the time when they
were invented, when the paper used did not permit much
subtlety or nuance. In contrast, an animated film such as
Bambi, which is composed of hundreds of minute variations of green and brown, is possible in 1941 because it JOHNSTON, 1981
is conceived for cinemas within a distribution practice in
which Technicolor checks and controls every single copy
before releasing it on the market. The tonalities of *Bambi*
would be unthinkable for TV, a medium that, because it
emits light, flattens, burns and simplifies the shading; to
say nothing of the fact that the colours would appear different on every different TV screen.

TV has a further difference from cinema inasmuch as
its viewers can decide the colour saturation, contrast and
brightness of the screen – and not knowing what an audi-
340 ence will actually see means that a margin of error must
be factored in, privileging the most marked chromatic
contrasts.

Since the 1960s the likes of Hanna-Barbera and Tezuka Osamu had grappled with the difficulties of cartoons made for the small screen,[2] simplifying their styles due to costs and to the demands of the medium. *The Simpsons* goes further and breaks the medium apart: in the process it deliberately embraces an elementary palette, reclaiming the limitations of TV as an aesthetic virtue. Both the protagonists and the scenography are filled with flat tints, originally on celluloid film, now computerized – a choice

2 Cartoons such as *The Flintstones* (1960) or *Astro Boy* (1963).

which was very anti-Disney, since the backgrounds of Disney cartoons always have painterly aspects due to the use of tempera or watercolour. In Springfield, everything is celluloid, technically and metaphorically: a production necessity becomes a stylistic factor that perfectly conveys the crudity of a vulgar and brutalized middle class. The palette is that of a hallucinatory stereotype in which all the lawns are green, the sky is blue and the clouds are white, as if the whole thing was made using a child's box of crayons. The Simpsons, therefore, are yellow for two reasons: on the one hand, to emphasize their acerbic and unhealthy aspect; on the other, to conform with a garish scheme composed only of hyper-saturated primaries, as if they were coloured with the palette of the monoscope with which broadcasters test the transmission signal. And since every TV viewer will see a different yellow, we can say that what we see in the Simpsons is not so much an exact colour as a default one. Reproduced on millions
of screens, on mugs and T-Shirts, comic books and toys,
BENJAMIN, 2000
Simpsons' yellow is slightly different every time, and yet
looks the same: it is a prototype of a colour, an approxi- 340
mation, sufficiently flexible and resistant to appear yellow
even when flung into the entropic vortex of televisual
reproduction.

In contrast, Giotto's yellow is a precise colour, as in
every work of art made as a single, unique piece, so that
if it is reproduced wrongly, it is no longer Giotto. 341

As we have explained, our contemporary theoretical model – that is to say the spectrum identified by Newton – presupposes that all the colours are moments in a sequence or a progression that contains them all. In this sequence, Simpsons yellow is not a precise point, it is rather a bandwidth, a segment of possible yellows. The fourteenth-century mind, on the other hand, has no idea of this whole, much less of a continuum, and the colours are isolated atoms that weave hierarchical and discontinuous relationships among themselves. Ultramarine blue is opposed to the other colours in a clear and peremptory way: a colour is ultramarine, or it is not. There is no middle way.

Today, however, with respect to the sensation it gives to the eye, a colour may be more or less similar to ultramarine; that is, we may have many progressive steps between violet and ultramarine, and between ultramarine and green, each one located at a point on the spectrum as demonstrated by the palettes of software graphics that are arranged in gradual, shading progression.

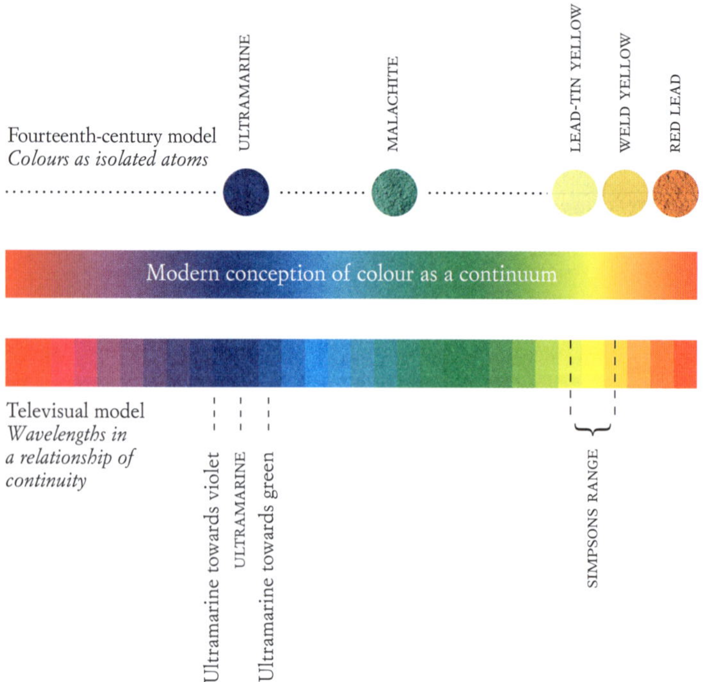

And so the 'Judas system' and the 'Simpsons system' present us with a yellow that is perceptually similar, but they are ultimately two matrices that if put together do not match. A comparison between the two reveals then that every culture elaborates its own universe of meanings linked to colours, but also that it may do so only by using the concrete colours at its disposal. Every context imposes specific limits to the palette, as if each one was only furnished with a limited vocabulary. The assortment depends on the techniques available, on the historical moment and on economics. And it is these material conditions that determine how we think, how we create and ultimately how we look at things.

An artist of the fourteenth century cannot think of a yellow that does not exist concretely, like the fluorescent one of marker pens, and for the same reason the creators of *The Simpsons*, operating within a TV format in the late 1980s, cannot use subtle variations of pastel tints, because the contrasts between them are weak and would be practically annulled when transmitted on screen.

PINOTTI, 2016

Today the majority of the images with which we engage emit light, just like an episode of *The Simpsons*. This gives colour a vivacity that it has never had before in the history of human artefacts, if we except Gothic glass – the exception that proves the rule. Thanks to screens, we experience colours that are vibrant and extremely brilliant, and that have become the parameter with which we evaluate the purity of all chromatic phenomena. Anyone who has experienced televisual colour can no longer see things with the eyes of the past. Perhaps we are not yet fully aware of the fact, but we have somewhere in our minds the yellow of the Simpsons, even when standing in front of a Renaissance fresco.

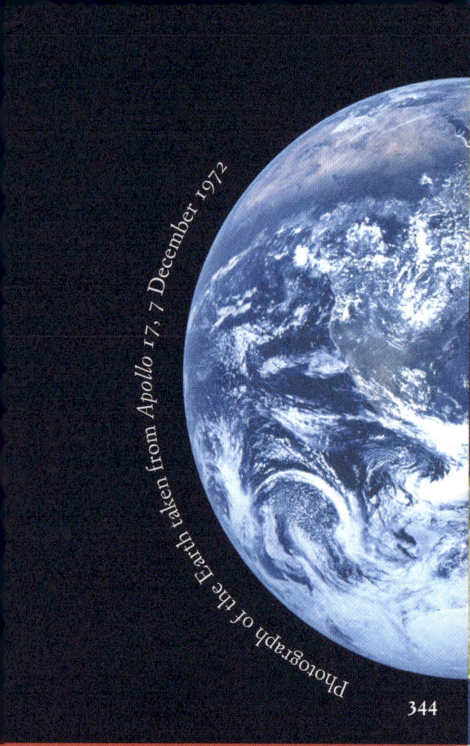

Photograph of the Earth taken from *Apollo 17*, 7 December 1972

344

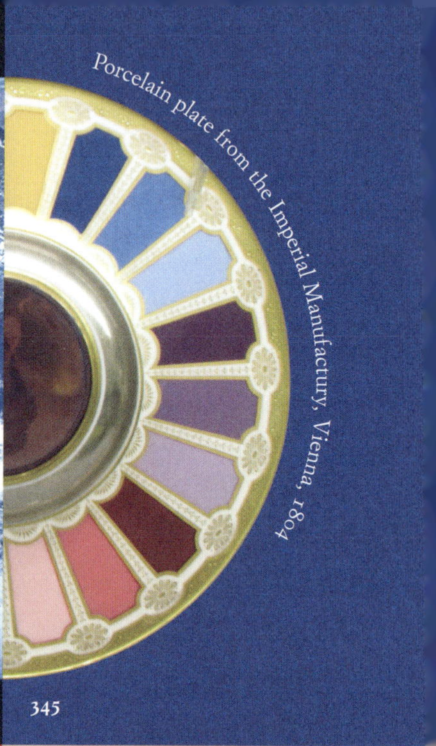

Porcelain plate from the Imperial Manufactury, Vienna, 1804

345

346

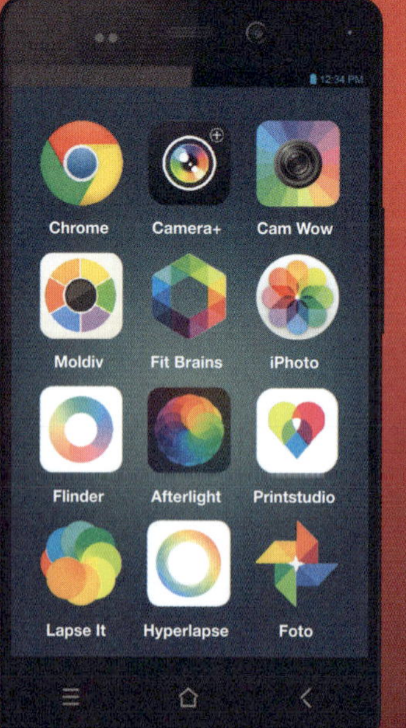

347

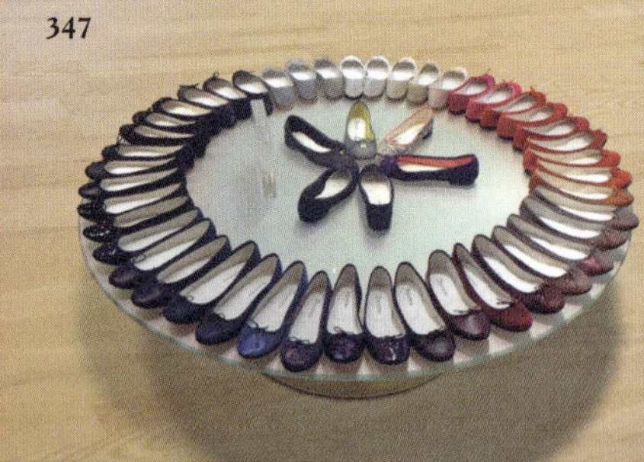

348

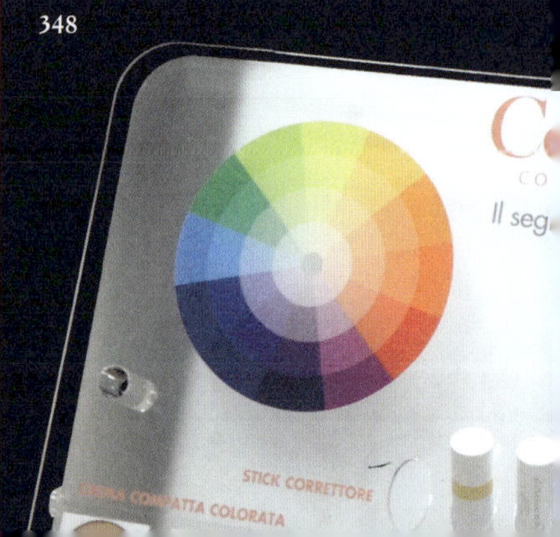

Epilogue

Colour as a Tool of the Mind

As soon as he set foot back on our planet, on 12 April 1961, the first man to have been into space revealed to the world something that was as unexpected as it was poetic. Seen from out there, the Earth is blue. Not because of the seas that cover it, but because of the atmosphere that envelops it.

MIRZOEFF, 2015

In all previous depictions of the Earth, it is differently coloured: often brown or green, similar to a geographical map or a globe. No one, before Yuri Gagarin actually saw it with his own eyes, had thought that it could be as blue and as bright as a moon.

In 1969, the Americans also made it into space, a year after the release of Stanley Kubrick's epochal *2001: A Space Odyssey*, the film that indelibly fixed our image of man in the cosmos. From this moment onwards, all subsequent representations of space changed: in cinema, in comic books, in video games, even in the shorthand of newscasters. This is how our collective imagination is constructed: an idea appears, takes shape, is liked, begins to be used by people, by artists, by designers and by directors, and gradually – perhaps because it is more suited than others to survive – it becomes a shared archetype.

Today, even for those who have never been close to leaving it, that the Earth is blue is merely a fact: one of those things that are just known and taken for granted – like the fact that grass is green and blood red. The difference with grass and blood, however, is that the blueness of the Earth is something that we have learned from the diffusion of images enabled by the mass media. It is something that we know, but that we have not seen and cannot see with the naked eye. This blue is a colour that we have never actually experienced, and that exists only thanks to a photographic intermediary. It might seem like a special case, but in truth today there is probably no colour that does not partake of this condition: that does not exist in our minds, in other words, by virtue of a technological mediation.

MOHOLY-NAGY, 2010

All societies have always formulated symbolic systems with which to recognize themselves, in which colour has played a central role: great epic and religious narratives, icons and figures to be devoted to, or to model oneself on; moral conventions and behavioural rules. What is new in the modern world is the framing of such practices within technological procedures and commercial exchanges that both amplify and standardize them.

BRUSATIN, 1983

It is for these reasons that colour is today not only a perception or a quality of things but a psychological category that exists bound up with ways of producing, distributing and narrating it.

PINOTTI, 2016

In the thirteenth century, in order to describe the perfection that was to be found in heaven, the poet Bonvesin de la Riva wrote that the colours are more brilliant up there, and that they never fade.[1] Such a description relies on the fact that at the time the fixing of textile dyes was virtually impossible. Today, in the age of highly and

[1] Bonsevin de la Riva, *De scriptura aurea* (circa 1274), verses 94–5.

indelibly colourful nylon and microfibre, one would never
think of using such a figure as a sign of divine perfection.
But we too have our chromatic metaphors and myths, ways
of saying things that would be meaningless to a medieval
man or woman.

Advertising imagery, for instance, often uses the colour
spectrum (or parodies of it) to convey an idea of technical
excellence: the rainbow is part of a well-established iconography for selling TVs, photocopying machines, printers
and smartphones, underlining the accuracy with which they
capture the colours of the world. The orderly progression
of the colours has become synonymous with completion
and vastness of choice, even in the most unexpected con-
MAROTTA, 1999
texts: from the shoe shop, where I have seen shoes placed 347
in a circle to demonstrate the variety of colours available,
to the pharmacy counter where I find a colour wheel used
to advertise the impeccability of cosmetics. Even the 348
Google Chrome logo is in the end a stylized colour wheel,
and dozens of variations are to be found in all the Apps
that process images. 346

If in the medieval era the important thing was that
colours should be durable, today it matters more for us
that there should be many of them. Sixteen million, no
less, as the producers of electronics boast – conveniently
ignoring the fact that the human eye cannot distinguish
more than 200. The colour wheel of Newton, Goethe and
Itten has become in the end a rhetorical figure, the myth
par excellence of our times: that of variety.

This association between the rainbow and colour com-
MIRZOEFF, 2005
pleteness seems obvious to us, and yet it is, precisely, a
myth: that a rainbow contains all of the colours is not only
not true, but it never formed part of the cultural baggage
of the past. If we look at representations of the rainbow
from late antiquity, it is composed of only two colours,

usually orange and green. Every era ultimately has its own perceptual regime, that is to say the way we look at what is around us. If in 10,000 years' time an archaeologist were to find a Pantone colour chart, this relic would testify to an important aspect of our civilization: colour as a regular system, in which the tints follow a sequence by gradation and are conceived and named for the most part as homogeneous backgrounds. A world made of atlases, circles and samples, useful for referencing, choosing and buying. A time when colour is so abstract that it can even 'become fashionable', or go out of fashion, regardless of the things that carry and exhibit it. But this is not the truth about colour. It is only a fragment from the cultural history of humanity.

At a certain point in history it was industry that defined chromatic priorities: deciding, for instance, that certain colours are more fundamental than others, to the point of treating these phantasmal 'primaries' as basic entities of nature rather than merely conventions or norms of production. It is an indication that technology can so strongly influence mentality as to be mistaken for a law of physics.

JORDAN, 2010

Only recently a group of researchers has discovered at the back of the eyes of certain women a fourth type of cone never noticed before. If this discovery was to be confirmed, it would substantially alter our view of the trichromatic model. It is probable that the fact of this cone's existence may have been overlooked partly because it was statistically rarer, partly because the theoretical model of the three primaries – invented for printing, formalized by physics and advanced by the arts – was for the whole of the nineteenth century an integral part of the cultural baggage of scientists. As we have seen, in 1801, while not being able to observe the back of the eye, and influenced by the typographic ideas of Le Blon, Thomas Young suspects that there are three visual receptors. And colour-blindness is diagnosed for the first time only in the industrial era, simply passing unobserved before the widespread availability of coloured objects. Perhaps only someone with lots of neckties can become aware that they are confusing colours.

And yet common and widespread credence is given to the myth that science operates beyond history, building a progress that happens in its own separate realm, with discoveries happening suddenly and to the surprise even of the researchers. In reality, as the most conscientious scientists confirm, there is always a theoretical hypothesis that guides research in the first place. We do not make experiments blind, hoping that something extraordinary will happen: we follow instead a line formulated within a specific culture.

KUHN, 1978

To mistake scientific facts for supra-historical truths is dangerous, since it may lead to the belief that the only possible world is the one in which we live – and this, paradoxically, can end up blocking the advancement of knowledge, including that of science.

ARNHEIM, 1997

For their part, art and design are dominated today by two powerful chromatic models. On the one hand, we have the legacy of the didactic, modernist, Gestalt tradition that comes from Itten, Albers and Arnheim, determining the way in which colour is taught in Western schools; on the other, there is the new knowledge being increasingly disseminated by neuroscience.[2] However fascinating and essential, neither one of these two approaches seems sufficient for understanding underlying, complex aesthetic languages. Art teaching addresses the functioning of colour *within* works, concentrating on the internal dynamics of compositions; neuroscience has instead shifted the interest from the works themselves

ZEKI, 2001

[2] Thanks in large part to the divulgatory writing and activities of scientists such as David Hubel, Margaret Livingstone and Semir Zeki.

to the brain, claiming that the experience of colour is within the mind of the beholder. In both cases, the two most important elements for understanding art are ignored: social context and history. A basic limitation arises if we think that the meaning and nature of our visual perception can be found intrinsically, within that perception itself, when on the contrary our gaze is always situated within a particular time and place. And the way in which we think changes with time and place

There is an object that can teach much about how the human mind works. In 1978, in Hochdorf, near Stuttgart, a princely burial site was discovered, full of gold and bronze artefacts, all made locally except for one large vessel that was obviously Greek in origin, and had no doubt found itself on Germanic soil after an involved series of adventures and vicissitudes. On the top of the vessel there are three lions couchant: two of them modelled in accordance
with Greek taste of the sixth century BC, whereas the third,
350 identical in its position, displays a different style.

It is likely that the original lion was lost or broken, and that, tasked with its reconstruction, a local artisan did so by employing the language that was most familiar to him. This Germanic lion is no less beautiful than its Greek counterparts, nor is it merely a copy. It is the fruit, however, of a different way of thinking and working.

Whereas the Greek sculptor concentrates on plastic
350A form and the interpenetration of volumes, the German
craftsman establishes the general mass of the body and
then incises the details – most probably because he is used
to working bronze as you would a necklace. The result is
350B that the face appears to be drawn rather than modelled.
The German artisan can recreate the lion only through
those technical and psychological procedures that he has

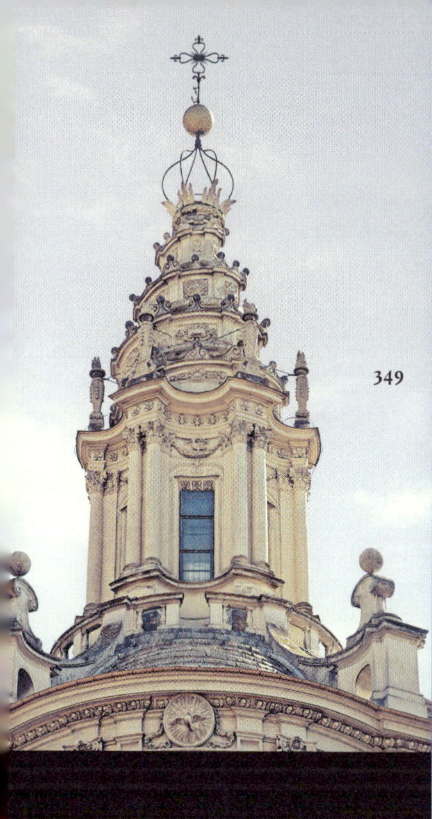

349

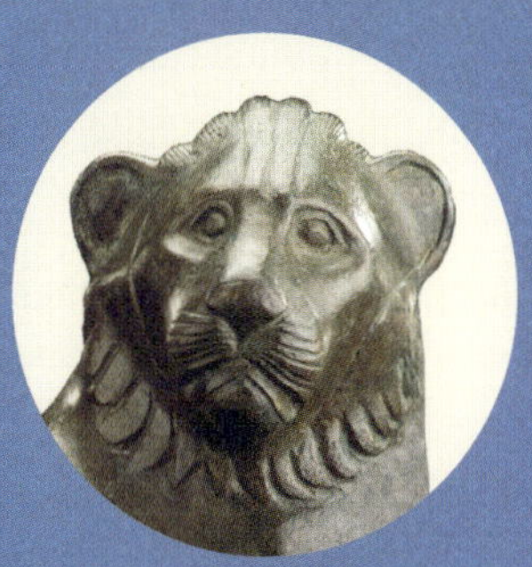

350A GREEK LION

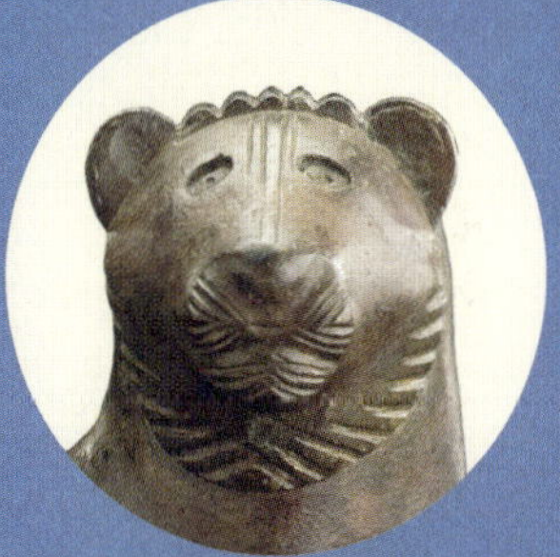

350B GERMANIC LION

↑

350

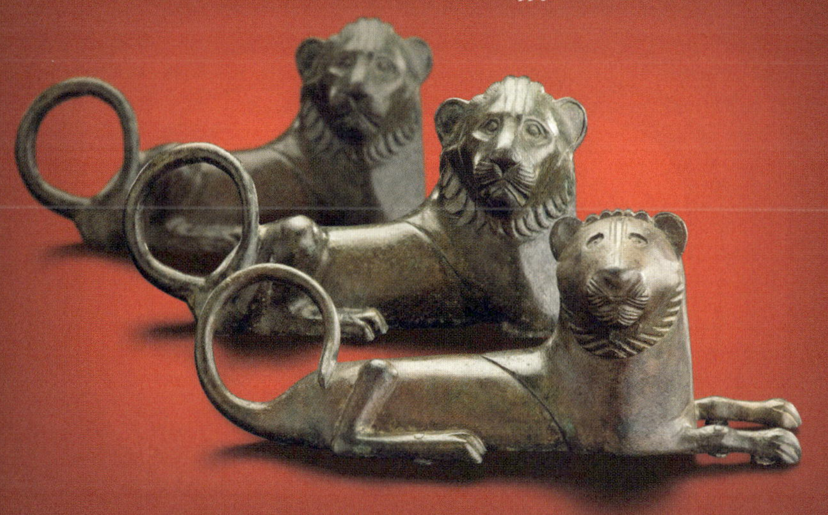

acquired over years of dealing with the specificities of his work. The result is that, even though they are made from the same material, the Greek lions are works of sculpture whereas the Germanic one is a piece of jewellery.

Comparing the lions shows how technique is not simply a means for achieving something but becomes over time the way in which we think about materials, according to the possibilities and limitations of the historical and geographical conditions in which we find ourselves living and operating.

GOODMAN, 2008

The sinuous and helical plastic forms of Francesco Bor-
349 romini's architecture, for example, were due to the fact that he studied the volumes of his buildings by modelling them in wax: certain curves can only be produced by moving the thumb in a malleable substance, and it would be highly unlikely that we could arrive at them by using a ruler and compass. The experience of working with wax feeds directly into technique, thought and invention. Ideas – whether they are artistic, to do with design, or stylistic – are not born in the abstract but in the process of confronting real problems. Borromini has acquired through actual practice and engagement with materials what we might call a 'mental tool'.

Unlike other categories, ideas or sentiments with which we think of the world, a mental tool is a way of reasoning that has a precise characteristic: it came from a concrete situation we had to deal with. It does not typically occur in the mind of an individual maker but is likely to involve an entire society.

In any case, a mental tool should not be thought of as something that sits between ourselves and our knowledge, like a filter that can be applied and removed, through which we see everything in an 'altered' way. Precisely because it is determined by historic contingencies, it is above all something in which we are *immersed*.

GARRONI, 1995

The philosopher Emilio Garroni has suggested with a striking image that the situation of those who know the world through their senses is like that of a fossil insect enclosed in amber. Like the insect, we are immersed in the medium through which we look, and we have no way of getting outside of it. The amber filters everything that we see and at the same time is the very condition of being able to see. It is our essential sensory environment: without amber, we would stop being fossil insects, we would stop being that which we are. We look through a filter from inside the filter, says Garroni.

Extending this metaphor to colour, we could say that our perceptual ambience is the set of collective historical, social and technical skills with which we live. In the end, just like the insect, we know colour through the layered knowledge of centuries of concrete practices. We cannot look at a Byzantine icon, for instance, and pretend that we do not know what a solid colour is. The concept of a solid colour is one of the filters with which we confront the icon. And indeed, we are able to appreciate the materiality of the surface and the uncertain tremulousness of gold precisely because we have an industrial idea of colour.

This is not to appeal to banal cultural relativism: it is not about minimizing the significance of the invention of primary colours, of the use of Pantone's system, of the Newtonian spectrum, of the discovery of retinal cones or of the trends of fashion. It is a call instead for us to always exercise a critical eye, enabling us to inhabit such knowledge in a complex and fruitful manner. If we cannot see the icon as a Byzantine viewer would have seen it, we can at least be aware of the way we see it today. Since we are unable to remove our own filter, so to speak, we can at least take its influence into account. And it is this consciousness of history that is the most important crux of any theory of colour that really wants to be modern: the only freedom that we have is to look while knowing that we are looking, and how.

KOYRÉ, 1967

The chromatic ideas of industrial society have one thing in common: they are attempts to rationalize colour. This also means standardizing our gaze, making it predictable in the process and potentially open to manipulation. Think of the predilection of many young girls for the colour pink, unquestionably influenced as it is by the pervasive model imposed on the market by toys and clothing. Or of the fact that veal will not sell unless it is very white, even artificially so. Or that yellow pencils are reputed to be more efficient than green ones. To believe that the responsibility of such prejudices is the fault of corporations or of consumerism would be simplistic and banal. A lot depends on us.

Every day we teach millions of children to mix blue with yellow, and tell them that what they obtain is green. We say this as if it were an indisputable fact. As if things had always been like this; as if all yellows and blues behaved in the same way. It seems like a game, like child's play, so to speak. But it is also a way of thinking. We are passing off technical and economic necessity as if it were a law of the universe. So we are offering those children a mental tool, while presenting it as simply a truth about colour and about the world.

All of this has far more concrete repercussions for our cultural future than might at first be apparent. Some recent controversies, for instance, have involved the restoration of works of the past and the way in which we have tried to reconstruct a lost colour.[3] With regard to painting, there is a European approach that defends a model based upon *conservation*, and accuses much of what happens in the US as tantamount to an alteration of the colours of works in the name of *renovation*. On paper, at least, European-style restoration represents an intervention that acknowledges that the past is not recoverable; whereas in the United States attempts are made to give us back the work as it looked when first painted. But is the way in which paintings would have been looked *at* in the Renaissance ever recoverable?[4]

In reality the criticism levelled at the American method is more subtle and touches a raw nerve. By increasing tone contrast and saturating colours we are not recovering historic truth so much as rendering a painting more chromatically appealing when reproduced in a catalogue, or in poster and postcard form. More often than not, transatlantic restoration does not so much conserve works for the future as refresh them so that they will work better in museum merchandizing.

Is this a bad thing? Are the Europeans in the right? Or perhaps, in the long run, is it not precisely such merchandizing that will guarantee the survival of cultural treasures?

Not wanting to see the technological and economic reality of colour means erasing an element that is crucial to our understanding and political consciousness. Technique has to do with history. Which is why the way in which we use it is always a moral problem.

[3] Something similar occurs in the restoration of classic films, where frames are cleaned one by one to eliminate trembling, dirt, dust – and adapt them to a new, crystal-clear digital vision.

[4] For centuries connoisseurs have appreciated the ageing process of paintings; the gradual darkening, as in seventeenth-century canvases that are painted with bituminous pigments which darken over time more than others. This patina was highly sought after as part of antiquarian taste, and was taken as a sure sign of a work that was valuable precisely because of its age. They called it the result of 'Time the painter', in order to indicate that centuries had altered the painting in an artistic way.

Designers and directors, artists and restorers, photographers and illustrators, curators of museums and newspaper editors, not to mention teachers and other educators, have precise responsibilities in contributing to the construction of both current and future ideas. To declare that cerulean or sky blue is 'the colour of the year' may be a marvellous proof of the human capacity to abstract and conceptualize – or just a terrible slogan dreamt up by an advertising firm. It all depends on the emphasis with which we say what we say. It's about knowing what you are doing and who you want to be, above all as citizens

Critical thinking can begin with some very small facts. And also with colour. Perhaps even when we teach children that green can be made by mixing together blue and yellow. We can demonstrate it. It really works. It is fascinating and amazing. It is one of the great triumphs of human history. But it is not the only way of making green. It is not the truth.

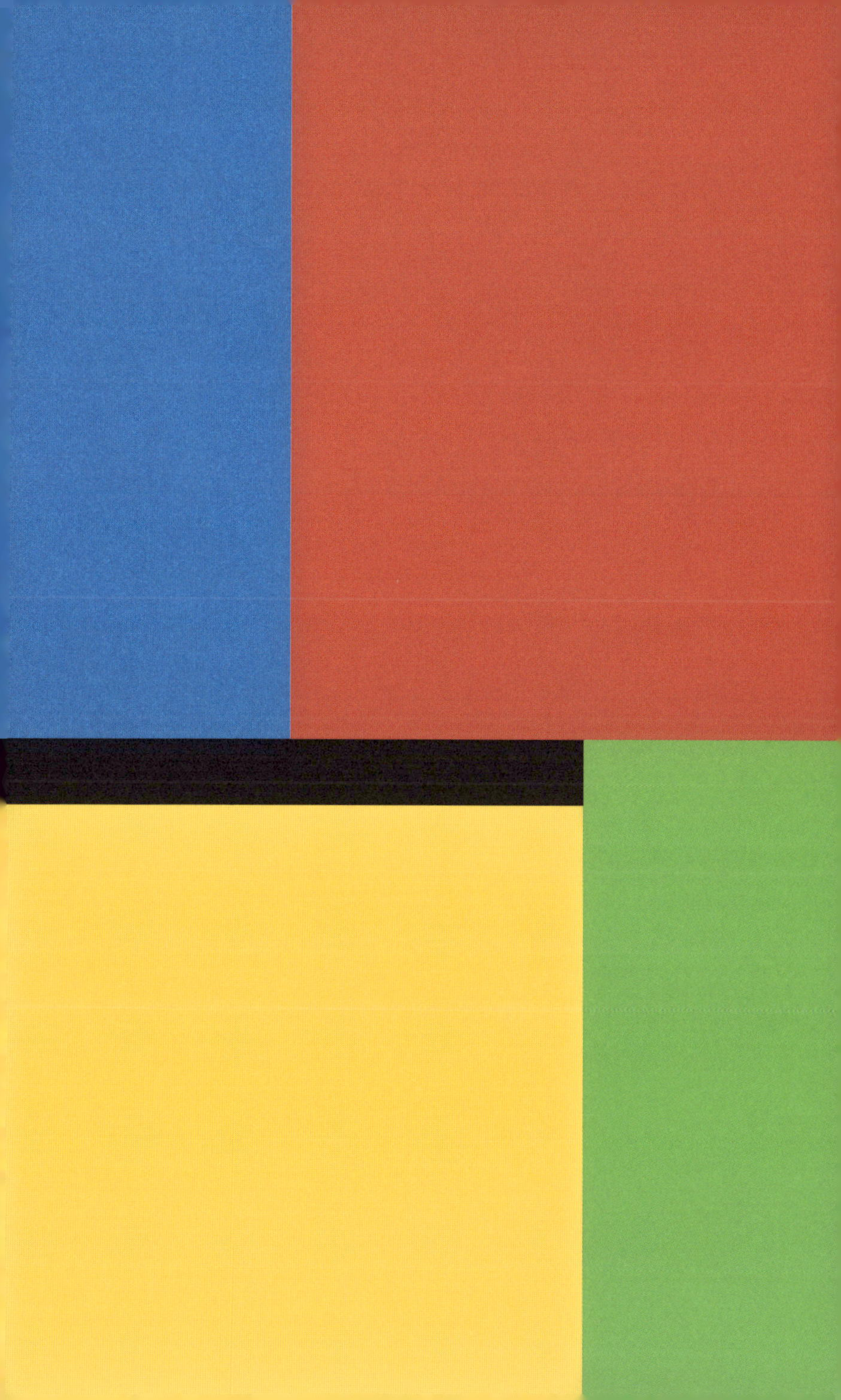

Appendix A
Scientific Concepts

FROVA, 2000

1.0 *Light and wavelengths.* About half the energy emitted by the Sun that reaches the Earth is visible **light**. Evolution has taken advantage of this quality: light transports rapidly and at great distance accurate information on the presence of things and their characteristics. It is a particular type of **electromagnetic radiation** the **wavelengths** of which are visible to us because the cells of our **retinas**, at the back of our eyes, are able to transform them into an electrochemical signal with which the brain constructs the sensation of seeing. Light as we know it is consequently a psychological fact.

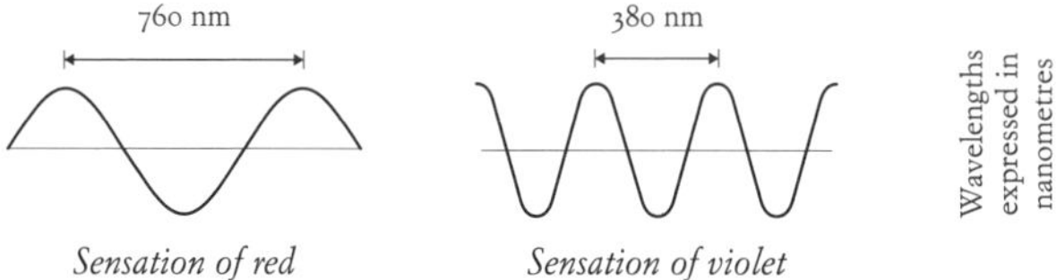

Wavelengths expressed in nanometres

1.1 For 200 years physicists asked themselves whether light was made up of **waves** or of **particles**. Isaac Newton was in no doubt that the answer was particles: for him the only waves were those of water and sound – not of light, given that it does not bend around obstacles. Today science explains that when light moves in space it may indeed be thought of as having the form of waves, while when it encounters matter it is better to imagine it like a swarm of particles moving in a straight line. In 1905, Einstein calls these particles **photons**, small packets of energy travelling in a manner similar to waves. Yet only recently have we been able to devise an experiment that would reveal at the same time both the undulatory and the corpuscular character of light.

1.2 From the point of view of physics, there is no qualitative difference between all electromagnetic radiation and the portion of it that we call light, in other words the portion between **380** and **760** **nanometres** that corresponds perceptually to the succession of colours

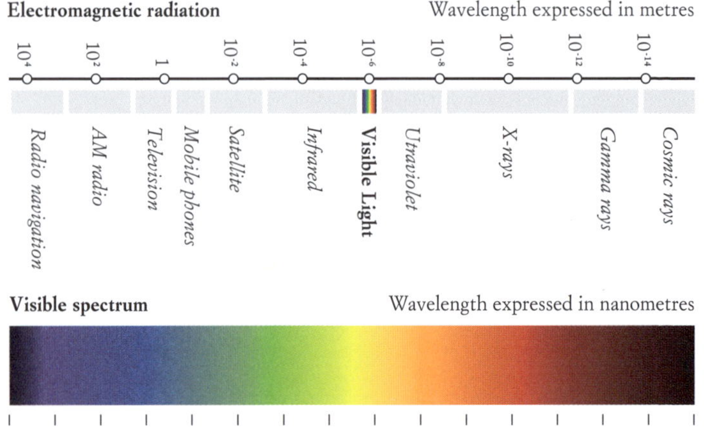

in the rainbow. The reason why we only see this part as light (and as colour) could be due to the fact that we are descended from creatures that used to live in turbid water, and this is the radiation that is capable of penetrating it. Other living beings, such as bees and some fish, see ultraviolet rays, while snakes see infrared. BRESSAN, 2007

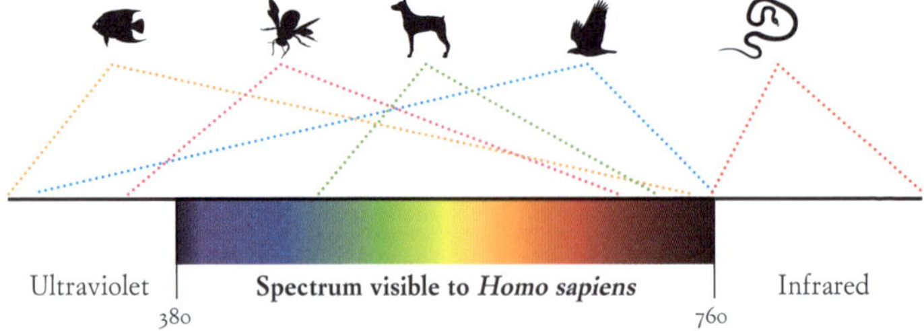

1.3 Every source of light, whether natural or artificial, emits photons of different wavelengths: the one that appears as a colour is the **dominant wavelength**. A **solid colour** is consequently one in which we do not see the presence of other colours, *not* one in which other wavelengths are absent. This is the case because everything in the world reflects a certain amount, however minimal, of all radiation. Our nervous system is not equipped to perceive single wavelengths but only their psychological result. In other words, a green radiation

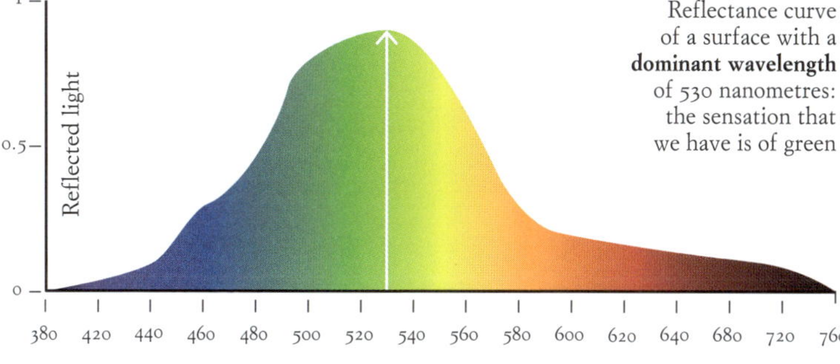

Reflectance curve of a surface with a **dominant wavelength** of 530 nanometres: the sensation that we have is of green

with a red overlaying appears to us as yellow, without any possibility of seeing its constituent parts.

From an electromagnetic point of view, **solid yellow** has been located between 568 and 583 nanometres; **solid green** between 498 and 530; **solid blue** between 468 and 487; while **solid red** is a colour that is outside of the spectrum and is described in **colorimetry** as the complementary of a turquoise of around 495 nanometres, indicated on the CIE diagram with a minus before it: −495 (see **10**). This is because in the spectrum there are reds with an orange tinge, but not what we might call red-red, such as that famously used by Coca-Cola for its brand.

OLEARI, 2008

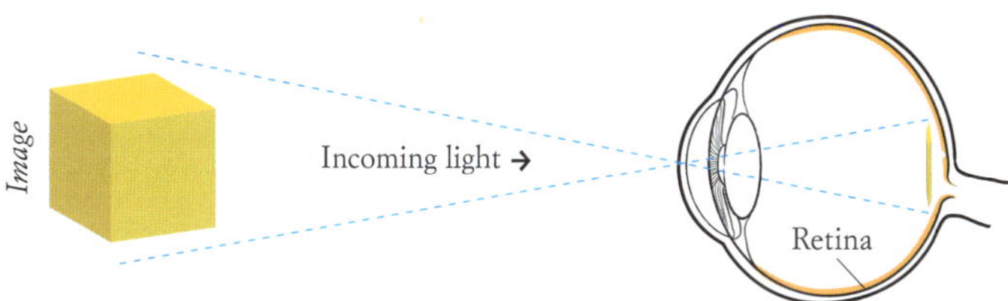

2.0 *The receptors and the spectrum.* The perception of the **light intensity** of a surface is given by the number of photons that hit the back of the eye. The electrical signal produced by the retina is in fact proportionate to the number of photons absorbed. The receptors that cover the retina are divided into four categories: the **rods**, sensitive to low illumination, that begin to function with darkness or penumbra (the greyscale version of vision); and three types of **cones**, each one with a different sensitivity curve for long, medium and short wavelengths that correspond more or less to the macro areas of reds, greens and blues – and for this reason are indicated with the letters L, M and S respectively. The green cones are in the majority, about 60 per cent

PURGHÉ, 1999

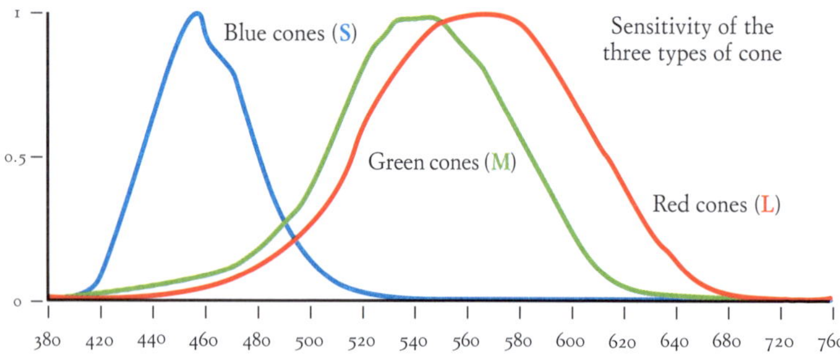

of the total; the reds account for 30 per cent and the blue for just 10. They are all responsive, however, to all wavelengths. Red cones have a slightly greater sensitiveness to redness but are also activated by the yellow, green and even blue wavelengths, albeit minimally. The contrast between these responses allows the construction of what we see as colour, by way of comparison rather than through mixing (see p. 194 and **3** below).

2.1 The spectral composition of a particular colour can be measured through an instrument called a **spectrophotometer** and presented as a **reflectance curve** (see illustrations below). It is the representation of a physical datum that does not take account of the particular sensitivity of cones or rods, which on the contrary is un-homogeneous in respect of the spectrum: in reality we see reds and greens better than other radiation (see point **8** diagram, below). On the abscissa axes the wavelengths are represented, on the ordinate ones are shown the percentages of reflected light. It is evident from the graphs that the things of this world always reflect a little of all wavelengths. This was already clear to Newton when he hypothesized that an object appears of a certain colour because there is an excess of a particular wavelength in relation to others (the point which is at the top of the curve). Monochromatic radiation that is less than 5 nanometres wide can only be obtained in a lab with a laser.

OLEARI, 2008

BERTAGNA, 2013

2.2 That the **tricolour system** of RGB monitors may be more suitable to the way our eye actually sees is a myth due a misunderstanding of how the retina works. The cones that cover it are in effect of three kinds; each one is more sensitive to a range of the spectrum – some to red, others to green, still others to blue – but they all respond to all the wavelengths. The red cones have a peak of sensitivity to red but are also activated by the other wavelengths, even if only minimally. The coming together of these responses allows the construction of

FIORENTINI, 1995

what we experience as a colour, through comparison rather than mixing. In contrast, the red LED of the monitor is *exclusively* concerned with and can only light that red. It may be more or less bright, but it can never be green. The monitor is substantially a system based on **optical mixing**, whereas the brain uses three measurements in order to effect a **comparison**.

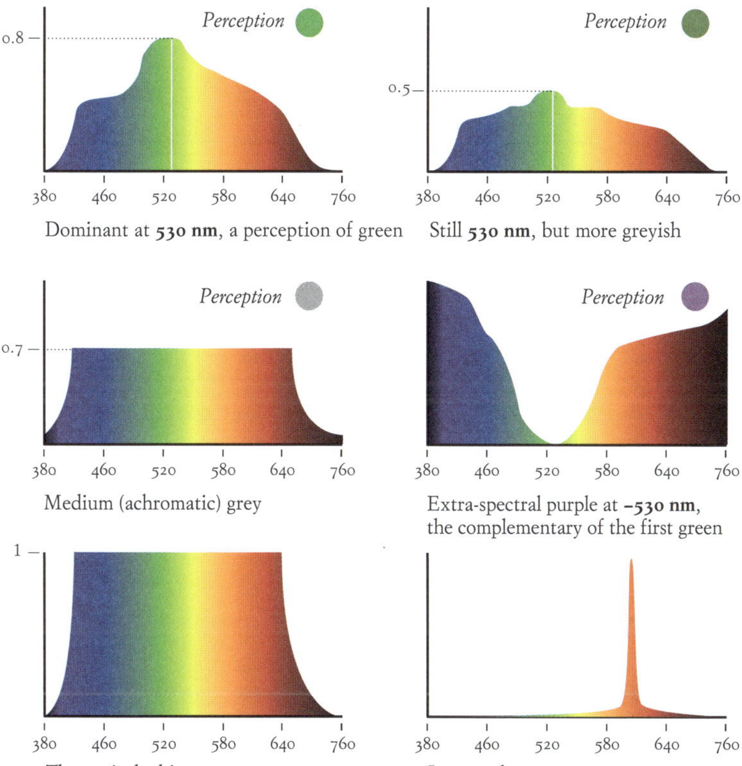

Dominant at **530 nm**, a perception of green

Still **530 nm**, but more greyish

Medium (achromatic) grey

Extra-spectral purple at **–530 nm**, the complementary of the first green

Theoretical white

Laser red

Note: The colouring of the diagrams has the sole purpose of emphasizing the presence of all the wavelengths from a single sensation, so as to make the concept clearer to the reader, but it has no mathematical justification.

Therefore the cones do not behave like inks or like an LED, and they should not be thought of as primary colours. In addition, whereas the three LED colours are present in equal quantities, in the retina the green cones are 60 per cent of the total against only 10 per cent of the blue (see **2.0**).

ZEKI, 1993

2.3 The elaboration of colour is articulated in phases: **assessment of the wavelength** in V1 (the primary visual cortex that sorts information) from data furnished from the retina; then we pass to V4, which weighs the relationship between closely related colours, guaranteeing **colour constancy** and extracting them from the spectrum (the V stands for vision and is the letter that precedes all the other areas in the brain involved in some aspect of seeing). Finally, there is a control of chromatic attribution that involves other areas such as the temporal cortex for the semantic sphere, and the hippocampus for memory. A banana appears more yellow than another object of the same yellow because we remember its prototypical colour.

Cross-section of the brain

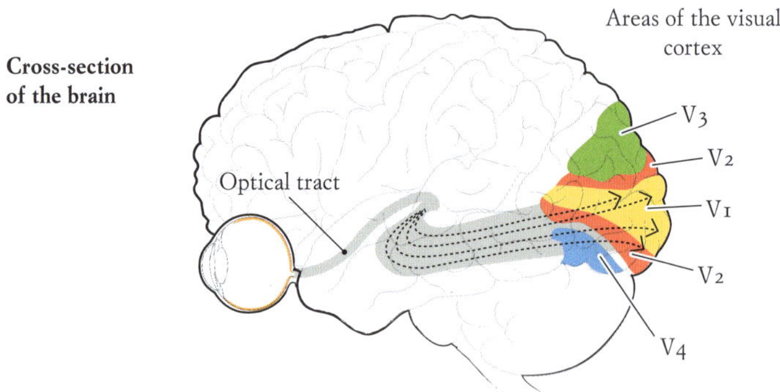

HUBEL, 1989

At a cellular level it goes through the following process: nearby receptors on the retina (cones and rods) communicate to a neuron above them that at that point something is happening; the neuron estimates the responses it receives and communicates to the level above it what it has come to know. Gradually, as we begin to rise, we find neurons that do not oversee a single point but an entire area, until we find in the higher levels neurons that become excited when they *see* a human face, not because they actually see it but because they interact with billions of cells beneath them that enable them to respond to precise configurations. Neurons all do the same thing: they respond to a signal, becoming excited or inhibited. What counts is not the quality of the neuron but only its position in the system.

3.0 *Theories of opposing signals*. The two classic models that have competed for the field since the eighteenth century are Young's **tri-colour theory** (elaborated by Helmholtz) and Hering's **opponent-process theory**. Taking inspiration from painters' ideas about mixing, Young hypothesizes that there are three receptors at the back of the eye, one for each of the three primaries which combine to produce the vision of all colours.

Young/Helmholtz tri-colour model

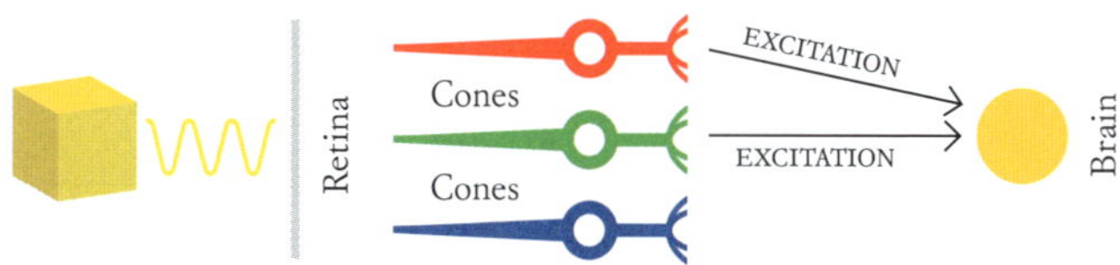

Hering maintains instead that yellow is autonomous (we do not experience/see it, in other words, as a combination of green and red), and speculates that the important thing is the relations that are created in the higher levels of the brain, and that there are four rather than three basic psychological colours (see pp. 195–7).

Hering's opponent-process model

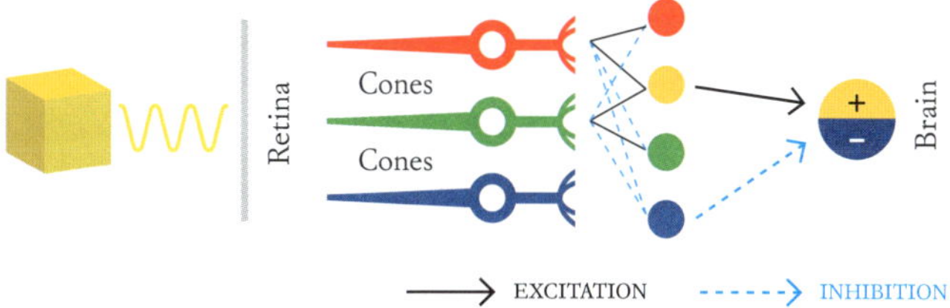

Young concentrates on the functioning of the retina, Hering on that of the brain. Recent scientific discoveries have justified the latter: the three cones that reveal the length of wave are precisely just instruments of measurement but do not participate in the actual construction of colour. This construction occurs higher up in the hierarchy of vision. The mechanism is the following: the signals coming from two or more cones flow into upper nerve cells (but always within the retina), exciting or inhibiting them. The cells excited by red cones may be inhibited by greens and vice versa; others instead become inhibited contemporaneously by reds and greens and excited by blue cones.

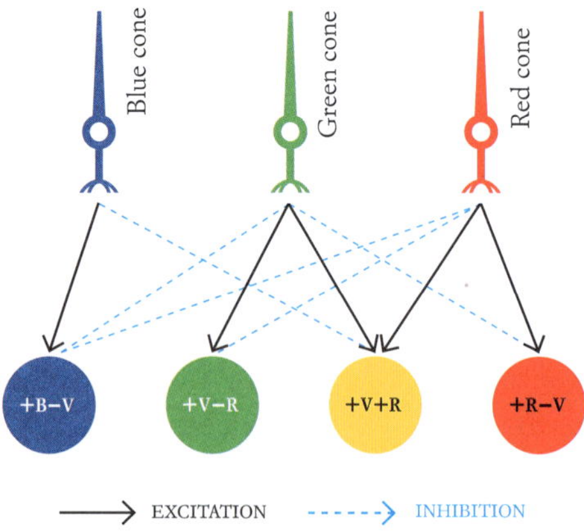

At this point the retina, with its calculations in place, sends to the cortex half a dozen pieces of already processed information in which it is not the wavelength that counts but its opposing signal: there is yellow, so there is no blue; the red increases, so the green diminishes, and so on.

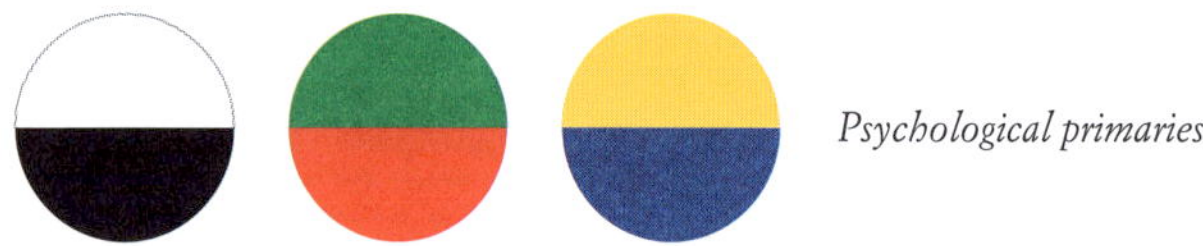

Psychological primaries

4.0 *The construction of colour.* The first reflections on the psychological construction of colour occurred in the eighteenth century when Gaspard Monge asked some university colleagues to look at two paper sheets, one white and the other red, through a plate of red glass. What happens in this experiment is counterintuitive: the two sheets appear to be the same colour. Basically the red sheet becomes desaturated and as luminous as the other one, so they both seem white. How is it possible, asks Monge, that an object that undoubtedly sends out red radiation appears to be white? The answer concerns the contrast with what it has around it: once the red glass is removed from the red sheet, the latter becomes one of the lighter elements of the scene, and so is interpreted by our brain as white.

4.1 An experimental verification of this concept was provided at the end of the 1950s by Edwin Land, to whom we owe the discovery of polarizing filters and the invention of the Polaroid. Land makes two slides of the same subject taken through two filters, one red and one green. The resulting images are devoid of colour because the film used was a black and white one; but in the first the red areas of the subject appear as light greys, whereas in the second the opposite occurs and the red areas come out almost black. At this point, with two separate projectors, Land projects the two slides so that they fit together perfectly. The resulting image is obviously black and white. But he then puts in front of the first projector the same red filter with which the first image was made, while leaving the light of the second projector white. And now, suddenly, the image appears in colour. We do not just see shades of pink, as we might be inclined to expect, but all colours. Land demonstrates a simple and vertiginous fact: we do not need to have colours present in order to see them.

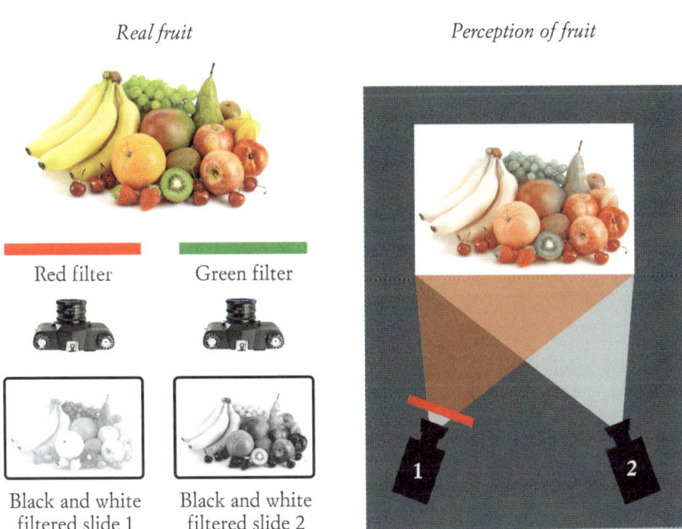

LAND, 1971

It was demonstrated that the cells that respond to a wavelength react to a surface of any colour, as long as it contains a minimum quantity of that wavelength. That the brain is capable of producing chromatic sensations with the absence of stimuli has been confirmed by the effects of LSD and other such psychotropic substances.

5.0 *Posthumous and complementary colours.* Theorized above all by Goethe, the **posthumous (or afterimage) colours** can be explained scientifically as due to the interaction between the retina and the processes that take place in the part of the visual cortex designated as V4 (see p.199). After having registered a certain wavelength, the groups of cells involved at a retinal level (cones) tend to send to the cortex a weaker signal, as if they were speaking in lowered voices – and this deceives the higher cells (V4) that end up constructing the sensation of complementary colour. If we look at the red square below for a few seconds and then move our gaze onto the black point, what we see appears to be ghosted by a square of turquoise, which is the complementary of red.

ZEKI, 2003

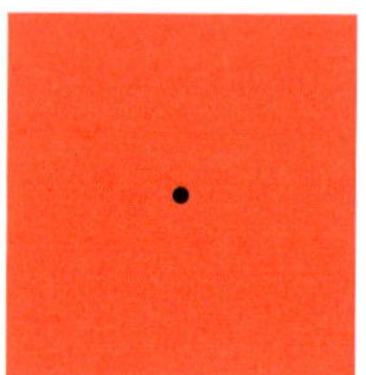

That this phenomenon depends on the cortex and not the retina was confirmed by a study of a patient with a partial cortical atrophy: he reported that after he had remade his bed using red sheets, he found himself for more than a minute with green hands. The defect, being partial, allowed him to see but slowed down the processes in V4 and produced a consecutive image that was abnormal.

BRESSAN, 2007

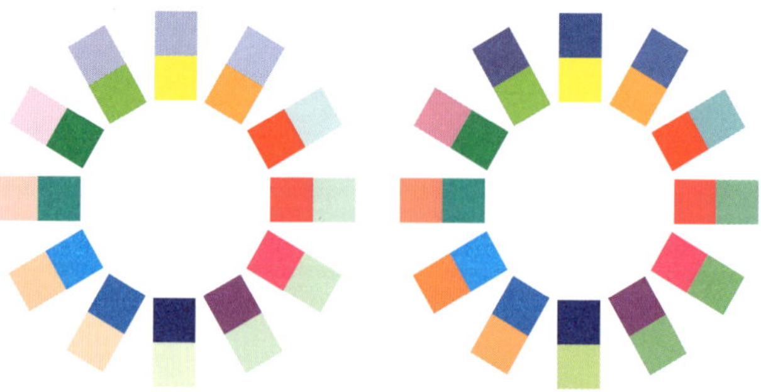

Circle of posthumous colours (paler ones on the outside)

Circle of complementary colours

It still remains a mystery as to why such a mechanism has evolved. It is probably an inevitable effect of the functioning of opposing signals that dominates the way we imagine colour, making us always think of it via opposed pairs (see p. 195).

5.1 A **complementary colour** may be defined in four distinct ways, in neurobiological, physical or artistic terms:

- Psychologically it is the posthumous perception that appears after we have looked at a certain colour for a few seconds (see **5.0**).
- In admixtures – both additive and subtractive – two colours are called complementary if they produce an achromatic one (white or grey) (see **6.3**).
- In the CIE chromaticity diagram (see **10.0**) two colours are complementary that are on opposite points of the perimeter, on a line passing through the centre of the white.
- In the colour wheels of artistic theory the complementary colours are on opposite sides of the circumference, even if this often leads to imprecise data: the complementary of strawberry red is in fact turquoise, whereas in Goethe's and Itten's circles it is leaf green (see Appendix B 16).

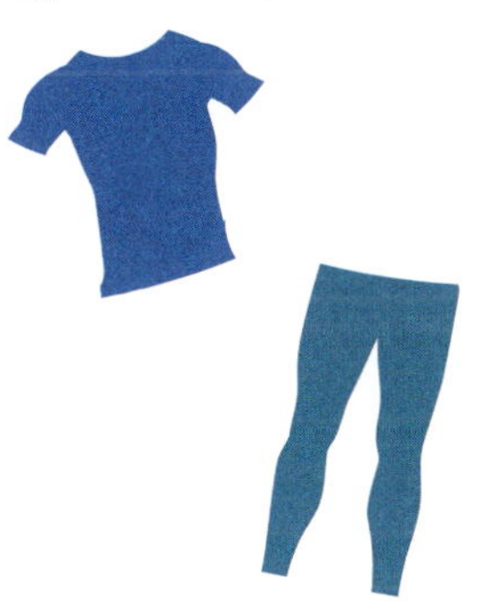

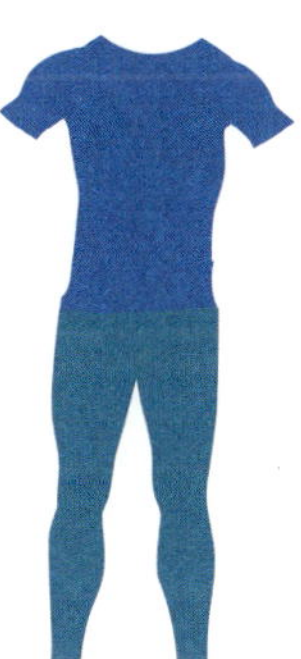

HOLTZSCHUE, 2011

A practical use for the contrast between complementaries is that of revealing a colour that we had not been properly aware of: if I take a blue jumper and a pair of blue trousers, for instance, they may seem similar, but if I contrast them then their difference is amplified with one seeming colder and the other warmer. Perhaps not everyone knows the technical definition, but in clothing shops it is a standard trick to juxtapose complementaries.

6.0 *Mixing.* Perceptually and operatively, colour mixing is of three types: **additive**, **subtractive** and **partitive**. It is important to underline that these adjectives refer to mixtures and not to colour: there are no 'subtractive colours' as one often finds oneself reading.

6.1 **Additive** mixing uses coloured lights: if I add to a green spotlight that of a red one, I obtain a colour more luminous than both, namely yellow. The term means to add light to light.

6.2 Subtractive mixing occurs when we subtract light, using solid colours such as paint from tubes or printing ink. In this case, yellow and blue give a kind of green which is darker, or with less light, than the two colours that generated it.

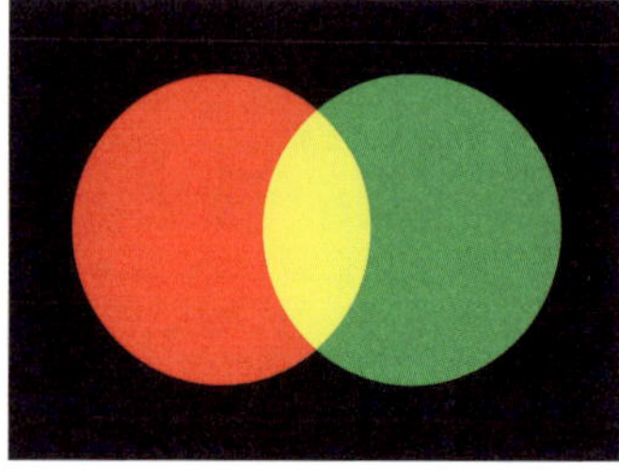

Additive mixing

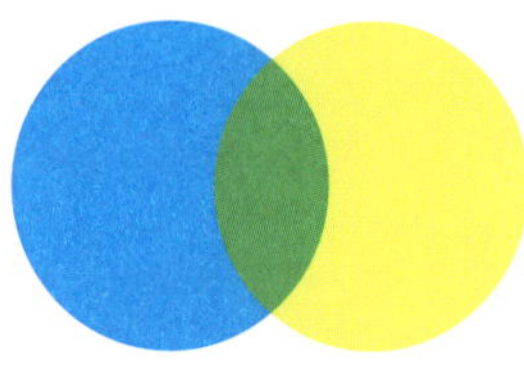

Subtractive mixing

6.3 Partitive mixing juxtaposes colours in a way that makes the result a product of visual perception, and is also called for this reason **spatial colour mixing**. A perfect example of this type of mixture is the grey hair of middle-aged people: in reality hair is either white or coloured, but seen from a distance the two colours may blur and appear grey to us. The effect depends on the resolution of the retina, that is on the quantity of cones involved: if I look closely, the retinal projection is greater and I can distinguish the two colours; from a distance the projection is smaller and the two colours blur in a new sensation.

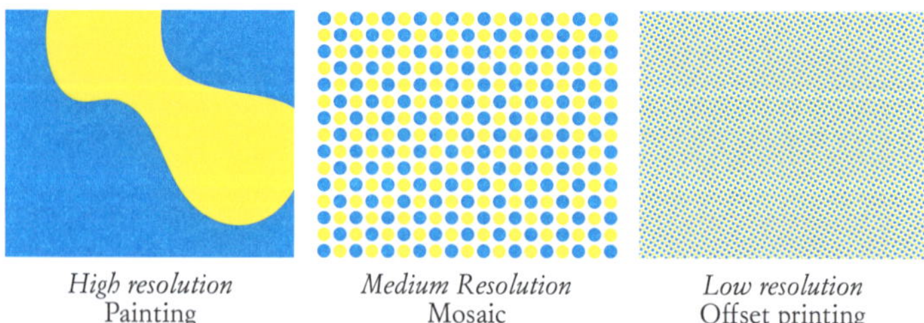

High resolution
Painting

Medium Resolution
Mosaic

Low resolution
Offset printing

Another example of partitive mixing is the mosaic: next to tiles which are yellow and blue I do not obtain green, as in tempera, but grey, because in this type of mixing the complementary colours behave as in additive mixing but with less luminosity. The televisual screen, on the other hand, made up of so many green, red and blue dots emitting light, produces a much clearer result: so if in the

GERRITSEN, 1983

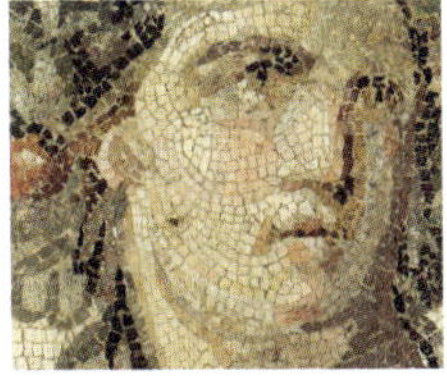
Mosaic

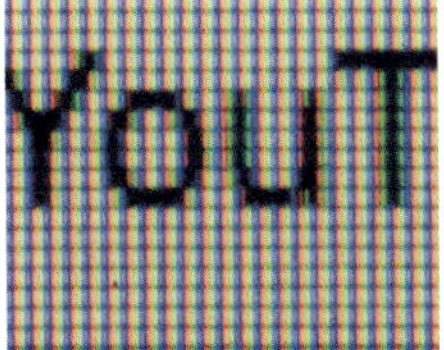

RGB screen

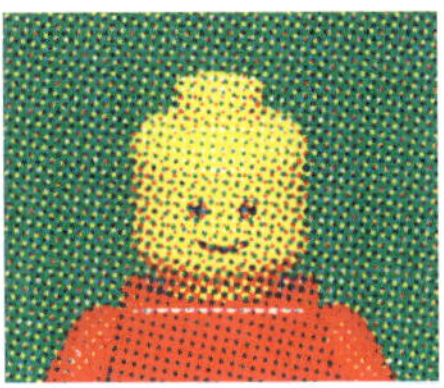
Screen-printing

mosaic green plus red gives ochre, in the television it gives yellow. Four-colour printing is instead both partitive and subtractive: it is partitive where the ink dots are side by side and blend optically; it is subtractive where the ink dots are layered as in a painting. When a cyan dot ends up over a yellow dot, we get green; when it ends up next to the yellow we obtain grey; when we have a little of one and a little of the other, we get a putrid green. Given this trio of outcomes, the use of black in four-colour printing helps to avoid an excessive greying of the darker tones. This mechanism should not be confused with pointillism in painting (as one reads wrongly in many art education manuals): Seurat's painting, like painting in general, is mostly the fruit of subtractive mixing; the juxtaposition of complementaries is used sparingly and only for the purpose of obtaining desaturated colours.

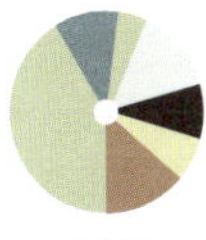
DISC

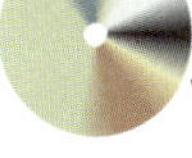
ROTATION

RESULTANT EFFECT

Another type of partitive mixing is the kind generated by movement, such as the rotation of Maxwell's spinning-tops: the velocity means that the eye no longer sees the discrete areas of colours but their mixture, and for this reason it is called **temporal colour mixing**.

7.0 *Nomenclature.* Colours are perceived in different **modes** according to the situation, and are named through psychological attributes.

7.1 One speaks of **isolated colour** when a colour is seen by itself without anything else around it: a disc of coloured light projected in a darkened room, for instance; or a homogeneous surface seen through a small hole (a reduction hole); or a traffic light in a dark street at night. The isolated colour is a particular experience in which a single homogeneous colour is surrounded by black. All of the colours when seen isolated (in the dark or against a dark background) appear saturated and luminous. An isolated brown is always perceived as yellow (see p. 200), while a piece of wood never appears yellow, because perfect isolation does not exist in nature: it is only possible to create it in a controlled context such as a lab. So in everyday life, colours are always **non-isolated**; we actually see them alongside many other colours. Besides, the cerebral cortex constructs the perception of colour by comparing the spectral composition of adjacent areas. A circle of coloured light in the dark (such as the one projected, or like the traffic light) is only an elementary case, a simple spatial relation, not coincidentally chosen as an object of study in a laboratory.

7.2 The principal and most common ways of seeing the appearance of colour are the so-called **object modes**, that is to say how colour manifests itself among the things we deal with in the world. There are three of these modes:

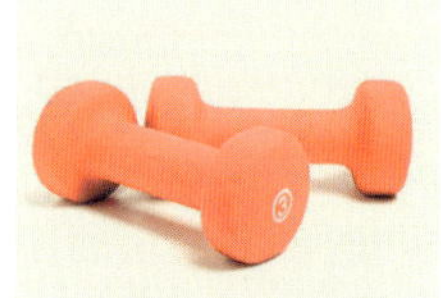

Surface mode
an opaque object
(reflection of light)

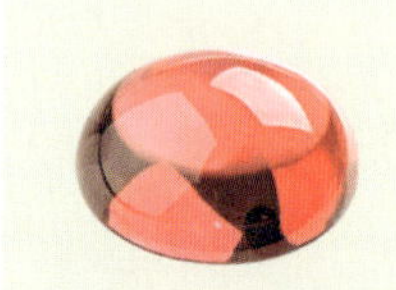

Volume mode
a transparent object
(transmission of light)

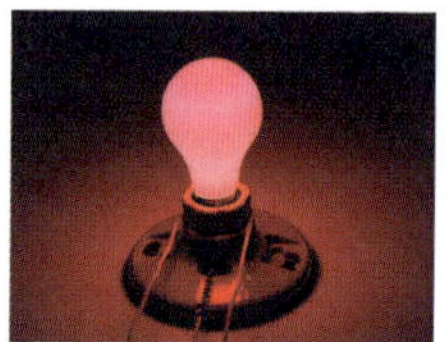

Illuminated mode
a luminous object
(emission of light)

The **surface mode** is that of any coloured object, such as a piece of paper or of plastic. It is a non-isolated form, visible in a context next to other colours. In the second case, called **volume mode**, colour is perceived thanks to the passage of light through the mass of the object, as in a glass of wine, for instance. The third case is the **illuminated mode**, where the colour has its source in a luminous entity, such as a coloured light bulb. The latter may appear isolated (the traffic light at night) or non-isolated (Christmas-tree lights, for example). Although they emit light, if they are not forcibly isolated the colours on monitors are seen by us as if they were surfaces, which is to say that the monitor is treated by our vision as if it were a painting.

Then there are the **non-object modes**. Respectively:

The **illuminating mode** is the colour attributed to light that predominates in a scene, as when we talk of an ambience of warm light. The **reduced mode** is colour perceived through an aperture which is

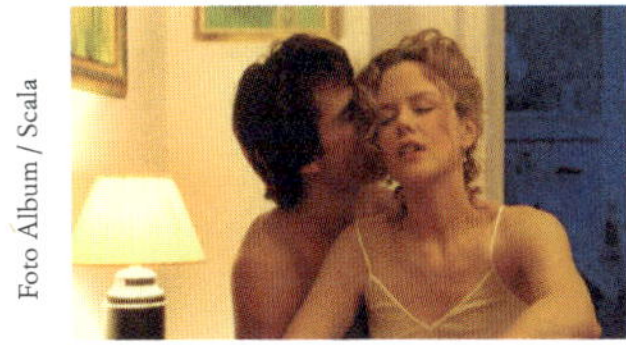
Foto Album / Scala

Illuminating mode
(chromatic light in a context)

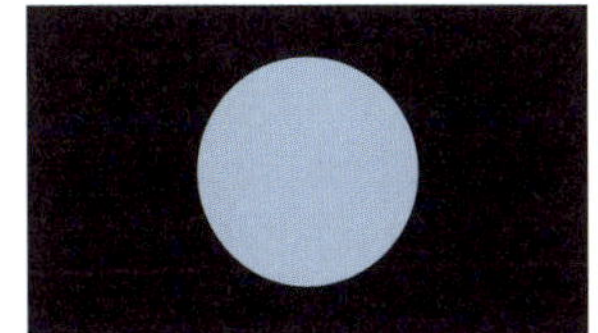

Reduced mode
(sky seen through a pinhole)

sufficiently small to make it appear homogeneous, as when looking through a tube with one eye. In everyday life, one of the few cases of reduced colour occurs when we look up at a cloudless sky and its colour appears to be solid, homogeneous, devoid of texture. In this case, we have an isolated colour par excellence.

7.3 Colour may be described through psychological attributes. The principal ones are **hue**, **brightness** and **saturation**. Others include the perception of what is clear, opaque, diaphanous, and so on. These are not measurable quantities, but ways of appearing before our gaze, qualitative evaluations.

7.3.1 The characteristic of a colour that makes it appear different from another one is its **hue**: red, blue, yellow are **hues**. The five circles below show five different hues of the same brightness or luminosity.

'Hue' is basically the term that distinguishes what we would actually call 'colour' when we feel that colour is present. All of the different hues are differences in wavelength, but not all differences between wavelengths entail differences in hue. That is to say, different spectral compositions can provoke in the brain the same perceptions: we can produce the same red by mixing wavelengths of different types (the discrepancy between physical quantities/measurements and sensations produced is one of the problematic cruxes of colour studies, whether scientific or philosophical).

Some colours are defined as **spectral** – the ones, in other words, that are contained in the rainbow. Others, not in the rainbow, such as purple or magenta, are **non-spectral**.

7.3.2 Every surface perceived has a precise **reflectance**, that is to say quantity of light that it reflects, which can be measured by a photometer. Objects with a reflectance of less than 10 per cent appear to us as black. The apparent reflectance, that is to say what is perceived by the human eye, is called **brilliance**, or more colloquially **brightness**, and is also a non-measurable psychological attribute. In the five following circles, the underlying hue remains the same but the brightness is altered.

PURGHÉ, 1999

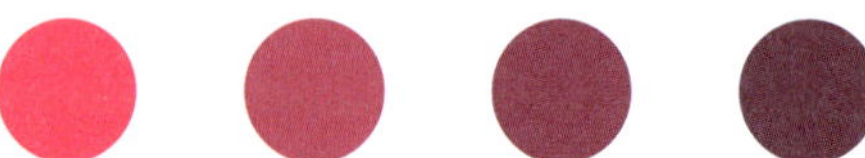

Technically speaking, the difference between red and pink is a difference in brightness. This is why these terms are psychological ones: from a physical point of view, pink should not be considered as a separate colour. Pink is simply a red to which 'more light' has been added, so red and pink – as long as it really is a treatment of the same electromagnetic curve – are effectively the same colour. From a linguistic, social, artistic and commercial point of view, on the other hand, red and pink are indeed considered to be two different colours. If an assistant in a clothes shop were to claim that two jumpers, one red and one pink, are in fact of the same colour and just different in brightness, this would hardly make sense, either in the lexicon of fashion or in everyday parlance.

Hue is consequently a **chromatic** attribute, which relates to the type of colour, whereas brightness is a **tonal** attribute, relating to the *quantity* of light. We call **clarity**, on the other hand, the perception relating to a non-isolated colour, seen in the midst of other colours. As a consequence, clarity is a form of brightness relative to context. So when dealing with a coloured lamp we can speak of its brightness, and when with a piece of paper on a table, of its clarity (in reality when we say that something is brighter than something else we are speaking of clarity).

7.3.3 In the following circles, tint and brightness remain constant while their depth changes, or what is more commonly called their **saturation**.

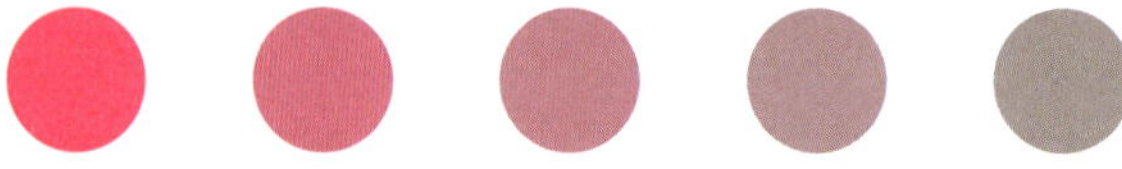

This term refers to the quantity of colour perceived, the fact that a vermillion red appears more *coloured* than an antique red. For isolated colours, the presence of hue is called **depth**. For a non-isolated colour, one that is therefore in relation to a scale, we speak of **chroma**, or purity of colour. In general, especially in a digital context, these terms are substituted by 'saturation', which instead should indicate the depth in relation to brightness. Dealing with a value linked to the quantity of light, the saturation would relate only to coloured light and not to reflective surfaces such as a piece of paper. Having said that, in common parlance we say that a colour is saturated in reference to the degree to which it differs from a grey of the same brightness.

8.0 *Perceived brightness of colours.* Colours can be ordered in a **chromatic sequence**, as happens with the spectrum, or in a **tonal sequence**, according to the amount of light they reflect and which our eye is most sensitive to.

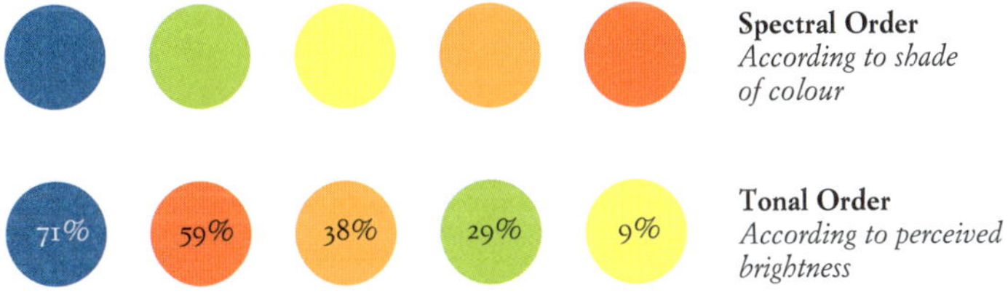

Spectral Order
According to shade of colour

Tonal Order
According to perceived brightness

If we convert a colour image to greyscale, as in a black and white photo, we see that every colour at its maximum saturation has a precise luminous quality that does not depend just upon physical facts but also upon the sensitivity of our visual apparatus. It is not the cortex, however, that is responsible for this factor: it is the structural quality of the retina. Our vision of yellow involves cones sensitive to greens and reds, which make up almost 90 per cent of the total, while for violet the minority blue cones are responsible.

Yellow therefore has a spectral composition that excites a major number of receptors and manifests itself as a major sensation of light. This sensitivity has a peak around the wavelength of yellow. If we had more blue cones, it is likely that we would be able to see (and to think) a violet more luminous than yellow. The perception of **intrinsic luminosity** in relation to colours and the capacity to compare them are the fundamental characteristics that enable the mind to evaluate volumes, depth and chromatic qualities. This also brings with it a greater capacity of discrimination as chromatic and luminous differences increase as well as the fundamental capacity to discern more or

83

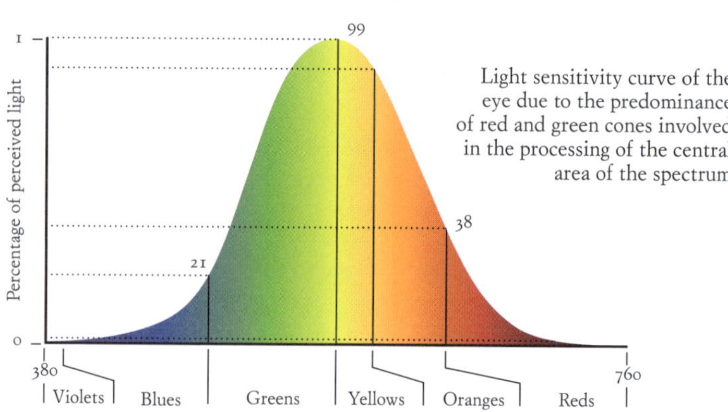

Light sensitivity curve of the eye due to the predominance of red and green cones involved in the processing of the central area of the spectrum

less high thresholds within tonal passages. Look at the following five circles, for instance:

Anyone is able order them according to the value of their luminosity:

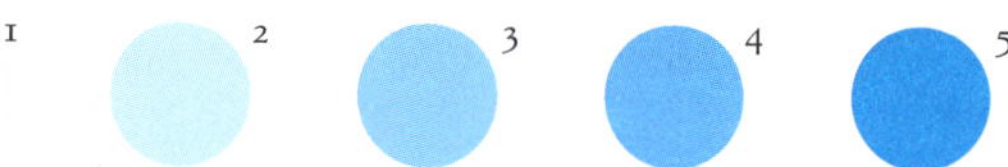

And if a sixth circle presented itself, we would know at which point in the line to position it. Hue and luminosity are therefore something we experience as a whole, but luminosity is also a precise quality that we associate with certain tints.

8.1 The relationship between colours and brightness, beyond painting, plays a key role in sign and informational systems. What matters is actually the capacity of colour to create a **margin** with what surrounds it that is sufficiently decipherable for our eye.

Unlike in other systems such as numerical or alphabetic ones, in the chromatic system the colours can be differentiated but not ordered. That is to say, in the map of the London Underground the colours distinguish the different lines but are not capable of establishing any sequence or hierarchy between them. The only way of creating order is to establish a shading through which they are seen as a series of successive steps – from light to dark, for instance, or from saturated to faded. This is what often happens with graphics for weather

BERTIN, 2011

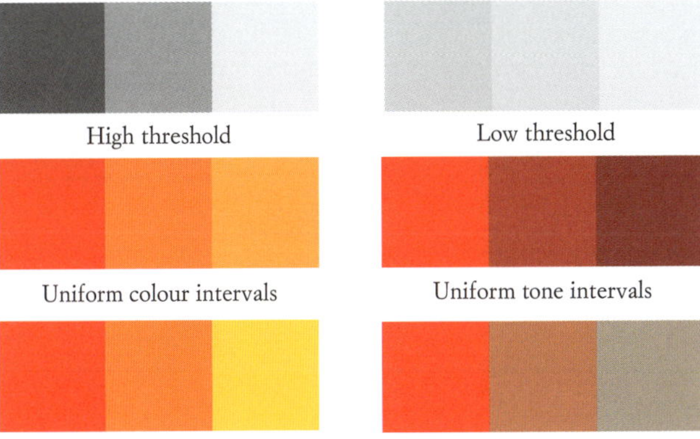

forecasts, where switching from blue to red represents an increase in temperatures. In all these cases it is clear that colour is always in need of a narrative to be able to signify.

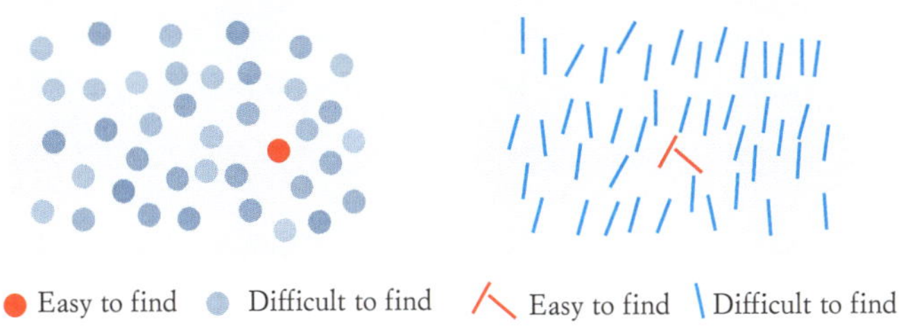

WARE, 2008

An extreme example is that of the transistor where colours indicate the power but need a reference to be read, since there are too many hues to be distinguished 'by eye'. Unlike such systems, the signs used for roads are purely perceptual: the red of prohibitions and the blue of directions speak directly to our eye without needing to resort to explanation or narrative. This is possible precisely because the differences are very marked and not too numerous. Colour, however, has the capacity to attract attention, so the choice of hues more or less saturated or bright depends largely on how much we want a certain element to 'catch the eye' more than others (for these qualities the internet has always used colour to indicate the clickable and the operable). In information systems we need to avoid figures in yellow against a white background, colours that are faded and not legible, and combinations of colours with little differentiation that on the one hand might get conflated in reproduction, and on the other be confused by readers with partial colour-blindness. In iconography, the priority of which is not expressive but informational, the problems of visual perception are always structural questions.

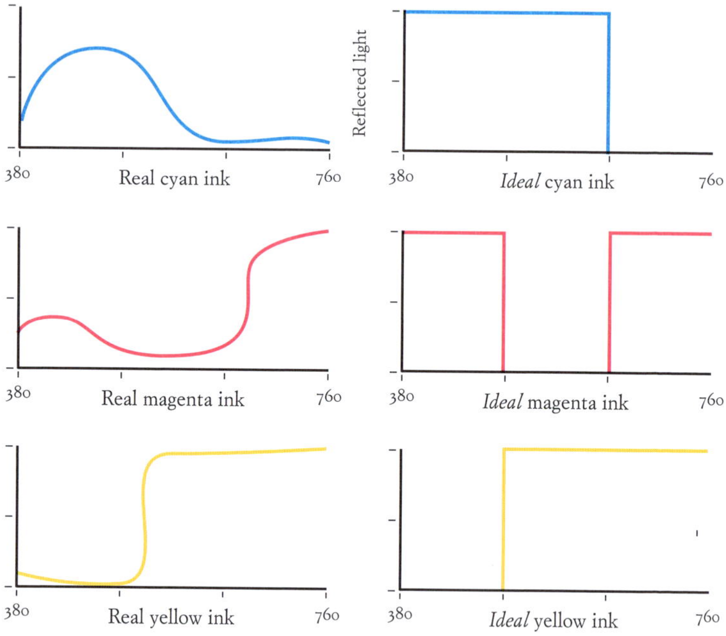

GERRITSEN, 1983

9.0 *Four-colour printing.* Also known as CMYK – from the initials of the three inks (cyan, magenta, yellow) plus the *k* that stands for *key*, because the black plate is the 'key' that allows each to be aligned with the others. In the parlance of the old typographers it was said that **cyan** and **magenta** make the image, **yellow** gives it transparency and **black** depth.

The mechanism is based on the choice of three colours, each of which does not reflect any of the wavelengths of the other two, thus guaranteeing the widest possible range once they have been mixed together. In reality, however, the inks reflect a little of all the wavelengths, and this is why the three primaries cannot reproduce all of the perceptible colours. Three ideal inks could do without the black, crowning the dream of Le Blon (see p. 138, note 9). Already in the second half of the nineteenth century, following the intuition of Maxwell, the colour was separated by photographing the subject three times through filters of complementary colour to that of print (see pp. 159–60).

10.0 *The CIE chromaticity diagram.* In 1931, the CIE (Commission Internationale de l'Éclairage) proposed a mathematically based chromatic model that allows for the definition of all colours visible to humanity by the use of three coordinates.

Unlike the circles, spheres and triangles favoured by the theorists of the past, what we end up with here is an irregular shape, similar to that of a bell, that gives a lot of space to some colours and less to others: more weight is given to yellows and greens, since all the visible colours are described by calibrating their wavelengths to the sensitivity of the human retina. The CIE of 1924 had in fact standardized the curve of sensitivity of the cones, evaluating electromagnetic radiation in relation to its capacity to stimulate the eye. Compared to the physics models of the nineteenth century that describe the world regardless of the person looking at it, and in which all the wavelengths have equal status, and respect the geometric regularity of artistic diagrams, what matters here is what is really visible. Not a simple coloured space, but colour as a thing that is seen. OLEARI, 2008

On the perimeter of the bell the wavelengths of the spectrum are distributed in a non-homogeneous manner (the distance between 500 and 480 nm is greater than that between 560 and 580 nm, even though we are dealing with the same physical magnitude), in accordance with the greater propensity of the retina towards the green range. The straight segment that forms the base of the bell, called the 'purple line', belongs instead to the reds not contained within the rainbow, which do not correspond to a monochromatic radiation but are the fruit of the sum of all the radiations at the extremities of the spectrum. Like all models, the CIE model is only able to define an isolated colour and cannot take account of actual perception in action, as phenomena such as **chromatic constancy** (see p. 199) or **simultaneous contrast** (see p. 95) involve too many variables to be mathematized. PURGHÉ, 1999

We are dealing with an exclusively theoretical model: a point on the graph shows nothing concrete: not an ink, not a wavelength, not a traceable value on a monitor. There is no technology capable of visualizing or producing the colours of the model, but at the same time there is now no technology that can do without it. We can think of it as a Platonic idea of all the colours potentially visible, of which our everyday monitors show only contingent manifestations (since it is a

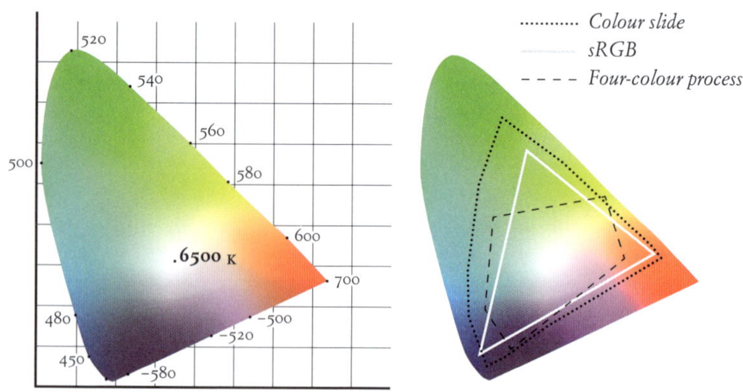

Wavelength expressed in nanometres, temperature expressed in kelvin

mathematical model, it is obviously not even representable; the figure is coloured only for didactic purposes). The idea of the model was born from many studies made after the First World War, when the impossibility of reproducing all colours by additive synthesis was noted, whatever triad of primaries were used and mixed. To construct the diagram, three imaginary primaries are identified, to which the vertices of a triangle containing the bell correspond: they serve as a mathematical reference allowing the expression of the rest of the values. Choosing three real primaries, that is three monochromatic lights at intervals of the spectrum, one becomes aware in fact that some colours will never be obtained by any possible combination of them. Every spectral colour can be the sum of three primaries as long as some of these can be expressed by a negative number. A technology capable of concretely producing all of the colours of the model does not currently exist.

11.0 *Munsell colour system.* In the Munsell tree, the trunk indicates the luminosity and going from the bottom upwards proceeds from darkness to light. Around this trunk the colours are arranged in circular fashion, while the branches represent the different degrees of saturation, and the further we go out on a branch the deeper the colour. The rule that governs the system is that the differences between one piece and another, in all three dimensions, are perceptually uniform. It is consequently a model built on the discernment capacities of the eye that defines the perceptible numerically through the three coordinates of luminosity, hue and saturation.

Foto Munsell Inc.

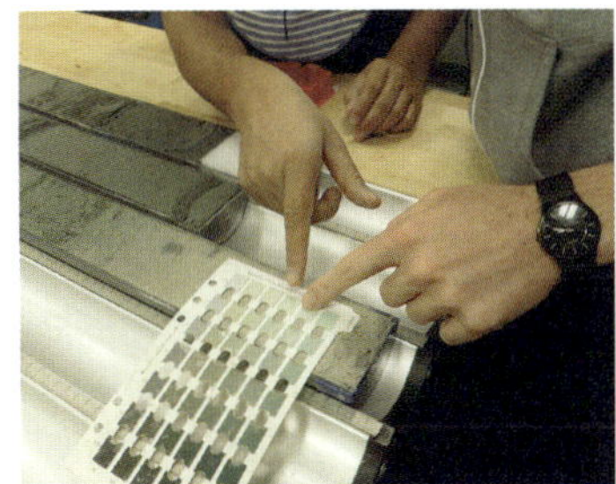

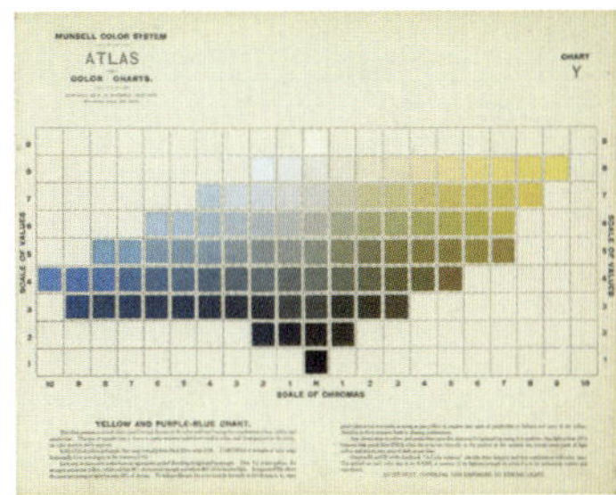

MUNSELL, 1921

Munsell's is the first structure based on homogeneous perceptual differences, and therefore on colour as it actually appears to us. It is mandatory that the perceived difference between two colours vertically, on the axis of luminosity, appears equal to the difference between two hues horizontally, on the axis of saturation (which Munsell calls 'chroma'). This implies that the distance of the saturated points from the centre should be different for each colour, inasmuch as it takes more steps to go from grey to red than from grey to blue. In this way, the tree has branches of different lengths and the resulting volume is irregular and not cylindrical.

Unlike Munsell's, Pantone's system is not based on any general theory: it is a simple communication protocol that does not establish relations between hues, and never defines a colour on the basis of geometric or perceptual parameters, but only on the basis of the quantity of mixture of eighteen inks. A worthy heir of Munsell's is the Swedish NCS or Natural Colour System, which articulates the relations starting from four basic colours according to ideas about opposition formulated by Hering. An analogue for industrial and architectural applications of Pantone is the RAL design system.

Appendix B
Principal Chromatic Models

Reconstruction of the models formulated from the beginning of the seventeenth century – the century in which the problem of rationalizing colour was first formulated. Hölzel's colour circle (16), developed following Goethe, is particularly noteworthy. Now virtually forgotten, Hölzel was an educator whose work has enormous influence in the twentieth century, determining many of the ideas of his pupil Johannes Itten.

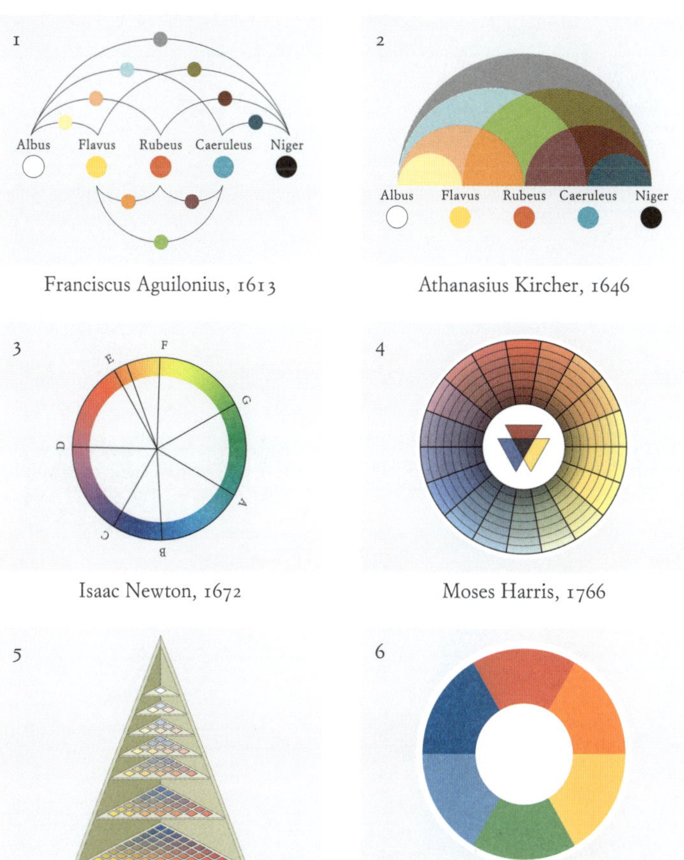

Franciscus Aguilonius, 1613

Athanasius Kircher, 1646

Isaac Newton, 1672

Moses Harris, 1766

Johann Heinrich Lambert, 1772

Johann Wolfgang von Goethe, 1810

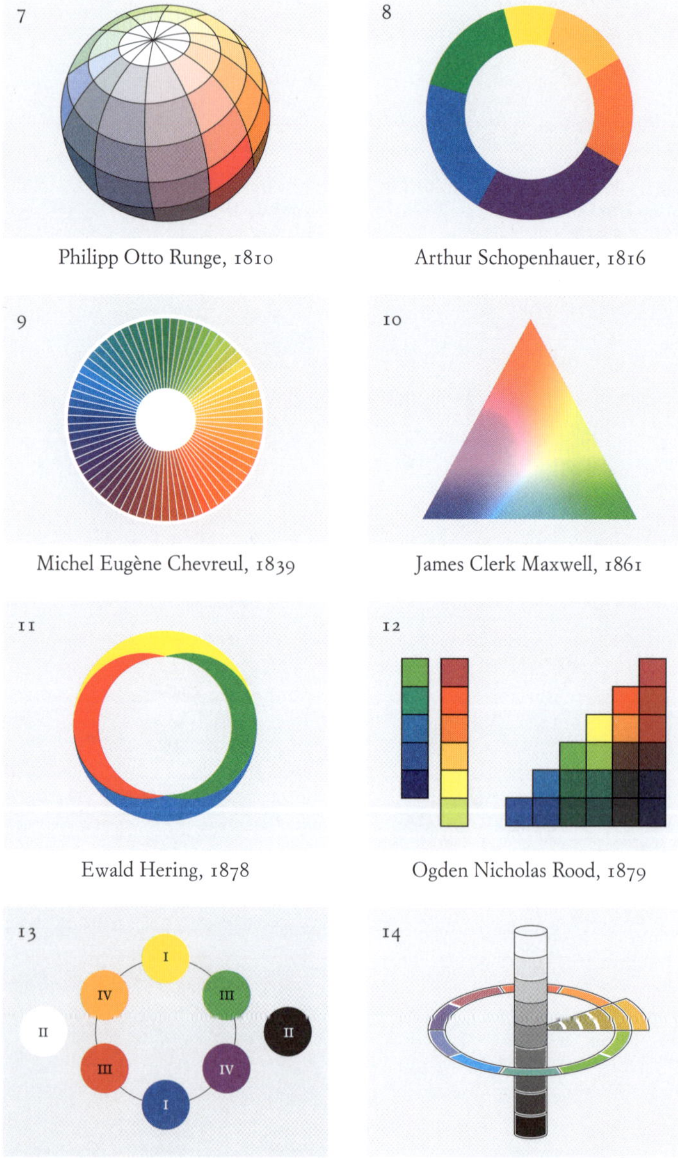

Philipp Otto Runge, 1810

Arthur Schopenhauer, 1816

Michel Eugène Chevreul, 1839

James Clerk Maxwell, 1861

Ewald Hering, 1878

Ogden Nicholas Rood, 1879

Vasilij Vasil'evič Kandinskij, 1912

Albert Munsell, 1915

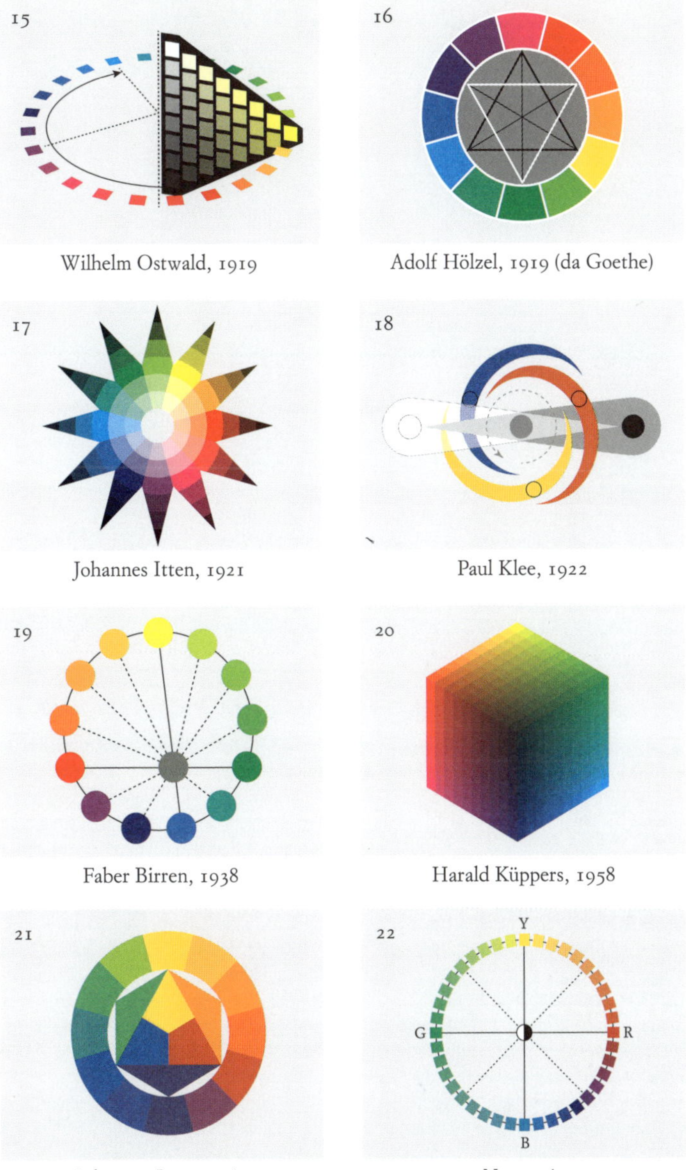

Wilhelm Ostwald, 1919

Adolf Hölzel, 1919 (da Goethe)

Johannes Itten, 1921

Paul Klee, 1922

Faber Birren, 1938

Harald Küppers, 1958

Johannes Itten, 1961

Ncs, 1969

A Note on the Illustrations

Unlike in the classic editorial model, in which works of art are reproduced in their entirety, in this book the images are presented in the form of details, sections or patches, and without any captions. A detail from a famous painting appears side by side with a technical procedure; a historical document finds itself next to a character from a film – suggesting assonances, appositions, and possible links between different worlds. The works involved are presented more as evidence of ways of thinking than as works of art. For this reason, the way in which the book is arranged is as an integral part of the text: its design is already a point of view on its subject. The idea is to provide a figurative apparatus running parallel to the text that will prompt an articulated look at the images, rendering fruitful the visual syncretism that is already the norm through use of the internet and social media. It is up to the reader, if they choose, to make further links – imaginative and personal – with the help of the works in the following list of illustrations.

List of Illustrations

Bibliography

ABRAMOV, I., GORDON, J., FELDMAN, O. e altri, *Sex and Vision*, in «Biology of Sex Differences», III (2012), n. 21.

ACTON, M., *Guardare un quadro*, Einaudi, Torino 2009.

AGNELLO, M., *Semiotica dei colori*, Carocci editore, Roma 2013.

AGRIPPA DI NETTESHEIM, H. C., *La filosofia occulta o la magia*, Edizioni Mediterranee, Roma 1972.

ALBERS, J., *Interazione del colore*, il Saggiatore, Milano 2005.

ALEXANDER, J. J. G., *Medieval Illuminators and Their Methods of Work*, Yale University Press, New Haven 1992.

ALGAROTTI, F., *Il newtonianismo per le dame, ovvero dialoghi sopra la luce e i colori*, Napoli 1737.

ALPERS, S. e BAXANDALL, M., *Tiepolo e l'intelligenza figurativa*, Einaudi, Torino 1996.

AMBROSE, G. e HARRIS, P., *Il manuale del graphic design*, Zanichelli, Bologna 2009.

ANDREUCCETTI, P. e LAZZARESCHI CERVELLI, I. (a cura di), *Il colore nel Medioevo. Arte simbolo tecnica*, Atti delle Giornate di Studi (Lucca, 5-6 maggio 1995), Lucca 1996.

ANTAL, F., *La pittura fiorentina e il suo ambiente sociale nel Trecento e nel primo Quattrocento*, Einaudi, Torino 1960.

ARGAN, G. C., *Il colore come rappresentazione dello spazio*, in «Colore», (1961), n. 7.

ARISTOTLE, *Parva naturalia*, Bompiani, Milano 2002.

ARNHEIM, R., *Arte e percezione visiva*, Feltrinelli, Milano 1997.

–, *Film come arte*, il Saggiatore, Milano 1960.

–, *Il pensiero visivo*, Einaudi, Torino 1974.

–, *La razionalizzazione del colore*, in *Intuizione e intelletto*, Feltrinelli, Milano 1987.

ASLAM, M. M., *Are You Selling the Right Colour?*, in «Journal of Marketing Communications», XII (2011), n. 1.

BALL, P., *Colore. Una biografia*, Rizzoli, Milano 2004.

–, CLARKE, M. e PARRAMAN, C., *Colour in the Making*, Black Dog Publishing, London 2013.

BANKEL, H. e altri, *I colori del bianco. Policromia nella scultura antica*, De Luca Editori d'Arte, Città del Vaticano-Roma 2004.

BARASCH, M., *Luce e colore nella teoria artistica del Rinascimento*, Marietti, Genova 1992.

BARTHES, R., *L'impero dei segni*, Einaudi, Torino 2002.

–, *Miti d'oggi*, Einaudi, Torino 2005.

BATCHELOR, D., *Cromofobia*, Bruno Mondadori, Milano 2001.

–, *The Luminous and the Grey*, Reaktion Books, London 2014.

BAUDRILLARD, J., *Il sistema degli oggetti*, Bompiani, Milano 2003.

BAXANDALL, M., *Ombre e lumi*, Einaudi, Torino 2003.

–, *Pittura ed esperienze sociali nell'Italia del Quattrocento*, Einaudi, Torino 2001.

BEAR, M. F., CONNORS, B. W. e PARADISO, M. A., *Neuroscienze*, Elsevier Masson, Milano 2002.

BENJAMIN, W., *I «passages» di Parigi*, Einaudi, Torino 2010.

–, *L'opera d'arte nell'epoca della sua riproducibilità tecnica*, Einaudi, Torino 2000.

BENSE, M., *Semiotica della forma e dei colori*, in «Versus», (1972), n. 3, pp. 60–73.

BERGER, J., *Questione di sguardi*, il Saggiatore, Milano 2009.

BERLIN, B. e KAY, P., *Basic Color Terms*, University of California Press, Berkeley 1969.

BERTAGNA, G. e BOTTOLI, A., *Scienza del colore per il design*, Maggioli Editore, Santarcangelo 2013.

BERTIN, J., *Semiology of Graphics. Diagrams, Networks, Maps*, Esri press, Redlands 2011.

BIANCO, L. (a cura di), *Le pietre mirabili. Magia e scienza nei lapidari greci*, Sellerio, Palermo 1992.

BILLOCK, V. A. e TSOU, B. H., *Vedere colori «impossibili»*, in «Le Scienze», 24 marzo 2010.

BIRREN, F., *Color and Human Response*, Van Nostrand Reinhold Company, New York 1978.

–, *Color, Form and Space*, Reinhold Publishing Corporation, New York 1961.

–, *Creative Color*, Schiffer Publishing, West Chester 1961.

–, *Light, Color & Environment*, Schiffer Publishing, West Chester 1988.

–, *Principles of Color*, Van Nostrand Reinhold Company, New York 1969.

BISSON, M., *A cosa serve il colore. Il ruolo del colore nello spazio costruito*, in *Colore e colorimetria. Contributi multidisciplinari*, Atti della Prima Conferenza Nazionale del Gruppo del Colore, Pescara 20-21 ottobre 2005, pp. 264–71.

– e BOERI, C., *Variazioni sul colore*, FrancoAngeli, Milano 2006.

BLUNT, A., *Le teorie artistiche in Italia. Dal Rinascimento al Manierismo*, Einaudi, Torino 1966.

BOATTO, A., *Di tutti i colori*, Laterza, Roma-Bari 2008.

BOCCARDI, L., *Colori. Simboli, storia, corrispondenze*, Marsilio, Venezia 2009.

BOERI, C. (a cura di), *Colore. Quaderni di cultura e progetto del colore*, Idc Colour Centre, Milano 2010.

BORDINI, S., *L'Ottocento. Le fonti per la storia dell'arte (1815-1880)*, Carocci editore, Roma 2013.

BOSCAROL, M., *Gestione digitale del colore nell'industria della stampa*, in *Colore e colorimetria* cit., pp. 22–9.

BRESSAN, P., *Il colore della luna. Come vediamo e perché*, Laterza, Roma-Bari 2007.

BRIGGS, A. e BURKE, P., *Storia sociale dei media*, il Mulino, Bologna 2010.

BRUCE, V., GREEN, P. R. e GEORGESON, M. A., *Visual Perception*, Psychology Press, New York 2003.

BRUNELLO, F. (a cura di), *«De arte illuminandi» e altri trattati sulla tecnica della miniatura medievale*, Neri Pozza, Vicenza 1975.

–, *L'arte della tintura nella storia dell'umanità*, Neri Pozza, Vicenza 1968.

BRUSATIN, M., *Colore*, in *Enciclopedia Einaudi*, Einaudi, Torino 1978, vol. III, pp. 388–409.

–, *Colore senza nome*, Marsilio, Venezia 2006.

–, *Lezioni sui colori*, Libreria Editrice Cafoscarina, Venezia 2005.

–, *Storia dei colori*, Einaudi, Torino 1983.

–, *Verde. Storie di un colore*, Marsilio, Venezia 2013.
– e COSTA, A., *Visione*, in *Enciclopedia Einaudi*, Einaudi, Torino 1981, vol. XIV, pp. 1110–41.
BUCCHETTI, V., *Packaging design. Storia, linguaggi, progetto*, FrancoAngeli, Milano 2012.
BURCKHARDT, T., *Alchimia*, Guanda, Milano 1986.
CALABI, D., «*Texture*» *Design*, in *Colore e colorimetria* cit., pp. 304–11.
CALABRESE, O., *Il problema del colore nei trattati d'arte del Cinquecento*, in «Versus», (1984), n. 37, pp. 19–33.
CALASSO, R., *Il rosa Tiepolo*, Adelphi, Milano 2006.
CALVESI, M., *Arte e alchimia*, Giunti, Firenze 1986.
CARDANO, G., *De Gemmis et coloribus*, 1562.
CARRIERA, R., *Maniere diverse per formare i colori*, Abscondita, Milano 2005.
CASTAGNOLA, G., *Come fotografare a colori*, Edizioni del Castello, Milano 1964.
CASTEL, L., *L'optique des couleurs*, Briasson, Paris 1740.
CASTELNUOVO, E., *Vetrate medievali*, Einaudi, Torino 1994.
CAUSSE, J.-G., *Lo stupefacente potere dei colori*, Ponte alle Grazie, Milano 2015.
CENNINI, C., *Il libro dell'arte*, Neri Pozza, Vicenza 1982.
CHEVREUL, M.-E., *De la loi du contraste simultané des couleurs*, Imprimerie Nationale, Paris 1889.
–, *The Principles of Harmony and Contrast of Colors*, Schiffer Publishing, West Chester 1987.
CLYDESDALE, F. M., *Color Perception and Food Quality*, in «Journal of Food Quality», I (1991), n. 14, pp. 61–74.
COCCIA, E., *Il bene nelle cose*, il Mulino, Bologna 2014.
CORONATO OCCOLTI, M., *Trattato dei colori*, Seth Viotto, Parma 1568.
COSTA, A., *La mela di Cézanne e l'accendino di Hitchcock*, Einaudi, Torino 2014.
DANTO, A., *Andy Warhol*, Einaudi, Torino 2010.
DAWSON, P., *Colour* in *Graphic Design Rules*, Frances Lincoln Limited, London 2012.
DE FUSCO, R., *Storia del design*, Laterza, Bari-Roma 2017.
DE GRANDIS, L., *Teoria e uso del colore*, Mondadori, Milano 1984.
DEL MORO, F. (a cura di), *Il colore nella grafica digitale*, Logos, Modena 2004.
DELACROIX, E., *Diario*, Einaudi, Torino 1994.
DELONG, M. e MARTINSON, B. (edited by), *Color and Design*, Berg, London 2012.
DESCARTES, R., *Opere scientifiche*, Utet, Torino 1966.
Design in 1000 oggetti, Gruppo editoriale l'Espresso, Roma 2008, vol. I–X.
DEUTSCHER, G., *La lingua colora il mondo*, Bollati Boringhieri, Torino 2013.
DI MONTAUTO, F., *Manuale di araldica*, Edizioni Polistampa, Firenze 1999.
DI NAPOLI, G., *Disegnare e conoscere*, Einaudi, Torino 2004.
–, *Il colore dipinto*, Einaudi, Torino 2006.
DI RENZO, M., *Il colore vissuto*, Edizioni Scientifiche Magi, Roma 1998.
– e WIDMANN, C. (a cura di), *La psicologia del colore*, Edizioni Scientifiche Magi, Roma 2001.
DOLCE, M. L., *Dialogo dei colori*, 1565.
DORFLES, G., *Introduzione al disegno industriale*, Einaudi, Torino 2001.
DREW, J. T. e MEYER, S. A., *Color Management*, Rotovision, Brighton 2005.

DRUCKER, J. e MCVARISH, E., *Graphic Design History*, Pearson Prentice Hall, Upple Saddle River 2009.

ECKSTUT, A. e ECKSTUT, J., *The Secret Language of Color*, Black Dog & Leventhal, New York 2013.

ECO, U., *Arte e bellezza nell'estetica medievale*, Bompiani, Milano 1987.

ECO-RAMGE, R. (a cura di), *Colore: divieti, decreti, dispute*, in «Rassegna», III (1985), n. 23.

EDWARDS, B., *L'arte del colore*, Longanesi, Milano 2006.

EHRNBERGER, K., *Visualising Gender Norms in Design. Meet the Mega Hurricane Mixer and the Drill Dolphia*, in «International Journal of Design», VI (2012), n. 3.

EISEMAN, L. e RECKER, K., *Pantone. Storia del XX secolo a colori*, Rizzoli, Milano 2011.

EISENSTEIN, E. L., *Le rivoluzioni del libro*, il Mulino, Bologna 2011.

ELKINS, J., *What Painting Is*, Routledge, New York-Abingdon 2000.

FAIRCHILD, M. D., *Color Appearance Models*, Addison Wesley Longman, Reading (Ma) 1998.

FALCINELLI, R., *Critica portatile al visual design*, Einaudi, Torino 2014.

–, *Guardare, pensare, progettare. Neuroscienze per il design*, Stampa Alternativa & Graffiti, Viterbo 2011.

FANTETTI, S. e PETRACCHI, C., *Il dizionario dei colori*, Zanichelli, Bologna 2001.

FAVRE, J.-P., *Color Sells Your Package*, ABC Verlag, Zürich 1969.

FEISNER, E. A., *Colour. How to Use Colour in Art and Design*, Laurence King Publishing, London 2001.

FIORENTINI, A. e MAFFEI, L., *Arte e cervello*, Zanichelli, Bologna 1995.

FLOCH, J.-M., *Identità visive*, FrancoAngeli, Milano 2015.

FLORENSKIJ, P., *Le porte regali*, Adelphi, Milano 1977.

FRANCALANCI, E. L., *Estetica degli oggetti*, il Mulino, Bologna 2006.

FRASER, T., *Colour in Design. Pocket Essentials*, Ilex, Lewes 2011.

FREUND, G., *Fotografia e società*, Einaudi, Torino 2007.

FRISBY, J. P. e STONE, J. V., *Seeing Color*, in *Seeing*, The Mit Press, Cambridge (Ma) 2010, pp. 397–418.

FROVA, A., *Luce colore visione*, Rizzoli, Milano 2000.

FUGA, A., *Tecniche e materiali delle arti*, Mondadori Electa, Milano 2004.

FUMAGALLI BEONIO BROCCHIERI, M., *L'estetica medievale*, il Mulino, Bologna 2002.

GAGE, J., *Color in Art*, Thames & Hudson, London 2006.

–, *Colore e cultura*, Istituto Poligrafico e Zecca dello Stato, Roma 2001.

–, *Colour and Meaning. Art, Science and Symbolism*, Thames & Hudson, London 2000.

GARAU, A., *Le armonie del colore*, Hoepli, Milano 1999.

GARFIELD, S., *Il malva di Perkin*, Garzanti, Milano 2002.

GARRONI, E., *Estetica. Uno sguardo attraverso*, Garzanti, Milano 1995.

GERBINO, W., *La percezione*, il Mulino, Bologna 1983.

GERRITSEN, F., *Evolution in Color*, Schiffer Publishing, West Chester 1988.

–, *Theory and Practice of Color*, Van Nostrand Reinhold Company, New York 1983.

GIANNINI, A. M., MARZI, T. e VIGGIANO M. P., *Design*, Giunti, Firenze 2011.

GILARDI, A., *Storia sociale della fotografia*, Bruno Mondadori, Milano 2000.

GLADSTONE, W. E., *Studies on Homer and the Homeric Age*, Oxford University Press, Oxford 1858.

GOETHE, J. W., *La storia dei colori*, Luni, Milano 2013.

–, *La teoria dei colori*, il Saggiatore, Milano 2008.

GOGUEN, J., (edited by), *Art and the Brain*, Imprint Academic, Exeter 1999.

GOMBRICH, E. H., *Arte e illusione. Studio sulla psicologia della rappresentazione pittorica*, Phaidon, Milano 2008.

–, *L'immagine e l'occhio. Altri studi sulla psicologia della rappresentazione pittorica*, Einaudi, Torino 1985.

–, *Il senso dell'ordine. Studio sulla psicologia dell'arte decorativa*, Einaudi, Torino 1979.

–, *Ombre*, Einaudi, Torino 1996.

GOODMAN, N., *I linguaggi dell'arte*, il Saggiatore, Milano 2008.

–, *Vedere e costruire il mondo*, Laterza, Roma-Bari 2008.

GOODWIN, C., *Il senso del vedere*, Meltemi, Roma 2003.

GRAMACCINI, N. e RAFF, T., *Iconologia delle materie*, in Castelnuovo, E. e Sergi, G. (a cura di), *Arti e storia nel Medioevo*, Einaudi, Torino 2003, vol. II.

GRAZIANI, M. P. e TORA, M., *Il colore come indicatore nelle scelte alimentari*, in *Colore e colorimetria* cit., pp. 351–8.

GREGORY, R. L. (a cura di), *Enciclopedia Oxford della Mente*, Sansoni, Firenze 1991.

–, *Eye and Brain*, Princeton University Press, Oxford 1997.

–, *Illusion in Nature and Art*, Macmillan, London 1980.

–, *Vedere attraverso le illusioni*, Raffaello Cortina Editore, Milano 2010.

GROSSMANN, M., *Colori e lessico*, Gunter Narr Verlag, Tübingen 1988.

GUALANDI, M. L., *L'antichità classica. Le fonti per la storia dell'arte*, Carocci editore, Roma 2014.

HALL, M. B., *Color and Meaning. Practice and Theory in Renaissance Painting*, Cambridge University Press, Cambridge 1994.

HARTHAN, J., *The History of the Illustrated Book*, Thames & Hudson, London 1997.

HOLLIS, R., *Graphic Design. A Concise History*, Thames & Hudson, London 2002.

HOLTZSCHUE, L., *Understanding Color*, John Wiley & Sons, Hoboken 2011.

HORNUNG, D., *Colour. A Workshop for Artists and Designers*, Laurence King, London, 2005.

HUBEL, D. H., *Occhio, cervello, visione*, Zanichelli, Bologna 1989.

– e altri, *I colori della vita*, Atti del Convegno Internazionale, Editrice La Stampa, Torino 1995.

– e LIVINGSTONE, M., *Segregation of form, Color, Movement, and Depth. Anatomy, Physiology, and Perception*, in «Science», CCXL (1988), n. 4853, pp. 740–9.

HUXLEY, A., *L'arte di vedere*, Adelphi, Milano 1989.

–, *Le porte della percezione*, Mondadori, Milano 1986.

INGS, S., *Storia naturale dell'occhio*, Einaudi, Torino 2008.

ITTEN, J., *Arte del colore*, il Saggiatore, Milano 1982.

–, *Design and Form. The Basic Course at the Bauhaus*, John Wiley & Sons, Hoboken 1975.

JARMAN, D., *Chroma*, Ubulibri, Milano 1995.

JOBLING, P. e CROWLEY, D., *Graphic Design. Reproduction and Representation since 1800*, Manchester University Press, Manchester 1996.

JOHNSTON, O. e THOMAS, F., *The Illusion of Life. Disney Animation*, Abbeville Press, New York 1981.

JORDAN, G., DEEB, S. S. e altri, *The Dimensionality of Color Vision in Carriers of Anomalous Trichromacy*, in «Journal of Vision», X (2010), n. 12.

KANDINSKI, V., *Lo spirituale nell'arte*, Se, Milano 2005.

–, *Punto, linea, superficie*, Adelphi, Milano 1968.

–, *Tutti gli scritti*, Feltrinelli, Milano 1989.

KANIZSA, G., *Grammatica del vedere. Saggi su percezione e Gestalt*, il Mulino, Bologna 1985.

KEMP, M., *The Science of Art. Optical Themes in Western Art from Brunelleschi to Seurat*, Yale University Press, New Haven 1992.

KEPES, G., *Language of Vision*, Dover Publications, New York 1995.

KLEE, P., *Quaderno di schizzi pedagogici*, Abscondita, Milano 2002.

–, *Teoria della forma e della figurazione*, Feltrinelli, Milano 1959.

KLEIN, R., *La forma e l'intelligibile*, Einaudi, Torino 1975.

KLIBANSKY, R., PANOFSKY, E. e SAXL, F., *Saturno e la melanconia*, Einaudi, Torino 2002.

KIRCHER, A., *Ars magna lucis et umbrae*, 1646.

KOYRÉ, A., *Dal mondo del pressapoco all'universo della precisione*, Einaudi, Torino 1967.

KRACAUER, S., *Film. Ritorno alla realtà fisica*, il Saggiatore, Milano 1962.

KRESS, G. e VAN LEEUWEN, T., *Reading Images. The Grammar of Visual Design*, Routledge, London 2006.

KÜPPERS, H., *The Basic Law of Color Theory*, Barron's Educational Series, New York 1981.

KUHN, T. S., *La struttura delle rivoluzioni scientifiche*, Einaudi, Torino 1978.

LAMB, T. e BOURRIAU, J. (a cura di), *Colour. Art & Science*, Cambridge University Press, Cambridge 1995.

LAND, E. e MCCANN, J. J., *Lightness and Retinex Theory*, in «Journal of the Optical Society of America», LXI (1971), n. 1, pp. 1–11.

LE BLON, J. C., *Coloritto*, London 1725.

LE CORBUSIER, *Verso una architettura*, Longanesi, Milano 2003.

LIVINGSTONE, M., *Vision and Art. The Biology of Seeing*, Abrams, New York 2002.

LOMAZZO, G. P., *Idea del tempio della pittura*, Paolo Gottardo Pontio, Milano 1590.

LOOMIS, A., *Creative Illustration*, Titan Books, London 2012.

LOOS, A., *Parole nel vuoto*, Adelphi, Milano 1972.

LUPTON, E. e MILLER, A. J., *The Abc's of the Bauhaus and Design Theory*, Princeton Architectural Press, New York 1991.

LÜSCHER, M., *Il test dei colori*, Astrolabio-Ubaldini, Roma 1976.

LUZZATTO, L. e POMPAS, R., *Colori e moda*, in *Colore e colorimetria* cit., pp. 336–42.

–, *Colore & colori*, Il Castello, Cornaredo 2009.

–, *I colori del vestire. Variazioni, ritorni, persistenze*, Hoepli, Milano 1997.

–, *Il significato dei colori nelle civiltà antiche*, Bompiani, Milano 2001.

MAFFEI, L. e MECACCI, L., *La visione dalla neurofisiologia alla psicologia*, Mondadori, Milano 1979.

MALTESE, C. (a cura di), *Le tecniche artistiche*, Mursia, Milano 1991.

MANCHIA, V., *Profondo come il blu. Per una lettura delle dinamiche dei colori nello Spirituale nell'arte di Wassily Kandinskij*, in «Ocula», (2004), n. 5.

MARCOLLI, A., *Teoria del campo*, Sansoni, Firenze 1971.

–, MACCHI, G., SILVESTRI, N. e SQUATRITI, F., *Arte e scienza. Spazio. Colore*, Mondadori Electa - La Biennale di Venezia, Milano - Venezia 1986.

MAROTTA, A., *Policroma. Dalle teorie comparate al progetto del colore*, Celid, Torino 1999.

MASSABÒ RICCI, I., CARASSI, M. e GENTILE, L. C. (a cura di), *Blu, rosso e oro. Segni e colori araldici in carte, codici e oggetti d'arte*, Mondadori Electa, Milano 1998.

MASSARI, S. e NEGRI ARNOLDI, F., *Arte e scienza dell'incisione*, Carocci editore, Roma 2008.

MASSIRONI, M., *Comunicare per immagini. Introduzione alla geometria delle apparenze*, il Mulino, Bologna 1989.

–, *Fenomenologia della percezione visiva*, il Mulino, Bologna 1998.

–, *The Psycology of Graphic Images*, Psychology Press, Abingdon 2001.

MATHIEU, V., *Goethe e il suo diavolo custode*, Adelphi, Milano 2002.

MEHL, R., *Playing with Color*, Rockport Publishers, Beverly (Ma) 2013.

MERLEAU-PONTY, M., *Fenomenologia della percezione*, Bompiani, Milano 2003.

–, *L'occhio e lo spirito*, Se, Milano 1989.

METHA, R. e ZHU, R. J., *Blue or Red? Exploring the Effect of Color on Cognitive Task Performaces*, in «Science», CCCXXIII (2009), n. 5918.

MIOTTO, E., *Luce e colori*, Fenice 2000, Milano 1994.

MIRZOEFF, N., *How to See the World*, Pelican, London 2015.

–, *Introduzione alla cultura visuale*, Meltemi, Roma 2005.

MOHOLY-NAGY, L., *Pittura Fotografia Film*, Einaudi, Torino 2010.

MONDRIAN, P., *Il Neoplasticismo*, Abscondita, Milano 2008.

–, *Tutti gli scritti*, Feltrinelli, Milano 1975.

MONTANARI, M., *Il riposo della polpetta*, Laterza, Roma-Bari 2009.

MONTANARI, T., *L'età barocca. Le fonti per la storia dell'arte (1600-1750)*, Carocci editore, Roma 2013.

MUNSELL, A. H., *A Grammar of Color*, The Strathmore Paper Company, Mittineague (Ma) 1921.

–, *Atlas of the Munsell Color System*, Wadsworth, Howland & Company, Boston 1915.

NEGRI ARNOLDI, F., *Tecnica e scienza*, in PREVITALI, G. (a cura di), *Storia dell'arte italiana*, Einaudi, Torino 1980, vol. IV.

NEWHALL, B., *Storia della fotografia*, Einaudi, Torino 1984.

NEWTON, I., *Scritti sulla luce e sui colori*, Rizzoli, Milano 2006.

NORDENFALK, C., *Storia della miniatura*, Einaudi, Torino 2012.

NOYES VANDERPOEL, E., *Color Problems*, Longmans, Green, and co., New York 1902.

OLEARI, C. (a cura di), *Misurare il colore*, Hoepli, Milano 2008.

ONIANS, J., *Neuroarthistory*, Yale University Press, New Haven 2008.

OSTWALD, W., *The Color Primer*, Van Nostrand Reinhold Company, New York 1969.

OTTMAN, K. (edited by), *Color Symbolism*, Spring Publication, Dallas 1977.

OVIO, G., *La scienza dei colori. Visione dei colori*, Hoepli, Milano 1987.

PÄCHT, O., *La miniatura medievale*, Bollati Boringhieri, Torino 2013.

PASTOUREAU, M., *Il colore*, in Castelnuovo e Sergi, *Arti e storia nel Medioevo* cit.

–, *Blu. Storia di un colore*, Ponte alle Grazie, Milano 2002.

–, *I colori dei nostri ricordi*, Ponte alle Grazie, Milano 2011.

–, *I colori del nostro tempo*, Ponte alle Grazie, Milano 2010.

–, *L'uomo e il colore*, Giunti, Firenze 1987.

–, *La stoffa del diavolo*, il Melangolo, Genova 2007.

–, *Medioevo simbolico*, Laterza, Roma-Bari 2005.

–, *Nero. Storia di un colore*, Ponte alle Grazie, Milano 2008.

–, *Rosso. Storia di un colore*, Ponte alle Grazie, Milano 2016.

–, *Verde. Storia di un colore*, Ponte alle Grazie, Milano 2013.

– e altri, *Il colore*, in «Le Scienze dossier», (2001), n. 9.

– e SIMONNET, D., *Il piccolo libro dei colori*, Ponte alle Grazie, Milano 2006.

PENDER, K., *Digital Colour in Graphic Design*, Focal Press, Oxford 1998.

PETROSKI, H., *The Pencil. A History of Design and Circumstance*, Knopf, New York 2002.

PIERANTONI, R., *L'occhio e l'idea. Fisiologia e storia della visione*, Bollati Boringhieri, Torino 1981.

PIEROTTI, F., *La seduzione dello spettro*, Le Mani, Genova 2012.

PINOTTI, A., *Estetica della pittura*, il Mulino, Bologna 2007.

– e SOMAINI, A., *Cultura visuale. Immagini, sguardi, media, dispositivi*, Einaudi, Torino 2016.

PLINY THE ELDER, *Storia delle arti antiche Naturalis Historia (Libri XXXIV-XXXVI)*, Rizzoli, Milano 2000.

POLANO, S. e ZALETTO, D. (a cura di), *Colore*, in «Multiverso», (2007), n. 4.

PURGHÉ, F., STUCCHI, N. e OLIVERO, A. (a cura di), *La percezione visiva*, Utet, Torino 1999.

QUONDAM, A., *Tutti i colori del nero. Moda e cultura nell'Italia del Cinquecento*, Angelo Colla Editore, Vicenza 2007.

RADIUS, E. (a cura di), *L'opera completa di Ingres*, Rizzoli, Milano 1968.

RAMACHANDRAN, V. S., *L'uomo che credeva di essere morto*, Mondadori, Milano 2012.

–, *Che cosa sappiamo della mente*, Mondadori, Milano 2004.

– e BLAKESLEE, S., *La donna che morí dal ridere*, Mondadori, Milano 1999.

– e HUBBARD, E. M., *Hearing Colors, Tasting Shapes*, in «Scientific American», CCLXXXVIII (2003), n. 5, pp. 52–9.

REWALD, J., *La storia dell'impressionismo*, Mondadori, Milano 1991.

RICCÒ, D., *Sentire il design*, Carocci editore, Roma 2008.

–, *Sinestesie del colore. Fra ricerca e sperimentazione didattica per il design di comunicazione*, in *Colore e colorimetria* cit., pp. 312–9.

–, *Sinestesie e progetto*, in «Progetto Grafico», V (2007), n. 10, pp. 152–3.

–, *Sinestesie per il design*, Rizzoli Etas, Milano 1999.

RILEY, C. A. II, *Color Codes*, University Press of New England, Lebanon (Nh) 1995.

RINALDI, S. (a cura di), *La fabbrica dei colori. Pigmenti e coloranti nella pittura e nella tintoria*, Il Bagatto, Roma 1986.

RONCHI, L. R., *Il processo del colore nel XXI secolo*, Fondazione Giorgio Ronchi, Firenze 2007.

ROOD, O. N., *Modern Chromatics*, Van Nostrand Reinhold Company, New York 1973.

RUNGE, P. O., *La sfera dei colori e altri scritti sul colore e sull'arte*, Abscondita, Milano 2008.

SACKS, O., *L'isola dei senza colore*, Adelphi, Milano 2004.

–, *Un antropologo su Marte*, Adelphi, Milano 1998.

SAGLIETTI, B., *Dal «clavecin oculaire» di Louis Bertrand Castel al «clavier à lumieres» di Alexandr Skrjabin*, in MESSINA, S. e TRIVERO, P., *Metamorfosi dei Lumi*, Accademia University Press, Torino 2002, vol. VI, pp. 187–205.

SAMBURSKY, S. e altri, *Il sentimento del colore*, Red Edizioni, Como 1990.

SAUNDERS, B., (a cura di), *The Debate about Colour Naming in 19th-Century German Philology*, Leuven University Press, Leuven 2007.

SAUSSURE, F. DE, *Corso di linguistica generale*, Laterza, Roma-Bari 2009.

SAXL, F., *La fede negli astri*, Bollati Boringhieri, Torino 2007.

SCARZELLA, P., *I colori del design. Il progetto del colore come fattore di successo dei prodotti industriali*, FrancoAngeli, Milano 2008.

SCHAPIRO, M., *L'impressionismo*, Einaudi, Torino 2008.

SCHOPENHAUER, A., *La vista e i colori e carteggio con Goethe*, Abscondita, Milano 2002.

SCULLY, K. e COBB, D. J., *Colour Forecasting for Fashion*, Laurence King, London 2012.

SEGRE MONTEL, C., *Miniatura*, in Castelnuovo e Sergi (a cura di), *Arti e storia* cit.

SHELTON, A. C., *Ingres*, Phaidon, London 2010.

SHERIN, A., *Design Elements. Color Fundamentals*, Rockport Publishers, Beverly (Ma) 2012.

SILVESTRINI, N. e TORNAGHI, A., *Colore. Codice e norma*, Zanichelli, Milano 1981.

SIMONDO, P., *Il colore dei colori*, La Nuova Italia, Firenze 1990.

SLOANE, P., *Colour. Basic Principles and New Directions*, Reinhold Book Corporation, New York 1967.

SNOWDEN, R., THOMPSON, P. e TROSCIANKO, T., *Basic Vision*, Oxford University Press, Oxford 2012.

SOLSO, R. L., *Cognition and the Visual Arts*, The Mit Press, Cambridge (Ma) 1996.

SPARKE, P., *An Introduction to Design and Culture. 1900 to the Present*, Routledge, London 2013.

–, *As Long as Is Pink*, Press of the Nova Scotia College of Art and Design, Halifax (Ns) 2010.

SQUILLACCIOTTI, M. (a cura di), *Sguardi sui colori*, Atti del Seminario Interdisciplinare dell'Università di Siena, Protagon Editori, Siena 2007.

STEWART, J., *Roy G. Biv. An Exceedingly Surprising Book about Colour*, Bloomsbury Publishing, New York - London - New Delhi - Sydney 2013.

STOICHITA, V. I., *Breve storia dell'ombra*, il Saggiatore, Milano 2000.

STONE, T. L., ADAMS, S. e MORIOKA, N., *Color Design Workbook*, Rockport Publishers, Beverly (Ma) 2006.

STORARO, V., *Scrivere con la luce, i colori, gli elementi*, Mondadori Electa, Milano 2002.

STURKEN, M. e CARTWRIGHT, L., *Practices of Looking. An Introduction to Visual Culture*, Oxford University Press, Oxford 2000.

SURACE, M., *Nero. La religione di un colore e i suoi fedeli laici*, Castelvecchi, Roma 2000.

TANIZAKI, J., *Libro d'ombra*, Bompiani, Milano 2000.

TEOFRASTO (PSEUDO ARISTOTELE), *I colori*, Ets, Pisa 1999.

TESTA, A., *Le vie del senso*, Carocci editore, Roma 2004.

TOLOMEO, C., *L'ottica*, Torino 1885.

TORNQUIST, J., *Colore e Luce. Teoria e pratica*, Istituto del Colore, Milano 2001.

TRIEDMAN, K., *Colour: The Professional's Guide. Understanding and Mastering Colour in Art and Design*, Ilex, London 2015.

TRUFFAUT, F., *Il cinema secondo Hitchcock*, il Saggiatore, Milano 2014.

TUFTE, E. R., *Beautiful Evidence*, Graphics Press, Cheshire 2006.

TURNER, M. (edited by), *The Artful Mind. Cognitive Science and the Riddle of Human Creativity*, Oxford University Press, Oxford 2006.

TWYMAN, M., *Printing 1770-1970. An Illustrated History of Its Development and Uses in England*, British Library, London 1998.

VERANI, G., *Combinazione e armonia dei colori (1748)*, Alfieri, Milano 1919.

VERITY, E., *Colour Observed*, Van Nostrand Reinhold Company, New York 1980.

VITTA, M., *Il progetto della bellezza. Il design fra arte e tecnica dal 1851 a oggi*, Einaudi, Torino 2011.

–, *Il rifiuto degli dèi. Teoria delle belle arti industriali*, Einaudi, Torino 2012.

WARE, C., *Information Visualization*, Morgan Kaufmann, Burlington (Ma) 2004.

–, *Visual Thinking for Design*, Morgan Kaufmann, Burlington (Ma) 2008.

WARHOL, A., *La filosofia di Andy Warhol*, Abscondita, Milano 2009.

WEINSCHENK, S. M., *100 cose che ogni designer deve conoscere sulle persone*, Pearson Italia, Milano 2011.

WHITE, J. V., *Color for Impact*, Strathmoore Press, Berkeley 1996.

WINGLER, H. M., *Il Bauhaus*, Feltrinelli, Milano 1972.

WITTGENSTEIN, L., *Esperienza privata e dati di senso*, Einaudi, Torino 2007.

–, *Osservazioni sui colori*, Einaudi, Torino 1981.

–, *Teoria fenomenologica dei colori*, in *Osservazioni filosofiche*, Einaudi, Torino 1976.

WÖLFFLIN, H., *Concetti fondamentali della storia dell'arte*, Abscondita, Milano 2012.

WRIGHT, A., *The Beginner's Guide to Color Psychology*, Kyle Cathie Limited, London 1995.

ZANCANI MONTUORO, P., *Colore*, in *Enciclopedia dell'arte antica classica e orientale*, Istituto dell'Enciclopedia Italiana, Roma 1959, vol. II.

ZECCHINA, A., *Alchimie nell'arte*, Zanichelli, Bologna 2012.

ZEKI, S., *A Vision of the Brain*, Wiley-Blackwell, Hoboken 1993.

–, *Artistic Creativity and the Brain*, in «Science Magazine», CCXCIII (2001), n. 5527.

–, *La visione dall'interno. Arte e cervello*, Bollati Boringhieri, Torino 2003.

– e MARINI, L.,*Three Cortical Stages of Colour Processing in the Human Brain*, in «Brain», (1998), n. 121, pp. 1669–85.

Acknowledgements.

This book is the fruit of eight years' work. My thanks go first to its Italian publishers: to Severino Cesari and Paolo Repetti, who believed in the project; to Rosella Postorino, who oversaw the editing, Raffaella Baiocchi for her work on the text, Daniela La Rosa for editorial coordination, Mauro Caprino for his indispensable technical help, and Monica Aldi for both aesthetic and legal assistance with the images. I am grateful to Marta Biddau, Cecilia Canziani, Emanuele Coccia, Marta Poggi and Stefano Vittori for discussions over the years about many problems related to art and design in contemporary society. Christian De Lorenzo and Valentina Manchia read the first draft, and it is thanks to them that it has taken its present form. Renato Bruni, Peppe Liberti and Benedetta Saglietti read the most scientifically technical passages, providing clarification where necessary. Ilenia Alesse, Daniele Balicco, Rita Benedetti, Emanuele Bevilacqua, Cristina Boeri, Andrea Bozzo, Giorgio Calandri, Marco Cassini, Anna Castagnoli, Aisha Cerami, Bruno Di Marino, Davide Ferri, Giovanni Lussu, Rachele Palmieri, Andrea Pescatori, Augusto Peroni, Daniela Piscitelli and Salvatore Zingale provided me with food for thought on the relationships between art, design and colour. Maria Teresa Carbone and Marco Filoni gave me in the columns of *Pagina99* the opportunity to write on many themes that were subsequently developed in the book. Roberto Casati and Barbara Carnevali allowed me to publicly air some of the ideas contained in the introduction, by inviting me to speak at the École Normale Supérieure in Paris. Michele Cornetto gifted me a rare and unobtainable text that proved to be invaluable. Cosimo Lorenzo Pancini designed the 'Coco' lettering used on the book's cover. Silvia Piombo of the Scala archive provided essential, fine-tuning legal advice concerning the illustrations. That great expert in the science of colour, Mauro Boscarol, helped me to dispel numerous technical and technological doubts. I am grateful to all the artists, publishers and collectors who gave permission for works to be reproduced, in particular: BlexBolex, Karin Ehrnberger, Milton Glaser, Gipi, Aoi Huber-Kono, Igort, Agostino Iacurci, Enzo Mari, Alessandro Mendini, Federico Novaro, Fausta Orecchio, Valeria Petrone, Emiliano Ponzi, Simone Rea, Marco Goran Romano, Shout, Anna Steiner, JeongMee Yoon and the 'Topipittori' (Paolo Canton and Giovanna Zoboli). Thanks also to the colleagues in my studio – Mauro Abbattista, Luca Martelli, Leonardo Magrelli, Nicola Bertelloni, Francesco Scagliarini, Chiara Nuvoli, Andrea Vendetti – who helped me in many ways, including practical ones, to finish the book. Special thanks to Livia Massaccesi for her elegant designs illustrating the chromatic conceits and motifs in *Vertigo*. And finally to my agent, Giulia Pietrosanti, who supported me throughout.